CONTEMPORARY AND EMERGING ISSUES IN TRADE THEORY AND POLICY

FRONTIERS OF ECONOMICS AND GLOBALIZATION

4

Series Editors:

HAMID BELADI
University of Texas at San Antonio, USA

E. KWAN CHOI
Iowa State University, USA

FRONTIERS OF ECONOMICS AND GLOBALIZATION VOLUME 4

CONTEMPORARY AND EMERGING ISSUES IN TRADE THEORY AND POLICY

Edited by

Sugata Marjit

Department of Economics and Finance, City University of Hong Kong, Hongkong

Eden S. H. Yu

Department of Economics and Finance, City University of Hong Kong, Hongkong

United Kingdom – North America – Japan
India – Malaysia – China

Emerald Group Publishing Limited
Howard House, Wagon Lane, Bingley BD16 1WA, UK

First edition 2008

British Library Cataloguing in Publication Data
A catalogue record for this book is available from the British Library

ISBN: 978-0-4445-3190-2
ISSN: 1574-8715

Printed and bound by MPG Books Ltd, Bodmin, Cornwall

ISOQAR QUALITY ASSURED ISO 9001 UKAS QUALITY MANAGEMENT 026
Certificate number 1985

Awarded in recognition of Emerald's production department's adherence to quality systems and processes when preparing scholarly journals for print

INVESTOR IN PEOPLE

To

Ram Kumar Marjit, Chitra Marjit,
Baisakhi Marjit

and

Mei Wo Sum Yu,
Chi Hou Yu

ABOUT THE SERIES:
FRONTIERS OF ECONOMICS AND GLOBALIZATION

This series is aimed at economists and financial economists worldwide and will provide an in depth look at current global topics. Each volume in the series will focus on specialized topics for greater understanding of the chosen subject and provide a detailed discussion of emerging issues. The target audiences are professional researchers, graduate students, and policy makers. It will offer cutting-edge views on new horizons and deepen the understanding in these emerging topics.

With contributions from leading researchers, each volume presents a fresh look at today's current topics. This series will present primarily original works, and employ references appropriate to the topic being explored.

Each volume will bring a set of highly concentrated articles that will provide in depth knowledge to a target audience, while the entire series will appeal to a wide audience by providing them with deeper knowledge on a broad set of emerging topics in the global economy.

The Frontiers of Economics and Globalization series will publish on topics such as:

- Frontiers of Trade Negotiations
- Frontiers of Derivative Pricing
- Frontiers of International Lending and Debt problems
- Frontiers of Economics Integration
- Frontiers of Trade and Environment
- Frontiers of Foreign Exchange
- Frontiers of International Finance
- Frontiers of Growth of Open Economies
- Frontiers of Futures Pricing
- Frontiers of International Financial Markets
- Frontiers of Investment Banking
- Frontiers of Mergers and Acquisitions
- Frontiers of Government Policy and Regulations
- Frontiers of Multi-Sector Growth Models
- Frontiers of Intellectual Property Rights
- Frontiers of Fragmentations and Outsourcing

Series Editors
Hamid Beladi
E. Kwan Choi

LIST OF CONTRIBUTORS

Rajat Acharyya	Department of Economics, Jadavpur University, Kolkata 700032, India
Mohammad Amin	Enterprise Analysis Unit, World Bank, Washington, DC, 20048, USA
Hamid Beladi	Department of Economics, College of Business, University of Texas at San Antonio, One UTSA Circle, San Antonio, Texas 78249-0633
Eric W. Bond	Department of Economics, Vanderbilt University, VU Station B #351819, 2301 Vanderbilt Place, Nashville, TN 37235, USA
Avik Chakrabarti	Department of Economics, 816 Bolton Hall, College of Letters and Science, University of Wisconsin-Milwaukee, P.O. Box 413, Wisconsin 53201
Brati Sankar Chakraborty	Economics Research Unit, Indian Statistical Institute, 203, B. T. Road, Kolkata-700108, India
Chi-Chur Chao	Department of Economics, Chinese University of Hong Kong, 9/F, Esther Lee Building, Chung Chi Campus, Shatin, Hong Kong
Sarbajit Chaudhuri	Department of Economics, University of Calcutta, 56A, B. T. Road, Kolkata 700050, India
Donald R. Davis	Department of Economics, Columbia University, 420 West 118th Street, New York, NY 10027, USA
Viet Do	Department of Economics, McGill University, 855 Rue Sherbrooke West, Montréal, Québec, H3A 2T7, Canada
Robert A. Driskill	Department of Economics, Vanderbilt University, VU Station B #351819, 2301 Vanderbilt Place, Nashville, TN 37235, USA
Stephen T. Easton	Department of Economics, Simon Fraser University, 8888 University Drive, Burnaby, B.C., Canada, V5A 1S6

Wilfred J. Ethier	Department of Economics, University of Pennsylvania, Philadelphia, PA 19104-6297, USA
Ronald Findlay	Economics Department, Columbia University, 1017 International Affairs Building, MC 3308, 420 West 118th Street, New York, NY 10027, USA
Yunfang Hu	Graduate School of International Cultural Studies, Tohoku University, 41 Kawauchi, Aoba-Ku, Sendai 980-8576, Japan
Jin Kenzaki	Economic and Market Analysis, Nikko Citigroup Limited, Shin-Marunouchi Building 1-5-1 Marunouchi, Chiyoda-ku, Tokyo 100-6520, Japan
Ulrich Kohli	Alternate Member of the Governing Board, Swiss National Bank, CH-8022, Zurich, Switzerland
Carsten Kowalczyk	The Fletcher School, Tufts University, 160 Packard Ave, Medford, MA 02155, USA
Jean-Pierre Laffargue	University of Paris I (Pantheon-Sorbonne) and CEPREMAP, 48 Boulevard Jourdan, 750143 Paris, France
Sajal Lahiri	Department of Economics, Southern Illinois University Carbondale, MC 4515, 1000 Faner Drive, Carbondale, IL, 62901, USA
Didier Laussel	University of Aix-Marseille 2, rue de la Charité, 13002 Marseilles, France
Ngo Van Long	Department of Economics, McGill University, 855 Rue Sherbrooke West, Montréal, Québec, H3A 2T7, Canada
Sugata Marjit	Centre For Studies in Social Sciences, R-1, Baishnabghata Patuli Township, Kolkata-700094, India
Tapan Mitra	Department of Economics, 448 Uris Hall, Cornell University, Ithaca, NY 14853, USA
Kazuo Nishimura	Institute of Economic Research, Kyoto University, Yoshida-Honmachi, Sakyo-ku, Kyoto 606-8501, Japan
Yoshiyasu Ono	Institute of Social and Economic Research, Osaka University, Osaka 567-0047, Japan
Raymond Riezman	Department of Economics, W360 PBB, University of Iowa, Iowa City, IA 52242, USA

Roy J. Ruffin	Department of Economics, University of Houston, Houston, TX 77204-5882, USA
Abhirup Sarkar	Economics Research Unit, Indian Statistical Institute, 203, B. T. Road, Kolkata-700108, India
Koji Shimomura	Research Institute for Economics & Business Administration, Kobe University, 2-1, Rokkodai-cho, Nada-ku, Kobe, 657-8501, Japan
Rika Takahashi	Faculty of Business Administration, Hosei University, 2-17-1 Fujimi, Chiyoda-ku, Tokyo 102-8160, Japan
An-Chi Tung	Institute of Economics, Academia Sinica, 130, Section 2 Academia Road, Taipei 11529, Taiwan
Henry Wan Jr	Department of Economics, Cornell University, 470 Uris Hall, Ithaca NY 14853-7601, USA
David E. Weinstein	Department of Economics, Columbia University, 420W 118th Street, MC 3308, New York, NY 10027, USA
Siu-kee Wong	Department of International Economics and Trade, Nankai University, 94 Wei Jin Road, Tianjin 300071, China
Shigemi Yabuuchi	Graduate School of Economics, Nagoya City University, Yamanohata, Mizuho, Nagoya 467-8501, Japan
Makoto Yano	Kyoto Institute of Economic Research, Kyoto University, Yoshida-Honmachi, Sakyo-ku, Kyoto 606-8501, Japan
Morihiro Yomogida	Department of Economics, Sophia University, 7-1 Kioi-cho, Chiyoda-ku, Tokyo 102-8554, Japan
Eden S.H. Yu	Department of Economics and Finance, City University of Hong Kong, 83 Tat Chee Avenue, Kowloon Tong, Hong Kong

CONTENTS

SECTION I

Introduction

Contemporary and Emerging Issues in Trade Theory and Policy

Sugata Marjit[a] and Eden S.H. Yu[b]

[a]*Centre for Studies in Social Sciences, R-1, Baishnabghata Patuli Township, Kolkata-700 094, India*
E-mail address: smarjit@hotmail.com
[b]*Department of Economics and Finance, City University of Hong Kong, 83 Tat Chee Avenue, Kowloon Tong, Hong Kong*
E-mail address: efedenyu@cityu.edu.hk

Section I – Editorial introduction

The collection of essays in this volume provides fairly comprehensive analyses of contemporary theoretical and policy issues in international trade. As technological revolution eliminates communications costs and the countries gear towards more open trade regimes through negotiations at the WTO, the world effectively gets smaller. The evolution of research in trade theory and policy has closely followed the trends in global economy. Issues such as how trade affects distribution of income across and within nations, generates resources for growth, leads to bilateral and multilateral cooperation and conflicts, and many others have been picked up and analyzed systematically in various chapters of this volume. Before we go into the details of the relevant sections and constituent chapters, it is worthwhile to emphasize two special features of this volume.

First, the volume deals extensively with a general equilibrium approach, although we do have a few very interesting partial equilibrium papers. This follows largely from the idea that a policy change at a sectoral level has economy wide implications. Hence, results that depend only on a partial view of the problem may fail to be robust.

Second, although the contributions are mainly theoretical, they are based upon widely observed real-life phenomena. Theoretical and preferably simple looking models go a long way in explaining and identifying the necessary elements required for empirical research. We are confident that the chapters contained in this volume will have a profound influence on young students and researchers.

Spawned from the 2006 APJAE Symposium on International Trade in Honor of Professor Ronald Jones at City University of Hong Kong, this volume brings together some of the finest minds in the discipline, and celebrates Professor Ronald Jones's 75th birthday. Professor Jones is a

Frontiers of Economics and Globalization
Volume 4 ISSN: 1574-8715
DOI: 10.1016/S1574-8715(08)04024-4

legendary figure in the field of International Trade. A Fellow of the Econometric Society and the US National Academy of Sciences, and a Member of American Academy of Arts and Sciences, Professor Jones continues to amaze the profession with his razor sharp analytical research. This is a tribute to his continuing legacy.

Section II – Perspective on trade models

This section deals primarily with the pattern of trade and resource allocation mechanisms drawing from traditional competitive as well as from imperfectly competitive models. The volume opens with the Findlay and Amin's chapter on national security and international trade focusing on a fairly contemporary area of research. It demonstrates how simple general equilibrium model of trade can be applied to reflect on the choice of national security and international trade, and examines the consequences of real income increase through gains from trade and the subsequent rise in demand for national security. Thus begins the second-round impact of trade on the national defense race through competition. The authors integrate the conventional competitive trade model in a set up where countries engage in two well-known forms of non-cooperative games, Cournot and Stackelberg. The countries can lose if they have to sacrifice a lot of consumption to match the defense initiative of the opponent.

The next chapter by Davis and Weinstein revisit the query whether the classic factor endowment models are consistent with intra-industry trade and whether it is necessary to use models of economies of scale and product differentiation in order to support empirical evidence that are readily available. Their rigorous empirical examination shows that the trade in factor services among northern nations are guided by differences in factor endowments, a finding that ascertains the validity of Heckscher–Ohlin–Samuelson type of framework for explaining North–North trade.

The next two chapters are related directly or indirectly with trading costs – costs that may render some goods non-traded. While Kohli extends the well-known Sanyal–Jones framework on middle products where every traded good has to have a non-traded component at the extreme downstream for local markets, Laussel and Riezman provide an analysis on how transportation costs alter the nature of the basic free trade equilibriums.

Kohli argues that the middle product model has some far-reaching consequences for the measurement of real value added, real domestic income, and productivity. This approach also presents the major advantage that it is fully consistent with national accounts data, and that it brings forward the role of a number of key price ratios such as the terms of trade, the real exchange rate, and the PPP exchange rate.

Laussel and Riezman argue that fixed transportation cost may not allow countries reap the benefits of trade as low volume of trade can entrap the economies in a stable, low-level equilibrium. Low trade volumes lead to large per unit transportation costs, which in turn reinforce the low volume of trade. The vicious cycle can only be broken if the countries are considerably far from one another and generate sufficient volume of trade, or if the transportation infrastructure is significantly improved.

In recent years, the world has seen remarkable growth in activities related to outsourcing, fragmentation of production and services, and off shoring of business. Ruffin explores the outsourcing incentives of firms under Cournot competition by allowing for any degree of competition along the spectrum of linkage. Vertical integration in the model can take place by vertical mergers, forward or backward integration. An interesting counter intuitive result is that vertical integration is highly profitable and always reduces the price of the final product. The cost-raising strategy of an integrated firm buying out unneeded component producers is profitable and detrimental to consumers only if the firm faces no competition from other integrated firms.

Section III – Factor rewards and trade theory

The impact of trade on factor rewards and the consequential relationship between trade and income distribution has been a topic of never-ending debates. If political authorities want to tilt their distribution of income in favor of a particular factor or a group of factors, they may not have to design sector-specific subsidies or other favors, they can achieve it indirectly by manipulating trade-related incentives. The three chapters included in this section reflect on these issues in some multi-dimensional cases from a theoretical perspective.

Easton revisits his own work with Jones on two good three-factor models and its relationship with the well-known Specific Factor model of trade, possibly one of the most cited works in trade and related literature. Picking up on two themes that run through Jones's "uneven" models is, first, a theoretical proposition that limits the extent of factor reward patterns in the general three by two framework, and second, a back to its roots economic history application of the specific factors model to a proposition about the origins of the industrial revolution in Britain.

Mitra and Wong both deal with the higher dimensional issues. While Mitra characterizes the inverse matrix of distributive shares, necessary for generalizing Stolper–Samuelson or Rybczynski type results, Wong studies the convergence of intercountry factor returns when endowments are fairly different.

Mitra argues that the inverse of the distributive share matrix must satisfy the following restriction: it cannot be anti-symmetric in its sign pattern. This means that one cannot partition the commodities into two groups (I and II) and factors into two groups (A and B), such that all factors in group A benefit (nominally) from all commodity price increases in group I, and simultaneously all factors in group B suffer from all commodity price increases in group II.

Wong's chapter specifies some conditions of the demand function in a two-factor, infinite-good model that guarantee partial equalization of the wage–rental ratio between two trading countries. Three cases are considered; the degree of substitutability between goods is assumed to be positively, negatively, and not correlated with the proximity of these goods in the factor-intensity ranking. In particular, when substitutability and the factor intensities ranking are independent, the factor price ratios are convergent. This generalizes the analysis in the literature, which is usually done under the assumption of Cobb–Douglas utility and production function.

Section IV – Dynamic issues

The specific factor model of international trade of Jones has been one of the possibly most cited works in trade, development, political economy, and history. Short and medium run adjustments needed to encounter the effects of foreign trade and investment may lead to general equilibrium repercussions, quite different from the ones one would expect in the longer run. The dynamic section of this volume deals separately with the generalization of this model in terms of two chapters.

Bond and Driskill extend the analysis of factor market distortions in a static two-sector general equilibrium model to a dynamic model of a small, open economy with capital accumulation. The static literature identified a number of paradoxical results that can arise, and Jones (1971) showed that a number of these paradoxes can be linked to the case where factor market distortions are sufficiently large so that the ranking of sectors by their capital/labor ratio ("physical" measure of capital intensity) differs from their ranking capital's share in unit costs ("value" measure of capital intensity). The chapter highlights the role of this reversal in generating paradoxical outcomes in the dynamic general equilibrium model.

Based on the Jones (1971) model, Hu, Nishimura, and Shimomura construct two dynamic models of international trade in which the rate of time preference is either constant or time-varying. The main purpose is to study whether and under what conditions the results derived in the Jones model still hold in the dynamic framework. It is shown that the results of dynamic models may be similar or different to those obtained in the static model. For example, it is possible that, in both static and dynamic models, an increase in the commodity price raises this commodity's output and the return to the specific factor in this sector. However, the effects on the wage rate and the welfare may be different due to the factor accumulation impact in the dynamic framework.

Section V – Trade and the developing economy

Trade and development as a topic of research has reached new heights with the entire developing world experimenting with market-based reforms and in the process getting exposed to economic and social turbulence. The first three chapters in this section deal with the issue of trade and resultant inequality. The last two talk about labor standards and fiscal policy in the context of a developing economy.

Marjit builds up a simple general equilibrium trade model where, in the absence of a credit market for human capital formation, initial distribution of capital endowment and relevant factor prices determine the size of the three income classes. The poor, with little capital, invest in traditional manufacturing, the middle-income group invest solely in human capital, and the rich invest in both. Chances are that such an economy will export both high-skilled and low-skilled goods, importing the middle one. Conventional wisdom suggests that greater skill premium encourages skill formation. In contrast we show that higher unskilled wage and lower degree of income inequality are consistent with greater skill formation. It shows that protection discourages skill formation and may aggravate inequality.

Chaudhuri and Yabucchi look at the impact of liberal investment policies on wage inequality in developing countries. They find that the inflow of foreign capital usually improves the wage inequality when the low-skill sector is capital-intensive. But the relative wage gap may widen if the high-skill sector is capital-intensive. When the non-traded sector produces a non-traded final commodity, wage inequality worsens if the low-skill sector is capital-intensive and employs only a very small proportion of the unskilled workforce and if the primary export sector is unskilled labor-intensive. Appropriate policy recommendations for improving the wage inequality have also been made.

Most of the models attempting to give an account of trade-induced symmetric increase in wage inequality have abandoned the factor price equalization (FPE) framework. Chakraborty and Sarkar identify a plausible route through which trade might increase wage inequality in both the trading countries in a standard FPE framework. There are two types of productive factors, skilled and unskilled labor and they differ with respect to their occupational options. Skilled labor can work both the skill-using sector and unskilled jobs, whereas unskilled labor is tied down to unskilled jobs. If the scale of operation of the IRS sector is limited by the size of the domestic market, then the skilled work force might remain underutilized. The model shows that trade can lead to a full utilization of skilled labor in all countries through exploiting the economies of scale. This, in turn, might increase the skill premium in all countries.

Acharyya critically examines the issue of child labor and product labeling. This chapter shows that if labels contain such information and the buyers react to this by offering increasingly lower prices for the varieties containing more child labor per unit of output, it may do more harm than helping the cause. That is, a trade sanction against child labor content of a good exported by developing countries may not be a good idea since it may, in fact, raise the incidence of child labor in those countries. This result is established in a simple general equilibrium framework where parents are altruist.

Does public investment necessarily increase employment in an open, developing economy? Chao, Laffargue, and Yu discuss this issue in great detail by considering public input provisioning for urban development. When a financing constraint is taken into account, an increase in public inputs may worsen urban unemployment and hence reduce welfare of the economy. Further, the optimal level of public input provision is larger (smaller) than that under full employment, if there exists a positive (negative) employment effect. The theoretical results are confirmed by numerical simulations.

Section VI – International factor mobility

This section addresses issues concerning international factor mobility and outsourcing.

Beladi and Chakrabarti compare the effects of frictions involved in immigration and international outsourcing have on the skilled–unskilled wage inequality. They conclude that the wedge between the wages of the skilled and unskilled workers widens as the frictions in immigration wear out and it also is sensitive to variations in contractual frictions in intermediates that affect international outsourcing.

Yomogida explores the impacts of international capital movements on income distribution within countries and the value of trade in goods. He extends Jones's 1980 model, in which sector-specific capital is introduced into a simple Ricardian setting, by introducing a simple structure of the demand for commodities, and shows how the pattern of demand plays a crucial role in the effects of capital movements on income distribution and goods trade.

Do and Long reveal how international outsourcing may worsen the welfare of the home country and reduce the profits of all firms, even when domestic wages are flexible. If wages are inflexible, outsourcing is welfare-improving if and only if the sum of the "trade creation" effect and the "exploitation effect" outshines the "trade diversion" effect. They also suggest that delaying outsourcing could be advisable because the fixed cost of outsourcing may fall over time. A social planner, therefore, would choose a different speed of outsourcing than that under *laissez-faire*.

Lahiri and Ono consider the effect of the environment on the level of foreign direct investment and on factor prices in the two countries by developing a $2 \times 2 \times 2$ model of international trade, in which one of the sectors is oligopolistic. The oligopolistic sector consists of a given number of *a priori* identical firms belonging to one of the two countries, but some deciding to locate in the other country so as to realize higher profits. The model also assumes that if a firm locates in the foreign country, its technological capability will go down due to the alien environment.

Section VII – International trade policy

Ethier contends that multilateral trade liberalization has reduced tariffs to historically low levels over the past 60 years, yet the dominant theory of multilateral trade agreements, based solely on terms-of-trade externalities between national governments, features two defects that render it inconsistent with reality. He proposes a simple formulation of the political economy of protection that dispenses with terms-of-trade externalities, predicts the properties that empirical work has confirmed, and is free of the counterfactual implications of the dominant approach.

Takahashi, Kenzaki, and Yano compare a competition policy with a partial tariff policy, in which tariffs are only imposed on a small range of imports. They find that if a country can impose a tariff on only a small part of the imports and at sufficiently low tariff rates, optimal partial tariff policy may not create as large a protective effect as optimal competition policy.

Kowalczyk offers a formal analysis of the economic welfare effects for large and small partners to free trade agreements. He derives the welfare for the large country for all possible small country sizes, and shows that the maximum possible loss for the large country is twice its tariff revenue. He also identifies the data necessary to estimate the welfare effects and consider how initial trade volumes, tariffs, and international price differences affect the large country's welfare.

Tung and Wan address the issue of how a country can industrialize under the WTO regime in the Jones–Kierzkowski world of fragmented production. They suggest that the generation of cross-border externalities, such as becoming the hub of a network of countries, can attract foreign investment with collective comparative advantage. The small, remote, and pre-industrial Singapore, for example, managed to organize a hub-spokes game and gained the most as the hub while presenting a win-win solution for all.

We would like to take this opportunity to express our gratitude to Charlotte Chen, Editorial Assistant of the *Asia-Pacific Journal of Accounting and Economics* (APJAE) and Archita Banik and Triparna Sinha of Centre for Studies in Social Sciences, Calcutta for their efforts and assistance in this project.

SECTION II

Perspective on Trade Models

CHAPTER 1

National Security and International Trade: A Simple General Equilibrium Model

Ronald Findlay[a] and Mohammad Amin[b]

[a]*Ragnar Nurkse Professor of Economics, Columbia University, USA*
E-mail address: ref2@columbia.edu
[b]*Enterprise Analysis Unit, World Bank, Washington, DC, 20048, USA*
E-mail address: m.amin@worldbank.org

Abstract
This chapter presents a general equilibrium model that embeds the issue of national security within a two-country Heckscher–Ohlin model of international trade. "National security" is defined as a public good that is an increasing function of a country's own defense expenditure and a decreasing function of the other country's defense expenditure. Defense is a non-traded public good produced by capital and labor, along with two tradable private goods in each country. The model is solved as a Nash equilibrium in defense expenditures and a Walrasian equilibrium for the two traded goods and the factors of production. It is shown that opening to international trade raises defense expenditures in each country since national security is a normal good in each of them. If defense is more capital-intensive than both tradable goods then trade lowers the cost of defense for the labor-abundant country and raises it for the capital-abundant country.

Keywords: General equilibrium model, national security, factor endowments, non-traded sector

JEL classifications: F10, H56

The world of nation states has always reflected a basic tension between the benign aspects of the mutually beneficial peaceful exchange of goods and ideas, on the one hand, and the threat of armed conflict over clashes of territorial interests and ideological differences on the other. Each of these aspects of international relations has developed its own tradition of analysis and reflection. The theory of international trade and factor movements was worked out by Adam Smith, David Ricardo, John Stuart Mill and others of the English Classical School and refined by their successors and others, in particular the Swedes Eli Heckscher and

Frontiers of Economics and Globalization
Volume 4 ISSN: 1574-8715
DOI: 10.1016/S1574-8715(08)04001-3

Bertil Ohlin. This literature has always ignored the "Hobbesian Problem" of how law and order is maintained between the participants in the world market. It is not enough to say that there are formal and informal treaties and agreements since, as Hobbes says, "covenants without the sword are but words". Domestic trade is taken to require a "magistrate" to hold the ring and enforce contracts but international trade is between sovereign nations, each of which controls the use of its own "sword".

The problem of "national security" in a world of competing nation-states is the main issue in the theory of international relations, which bears an analogous relation to the discipline of political science that the theory of international trade does to economics. The question of what "force level" to deploy by each nation-state, relative to the force levels of the others, is however also an economic problem, one that has been surprisingly neglected by economists. Theorists of international relations, such as Waltz (1959), while conscious of the economic aspects of national security concerns, have concentrated on the military and diplomatic aspects of the problem.

The field of "defense economics" which has arisen since World War II has been surveyed extensively in the volumes edited by Hartley and Sandler (1995) and in an advanced text by Sandler and Hartley (1995). The reader is referred to these works for detailed exposition and references to the relevant literature of this field. More specifically, the relation between national security and international trade has been explored in a variety of special contexts. One of these is the "national defense" argument for tariffs, the subject of a valuable article by Mayer (1977). Another topic on which an extensive literature has arisen is the problem of sharing the burden of defense expenditure within a military alliance such as NATO, to which the recent article by Wong (1991) is a major contribution. Polachek (1980) is an important empirical investigation of the relationship between international trade and conflict between the trading partners. Skaperdas and Syropoulos (1996) is another notable reference.

The purpose of the present chapter is to make a modest contribution to this area of common interest by constructing a simple general equilibrium model that will consider both national security and international trade in a simplified world of two sovereign nation-states. Trade levels and force levels will be simultaneously determined by the relevant preferences and technology, in conjunction with factor endowments. The model that we use is the familiar two-factor, two good Heckscher–Ohlin–Samuelson model, augmented with a non-traded sector as introduced by Komiya (1967), which will be identified with "defense", an assumption that is also made by Wong (1991). Thus we have three goods denoted X, Y and D with production functions

$$X = X(K_x, L_x) \tag{1}$$

$$Y = Y(K_y, L_y) \tag{2}$$

$$D = D(K_D, L_D) \tag{3}$$

With resource constraints

$$K_x + K_y + K_D = \overline{K} \tag{4}$$

$$L_x + L_y + L_D = \overline{L} \tag{5}$$

All three production functions are assumed to be of the usual neo-classical type and to exhibit constant returns to scale. The nominal prices of the three goods are P_x, P_y and P_D and we define

$$p = \frac{P_x}{P_y}$$

$$\pi = \frac{P_D}{P_y}$$

so that Y is the *numeraire*.

The real wage and real rental are denoted w and r, respectively, and θ is the wage–rental ratio.

We make the strong factor-intensity assumption that

$$k_x(\theta) < k_y(\theta) < k_D(\theta) \tag{6}$$

where k_x, k_y and k_D are the capital–labor ratios chosen in each of the three respective sectors as functions of the wage–rental ratio θ.

The fact that the defense sector is assumed to be the most capital-intensive is not necessary for the subsequent analysis but it does serve to simplify and sharpen the results.

We now turn to the specification of preferences. The tradable goods X and Y are "normal" private consumer goods and can be introduced as arguments of a homothetic utility function

$$U = U(C_x, C_y) \tag{7}$$

where C_x and C_y are per capita consumption of X and Y, respectively.

The defense good, however, is a component of what we call "national security", which is a public good, having properties of being "non-rivalrous" and "non-excludable" and is defined as

$$S = S(D, D^*) \tag{8}$$

where D^* is the defense level of the foreign country and

$$\frac{\partial S}{\partial D} > 0, \quad \frac{\partial S}{\partial D^*} < 0$$

i.e. national security is an increasing function of one's own defense level and a decreasing function of the other country's defense level. This formulation is consistent with the concept of "security function" discussed in Sandler and Hartley (1995, p. 55), which also gives references to earlier work by Ron Smith, Neil Bruce and others.

Over-all welfare is specified as

$$W = W\left[U(C_x, C_y), S(D, D^*)\right] \tag{9}$$

which therefore has two separable components, ordinary utility from consumption of private goods and national security, the public good that increases in the level of domestic defense, given the level of defense of the foreign country.

Technology, preferences and endowments of the foreign country are all analogous to those of the home country. It will be convenient, but by no means necessary, to make the familiar Heckscher–Ohlin–Samuelson assumption that technology and preferences of the two countries are identical. The home country will be taken as capital-abundant relative to the foreign country so that we have

$$\overline{k} \equiv \frac{\overline{K}}{\overline{L}} > \frac{\overline{K^*}}{\overline{L^*}} \equiv \overline{k^*}$$

Suppose initially that the countries do not engage in any trade at all but are mutually interdependent through the level of defense that each country chooses to maintain, which therefore influences the national security of the other country. We seek first to establish the general equilibrium solution to this Hobbesian problem in the absence of trade between the nations. The subsequent sections will introduce international trade and examine its impact on the interdependent defense levels of the solution to the present problem.

To solve this problem we proceed by asking what the optimal level of domestic defense D will be for any given foreign defense level D^*. The analogous exercise for the foreign country will give us the familiar "reaction functions" $D(D^*)$ and $D^*(D)$ of the two countries, enabling us to find an appropriate Nash equilibrium, i.e. what is the optimal level of D, given D^* and of D^*, given D.

We first observe that for any value of the relative price p of X and Y, we obtain $w(p)$, $r(p)$ and therefore $\theta(p)$ by the familiar Stolper–Samuelson relationship from goods to factor prices. Since the prices of the two inputs are determined by the relative product prices of X and Y, the relative price π of a unit of defense is also determined as a function of that variable, so that we have $w(p)$, $r(p)$, $\theta(p)$ and $\pi(p)$ all determined once a value of p is specified.

Let the economy consist of N agents, all of who have the same over-all welfare function W as given by (9) and equal per capita endowment of capital $\bar{k}$. Then, for any level of foreign defense D^* and the given price p we can determine the optimal levels of C_x, C_y and D by maximizing the objective function W subject to the budget constraint

$$pC_x + C_y + \frac{\pi(p)}{N}D = w(p) + r(p)\bar{k} \tag{10}$$

where $\pi(p)/N$ is the per capita share of the cost of a unit of defense, which is a public good. The first order conditions for this maximization problem are

$$\text{MRS}_{xy} = p \tag{11}$$

$$N(\text{MRS}_{Dy}) = \pi(p) \tag{12}$$

where (12) is seen to be the familiar Lindahl–Samuelson criterion that the optimal supply of a public good be at the level where the vertical sum of the marginal valuations of all the individuals is equal to the marginal cost of supplying the public good, which is $\pi(p)$.

Equations (10)–(12) can be solved to determine the three unknowns C_x, C_y and D. The aggregate consumption levels of C_x and C_y are the corresponding per capita values multiplied by N. Thus the consumption levels of C_x, C_y and D are all determined for the given values of D^* and p.

The production of D can be set equal to the desired consumption level. The amounts of capital and labor, K_D and L_D, required to do this can be determined by the level of D and the optimal capital–labor ratio $k_D[\theta(p)]$, determined by the given value of p and corresponding value of the wage–rental ratio $[\theta(p)]$. The endowments left over to produce the private goods X and Y are $(\bar{K} - K_D)$ and $(\bar{L} - L_D)$. Letting $\tilde{k}$ stand for the ratio of these two variables we have

$$\lambda k_x[\theta(p)] + (1 - \lambda)k_y[\theta(p)] = \tilde{k} \tag{13}$$

where λ and $(1-\lambda)$ are the fractions of $(\bar{L} - L_D)$ devoted to X and Y, respectively. Solving (13) for λ in conjunction with $(\bar{L} - L_D)$ gives us the production levels $X(p)$ and $Y(p)$ corresponding to the given values of p and D^*.

We can thus determine the *excess supply* of X and Y corresponding to the given value of p from the budget constraint as

$$Ex \equiv [X(p) - C_x(p)] = -\frac{1}{p}\left[C_y(p) - Y(p)\right] = -\frac{1}{p}E_y \tag{14}$$

In deriving (14) from the over-all budget constraint we subtract the value of defense output (equal to "consumption" of defense) from both sides. Each individual is assessed a lump-sum tax equal to his desired level of defense. We of course abstract here from the problem of revelation of preferences for public goods.

Since both D^* and p were set at arbitrary levels there is no reason for supply and demand to balance in the markets for X and Y. We therefore proceed by keeping D^* constant but varying p. From the factor-intensity hypothesis it follows that

$$w'(p) > 0, \quad r'(p) < 0, \quad \pi'(p) < 0$$

The first two are just the Stolper–Samuelson Theorem, while the fall in the relative price of defense is simply a consequence of the assumption that it is the most capital-intensive of the three goods that are produced.

The fall in π with D^* constant means that consumers will want to "buy" more defense, if national security is a "normal" good, as is entirely plausible. The demand and therefore the supply of defense will rise. The rise in p raises the wage–rental ratio θ and consequently all the capital–labor ratios k_x, k_y and k_D as well.

This rise in D as well as k_D implies that the capital–labor ratio $\tilde{k}$ for the non-defense sector as a whole must fall. At constant relative product prices this must imply, by the Rybczynski Theorem, that the output of X rises relative to that of Y, a tendency that is reinforced by the shift in p itself in favor of X. With the opposite tendency in consumption of C_x and C_y induced by the rise in p it follows that the excess supply of X must rise in response to the rise in p.

For the given level of D^* we have therefore shown that the excess supply function for X

$$E_x = E_x(p, D^*) \tag{15}$$

has the property

$$\frac{\partial E_x}{\partial p} > 0$$

We can find the value of p that makes

$$E_x(p, D^*) = 0 \tag{16}$$

This value of p then determines $w(p)$, $r(p)$, $\theta(p)$ and $\pi(p)$, as well as the levels of X, Y and D that maximize W subject to the given value of D^*. In other words we have determined a point on the domestic reaction function $D(D^*)$.

Next we need to determine the consequences of a rise in D^* on D and all the other variables. To do this we hold p constant initially.

The rise in D^* with p held constant means that national security $S(D, D^*)$ will be reduced. In the over-all welfare function (9) the marginal utility of national security will therefore rise while that of consumption remains constant. Optimization therefore requires an increase in D and a reduction of expenditure on X and Y. The increase in D with $k_D[\theta(p)]$

constant (because p is being held constant) implies that $\tilde{k}$ will fall. The Rybczinski Effect therefore raises the output of X relative to Y while on the demand side the consumption of both declines in the same proportion since p is held constant and $U(C_x, C_y)$ is homothetic. The excess supply of X must therefore increase in response to the rise in D^* if p is held constant. We have therefore shown that

$$\frac{\partial E_x}{\partial D^*} > 0$$

To clear the market p must therefore fall in response to the rise in D^*. The fall in p must result in a rise in π, the unit cost of defense, because $\pi'(p)$ is negative. Thus the rise in the marginal cost and hence the price of defense will dampen the rise in D though it cannot of course reverse it. Successive increases in D^*, however, will induce a continuously rising marginal cost of D as it rises in response. The domestic reaction function $D(D^*)$ will therefore be positively sloped and convex, reflecting the increasing marginal cost of domestic defense as D^* rises.

Symmetric reasoning establishes that the foreign reaction function $D^*(D)$ will also be positively sloped and convex. Figure 1 displays both

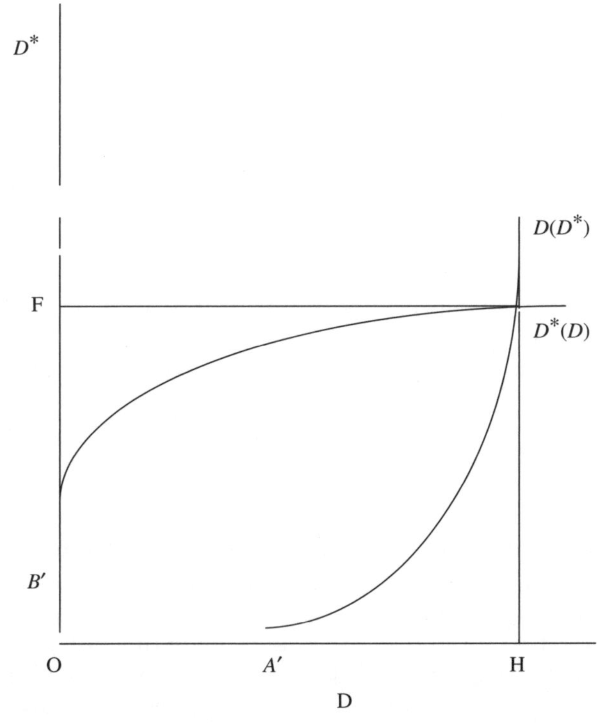

Fig. 1. Domestic and foreign reaction functions.

reaction functions and their unique intersection that determines the optimal level of each country's defense and thus the corresponding values of all other variables.

One important question is the optimal level of defense if the other country's defense level were to be zero. In Figure 1 we have shown each defense level as positive even if the other's is zero. Our justification for doing this is the plausible fact that each country would be concerned that even if the observed level of the other's defense were to be zero it might nevertheless be prudent to maintain its own defense at a positive level, in view of possible future surprise attacks or lags in mobilization efforts. Thus the origin (0,0) is ruled out as a possible, even if Utopian, solution.

It is readily seen that the solution with optimal domestic defense at OH and foreign defense at OF is stable as well as unique.

We now introduce international trade into the model, along with the interdependent defense expenditures that we have been considering. At the purely formal level this is not difficult to do. We can still construct the reaction functions $D(D^*)$ and $D^*(D)$ as before, the only modification being that for any given level of the other country's defense the optimal response is calculated at a relative price p that clears *world* excess supply of X instead of just the corresponding *national* excess supply.

Thus, given D^*, we construct the home excess supply function for X at this level of D^* just as before. To construct the foreign excess supply of X we keep the foreign defense level at D^* and the home defense level at whatever is optimal at each price and the foreign defense level at D^*.

To express this more formally, in the absence of international trade we construct the domestic reaction function for each level of foreign defense expenditure $\overline{D^*}$ by setting

$$E_x\left[p, D(p, \overline{D^*})\right] = 0 \tag{17}$$

and finding the D that is determined by $D(p, \overline{D^*})$ for the value of p that solves (17).

In the presence of international trade we find that the value of D determined by $D(p, \overline{D^*})$ for the value of p that solves

$$E_x\left[p, D(p, \overline{D^*})\right] + E_x^*\left[p, D(p, \overline{D^*}), \overline{D^*}\right] = 0 \tag{18}$$

The reaction function of the foreign country $D^*(D)$ in the presence of international trade is of course determined by a symmetric procedure to that of the domestic reaction function.

The intersection of the two reaction functions determines simultaneously the optimal defense levels D and D^* as well as all product and factor prices and the volume of international trade. With identical constant returns to scale technology for all three goods, commodity price equalization for the two tradable goods X and Y also equalizes the price of the non-traded defense good and both factors of production in the two countries. We also need to assume that neither country is completely specialized on either one of the tradable goods for factor price equalization and commodity price equalization for the non-traded good to hold.

This model of a Nash equilibrium in defense expenditures is obviously related to the classic "arms race" model of Richardson (1960), extended by Intriligator (1975) and others.

A key question that now arises is the impact of free trade on the optimal defense levels of the two countries under autarky, as determined earlier. A direct comparison of the two cases does not yield any insight and so we must proceed in a more step-by-step fashion in order to answer the question.

First let us enquire what the effects of free trade will be if the optimal autarky defense levels are kept frozen. In this case it is clear that free trade will make each country better off, for the usual reasons. The capital-abundant home country will export the capital-intensive good Y and import the labor-intensive good X. The relative price p of X will fall at home and rise abroad. Since the defense good is the most capital-intensive and $\pi'(p)$ is negative, the marginal cost of a unit of defense will rise at home and fall abroad.

With higher real income due to the gains from trade and a fall in the marginal cost of defense the labor-abundant foreign country will want to take some of its higher real income in the form of enhanced security and so will want to increase the level of its defense. The home country will thus face a situation where it has higher real income from consumption, due to the gains from trade, but a decline in the national security component of its welfare because of the incipient rise in the foreign country's defense level. It will then be optimal for the home country also to raise its level of defense in response, to mitigate the decline in its national security, thus sacrificing some of the gains from trade on consumption. To equate the marginal contribution to welfare from the two components both must either increase or decrease. Either result is possible depending upon the magnitude of the gains from trade relative to the negative impact on national security.

Thus, opening to free trade raises both defense levels as both countries try to take some of the gains from trade in the form of higher national security by spending more on defense, thus each imposing negative externalities on the other. The labor-abundant country enjoys an advantage in this process since the rise in the relative price of its labor-intensive exportable X lowers the marginal cost of defense whereas it rises for the capital-abundant home country.

Thus the labor-abundant foreign country is necessarily better off, both in terms of consumption and national security. The capital-abundant home country *could be worse off*, if the decline in security were sufficiently great so that the gains from trade did not suffice to enable the level of defense to be raised adequately to offset the higher defense level of the foreign country.

Finally, we must take account of the secondary relative price adjustment necessary to clear the world market in response to the changes in the defense levels of the two countries at constant terms of trade. Since defense is the most capital-intensive good and it rises in both countries the world capital–labor ratio for the production of the two tradables X and Y must fall. By the Rybczynski Theorem this must increase the excess supply of the labor-intensive good X, the relative price of which must therefore fall. The final terms of trade of the labor-abundant foreign country will therefore not be as favorable as with both defense levels held constant but the relative price of its labor-intensive export must still rise by comparison with autarky.

Let us now consider the "optimum tariff" argument in the presence of interdependent defense expenditures by the two trading nations, which adds a significant dimension to the standard analysis. Since the home country possesses a degree of monopoly power it can raise its over-all welfare by imposing a tariff on its labor-intensive imports from the foreign country. A tariff will raise the price of X at home and lower it in the foreign country. Since $\pi'(p)$ is negative this means that the marginal cost of defense will fall at home and rise abroad. This national security advantage of a tariff to the home country is thus an *additional* benefit. Furthermore, the higher real income of the tariff-imposing country increases its optimal defense spending which is capital-intensive. The capital–labor ratio in the tradable sector therefore falls, raising its production of the labor-intensive good X relative to Y. The increased world excess supply of X thus lowers the price of X further, reinforcing the improvement in the home country's terms of trade. The foreign country, however, loses welfare both in terms of utility from consumption and in terms of national security.

The "terms of trade" argument and the "national security" arguments that have both been advanced for tariffs thus merge into one in the present model where they can be balanced against each other to produce a single tariff that optimizes over-all national welfare at the expense of the foreigner.

Up to now we have treated the problem of interdependent defense expenditures by the two nations in a "Nash" or "Cournot" fashion, i.e. each takes the other's level as given and makes its own optimal response to that particular level, with equilibrium established at a point where each response is optimal, given the level of the other. We now investigate the "Stackelberg" solution, where one country takes the entire reaction function of the other as given and determines which point on the other's reaction will maximize its own welfare.

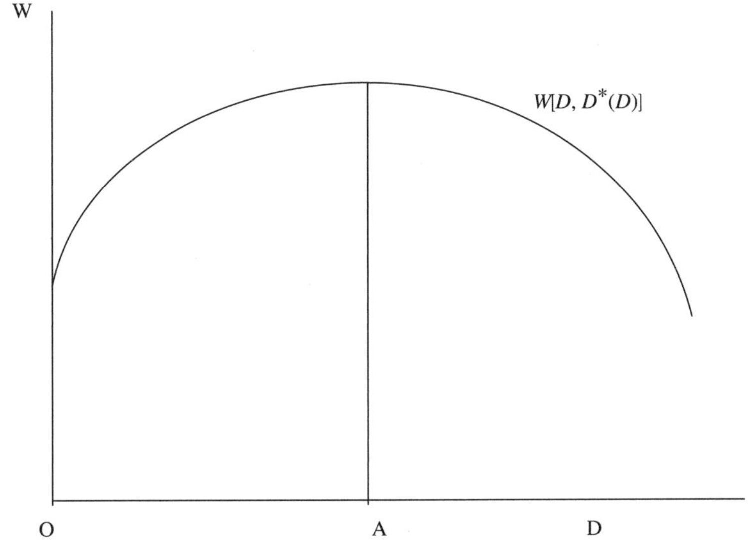

Fig. 2. Stackelberg optimum defense level.

The Stackelberg Problem for the home country is therefore to maximize its welfare function W, which is a function of both D and D^*, subject to the reaction function $D^*(D)$ of the foreign country. In Figure 2 we plot W as a function of D, with D^* being determined from $D^*(D)$ for each level of D. As D rises $U = U(C_x, C_y)$, utility from consumption, clearly falls but national security $S = S(D, D^*)$ can rise more than sufficiently to offset this fall, even though D^* rises in response along the reaction function $D^*(D)$. Eventually, however, the marginal welfare loss from declining consumption must rise sufficiently to more than offset any increase in national security, so that over-all welfare declines. The Stackelberg optimum for D is therefore the point at which $W(D)$ reaches a maximum, as at the level OA in Figure 2.

The Stackelberg optimum for the home country *also makes the foreign country better off*. This is not really paradoxical since the Nash equilibrium in optimal defense levels when each takes the other's defense level as given is clearly inefficient from a world standpoint. Thus we have a situation where *partial unilateral disarmament* by the Stackelberg leader raises the follower's welfare as well and is then clearly an improvement in world efficiency leaving more resources for consumption for both countries.

A bilateral defense agreement could of course reduce both defense levels even further and hence make both parties still better off.

The present framework can clearly be extended to cover issues such as burden-sharing between allies in a multi-country context, as examined by Wong (1991) and others.

References

Hartley, K., Sandler, T. (Eds.) (1995). *Handbook of Defense Economics*. Elsevier, Amsterdam.
Intriligator, M.D. (1975), Strategic considerations in the Richardson model of arms races. *Journal of Political Economy* 83 (2), 339–353.
Komiya, R. (1967), Non-traded goods and the pure theory of international trade. *International Economic Review* 8, 132–152.
Mayer, W. (1977), The national defense tariff argument reconsidered. *Journal of International Economics* 7, 363–377.
Polachek, S.W. (1980), Conflict and trade. *Journal of Conflict Resolution* 24, 55–78.
Richardson, L.F. (1960), *Arms and Insecurity: A Mathematical Theory of the Causes and Origins of War*. Homewood, Pittsburgh.
Sandler, T., Hartley, K. (1995), *The Economics of Defense*. Cambridge University Press.
Skaperdas, S., Syropoulos, C. (1996), Competitive trade with conflict. In: Garfinkel, M.R., Skaperdas, S. (Eds.), *The Political Economy of Conflict and Appropriation*. Cambridge University Press, (Chapter 5).
Waltz, K.N. (1959), *Man, the State and War*. Columbia University Press.
Wong, K.Y. (1991), Foreign trade, military alliance and defense-burden sharing. *Defense Economics* 2, 83–103.

CHAPTER 2

Do Factor Endowments Matter for North–North Trade?

Donald R. Davis[a] and David E. Weinstein[b]

[a]*Kathryn and Shelby Cullom Davis Professor of Economics and International Affairs, Department of Economics, Columbia University, USA*
E-mail address: drd28@columbia.edu
[b]*Carl S. Shoup Professor of the Japanese Economy, Department of Economics, Columbia University, USA*
E-mail address: dew35@columbia.edu

Abstract
The dominant paradigm of world trade patterns posits two principal features. Trade between North and South arises due to traditional comparative advantage. Trade within the North, largely intra-industry trade, is based on economies of scale and product differentiation. The paradigm specifically denies an important role for endowment differences in determining North–North trade. We demonstrate that trade in factor services *among* countries of the North is systematically related to endowment differences and large in economic magnitude. Intra-industry trade, rather than being a puzzle for a factor endowments theory, is instead the conduit for a great deal of this factor service trade.

Keywords: Comparative advantage, Intra-industry trade, endowment differences

JEL classifications: F1, F11, D5

1. Introduction

The new trade theory of the 1980s is primarily recognized for its novel contributions regarding increasing returns, product differentiation, and imperfect competition.[1] Yet the influence of this literature goes beyond simply adding a few new models to the canon. In a pair of influential papers, Krugman (1981) and Helpman (1981) articulated a vision of world

[1] See the seminal papers of Krugman (1979) and Lancaster (1980).

Frontiers of Economics and Globalization
Volume 4 ISSN: 1574-8715
DOI: 10.1016/S1574-8715(08)04002-5

trade patterns that integrated the new trade theory with the traditional factor endowments theory of Heckscher–Ohlin. In this formulation, each theory plays a role, but the roles differ. Trade among rich countries of the North is intra-industry and takes advantage of gains from specialization in a world of scale economies. Trade between North and South is inter-industry based on differences in factor endowments. This hybrid paradigm is now the professions dominant vision of the determinants of world trade patterns.

In arguing for the empirical relevance of the scale economies element of this paradigm, Krugman (1981) cited two seeming paradoxes in world trade patterns when viewed through a factor endowments lens: "First, much of world trade is between countries with similar factor endowments. Second, a large part of trade is intra-industry in character – that is, it consists of two-way trade in similar products."[2] The new paradigm specifically denied that factor endowment differences are important for understanding trade *among* the rich countries of the North, for which instead it turns to the new trade theory. And the predominance of intra-industry trade is also viewed as a puzzle, because this is viewed as trade in goods of similar factor intensity.[3] In effect, the new paradigm integrated the traditional and new theories by saying that the traditional theories explained the small part of world trade that is North–South while the new theories accounted for the large share of trade that is North–North.

The present chapter examines whether such a neat division is tenable. It provides the first sound empirical scrutiny of the role of factor endowments in determining North–North trade. It has not been possible to examine this empirical issue previously because the literature on trade in factor services was dominated by anomalies and conundrums, such as Trefler's (1995) "mystery of the missing trade" and Gabaix's (1997) "rejection of the Heckscher–Ohlin–Leontief hypothesis," rather than models that match well with the data.[4] Recently, Davis and Weinstein (2001) have provided a simple theoretical framework that provides a

---

[2] These observations about trade patterns were offered specifically to motivate a move to the new trade theory view which could account for these facts even among countries with identical endowments. Krugman (1980) also appealed to one element apart from trade patterns: an apparent absence of substantial distributional impact of trade reform.

[3] The work of Grubel and Lloyd (1975) played a fundamental role is focusing attention on the salience of intra-industry trade. Helpman and Krugman (1985, p. 2) discuss this issue as follows: "In particular, countries should export goods whose factor content reflects their underlying resources. This is in fact by and large true of countries' net exports. But to casual observation, and on more careful examination, actual trade patterns seem to include substantial two-way trade in goods of similar factor intensity. This 'intra-industry' trade seems both pointless and hard to explain from the point of view of a conventional trade analysis." This perspective is evident as well in virtually all recent editions of trade textbooks. See also Davis (1997) for a discussion.

[4] Cf. Bowen *et al.* (1987), Trefler (1995), and Gabaix (1997).

surprisingly strong match between prediction and data for trade in factor services. This is the starting point for the present chapter.

We will say that endowment differences are important for North–North trade if two criteria are met: (1) Factor service trade among countries of the North is *systematically* related to endowment differences and (2) The magnitude of factor service trade is economically large. Our results show that both criteria are met.

This implies that the core vision of the determinants of world trade patterns needs to be amended, particularly as it pertains to trade among the rich countries of the North. As the current paradigm suggests, scale economies and product differentiation may well be important for trade within the North – nothing that we do contests this. What we show is that endowments matter not only for North–South trade, but for trade *within* the North as well. Factor service trade for countries of the North is systematic, economically large, and frequently more intensively directed toward other countries of the North than toward the South.

Moreover, our work forces a reconsideration of the role of intra-industry trade. Conventionally its importance for bilateral trade among countries of the North is taken as evidence that endowments do not matter for this trade. What we show instead is that, when properly conceived and measured, intra-industry trade is instead one of the principal conduits of factor service trade for countries of the North.

The present work builds on Davis and Weinstein (2001), although it goes beyond that work in a number of dimensions. It develops new theoretical predictions about net factor content of trade to subsets of trading partners, including identifying cases in which the qualitative nature of this trade may differ by partner. It decomposes the net factor content of trade into analytically distinct components, which helps to understand on a deeper level the failure of factor content tests in so much of the prior literature. While it is based on the same data as Davis and Weinstein (2001), it departs from the estimation context of technology matrices in that paper because it wants a more exact detailing of the precise factor service flows and how prior work failed to make sense of them.

We develop this chapter in three additional sections. Section 2 articulates our basic theoretical framework, develops some new results regarding factor service trade with well-defined classes of countries, and provides a theoretical decomposition relating our measures to those employed in previous empirical work. Section 3 derives the principal empirical results. Section 4 concludes.

2. *Theory*

The starting point for an investigation of the role of trade in factor services must be measurement. The classic framework for measuring trade in factor services is due to Vanek (1968). Trefler (1993, 1995) amends this in an adjusted factor price equalization framework to allow either for factor-augmenting or for Hicks-neutral technical differences. Deardorff (1982) and Helpman (1984) develop versions that are highly relevant for our work here, which allow for differences in relative factor prices across countries that cannot be handled as simple factor-augmenting differences. Davis and Weinstein (2001) develop a variant of the Deardorff–Helpman model with explicit consideration of the nature of technical differences, as well as the presence of non-traded goods, and show that such a model has substantial empirical support.

Here our concern is to move beyond a test of the theory to understand some key questions for which magnitudes matter. Is factor service trade important for countries of the North? If so, what is the relative importance in this trade of trade with other countries of the North? Is this factor service trade systematic, even among countries of the North? How does the fact that much trade within the North is intra-industry affect our view of factor service trade among these countries? Is intra-industry trade truly trade in goods of similar factor intensity? Over all, how important is intra-industry trade in the net exchange of factor services among countries of the North? To answer these questions, we specify a model that builds on Davis and Weinstein (2001).

The theoretical framework that we employ is exceedingly simple. We assume that we are in a Heckscher–Ohlin world with many goods, factors, and countries. Technologies are constant returns to scale. Preferences are identical and homothetic. Any technological differences are assumed to be of the factor-augmenting variety, so can be subsumed by converting factors to efficiency units. Factor price equalization is assumed not to hold for any pair of countries in our sample. The number of goods produced is assumed to be sufficiently large that we can safely ignore "boundary" goods produced by more than one country. In short, this is a standard multi-cone Heckscher–Ohlin model with specialization in traded goods. When considered in a two-factor framework, this model receives strong empirical support in Davis and Weinstein (2001).

In this chapter, a prime concern will be tracking the factor content of trade. A standard way for measuring this in the case of No FPE is developed in Deardorff (1982) and Helpman (1984).[5] The key insight is

---

[5] This is very close to what Deardorff (1982) termed the "actual factor content of trade," which allowed him his most general results. To make our measure and his coincide exactly would have required an iteration procedure that traces back factor contents of intermediates used in exports, the factor content of imported intermediates used in the production of those intermediates, etc. Because a great deal of the factor content comes from use of non-tradables and because imports are typically a small portion of usage even in tradable sectors, we judged these issues to be of second order for our purposes. Note that Deardorff and Helpman used these measures to derive restrictions on comparative costs, whereas we will be concerned more directly with the measures of factor content themselves.

that when techniques of production vary across countries, as is the case when FPE fails, factor contents should be measured using the producer's technology. Allowing c and c' to index countries, $\mathbf{B}_{fc}$ to be the fth row of the total factor input matrix of country c, $\mathbf{E}_c$ to be gross exports from c, and $\mathbf{M}_{cc'}$ to be gross imports by c from c', the Deardorff–Helpman measure of the factor content of trade for country c in this case with No FPE is:

$$\mathbf{F}_{fc} \equiv \mathbf{B}_{fc}\mathbf{E}_c - \sum_{c'} \mathbf{B}_{fc'}\mathbf{M}_{cc'} \tag{1}$$

Note that for the case with FPE, $\mathbf{B}_{fc} = \mathbf{B}_{fc'}$, so this reduces to the standard Heckscher–Ohlin–Vanek (HOV) measure.

An extremely important question is how the analytically correct Deardorff–Helpman measure of the net factor content of trade compares to the conventional measures of net factor trade that have been employed in the empirical literature. The conventional approach has been to assume that the appropriate measure of a country's net factor trade is the product of a common technology matrix, typically that of the United States, and the country's net trade vector. This is easily accomplished via a decomposition of the appropriate measure into two components, one reflecting the conventional measure, and the second reflecting various types of measurement errors inherent in the conventional measure.

To do the decomposition, it is useful to start with a few key concepts. First, let $\mathbf{T}_{cc'}$ be the vector of net exports by industry between countries c and c'. Positive elements correspond to industries in which c is a net exporter to c' and negative elements indicate those industries in which it is a net importer. It is convenient to divide up the net export vector into these two components. Define a variable $\mathbf{T}^{+}_{cc'}$ to be the level of net *exports* where this is positive, and to be zero elsewhere. Correspondingly, define $\mathbf{T}^{-}_{cc'}$ to be the level of net *imports* where c is a net importer (hence a negative number) and to be zero elsewhere. Then, it follows that:

$$\mathbf{T}_{cc'} \equiv \mathbf{T}^{+}_{cc'} + \mathbf{T}^{-}_{cc'}$$

It is also convenient to define a variable we can call "matched intra-industry trade." In bilateral trade, it is the positive quantity of imports within an industry that can be exactly matched with the bilateral exports within the same industry. Using the mnemonic of Grubel–Lloyd, matched intra-industry trade is defined for industry i as:[6]

$$\mathbf{G}^{i}_{cc'} \equiv \min\{\mathbf{E}^{i}_{cc'}, \mathbf{M}^{i}_{cc'}\}$$

---

[6] Grubel and Lloyd (1975) provided an influential early documentation of the predominance of intra-industry trade, particularly among countries of the North.

Using this concept of matched intra-industry trade, it is possible to decompose the gross export vector into two components. Some goods we import on net, so that our gross exports equal precisely the level of matched intra-industry trade, $\mathbf{G}^{i}_{cc'}$. Others we export on net, so our gross exports are the sum of matched intra-industry trade plus the net exports. Our gross exports can then be written as:

$$\begin{aligned}\mathbf{E}_{cc'} &\equiv \mathbf{G}_{cc'} + \mathbf{T}^{+}_{cc'} \\ &\equiv \text{Matched intra-industry trade} + \text{(positive) net exports}\end{aligned}$$

We can do a similar decomposition for our net imports:

$$\begin{aligned}\mathbf{M}_{cc'} &\equiv \mathbf{G}_{cc'} - \mathbf{T}^{-}_{cc'} \\ &\equiv \text{Matched intra-industry trade} - \text{(negative) net imports}\end{aligned}$$

Just to tie this down, note that the net trade vector between c and c' is then:

$$\mathbf{T}_{cc'} \equiv \mathbf{E}_{cc'} - \mathbf{M}_{cc'} \equiv \left(\mathbf{G}_{cc'} + \mathbf{T}^{+}_{cc'}\right) - \left(\mathbf{G}_{cc'} - \mathbf{T}^{-}_{cc'}\right) \equiv \mathbf{T}^{+}_{cc'} + \mathbf{T}^{-}_{cc'}$$

Now we can turn to the decomposition of our appropriate measure of net factor trade. Since most previous studies employed the US technology matrix, we will use it for the decomposition.Recall that the conventional measure of country c's factor content of trade has been:

$$\mathbf{F}^{\text{Conv}}_{fc} \equiv \mathbf{B}_{f\text{US}}\mathbf{T}_{c}$$

If we add and subtract this from our appropriate measure from Equation (1) above, we obtain the desired decomposition:

$$\begin{aligned}\mathbf{F}_{fc} \equiv \mathbf{F}^{\text{Conv}}_{fc} &- \left[\sum_{c'}(\mathbf{B}_{f\text{US}} - \mathbf{B}_{fc})\mathbf{T}^{+}_{cc'}\right] - \left[\sum_{c'}(\mathbf{B}_{f\text{US}} - \mathbf{B}_{fc'})\mathbf{T}^{-}_{cc'}\right] \\ &+ \left[\sum_{c'}(\mathbf{B}_{fc} - \mathbf{B}_{fc'})\mathbf{G}_{cc'}\right] \\ &\equiv \mathbf{F}^{\text{Conv}}_{fc} + \varepsilon^{\text{NE}}_{fc} + \varepsilon^{\text{NI}}_{fc} + \varepsilon^{\text{MIT}}_{fc}\end{aligned}$$

The first term is the conventional measure of the factor content of trade employed in previous studies, based on all countries using US technology. The remaining three terms identify systematic errors associated with the conventional measure, and are straightforward to interpret. The first error arises when the factor content of country c's net exports (NE) is incorrectly measured with the US technology matrix rather than the appropriate matrix from country c. The second source of error comes similarly from the fact that the factor content of net imports (NI) is incorrectly measured with the US technology matrix rather than that of the producer, country c'. The final error arises because the use of any common technology matrix defines matched intra-industry trade (MIT) to have zero factor content, whereas the true factor content of trade must take account of the fact that even matched intra-industry trade will contribute to the net factor content, the magnitude of this error depends on the volume of matched intra-industry trade and the difference in production techniques employed by c and c'.

So far we have been working with a country's trade with the rest of the world. The standard theory typically makes no prediction about *bilateral* factor contents because the bilateral pattern of goods trade may not be uniquely defined. Here, however, the assumptions of specialization and identical homothetic preferences allow us to make bilateral factor content predictions. Because of specialization, there is little harm in thinking of each country producing a single composite good using all of its factors, which it both consumes and exports. Thus the net factor content of trade in factor f between country c and c', denoted $\mathbf{F}_{fcc'}$, will be the difference between the exports of f from c and the imports of f by c:

$$\mathbf{F}_{fcc'} = \mathbf{s}_{c'}\mathbf{V}_{fc} - \mathbf{s}_c\mathbf{V}_{fc'}$$

Simple manipulation of this implies that country c will be a net exporter of factor f bilaterally to any country such that:

$$\frac{\mathbf{V}_{fc}}{\mathbf{s}_c} > \frac{\mathbf{V}_{fc'}}{\mathbf{s}_{c'}}$$

In the reverse case it will be a bilateral net importer.

This last point is worth emphasizing. The typical country, one not at the extremes of abundance for a particular factor, will find that it is a net exporter of a factor to those less abundant than it as measured by $\mathbf{V}_{fc}/\mathbf{s}_c$ and a net importer of those factor services in the reverse case. The measure of the net factor content of trade with the world as a whole tends to obscure this systematic feature of the model because the positive and negative bilateral net factor trades may be canceling out. Moreover, it is important to stress that even if the total net factor trade is driven toward zero, this does not mean that the gains from being able to engage in these trades are likewise heading toward zero. Rather, there are gains from trading both with those more and less well endowed with the factor.

This motivates separating out for each factor and country the set of countries that are more or less well endowed with a factor. Let $\Omega(f, c)$ be defined as the set of countries c' more abundant in factor f than country c, i.e. in which $\mathbf{V}_{fc}/\mathbf{s}_c < \mathbf{V}_{fc'}/\mathbf{s}_{c'}$. Similarly, we can define $\omega(f, c)$ as the set of countries for which c is more abundant in f, i.e. $\mathbf{V}_{fc}/\mathbf{s}_c > \mathbf{V}_{fc'}/\mathbf{s}_{c'}$. This allows us to calculate the factor content of trade separately for each country and factor with respect to those with which that country is a net exporter vs. importer of the factor services. Hence define:

$$\mathbf{F}_{fc}^{+} \equiv \sum_{c' \in \Omega(f,c)} \mathbf{B}_{fc}\mathbf{E}_{cc'} - \sum_{c' \in \Omega(f,c)} \mathbf{B}_{fc'}\mathbf{M}_{cc'} \quad \text{and}$$

$$\mathbf{F}^{-}_{fc} \equiv \sum_{c' \in \omega(f,c)} \mathbf{B}_{fc}\mathbf{E}_{cc'} - \sum_{c' \in \omega(f,c)} \mathbf{B}_{fc'}\mathbf{M}_{cc'}$$

Finally, having spent so much time-developing measures of the factor content of trade, we should say a few words about what we hope to learn from these measures. Deardorff and Staiger (1988) develop conditions under which it is possible to convert from factor content measures to welfare measures. The required restrictions are strong and do not hold in the present context. This makes it difficult to make strong normative statements based on the findings. Nonetheless, we do feel that the measures can be informative. First, the theory that we have developed actually places much stronger restrictions on the data than the traditional HOV theory, including predictions bilaterally and to theoretically identified subsets of countries. Hence it will be informative to see if the measures conform to these predictions. Second, the predictions and measures of net factor trade with the distinct groups of countries provide at least some coarse insight about the likely magnitude of impact on local factor markets of trade with the distinct groups of countries. Lastly, they will also provide again at least a coarse guide to how important trade in factor services is within the OECD as opposed to with the remainder of the world.

3. *Measuring net factor trade*

3.1. Data

All of our direct and indirect technology matrices for our OECD countries are constructed using information available in the STAN, ISDB, and OECD input–output databases. Each country's economy is divided into 34 sectors which yields industry definitions that are equivalent to ISIC three- or four-digit data. Endowment data are taken from these sources for our sample of 10 OECD countries and from the Penn World Tables version 5.6. Trade data are taken from the OECD and from Feenstra *et al.* (1997). The exact methods used to construct our technology matrices are often complex and details are described in detail in the data appendix to Davis and Weinstein (2001). An important difference between the data used in that paper and the data in this chapter, is that all trade tests in the former work are conducted using estimated technology matrices. In this chapter, we only work with the actual technology matrices.[7] All other data are identical in the two papers.

[7] The technology matrix for the composite rest of the world corresponds to the one used in specification T6 in Davis and Weinstein (2001). This matrix satisfies the full employment condition for the rest of the world.

All technology matrices and endowments were adjusted so that factor service flows are in efficiency units. This entails deflating each element of $\mathbf{B}_c$ and $\mathbf{V}_c$ by a Hicks-neutral parameter, λ_c, corresponding to the productivity of factors in that country. The parameter λ_{US} is normalized to unity. Each of these λ_c is calculated according to specification P5 in Davis and Weinstein (2001). Since $\mathbf{B}_c\mathbf{Y}_c = \mathbf{V}_c$, it must also be the case that we have full employment in efficiency units, i.e. $\mathbf{B}_c^E\mathbf{Y}_c \equiv (1/\lambda_c)\, \mathbf{B}_c\mathbf{Y}_c = (1/\lambda_c)\, \mathbf{V}_c \equiv \mathbf{V}_c^E$. To keep the notation simple, however, we have suppressed the efficiency unit superscript (E) in subsequent sections.

3.2. True and conventional measures of net factor trade

In the theoretical section, we note that the starting point for our analysis is the Deardorff–Helpman measure of the factor content of trade in a No-FPE world. We also noted that this measure of the true factor content of trade can be decomposed into the conventional measure plus three sources of error. To place this in context, it is useful to think about what role might have been played by this measurement issue in the phenomenon that Trefler (1995) memorably termed the "mystery of the missing trade." The mystery concerns a feature of the data under the conventional empirical implementation of HOV:

$$\mathbf{F}_{fc}^{\text{Conv}} \equiv \mathbf{B}_{f\text{US}}\mathbf{T}_c = \mathbf{V}_{fc} - s_c\mathbf{V}_{fW}$$

In simple terms, the mystery in the data is that the measured net factor trade on the LHS is an order of magnitude smaller than the predicted factor trade based on endowments on the RHS.

The major thrust of Trefler's effort to solve this anomaly was to take the LHS as given and ask what amendments on the RHS would help. His preferred specification featured Hicks-neutral efficiency differences across countries and a home bias in demand. The assumption of a home bias directly scales down the RHS, but the efficiency difference will affect both sides of the equation.

Davis and Weinstein (2001) and Helpman (1999) argue that the conventional measure of net factor trade, $\mathbf{F}_{fc}^{\text{Conv}}$, is likely to be biased toward zero. The reasoning is quite straightforward. In a No-FPE world, factor prices vary inversely with factor abundance. This leads countries to specialize in the production of goods that use their abundant factors intensively and not to produce goods that use their scarce factors intensively. Since a country's technology matrix is based on what is actually produced in that country, countries that are abundant in a factor will use techniques that use more of their abundant factors. Applying this matrix to imports from less endowed countries will overstate the measured factor content of imports for abundant factors and understate it for less abundant factors. This will cause $\mathbf{F}_{fc}^{\text{Conv}}$ to be biased toward zero because we erroneously think that our imports are produced using the same technologies employed at home.

Although Davis and Weinstein (2001) demonstrate that $\mathbf{F}_{fc}^{\text{Conv}}$ is much smaller than predicted factor trade and that these predicted biases in the technology matrices exist, the chapter did not directly examine whether these biases were critical to understanding the missing trade phenomenon. This is because in the Davis and Weinstein work, both the LHS and RHS change in the move across specifications. In this section, we show that measurement error alone suffices to generate the "mystery of the missing trade."

Rather than work with estimated technology matrices as in our earlier work, we compare $\mathbf{F}_{fc}^{\text{Conv}}$ with the correct Deardorff–Helpman measure of $\mathbf{F}_{fc}$, calculated using the true technology matrices. A plot appears as Figure 1. If the conventional measure of net factor content is close to the true factor content, all of the data will lie on the 45 degree line, or more weakly, will lie in quadrants one and three. A quick scan of the plot reveals this is very much at odds with the data. The magnitude of the conventional

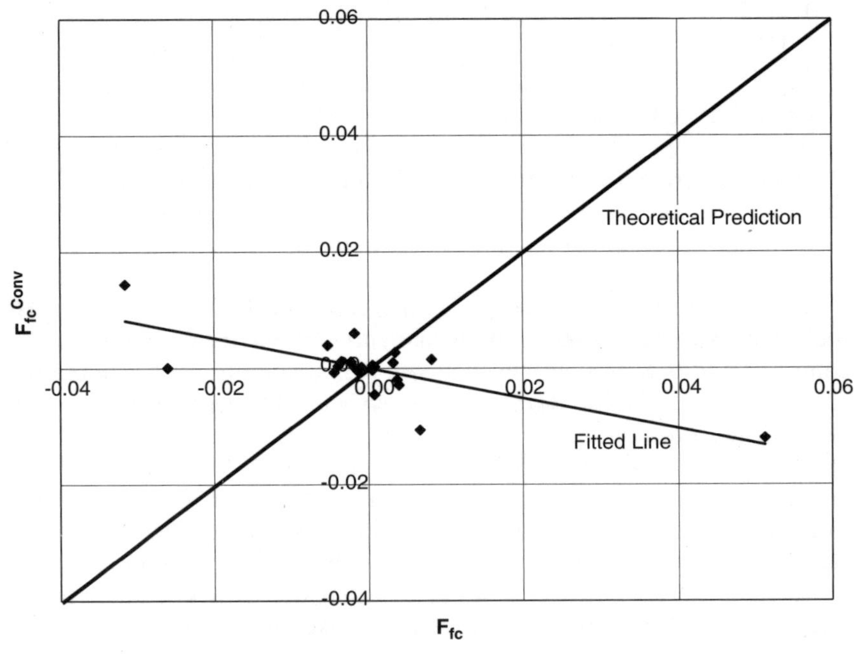

$\mathbf{F}_{fc}^{\text{Conv}} \equiv \mathbf{B}_{f,\text{US}}\mathbf{T}^{c}$ is the conventional measure of the factor content of trade.

$\mathbf{F}_{fc} \equiv \mathbf{B}_{fc}\mathbf{E}_{c} - \sum_{c' \neq c} \mathbf{B}_{fc'}\mathbf{M}_{cc'}$ is the Deardorff–Helpman measure of the factor content of trade.

This figure shows that conventionally measured net factor service trade is negatively correlated with actual net factor service trade.

Fig. 1. ***F_{fc}^{Conv} vs. true factor content of trade, F_{fc}.***

measure of net factor trade is much smaller than true net factor trade. The variance of the former is only one-eighth as large as the latter. More surprising yet is that there is, if anything, a *negative* relation between conventional and true net factor trade. Less than one third of the points lie in quadrants one and three.

The fact that the conventional measure of net factor trade is much smaller than the true measure, and the fact that the relation is negative, carries an important message. Efforts to reconcile measured and predicted net factor trade by hypotheses that would alter predicted net factor trade were ultimately doomed. The attenuation bias is so severe that this sufficed to generate the mystery of the missing trade, quite apart from other problems in theory or measurement.

A natural question arises at this point. Nearly all of the studies have used only the US technology matrix. Yet from the theory, there are reasons to believe that the adoption of *any* common technology matrix will lead to attenuation, for example because it excludes the possibility that there is factor content in intra-industry trade. Hence it is reasonable to ask whether this crippling mis-measurement of net factor trade is a consequence of using the US technology matrix, or of using any common technology matrix. This is easy to resolve by simply substituting the technology matrices of other countries for that of the US and repeating the experiments. A plot using all available technology matrices appears as Figure 2. The results bear a striking resemblance to those based on the US technology matrix. The conventional measures understate the magnitude of true net factor trade, and indeed maintain the negative relation between the conventional and true measures. The severe mis-measurement of net factor trade is not simply a consequence of the choice of the US technology matrix.

A third issue arises regarding the conventional measure of net factor trade. Theory suggests that the mis-measurement of the factor content of imports is a critical element in generating the attenuation. Hence we should observe the bias even if we apply a country's technology matrix only to its own net trade vector. It is again simple to investigate this by restricting the sample from the last exercise to the cases in which there is a match between the country whose technology matrix is in use and the net trade vector we look at. The plot appears as Figure 3. From the standpoint of the previous literature, the result is very discouraging. The conventional measure and true net factor trade are no more strongly related even when we restrict the sample to the country whose technology matrix we employ.

3.3. Decomposition of net factor trade and the role of intra-industry trade

So far we have been looking only at the relation between conventional and true measures of net factor trade. Our results suggest that insofar as there

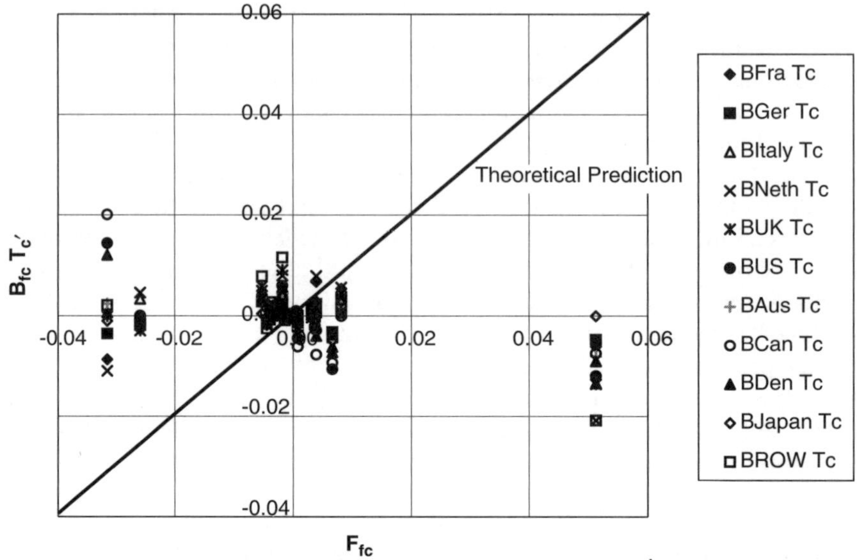

$\mathbf{B}_{fc}\mathbf{T}_{c'}$ is a conventional measure of the factor content of country c''s trade vector evaluated using country c's technology matrix. The difference is that rather than assume everyone uses the US technology matrix, we calculate this respectively assuming all use the technology of France, then Germany, and so on. $\mathbf{F}_{fc} \equiv \mathbf{B}_{fc}\mathbf{E}_c - \sum_{c' \neq c} \mathbf{B}_{fc'}\mathbf{M}_{cc'}$ is the Deardorff–Helpman measure of the actual factor content of trade. This figure shows that the negative correlation between conventionally measured net factor service trade and actual net factor service trade does not depend on the technology matrix used.

Fig. 2. Conventional measure vs. true factor content of trade using various countries' technology matrices as the base.

is a relation, it is negative. We now turn to a more formal decomposition in the data. We have noted there are three sources of error. For simplicity of reference, we repeat the decomposition here:

$$
\begin{aligned}
\mathbf{F}_{fc} \equiv \mathbf{F}_{fc}^{\mathrm{Conv}} &- \left[\sum_{c'} (\mathbf{B}_{f\mathrm{US}} - \mathbf{B}_{fc})\mathbf{T}_{cc'}^{+}\right] - \left[\sum_{c'} (\mathbf{B}_{f\mathrm{US}} - \mathbf{B}_{fc'})\mathbf{T}_{cc'}^{-}\right] \\
&+ \left[\sum_{c'} (\mathbf{B}_{fc} - \mathbf{B}_{fc'})G_{cc'}\right] \\
\equiv \mathbf{F}_{fc}^{\mathrm{Conv}} &+ \varepsilon_{fc}^{\mathrm{NE}} + \varepsilon_{fc}^{\mathrm{NI}} + \varepsilon_{fc}^{\mathrm{MIT}}
\end{aligned}
$$

Our discussion will emphasize the last of these errors. It is a commonplace in the theory that the defining characteristic of intra-industry trade is that it is in goods of the same factor intensity because of the assumption that we are producing the same goods with the same

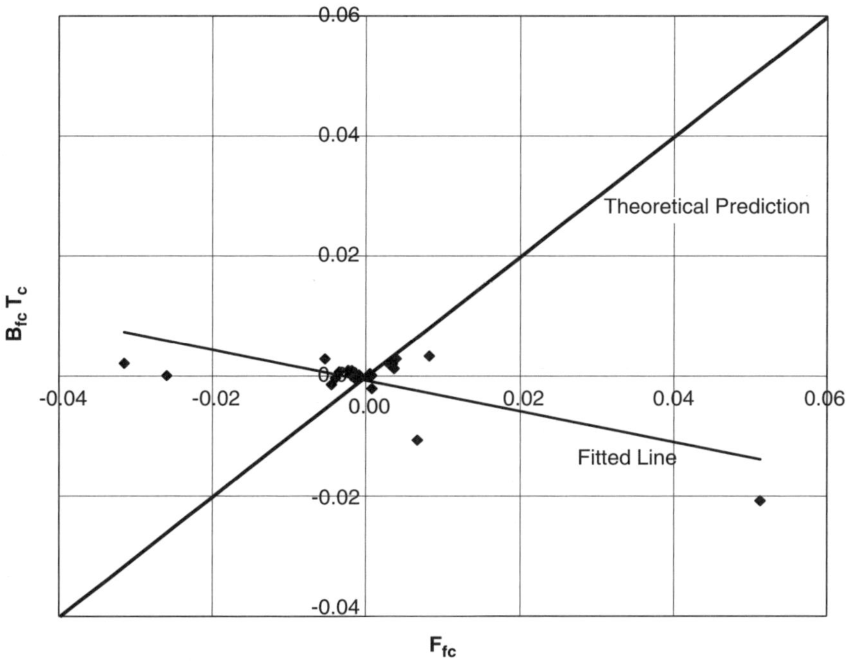

Here we apply each country's technology matrix only to its own net trade vector. That is, $\mathbf{B}_{fc}\mathbf{T}_c$ is the factor content of country c 's trade vector evaluated using its own technology matrix. $\mathbf{F}_{fc} \equiv \mathbf{B}_{fc}\mathbf{E}_c - \sum_{c' \neq c} \mathbf{B}_{fc'}\mathbf{M}_{cc'}$ is the Deardorff–Helpman measure of the factor content of trade. This figure shows that even if one applies each country's technology matrix to their own net trade vector, the measured net factor content of trade is still quite small compared with the (Deardorff–Helpman) measure of actual factor service flows.

Fig. 3. Measured factor trade using own technology matrix vs. actual factor trade.

technologies and factor prices.[8] Hence, matched intra-industry trade, where exports identically equal imports, should have zero factor content. In fact, this relation has been *imposed* in previous empirical tests of HOV, which look only at countries' *net* commodity trade vector. Yet by examining the equation above, and from the fact already observed that countries' technology matrices differ, we can see that this would not be precisely right.

This raises the question of how important a role intra-industry trade plays in carrying out net factor trade. Conventional wisdom based on integrated equilibrium models holds that this term should be small, for two

[8] That is, we are in an "integrated equilibrium" in the sense of Helpman and Krugman (1985).

reasons. First, where technologies differ greatly, as in North–South trade, we know there is little intra-industry trade. Second, where we know there is a great deal of intra-industry trade, as in North–North trade, the input coefficients should differ either trivially or randomly. Hence, for intra-industry trade to contribute importantly to true net factor trade, it must be the case that the technology differences are both large and systematic. The conventional wisdom, however, does not hold up if there is specialization of goods within industries and a failure of factor price equalization. In this case, intra-industry trade is likely to be an important conduit of factor service trade because even within industries goods are being produced with different factor proportions.

A simple approach to assessing the importance of intra-industry trade in the export of factor services is to plot the factor content of intra-industry trade, $\varepsilon_{fc}^{\mathrm{MIT}}$, against the factor content of trade, $\mathbf{F}_{fc}$. If intra-industry trade is unimportant as a communicator of net factor content, then the data should lie along the horizontal axis. In the unlikely case that all net factor content is carried out through intra-industry trade, the data will lie on the 45-degree line. The plot appears as in Figure 4. It is striking that intra-industry trade has a much more systematic relation to true net factor content than our traditional measure does. Moreover, the slope of the line is 0.42, indicating that, on average, more than 40 percent of all net factor trade is carried out through intra-industry exchange.

A more detailed view is revealed by examining the role of intra-industry trade in total net factor trade for individual countries. There is no *a priori* reason that these terms must have the same sign. But when they do, and when their ratio is less than unity, there is a natural interpretation of this ratio as the share of intra-industry trade in a country's total net trade in a factor. The results appear in Table 1. As it turns out, in 19 of 22 cases, the factor content of intra-industry trade is the same as the overall factor content of trade. By contrast, this was true for only 7 of 22 cases with the conventional measure of net factor trade. The median ratio of factor content of intra-industry trade relative to $\mathbf{F}_{fc}$ is 34 percent. This actually understates the importance of intra-industry trade for many countries. In half of the rich OECD countries in our sample, intra-industry trade is more important than inter-industry trade in the net export or import of factor services. Moreover, for France, the UK, and the US, the factor content of intra-industry trade is at least two-thirds as large as total net factor service trade.

This suggests that the profession has operated under a serious misconception. The prevalence of intra-industry trade has been taken as evidence that the factor content of North–North trade is minimal. An unexpected converse is closer to the truth: intra-industry trade is in fact one of the principal conduits of net factor trade. This is true even for the rich OECD countries.

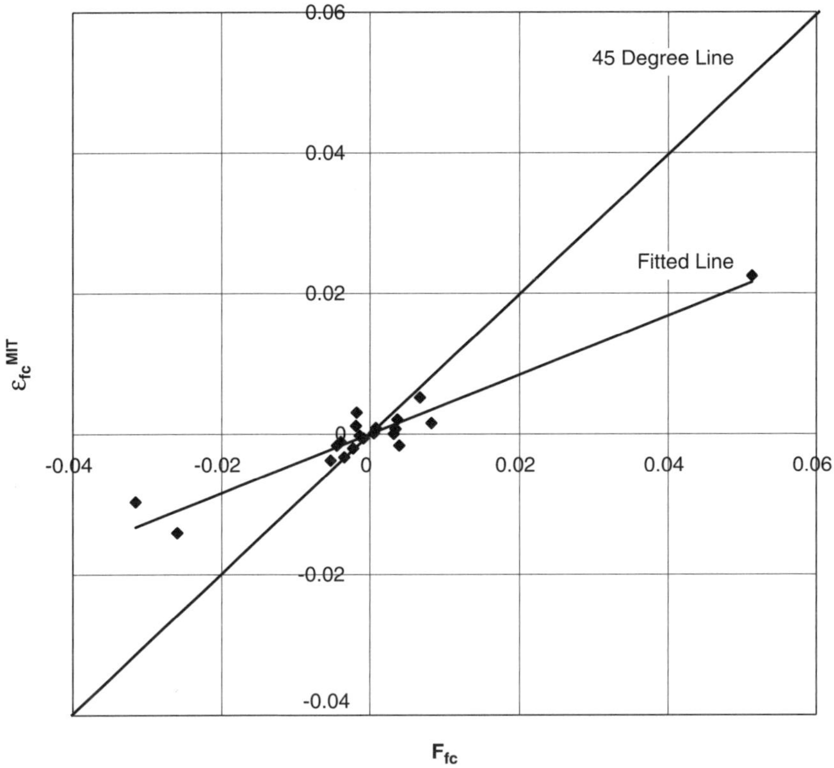

$\varepsilon_{fc}^{MIT} \equiv \sum_{c'} \left[\mathbf{B}_{fc} - \mathbf{B}_{fc'} \right] \mathbf{G}_{cc'}$ is the factor content of matched intra-industry trade.

$\mathbf{F}_{fc} \equiv \mathbf{B}_{fc}\mathbf{E}_{c} - \sum_{c' \neq c} \mathbf{B}_{fc'}\mathbf{M}_{cc'}$ is the Deardorff–Helpman measure of the factor content of trade. This figure shows that the factor content of intra-industry trade is quite large as a share of, and highly correlated with, total factor service trade.

Fig. 4. Factor content of intraindustry trade vs. true F_{fc}.

3.4. Are factor service flows important?

The previous section shows that the conventional measure of factor service flows is quite small relative to actual flows. This still leaves open the question of how important actual factor service flows are. As we noted earlier, theory does not provide a uniquely appropriate measure. Here we will provide a variety of metrics that will throw light on various facets of the question.

We begin with a simple and intuitive measure. We just scale the absolute value of the net factor trade by the national endowment of a factor. This may roughly be interpreted as the share of the national endowment exported or imported on net. The results of this experiment appear in Table 2. The median in our sample of 10 OECD countries is a net trader of

Table 1. The factor content of matched intra-industry trade as a share of total factor content trade

	$\frac{\varepsilon_{fc}^{\text{MIT}}}{\mathbf{F}_{fc}}$		
	Capital	Labor	Average
Australia	0.24	0.17	0.21
Canada	0.01	−0.61	−0.30
Denmark	0.23	0.68	0.45
France	0.56	0.96	0.76
Germany	0.19	0.71	0.45
Italy	0.84	0.28	0.56
Japan	−0.42	−1.70	−1.06
The Netherlands	0.21	0.90	0.56
UK	1.11	0.36	0.74
USA	0.78	0.54	0.66
ROW	0.31	0.44	0.37
Median	0.24	0.44	0.34

$\varepsilon_{fc}^{\text{MIT}} \equiv \sum_{c'} \left[\mathbf{B}_{fc} - \mathbf{B}_{fc'}\right] \mathbf{G}_{cc'}$ is the factor content of matched intra-industry trade.
$\mathbf{F}_{fc} \equiv \mathbf{B}_{fc}\,\mathbf{E}_c - \sum_{c' \neq c} \mathbf{B}_{fc'}\mathbf{M}_{cc'}$ is the Deardorff–Helpman measure of the factor content of trade. This table shows that the factor content of intra-industry trade is large relative to total the total net factor content of trade for most countries and factors.

Table 2. Net factor service flows as a share of national endowments

	Capital	Labor
Median Abs($\mathbf{F}_{fc}/\mathbf{V}_{fc}$)	0.077	0.102
Median Abs($\mathbf{F}_{fc}/\mathbf{V}_{fc}$) G10 only	0.048	0.089
Median Abs($\mathbf{F}_{fc}/\mathbf{V}_{fc}^{\text{tradable}}$)	0.181	0.357
Median {Abs(($\mathbf{F}_{fc}^{+}/\mathbf{V}_{fc}$)+($\mathbf{F}_{fc}^{-}/\mathbf{V}_{fc}$))}	0.098	0.123

Notes: G10 refers to the sample of 10 OECD countries for which we have technology matrices.
$\mathbf{F}_{fc} \equiv \mathbf{B}_{fc}\mathbf{E}_c - \sum_{c' \neq c} \mathbf{B}_{fc'}\mathbf{M}_{cc'}$ is the Deardorff–Helpman measure of the factor content of trade. $\mathbf{F}_{jc}^{+}$ is net factor trade with more abundant countries; $\mathbf{F}_{jc}^{-}$ is net factor trade with less abundant countries; and $\mathbf{V}_{fc}$ are endowments of factor f in country c. This table shows that net factor service flows are quite large relative to national endowments. This is especially true when considering the magnitudes of these flows relative to endowments used in the production of tradables or when correcting for the attenuation bias arising from the fact that countries systematically are net exporters of factor services to less abundant countries and net importers from more abundant countries.

approximately 5 percent of its total capital and 9 percent of its total labor. These shares are much higher for the Netherlands and Denmark, which export capital services equal to over 10 percent of their capital and import labor services equal to over 15 percent of their labor.

In recent papers, Irwin (1996) and Feenstra (1998) have argued that scaling by a country's total resources (in their case, GDP) may be seriously misleading about the influence of trade within the tradable sectors. This point is underscored by the observation in Davis and Weinstein (2001) that the interaction between non-tradable sectors and the failure of FPE is very important in reconciling predicted and measured net factor trade. These considerations suggest the value of considering a scaling by national endowments net of resources devoted to non-traded production.[9] This is implemented easily. If we pre-multiply non-traded output by the relevant technical coefficients, we get the commitment of resources to non-traded sectors, which can be subtracted from national endowments to yield the desired endowments committed to traded sectors.

The results from scaling total net factor trade by endowments devoted to tradables are presented in Table 2. The median country is an absolute net trader of 18 percent of its capital endowment and 36 percent of its labor endowment devoted to tradables. This indicates that for the typical country, net factor trade looms quite large relative to total resources devoted to production of tradables.

3.5. Special properties of net factor trade in a No-FPE world

This chapter has taken relatively little advantage thus far of the special structure of the underlying theoretical assumption of No-FPE. As it turns out, this assumption imposes a great deal more structure on our predictions than would the conventional HOV model. In the conventional HOV model, a country's net factor trade is well defined relative to all remaining countries taken together, but not typically to any subset of countries. We showed in the theoretical section that in the No-FPE world, there are very definite predictions of the model both bilaterally and relative to subsets of the remaining countries. In particular, it stresses that a Vanek-type chain can be formed, factor-by-factor, dividing the countries according to whether they are more or less well endowed with a factor than the country in question. The important fact for us here is that the typical

[9] Unfortunately, we do not have a perfect breakdown of tradable and non-tradable goods. If we define tradables to include all manufacturing, mining, and agricultural sectors, and define all other sectors as non-tradables, we obtain a rough division. The division is rough because many sectors that we label tradable contain goods traded only with great difficulty (e.g. concrete), and our non-tradable goods sectors contain some that are traded (e.g. Transport and Communication and Finance and Insurance). Even so, using this organization scheme, the median import to domestic-absorption ratio is 0.254 for the tradable sectors and 0.004 for the non-tradables sectors. Furthermore, when looking at the data on a sector-by-sector basis we find that the median import to domestic-absorption ratio is always above 0.12 for our tradables sectors and below 0.05 for non-tradables. This suggests that our classification scheme appropriately captures the differential tradability.

Table 3. Sign tests for trade with more and less abundant countries

	Proportion correct in world		Proportion correct in G10	
	Capital	Labor	Capital	Labor
Aggregate data				
Imports factors from more abundant countries	0.700	1.000	0.667	1.000
Exports factors to less abundant countries	1.000	0.800	1.000	0.700
Total	0.850	0.900	0.842	0.858
p-value	0.001	0.000	0.002	0.002
Bilateral country data				
Imports factors from more abundant partners or exports factors to less abundant partners	0.673	0.746	0.600	0.689
p-value	0.007	0.000	0.116	0.008
Overall	0.709		0.644	
p-value	0.000		0.000	

Notes: G10 refers to the sample of 10 OECD countries for which we have technology matrices. The first panel of this table shows that countries systematically are net exporters of factors to the set of less abundant countries and net importers from the set of more abundant countries. The second panel shows that even bilateral trade reflects endowment differences.

country is predicted to be a net exporter of a factor's services to all countries, separately or together, who are less well endowed with this factor, and a net importer of services of this factor from any and all of the countries better endowed with this factor. This special structure allows us to further investigate the empirical robustness of our theoretical model.

The results of this exercise are presented in Table 3. With two factors and two groups for our sample of 10 OECD countries and the composite Rest of the World, there are 40 observations.[10] In nearly 90 percent of the cases, the model correctly predicts the direction of net factor trade. This is significantly different from a random outcome at all conventional significance levels. This is particularly impressive given that we are predicting that each country will be a net exporter of a factor to one group of countries and a net importer of the same factor from a separate group of countries.

This also suggests one further amendment in our calculation of the role of net factor trade in a No-FPE world. A simple example will make the relevant analytic point. Consider the case of a country that happens to have endowments in nearly the same proportion as the world as a whole. The factor content of its production is nearly proportional to world endowments by market clearing. But identical and homothetic preferences

[10] Countries at the extremes of the abundance distribution always have no trade with more extreme partners so we lose two observations per factor.

insure that its absorption of factor services is exactly proportional to world endowments. With equal endowment mass both above and below the world diagonal, its net factor trade may be quite small. Yet this may mask the fact that it is engaging in a great deal of factor trade both with countries above the world diagonal as well as those below it.[11]

This example suggests breaking up the world into the same two groups, according to whether they are more or less abundant in a factor than a particular country. Absolute net factor contents would then be calculated for the two groups separately and added before scaling. The hope is that this will provide a more appropriate measure of the true role of net factor trade in a No-FPE world. The results of this exercise are presented in Table 3. The results show that this exercise raises measured net factor trade by approximately one-quarter, to a median of approximately 10 percent of total national endowments for capital and 12 percent for labor. If we were instead to scale by endowments in the tradable sectors, the corresponding figures would be 38 percent for capital and 49 percent for labor. These numbers indicate that OECD countries engage in large amounts of factor service trade.

3.6. Net factor trade within the North

It is often suggested that factor service trade among wealthy countries is relatively unimportant. There is no question that a majority of factor service trade is North–South. However, this does not mean that North–North factor service trade is unimportant. First, when we exclude trade with the rest of the world from our sample, we find the same general pattern of exporting factors to less abundant countries and importing factors from more abundant countries. Indeed in 85 percent of the cases we observe, these OECD countries are displaying this trade pattern. Hence we easily reject the notion that factor endowments are unimportant for understanding North–North trade.

More surprising is the importance of factor service trade within the North. In order to measure this, we calculate the following ratio:

$$\frac{\sum_{c' \in G10} \left|\mathbf{F}_{fcc'}\right|}{\sum_{c'} \left|\mathbf{F}_{fcc'}\right|}$$

[11] This example has one trick. Even if the country's endowment were exactly proportional to the world endowment, this would not drive its net factor trade to exactly zero. In fact, the country would be a net importer of both factors! The trick is that this country has a higher share of world income than it would in an integrated equilibrium. We know this by the fact that it has gains from trade although it could replicate (in miniature) the integrated equilibrium. Hence it will be a net importer of both factor services.

Table 4. Bilateral net factor service trade among the G10 as a share of total net factor service trade

	Capital	Labor
Australia	0.40	0.62
Canada	0.67	0.37
Denmark	0.69	0.37
France	0.26	0.24
Germany	0.37	0.31
Italy	0.81	0.24
Japan	0.82	0.45
The Netherlands	0.50	0.30
UK	0.47	0.40
USA	0.39	0.43
Median	0.48	0.37

Notes: G10 refers to the sample of 10 OECD countries for which we have technology matrices. This table shows that net factor service flows within the North constitute a large proportion of the net factor service flows of these countries.

where $\mathbf{F}_{fcc'}$ is the net factor service exports of factor *f* from *c* to *c'*. Since the numerator is the sum of the absolute value of each country's net bilateral factor service trade in factor *f* with the nine other Northern countries (note $\mathbf{F}_{fcc'} = 0$) and the denominator indicates the absolute value of all of its net factor service trade, this ratio tells us what share of net factor service trade is with other Northern countries. The results in Table 4 indicate that, for the median country, between one-third and one-half of all of its factor trade is with other members of our 10-country OECD sample. For 6 of the 10 countries, factor service trade, in volume terms, is actually more important within our set of 9 other OECD countries than outside for at least one factor. This result is more surprising when we recall that all trade with the remaining 13 OECD members not part of our 10 countries is treated here as trade with the ROW.

3.7. Bilateral net factor trade country-by-country

Thus far we have considered trade flows between any given country and the set of countries that are more or less abundant. Our theory, however, suggests that we should be able to cut the data even more finely. When examining bilateral trade between any two countries, the No-FPE model suggests that the net factor service flows should reflect the relative abundance of the two countries in question. If FPE obtains, then there would be no reason to think that relative abundances would be reflected in bilateral factor trade flows. In Table 3 we examine whether

Sign $(\mathbf{F}_{fcc'}) = \text{Sign } (\mathbf{V}_{fc}/\mathbf{s}_c - \mathbf{V}_{fc'}/\mathbf{s}_{c'})$, where $\mathbf{F}_{fcc'}$ is country c's net factor exports to country c'.

As one might expect, there is a slight deterioration in the percentage of sign matches.[12] Overall, we find that bilateral country factor trade is correctly predicted in 71 percent of the cases. This is significantly different from a coin flip at all conventional levels of significance, indicating that one can reject the hypothesis that endowments are not a factor in determining *bilateral* trade flows. This result by itself is perhaps not that surprising because few would argue that endowment differences are not important in explaining North–South trade. A stronger null hypothesis is to ask whether one should think of bilateral North–North trade as devoid of factor content. If bilateral North–North trade is devoid of factor content, then the factor content of bilateral North–North trade should be random. In Table 3 we repeat our experiment on bilateral factor content of trade by excluding all trade with the ROW. Whereas this result is only significant at the 11 percent level for capital, it is highly significant for labor and for both factors considered jointly, with correct signs in two-thirds of the cases overall. The results indicate that endowments help us to understand even bilateral trade in the North.

4. Conclusion

The central paradigm for explaining international trade flows relies on a dichotomy. Trade between North and South is explained by endowment differences. Trade within the North is explained by economies of scale and product differentiation. This paradigm specifically rejects an important role for endowment differences in explaining trade within the North.

We subject this paradigm to empirical scrutiny. We posit that endowments matter for North–North trade if two criteria are met. (1) Net factor service trade is systematically related to endowment differences and (2) The economic magnitudes of this net factor service trade are large. Our empirical work shows that both criteria are met.

We would like to stress that nothing that we have done excludes the possibility that product-level Ricardian differences or scale economies will

---

[12] There are several reasons to believe that the results are likely to be weaker as we move to considering bilateral country data. The first is that we are likely to encounter more noise due to bilateral trade barriers, both political and geographic. Second, it is not clear how to handle trade surpluses and deficits. Large surpluses and deficits in countries like the Japan and the US that occurred at this time are likely to cause problems with factor content calculations among relatively similar countries. Third, the previous results implicitly weighted the results by the size of the factor content of trade. Small errors in bilateral factor content of trade would be offset as along as on average countries export their abundant factors to less abundant countries. This final specification treats small errors the same as large correct predictions.

be important elements of a complete picture of world trade patterns. Indeed, our priors are that such a complete model will almost certainly draw on each of these elements, although identifying the contribution of each must await formal empirical work that places them in a common framework. Our aim here has been more modest: to show that the paradigm of world trade patterns needs to be broadened to acknowledge that differences in endowments do indeed matter for trade patterns even among countries of the North.

Acknowledgements

We are grateful to the National Science Foundation for support of this research. Helpful comments from members of the NBER International Trade and Investment group are appreciated.

References

Bowen, H.P., Leamer, E.E., Sveikauskas, L. (1987), Multifactor, multicountry tests of the factor abundance theory. *American Economic Review* 77 (5), 791–809.

Davis, D.R. (1997), Critical evidence on comparative advantage? North-North trade in a multilateral world. *Journal of Political Economy* 105 (5), 1051–1060.

Davis, D.R., Weinstein, D.E. (2001), An account of global factor trade. *American Economic Review* 91, 1423–1453.

Deardorff, A.V. (1982), The general validity of the Heckscher-Ohlin theorem. *American Economic Review* 72 (4), 683–694.

Deardorff, A.V., Staiger, R.W. (1988), An interpretation of the factor content of trade. *Journal of International Economics* 24 (1–2), 93–107.

Feenstra, R.C. (1998), Integration of trade and disintegration of production in the global economy. *Journal of Economic Perspectives* 12 (4), 31–50.

Feenstra, R.C., Lipsey, R.E., Bowen, H.P. (1997), World trade flows, 1970–1992, with production and tariff data. NBER Working Paper No. 5910, January.

Gabaix, X. (1997), The Factor Content of Trade: A Rejection of the Heckscher-Ohlin-Leontief Hypothesis. Mimeo, Harvard University.

Grubel, H.G., Lloyd, P.J. (1975), *Industry Trade: The Theory and Measurement of International Trade in Differentiated Products*. Wiley, New York.

Helpman, E. (1981), International trade in the presence of product differentiation, economies of scale and monopolistic competition: a Chamberlin-Heckscher-Ohlin approach. *Journal of International Economics* 11, 305–340.

Helpman, E. (1984), The factor content of foreign trade. *Economic Journal* 94 (373), 84–94.

Helpman, E. (1999), The structure of foreign trade. *Journal of Economic Perspectives* 13 (2), 121–144.

Helpman, E., Krugman, P.R. (1985), *Market Structure and Foreign Trade*. MIT Press, Cambridge.

Irwin, D.A. (1996), The United States in a new global economy? A century's Perspective. *American Economic Review* 86 (2), 41–46.

Krugman, P.R. (1979), Increasing returns, monopolistic competition, and international trade. *Journal of International Economics* 9 (4), 469–479.

Krugman, P.R. (1980), Scale economies, product differentiation, and the pattern of trade. *American Economic Review, American Economic Association* 70 (5), 950–959.

Krugman, P.R. (1981), Intraindustry specialization and the gains from trade. *Journal of Political Economy* 89 (5), 959–973.

Lancaster, K. (1980), Intra-Industry trade under perfect monopolistic competition. *Journal of International Economics* 10 (2), 151–175.

Trefler, D. (1993), International factor price differences: Leontief was right! *Journal of Political Economy* 101 (6), 961–987.

Trefler, D. (1995), The case of the missing trade and other mysteries. *American Economic Review* 85 (5), 1029–1046.

Vanek, J. (1968), The factor proportions theory: the n-factor case. *Kyklos* 21, 749–755.

CHAPTER 3

A Simple Vertical Competition Model: Structure and Performance

Roy J. Ruffin

Department of Economics, University of Houston, Houston, TX, USA
E-mail address: rruffin@uh.edu

This chapter investigates the structure of a simple vertical competition model by exhibiting the competitive links among assemblers, component producers, and integrated firms in a generalization of Cournot's model of the vertical integration by allowing any degree of competition among cohorts. Vertical integration in the model can take place by vertical mergers, forward or backward integration. Vertical integration is highly profitable and always reduces the price of the final product. The cost-raising strategy of an integrated firm buying out unneeded component producers is profitable and detrimental to consumers only if the firm faces no competition from other integrated firms.

Keywords: Vertical integration, outsourcing, oligopoly

JEL classifications: D40, L13, L22

It is a pleasure once again to honor Professor Ronald Jones for his extensive work in international trade theory. This chapter deals with the general theory of vertical markets, but does not apply it to international trade theory. It is not surprising that Jones (2000) has devoted considerable attention to the issue of the international fragmentation of production. Here I abstract from all issues of comparative advantage or economies of scale, and simply look at the incentive to vertically integrate under any degree of competition along the production chain. I will show that fragmentation does not occur under these circumstances, so Jones' emphasis on comparative advantage and economies of scale is well placed.

Every business brings together separate operations. What constitutes vertical integration means that particular products or services in the sequence of operations leading to a final product also have active markets. In 1838, Antoine Augustin Cournot established the proposition that an

Frontiers of Economics and Globalization
Volume 4 ISSN: 1574-8715
DOI: 10.1016/S1574-8715(08)04003-7

association of monopolists producing component inputs of a composite product is in the interest of consumers unlike an association of producers of competing products (Cournot, 1960, p. 103). The reason is that the independent producers of complementary inputs run into the free rider problem. Thus, if an integrated monopolist is broken up into its component parts, consumers suffer. Cournot's theorem is now well-known in the economics literature (Baumol, 2001; Economides and Salop, 1992).

However, Cournot assumed that (1) component producers face no competition, (2) there is perfect competition in the downstream markets, and (3) the vertically integrated firm faces no competition. If component producers face competition, their prices will be lower and the incentive to integrate backwards will be lessened. If downstream producers face less competition, their prices and profits will be higher and, again, the incentive to integrate backwards will be lessened. Finally, if the resulting integrated firm is to face some competition, its prospective profits will be lowered, so the incentive to integrate will be smaller. I show that none of these concerns affects Cournot's theorem involving only vertical mergers. Obviously, we must make a set of technological and behavioral conditions that mirror those made by Cournot in order to give the theorem a fair chance of surviving a generalization. Indeed, only one additional and very mild behavioral assumption needs to be introduced.

The Cournot approach is the simplest possible model that can portray the complementary and competitive links between the different cohorts that occupy the various links in the chain from component production to the delivery of the final product to the consumer. Some writers have introduced differentiated products (Economides and Salop, 1992; Ordover *et al.*, 1990) while others have described the role of economies of scale and scope, the costs of searching for partners, and the governance problems facing large firms (Grossman and Helpman, 2002; Williamson, 1986). These factors will clearly make outsourcing more of a viable alternative. Jean Tirole (1988, p. 169) has remarked that "vertical relationships among firms are often much richer and more complex than those between a firm and its consumers." But complex models are difficult to analyze, and may lose sight of the bigger picture that may have been picked up by the simple Cournot model, namely, that vertical integration is widespread. In addition, the flat landscape adopted herein allows us to derive other theorems that may well hold in a more realistic, but difficult to analyze, setting. For example, is forward or backward integration more beneficial to consumers than vertical mergers? Or, what are the anti-trust implications of integrated firms buying up unneeded component firms?

Section 1 of this chapter reprises the original Cournot theorem. Section 2 investigates the structure of vertical competition by developing a simple model that includes oligopolistic assemblers of components, oligopolistic producers of components, and oligopolistic integrated firms. Except for the numbers of firms, the same assumptions are made as in the original Cournot theorem. In fact, it is shown that the key Cournot assumption, while implausible with large numbers, actually makes vertical integration less profitable but, nevertheless, highly profitable. Section 3 provides a simple numerical example to illustrate the profitability of anti-competitive behavior by a vertically integrated firm buying out component manufacturers to raise costs to their downstream customers. Section 4 discusses the empirical implications of the model and shows that simple models still have a role to play in understanding industry structure.

1. Cournot's forward integration model

This section summarizes Cournot's simple model of forward integration (Cournot, 1960, pp. 99–103) A good is produced with two components, each produced by a monopoly. Costs of production are assumed to be zero, both for assembly and for component production. The assembly industry is perfectly competitive. The price of the good is P; the price of each component is q_i. One unit of each component is required per unit of the good. Since the assembly industry is competitive, $P = q_1 + q_2$. Market demand is $D(P)$. Components can only be produced inside a firm. An integrated monopoly will simply maximize $PD(P)$ resulting in

$$PD'(P) + D(P) = 0. \tag{1}$$

This is the familiar monopoly solution. If the industry is vertically fragmented, then each component producer will maximize $q_iD(q_1 + q_2)$. Each component producer behaved independently, and so the first-order condition for each would be

$$q_iD'(P) + D(P) = 0. \tag{2}$$

Adding (2) over the two firms gives us

$$PD'(P) + 2D(P) = 0. \tag{3}$$

It is plausible in these circumstances for component producers to assume an additional component will result in assemblers producing one more unit of the final good. As Cournot pointed out, the "very remarkable difference" is that the root of Equation (3) will be higher than the root of Equation (1). Thus, "the composite commodity will always be made more expensive, by reason of separation of interests than by reason of the fusion of interests" (Cournot, 1960, p. 103). The economics is clear comparing (2) with (1): at the same price P, if (1) is zero it would still be the case that condition (2) would be positive so that each component producer would still want to raise the price. This is a free rider problem.[1] Thus, we can see

[1] We shall later see that this result may not hold with more producers of components if there is also a degree of horizontal merger.

that fragmented production must lead to a higher composite good price, making consumers and society worse off. Cournot then pointed out that with r components the solution would be

$$PD'(P) + rD(P) = 0. \tag{4}$$

The price of each component will be $q = P/r$. Equation (4) shows that as r approaches infinity, the free rider problem becomes so serious that the market would shut down at the price P^*, where $D(P^*) = 0$.

It is interesting to note that there is enormous market foreclosure taking place in Cournot's case, since the competitive assembly industry is being completely shut down by the forward integration of the component producers.

2. *The model*

In the Cournot model, there is perfect competition in the assembly of components and no competition among the potential producers of the components. This section develops a model in which there is oligopoly among each cohort of producers: component producers, assemblers, and integrated firms. The following assumptions characterize the model:

- A1. Each unit of a composite good requires one unit each of $r \geqslant 1$ components.
- A2. Integrated firms produce all necessary components and assemblers produce no components and purchase only from the non-integrated component firms. There are n_1 integrated firms, n_2 producers of *each* component, and n_3 assembly firms.
- A3. There is a single market for the composite good and each component. The sth component sells at the price q_s.
- A4. All firms know the direct market demand function for the composite good $D(P)$, where P is the price of the assembled good to consumers, $D'(P) < 0$, and the price elasticity of demand $\varepsilon(P) = -D'(P)P/D$ is non-decreasing in price.
- A5. Marginal and average costs are constant. The cost of assembly for any firm is c_1; and for simplicity the cost of producing any of the r components is c_2.
- A6. Integrated and assembly firms engage in Cournot quantity competition and know the market demand function.
- A7. Each component firm makes the assumption that the output of its rival component producers and the outputs of all integrated firms are constant, but if it raises its output by one unit so will the output of the final good by the assembly firms.
- A8. All decisions are made simultaneously.

These assumptions mirror Cournot's analysis. Assumption A1 rules out substitution possibilities among components. For example, a car requires an engine, a set of spark plugs, and a set of tires. It would be difficult to make substitutions such as a little larger engine for one of the tires! Variable proportions make the analysis considerably more difficult, but has been shown by others not to be a critical assumption as long as one does not mix horizontal with vertical integration (Abiru, 1988). Assumption A2 considerably simplifies the analysis. There is no incentive for integrated firms to purchasc components in the market; and assemblers must acquire components from the producers of such goods. It might appear that integrated firms are prohibited from selling components to assemblers, but they can do so by setting up a separate component firm in each component. The key requirement that simplifies the analysis is that there is the same degree of competition in each component sub-industry. We could assume that there are different degrees of competition among the various component producers, but the model would lose all of its simplicity. Assumption A5 rules out economies or diseconomies of scale or scope as well as comparative advantages some firms might enjoy over other firms.[2] George Stigler (1951) has conjectured that economies of scale can lead to less integration. To assume that the cost of producing each component to be the same is not critical, and, like the assumption of the same degree of competition in each component sub-industry, simplifies the analysis without affecting the key results.[3]

Assumption A7 may appear critical and, like Cournot's oligopoly model, can be argued to be unsophisticated or unrealistic. It says that the producer of spark plugs must assume that another set of spark plugs will result in another car on the market, and that the spark plug producer knows the market demand for cars. This is the assumption that we must make to exactly mirror Cournot's model. However, it is not at all necessary. Note that if component producers are optimistic, and assume a unit increase in their output only increases industry output by some fraction θ, the incentive to vertically integrate will be larger because assembly prices will be higher. For example, in that case Cournot's Equation (3) would have been $P\theta D'(P) + 2D(P) = 0$. The root of this equation will again be higher than (1) if $\theta < 1$. But I do not wish to include any assumption that increases the incentive to vertically integrate. Thus, in order not to bias the results toward vertical integration and for the sake of simplicity, I assume $\theta = 1$.

Assumption A8 rules out a multiple stage game. I see no compelling economic reason to suppose that component production must occur

---

[2] For example, Robert Crandall (1968) argues that in automobile production economies of scope in the production of components are limited. See also Stigler (1951).

[3] A similar set-up chooses to start from the standard Cournot oligopoly model rather than Cournot's vertical integration model and, thus, assumes that the number of components $r = 1$ [18]. This abstracts from the free riding problem.

before assembly firms make their decisions because in the real world the production of components and final product is continuous.

Since all firms within a cohort face the same costs, the cost of producing each component is the same, and each unit of final product requires exactly one of each component, firms in each cohort are identical. The unit cost of production for an integrated producer is $c_1 + rc_2$; and the unit cost of production for any fragmented producer is simply c_2. Let q_s denote the price of the sth ($s = 1, \ldots, r$) component sold by component producers. The cost of production to an assembly firm is $c_1 + \Sigma_s q_s$.

Consider now the profits of each of the cohorts. Let x_{1i} ($i = 1, \ldots, n_1$), x^s_{2j} ($j = 1, \ldots, n_2$; $s = 1, \ldots, r$), and x_{3k} ($k = 1, \ldots, n_3$) denote their respective outputs of integrated firms, component producers, and assemblers. A firm other than the ith integrated firm, jth component firm, or kth assembly firm is indexed by i', j', and k'.

The profit of the ith integrated firm is

$$\pi_{1i} = (P - c_1 - rc_2)\left[D(P) - \sum\nolimits_{i' \neq i} x_{1i'} - \sum\nolimits_k x_{3k}\right], \tag{5}$$

where of course the firm's output x_{1i} is given by the term in brackets. Each integrated firm will assume that the outputs of all rival firms are constant. It indirectly controls the price of the product by altering its output; accordingly, the firm's first-order condition is simply

$$(P - c_1 - rc_2)D'(P) + x_{1i} = 0. \tag{6}$$

The jth component firm producing component s has profit

$$\pi^s_{2j} = (q_s - c_2)\left[D(P) - \sum\nolimits_{j' \neq j} x^s_{2j'} - \sum\nolimits_i x_{1i}\right]. \tag{7}$$

Note that the demand facing firm j in component s, x^s_{2j}, is total demand minus what its rivals and the integrated firms are producing, recalling that each unit of the final product requires precisely one unit of component s. We do not count the output of the assembly firms because that would be double-counting (already implied by the outputs of the component firms). What is critical is that the component firm, say, increases its output, it naively supposes (by A7) that industry output increases by exactly the same amount, so that $D'(P) = \mathrm{d}x^s_{2j}/\mathrm{d}q_s$. Thus, the first-order condition for each component firm is simply

$$(q_s - c_2)D'(P) + x^s_{2j} = 0. \tag{8}$$

There are rn_2 of such equations.

Finally, we have the profit of each assembly firm:

$$\pi_{3k} = (P - c_1 - \sum\nolimits_s q_s)\left[D(P) - \sum\nolimits_i x_{1i} - \sum\nolimits_{k' \neq k} x_{3k'}\right]. \tag{9}$$

For assembly firms, the first-order condition is simply

$$(P - c_1 - \sum\nolimits_s q_s)D'(P) + x_{3k} = 0. \tag{10}$$

Market-clearing in the final goods market requires that the outputs of all the assembly firms and integrated firms equal final demand:

$$D(P) = \sum_k x_{jk} + \sum_i x_{1i}. \tag{11}$$

Market-clearing in each component market requires

$$\sum_k x_{3k} = \sum_j x^s_{2j}. \tag{12}$$

Equations (6), (8), (10)–(12) represent $n_1 + rn_2 + n_3 + r + 1$ equations in the same number of unknowns. Clearly, it is not really necessary to suppose identical costs across firms; however, this assumption enables us to easily calculate the solution. Obviously, it will be the case that $x_{1i} = x_1$ for all i; $x^s_{2j} = x_2$ for all j and s; $x_{3k} = x_3$ for all k; and $q_s = q$ for all s.

We can thus see that in equilibrium the model reduces to

$$(P - c_1 - rc_2)D'(P) + x_1 = 0, \tag{13}$$

$$(q - c_2)D'(P) + x_2 = 0, \tag{14}$$

$$(P - c_1 - rq)D'(P) + x_3 = 0, \tag{15}$$

$$D(P) = n_1 x_1 + n_3 x_3, \tag{16}$$

$$n_2 x_2 = n_3 x_3. \tag{17}$$

Clearly, if we substitute the first-order conditions into (13)–(15) into the market-clearing Equations (16) and (17), we obtain two equations in P and q. Thus, Equation (16) is

$$n_1(P - c_1 - rc_2) + n_3(P - c_1 - rq) = -\frac{D(P)}{D'(P)} = \frac{P}{\varepsilon(P)}, \tag{18}$$

where $\varepsilon(P)$ is the elasticity of demand, $-D'(P)P/D(P)$. Equation (17) may be similarly rewritten as

$$(q - c_2)n_2 = (P - c_1 - rq)n_3. \tag{19}$$

Solve (19) for q and then substitute (19) into (18) to solve for an equation in P, yielding

$$\varepsilon(P)\left[\frac{1 - (c_1 + rc_2)}{P}\right] = \frac{1}{n_1 + n_2 n_3/(n_2 + rn_3)}. \tag{20}$$

The term in brackets on the left-hand side is the profit rate of an integrated firm; this profit rate times the elasticity of demand for the product must be less than unity. Suppose $n_2 = n_3 = n$, then the right-hand side would reduce to $1/[n_1 + n/(1+r)]$. Suppose $r = 9$ and $n = 10$, then 100 assembly and component firms would be necessary to reduce the price to the level generated by a single integrated firm! This gives some indication of the effectiveness of vertical integration in the model.

Equation (20) is my fundamental result and shows that this particular theory of simple vertical integration is not much more complicated than Cournot oligopoly! We make the plausible assumption that as the price of composite good rises, the elasticity of demand does not fall, that is, $\varepsilon'(P) \geq 0$. Cournot's simple model did not require this assumption. The term in brackets, $[1-(c_1+rc_2)/P]$, is strongly increasing in the price. This means that the left-hand side of (20) must be monotonically increasing in the price even if $\varepsilon'(P)=0$ and can be increasing in P even if $\varepsilon'(P)<0$. Adding costs to the model gives it more robustness. The equilibrium price will rise or fall as the right-hand side of (20) rises or falls. Cournot's free rider problem shows up in the fact that a higher r must raise the price of the final good because the component firms set higher prices, driving up the costs to assembly firms.

I will define a vertical merger as a merger between an assembly firm and single set of r component firms ($\Delta n_1=1$, $\Delta n_2=-1$, $\Delta n_3=-1$). I will consider a forward integration to occur when a single set of r component firms merge and start producing the final product ($\Delta n_1=1$, $\Delta n_2=-1$, $\Delta n_3=0$). Finally, a backward integration takes place if an assembly firm starts producing the components ($\Delta n_1=1$, $\Delta n_2=0$, $\Delta n_3=-1$). I define vertical integration to be one of these cases.

Denote the denominator of (20) as $Z=n_1+n_2n_3/(n_2+rn_3)$. We need to show that vertical integration increases Z in order to show that price falls. To simplify, I consider continuous values for the n_is. Let $\partial Z/\partial n_i=Z_i$. Denote $v=(n_2+rn_3)$. It is straightforward to show that $Z_2=rn_3^2/v^2$ and $Z_3=n_2^2/v^2$. Since every Z_i is positive, it follows that an increase in competition in any cohort reduces the price of the product.

When a vertical merger occurs,

$$Z_1-Z_2-Z_3=\frac{n_3^2r(r-1)+2rn_2n_3}{v^2}>0. \tag{21}$$

When a backward integration occurs,

$$Z_1-Z_3=\frac{r^2n_3^2+2rn_2n_3}{v^2}>0. \tag{22}$$

When a forward integration occurs,

$$Z_1-Z_2=\frac{n_3^2r(r-1)+2rn_2n_3+n_2^2}{v^2}>0. \tag{23}$$

These calculations show that in every case Z increases and, therefore, any vertical integration lowers the price. Note that forward and backward integrations have the largest impact on price. Since it is likely that $Z_2>Z_3$ (because $r>1$), a backward integration will lower the price more than a forward integration. Summarizing:

Proposition 1. *If $\varepsilon'(P)\geq 0$, a vertical merger, a backward integration, and a forward integration result in a lower price; a backward integration will* *generally lower the price more than a forward integration and both will lower the price more than a vertical merger.*

This is my basic theorem in the simple theory of vertical integration.[4] Clearly, a model-builder could reach a different result by inadvertently assuming that $\varepsilon'(P)<0$ and zero costs and, thus, conclude that perhaps other features of the model were responsible.

There are two interesting special cases. Consider a completely fragmented industry in which $n_1 = 0$ and there is a perfectly competitive assembly industry. Then (20) becomes

$$\varepsilon\left[\frac{1-(c_1+rc_2)}{P}\right] = \frac{r}{n_2}. \tag{24}$$

Now we see that if $r = n_2$, an industry that is completely fragmented with a perfectly competitive assembly industry will have a composite good price equal to that of a single firm monopoly because when the right-hand side of (24) is unity we have the monopoly solution. But if $n_2 > r$, the price of the composite good price will be less than the monopoly price; and if $n_2 < r$, the composite good price will exceed the monopoly price. Thus,

PROPOSITION 2. *If $\varepsilon'(P) \geq 0$ and there is a perfectly competitive assembly industry, thenif a completely fragmented industry ($n_1 = 0$) is vertically and horizontally integrated into a monopoly, the price will rise if and only if $n_2 > r$; the price will fall if and only if $n_2 < r$.*

The source of this result is the fact that the degree of competition in each component industry mitigates the free rider problem arising from the Nash pricing of each component.[5] Note that had Cournot assumed two competing component firms in each of the two components, the vertical and horizontal merger would not have lowered the price! Was he lucky or did he just have great intuition about what generalizations mattered?

Another special case include the double marginalization model (Spengler, 1950). To see this, assume that $n_2 = n_3 = n$. Then (20) becomes

$$\varepsilon(P)\left[\frac{1-(c_1+rc_2)}{P}\right] = \frac{1}{n_1+n/(r+1)}. \tag{25}$$

---

[4] Proposition 1 holds for any r. Michael Salinger (1988) considers a special case ($r = 1$) and concludes that a vertical merger may increase or lower the price. This is due to his use of linear demand, which with positive costs leads to a very complicated expression and appears to hide the central result. I note this expression later.

[5] A similar result for differentiated products and assuming that the number of components equals the number of firms is found in Economides and Salop (1992).

The model is now so simple that we can prove Proposition 1 by simple inspection. If *one* set of r component firms and *one* assembly firm merge into a single integrated firm, then we would have the result that n_1 rises by *one* unit while n falls by *one* unit, decreasing the right-hand side of Equation (25). Hence, a vertical merger must lower the price. The original case of double marginalization is even simpler and involves an initial $n_1 = 0$, $n = 1$, and $r = 1$.

Is vertical integration profitable? It may appear that this question cannot be answered without a specific demand function.[6] But integration is so profitable that the simple economics of the question shows that there is a strong presumption of profitability. Let $m_1 = P - c_1 - rc_2$, $m_2 = q - c_2$, and $m_3 = P - c_1 - rq$ denote the profit margins of our three cohorts. But multiply m_2 by r and add the result to m_3 and we obtain m_1; accordingly,

$$m_1 = rm_2 + m_3. \tag{26}$$

This means that the profit *margin* of each integrated firm exceeds the profit *margin* of any assembly firm by precisely the sum of the profit *margins* of all the component firms. This can be used to show the extreme profitability of vertical integration in our rather flat landscape. Now the first-order condition for any firm is $m_i D'(P) + x_i = 0$. Letting $b = -D'(P)$, profit is always $\pi_i = bm_i^2$. Units can always be chosen so that $b = 1$. By squaring both sides of (26) we can therefore see that

$$\pi_1 = r^2\pi_2 + \pi_3 + 2rm_2m_3 = r\pi_2 + \pi_3 + 2rm_2m_3 + r(r-1)\pi_2. \tag{27}$$

The above equation shows that vertical integration is highly profitable, especially if r is large. If component production is perfectly competitive, the gains from vertical integration vanish because $\pi_2 = 0$, implying that $\pi_1 = \pi_3$. With oligopolistic competition between component producers, when a single set of r component firms (with profit $r\pi_2$) and a single assembly firm (with profit π_2) gaze longingly upon the superior profits of an integrated firm, either singly or jointly, the incentive to merge or integrate is enormous. While vertical integration lowers π_1, the fall will be small relative to the term $2rm_1m_2 + r(r-1)\pi_2$. And it will always be the case, with large enough r, that a vertical merger or integration will increase profits.

PROPOSITION 3. *There is a strong presumption that a vertical integration is always profitable and must be with sufficiently large r.*

We now turn to complementary competition between cohorts. First, note from the first-order conditions it follows that

$$x_1 = rx_2 + x_3. \tag{28}$$

[6] Horizontal mergers are quite different (Salant *et al.*, 1983). Such mergers are (slightly) unprofitable and so require a specific demand function.

In our flat landscape, the output of an integrated firm equals the output of each of the component firms of the r components and any assembly firm. Admittedly, this is unrealistic in the real world of economies of scale, comparative advantages, and other assorted advantages of outsourcing. But it has an interesting implication that does make sense. Since the Z_is are positive, any increase in competition in any cohort must reduce the price of the composite good (cf. Ruffin, 1971). This, of course, will decrease the output of any integrated firm. This follows from the first-order condition for such a firm, (13). Now, substituting (28) and (17) into (16) yields

$$x_2(rn_1 + n_2) + n_1 x_3 = D(P). \qquad (29)$$

Using (20), since an increase in any n_i lowers P, an increase in n_3 will increase $D(P)$. Since x_3 then falls with more assembly firms, it must be that x_2 rises or that the component firms are benefited! Substituting (17) again into (29) to eliminate $n_2 x_2$ we get

$$x_2 r n_1 + x_3(n_1 + n_3) = D(P). \qquad (30)$$

From (30), it is also the case that an increase in n_2 will lower x_2 and thus increases x_3.

Proposition 4. *Competition between assemblers or component producers and integrated firms is competitive, but competition between assemblers and component firms is complementary.*

Thus, we see that by abstracting from the complications arising from comparative advantages, economies and diseconomies of scale and scope, and so forth, we can easily derive a proposition that is eminently reasonable and probably holds in a far more general setting, but perhaps difficult to prove.

3. A numerical example: anti-trust issues

The anti-trust literature has been concerned with the implications cost-raising strategies. To illustrate the usefulness of the model, a numerical example shows that it pays a monopolist integrated firm to purchase an unneeded set of component firms, driving up component prices to assemblers. However, it may not pay an oligopolistic integrated firm to engage in such anti-competitive behavior. Therefore, a simple rule emerges from our analysis. Ignore vertical mergers of all types except those that involve pure cost-raising by an integrated firm facing no competition from other integrated firms.

Assume a linear demand curve $D(P) = a - bP$ and, for simplicity, zero costs. The assumption of positive costs leads to complicated expressions.[7]

---

[7] With positive costs the solution is $P = [av + bv(c_1 n_3 + c_1 + rc_2) + (n_2 c_2 - n_3 c_1) n_3 rb]/bA$, where $v = (rn_3 + n_2)$ and $A = [n_2 n_3 + (n_1 + 1)(rn_3 + n_2)]$.

In terms of the profit margins the solutions are then

$$P = m_1 = \frac{a(rn_3 + n_2)}{bA}, \tag{31}$$

$$q = m_2 = \frac{an_3}{bA}, \tag{32}$$

$$P - rq = m_3 = \frac{an_2}{bA}, \tag{33}$$

where $A = n_2 n_3 + (n_1 + 1)(rn_3 + n_2)$.

As a benchmark, suppose that $n_1 = n_2 = n_3 = r = 2$, then $A = 4 + (3)(6) = 22$. Let us assume also that $b = 1$ without loss of generality. Then assuming that $a = 220$, we have

$$P = m_1 = \$60; \quad q = m_2 = \$20; \quad \text{and} \quad m_3 = \$20.$$

The profits of each type of firm are simply

$$\pi_1 = 3600, \quad \pi_2 = 400, \quad \text{and} \quad \pi_3 = 400.$$

Total profit $\Pi = n_1\pi_1 + rn_2\pi_2 + n_3\pi_3 = \$9600$ and consumer surplus is \$12,800, so that total welfare in this case is $W = \$22{,}400$.

Now consider the possibility of "anti-competitive" behavior. Assume an integrated firm purchases a set of component firms in the knowledge that this will drive up the costs of assembly firms, benefiting them. Will the cost of the firms they purchase exceed or fall short of the boost to profits? Starting from the benchmark, we may now assume that $n_1 = 2$, $n_3 = 2$, $r = 2$, and now $n_2 = 1$. Then $A = 2 + (3)(4 + 1) = 17$. Thus,

$$P = m_1 = \frac{220(5)}{17} = \$64.70; \; m_2 = \frac{220(2)}{17} = \$25.89, \; \text{and} \; m_3 = \$12.95.$$

Now, their profits are

$$\pi_1 = \$4186; \quad \pi_2 = \$670; \quad \text{and} \quad \pi_3 = \$168.$$

Clearly, while the profits of each integrated firm rise by \$586 to \$4186, the cost of the buyout is at least $r\pi_2 = \$1340$. Thus, it does not pay a single firm to buyout a set of component firms whose collective profits of the component firms prior to the purchase was \$800. Thus, such anti-competitive behavior is not profitable. Total welfare would also fall because the price rises.

However, total profits of the integrated firms have risen by \$1172 suggesting that a single integrated firm would find such a buy-out profitable. Indeed, if $n_1 = 1$, $n_2 = n_3 = r = 2$, then the profits are (before buy-out):

$$\pi_1 = 4356 \quad \text{and} \quad \pi_2 = 484, \quad \text{and} \quad P = \$66.$$

Now, if the single integrated firm buys out one set of component firms for \$968, the new solution for $n_1 = n_2 = 1$ and $n_3 = r = 2$ is:

$$\pi_1 = \$8403 \text{ with } P = \$92.$$

Clearly, the single integrated firm can afford to purchase one set of component firms.[8]

4. Empirical implications

The above model has clear empirical implications. The main alternative to the model is the transaction costs approach pioneered by Oliver Williamson (1986). But the model has the advantage of being quantitative and less subject to interpretation. For example, it has been reported that Ronald Coase disputes the notion that opportunistic behavior plays a role in backward integration (Klein, 1988).

There are six key implications of the above theory. First, vertical integration should lower the price or, in a more extended case, raises quality.[9] The second implication is that more components make vertical integration more profitable. The extant literature gives some anecdotal evidence in favor of this result (Monteverde and Teece, 1982; Stigler, 1950). One way of testing the present model against the transaction costs alternative is the role of the number of components. The transaction cost approach has been interpreted as suggesting that more components increases the cost of transactions and, therefore, should reduce the benefits of vertical integration (Levy, 1985). With two conflicting hypotheses to test, the empirical issue becomes more interesting and more work is certainly required. The third key implication is that greater concentration increases the benefits of vertical integration. There is statistical evidence in favor of this implication (Levy, 1985).

Fourth, the model casts serious doubt on the widespread use of the ratio value-added to sales as a measure of vertical integration (Stigler, 1951). While all writers have been uncomfortable with this measure, the problem with the measure is that it mostly reflects the elasticity of demand for the product. Since vertical integration always lowers price, if demand is inelastic the dollar value of sales will fall, causing the measure to presumably fall if material costs are constant.

Proposition 1 carries a fifth implication: forward or backward integration should provide more consumer surplus than a vertical merger. I know of no evidence against or in favor of this implication.

A sixth implication is derived from Proposition 4. Everything else equal, the stock market values of component or assembly firms should have a higher correlation with the stock market values of integrated firms than the correlation between component and assembly firms. Indeed, I would

---

[8] I am indebted to Steve Brown and Nathan Balke for this application of the model.

[9] For evidence see Chipty (2001), De Vany and Eckert (1991), McBride (1983), and Whitney (1955).

expect a negative correlation of the *first differences* of the stock market returns of component and assembly firms.

Acknowledgments

The chapter has benefited from the remarks of participants of the Southeast Economic Theory and International Trade Conference in October 2000, and seminar participants at the Wirtschaftsuniversität Wien, and the Federal Reserve Bank of Dallas. I wish to thank Nathan Balke, William Baumol, Steve Brown, Arthur De Vany, Martin Summer, Eva Pichler, Joel Sailors, and Roger Sherman for helpful comments; they are not responsible for its contents. I also wish to thank the Bundesbank for research support as the Bundesbank Professor at the Free University of Berlin in the summers of 2001 and 2002.

References

Abiru, M. (1988), Vertical integration, variable proportions and successive oligopolies. *Journal of Industrial Economics* 36, 315–325.

Baumol, W.J. (2001), When is inter-firm coordination beneficial? The case of innovation. *International Journal of Industrial Organization* 19, 727–737.

Chipty, T. (2001), Vertical integration, market foreclosure, and consumer welfare in the cable television industry. *American Economic Review* 91 (3), 428–453.

Cournot, A. (1960), *Researches into the Mathematical Principles of the Theory of Wealth*, originally published 1838, translated by Nathaniel T. Bacon. Augustus Kelly, New York.

Crandall, R. (1968), Vertical integration and the market for repair parts in the United States Automobile Industry. *Journal of Industrial Economics* 16, 212–234.

De Vany, A., Eckert, R. (1991), Motion picture antitrust: the paramount cases revisited. *Research in Law and Economics* 14, 51–112.

Economides, N., Salop, S.C. (1992), Competition and integration among complements, and network market structure. *Journal of Industrial Economics* 40, 105–123.

Grossman, G., Helpman, E. (2002), Integration versus outsourcing in industry equilibrium. *Quarterly Journal of Economics* 117, 85–120.

Jones, R.W. (2000), *Globalization and the Theory of Input Trade*. MIT Press, Cambridge.

Klein, B. (1988), Vertical integration as organizational ownership: the fisher-body-general motors relationship revisited. *Journal of Law and Economic Organization* 4, 199–213.

Levy, D.T. (1985), The transaction costs approach to vertical integration: an empirical examination. *Review of Economics and Statistics* 67, 438–445.

McBride, M.E. (1983), Spatial competition and vertical integration: cement and concrete revisited. *American Economic Review* 73, 1011–1022.

Monteverde, K., Teece, D.J. (1982), Supplier switching costs and vertical integration in the automobile industry. *Bell Journal of Economics* 13, 206–213.

Ordover, J., Saloner, G., Salop, S.C. (1990), Equilibrium vertical foreclosure. *American Economic Review* 80, 127–142.

Ruffin, R.J. (1971), Cournot oligopoly and competitive behavior. *Review of Economic Studies* 38, 493–502.

Salant, S., Switzer, W., Swisher, S., Reynolds, R. (1983), Losses from horizontal merger: the effects of an exogenous change in industry structure on Cournot-Nash equilibrium. *Quarterly Journal of Economics* 98, 185–199.

Salinger, M.A. (1988), Vertical mergers and market foreclosure. *Quarterly Journal of Economics* 102, 335–356.

Spengler, J.J. (1950), Vertical integration and antitrust policy. *Journal of Political Economy* 58, 347–352.

Stigler, G.J. (1950), Monopoly and oligopoly by merger. *American Economic Review* 40, 23–34.

Stigler, G.J. (1951), The division of labor is limited by the extent of the market. *Journal of Political Economy* 59, 185–193.

Tirole, J. (1988), *The Theory of Industrial Organization*. MIT Press, Cambridge.

Whitney, S.N. (1955), Vertical disintegration in the motion picture industry. *American Economic Review* 45, 491–498.

Williamson, O.E. (1986), Vertical integration and relation variations on a transaction-cost economics theme. In: Stiglitz, Mathewson (Eds.), *New Developments in the Analysis of Market Structure*. Macmillan Press, London.

CHAPTER 4

Globalization, Trade in Middle Products, and Relative Prices

Ulrich Kohli

Alternate Member of the Governing Board, Swiss National Bank, CH-8022, Zurich, Switzerland
E-mail address: Ulrich.Kohli@snb.ch

Abstract
Nearly all international trade takes place in *middle products*, rather than in finished goods as it is assumed in most models of international trade theory. Recognition of this fact has some far-reaching consequences for the measurement of real value added, real domestic income, and productivity, and it brings forward the role of a number of related, yet distinct, key price ratios: the terms of trade, the real exchange rate, and the trading gains. Production theory, rather than consumer theory, is therefore the appropriate setting for analyzing issues such as openness, trade imbalances, and income distribution.

Keywords: Globalization, middle products, imbalances, terms of trade, real exchange rate, trading gains, income distribution

JEL classifications: C43, D33, F11, O47

1. Introduction

Three ongoing trends that characterize the U.S. economy are receiving much attention of late, from economists, policy makers, and the public alike. Indeed, two of these were featured very prominently in the Spring 2007 issue of the International Monetary Fund's *World Economic Outlook*.[1] All three developments are thought to be linked, to some extent at least, to globalization and the increasing international fragmentation of production.[2] First, there is the falling income share of labor. As shown by Figure 1, U.S. labor income has fallen from close to 66% of total factor

[1] See International Monetary Fund (2007), Chapters 3 and 5.
[2] The term fragmentation of production was coined by Jones (2000).

Frontiers of Economics and Globalization
Volume 4 ISSN: 1574-8715
DOI: 10.1016/S1574-8715(08)04004-9

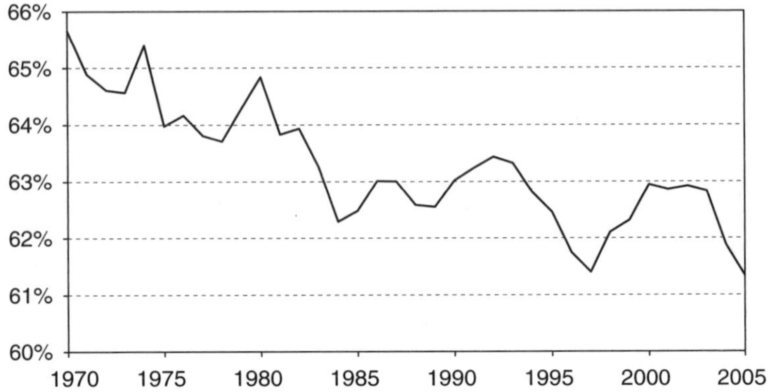

Fig. 1. Labor share.

income to little more than 61% between 1970 and 2005.[3] Second, there is the remarkable increase in the openness of the U.S. economy. As depicted in Figure 2, the share of foreign trade in gross domestic product (GDP) has increased from about 5% in 1970 to over 13% in 2005.[4] And third, there is the large increase in the U.S. trade deficit. Whereas trade was still pretty much balanced as recently as the early 1990s, the deficit had grown to nearly 6% of GDP by 2005 (Figure 3).[5]

The question of the distribution of income between labor and capital is usually analyzed from the standpoint of production theory. The declining labor share is then found to be mostly due to changes in relative factor endowments, technology, and the output mix, with the extent of the substitution possibilities between labor and capital playing a prominent role.

Analyses of openness and trade imbalances, however, are typically imbedded in consumer theory. The volumes of imports and exports are generally viewed as being demand determined, with (domestic, respectively foreign) income and relative prices playing a key role.[6] Advances in transportation, computing, and communication technologies, international transfers of technology, and lower trade barriers have led to significant reductions in the relative prices of imports, at home and abroad. This and the fact that many foreign-made goods are perceived as superior (in the

---

[3] See the Appendix for a description of the data. The same phenomenon holds in many other industrialized countries; see International Monetary Fund (2007), Chapter 5.

[4] The foreign trade share is defined as the arithmetic average of the export and import shares (the latter in absolute value). The increasing trade integration of many countries has also been documented by the *World Economic Outlook* in the past; see International Monetary Fund (1997, 2002) for instance.

[5] While there are many other countries that register trade deficits, the U.S. deficit absorbs about three quarters of available world surpluses; see International Monetary Fund (2007), Chapter 3.

[6] This is the so-called *elasticity approach*; see Marquez (2002) for a good review.

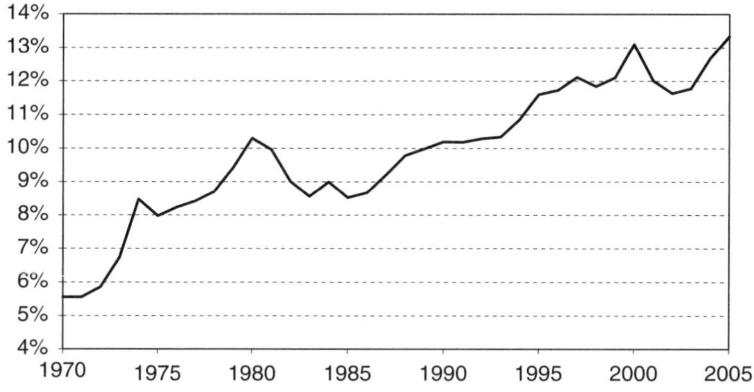

Fig. 2. Openness.

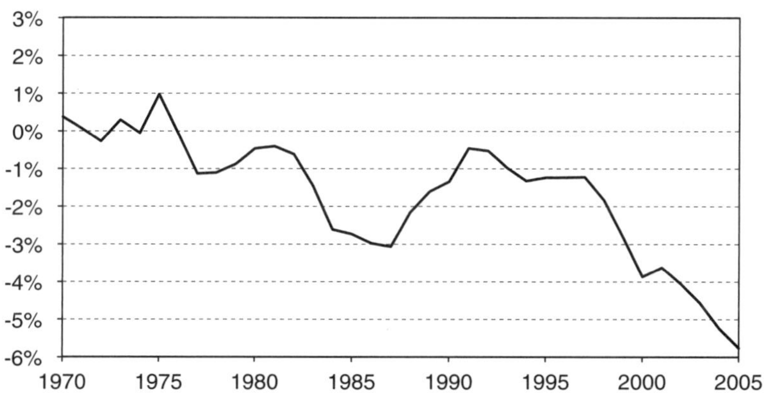

Fig. 3. Trade balance.

sense that their income elasticity of demand is greater than one) have had a marked impact on the volume of international trade, thereby explaining the increase in the global integration of the U.S. economy. As to the trade deficit that has developed over time, it is generally thought to be due to a real overvaluation of the U.S. dollar and to the relatively large income elasticity of the U.S. demand for foreign goods.[7]

Although large imbalances are not necessarily a cause for concern, for trade deficits and surpluses are simply a manifestation of intertemporal trade and there should be no presumption that this situation is suboptimal

---

[7] The U.S. savings–investment imbalance is often also mentioned as a possible cause. However, in the context of the model developed in this chapter, this is essentially another way to look at the exchange rate mechanism: an increase in domestic absorption will, *ceteris paribus*, lead to an increase in the price of nontraded goods, which is equivalent to a real appreciation of the domestic currency.

(the "consenting adults" view), the debate has nonetheless focused on the real exchange rate adjustment necessary to have a significant impact on trade balances.[8] As suggested by the standard open economy macro model (the Fleming–Mundell model), a real depreciation of the U.S. dollar would make U.S. exports more competitive on foreign markets and it would discourage imports.[9] One drawback of this type of analysis, though, is that, by being very Keynesian in spirit, it focuses almost exclusively on demand, with little regard for supply conditions. In a neoclassical setting, assuming that the home economy is small compared to the rest of the world, it may be adequate to assume that the foreign supply of imports is infinitely elastic, but then, by the same token, the foreign demand for the home product should probably be treated as infinitely elastic as well.[10] In other words, as far as exports are concerned it should be the domestic supply of exports, rather than the foreign demand for them, that matters. This suggests that production theory, rather than consumer theory, is the proper setting for explaining the volume of exports.

Another drawback of the Fleming–Mundell approach is that, given that there are only two goods in the model (a domestic one and a foreign one), it does not allow for the distinction between a country's real exchange rate and its terms of trade. The two terms are therefore often used interchangeably in the literature, even though they are really quite different concepts. Admittedly, standard neoclassical trade theory – such as the Heckscher–Ohlin–Samuelson (HOS) model – is not well equipped either to deal with exchange rate analysis, not even in the small open economy case. There is little place for the real exchange rate in that model, with a change in the relative price of exportables to importables meaning a change in the terms of trade, rather than in the exchange rate. The way a depreciation of the home currency might work in such a model is through absorption, thanks to a monetary channel: a depreciation of the home currency, by increasing the prices of both importables and exportables, will tend to reduce real balances and thus incite domestic households to save more and absorb less.

To be able to bring the real exchange rate into the analysis without adding a monetary sector one can add a third type of good, a nontradable good. A change in the real exchange rate can then be thought of as a change in the price of tradables relative to nontradables, without requiring any change in the price of exportables relative to importables (the terms of trade). A depreciation, by making tradable goods more expensive relative to nontradables, will encourage the production and discourage the absorption of tradables, thereby increasing net exports. For given factor

---

[8] See Obstfeld and Rogoff (2004, 2005), for instance. The 2007 Spring edition of the IMF's *World Economic Outlook* (Chapter 3) is no exception.

[9] See Fleming (1962) and Mundell (1963).

[10] If the foreign demand for domestic exports were less than perfectly elastic, this would indicate that the home country has some market power, i.e. it is not truly small.

endowments, the production (and hence absorption) of nontradables will necessarily decline. This adjustment mechanism is captured by the so-called *Australian model*, where the terms of trade are typically held constant, thereby making it possible to focus on the real exchange rate effect.[11]

Most theoretical international trade models, such as the HOS model and the specific factors model,[12] assume that trade takes place in final products. An improvement in the terms of trade is welfare enhancing because it allows the country to reach a higher social indifference curve,[13] even though real GDP (i.e. the position of the production possibilities frontier) does not change.[14] This hypothesis does not match the facts, however, since most international trade is in raw materials and nonfinished products. The international fragmentation of production, by making it possible for countries to exploit their comparative advantages even further at the component level, has accentuated this.[15] Furthermore, even most so-called finished products that are traded are not ready to meet final demand since they must still go through a number of domestic changes, such as unloading, storing, insuring, financing, repackaging, wholesaling, transporting, assembling, cleaning, advertising, retailing, and so on. The price that is charged to the final user is typically much higher than the price of the good when it first entered the country. The difference is accounted for by domestic value added.[16] If imports are to be treated as intermediate products, then the same must hold for exports since these must still be processed by foreign producers before being able to satisfy final demand. As such, exports are conceptually different from goods intended for the domestic market, which are essentially nontraded.[17] Trade thus takes place in middle products, to use the terminology of Sanyal and Jones (1982). It is a fact that most import decisions are made by firms, not by households.

---

[11] See Salter (1959), Dornbusch (1980), and Corden (1992), for instance.

[12] For the specific factors model, see Jones (1971).

[13] Some income redistribution might be needed for welfare to increase in the Pareto sense; see Krueger and Sonnenschein (1967) and Woodland (1982), for instance. Note that the impact of an improvement in the terms of trade on welfare and future growth may be ambiguous in the presence of distortions such as trade and production taxes or subsidies, in case of departures from perfect competition in the products or factor markets, or under uncertainty; see Pattanaik (1970), Batra and Scully (1971), and Lahiri and Sheen (1990), for instance.

[14] Note, however, that if real GDP is computed as a Laspeyres quantity index, as it is often the case, real GDP will tend to fall, irrespective of whether the terms of trade improve or worsen, whereas a Paasche index of real GDP would necessarily register an increase; see Kohli (1983). If real GDP is computed using a functional form that is exact for the underlying technology, real GDP will remain unchanged.

[15] See Obstfeld (2002).

[16] The same is true for reexports (entrepot trade), which typically contain a substantial proportion of domestic value added; see Hanson and Feenstra (2004), for instance.

[17] Needless to say, nontraded goods may contain traded components to various degrees, just like exports may contain traded as well as nontraded elements; see Burstein (2005a, 2005b), for instance.

Thus, production theory, rather than consumer theory, would appear to be the proper setting to derive, not just the supply of exports as we argued earlier, but the demand for imports as well.[18] This also suggests that the three issues that were identified above – regarding the labor share, openness, and trade imbalances – are all related. In fact, as we shall see, the three shares can be derived jointly from the same optimization problem.

Treating traded goods as middle products also has far-reaching consequences for the measurement of real value added, which we define as the real income realized from domestic production inclusive of trading gains. Indeed, in the HOS model trade is pictured as taking place almost as an afterthought, i.e. after production has been completed. Any gains from trade benefit households, but have little to do with production and output. If trade is modeled as taking place in middle products, then it must be true that trade takes place *during* the production process. It is then an intimate part of production, and the extra value that it generates must be taken into account when computing the economy's total value added. A change in the terms of trade or in the real exchange rate tends to affect real value added. In that sense, these are very similar to a technological change.[19] Real GDP is therefore no longer the appropriate measure of real value added. Instead, one should focus on real gross domestic income (GDI), i.e. nominal GDP (or GDI) deflated by the price of domestic absorption.[20]

The purpose of this chapter is to show how, using a real GDI function for the United States under the assumption that trade is in middle products, our measures for the labor income share, openness, and trade imbalances – as depicted in Figures 1–3 – can be derived and estimated jointly. Changes in these shares can be explained by changes in the terms of trade and the real exchange rate, together with changes in relative factor endowments and technological progress.[21] Our econometric estimates also make it possible to get a sense as to how large a change in the terms of trade and/or the real exchange rate would be necessary to make a significant dent into the U.S. trade deficit.

---

[18] See Burgess (1974) and Kohli (1978, 1991).

[19] See Diewert and Morrison (1986), Kohli (1990, 2004a), and Feenstra *et al.* (2005).

[20] In a recent paper, Feenstra *et al.* (2004) draw a distinction between two measures of real GDP: an output side measure, which they denote by GDP^o, and an expenditure side measure, which they denote by GDP^e. The former is obtained by deflating nominal GDP by a price index for output (the usual GDP deflator), while the latter is obtained by using instead a price index for expenditures (a domestic absorption price index). The distinction between GDP^o and GDP^e is thus essentially the same as between real GDP and real GDI.

[21] We use the term "technological progress" in a broad sense: it includes technological advances in the production of goods and services as well as improvements in institutions and enhancements in economic (including trade) policies.

2. Real GDP, real GDI, and relative prices

Trade in middle products means that trade must be modeled as part of the production process, rather than as taking place after production has been completed. In the spirit of Sanyal and Jones (1982), let us assume that production involves two primary inputs – labor (L) and capital (K) – and that these are used together with imports (M) to produce two outputs, one intermediate output (X) that is exported and one final, nontraded good (N) that is absorbed domestically.[22] Let $x_{j,t}$ and $w_{j,t}$ denote the endowment and the rental price of factor j ($j \in \{K,L\}$) at time t, respectively. The price and the quantity of good i ($i \in \{N,X,M\}$) at time t are denoted $p_{i,t}$ and $q_{i,t}$.

We begin with some definitions, starting with nominal GDP (Π_t):

$$\Pi_t \equiv p_{N,t}q_{N,t} + p_{X,t}q_{X,t} - p_{M,t}q_{M,t}. \tag{1}$$

Let $p_{Y,t}$ be the price of GDP. We measure it as a Törnqvist chained price index:[23]

$$p_{Y,t} \equiv p_{Y,t-1} \cdot \exp\left[\sum_i \pm \frac{1}{2}(s_{i,t} + s_{i,t-1}) \ln \frac{p_{i,t}}{p_{i,t-1}}\right], \quad i \in \{N, X, M\}, \tag{2}$$

where the sign is negative for imports and positive otherwise, and $s_{i,t}$ is the GDP share of component i:

$$s_{i,t} \equiv \frac{p_{i,t}q_{i,t}}{\Pi_t}, \quad i \in \{N, X, M\}. \tag{3}$$

Real GDP ($q_{Y,t}$) can then be obtained by deflation:[24]

$$q_{Y,t} \equiv \frac{\Pi_t}{p_{Y,t}}. \tag{4}$$

Real GDI ($q_{Z,t}$), on the contrary, can be obtained by deflating nominal GDP by the price of domestic absorption:

$$q_{Z,t} \equiv \frac{\Pi_t}{p_{N,t}}. \tag{5}$$

As argued earlier, if trade is in middle products real GDI is a better measure of domestic real value added than real GDP, since the latter ignores the changes in real value added resulting from movements in the

---

[22] This good can be thought of as an aggregate of consumption, investment, and government purchases. The Sanyal and Jones model is somewhat more general in that it allows for two nontraded goods. However, the production structure it stipulates, by containing many elements of nonjointness and disjointness, is quite restrictive; see Kohli (2001a).

[23] Like for other price indices, the base period price (e.g. the price of period 0, $p_{Y,0}$) is typically set to unity.

[24] Real GDP so defined has the implicit Törnqvist form; see Kohli (2004b). It is a superlative index in the sense of Diewert (1976).

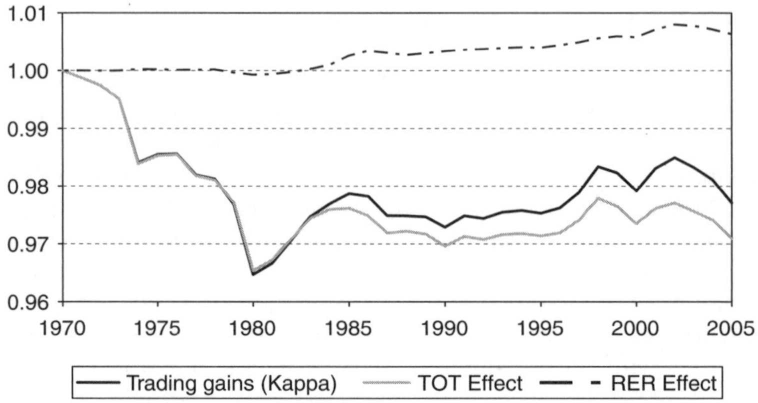

Fig. 4. Trading gains: terms of trade and real exchange rate effects.

terms of trade and in the real exchange rate. The relationship between real GDI and real GDP is captured by κ_t, which is defined as

$$\kappa_t \equiv \frac{q_{Z,t}}{q_{Y,t}}. \tag{6}$$

κ_t can be thought of as an index of the trading gains; see Kohli (2006). Its path is depicted in Figure 4. The trading gains index fell significantly during the 1970s, from 1.00 to about 0.965. This means that real GDP overestimated the growth of U.S. real value added by about 3.5% over the course of that decade. After recovering somewhat during the early 1980s, the index has mostly moved sideways. Nonetheless, there were individual years when the trading gains or losses were nontrivial, such as in 1987, when real GDP growth overestimated the growth in real value added by about 0.3%, or in 1998 and 2001, when it underestimated it by about 0.4%.

We next define the price of traded goods ($p_{T,t}$) as the geometric mean of the prices of exports and imports:

$$p_{T,t} \equiv p_{X,t}^{1/2} p_{M,t}^{1/2}. \tag{7}$$

We can now identify several important price ratios that will be relevant for the analysis that follows. We begin with the real exchange rate (ε_t), also known as the Salter ratio, which is defined as the relative price of traded vs. nontraded goods:[25]

$$\varepsilon_t \equiv \frac{p_{T,t}}{p_{N,t}}. \tag{8}$$

[25] See Salter (1959), Dornbusch (1980), Frenkel and Mussa (1984), Corden (1992), and the literature on the Australian model. An increase in ε signals a real depreciation of the home currency.

Note that the real exchange rate so defined does not coincide exactly with another common definition of the real exchange rate – sometimes called the purchasing power parity (PPP) real exchange rate – namely the nominal exchange rate adjusted for price-level differentials.[26] To see this, let $p^*_{N,t}$ be the price of foreign absorption (expressed in foreign currency) and let E_t be the nominal exchange rate (the price of foreign exchange). The PPP (nominal) exchange rate can then be defined as

$$\pi_t \equiv \frac{p_{N,t}}{p^*_{N,t}}, \tag{9}$$

whereas the PPP real exchange rate can be written as

$$e_t \equiv \frac{E_t p^*_{N,t}}{p_{N,t}} = \frac{E_t}{\pi_t}. \tag{10}$$

Comparing (8) with (10), the difference between ε_t and e_t is obvious: the former refers to the domestic prices of traded and nontraded goods, whereas the latter makes an international comparison between the prices of nontraded goods. As we shall see below, neither π_t nor e_t are relevant for domestic production decisions.[27]

Next, we consider the terms of trade (τ_t), defined as the price of exports relative to the price of imports:

$$\tau_t \equiv \frac{p_{X,t}}{p_{M,t}}. \tag{11}$$

The paths of ε_t and τ_t are depicted in Figure 5. It is striking that over the last 25 years ε_t has fallen substantially, by over 40%. That is, the price of traded goods has increased much less rapidly than the price of nontraded goods. This amounts to a substantial real appreciation of the U.S. dollar. Without wanting to draw any definite conclusions at this stage, the fall in the real exchange rate might help to explain why U.S. production has tilted towards the production of nontraded goods and away from the production of traded goods, whereas absorption has done exactly the reverse, thereby leaving a large gap between the production and the absorption of traded goods. The figure also shows the terms of trade. Its path is clearly distinct from that of the real exchange rate. The U.S. terms of trade have been fairly steady over the past 25 years. They did deteriorate significantly during the 1970s following the two oil shocks, thereby reducing real GDI at that time.

We may note from (4) and (5) that κ_t as defined by (6) can also be expressed as a price ratio, namely the price of GDP relative to the price of

---

[26] See Edwards (1989) for a review of competing definitions of the real exchange rate.

[27] Note that in the absence of transportation costs and of any barriers to trade, one would expect the law of one price to hold: $p_{T,t} = E_t p^*_{T,t}$. In that case, the PPP real exchange rate can also be expressed as $e_t = \varepsilon_t/\varepsilon^*_t$, where $\varepsilon^*_t \equiv p^*_{T,t}/p^*_{N,t}$ is the foreign Salter ratio; ε^*_t plays no role in our analysis.

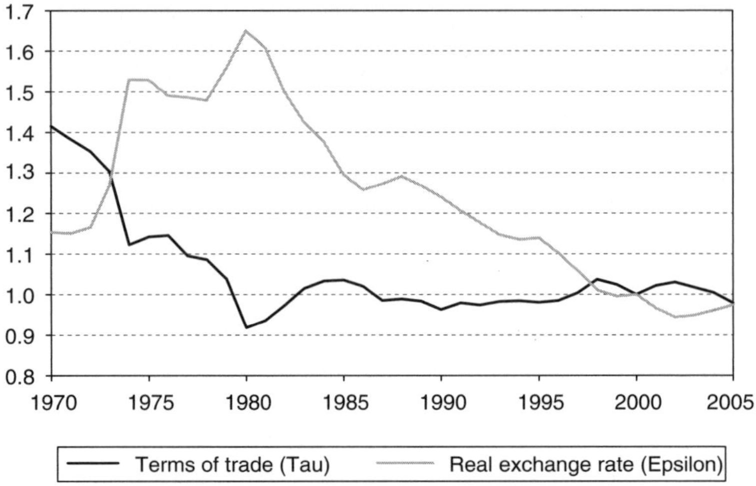

Fig. 5. Terms of trade and real exchange rate.

domestic absorption:

$$\kappa_t = \frac{p_{Y,t}}{p_{N,t}}. \tag{12}$$

It is noteworthy that ε_t, τ_t, and κ_t are not fully independent of each other. Indeed, definitions (7), (8), and (11) imply that

$$\frac{p_{X,t}}{p_{N,t}} = \varepsilon_t \tau_t^{1/2} \tag{13}$$

and

$$\frac{p_{M,t}}{p_{N,t}} = \varepsilon_t \tau_t^{-1/2}. \tag{14}$$

It thus follows from (2) and (12) that

$$\kappa_t = \kappa_{t-1} \cdot \exp\left[\frac{1}{2}(s_{A,t} + s_{A,t-1}) \ln \frac{\tau_t}{\tau_{t-1}} + \frac{1}{2}(s_{B,t} + s_{B,t-1}) \ln \frac{\varepsilon_t}{\varepsilon_{t-1}}\right], \tag{15}$$

where $s_{A,t} \equiv (s_{X,t} + s_{M,t})/2$ is the average foreign trade share (the measure of openness depicted in Figure 2) and $s_{B,t} \equiv s_{X,t} - s_{M,t}$ is the trade balance relative to GDP as shown in Figure 3. Expression (15) provides a convenient decomposition of the trading gains into terms of a trade effect and a real exchange rate effect.[28] This is shown in Figure 4, using 1970 as a

[28] See Kohli (2008b). The terms of trade effect defined by the first term in the square brackets of (15) does not coincide exactly with the terms of trade effect as defined by Diewert and Morrison (1986) and Kohli (1990); see Kohli (2006) for details.

reference period. It can be seen that the real exchange rate effect has been slightly positive over the entire period. Indeed, the drop in the (relative) price of tradables has had a positive income effect given that the U.S. trade account was in a deficit position for most of the period: the fall in export revenues has been more than compensated by the reduction in the import bill. The terms of trade effect, on the other hand, has been negative on balance.

3. Description of the aggregate technology

Let Ψ_t be the production possibilities set (i.e. the set of all feasible input and output combinations) at time t.[29] We assume that Ψ_t is a convex cone. An illustration of such a technology, drawn in the nontraded good, exports, and import quantity space, for three different levels of domestic factor endowments, is shown in Figure 6.[30]

The aggregate technology can then be described by a real GDI function defined as[31]

$$q_{Z,t} = z(\tau_t, \varepsilon_t, x_{K,t}, x_{L,t}, t) \equiv \max_{q_N, q_X, q_M} \left\{ \begin{array}{c} q_N + \varepsilon_t \tau_t^{1/2} q_X - \varepsilon_t \tau_t^{-1/2} q_M : \\ (q_N, q_X, q_M, x_{K,t}, x_{L,t}) \in \Psi_t \end{array} \right\}. \tag{16}$$

One can show that the real GDI function has the following slope properties:[32]

$$\frac{\partial z(\cdot)}{\partial \tau} = \frac{1}{2} \frac{\varepsilon_t}{\tau_t} (\tau_t^{1/2} q_{X,t} + \tau_t^{-1/2} q_{M,t}), \tag{17}$$

$$\frac{\partial z(\cdot)}{\partial \varepsilon} = \tau_t^{1/2} q_{X,t} - \tau_t^{-1/2} q_{M,t}, \tag{18}$$

$$\frac{\partial z(\cdot)}{\partial x_K} = \frac{w_{K,t}}{p_{N,t}}, \tag{19}$$

---

[29] Throughout this chapter we assume that resources are fully employed and freely mobile between activities.

[30] For the purpose of this illustration the transformation function $\psi(\cdot)$ has been assumed to be as follows: $\psi(q_N, q_X, q_M, x) = (q_N^2 + q_X^2) - q_M x = 0$, where x is an aggregate of labor and capital, and it takes on the values of 2/3, 1, and 2. For simplicity, we have thus assumed that the technology is globally separable (i) between the domestic factors and the three products, and (ii) between the composite domestic factor and imports, on one hand, and exports and nontraded goods, on the other. These restrictions are not imposed in our empirical work.

[31] The real GDI function can be viewed as a modified nominal GDP function; see Kohli (1978, 1991, 2004a, 2007), Woodland (1982), and Harrigan (1997).

[32] See Kohli (2007).

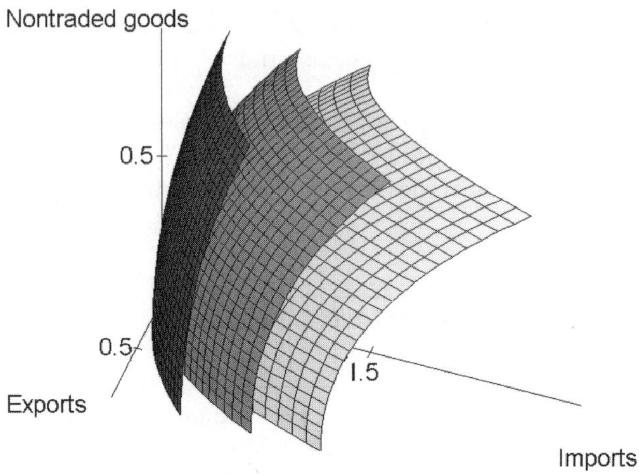

Fig. 6. Three good production possibilities surface for alternative domestic factor endowments.

$$\frac{\partial z(\cdot)}{\partial x_L} = \frac{w_{L,t}}{p_{N,t}}, \tag{20}$$

and

$$\frac{\partial z(\cdot)}{\partial t} = \mu_t q_{Z,t}, \tag{21}$$

where μ_t is the instantaneous rate of technological change.

For the empirical implementation we need a functional form to describe (16). One form well suited for our purposes is the Translog function.[33] It provides a second-order approximation in logarithms of an arbitrary real GDI function:

$$\begin{aligned} \ln q_{Z,t} = {} & \ln x_{L,t} + \alpha_0 + \alpha_\tau \ln \tau_t + \alpha_\varepsilon \ln \varepsilon_t + \beta_K \ln k_t + \beta_T t \\ & + \frac{1}{2}\gamma_{\tau\tau} \ln \tau_t^2 + \gamma_{\tau\varepsilon} \ln \tau_t \ln \varepsilon_t + \frac{1}{2}\gamma_{\varepsilon\varepsilon} \ln \varepsilon_t^2 \\ & + \frac{1}{2}\phi_{KK} \ln k_t^2 + \phi_{KT} \ln k_t \, t + \frac{1}{2}\phi_{TT}\, t^2 \\ & + \delta_{\tau K} \ln \tau_t \ln k_t + \delta_{\varepsilon K} \ln \varepsilon_t \ln k_t + \delta_{\tau T} \ln \tau_t t + \delta_{\varepsilon T} \ln \varepsilon_t \, t, \end{aligned} \tag{22}$$

where k_t is the capital/labor ratio:

$$k_t \equiv \frac{x_{K,t}}{x_{L,t}}. \tag{23}$$

[33] See Christensen *et al.* (1973), Diewert (1974), and Kohli (1978, 1991, 2004a).

In the case of (22) the first-order conditions (17)–(21) can best be expressed in share form through logarithmic differentiation:

$$s_{A,t} = \alpha_\tau + \gamma_{\tau\tau} \ln \tau_t + \gamma_{\tau\varepsilon} \ln \varepsilon_t + \delta_{\tau K} \ln k_t + \delta_{\tau T} t, \quad (24)$$

$$s_{B,t} = \alpha_\varepsilon + \gamma_{\tau\varepsilon} \ln \tau_t + \gamma_{\varepsilon\varepsilon} \ln \varepsilon_t + \delta_{\varepsilon K} \ln k_t + \delta_{\varepsilon T} t, \quad (25)$$

$$s_{K,t} = \beta_K + \delta_{\tau K} \ln \tau_t + \delta_{\varepsilon K} \ln \varepsilon_t + \phi_{KK} \ln k_t + \phi_{KT} t, \quad (26)$$

$$s_{L,t} = 1 - \beta_K - \delta_{\tau K} \ln \tau_t - \delta_{\varepsilon K} \ln \varepsilon_t - \phi_{KK} \ln k_t - \phi_{KT} t, \quad (27)$$

and

$$\mu_t = \beta_T + \delta_{\tau T} \ln \tau_t + \delta_{\varepsilon T} \ln \varepsilon_t + \phi_{KT} \ln k_t + \phi_{TT} t. \quad (28)$$

Before turning to the estimation of the model, we must note that one of (26) and (27) is superfluous, since the two factor shares add up to unity. Note also that μ_t is not directly observable. In what follows, we will adopt the procedure of Kohli (1991) and approximate μ_t by the average rate of total factor productivity (TFP) between periods $t-1$ and $t+1$. The system of Equations (24)–(25) and (27)–(28) is estimated together with the real GDI function (22) itself. Note that the three Equations (24), (25), and (27) directly yield the three variables that were flagged in the introduction, namely openness, the trade balance, and the labor share. According to our model all three are functions of the real exchange rate, the terms of trade, the capital/labor ratio, and the passage of time.

As indicated by (24)–(28), and as to be expected from neoclassical trade theory, domestic relative factor endowments do matter as well. The U.S. capital–labor ratio has been increasing substantially over time, increasing by over 50% between 1970 and 2005; see Figure 7. Yet, the capital intensity variable has often been ignored in the current debate about globalization, trade imbalances, and income distribution.

It should be noted that Sanyal and Jones (1982) made quite explicit assumptions about the production structure of their model, i.e. about the way inputs are transformed into outputs. Their model contained many elements of nonjointness and disjointness in production. Such hypotheses often lead to strong and unambiguous comparative statics results, but they also severely restrict the flexibility of the technology. Our model does not rely on any such restrictions: real GDI function (22) is fully flexible and perfectly compatible with joint production.[34]

[34] See Kohli (2001a, 2001b) for an empirical implementation and a test of the restrictions imposed by the Sanyal and Jones production structure.

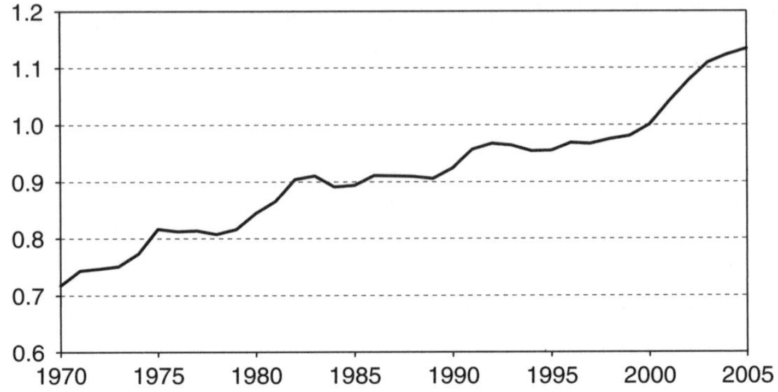

Fig. 7. Capital–labor ratio.

4. Estimation results

The model was first estimated by iterative Zellner (IZEF) as implemented in TSP, version 4.3A. The parameter estimates are reported in the first column of Table 1, together with their *t*-values. It can be seen that most parameters are determined with a relatively high degree of precision. We also verified that these estimates satisfy all required regularity (curvature and monotonicity) conditions for all observations. Conventional R^2 for the five equations are reported at the bottom of the table, but these must be interpreted with care since they are not derived from ordinary least squares estimates. The goodness of fit seems particularly low for the technological change equation, but this is quite typical, since, as shown by (38) and (39) below, the dependent variable consists of an underlying rate of technological progress – that is quite steady over time – and a random element.[35]

Although we assume that relative output prices and domestic factor endowments are exogenous to production decisions, this is unlikely to be true in an econometric sense in the case of the United States given its size, and in view of the fact that consumption/savings decisions by households are likely to affect the price of nontraded goods. We have therefore reestimated the model by iterative three stage least squares (I3SLS). The instruments that we have used are: the lagged values of the terms of trade and of the real exchange rate, the domestic factor endowments, the government purchases of goods and services (all of these in logarithms), the government budget deficit, the federal funds rate, the unemployment rate, time, time squared, and a constant term. The resulting parameters are shown in the second column of Table 1. We have verified that these estimates too fulfill all regularity conditions for all observations.

[35] See Kohli (1991) for a similar result.

Table 1. Parameter estimates (t-values in parentheses)

	IZEF	I3SLS
$\hat{\alpha}_0$	9.19444	9.19405
	(3363.00)	(3356.97)
$\hat{\alpha}_\tau$	0.12147	0.12249
	(104.15)	(89.64)
$\hat{\alpha}_\varepsilon$	−0.03109	−0.03007
	(−10.47)	(−11.07)
$\hat{\beta}_K$	0.38055	0.37901
	(205.19)	(187.69)
$\hat{\gamma}_{\tau\tau}$	0.09513	0.09309
	(4.41)	(3.16)
$\hat{\gamma}_{\tau\varepsilon}$	0.11507	0.11630
	(6.87)	(5.28)
$\hat{\gamma}_{\varepsilon\varepsilon}$	0.07778	0.07972
	(3.74)	(3.74)
$\hat{\phi}_{KK}$	−0.13730	−0.08265
	(−4.03)	(−2.12)
$\hat{\delta}_{\tau K}$	−0.07940	−0.11114
	(−4.17)	(−5.01)
$\hat{\delta}_{\varepsilon K}$	−0.01182	−0.04113
	(−0.69)	(−2.22)
$\hat{\delta}_{\tau T}$	0.00470	0.00505
	(10.10)	(9.00)
$\hat{\delta}_{\varepsilon T}$	0.00063	0.00099
	(1.30)	(1.97)
$\hat{\phi}_{KT}$	0.00168	0.00052
	(2.79)	(0.85)
$\hat{\beta}_T$	0.01237	0.01219
	(30.25)	(29.07)
$\hat{\phi}_{TT}$	0.00022	0.00022
	(6.61)	(6.65)
R_Z^2	0.99895	0.99894
R_A^2	0.95832	0.96243
R_B^2	0.53118	0.54667
R_L^2	0.58015	0.58700
R_T^2	0.13936	0.13835

Looking at share Equations (24), (25), and (27), we find that an improvement in the terms of trade (a rise in τ_t) tends to favor openness, improve the trade balance, and increase the income share of labor. The same holds true for a real depreciation of the currency (an increase in ε_t). An increase in capital intensity (an increase in k_t) also leads to an increase in the labor share,[36] but it tends to hinder openness and worsen the trade balance.

---

[36] This is the manifestation of a Hicksian elasticity of complementarity between capital and labor that is greater than one: its estimate oscillates between 1.35 and 1.37 over the sample period.

Technological change (the passage of time), finally, favors openness and tends to improve the trade account, but it is biased against labor.

Before examining what light our estimates might shed on the recent experience of the United States in terms of openness, trade imbalances, and income distribution, it is worthwhile computing the standard price and quantity elasticities that our production model allows us to identify.[37] 2005 values (I3SLS estimates) are reported in expression (29):

$$\begin{bmatrix} d\ln q_X \\ d\ln q_M \\ d\ln q_N \\ d\ln w_K \\ d\ln w_L \\ d\mu \end{bmatrix} = \begin{bmatrix} 1.168 & -0.802 & -0.366 & -0.807 & 1.807 & 0.063 \\ 0.612 & -1.124 & 0.512 & -0.245 & 1.245 & 0.044 \\ -0.039 & -0.072 & 0.112 & 0.414 & 0.586 & 0.012 \\ -0.240 & 0.095 & 1.146 & -0.846 & 0.846 & 0.015 \\ 0.322 & -0.291 & 0.969 & 0.507 & -0.507 & 0.012 \\ 0.006 & -0.005 & -0.001 & 0.001 & -0.001 & 0.000 \end{bmatrix} \begin{bmatrix} d\ln p_X \\ d\ln p_M \\ d\ln p_N \\ d\ln x_K \\ d\ln x_L \\ dt \end{bmatrix}. \tag{29}$$

Each entry of the square matrix can be viewed as the partial derivative of one of the six endogenous variables with respect to one of the six exogenous variables. Thus, the first entry in the northwest corner (1.168) is the own price elasticity of the supply of exports, $\partial \ln q_X / \partial \ln p_X$. We can see that the own price elasticities of the supply of exports and of the demand for imports are both greater than one in absolute value. Looking at the cross price elasticities of output supply, we find that an increase in the price of exports discourages the production of nontradables, but it has a stimulating effect on the demand for imports. Similarly, an increase in the price of nontradables also encourages imports, and it shifts resources away from the production of exports. An increase in the price of imports has a negative impact on the production of both exports and nontradables. The inverse price elasticities of the demand for labor and for capital (rows and columns 4–5) show that an increase in the endowment of either factor depresses its own rental price by a small amount and favor the other factor. The implied value for the Hicksian elasticity of complementarity between labor and capital is 1.353. Of considerable interest also are the Stolper–Samuelson elasticities (rows 4 and 5, columns 1–3). They show that an increase in export prices and a drop in import prices heavily favor labor at the expense of capital, and that an increase in the price of nontradables leads to an increase in the nominal rental price of both factors, although in real terms it makes labor slightly worse off. The Rybczynski elasticities (rows 1–3, columns 4–5) convey the same message translated into the quantity space: an increase in the endowment of labor heavily favors foreign trade, whereas an increase in the capital stock, other things equal, actually reduces the supply of exports and the demand for

[37] See Kohli (1978, 1991) for further explanations, and Kohli (2004a) for the link between a real GDI function and a nominal GDP function.

imports. The last column of the square matrix shows that technological change has a positive impact on the demand for imports and on the supply of exports and nontradables (although it is biased in favor of foreign trade) and that, although it benefits both factors, it is biased in favor of capital. The last row, finally, indicates that an improvement in the terms of trade or an increase in the capital–labor ratio stimulate technological change.

5. *Accounting for changes in openness, imbalances, and income shares*

As time passes, technological progress and changes in relative factor endowments shift the production possibilities frontier. To the extent that the shift is non-neutral, the input–output mix would change even if relative prices did not. Of course, over time relative prices (the terms of trade and the real exchange rate) will tend to change too: this leads to further changes in the input–output mix, as the production point moves along the production possibilities frontier. The changes in openness, in the trade balance and in the labor share that we observe over time reflect the summation of these four effects. To disentangle these forces, we can take the first differences of Equations (24), (25), and (27):

$$\Delta s_{A,t} = \hat{\gamma}_{\tau\tau}\Delta \ln \tau_t + \hat{\gamma}_{\tau\varepsilon}\Delta \ln \varepsilon_t + \hat{\delta}_{\tau K}\Delta \ln k_t + \hat{\delta}_{\tau T} + u_{A,t}, \tag{30}$$

$$\Delta s_{B,t} = \hat{\gamma}_{\varepsilon\tau}\Delta \ln \tau_t + \hat{\gamma}_{\varepsilon\varepsilon}\Delta \ln \varepsilon_t + \hat{\delta}_{\varepsilon K}\Delta \ln k_t + \hat{\delta}_{\varepsilon T} + u_{B,t}, \tag{31}$$

and

$$\Delta s_{L,t} = -\hat{\delta}_{\tau K}\Delta \ln \tau_t - \hat{\delta}_{\varepsilon K}\Delta \ln \varepsilon_t - \hat{\phi}_{KK}\Delta \ln k_t - \hat{\phi}_{KT} + u_{L,t}, \tag{32}$$

where Δ is the first difference operator, the hats (ˆ) signal estimated values, and the u's denote unexplained residuals.

Our results for the period 1970–2005 are summarized in Table 2. As was already illustrated by Figure 1, openness increased substantially over the time period, by about 7.8 percentage points relative to GDP. This increase is due exclusively to technological progress, for the increase in capital intensity, the worsening in the terms of trade, and the real appreciation of the currency all three pushed in the opposite direction. Technological progress typically leads to an outward shift in the production possibilities frontier. Our results indicate that in the U.S. case, this shift is biased, i.e. it is accompanied by a twist that favors the production of exports and the use of imports over the production of nontraded goods.[38]

As to the deterioration of the trade balance (about 6.1 percentage points over the time interval), it is mostly due to the worsening of the terms of trade, followed by the increase in U.S. capital intensity and the real appreciation of the currency. The increase in capital intensity led to a twist

[38] This is confirmed by the estimates of $\partial \ln q_X/\partial t$, $\partial \ln q_M/\partial t$, and $\partial \ln q_N/\partial t$ reported in (29).

Table 2. Cumulated effects of changes in the terms of trade, the real exchange rate, capital intensity, and technology on openness, the trade balance, and the labor share 1970–2005

	Openness (s_A)	Trade balance (s_B)	Labor share (s_L)
Terms of trade (τ)	−0.034	−0.043	−0.041
Real exchange rate (ε)	−0.020	−0.013	−0.007
Capital/labor ratio (k)	−0.051	−0.019	0.038
TFP (t)	0.177	0.035	−0.018
Residual	0.006	−0.021	−0.015
Total (1970–2005)	0.078	−0.061	−0.043

in the production possibilities that, for given relative prices, heavily favored the production of nontraded goods as the expense of exports; see the elasticity estimates contained in (29). The demand for imports was penalized as well, but much less so than the supply of exports. Far from being offset by changes in relative prices, this change in the input–output mix was actually reinforced by the worsening in the terms of trade and the fall in the relative price of traded goods. Technological change had a substantial effect too, but it acted in the opposite direction. It must be noted, though, that about one third of the deterioration of the trade balance cannot be explained by the model.

With regards to the labor share, finally, the observed 4.3 percentage point fall is explained mostly by the worsening in the terms of trade and by technological change. The real appreciation that took place had a small negative effect only. The increase in capital intensity, however, contributed to contain the fall in the labor share. If it were not for that positive influence, the fall in the labor share would have been nearly twice as high. The negative impact that the worsening in the terms of trade had on the labor share can probably best be understood by considering the complementarity relationship (in the Hicksian sense) that exists between imports and labor: if the use of imports is curtailed as the result of the increase in their relative price, it impacts negatively on the marginal product of labor. Admittedly, about one third of the fall in the income share of labor is not accounted for by the model.

In summary, the worsening in the United States' terms of trade followed by the increase in capital intensity that appears to be biased in favor of the production of nontradables appear to be the main reasons for the deterioration in the trade account. Technological change, however, favors net exports and openness. As for labor, capital is its best friend. An improvement in the terms of trade would also do much to lift the labor share.

What would it take to make a significant dent into the U.S. trade deficit? According to the estimates reported in Table 1, column 2, it would require a 9.0% real depreciation (i.e. an increase in the relative price of traded goods) to reduce the deficit relative to GDP by one percentage point. It would take an 11.3% improvement in the U.S. terms of trade to achieve the same result. A joint 10% real depreciation and 10% improvement in the terms of trade would reduce the deficit by 1.9 percentage points.[39] This would also increase openness by about 2.0 percentage points and raise the labor share by 1.5 percentage points. Over time, regarding the offsetting influences of capital accumulation and technological change on the trade balance and the labor share, it would take increases in the capital–labor ratio at rates between 0.6% and 2.4% (vs. the historical average of 1.3%) to increase both shares.

6. *Productivity*

As we have seen, the view that all trade takes place in middle products has profound implications for the measurement of real value added. It should therefore come as no surprise that it also has significant consequences for the measurement of productivity, in particular the measurement of average labor productivity.[40] Indeed, the appropriate numerator should be real GDI rather than real GDP when measuring real value added per unit of labor. Let $\Theta_{t,t-1}$ be the index of average labor productivity between times $t-1$ and t:

$$\Theta_{t,t-1} \equiv \frac{q_{Z,t}/x_{L,t}}{q_{Z,t-1}/x_{L,t-1}}. \tag{33}$$

Real GDI function (22) provides a natural starting point for our analysis. Subtracting $\ln x_{L,t}$ from both sides of (22), taking first-order differences, and making use of (24)–(28) we get:

$$\Theta_{t,t-1} = \Theta^{\tau}_{t,t-1} \cdot \Theta^{\varepsilon}_{t,t-1} \cdot \Theta^{k}_{t,t-1} \cdot \Theta^{T}_{t,t-1} \cdot \Theta^{u}_{t,t-1}, \tag{34}$$

where

$$\Theta^{\tau}_{t,t-1} \equiv \exp\left[\frac{1}{2}(\hat{s}_{A,t} + \hat{s}_{A,t-1}) \ln \frac{\tau_t}{\tau_{t-1}}\right], \tag{35}$$

$$\Theta^{\varepsilon}_{t,t-1} \equiv \exp\left[\frac{1}{2}(\hat{s}_{B,t} + \hat{s}_{B,t-1}) \ln \frac{\varepsilon_t}{\varepsilon_{t-1}}\right], \tag{36}$$

---

[39] For a given price of nontraded goods, this would require import prices to increase by 4.9% and export prices to increase by 15.4%.

[40] For an analysis of the relationship between the average and the marginal measures of labor productivity, see Kohli (2008a).

$$\Theta^k_{t,t-1} \equiv \exp\left[\frac{1}{2}(\hat{s}_{K,t} + \hat{s}_{K,t-1})\ln\frac{k_t}{k_{t-1}}\right], \tag{37}$$

$$\Theta^T_{t,t-1} \equiv \exp\left[\frac{1}{2}(\hat{\mu}_t + \hat{\mu}_{t-1})\right], \tag{38}$$

and

$$\Theta^u_{t,t-1} \equiv \frac{q_{Z,t}/q_{Z,t-1}}{\hat{q}_{Z,t}/\hat{q}_{Z,t-1}}. \tag{39}$$

The hats (ˆ) in (35)–(39) denote fitted – as opposed to observed – values. The growth in average labor productivity can thus be decomposed into five terms: the contributions of changes in the terms of trade, in the real exchange rate and in capital intensity, the effect of technological progress, and an unexplained residual. The first two terms together account for the trading gains; see expression (15). The last two terms together capture the full change in TFP: it consists of an underlying, persistent term ($\Theta^T_{t,t-1}$) and of an unexplained, random residual ($\Theta^u_{t,t-1}$). Note that (35)–(37) could also be computed on the basis of observed rather than fitted shares. In that case TFP would have to be computed as a residual, however, and it would not be possible to distinguish between $\Theta^T_{t,t-1}$ and $\Theta^u_{t,t-1}$.[41]

Decomposition (34) is documented by Figure 8 that shows the cumulated sums of these effects. The lowest line (denoted TG) represents the trading gains.[42] For the second line up (TG & KL) we have added the capital intensity effect, and then, for the third line (TG & KL & TC), the technological change effect. Adding finally the unexplained component one obtains the observed labor productivity line (denoted QZ/XL). One sees that average labor productivity has increased by nearly 70% over the sample period. Technological change was clearly the driving force, with the increase in capital intensity nonetheless responsible for close to one third of the increase. As indicated earlier, the trading gains have been negative on average, holding back average labor productivity by about 2.5%.

7. *Conclusions*

Ron Jones's insight that most trade is in middle products has far-reaching consequences for the measurement of real value added and productivity,

---

[41] Note that, in any case, TFP is a catchall term: it includes the effects of technological progress, changes in institutions, adjustments in policy, and so on. It is not possible to assess the relative importance of each one of these factors.

[42] In order not to overburden the graph, we do not represent the terms of trade effect and the real exchange rate effect separately. The decomposition of the trading gains was shown in Figure 4. Note, however, that the decomposition shown in Figure 4 was based on observed rather than fitted shares, but the difference is numerically very small.

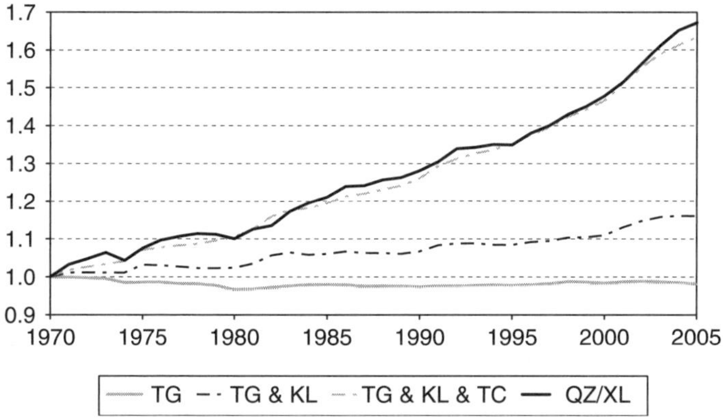

Fig. 8. Average labor productivity.

and for the modeling of international trade. It implies that production theory is the proper setting for the analysis of issues such as openness, trade imbalances, and income distribution, and that certain key ratios, such as the terms of trade, the price of traded vs. nontraded goods, and capital intensity are the driving forces. It also suggests that the emphasis on the PPP real exchange rate, which compares the prices of final goods at home and abroad, might be misplaced.

Our empirical results indicate that technological change has been a major force in the changes that have taken place in recent decades, be it in terms of openness, trade imbalances, or income distribution. The observed increase in the average productivity of labor, itself, has been largely driven by the growth in TFP.

Our results also suggest that a large increase in the relative price of traded goods is likely to be required to make a significant dent into the U.S. trade deficit. Ideally, the increase in export prices should exceed the increase in import prices, thereby also improving the U.S. terms of trade. This would not only alleviate some of the anxieties regarding the large trade deficit, but it would also be beneficial to the United States from a welfare perspective. Thus, a 15% increase in export prices accompanied by a 5% rise in import prices would reduce the deficit by about two percentage points. Admittedly, these calculations should only be viewed as rough estimates, but they do suggest that a sizable increase in the traded to nontraded good price ratio would be required for the U.S. current account deficit to shrink significantly. A drop in nontraded service prices and in housing prices could contribute to the adjustment.

Admittedly, the model has nothing to say about the causes of the changes in the terms of trade and the real exchange rate, and what kind of shock, if any, would trigger an adjustment. Without doubt, the observed changes in relative prices reflect shifts in world demand and supply conditions, factor endowments, technology, tastes, demography, and so on. One should not necessarily think in terms of causality either, for in a general equilibrium situation, prices and quantities are determined simultaneously. However, one might argue that more attention needs to be paid to the terms of trade and to the relative prices of traded and nontraded goods when analyzing issues related to globalization.

Acknowledgment

I am grateful to Pierre Duguay, Matthias Lutz, and Marshall Reinsdorf for helpful comments and suggestions, but they are obviously not responsible for any errors or omissions.

Appendix: Description of the data

All data are annual for the period 1970–2005. The prices and quantities of all inputs and outputs are required. The data for GDP and its components, and the corresponding prices, are taken from the *Bureau of Economic Analysis* website. Quantities are then obtained by deflation. Data on the capital stock, labor compensation, and gross domestic factor income are also derived from *BEA* sources. The quantity of capital services is assumed to be proportional to the stock. Capital income is defined as gross domestic factor income minus labor compensation. The quantity of labor services is computed by multiplying the total number of employees on nonfarm payrolls by an index of the average number of weekly hours worked in the nonfarm business sector. Both these series are taken from the *Bureau of Labor Statistics* website. The user costs of labor and capital are then obtained by dividing labor and capital income by the corresponding quantity series. The price of nontradables is computed as a Törnqvist price index of the deflators of consumption, investment, and government purchases. All output (including import) prices and both domestic input quantities are set to unity in 2000; t is defined as a time trend with unit annual increments, and it is set to zero for the year 2000.

References

Batra, R.N., Scully, G.W. (1971), The theory of wage differentials: welfare and immiserizing growth. *Journal of International Economics* 1, 241–247.

Burgess, D.F. (1974), Production theory and the derived demand for imports. *Journal of International Economics* 4, 103–117.

Burstein, A., Eichenbaum, M., Rebelo, S. (2005a), Large devaluations and the real exchange rate. *Journal of Political Economy* 113, 742–784.

Burstein, A., Eichenbaum, M., Rebelo, S. (2005b), The importance of nontradable goods' prices in cyclical real exchange rate fluctuations. NBER Working Paper 11699.

Christensen, L.R., Jorgenson, D.W., Lau, L.J. (1973), Transcendental logarithmic production frontiers. *Review of Economics and Statistics* 55, 28–45.

Corden, W.M. (1992), *Dependent Economy Model of the Balance of Payments. New Palgrave Dictionary of Money and Finance*. Macmillan, London.

Diewert, W.E. (1974), Applications of duality theory. In: Intriligator, Kendrick (Eds.), *Frontiers of Quantitative Economics* vol. 2, North-Holland, Amsterdam.

Diewert, W.E. (1976), Exact and superlative index numbers. *Journal of Econometrics* 4, 115–145.

Diewert, W.E., Morrison, C.J. (1986), Adjusting output and productivity indexes for changes in the terms of trade. *Economic Journal* 96, 659–679.

Dornbusch, R. (1980), *Open Economy Macroeconomics*. Basic Books, New York.

Edwards, S. (1989), Economic liberalization and the equilibrium real exchange rate in developing countries. In: Calvo, Findlay, Kouri, Braga de Macedo (Eds.), *Debt, Stabilization and Development*. Blackwell, Oxford.

Feenstra, R.C., Heston, A., Timmer, M.P., Deng, H. (2004), Estimating real production and expenditure across nations: a proposal for improving the Penn world tables. NBER Working Paper 10866.

Feenstra, R.C., Reinsdorf, M.B., Slaughter, M.J., Harper, M. (2005), Terms of trade gains and U.S. productivity growth. Unpublished.

Fleming, J.M. (1962), Domestic financial policies under fixed and under floating exchange rates. IMF Staff Papers 9, pp. 369–380.

Frenkel, J.A., Mussa, M. (1984), Asset markets, exchange rates, and the balance of payments: a reformulation of doctrine. In: Jones, Kenen (Eds.), *Handbook of International Economics*. North-Holland, Amsterdam.

Hanson, G.H., Feenstra, R.C. (2004), Intermediaries in entrepot trade: Hong Kong re-exports of Chinese goods. *Journal of Economics & Management Strategy* 13, 3–35.

Harrigan, J. (1997), Technology, factor supplies and international specialization: estimating the neoclassical model. *American Economic Review* 87, 475–494.

International Monetary Fund. (1997), *World Economic Outlook, May 1997*. International Monetary Fund, Washington, DC.

International Monetary Fund. (2002), *World Economic Outlook, September 2002*. International Monetary Fund, Washington, DC.

International Monetary Fund. (2007), *World Economic Outlook, April 2007*. International Monetary Fund, Washington, DC.

Jones, R.W. (1971), A three-factor model in theory, trade, and history. In: Bhagwati, Jones, Mundell, Vanek (Eds.), *Trade, Balance of Payments, and Growth: Essays in Honor of Charles P. Kindleberger*. North-Holland, Amsterdam.

Jones, R.W. (2000), *Globalization and the Theory of Input Trade*. MIT Press, Cambridge, MA.

Kohli, U. (1978), A gross national product function and the derived demand for imports and supply of exports. *Canadian Journal of Economics* 11, 167–182.

Kohli, U. (1983), Technology and the demand for imports. *Southern Economic Journal* 50, 137–150.

Kohli, U. (1990), Growth accounting in the open economy: parametric and nonparametric estimates. *Journal of Economic and Social Measurement* 16, 125–136.

Kohli, U. (1991), *Technology, Duality, and Foreign Trade: The GNP Function Approach to Modeling Imports and Exports*. University of Michigan Press, Ann Arbor, MI.

Kohli, U. (2001a), Sanyal and Jones on trade in middle products. *Journal of International Trade and Economic Development* 10, 39–63.

Kohli, U. (2001b), Sanyal and Jones on fragmentation and trade: empirical evidence for South Korea. In: Cheng, Kierzkowski (Eds.), *Global Production and Trade in East Asia*. Kluwer Academic Publishers, Norwell, MA.

Kohli, U. (2004a), Real GDP, real domestic income, and terms-of-trade changes. *Journal of International Economics* 62, 83–106.

Kohli, U. (2004b), An implicit Törnqvist index of real GDP. *Journal of Productivity Analysis* 21, 337–353.

Kohli, U. (2006), Real GDP, real GDI, and trading gains: Canada, 1981–2005. *International Productivity Monitor* 13, 46–56.

Kohli, U. (2007), Terms-of-trade changes, real GDP, and real value added in the open economy: reassessing Hong Kong's growth performance. *Asia-Pacific Journal of Accounting & Economics* 14, 87–109.

Kohli, U. (2008a), Labour productivity: average vs. marginal. In: Diewert, W.E., Balk, B.M., Fixler, D., Fox, K.J., Nakamura, A.O. (Eds.), *Price and Productivity Measurement*. Trafford, Victoria, BC, forthcoming.

Kohli, U. (2008b), Real GDP, real GDI, and trading gains. In: Diewert, W.E., Balk, B.M., Fixler, D., Fox, K.J., Nakamura, A.O. (Eds.), *Price and Productivity Measurement*. Trafford Press, Victoria, BC, forthcoming.

Krueger, A.O., Sonnenschein, H. (1967), The terms of trade, the gains from trade and price divergence. *International Economic Review* 8, 121–127.

Lahiri, S., Sheen, J. (1990), Terms of trade vulnerability and national welfare in a small open economy. Oxford Economic Papers, New Series, vol. 42, pp. 526–543.

Marquez, J. (2002), *Estimating Trade Elasticities*. Kluwer Academic Publishers, Boston, MA.

Mundell, R. (1963), Capital mobility and stabilization policy under fixed and flexible exchange rates. *Canadian Journal of Economics and Political Science* 29, 475–485.

Obstfeld, M. (2002), Exchange rates and adjustment: perspectives from the new open economy macroeconomics. *Monetary and Economic Studies* 20, 23–46.

Obstfeld, M., Rogoff, K. (2004), The unsustainable US current account position revisited. NBER Working Paper 10869.

Obstfeld, M., Rogoff, K. (2005), Global current account imbalances and exchange rate adjustments. Brooking Papers on Economic Activity.

Pattanaik, P.K. (1970), Domestic distortions and the gains from trade. *Economic Journal* 80, 638–649.

Salter, W.E.G. (1959), Internal and external balance: the role of price and expenditure effects. *Economic Record* 35, 226–238.

Sanyal, K.K., Jones, R.W. (1982), The theory of trade in middle products. *American Economic Review* 72, 16–31.

Woodland, A.D. (1982), *International Trade and Resource Allocation*. North-Holland, Amsterdam.

CHAPTER 5

Fixed Transport Costs and International Trade

Didier Laussel[a] and Raymond Riezman[b]

[a]*University of Aix-Marseille 2, rue de la Charité, 13002 Marseilles, France*
E-mail address: laussel@univ-aix.fr
[b]*Department of Economics, W360 PBB, University of Iowa, Iowa City, IA 52242, USA*
E-mail address: raymond-riezman@uiowa.edu

Abstract
We develop a simple two-country model of international trade that assumes that there is a fixed cost of doing international trade. We show that this leads to multiple equilibria that can be Pareto-ranked. We examine the stability properties of these equilibria.

Keywords: Fixed cost, international trade, multiple equilibria, Pareto-ranked

JEL classifications: F1, F11

1. Introduction

Explicit treatment of transportation costs has received relatively little attention in the international trade literature. Samuelson (1954), in an analysis of the transfer problem, developed what has become known as the "iceberg" model of transport costs. In the iceberg model, transporting goods costs some proportion of either the goods' value or the physical quantity. The advantage of this approach is that transportation costs simply act as a kind of simple tax for which there is no revenue produced. In international trade models, its like there is a tariff that produces no revenue. In these models the standard trade theorems hold.

The next major theoretical advance in modeling transportation costs was by Falvey (1976). He treats transportation as services that need to be consumed in order for international trade to take place. Falvey explicitly models a transportation sector and shows that in a Heckscher–Ohlin framework the main trade theorems go through and the analysis is modified in straightforward ways. Despite these theoretical developments recent empirical work on transportation costs point in another direction.

Frontiers of Economics and Globalization
Volume 4 ISSN: 1574-8715
DOI: 10.1016/S1574-8715(08)04005-0

Hummels and Skiba (2004) in a paper about whether high- or low-quality goods are more likely to be exported find that, "… we provide strong evidence against a widely used assumption in the trade literature: that transportation costs are of the 'iceberg' form, proportional to goods prices." In a different context, Hummels and Skiba (2002) argue that economies of scale in transport are important and in part, these economies may derive from large fixed costs of trade. Our purpose here is to explore a model in which there are economies of scale in transport. For simplicity we do this by introducing fixed costs of transportation into a model of international trade and work out the implications.

We develop a simple two-country model of international trade that assumes that there is a fixed cost of doing international trade. We show that this leads to multiple equilibria that can be Pareto-ranked. There are high volume of trade, medium volume of trade and no trade (autarky) equilibria. The high trade equilibrium is best and autarky is worst. Then, we examine the stability properties of these equilibria and show that the high trade equilibrium and autarky are stable while the medium volume of trade equilibrium is unstable. We argue that some countries could be in an autarky trap since in the neighborhood of autarky, because of the fixed transportation cost, they would have no incentive to engage in international trade.

The model is developed in Section 2, offer curves are derived in Section 3, equilibrium solved for in Section 4, a ricardian example is developed in Section 5, stability and efficiency are discussed in Section 6 and policy conclusions are discussed in Section 7.

2. *The general model*

We consider a model in which two goods, labeled 1 and 2, are exchanged between two countries, a home country and a foreign country. All foreign country variables are indicated by asterisks (*): The two goods are produced within each country under perfect competition and with constant returns to scale production functions with the help of $m \geq 1$ internationally immobile factors. The domestic (respectively foreign) prices of the goods 1 and 2 are denoted by p_1 and p_2 (respectively p_1^* and p_2^*). Assuming that the production functions exhibit the usual properties (such as the Inada conditions in the two-factor case) the *autarkic* supply functions (i.e., when no resources are used for transportation) are written as $S_i(p_i/p_j)$ and $S_i^*(p_i^*/p_j^*)$, $i,j = 1,2$, $i \neq j$, respectively in the home and foreign countries with $S_i' > 0$ and $S_i^{*\prime} > 0$.

The role of transportation costs is central in our model. In particular, we are interested in the effect of fixed costs of transportation that may be associated with international trade. These may include the costs of shipping goods from one country to the other or costs of setting up distribution and marketing networks. We focus here on the case when the transportation costs include only fixed (but not sunk) costs.[1] For simplicity, we suppose that shipping goods from the home (respectively foreign) country to the foreign (respectively home) country requires investing a fraction β (respectively β^*) of all the domestic (respectively foreign) factor resources whatever be the (strictly positive) volume of trade. Together with constant returns to scale (CRS), this assumption allows us to rule out any effect of transportation activities on factor prices. The effect of opening the economy is simply to reduce proportionally by a factor β (β^*) the stocks of factors available for production activities. Since the CRS assumption rules out size effects, it is clear that at given domestic (respectively foreign) prices the factor prices are the same in free trade as in autarky. It follows that the total domestic (respectively foreign) factor income Y (respectively Y^*) equals its autarkic value, itself equal to the value of the *autarkic* domestic (respectively foreign) output valued at (the same) domestic (respectively foreign) prices:

$$Y = p_1 S_1\left(\frac{p_1}{p_2}\right) + p_2 S_2\left(\frac{p_2}{p_1}\right) \tag{1}$$

$$Y^* = p_1^* S_1^*\left(\frac{p_1^*}{p_2^*}\right) + p_2^* S_2^*\left(\frac{p_2^*}{p_1^*}\right) \tag{2}$$

We assume average cost pricing in transportation activities. These fixed transport costs could be financed in a variety of ways, and while we acknowledge that the method of financing these activities is potentially important, we wish to keep the model as simple as possible in order to focus on the effects of the fixed costs. Accordingly, we assume that when there is international trade the difference between the foreign and the domestic prices of the exported goods times the volume of exports exactly covers the fixed transportation cost expenditures. This can be thought of as an equilibrium condition: the home (respectively foreign) firms must be indifferent between selling on the home and on the foreign markets.

The equilibrium profits are zero and the total domestic (respectively foreign) income is then equal to the factor income Y (respectively Y^*). Finally the domestic and foreign *free trade* supply functions may be written, respectively, as $(1-\beta)\ S_i(p_i/p_j)$ and $(1-\beta^*)\ S_i^*(p_i/p_j)$, $i,j = 1,2$, $i \neq j$, i.e. as fixed fractions of the autarkic supplies.

The consumption demands in the home and foreign countries are derived from the maximization of two thrice continuously differentiable concave utility functions $U(C_1,C_2)$ for the home country and $U^*(C_1^*, C_2^*)$ for the foreign country subject to the budget constraints which are respectively

$$p_1 C_1 + p_2 C_2 = Y \tag{3}$$

[1] Adding variable costs would not change the results in any significant way.

and

$$p_1^* C_1^* + p_2^* C_2^* = Y^* \tag{4}$$

We obtain twice-continuously differentiable demand functions:

$$C_i = D_i\left(\frac{Y}{p_i}, \frac{p_j}{p_i}\right), i,j = 1,2, \quad i \neq j \tag{5}$$

and

$$C_i^* = D_i^*\left(\frac{Y^*}{p_i^*}, \frac{p_j^*}{p_i^*}\right), i,j = 1,2, \quad i \neq j \tag{6}$$

We assume that the first derivatives of these demand functions are strictly positive, i.e. that the two goods are normal. Notice that, given Equations (1) and (2) these demands depend only on relative good prices and that they are more conveniently written as

$$D_i\left(\frac{Y}{p_i}, \frac{p_j}{p_i}\right) = d_i\left(\frac{p_j}{p_i}\right) \tag{7}$$

$$D_i^*\left(\frac{Y^*}{p_i^*}, \frac{p_j^*}{p_i^*}\right) = d_i^*\left(\frac{p_j^*}{p_i^*}\right) \tag{8}$$

As is well known the income and substitution effects have the same sign in the case of exports so that, if i is an exported good, $d_i'(p_j/p_i) > 0$ ($d_i^{*\prime}(p_j/p_i) > 0$). The signs of the two effects are opposite in the case of imports so that one cannot say *a priori* anything on the sign of the above derivatives.

Notice that for given relative prices, these demand functions do not depend on β or β^*. This means that transportation costs have no direct effect on demand.

For convenience, we assume that if trade takes place the home country exports good 1. Hence,

$$X_1(p, \beta) = (1 - \beta)S_1(p) - d_1(p)$$

and

$$M_2(p, \beta) = d_2(p) - (1 - \beta)S_2(p)$$

are the export supply and import demand functions of the home country and $p = p_1/p_2$. For the foreign country

$$X_2^*(p^*, \beta^*) = (1 - \beta^*)S_2^*(p^*) - d_2^*(p^*)$$

and

$$M_1^*(p^*, \beta^*) = d_1^*(p^*) - (1 - \beta^*)S_1^*(p^*)$$

are the export supply and import demand functions, respectively and $p^* = p_1^*/p_2^*$.

Average cost pricing in the transportation industries implies that

$$(p_1^* - p_1)X_1(p, \beta) = \beta(p_1 S_1(p) + p_2 S_2(p)) \tag{9}$$

and

$$(p_2 - p_2^*)X_2^*(p^*, \beta^*) = \beta^*(p_1^* S_1^*(p^*) + p_2^* S_2^*(p^*)) \tag{10}$$

From Equations (1) and (3) we obtain

$$p_1 X_1(p, \beta) = p_2 M_2(p, \beta) + \beta(p_1 S_1(p) + p_2 S_2(p))$$

Together with Equation (9) we now obtain

$$vX_1(p, \beta) = M_2(p, \beta) \tag{11}$$

where $v = p_1^*/p_2$ denotes the ratio between the c.a.f. prices of the two goods. By a similar argument Equations (2), (4) and (10) imply that

$$vM_1^*(p^*, \beta^*) = X_2^*(p^*, \beta^*) \tag{12}$$

It is worth noting that these "balance of trade" equilibrium conditions (Equations (11) and (12)), contrary to the standard model of international trade without transportation costs, do not simply follow from the domestic and the foreign budget constraints. To derive them, we have assumed condition (9) and condition (10). These two conditions already have an equilibrium interpretation: they imply that the domestic (respectively foreign) firms are indifferent between selling on the domestic or the foreign market. If they hold, then international trade is possible and that means that essentially there is now one world market for each good.

3. *The offer curves*

We are now able to construct the home and foreign "offer curves" that specify the amount of exports a country is willing to supply in exchange for each possible level of imports. Given our previous assumptions if there is international trade then, the home country exports good 1 and exports good 2, while this is the reverse for the foreign country.

For international trade to take place each country has to gain enough from trade to cover the fixed transportation costs. For example, the home country is willing to trade if and only if the home *domestic* relative export price p is not lower than the critical value $\underline{p}(\beta)$ which is unambiguously defined by $X_1(\underline{p}(\beta), \beta) = 0$.[2] This critical price is easily proved to be an increasing function of β. Accordingly, the minimum volume of imports below which the home country is not willing to trade at all is $\underline{M}_2(\beta) = M_2(\underline{p}(\beta), \beta)$, where $\underline{M}_2$ is itself strictly increasing in β. Since M_2 is a strictly increasing function of p we may use the inverse function

[2] Given Equation (15) it is easy to show $\underline{p}(\beta) \geq p^A$.

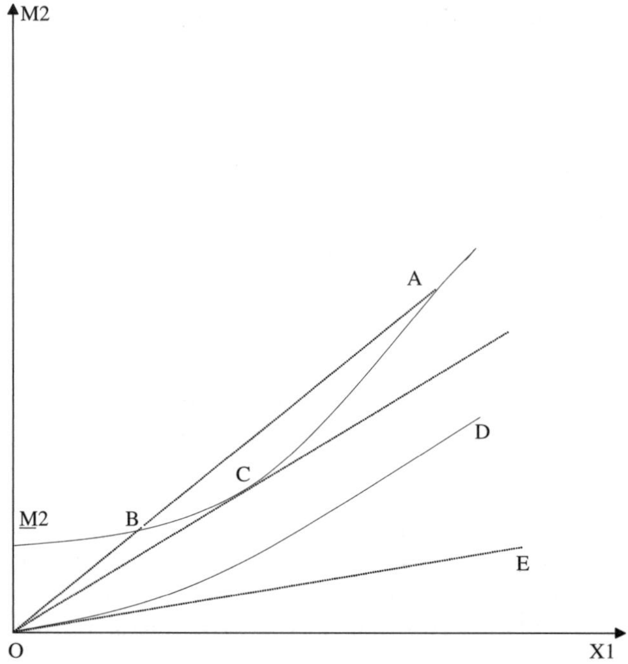

Fig. 1. Home offer curve with fixed costs.

theorem which guarantees the existence of an inverse function $\rho \equiv M_2^{-1}$. The offer curve of the home country is now simply defined as

$$X_1 = f(M_2, \beta) = \max\{0, X_1(\rho(M_2, \beta), \beta)\} \tag{13}$$

Obviously, $f(M_2,\beta) = 0$ for all $M_2 \leq \underline{M}_2(\beta)$. Moreover $(\partial f(M_2,\beta)/\partial\beta) < 0$. To see how the offer curve is affected by fixed transportation costs consider Figure 1. The usual domestic offer curve with no fixed transportation costs ($\beta = 0$) is OD. It is convex since to a given domestic price ratio p must correspond under the usual assumptions to one and only one couple (X_1,M_2). We assume that it is *strictly* convex.[3] The slope of the tangent OE to OD at the origin is equal to the autarkic equilibrium price ratio p^A.

Now consider the home country offer curve when there are fixed transport costs. The home country offer curve corresponding to some $\beta > 0$ is $O\underline{M}_2A$. At any point A on the home country offer curve we deduce from Equation (11) that the value of the international relative price v equals the

[3] This amounts to ruling out *flat* parts of the usual offer curves as occur in the Ricardian case. This assumption ensures that for low transport costs and a volume of imports above a given minimum the home offer curve is convex. However as shown in Section 5 for the Ricardian case, this assumption is too strong: in this case indeed the home offer curve is unambiguously convex for any value of β provided that $M_2 > \underline{M}_2(\beta)$.

slope of OA. For sufficiently low values of β it must be *convex* for all $M_2 > \underline{M}_2(\beta)$ as pictured above. A necessary condition for the home country being willing to trade is obviously that the international relative price v of good 1 be larger than a value $\underline{v}(\beta)$ equal to the slope of OC which is itself strictly larger than the autarkic equilibrium price ratio p^A. Thus, with fixed transportation costs the domestic country requires more gains from trade (a higher relative price for good 1) before it is willing to engage in international trade. Of course $\underline{v}(\beta)$ tends toward p^A as β tends toward 0. Notice that for any value of v larger than $\underline{v}(\beta)$ there correspond two points on the home offer curve and hence two possible trade vectors and two possible values of the domestic relative price p.

The foreign offer curve is affected in the same way. The foreign country is willing to trade if and only if the foreign domestic relative price of imports p^* is not larger than a critical value $\bar{p}^*(\beta^*)$ unambiguously defined by $X_2^*(\bar{p}^*(\beta^*), \beta^*) = 0$. Accordingly, the minimum volume of imports below which the foreign country is not willing to trade is $\underline{M}_1^*(\beta^*) = M_1^*(\bar{p}^*(\beta^*), \beta^*)$ and is strictly increasing in β^*. M_1^* being a strictly decreasing function of p^*, we may use the inverse function theorem which guarantees the existence of $M_1^{*\,-1} \equiv \sigma$. The offer curve of the foreign country is then simply

$$X_2^* = f^*(M_1^*, \beta^*) = \max\{0, X_2^*(\sigma(M_1^*, \beta^*), \beta^*))\} \tag{14}$$

Notice that $f^*(M_1^*, \beta^*) = 0$ for all $M_1^* \leq \underline{M}_1^*(\beta^*)$ and that $(\partial f^*(M_1^*, \beta^*)/\partial \beta^*) < 0$.

Figure 2 shows foreign country offer curves for $\beta^* = 0$ and $\beta^* > 0$. At any point A on this curve it follows from Equation (12) that the corresponding international price ratio v equals the slope of OA. By the same argument used above for establishing the convexity of the home offer curve, the foreign offer curve is concave for sufficiently low values of β^* and for values of M_1^* larger than $\underline{M}_1^*(\beta^*)$. The foreign country is willing to trade if and only if the international price ratio v is lower than the critical value $\bar{v}(\beta^*)$ corresponding to the slope of the tangent OC* to the offer curve from the origin. Of course $\bar{v}(\beta^*)$ is lower than the foreign autarkic price ratio p^{A*} given by the slope of OE*.

4. The Equilibria

The *autarkic equilibrium* (relative) prices p^A and p^{*A} satisfy the market-clearing conditions (from Walras Law equilibrium on the first market entails equilibrium on the second market) :

$$S_1(p^A) = d_1\left(\frac{1}{p^A}\right)$$

$$S_1^*(p^{A*}) = d_1\left(\frac{1}{p^{A*}}\right) \tag{15}$$

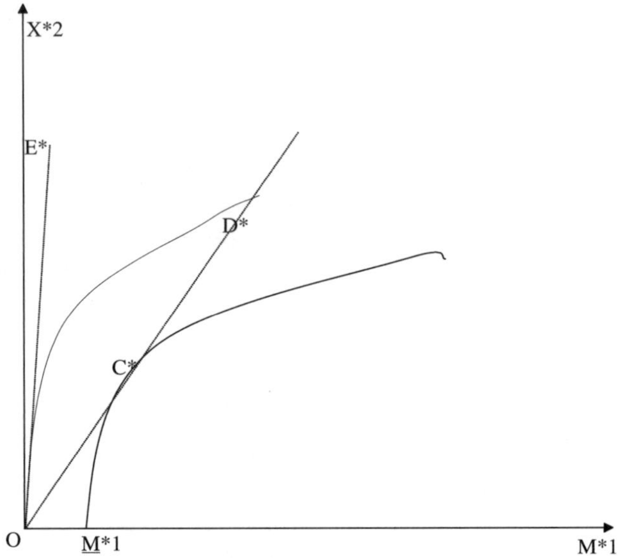

Fig. 2. Foreign offer curve with fixed costs.

We assume without loss of generality that $p^A < p^{A*}$, i.e. that the home country has a comparative advantage in good 1.

Whenever the fixed transportation costs are both strictly positive (i.e., whenever $\beta > 0$ and/or $\beta^* > 0$) *autarky is an equilibrium of our model.* When the volume of trade is arbitrarily low no firm expects to be able to cover the fixed cost expenditures which it would have to make in order to enter the transportation industry. Put another way, at autarky, the prices of transportation services per unit of good shipped are so large as to discourage any trade.[4] This looks like a "low-level equilibrium trap": there is no trade because at the margin transportation costs are very large but the transportation costs are large because there is no trade. However, it remains to show that there may also exist equilibria with positive volumes of trade.

An *international* (i.e., with positive trade) *equilibrium* of this model is formally a triple of relative prices (p, p^*, v) such that (i) the two goods markets clear and (ii) the two transportation industries break even. As usual, owing to Walras Law, one of these conditions is redundant so that one is left with three equations in three unknowns. Interestingly enough the two goods market clearing equations are

$$(1-\beta)S_1(\hat{p}) + (1-\beta^*)S_1^*(\hat{p}^*) = d_1\left(\frac{1}{\hat{p}}\right) + d_1^*\left(\frac{1}{\hat{p}^*}\right) \qquad (16)$$

[4] They indeed tend toward infinity.

and

$$(1-\beta)S_2\left(\frac{1}{\hat{p}}\right)+(1-\beta^*)S_2^*\left(\frac{1}{\hat{p}^*}\right)=d_2(\hat{p})+d_2^*(\hat{p}^*) \tag{17}$$

These equations determine the domestic relative prices in the home and foreign countries and thereby all the relevant quantities (output, consumption, import and export levels) *independently of the budget balance conditions for the transportation industries*. Then either condition (11) or condition (12) determines the international price ratio v so as to satisfy budget balance in the transportation industry.

To see how the model works it helps to first consider the classical case without transportation costs ($\beta=\beta^*=0$). Here, at free trade, the two relative prices, home and foreign, must coincide in equilibrium ($p=p^*=v$) and conditions (11) and (12) are automatically satisfied. Moreover, from Walras Law, the second market clears if the first one does (and reciprocally) so that we are left with only one equilibrium condition, say Equation (16), which may be written as $E_1(v)=d_1(1/v)+d_1^*(1/v)-S_1(v)-S_1^*(v)=0$. Under standard assumptions the excess demand for good 1 (E_1) is a continuous function of v, is positive when $v=0$, and tends toward a strictly negative value when v tends toward infinity. This ensures the existence of at least one equilibrium, i.e. of a value $\hat{v}$ such that $E_1(\hat{v})=0$. As is well known, this equilibrium is unique whenever the condition below is satisfied.

Condition 1 (*Marshall–Lerner*). $\varepsilon(v)+\varepsilon^*(v)>1$

where $\varepsilon(v)$ and $\varepsilon^*(v)$ are respectively the home and foreign price-elasticities of imports. Recalling that home imports of good 2 are $M_2=C_2-S_2$ and foreign imports of good 1 are $M_1^*=C_1^*-S_1^*$, then $\varepsilon(v)=vM_2'(v)/M_2(v)$ and $\varepsilon^*(v)=-(vM_1^{*\prime}(v)/M_1^*(v))$.

We next turn to determining equilibrium. Equilibrium occurs when the two offer curves intersect since that is where import demands are equal to export supplies. In the case without transportation costs (dotted curves in Figure 3), the Marshall–Lerner condition ensures that the offer curves cut only twice, at O (autarky) and at E (free trade equilibrium.) However, only E corresponds to an equilibrium since at O the relative prices p^A and p^{A*} differ, giving rise to the possibility of costless and profitable trade.

When there exist small but strictly positive transportation costs a simple continuity argument shows that there now exist two international equilibria with positive amounts of trade, a "high" equilibrium at H, near E, and an "intermediate" equilibrium at I, near O with an international equilibrium price ratio respectively equal to the slopes of OH and OI. Moreover, as shown above autarky now becomes an equilibrium with equilibrium home and foreign autarkic relative prices equal to the slopes of OE and OE*.

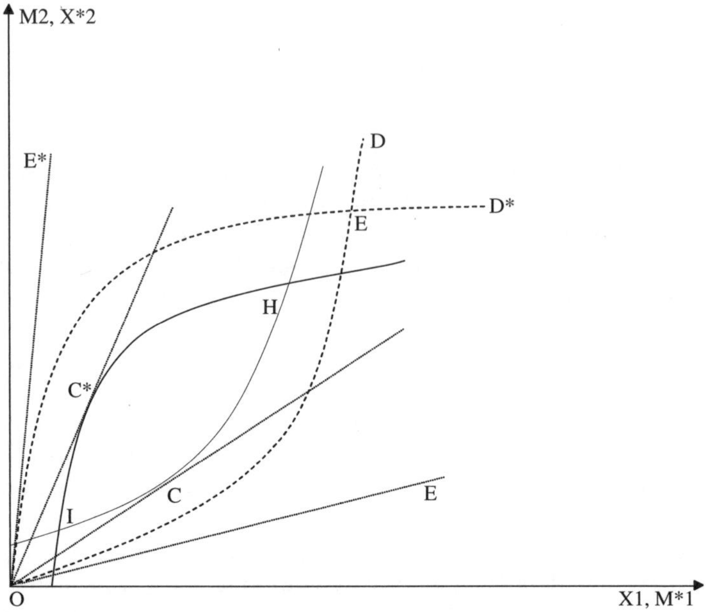

Fig. 3. Equilibria with fixed costs.

PROPOSITION 1. *For small enough values of β and β^*, such that at least β or $\beta^* > 0$, there exist three equilibria which are ranked by increasing volumes of trade: autarky, an "intermediate trade" equilibrium and a "high trade" equilibrium.*

To illustrate how the equilibrium works we consider an example of a Ricardian economy.

5. The Ricardian case

Here labor is the only factor both in production and transportation activities. The unit labor requirement in the production of good i in the home country is a_i. All foreign country variables are indicated by asterisks (*). Without loss of generality we assume as in the previous Sections that *the home country has a comparative advantage in the production of good* 1, or, equivalently, that the foreign country has a comparative advantage in the production of good 2, i.e.

ASSUMPTION 1. $(a_1/a_2) < (a_1^*/a_2^*)$.

Straightforwardly, here if $p = (a_1/a_2)$

$$S_i(p) \in \left[0, \frac{L}{a_1}\right], \quad i = 1, 2$$

$$Y = \frac{L}{a_1}\frac{a_1}{a_2}$$

and

$$\begin{aligned} &M_2 \in \left[0, d_2\left(\frac{a_1}{a_2}\right)\right] \\ &X_1 = M_2\frac{a_2}{a_1} - \frac{\beta L}{a_1} \end{aligned} \tag{18}$$

If $p \geq (a_1/a_2)$

$$\begin{aligned} S_1(p) &= \frac{L}{a_1} \\ S_2(p) &= 0 \\ Y &= \frac{L}{a_1}p \end{aligned}$$

and

$$\begin{aligned} &M_2 = d_2(p) \\ &X_1 = pd_2(p) - \frac{\beta L}{a_1} \end{aligned} \tag{19}$$

It is then easy to build the home offer curve as

$$X_1 = 0 \text{ when } M_2 \in \left[0, \frac{\beta L}{a_2}\right] \tag{20}$$

$$X_1 = M_2\frac{a_2}{a_1} - \frac{\beta L}{a_1} \text{when } M_2 \in \left[\frac{\beta L}{a_2}, d_2\left(\frac{a_1}{a_2}\right)\right]$$

$$X_1 = \frac{M_2}{d_2^{-1}(M_2)} - \frac{\beta L}{a_1} \text{when } M_2 \geq d_2\left(\frac{a_1}{a_2}\right) \tag{21}$$

Figure 4 illustrates the determination of country A's offer curve OABC. Note that OA $= F/a_2$, OR $= -(F/a_1)$ and OE $= g_{A2}(a_1/a_2)$. The slope of OB equals a_1/a_2. The coordinates of point D for instance give the amounts of exports of good 1 and imports of good 2 which country A wants to trade when the domestic price ratio p_1/p_2 equals the slope of RD. The specificity of the Ricardian case is the existence of a flat part of the offer curves (AB in Figure 2).

Using similar arguments the foreign offer curve is then derived as:

$$X_2^* = 0 \text{ when } M_1^* \in \left[0, \frac{\beta^* L^*}{a_1^*}\right] \tag{22}$$

$$X_2^* = M_1^*\frac{a_1^*}{a_2^*} - \frac{\beta^* L^*}{a_2^*} \text{when } M_1^* \in \left[\frac{\beta^* L^*}{a_1^*}, d_1^*\left(\frac{a_2^*}{a_1^*}\right)\right]$$

$$X_2^* = \frac{M_1^*}{d_1^{*-1}(M_1^*)} - \frac{\beta^* L^*}{a_2^*} \text{when } M_1^* \geq d_1^*\left(\frac{a_2^*}{a_1^*}\right) \tag{23}$$

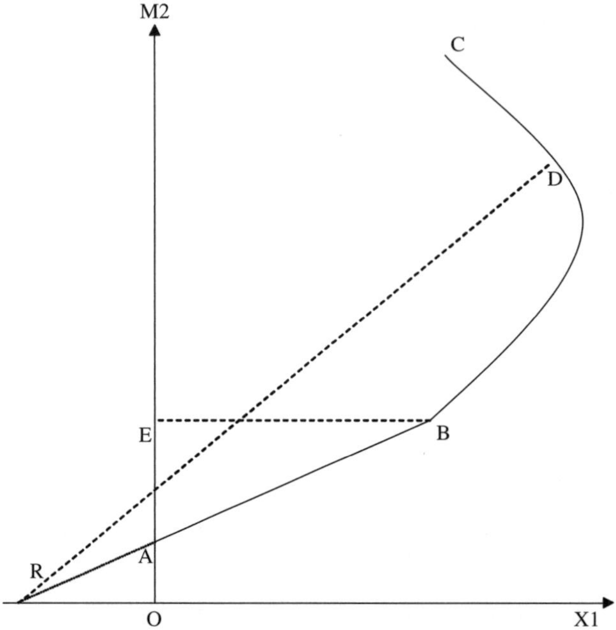

Fig. 4. Home offer curve–Ricardian case.

If and only if the values of β and β^* are low enough so as to satisfy the inequalities below

$$\frac{\beta^* L^* a_2 + \beta L a_2^*}{a_1^* a_2 - a_1 a_2^*} \le d_1^*\left(\frac{a_2^*}{a_1^*}\right)$$

and

$$\frac{\beta^* L^* a_1 + \beta L a_1^*}{a_1^* a_2 - a_1 a_2^*} \le d_2\left(\frac{a_1}{a_2}\right)$$

there exists an intermediate equilibrium where the flat parts of the two offer curves intersect: at this equilibrium the two countries produce the two goods[5] and the relative internal equilibrium prices equal their respective autarkic values, i.e. $p = (a_1/a_2)$ and $p^* = (a_2^*/a_1^*)$. At this equilibrium $X_1 = M_1^* = (\beta^* L^* a_2 + \beta L a_2^*)/(a_1^* a_2 - a_1 a_2^*)$ and $X_2^* = M_2 = (\beta^* L^* a_1 + \beta L a_1^*)/(a_1^* a_2 - a_1 a_2^*)$. The welfare at this intermediate equilibrium is the same in both countries as at the autarkic equilibrium. This follows simply from the fact that the relative internal prices and hence the consumption levels are identical. It is indeed easy to see that the amounts of labor which are saved in the two countries by having each of them

[5] Whereas efficiency requires that one country at least be fully specialized.

produce more of the good in which it has a comparative advantage and less of the other are exactly equal to the quantities of labor required in order to ship the goods between countries, namely $M_1^*(a_1^* - a_1) + M_2(a_2 - a_2^*) = \beta L + \beta^* L^*$. From the general Proposition 1 for small enough values of β and β^* there also exists a high equilibrium. At this equilibrium at least country is fully specialized. This is pictured in Figure 5 below for the case where both countries are fully specialized at H.

We next turn to consideration of the properties of these three equilibria.

6. Stability and Efficiency

6.1. Stability

In this section we confine ourselves to the case of positive fixed transport costs of trade ($\beta > 0$ and $\beta^* > 0$). We begin by investigating the (local) Walrasian stability of the three equilibria. The essential idea of Walrasian stability is that an equilibrium is stable if, when price is above the equilibrium price, then supply exceeds demand. If the price is below the equilibrium price, then demand exceeds supply. We are willing to define here stability along these lines. An international equilibrium has been defined above as a triple of relative prices. To analyze a simple *tâtonnement*

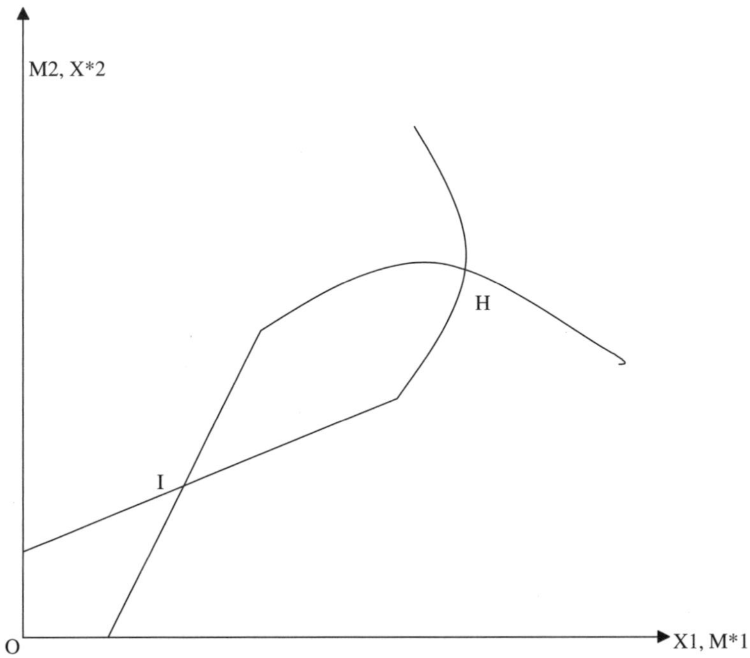

Fig. 5. Equilibria–Ricardian case.

process in a neighborhood of an international equilibrium we require that conditions (11) and (12) be satisfied everywhere, i.e. there is average cost pricing of transportation services even out of equilibrium. Under this assumption there are, in a neighborhood of an international equilibrium like H or I, two one to one correspondences, defined by (11) and (12), between the international price ratio v and, respectively, the home and foreign domestic price ratios p and p^*. It follows that the value of v completely determines the initial conditions of the *tâtonnement* process in a neighborhood of an international equilibrium

DEFINITION. Equilibrium price v^0 is a locally *stable international equilibrium price* if the following two conditions hold:

a. $v \geq v^0 \Rightarrow X_1(v) \geq M_1^*(v)$ and $M_2(v) \geq X_2^*(v)$

b. $v \leq v^0 \Rightarrow X_1(v) \leq M_1^*(v)$ and $M_2(v) \leq X_2^*(v)$.

Using this definition we determine which of the two international equilibria we have is stable. The three equilibria are illustrated in Figure 6. We have the "high" equilibrium at H, the "intermediate" equilibrium at I and autarky at 0. First, consider the high equilibrium. Suppose that the international price v is less than the equilibrium price v^0 At that price the home country will trade at point B and the foreign country at point C. It is clear from Figure 6 that the foreign demand for imports of good 1 exceeds

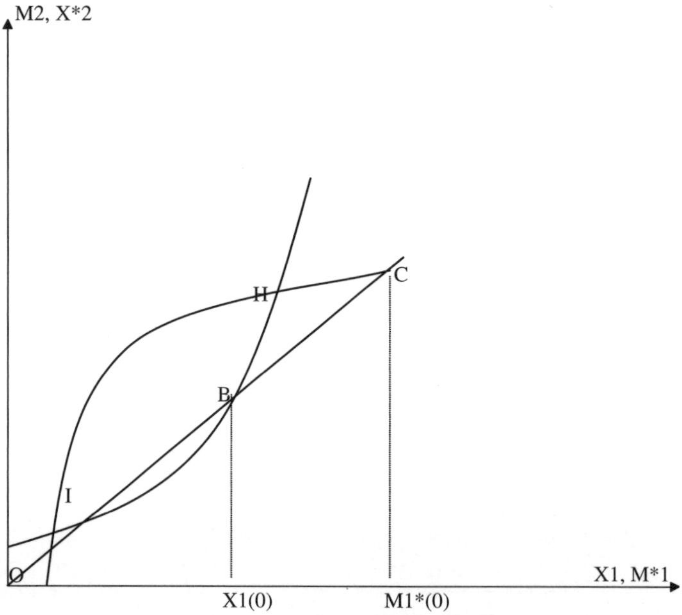

Fig. 6. Stability of H.

the home supply of exports of good 1 and in the market for good 2, foreign export supply exceed home import demand. That is, when $v \leq v^0 \Rightarrow X_1(v) \leq M_1^*(v)$ and $M_2(v) \leq X_2^*(v)$, hence condition b is satisfied. If we consider prices above equilibrium, it is also clear that the reasoning above is simply reversed and condition a is satisfied. Therefore, *H is a stable equilibrium.*

Next consider equilibrium point I. If we consider a price below equilibrium then the home country would trade at B in Figure 7 and the foreign country would trade at A. That means when the price is below the equilibrium the foreign demand for imports of good 1 is less than the home supply of exports of good 1 and in the market for good 2, foreign export supply falls short of home import demand. Thus, if $v \leq v^0 \Rightarrow X_1(v) > M_1^*(v)$ and $M_2(v) \geq X_2^*(v)$ and condition b is violated. The reader can easily verify that condition a also fails and therefore, *the equilibrium at I is unstable.*

Finally, and perhaps, most importantly, consider autarky. In the case of autarky we have to consider the relative prices in each country. Stability of autarky requires that in the home country for a value of p larger (respectively lower) than p^A, there is an excess supply of (respectively excess demand for) good 1 and an excess demand for (respectively excess supply of) good 2 on the home markets and symmetrically in the foreign country. This turns out to be true in a neighborhood of autarkic prices since $p^A < \underline{p}(\beta)$ and $p^{*A} > \bar{p}^*(\beta^*)$. When the domestic price ratios p and p^*

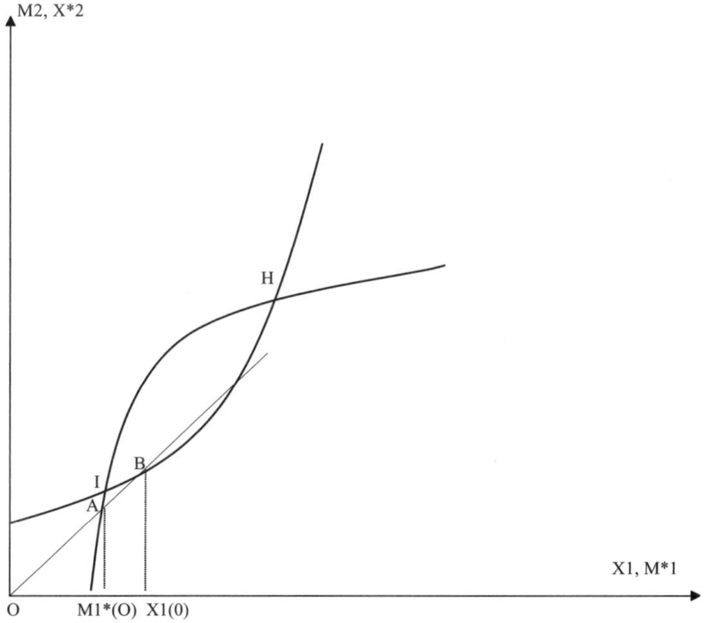

Fig. 7. Stability of I.

do not differ significantly from their autarkic equilibrium values the two countries do not want to trade. Due to the fixed transport costs the excess of production over domestic demand of some good does not translate into some positive export supply.

We summarize these results in a proposition.

PROPOSITION 2 *(Stability). The high trade equilibrium and autarky are stable equilibria. The low trade equilibrium is unstable.*

6.2. Efficiency

We next consider efficiency. The central question we ask is whether the three equilibria can be ranked? We are able to show that in fact, all three equilibria can be Pareto-ranked.

PROPOSITION 3 *(Efficiency). With fixed costs of transportation the three equilibria can be Pareto-ranked. The high trade equilibrium Pareto-dominates the intermediate trade equilibrium which in turn, Pareto-dominates the autarkic equilibrium.*

PROOF. First, consider the home offer curve. It follows from convexity assumptions made earlier that, moving from the left to the right on the home offer curve means M_2 is increasing as is p. So, M_2 is increasing in p. By the same argument M_1^* is decreasing in p^* moving from the left to the right on the foreign offer curve. It follows then, that at the high equilibrium point H, p is higher and p^* is lower than at the intermediate equilibrium point I. This means that the wedge between the internal home and foreign relative prices is lower at H than at I. This reasoning also shows that the wedge is lower at I than it is at O. The second step is now to show that the home welfare $W(p) = U(C_1(p), C_2(p))$ is increasing in p while the foreign welfare $W^*(p^*) = U^*(C_1^*)(p^*), C_2^*(p^*))$ is decreasing in p^*: We obtain

$$W'(p) = U_1'(C_1(p), C_2(p))C_1'(p) + U_2'(C_1(p), C_2(p))C_2'(p)$$

and then, using the first-order conditions of the home consumer's problem

$$W'(p) = U_2'(C_1(p), C_2(p))\left[pC_1'(p) + C_2'(p)\right]$$

From Equations (1) and (3)

$$pC_1'(p) + C_2'(p) + C_1(p) = pS_1'(p) + S_2'(p) + S_1(p)$$

Since at equilibrium the home national income is maximized $pS_1'(p) + S_2'(p) = 0$ and we can safely conclude that

$$W'(p) = U_2'(C_1(p), C_2(p))\ [S_1(p) - C_1(p)] > 0$$

By the same argument

$$W^{*'}(p^*) = -\frac{U_1^{*'}(C_1^*(p), C_2^*(p))}{p^{*^2}}\left[S_2^*(p^*) - C_2^*(p^*)\right] < 0$$

REMARK. Though the "high trade equilibrium", when it exists, Pareto-dominates both the intermediate and the autarkic equilibrium it is not Pareto-efficient. Efficiency would indeed require that prices equal marginal costs.

Specifically, since the marginal transport costs are zero in this model there should be no difference between home and foreign prices. This is not the case here owing to average cost pricing in the transportation industries: import prices are above marginal costs in both countries and the levels of consumption of imported (respectively exported) goods are accordingly below (respectively above) their optimal levels.

7. Concluding remarks and extensions

The basic message of this chapter is clear. While there may exist some scope for mutually profiable North–South (interindustry) trade based on comparative advantage the world may well be trapped in some low-level equilibrium (here the autarkic one) where, due to the existence of fixed transportation costs, low trade volumes lead to large unit transport prices which themselves induce in turn low trade volumes. The dimension of this "trap" can be informally measured by the distance between this (stable) low-level equilibrium and the (unstable) intermediate equilibrium, a distance which is increasing in the fixed transportation costs. One could think that getting out of this trap may require some kind of "big push", for instance some public investments in transport infrastructures: by doing so one could expect the emergence of a "high trade" equilibrium. Moreover, if these investments be financed by lump-sum taxation, an additional source of inefficiency, the divergence between the home and foreign relative prices, could be eliminated. Notice, however, that such a move would require some coordination between the governments of the two countries.

References

Falvey, R. (1976), Transport costs in the pure theory of international trade. *The Economic Journal* 86, 536–550.

Hummels, D., Skiba, A. (2002), A virtuous circle? Regional tariff liberalization and scale economies in transport, mimeo.

Hummels, D., Skiba, A. (2004), Shipping the good apples out? An empirical confirmation of the Alchain-Allen conjecture. *Journal of Political Economy* 112, 1384–1402.

Samuelson, P. (1954), The transfer problem and transport costs, II: analysis of effects of trade impediments. *The Economic Journal* 64, 264–289.

SECTION III

Factor Rewards and Trade Theory

CHAPTER 6

Something New for Something Old: Reflections on a Model with Three Factors and Two Goods

Stephen T. Easton

Department of Economics, Simon Fraser University, Canada
E-mail address: easton@sfu.ca

Abstract
Regardless of extent of substitutability and complementarity in a conventional general equilibrium model with three factors and two sectors, there is no possibility that factor rewards of the extreme factors will reverse their ranking in response to a change in relative prices.

Keywords: General equilibrium model, factor rewards, relative prices

JEL classification: F11

1. Introduction

My first exposure to Ron Jones was at a 1971 summer seminar at the University of Wisconsin run by Jeffrey Williamson and Peter Lindert on the topic of general equilibrium and economic history. I was a graduate student studying international trade at the University of Chicago with Harry Johnson and much of our analysis emphasized geometry. Ron's presentation and elaborations of the structures of simple general equilibrium (Jones, 1965) and the specific factors model (Jones, 1971) at the seminar was to me a revelation. In clear intuitive algebra Ron was able to bring general equilibrium to useable life. I was hooked. Ron let me see a preproduction copy of the new Caves and Jones textbook, and my understanding of international trade was immeasurably enhanced. I raced home, and for the rest of that summer immersed myself in learning the algebra by extending the specific factors model to a world of technical progress in the context of the British Industrial Revolution. My rather traditional European history instructor was bemused when he received the paper later that year. Two years later, coincidentally Ron and I met again in London where we both were living for the year. By the time the year was

Frontiers of Economics and Globalization
Volume 4 ISSN: 1574-8715
DOI: 10.1016/S1574-8715(08)04006-2

over I had gotten to know Ron and had come to benefit, both professionally and personally, from his vast store of knowledge and his generosity in sharing his insights. In 1980, while I visited Rochester, we wrote our first piece together (Jones and Easton, 1983) and since then have collaborated on several more (Jones and Easton, 1986, 1989, 1990; Easton and Jones, 1992). The analysis I develop below goes back to that first paper on factor substitutability and complementarity in the context of a two-sector three-factor model and extends some of our initial results. In particular, I look more closely on what patterns of factor rewards cannot occur even with extreme examples of substitutability and complementarity.

2. The issues

In approaching the issues of factor complementarity and substitutability the minimum model for such an analysis includes three factors of production. Unlike the specific factors model (Jones, 1971) which has three factors but requires only two to be used in each industry, to discuss complementarity our analysis requires a more general approach and consequently uses three factors in each of the two industries. This framework is a natural extension to the legacy of Heckscher–Ohlin–Samuelson and the specific factors model, and its development[1] has become an active niche in the profession that has produced both theoretical and empirical applications in a variety of contexts.[2] The general approach that we used gave rise to a number of results. Among the more interesting is the general proposition that for factor rewards, substitutability attracts and complementarity repels. By this what is meant is that as factors become better substitutes for each other, the consequences of a change in commodity prices is to cause the factor rewards of better substitutes to change in ways that more closely resemble one another. When factors are complements, the opposite occurs. The more the complementarity, the more the rewards of complements tend to move farther apart in response to a commodity price change. The way in which this is expressed is through the magnification effects that rank the consequences to factor rewards in response to changes in commodity prices.

What we did not do, however, was push our results to ask what was not possible. For example, could factor prices reverse in the sense that an exteme factor in whose industry the relative price has risen actually fall by as much as (or more than) the factor that is extreme in the industry whose relative commodity price has fallen (Takayama, 1982). We also had one definition of complementarity that while reasonable, is not the only possible definition. The structure of this chapter is to review the model

[1] Early work included Thakkar (1971), Batra and Casas (1976), Ruffin (1981), and Suzuki (1981, 1983).

[2] See for example Takeda (2005) or Thompson (1983, 1985, 1990, 1993, 1995), for illustrations of the breath of use of the more general three-factor two-sector framework.

with an eye toward discovering whether the magnification results we described in 1983 were exhaustive or could we have missed some?

3. The model

The general model that we use to develop the issue has two linear homogeneous industries that each use three factors of production to produce outputs. Both commodity and factor markets are competitive. Such a standard setup gives rise to a five-equation system in which overall factor quantities, V_1, V_2, and V_3 and commodity prices, p_1 and p_2 are treated as exogenous and equal to unit costs in the determination of factor rewards w_1, w_2, and w_3 and commodity outputs, x_1 and x_2. Writing factor input per unit output as $a_{ij} = V_i/x_j$ lets us summarize the framework as

$$a_{11}x_1 + a_{12}x_2 = V_1, \tag{1}$$

$$a_{21}x_1 + a_{22}x_2 = V_2, \tag{2}$$

$$a_{31}x_1 + a_{32}x_2 = V_3, \tag{3}$$

$$a_{11}w_1 + a_{21}w_2 + a_{31}w_3 = p_1, \tag{4}$$

and

$$a_{12}w_1 + a_{22}w_2 + a_{32}w_3 = p_2. \tag{5}$$

Equations (1)–(3) may be thought of as equations of supply and demand for each of the factors of production, with supply V_i being equated to demands arising from the intensive (a_{ij}) and extensive (x_j) margins.

The model needs one more important ingredient that characterizes the difference intensities with which factors are used in the different industries. These factor intensity differences are written as

$$\frac{a_{11}}{a_{12}} > \frac{a_{31}}{a_{32}} > \frac{a_{21}}{a_{22}}. \tag{6}$$

For expositional convenience factor one denotes the extreme factor in industry one, and factor two indicates the extreme factor in industry two. Being the extreme factor in industry one means that factor one will always be used relatively more intensively in industry one than in industry two for all factor prices. There is, however, another intensity in the model. Middle factor intensity, factor three in our numbering, is a concept that plays an important part in understanding the outcomes of the model. A more convenient expression of the factor intensities can be seen by multiplying each a_{ij} by the wage and dividing by the price of output so that, for example, from a_{11}/a_{12}, we have $((a_{11}w_1)/p_1)/((a_{12}w_1)/p_2) = \theta_{11}/\theta_{12}$, so that we have the ranking

$$\frac{\theta_{11}}{\theta_{12}} > \frac{\theta_{31}}{\theta_{32}} > \frac{\theta_{21}}{\theta_{22}}, \tag{7}$$

in which the θ_{ij}s are the distributive share of factor i in commodity output j. The intensity with which the middle factor is used means that if $\theta_{31} > \theta_{32}$, we say that industry one is relatively intensive in using the middle factor.

3.1. Comparative statics

The important propositions of any model appear when the system is perturbed by changes in the exogenous variables. Looking first at Equations (4) and (5) (because they are relatively straightforward) we can take percentage changes and write them as

$$\theta_{11}\widehat{w}_1 + \theta_{21}\widehat{w}_2 + \theta_{31}\widehat{w}_3 = \widehat{p}_1 \tag{8}$$

and

$$\theta_{12}\widehat{w}_1 + \theta_{22}\widehat{w}_2 + \theta_{32}\widehat{w}_3 = \widehat{p}_2, \tag{9}$$

where the "^" denotes the percentage change operator and use has been made of cost minimization.[3] In a sense the two equations give us two out of three of the factor rewards, so we still need one more equation. This can be found in the factor markets by solving Equations (1) and (2) for x_1 and x_2 and substituting the solutions into Equation (3).[4] Equation (3) can then be proportionally differentiated and simplified to

$$\xi_1\widehat{w}_1 + \xi_2\widehat{w}_2 + \xi_3\widehat{w}_3 = \widehat{V}_3 - \alpha_1\widehat{V}_1 - \alpha_2\widehat{V}_2, \tag{10}$$

in which the $\alpha_1 = (\lambda_{31} - \lambda_{21})/(\lambda_{11} - \lambda_{21})$, $\alpha_2 = (\lambda_{11} - \lambda_{31})/(\lambda_{11} - \lambda_{21})$, and the $\lambda_{ij} = a_{ij}x_j/Vi$ are the physical share of factor i that are used in industry j.[5] The right-hand side of Equation (10) gives the excess demand for factor three at constant factor prices if there is a change in factor quantities. The left-hand side of Equation (10) provides the substitution effects in the factor markets as each a_{ij} is a function of all factor rewards: $a_{ij} = a_{ij}(w_1, w_2, w_3)$. To get to Equation (10) recall we substituted the solutions for x_j into the third factor's equation. Consequently when a factor price changes, ξ_i reports the effect of factor price i's change on the excess demand for factor three: $\xi_i = \sigma_3^i - \left(\alpha_1\sigma_1^i + \alpha_2\sigma_2^i\right)$. The σ_i^k is the (economy-wide) elasticity of substitution of factor i with respect to a change in factor price k.[6] Notice that the α_js weight the extreme factors'

---

[3] That is $\theta_{11}\hat{a}_{1j} + \theta_{21}\hat{a}_{2j} + \theta_{31}\hat{a}_{3j} = 0$.

[4] Jones and Easton (1983, pp. 73–77) develop the solutions in full.

[5] From Equation (7) we know that $\lambda_{11} > \lambda_{31} > \lambda_{21}$ so that α_j will always be a fraction. For those interested in analogies, in the specific factors model, the value of $\lambda_{11} = 1$ and $\lambda_{21} = 0$. Consequently $\alpha_1 = \lambda_{31}$ and $\alpha_2 = \lambda_{32}$ which will leave us with the familiar $\widehat{V}_3 - \lambda_{31}\widehat{V}_1 - \lambda_{32}\widehat{V}_2$ as the excess demand for factor 3 at constant factor prices.

[6] The σ_i^k draws together the effects of a factor k price change on the demand for factor i in each industry weighted by the share of the factor used in that industry. Thus $\sigma_i^k = \lambda_{i1}E_{i1}^k + \lambda_{i2}E_{i2}^k$, and is the economy-wide demand for factor i when factor price k changes.

effects against the middle factor both at the extensive margin in Equation (10) and at the intensive margin reflected in the terms comprising ξ_i.

From Equations (8) to (10), we are in a position to solve algebraically for the equilibrium responses of factor prices to changes in factor endowments.[7] This is done in Jones and Easton (1983, p. 20) and will not be reviewed here. Instead the next step is to develop a figure that will make it possible to interpret the results in a way that can be exploited systematically to review the consequences of changes in substitutability and complementarity.

3.2. The geometry of solving for factor rewards when commodity prices change

To understand the consequences of commodity price changes on factor prices, the diagram that proves most useful makes factor price three, the middle factor, the numeraire.[8] Since we are interested in the behavior of factor prices, factor price w_1 is written along the horizontal axis and w_2 along the vertical – as in Figure 1. To characterize the initial equilibrium, we have our three basic relationships to plot: commodity prices in Equations (8) and (9) and our factor market equilibrium relationship, Equation (10). Looking first at Equations (8), since w_3 is the numeraire, we want to plot combinations of w_1 and w_2 along which $\widehat{p}_1 = 0$. This is done as line P_1 in the figure. Similarly we can plot the intital level of $\widehat{p}_1 = 0$ which is denoted as P_2 in the figure. The slope of P_1 is steeper than the slope of P_2 since P_1 is more intensive in the use of extreme factor one.[9] The two schedules cross at E_0. As this is the initial equilibrium, it is also the intersection of the V-locus which (from Equation (10)) describes equilibrium in the factor markets. For a fixed w_3 and unchanged factor endowments, all $\widehat{V}_i = 0$, the V-locus represents combinations of w_1 and w_2 that keep the factor market in equilibrium. The slope of the V-locus depends on the responses of excess demands to changes in the factor rewards as captured by the expression

$$-\frac{\widehat{w}_2}{\widehat{w}_1} = \frac{\xi_1}{\xi_2}, \tag{11}$$

[7] Since we know from Samuelson's reciprocity theorem (Samuelson, 1953) that $(\delta x_j/\delta V_i) = (\delta w_i/\delta p_j)$, solving for factor reward changes as a consequence of commodity price changes goes a long way toward describing the behavior of commodity outputs in response to changes in factor inputs, the relative ease of dealing with price changes is a natural way to look at the model.

[8] Choosing the middle factor as the numeraire is only for graphical convenience. It has no substantive effect on the magnification effect rankings.

[9] The slope of P_1 is, $\widehat{w}_2/\widehat{w}_1 = -\theta_{11}/\theta_{21}$ while the slope of P_2 is $\widehat{w}_2/\widehat{w}_1 = -\theta_{12}/\theta_{22}$.

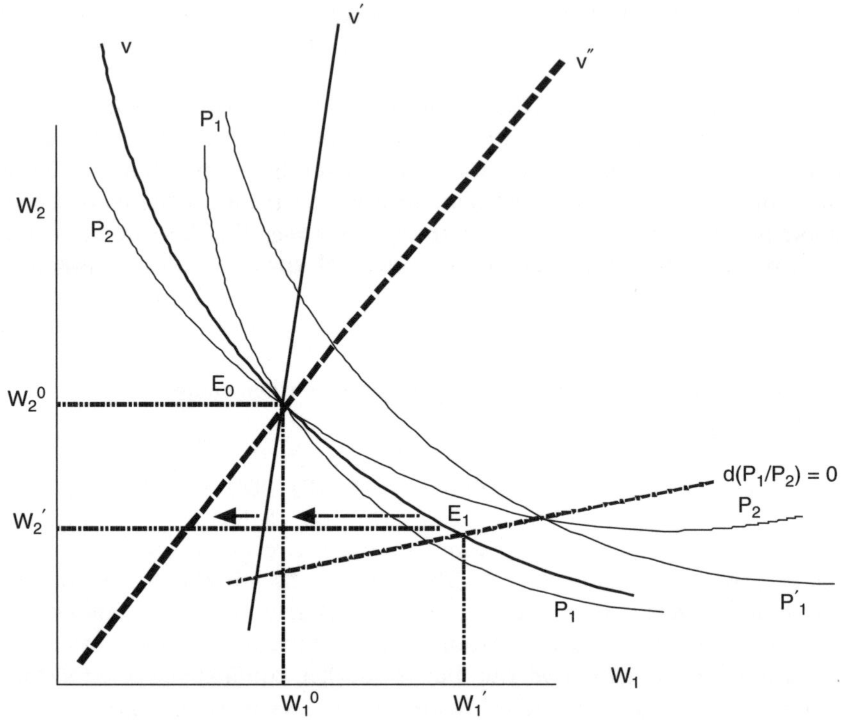

Fig. 1.* *The determination of factor rewards.

which depends on the elasticities of substitution among the different factor rewards which are discussed below in Section 3.3. We will assume initially that the *V*-locus lies between the P_1 and P_2 loci.

To illustrate how the model works to determine factor prices, begin with an increase in the price of good one to P_1'. The point at which P_1' intersects P_2 establishes the new relative price ratio and factor rewards w_1 and w_2 can be read from the diagram. However, the commodity prices P_1' and P_2 in this new relative price ratio are not consistent with equilibrium in the factor markets along the *V*-locus. The higher wage rates for both factors one and two give rise to an excess demand for factor three. In effect the absolute returns to the extreme factors are too high. To reestablish equilibrium in the factor markets, reduce both w_1 and w_2 along a ray that keeps the relative price ratio constant: $d(P_1/P_2) = 0$.[10] Equilibrium is established at point E_1 where the reduction in both returns is consistent

[10] The slope of the ray holding relative prices constant at a constant w_3 is $(\theta_{11} - \theta_{12})/(\theta_{22} - \theta_{21})$. It thus depends upon the middle factor intensity. In the case depicted in the figure good one is middle factor intensive: $\theta_{31} > \theta_{32}$.

with equilibrium in the factor markets as the point lies on both price loci and the V-locus.

From the lack of jointness in production we know that at least one factor reward must exceed the relative commodity price increase, and one factor reward must fall by more than the greatest decrease in the relative commodity price. At this point we have established that: w_1 has risen unambiguously to w_1', that w_2 has fallen to w_2', that the relative price of good one has increased and is higher than it was initially, and that the price of good two has fallen from its initial value – that is, it has decreased along the constant price ratio line to E_1, and that the return to factor two has fallen. These can be summarized in the (Jones') magnification effects:

$$\widehat{w}_1 > \widehat{p}_1 > \widehat{w}_3\ (=0) > \widehat{p}_2 > \widehat{w}_2. \tag{12}$$

The fact that w_3 is held constant is a convenience for the diagram but does nothing to affect the relative rankings. Notice that factor one gains and factor two loses in real terms. Factor three, the middle factor, may gain or lose depending on the extent to which it consumes good one or two: this is the neoclassical ambiguity (Ruffin and Jones, 1977).

3.2.1. Rotating the V-locus

The aspect of the geometry that is important for our analysis is embedded in the slope of the V-locus. In the example above the key feature of the V-locus is that it lies between the price loci, P_1 and P_2.[11] As a matter of geometry this obviously does not need to be the case. Consider for example if the V-locus were to lie outside the boundary of the P-loci. In particular, if the V-locus were to continue to have a negative slope passing through E_0, but now assume it lies below the P_1-locus. In this case (not shown) w_1 will increase and w_2 will fall, but the fall in both prices along the $d(P_1/P_2) = 0$ locus gives rise to the magnification effect in (13):

$$\widehat{w}_1 > \widehat{w}_3\ (=0) > \widehat{p}_1 > \widehat{p}_2 > \widehat{w}_2 \tag{13}$$

so that both the first factor and third factors gains in real terms from the increase in the relative price of good one.

If the V-locus is rotated still further, past the vertical (at which point it is clear that $\widehat{w}_1 = \widehat{w}_3\ (=0) > \widehat{p}_1 > \widehat{p}_2 > \widehat{w}_2$) and enter the realm in which the V-locus has a positive slope, the interesting feature of the analysis is to suggest that the reward to factor one is falling. Consider the slope in the figure V'. With this slope, w_1 is actually declining relative to w_3. This leads to the following sequence of returns identified in Jones and Easton (1983):

$$\widehat{w}_3\ (=0) > \widehat{w}_1 > \widehat{p}_1 > \widehat{p}_2 > \widehat{w}_2, \tag{14}$$

[11] This is always the case in the specific factor model, so consequently the magnification effect described in (12) is the only possible outcome.

$$\widehat{w}_3\ (=0) > \widehat{p}_1 > \widehat{w}_1 > \widehat{p}_2 > \widehat{w}_2, \tag{15}$$

and

$$\widehat{w}_3\ (=0) > \widehat{p}_1 > \widehat{p}_2 > \widehat{w}_1 > \widehat{w}_2, \tag{16}$$

each of which is consistent with a positively sloped *V*-locus which continues to rotate clockwise.

The diagram has revealed that the pattern of factor rewards can be tied to the slope of the *V*-locus. The next step is to understand what causes the *V*-locus to rotate.[12]

3.3. The economic meaning of the slope of the *V*-locus

The slope of the *V*-locus is central to understanding the issues of substitutability in the model. The slope links the substitutions that take place when factor prices change. Written most intuitively:

$$-\frac{\widehat{w}_2}{\widehat{w}_1} = \frac{\xi_1}{\xi_2} = \frac{\sigma_3^1 - \left(\alpha_1\sigma_1^1 + \alpha_2\sigma_2^1\right)}{\sigma_3^2 - \left(\alpha_1\sigma_1^2 + \alpha_2\sigma_2^2\right)}, \tag{17}$$

the slope identifies the elasticity of substitution of each of the extreme factors for the middle factor, σ_3^1 and σ_3^2, and a weighted sum of the own price and elasticity of substitution between the two extreme factors. One more complicated, but ultimately more revealing characterization of the slope is found by rewriting (17) as (Jones and Easton, 1983, p. 85)

$$\frac{\xi_1}{\xi_2} = \left(\frac{\theta^1}{\theta^2}\right)\left(\frac{\omega_1\sigma_1^3 + (\omega_1 - \omega_2)\sigma_1^2}{\omega_2\sigma_2^3 - (\omega_1 - \omega_2)\sigma_2^1}\right), \tag{18}$$

in which θ^i is the share of factor *i* in national income, $\omega_i = (1/\theta^3) + \alpha_i/\theta^i$, and the difference $(\omega_1 - \omega_2) = (\alpha_1/\theta^1) - (\alpha_2/\theta^2)$ which is positive if and only if industry one is middle factor intensive (our assumption). The critical mix between algebra and geometry can be seen initially by considering what would happen if the elasticity of substitution between the extreme factors increased. Assume initially that both the numerator and denominator are positive as would be the case in the figure if the *V*-locus had a negative slope. In the case of a now higher elasticity of substitution of the extreme factors for one another, both σ_1^2 and σ_2^1 increase.[13] Ignoring the other terms for the moment, the numerator gets increasingly positive while the denominator becomes smaller. As we continue to increase the substitutability, the slope becomes undefined as the denominator equals

---

[12] It is important to note that the *V*-locus does not rotate as a consequence of some experiment in the model. Every economy has a *V*-locus with a particular slope. When we "rotate" the *V*-locus, we are looking at a different economy, not performing an experiment in one particular economy.

[13] We know that $\sigma_2^1 = (\theta^1/\theta^2)\sigma_1^2$.

zero, and then continues to rotate as higher values of the extreme factor substitutability lead to a negative denominator. Thus higher elasticities of substitution between extreme factors causes the *V*-locus to rotate clockwise to positions such as those represented by *V'* in the diagram. Similarly, if we consider lower elasticities of substitutability becoming elasticities of complementarity between the middle factor and factor two, a similar sort of rotation will take place.

4. *Two extreme cases*

When we looked at the possible outcomes of increasing substitutability between the extreme factors, we reported ranking like those of Equation (16). One question that has not been asked is whether there is any reason why the rankings might not permit the changes in $\widehat{w}_1$ to be equal to or less than $\widehat{w}_2$. Indeed, is there any limit to the extent to which the *V*-locus can rotate? Can it rotate through a ray from the origin – as illustrated by the dotted *V''*-locus in the figure – or can it rotate even further? If these configurations of the *V*-locus are possible then there is at least one set of magnification effects that has been ignored. In the context of industry one being middle factor intensive, there are two cases that are interesting: extremely high elasticities of substitution between the extreme factors, and a high degree of complementarity between factors two and three, an extreme factor, and the middle factor as these are configurations most closely associated with a positively sloped *V*-locus.

Let us begin with the case of high degrees of substitutability between factors one and two. Our assumption is that we can have very large values of σ_2^1, but these must be less than infinite. If there is an infinite substitutability between the two factors, then it is difficult to assign meaning to the intensity assumptions that we have made as there are really only two factors in the model. To look at this high elasticity of substitution case, rewrite Equation (18) by substituting for σ_1^2 by using the relationship $\theta^1\sigma_1^2 = \theta^2\sigma_2^1$ and divide both the numerator and denominator by σ_2^1:

$$\frac{\xi_1}{\xi_2} = \left(\frac{\theta^1\omega_1(\sigma_1^3/\sigma_2^1) + (\omega_1 - \omega_2)\theta^2}{\theta^2\omega_2(\sigma_2^3/\sigma_2^1) - (\omega_1 - \omega_2)\theta^2}\right). \tag{19}$$

Now if the σ_2^1 gets large, then the first term in both the numerator and the denominator get as small as we like and were they to approach a limit of zero, then the slope would be unity (recall it is the negative of ξ_1/ξ_2 that is the slope). As a result, with a finite value for σ_2^1, it is clear that the elasticity of the *V*-locus in this case is warded away from unity and consequently we can rule out the possibility that $\widehat{w}_1 = \widehat{w}_2$ and *ipso facto* potential cases in which $\widehat{w}_1 < \widehat{w}_2$.

This extreme case illustrates that substitutability attracts in the sense that the changes in factor rewards move toward each other in our ranking as factors one and two becomes increasingly good substitutes within the production technology. So what is happening? The better the degree of substitutability, the less easily are the factor rewards separated. Consequently when industry one's relative price increases, some factor reward must increase, and in this case with industry one middle factor intensive, it is the reward to the middle factor that rises to absorb in price increase.

Alternatively, putting the issue directly, if all factors are substitutes, can $(\xi_1/(-\xi_2)) = 1$? To see that this is not possible, draw from Equation (17) and assume that $(\xi_1/(-\xi_2)) = 1$, so that

$$\sigma_3^1 - \left(\alpha_1\sigma_1^1 + \alpha_2\sigma_2^1\right) = -\left[\sigma_3^2 - \left(\alpha_1\sigma_1^2 + \alpha_2\sigma_2^2\right)\right]. \tag{20}$$

Rearranging the terms

$$\left(\sigma_3^1 + \sigma_3^2\right) = \alpha_1\left(\sigma_1^2 + \sigma_1^1\right) + \alpha_2\left(\sigma_2^2 + \sigma_2^1\right), \tag{21}$$

which in turn means that:[14]

$$\left(\sigma_3^3\right) = \alpha_1\left(\sigma_1^3\right) + \alpha_2\left(\sigma_2^3\right). \tag{22}$$

But since all goods are substitutes, this is a contradiction since the own factor price must be negative, $\sigma_3^3 < 0$, while $\sigma_1^3 > 0$ and $\sigma_2^3 > 0$.

The second case of interest is one in which the elasticity of complementarity is between factors two and three: the extreme factor and the middle factor. In Jones and Easton (1983) perfect complementarity is defined as existing when for any change in factor prices, the relative proportions in which the factors that are perfect complements are held constant. Thus complementarity between extreme factors looks like: $\sigma_1^k = \sigma_2^k$, and complementarity beween the middle factor and an extreme factor (two in this case) looks like: $\sigma_3^k = \sigma_2^k$. With perfect complementarity between the two extreme factors, their factor rewards are "repelled", and the ranking of rewards leaves the middle factor in the middle: $\widehat{w}_1 > \widehat{p}_1 > \widehat{w}_3 > \widehat{p}_2 > \widehat{w}_2$. However, when the middle factor is a perfect complement to extreme factor two, the ranking switches as the middle factor and extreme factor two are pushed as far apart as possible: $\widehat{w}_3 > \widehat{p}_1 > \widehat{w}_1 > \widehat{p}_2 > \widehat{w}_2$. The import of these two extreme cases is to make it clear that in the case of extreme substitutability and perfect complementarity, there is no possibility that the *V*-locus will reach a ray from the origin. Thus there is no possibility that $\widehat{w}_1 = \widehat{w}_2$.

[14] Homogeneity implies that $\sigma_i^1 + \sigma_i^2 + \sigma_i^3 = 0$ as a common increase in all factor prices leaves demands unchanged.

4.1. More than perfect complementarity

The extension that I wish to consider has to do with the definition of perfect complementarity. Suppose that we define complementarity such that for an increase in the price of (say) factor three, the amount of factor two used falls: we do not put any constraint on the effect of factor price change on the proportions in which the factors are used. For example, we can imagine that an increase in the price of factor two causes a greater fall in the usage of factor three than in factor two: a sort of "super" complementarity – after all, we need something beyond "perfect". To set ideas, imagine initially that both industries have the same middle factor intensity. This means that $\omega_1 = \omega_2$. From (18) we know that

$$\frac{\xi_1}{\xi_2} = \left(\frac{\theta^1}{\theta^2}\right)\left(\frac{\omega_1\sigma_1^3}{\omega_2\sigma_2^3}\right). \tag{23}$$

Substituting[15] for σ_1^3 and rearranging leaves an expression:

$$\frac{\xi_1}{\xi_2} = -1 - \frac{\theta^3\sigma_3^3}{\theta^3\sigma_2^3}, \tag{24}$$

where both the substitution elasticities are negative so that the entire expression is again warded away from -1. Such a result suggests that as the value of σ_2^3 becomes increasingly negative, the slope of the V-locus can get arbitrarily close to -1. Thus complementarity defined in the sense discussed here permits a ranking of $\widehat{w}_3 > \widehat{p}_1 > \widehat{p}_2 > \widehat{w}_1 > \widehat{w}_2$.

But can complementarity even in this sense lead to an equality of the wage change of the extreme factors? Happily, again, the answer is "No". To see this start with Equation (23) which embodies the assumption that the elasticity of the V-locus is unity so that $\widehat{w}_1 = \widehat{w}_2$. Since unit costs are minimized, $\theta^1\sigma_1^i + \theta^2\sigma_2^i + \theta^3\sigma_3^i = 0$. Substitute for σ_1^3 and rearrange so that

$$\sigma_3^3\left(1 + \frac{\theta^3}{\theta^1}\right) = \theta^2\left(\frac{\alpha_2}{\theta^2} - \frac{\alpha_1}{\theta^1}\right)\sigma_2^3, \tag{25}$$

but this is a contradiction. We assumed that $\sigma_2^3 < 0$ and we know that the own price elasticity of substitution is always negative, $\sigma_2^3 < 0$. The term in brackets $((\alpha_2/\theta^2) - (\alpha_1/\theta^1)) < 0$ as a matter of our assumed factor intensity. Thus it is clear that even with this extended definition of complementarity that allows for changes in factor use unlimited by the own factor usage, we will still not see a positional switch in the factor prices of the extreme factors.

---

[15] We know that $\theta^1\sigma_1^k + \theta^2\sigma_2^k + \theta^3\sigma_3^k = 0$.

5. Conclusion

By extending and developing the frameworks and techniques that he pioneered, we can honor Ron Jones' contribution to economics. Although he has contributed to a host of literatures, the proof of his contributions is high. In this one example that we have taken, the general three-factor two-sector framework is a model that has many uses. It generates a variety of outcomes that are not possible in the specific factor model. However, not all outcomes are possible. We have seen that it permits a wide range of factor reward rankings depending on the intensity of middle factor usage and the configuration of three basic elasticities: the elasticity of substitution of the middle factor against each of the extreme factors and of the elasticity of substitution of the extreme factors toward one another. Although somewhat more complex than the specific factor model, it should be a workhorse for small-scale general equilibrium analysis. Many activities use the same factors to produce outputs, and the richness of three factors provides a more complete backdrop to understand behavior. By firming up the kinds of outcomes that are not possible and extending the definition of what we call complementarity, we can encourage its use. This will be the most fitting tribute to Ron Jones' contributions.

References

Batra, R.N., Casas, F.P. (1976), A synthesis of the Heckscher-Ohlin and the neoclassical models of international trade. *Journal of International Economics* 6, 21–38.

Easton, S.T., Jones, R.W. (1992), Wage agreements and optimal international factor flows. In: Giersch, H. (Ed.), *Money, Trade and Competition: Essays in memory of Egon Sohmen*. Springer, New York, pp. 151–165.

Jones, R.W. (1965), The structure of simple general equilibrium models. *Journal of Political Economy* 73, 557–572.

Jones, R.W. (1971), A three factor model in theory, trade and history. In: Bhagwati, Jones, Mundell, Vanek (Eds.), *Trade, Balance of Payments and Growth: Essays in Honor of C. B. Kindleberger*. North-Holland, Amsterdam, pp. 3–21.

Jones, R.W., Easton, S.T. (1983), Factor intensities and factor substitution in general equilibrium. *Journal of International Economics* 15, 65–99.

Jones, R.W., Easton, S.T. (1986), The theory of international factor flows: the basic model. *Journal of International Economics* 20, 313–327.

Jones, R.W., Easton, S.T. (1989), Perspectives on 'buy-outs'and the Ramaswami effect. *Journal of International Economics* 27, 363–371.

Jones, R.W., Easton, S.T. (1990), Foreign investment and migration: analytics and extensions of the basic model. *Keio Economic Studies* 27, 1–20.

Ruffin, R.J. (1981), Trade and factor movements with three factors and two goods. *Economics Letters* 7, 177–182.

Ruffin, R.J., Jones, R.W. (1977), Protection and real wages: the neoclassical ambiguity. *Journal of Economic Theory* 14, 337–348.

Samuelson, P.A. (1953), Prices of factors and goods in general equilibrium. *The Review of Economic Studies* 21, 1–20.

Suzuki, K. (1981), The extension of international trade theory to 'three-ness'. Unpublished doctoral dissertation, University of Rochester.

Suzuki, K. (1983), A synthesis of the Hecksher-Ohlin and neoclassical models of international trade: a comment. *Journal of International Economics* 14, 141–144.

Takayama, A. (1982), On theorems of general competitive equilibrium of production and trade – a survey of some recent developments in the theory of international trade. *Keio Economic Studies* 19, 1–37.

Takeda, S. (2005), The effect of differentiated emission taxes: does an emission tax favor industry? *Economics Bulletin* 17 (3), 1–10.

Thakkar, R. (1971), Structure of a two-sector three-factor economy – production, trade and growth. Unpublished doctoral dissertation, University of Rochester.

Thompson, H. (1983), Factor migration and income redistribution in international trade. *Keio Economic Studies* 2, 65–70.

Thompson, H. (1985), Complementarity in a simple general equilibrium model. *Canadian Journal of Economics* 18, 616–621.

Thompson, H. (1990), Simulating a multifactor general equilibrium model of production and trade. *International Economic Journal* 4, 21–34.

Thompson, H. (1993), The magnification effect with three factors. *Keio Economic Studies* 30, 57–64.

Thompson, H. (1997), Free trade and income redistribution in a three factor model of the US economy. *Southern Economic Journal* 63, 1074–1093.

CHAPTER 7

On Commodity Prices and Factor Rewards: A Close Look at Sign Patterns

Tapan Mitra

Department of Economics, Cornell University, Ithaca, NY, USA
E-mail address: tm19@cornell.edu

Abstract
The effect of changes in commodity prices on factor rewards is studied in the multi-commodity, multi-factor case. It is shown that the inverse of the distributive share matrix must satisfy the following restriction: it cannot be *anti-symmetric in its sign pattern*. This means that one cannot partition the commodities into two groups (I and II) and factors into two groups (A and B), such that all factors in group A benefit (nominally) from all commodity price increases in group I, and simultaneously all factors in group B suffer from all commodity price increases in group II. It turns out that this is also the *only* sign-pattern restriction imposed by the general nature of the relationship of commodity prices and factor rewards.

Keywords: Stolper-Samuelson result, factor rewards, distributive share matrix, sign-pattern restriction

JEL classifications: C65, C67, D33, D51, F11

1. Introduction

The relation between commodity prices and factor rewards is an enduring theme in the contributions of Ron Jones to the pure theory of international trade. From his famous 1965 paper, "On the Structure of Simple General Equilibrium Models" (Jones, 1965) to his 2006 expository piece, "'Protection and Real Wages': The History of an Idea," (Jones, 2006) we see in his research on this topic a sustained interest that is truly remarkable. Inspired by the original Stolper–Samuelson (1941) paper, this topic came to represent for him the essence of the applicability of international trade theory to policy issues, as well as a leading test case of the importance of general equilibrium analysis.

Frontiers of Economics and Globalization
Volume 4 ISSN: 1574-8715
DOI: 10.1016/S1574-8715(08)04007-4

If one follows the development of his ideas on this topic over this 40-year period, one can discern at least two distinct themes.[1] The first is concerned primarily with the Stolper–Samuelson *result*, and its generalizations to the case of many commodities and many factors. This line of his research has identified *particular* production structures, in the many commodity, many factor case, for which the Stolper–Samuelson result continues to hold; they include the "produced mobile factor structure" discussed in Jones (1975) and Jones and Marjit (1985), and the "neighborhood production structure" analyzed in Jones and Kierzkowski (1986).[2] It has also identified *sufficient conditions* on the share matrix for *general* production structures which ensure the Stolper–Samuelson result in either its strong form (see Jones *et al.*, 1993) or its weak form (see Mitra and Jones, 1999).[3]

The second theme is concerned with the Stolper–Samuelson *idea* that the impact of changes in commodity prices on factor rewards can be studied by systematic use of general equilibrium analysis. In this theme, the emphasis is less on the original Stolper–Samuelson result, and more on identifying useful predictions that can be made about changes in the distribution of income, following changes in commodity prices. Pioneered by Ethier (1974), this line of research has been pursued by, among others, Kemp and Wan (1976), Jones and Scheinkman (1977), Chang (1979) and Jones (1985).[4] While appropriate conditions on factor intensities figure prominently in the first theme (following, notably, the contributions of Chipman (1969) and Kemp and Wegge (1969)), they play no role in the second.

The results I will be discussing in this chapter belong to the second theme. We consider the setting which involves the active production in competitive markets of n commodities, each produced non-jointly by the use of n distinct factors of production (known as the "even case") in processes that are linearly independent of each other at prevailing factor prices. The distributive share of factor i in industry j denoted by α_{ij} is assumed to be strictly positive for all i, j.[5]

---

[1] To be sure, this statement is a gross oversimplification. But, since it helps me to a certain extent in fitting my own contribution in his scheme of ideas, I will maintain it.

[2] The analysis of the shape of "share ribs" in Jones and Mitra (1995) was used to unify these results in a common (but still special) production structure.

[3] These conditions, though strong, can be directly verified using only the information about the share matrix, and are to be distinguished in this respect from more general conditions, which have been proposed in the literature, but which are not verifiable in the same way; see, especially, the well-known papers by Uekawa (1971) and Inada (1971).

[4] For useful surveys of the relevant literature, we refer the reader to Ethier (1984) and Jones and Neary (1984).

[5] The equality of the number of factors and the number of commodities, as well as the positivity of all α_{ij}, are strong assumptions of this framework. More general frameworks, in which the number of commodities need not be equal to the number of factors, and some of the α_{ij} can be zeroes, have been studied by, among others, Jones and Scheinkman (1977) and Chang (1979).

The inverse of the column-stochastic matrix (α_{ij}) denoted by (β_{ij}), where $\beta_{ij} = [\partial w_j(p)/\partial p_i][p_i/w_j]$, is a column-stochastic matrix which provides the full information of the effects of commodity prices (p_i) on factor rewards (w_j). It can be seen easily that the matrix (β_{ij}) must satisfy the restriction (referred to as (R) in Section 3) that every row and every column of it must have both positive and negative elements. The implications that have been drawn from this information can be summarized as follows:

(i) For each factor, there is some commodity, such that (*ceteris paribus*) an increase in price of that commodity leads to a decrease in the factor's reward.

(ii) For every commodity, there is some factor, such that (*ceteris paribus*) an increase in price of the commodity leads to a decrease in that factor's reward.

(iii) For every commodity, there is some factor, such that (*ceteris paribus*) an increase in price of the commodity leads to an increase in that factor's *real* reward.

(iv) For each factor, there is some commodity, such that (*ceteris paribus*) an increase in price of that commodity leads to a *nominal* increase in the factor's reward.

(v) For each factor, there is some *set* of commodities such that an equiproportionate increase in the prices of all commodities in that set, other prices being constant, will increase the *real reward* of the factor.

We now ask whether these implications characterize the qualitative information that can be derived regarding the relationship of commodity prices to factor rewards in this framework. Apparently not, because the matrix

$$T = \begin{bmatrix} 1.5 & -1 & -1 & -1 \\ -1 & 1.5 & -1 & -1 \\ 0.25 & 0.25 & 4 & -1 \\ 0.25 & 0.25 & -1 & 4 \end{bmatrix}$$

is a column-stochastic matrix, which satisfies restriction (R) and all the properties listed in (i)–(v), but T *cannot* be generated as the inverse of any distributive share matrix (in our framework). In other words, the dependence of factor rewards on commodity prices exhibiting the behavior displayed in T cannot be rationalized in terms of our framework.

It is possible to reach this conclusion without performing extensive calculations, but by simply observing the *sign pattern* of the matrix T, and applying Theorem 1, stated in Section 3 of this chapter. But, the reader is asked to refrain from skipping ahead to Section 3, and encouraged to try to figure out this conclusion based on the information provided above.[6]

Theorem 1 in this chapter develops a condition (referred to as Condition C in Section 3) on the sign pattern of T which *must be violated* if T is to be the inverse of a distributive share matrix. Further, given the restriction (R), the violation of Condition C captures all the qualitative restrictions imposed by our framework on the relationship between commodity prices and factor rewards. This is reported in Theorem 2.

The principal use of Theorem 1 is to rule out some kinds of behavior of factor rewards following commodity price changes, as illustrated in the above example of T, which are not already ruled out by the restriction (R). The principal use of Theorem 2 is that it gives us an easy way to rationalize a variety of behavior of factor reward changes following commodity price changes.

2. *Preliminaries*

2.1. Notation

For vectors $x, y \in \mathbb{R}^n$, $x \geq y$ means $x_i \geq y_i$ for $i = 1, \ldots, n$; $x > y$ means $x \geq y$ and $x \neq y$; $x \gg y$ means $x_i > y_i$ for $i = 1, \ldots, n$. The set $\{x \in \mathbb{R}^n : x \geq 0\}$ is denoted by $\mathbb{R}^n_+$; the set $\{x \in \mathbb{R}^n : x \gg 0\}$ is denoted by Ω.

The n unit vectors in $\mathbb{R}^n$ are denoted by $e^1, \ldots, e^n$; the vector $(1, 1, \ldots, 1) \in \mathbb{R}^n$ is denoted by u.

Let $A = (a_{ij})$ be an $n \times n$ real matrix. Then A is called a *positive matrix* if $a_{ij} > 0$ for all $i, j = 1, \ldots, n$. It is called a *positive diagonal matrix* if it is a diagonal matrix, and $a_{ii} > 0$ for all $i = 1, \ldots, n$.

2.2. The framework

Consider an n-commodity, n-factor model of production (with $n \geq 2$), in which y_j denotes the output of the jth commodity and x_{ij} the amount of the ith factor used in the production of the jth commodity (where $i, j = 1, 2, \ldots, n$).

For each commodity j, the output level y_j is determined by input levels $(x_{1j}, \ldots, x_{nj})$ of the n factors, according to a production function f_j from $\mathbb{R}^n_+$ to $\mathbb{R}_+$:

$$y_j = f_j(x_{1j}, \ldots, x_{nj}) \quad \text{for } j = 1, \ldots, n. \tag{1}$$

[6] I must confess that, to me, the conclusion is not immediately obvious, and not obvious even after a great deal of thought.

For each $j = 1, \ldots, n$, assume:[7]

(F.1) f_j is non-decreasing, continuous and homogeneous of degree one on $\mathbb{R}^n_+$.
(F.2) $f_j(x) > 0$ if and only if $x \gg 0$.
(F.3) f_j is strictly quasi-concave on Ω.

For each commodity j, given an output level $y > 0$, and a vector of factor prices $w = (w_1, \ldots, w_n) \gg 0$, consider the cost-minimizing problem:

$$\left.\begin{array}{ll} \text{Minimize} & wx \\ \text{subject to} & f_j(x) \geq y \\ \text{and} & x \in \mathbb{R}^n_+ \end{array}\right\} \text{(CM)}.$$

Problem (CM) has a unique solution, $x_j(w, y) = (x_{1j}(w, y), \ldots, x_{nj}(w, y))$ in Ω. These are the *conditional input demands* in the production of commodity j. The *cost* function $c_j(w, y)$ is then $wx_j(w, y)$. Since the production function f_j is homogeneous of degree one, we have for each j,

$$c_j(w, y) = yc_j(w, 1); \quad x_j(w, y) = yx_j(w, 1).$$

Denote the *unit cost* functions $c_j(w,1)$ by $g_j(w)$, and the *unit conditional demand* functions $x_j(w,1)$ by $a_j(w) = (a_{1j}(w), \ldots, a_{nj}(w))$. Thus, for each j,

$$g_j(w) = \sum_{i=1}^{n} a_{ij}(w) w_i. \tag{2}$$

It is known that for $i, j = 1, \ldots, n$, the functions $a_{ij}(w)$ are continuous on Ω. Also, for each $j = 1, \ldots, n$, the function $g_j(w)$ has continuous partial derivatives on Ω, and we have ("Shephard's Lemma"):[8]

$$\frac{\partial g_j(w)}{\partial w_i} = a_{ij}(w) \quad \text{for } i = 1, \ldots, n. \tag{3}$$

If the n commodities are traded in a competitive market under a price system $p \in \Omega$, the price of the jth commodity must equal its unit cost $g_j(w)$ if it is positively produced in equilibrium. Proceeding under the assumption that given the price vector $p^0 \in \Omega$, the economy is in an incomplete specialization equilibrium at factor prices $w^0 \in \Omega$, we then have

$$\left.\begin{array}{l} \text{(i) } a_{ij}(w^0) > 0 \quad \text{for } i = 1, \ldots, n \text{ and } j = 1, \ldots, n \\ \text{(ii) } g_j(w^0) = p_j^0 \quad \text{for } j = 1, \ldots, n \end{array}\right\}. \tag{4}$$

Assume that the Jacobian of $g(w) = (g_1(w), \ldots, g_n(w))$ is non-zero at $w = w^0$. Then, by the inverse function theorem, there is a neighborhood

[7] The assumptions, in fact, imply that each f_j is concave on $\mathbb{R}^n_+$.
[8] See, especially, Nikaido (1968, p. 357).

U of w^0 and a neighborhood V of p^0, and a unique mapping $h: U \to V$ satisfying

$$h(g(w)) = w \text{ for all } w \in U. \tag{5}$$

Furthermore, h has continuous partial derivatives on V, and

$$[Dh(p^0)] = [Dg(w^0)]^{-1}, \tag{6}$$

where $[Dg(w^0)]$ is the Jacobian matrix of g at w^0 and $[Dh(p^0)]$ the Jacobian matrix of h at p^0 (See, especially, Apostol, 1957, p. 144).

If we denote the positive matrix $(a_{ij}(w^0))$ by $A \equiv A(w^0)$, then by (3) and (6) respectively, we have

$$[Dg(w^0)]' = A \tag{7}$$

and

$$[Dh(p^0)]' = A^{-1} = (b_{ij}). \tag{8}$$

Recalling (5), we can rewrite (8) as

$$\left[\frac{\partial w_j(p^0)}{\partial p_i}\right] = (b_{ij}) = A^{-1}. \tag{9}$$

Define the matrix of *distributive shares*, $S = (\alpha_{ij})$ by

$$\alpha_{ij} = \frac{w_i^0 a_{ij}(w^0)}{p_j^0} \quad \text{for } i = 1, \ldots, n \text{ and } j = 1, \ldots, n. \tag{10}$$

Then, by using (2) and (4), we have

$$\left.\begin{array}{l} \text{(i) } \alpha_{ij} > 0 \quad \text{for } i = 1, \ldots, n \text{ and } j = 1, \ldots, n \\ \text{(ii) } \sum_{i=1}^{n} \alpha_{ij} = 1 \quad \text{for each } j = 1, \ldots, n \end{array}\right\}. \tag{11}$$

That is, each column sum of S is equal to 1.

Define P to be the diagonal matrix with $(p_1^0, \ldots, p_n^0)$ on its diagonal; define W to be the diagonal matrix with $(w_1^0, \ldots, w_n^0)$ on its diagonal. Then, (10) implies that

$$S = WAP^{-1}. \tag{12}$$

So, S has an inverse, and denoting the inverse of S by T, we have

$$T = PA^{-1}W^{-1}. \tag{13}$$

Denoting by (β_{ij}) the matrix T, we observe from (9) and (13),

$$\beta_{ij} = \left[\frac{\partial w_j(p^0)}{\partial p_i}\right]\left[\frac{p_i^0}{w_j^0}\right] \quad \text{for } i = 1, \ldots, n \text{ and } j = 1, \ldots, n. \tag{14}$$

We are principally interested in making predictions about β_{ij}.

Denoting the column vector (1, 1, ..., 1) in $\mathbb{R}^n$ by u, we observe that by (11), we have

$$u'S = u'. \tag{15}$$

So, post-multiplying both sides of (15) by T, we get

$$u' = u'T. \tag{16}$$

That is, each column sum of T is equal to 1, and consequently,

$$\sum_{i=1}^{n} \beta_{ij} = \sum_{i=1}^{n} \left[\frac{\partial w_j(p^0)}{\partial p_i}\right]\left[\frac{p_i^0}{w_j^0}\right] = 1 \quad \text{for each } j = 1, \ldots, n. \tag{17}$$

In what follows, we suppress the factor prices w^0 and commodity prices p^0 at which our analysis is carried out. Thus, our analysis is explicitly *local* in a neighborhood of the equilibrium given by (p^0, w^0).

3. Effects of commodity price changes on factor rewards

3.1. Review of the literature

We review what is known about the effect of commodity prices on factor returns, that is about β_{ij}. Since

$$ST = TS = I \tag{18}$$

and S is a positive matrix, we have the following restriction:

(R) Every column and every row of T must have positive as well as negative entries.[9]

One can elaborate on the implications of the restriction (R) as follows:

(i) For each j, there is some i such that

$$\beta_{ij} = \left[\frac{\partial w_j(p^0)}{\partial p_i}\right]\left[\frac{p_i^0}{w_j^0}\right] < 0;$$

that is, for each factor j, there is some commodity i such that an increase in price of commodity i alone leads to a decrease in factor j's reward.[10]

---

[9] If the ith column of T has only non-positive elements, then $S_i T^i \leq 0$, since S is a non-negative matrix. Here S_i is the ith row of S and T^i is the ith column of T. But, by (18), $S_i T^i = 1$, a contradiction.

Suppose the ith column of T has only non-negative elements. Using (18), we have $S_j T^i = 0$ for $j \neq i$, and so the ith column of T has only zero elements, since S is a positive matrix. Thus, we must have $S_i T^i = 0$. But, by (18), $S_i T^i = 1$, a contradiction.

Analogous arguments with the rows of T yield the remaining results claimed in (R).

[10] To use the terminology of Ron Jones, each factor has a commodity enemy.

(ii) For each i, there is some j such that

$$\beta_{ij} = \left[\frac{\partial w_j(p^0)}{\partial p_i}\right]\left[\frac{p_i^0}{w_j^0}\right] < 0;$$

that is, for every commodity i, there is some factor j such that an increase in price of commodity i alone leads to a decrease in factor j's reward.[11]

(iii) For each i, there is some j such that

$$\beta_{ij} = \left[\frac{\partial w_j(p^0)}{\partial p_i}\right]\left[\frac{p_i^0}{w_j^0}\right] > 1;$$

that is, for every commodity i, there is some factor j such that an increase in price of commodity i alone leads to an increase in factor j's *real* reward.[12]

(iv) For each j, there is some i such that

$$\beta_{ij} = \left[\frac{\partial w_j(p^0)}{\partial p_i}\right]\left[\frac{p_i^0}{w_j^0}\right] > 0;$$

that is, for each factor j, there is some commodity i such that an increase in price of commodity i alone leads to a *nominal* increase in factor j's reward. It is important to note that this conclusion is not symmetric to (iii). The *real* reward of factor j can go down, since the price of some commodity has gone up.[13]

If one combines implication (i) with (17), one may, however, note a further implication (this is due to Jones (1985)).

(v) For each j, there is some set $F \subset \{1, 2, \ldots, n\}$, such that

$$\sum_{i \in F} \beta_{ij} = \sum_{i \in F}\left[\frac{\partial w_j(p^0)}{\partial p_i}\right]\left[\frac{p_i^0}{w_j^0}\right] > 1.$$

The set F can be taken to be the set of indices i (non-empty, by implication (iv)) for which $\beta_{ij} > 0$. This means that an equiproportionate increase in the prices of all commodities with indices

[11] Each commodity is an enemy of some factor.

[12] This important observation is due to Ethier (1974): every commodity is a friend of some factor.

Given any i, donate by G the set of indices j for which $\beta_{ij} > 0$. This set is non-empty, and a strict subset of $\{1, \ldots, n\}$ by (R). Then, we have, by (11), (18) and (R),

$$1 = \sum_{j=1}^{n} \beta_{ij}\alpha_{ji} < \sum_{j \in G} \beta_{ij}\alpha_{ji} \leq \left[\max_{j \in G} \beta_{ij}\right] \sum_{j \in G} \alpha_{ji} < \left[\max_{j \in G} \beta_{ij}\right]$$

[13] So, in general, every factor need not have a commodity friend.

i in the set F, other prices being constant, will increase the *real reward* of factor j.[14]

3.2. A result on sign patterns

Implications (i)–(v), which have been discussed in the literature, follow from (11), (17) and (18). So, a legitimate question is whether these implications exhaust all the restrictions contained in (11), (17) and (18).

In this subsection, we establish a result which shows that there is a restriction on the *sign patterns* of $T \equiv (\beta_{ij})$ that follows from (11), (17) and (18). We describe the result in words before proceeding with a formal discussion. The result shows that the inverse of the distributive share matrix *cannot* be *anti-symmetric* in its sign pattern. This means that one cannot partition the commodities into two groups (I and II) and factors into two groups (A and B), such that all factors in group A benefit (nominally) from all commodity price increases in group I, and simultaneously all factors in group B suffer from all commodity price increases in group II.

To illustrate the nature of the restriction, one may note that (for $n = 4$) the matrix (β_{ij}) *cannot* be of the following form:

$$\begin{bmatrix} * & * & - & - \\ * & * & - & - \\ + & + & * & * \\ + & + & * & * \end{bmatrix}. \tag{19}$$

[Here, and in what follows, a "+" indicates that the entry in the cell is ≥ 0, and a "–"indicates that the entry in the cell is ≤ 0]. In (19), commodities have been partitioned into two groups, I and II, with I consisting of commodities {3, 4} and II consisting of commodities {1, 2}. Factors have been partitioned into two groups, A and B, with A consisting of factors {1, 2} and B consisting of factors {3, 4}. Then the sign pattern in (19) indicates that all factors in group A benefit nominally from all commodity price increases in group I, and all factors in group B suffer from all commodity price increases in group II.

---

[14] Every factor has a group of good friends. The pun is, of course, intended. Given any j, denote by F the set of indices i for which $\beta_{ij} > 0$. The set F is non-empty, and a strict subset of $\{1, \ldots, n\}$ by (R). Then, by (11), (17), (18) and (R), we have

$$1 = \sum_{i=1}^{n} \beta_{ij}\alpha_{ji} < \sum_{i \in F} \beta_{ij}\alpha_{ji} \leq \left[\max_{i \in F} \alpha_{ji}\right] \sum_{i \in F} \beta_{ij} < \sum_{i \in F} \beta_{ij}$$

In this proof, I have deliberately refrained from referring to Samuelson's duality theorem, which is usually invoked to establish this result. Instead, I have tried to keep the proof similar to the proof of implication (iii) above.

In particular, in the example described in Section 1, the sign pattern described in (19) occurs. Thus, without consulting any other quantitative details of the matrix in that example, one can conclude that it *cannot* be the inverse of a distributive share matrix (in our maintained framework). That is, the behavior described in the matrix $T = (\beta_{ij})$ in that example cannot be rationalized in terms of our maintained framework, even though it clearly satisfies *all* the restrictions described in (i)–(v) of the last section.[15]

THEOREM 1. *Let $T = (\beta_{ij})$ denote the inverse of a distributive share matrix $S = (\alpha_{ij})$. Then T cannot satisfy the following condition.*

CONDITION C. *There exist integers k,m, with $1 \le k < n$, and $1 \le m < n$, such that the following inequalities hold simultaneously:*

(i) $\beta_{ij} \le 0$ for all $i = 1, \ldots, k$ and $j = m+1, \ldots, n$, and
(ii) $\beta_{ij} \ge 0$ for all $i = k+1, \ldots, n$ and $j = 1, \ldots, m$.

PROOF. Suppose, on the contrary, that $T = (\beta_{ij})$ satisfies Condition C. Then, there exist integers k,m, with $1 \le k < n$ and $1 \le m < n$, such that the inverse of the distribution matrix, $T = (\beta_{ij})$ satisfies (i) and (ii) simultaneously.

Focus on the distributive shares of the first industry; that is, on the first column of S. For $i = 1$, we have by (18),

$$\sum_{j=1}^{m} \beta_{ij}\alpha_{j1} + \sum_{j=m+1}^{n} \beta_{ij}\alpha_{j1} = 1. \tag{20}$$

And, for each $i \in \{2, \ldots, k\}$ (if any), we have, by (18)

$$\sum_{j=1}^{m} \beta_{ij}\alpha_{j1} + \sum_{j=m+1}^{n} \beta_{ij}\alpha_{j1} = 0. \tag{21}$$

Using (11) and (i), we know that the second term on the left-hand side of (20) and (21) must be non-positive, and so

$$\begin{bmatrix} \sum_{j=1}^{m} \beta_{1j}\alpha_{j1} \\ \cdots \\ \cdots \\ \sum_{j=1}^{m} \beta_{kj}\alpha_{j1} \end{bmatrix} \ge \begin{bmatrix} 1 \\ 0 \\ \cdots \\ 0 \end{bmatrix}, \tag{22}$$

where each vector in (22) has k co-ordinates.

[15] In fact, the matrix $T = (\beta_{ij})$ in the example demonstrates (to use the terminology of Chipman (1969)) strong Stolper–Samuelson properties in response to increase in prices of commodities 1 and 2, and weak Stolper–Samuelson properties in response to increase in prices of commodities 3 and 4.

Define γ to be the column vector in $\mathbb{R}^n$, given by $\gamma = [\alpha_{11}, \ldots, \alpha_{m1}, 0, \ldots, 0]$. That is, it differs from the first column of S in that the last $(n-m)$ entries are zeroes. Then, denoting the n rows of the (β_{ij}) matrix by $(\beta_1, \ldots, \beta_n)$, we can use (22) to write

$$\begin{bmatrix} \beta_1\gamma \\ \cdots \\ \cdots \\ \beta_k\gamma \end{bmatrix} = \begin{bmatrix} \sum_{j=1}^{m} \beta_{1j}\alpha_{j1} \\ \cdots \\ \cdots \\ \sum_{j=1}^{m} \beta_{kj}\alpha_{j1} \end{bmatrix} \geq \begin{bmatrix} 1 \\ 0 \\ \cdots \\ 0 \end{bmatrix}, \tag{23}$$

where each entry in the vector on the left is an inner product of two vectors in $\mathbb{R}^n$.

Using (ii), we also have

$$\begin{bmatrix} \beta_{k+1}\gamma \\ \cdots \\ \beta_n\gamma \end{bmatrix} \geq \begin{bmatrix} 0 \\ \cdots \\ 0 \end{bmatrix} \tag{24}$$

where each vector in (24) has $(n-k)$ co-ordinates. Thus, combining (23) and (24), we obtain:

$$\begin{bmatrix} \beta_1\gamma \\ \cdots \\ \cdots \\ \beta_n\gamma \end{bmatrix} \geq \begin{bmatrix} 1 \\ 0 \\ \cdots \\ 0 \end{bmatrix}, \tag{25}$$

where each vector in (25) has n co-ordinates. Clearly, (25) is the same as writing

$$T\gamma \geq e^1 > 0. \tag{26}$$

Since S is a positive matrix (see (11)), we obtain from (26),

$$S(T\gamma) \geq Se^1 \gg 0. \tag{27}$$

But, since $S(T\gamma) = (ST)\gamma = \gamma$ (by using (18)), (27) implies that $\gamma \gg 0$. This is clearly a contradiction, since the last $(n-m) \geq 1$ entries of γ are zeroes.

Remarks.

(i) The theorem can be derived by using the mathematical result obtained by Johnson *et al.* (1979, Theorem, p. 76) and Fiedler and Grone (1981, Theorem, p. 240). Those results relate to the general problem of characterizing matrices whose inverses are positive matrices, known as the "inverse-positive matrix problem." They are not explicitly concerned with column-stochastic matrices (as we are), but the translation of the results can clearly be made to that sub-class. Johnson *et al.* (1979) use stronger hypotheses, in which (i) and (ii) of Condition C are required to hold with strict inequalities, although their approach indicates that the weaker hypotheses made here suffice. Our proof is slightly different and a bit simpler, and is presented primarily to keep our exposition self-contained.

(ii) Since the numbering of factors and commodities has played no role in our analysis, the (β_{ij}) matrix, *after any independent renumbering of factors and commodities*, cannot exhibit an anti-symmetric sign pattern in the sense described in Condition C of the theorem.

(iii) The theorem would, of course, be valid under any *strengthening* of Condition C. In particular, inequalities (ii) can be strengthened to

$$\text{(ii}'\text{)}\ \beta_{ij} \geq 1 \text{ for all } i = k+1, \ldots, n \text{ and } j = 1, \ldots, m,$$

which can be interpreted in terms of the effects of changes in commodity prices on *real* factor rewards.

(iv) From the perspective of the result contained in Theorem 1, the original Stolper–Samuelson result in the 2×2 case can be viewed as one which *rules out* the patterns of behavior of (β_{ij}), where $\beta_{ij} = [\partial w_j(p)/\partial p_i][p_i/w_j]$, given by

$$(\beta_{ij}) = \begin{bmatrix} * & - \\ + & * \end{bmatrix}$$

and its variations, described in remark (ii) above. We elaborate further on the low-dimensional cases (that is, $n = 2$ and $n = 3$) in the next subsection.

3.3. Discussion of low-dimensional cases

The sign-pattern restriction (obtained in Theorem 1) on the inverse of the distributive share matrix is clearly an *additional* restriction that goes beyond the implications (i)–(v) in the case $n = 4$ as our example shows.

We now note that for $n = 2$ and for $n = 3$, it is *not* an additional restriction; that is, for $n = 2$ and $n = 3$, we show that the restriction (R) implies that Condition C cannot hold.

Consider a 2×2 matrix $T = (\beta_{ij})$, which satisfies Condition C. Then, it must be of the form

$$T = (\beta_{ij}) = \begin{bmatrix} * & - \\ + & * \end{bmatrix}. \tag{28}$$

If $\beta_{11} \leq 0$, then row 1 violates (R). However, if $\beta_{11} > 0$, then column 1 violates (R). Thus, in either case, (R) would be violated if Condition C holds.

Consider a 3×3 matrix $T = (\beta_{ij})$, which satisfies Condition C. Then, it can be of several forms. But, it is easy to check that the analysis in all cases can be reduced to the cases depicted in the following two forms:

$$\text{(i) } T = (\beta_{ij}) = \begin{bmatrix} * & * & - \\ + & + & * \\ + & + & * \end{bmatrix} \text{ or (ii) } T = (\beta_{ij}) = \begin{bmatrix} * & * & - \\ * & * & - \\ + & + & * \end{bmatrix}. \tag{29}$$

Consider (29)(i) first. For (R) to hold, we must clearly have $\beta_{11} < 0$ and $\beta_{12} < 0$. But, then the first row of T would violate (R).

Next, consider (29)(ii). If $\beta_{33} \leq 0$, then the third column of T violates (R). However, if $\beta_{33} > 0$, then the third row of T violates (R).

3.4. A converse result on sign patterns

We now investigate whether the sign-pattern restriction described in Theorem 1, together with (R), exhaust all the restrictions imposed by our framework on the relationship between commodity prices and factor rewards. Qualitatively, it does, as the following result notes.

THEOREM 2. *Let $T = (\beta_{ij})$ be an $n \times n$ non-singular matrix, whose column sums are equal to 1. Suppose T satisfies (R), and does not satisfy Condition C of Theorem 1, even after all possible independent renumberings of its rows and columns. Then, there is an $n \times n$ positive non-singular matrix $S = (\alpha_{ij})$, whose column sums are equal to 1, such that the inverse of S has the same sign pattern as T.*

PROOF. We can apply the theorem of Fiedler and Grone (1981, p. 240)[16] to obtain an $n \times n$ positive non-singular matrix $A = (a_{ij})$; such that the inverse of A (denoted by $B = (b_{ij})$) has the same sign pattern as T.

Define, for each $j \in \{1, \ldots, n\}$:

$$\sigma_j = \sum_{i=1}^{n} a_{ij} \tag{30}$$

and denote by Z the diagonal matrix, with $(1/\sigma_1, \ldots, 1/\sigma_n)$ on its diagonal. Then, AZ is an $n \times n$ positive non-singular matrix, whose column sums are equal to 1, by (30). Define $S = AZ$. Then,

$$S^{-1} = Z^{-1}A^{-1} = Z^{-1}B. \tag{31}$$

---

[16] Use the equivalence of statements (i) and (ii) in their theorem.

Since Z^{-1} is a diagonal matrix with $(\sigma_1, \ldots, \sigma_n)$ on its diagonal, the sign pattern of S^{-1} is the same as the sign pattern of B, which is the same as the sign pattern of T.

REMARK. The matrix S obtained in Theorem 2 can be interpreted as a distributive share matrix, arising from the framework described in Section 2, whose inverse exhibits the sign pattern of T. That is, this distributive share matrix, S, would yield precisely the same qualitative features regarding the effect of commodity prices on factor rewards as indicated by the sign pattern of T. In this sense, the sign pattern of T can be rationalized by the distributive share matrix S.

References

Apostol, T. (1957), *Mathematical Analysis*. Addison-Wesley, Reading, MA.

Chang, W.W. (1979), Some theorems of trade and general equilibrium with many goods and factors. *Econometrica* 47, 709–726.

Chipman, J.S. (1969), Factor price equalization and the Stolper-Samuelson theorem. *International Economic Review* 10, 399–406.

Ethier, W. (1974), Some of the theorems of international trade with many goods and factors. *Journal of International Economics* 4, 199–206.

Ethier, W. (1984), Higher Dimensional Issues in Trade Theory. In: Jones, R.W., Kenen, P.B. (Eds.), *Handbook of International Economics, Volume 1: International Trade Theory*. North-Holland, Amsterdam, pp. 131–184.

Fiedler, M., Grone, R. (1981), Characterizations of sign patterns of inverse-positive matrices. *Linear Algebra and Its Applications* 40, 237–245.

Inada, K.I. (1971), The production coefficient matrix and the Stolper-Samuelson condition. *Econometrica* 39, 219–240.

Johnson, C.R., Leighton, F.T., Robinson, H.A. (1979), Sign patterns of inverse-positive matrices. *Linear Algebra and Its Applications* 24, 75–83.

Jones, R.W. (1965), The structure of simple general equilibrium models. *Journal of Political Economy* 73, 557–572.

Jones, R.W. (1975), Income distribution and effective protection in a multicommodity trade model. *Journal of Economic Theory* 11, 1–15.

Jones, R.W. (1985), Relative prices and real factor rewards: a reinterpretation. *Economics Letters* 19, 47–49.

Jones, R.W. (2006), "Protection and real wages": the history of an idea. *Japanese Economic Review* 57, 1–21.

Jones, R.W., Kierzkowski, H. (1986), Neighborhood production structures with an application to the theory of international trade. *Oxford Economic Papers* 38, 59–76.

Jones, R.W., Marjit, S. (1985), A simple production model with Stolper-Samuelson properties. *International Economic Review* 26, 565–567.

Jones, R.W., Marjit, S., Mitra, T. (1993), The Stolper-Samuelson theorem: links to dominant diagonals. In: Becker, R.A., Boldrin, M., Jones, R.W., Thomson, W. (Eds.), *General Equilibrium, Growth and Trade*, vol. II. Academic Press, New York, pp. 429–441.

Jones, R.W., Mitra, T. (1995), Share ribs and income distribution. *Review of International Economics* 3, 36–52.

Jones, R.W., Neary, J.P. (1984), The positive theory of international trade. In: Jones, R.W., Kenen, P.B. (Eds.), *Handbook of International Economics, Volume 1: International Trade Theory*. North-Holland, Amsterdam, pp. 1–62.

Jones, R.W., Scheinkman, J.A. (1977), The relevance of the two-sector production model in trade theory. *Journal of Political Economy* 85, 909–935.

Kemp, M.C., Wan, H.Y. (1976), Relatively simple generalizations of the Stolper-Samuelson and Samuelson-Rybczynski theorems. In: Kemp, M.C. (Ed.), *Three Topics in the Theory of International Trade*. North-Holland, Amsterdam, pp. 49–59.

Kemp, M.C., Wegge, L.L. (1969), On the relation between commodity prices and factor rewards. *International Economic Review* 10, 407–413.

Mitra, T., Jones, R.W. (1999), Factor shares and the Chipman condition. In: Moore, J., Riezman, R., Melvin, J. (Eds.), *Trade, Theory and Econometrics: Essays in Honor of John S. Chipman*. Routledge, London, pp. 125–133.

Nikaido, H. (1968), *Convex Structures and Economic Theory*. Academic Press, New York.

Stolper, W., Samuelson, P.A. (1941), Protection and real wages. *Review of Economics Studies* 9, 58–73.

Uekawa, Y. (1971), Generalization of the Stolper-Samuelson theorem. *Econometrica* 39, 197–217.

CHAPTER 8

Comparative Statics in a Two-Factor Multi-Commodity Model without Factor Price Equalization

Siu-kee Wong

Department of International Economics and Trade, Nankai University, China
E-mail address: ecswsk@nus.edu.sg

Abstract
When the factor endowments of two trading countries do not lie in the same diversification cone, trade in commodities may not reduce the international factor return differentials. This chapter specifies some conditions of the demand function in a two-factor, infinite-good model that guarantee partial factor price equalization. The wage-rental ratios of two trading countries are convergent if goods farther apart are poorer substitutes than goods closer together in the factor-intensity ranking. This generalizes the result in the literature, which is usually obtained under the assumption of Cobb–Douglas utility and production functions.

Keywords: Factor price equalization, comparative statics, factor-intensity ranking, infinite-good model

JEL classification: F11

1. Introduction

Factor price equalization (FPE) has been used as a simplifying assumption in many theoretical and empirical models. Although FPE may not be a good approximation to the real world economy, it is often assumed for convenience. Increasingly, the restrictiveness of the FPE assumption is noticed in both empirical and theoretical works. Once the FPE assumption is dropped, changes in specialization pattern have to be taken into account and the results in comparative statics analyses may not be the same. For example, Jones (2002) stressed that how technical progress affects factor prices crucially depends on whether the production pattern of a country is altered. In this chapter, I will examine a comparative static problem

Frontiers of Economics and Globalization
Volume 4 ISSN: 1574-8715
DOI: 10.1016/S1574-8715(08)04008-6

in a full-fledged general equilibrium model without assuming FPE. In particular, would international trade bring the factor prices of the trading countries closer to each other? Some earlier discussions like Ohlin (1952, Chapter 2) argued that international trade would only partially equalize factor prices between trading countries even if all countries use the same production techniques. Not much work has been done to examine the conditions for partial FPE. Pearce (1970, Chapter 16), Uzawa (1959), Deardorff (1986) and Falvey (1999) are exceptions.[1]

It is well known that the demand condition can drive trading countries to different specialization patterns and FPE does not hold as a result. Using a two-factor, four-commodity example, Deardorff (1986) argued that international trade in consumption goods may lead to divergence of the factor price ratios. In the example, the utility function takes the form $u(x_1 + x_3, x_2 + x_4)$, where goods are indexed in ascending labor intensity. Since there are two pairs of perfect substitutes, the model can be analyzed in terms of two composite goods. This would create factor intensities reversal in the technology of the two composite goods and commodity trade might lead to divergence of the factor price ratios of these two countries. Deardorff also showed that for Cobb–Douglas production and utility functions, trade in consumption goods would reduce the international factor price differentials. Using similar assumptions, Xu (1993) also showed partial FPE in a continuum good model. In a model with general production structure, Falvey (1999) found that for two countries with small endowment differences and identical production technology, commodity trade tends to bring factor price convergence. It would be interesting to know whether the partial FPE result holds without the assumptions of Cobb–Douglas utility and production functions or small endowment differences.

This chapter considers partial FPE between two countries with large endowment differences in a two-factor, multi-commodity model for rather general production technology. It is assumed that preferences are homothetic and goods closer together in the factor intensities ranking are better substitutes than goods farther apart. The endowments are parameterized in the model such that the autarky and trading equilibria become special cases. It is assumed that there is a continuum of consumption goods so that the specialization pattern and thus the derived demand for factors would change smoothly along the adjustment path.

[1] In contrast, complete FPE has been analyzed in many different ways. Samuelson (1953) studied the FPE problem by considering the inversion of the cost functions. Gale and Nikaido (1965) showed that global univalence of the cost functions holds if the Jacobian of the cost functions is a P-matrix. McKenzie (1955) showed that given factor supplies, factor prices are uniquely determined by good prices and FPE holds when the endowments of the two countries lie in the same diversification cone. The integrated equilibrium approach treats FPE as replication of the integrated equilibrium through international trade. A large volume of works have followed these approaches and searched for conditions for FPE.

Analogous to the analysis in the one-factor model in Wilson (1980), the change in the factor demand is decomposed into several effects to identify what changes have taken place. The change in factor demand due to changes in specialization pattern is referred to as the specialization effect. The output effect and factor substitution effect capture the variations in the factor demand caused by changes in outputs and production techniques, respectively. It will be shown that the factor price ratios of the two trading countries change monotonically towards each other along a path connecting the autarky equilibrium and the trading equilibrium.

The chapter is organized as follows. In Section 2, the model and the assumptions will be specified. In Sections 3 and 4, I examine the comparative statics for the equilibria with and without FPE, respectively. In Section 5, I consider the global structure of the path connecting the autarky equilibrium and the trading equilibrium. In Section 6, some concluding remarks will be drawn. The proofs are provided in the Appendix.

2. *The model*

The model is similar to the one in Dornbusch *et al.* (1980). Let there be two countries, home and foreign. The variables associated with the foreign country would be indicated with asterisk. There is a continuum of consumption goods and let [0,1] be the set of consumption goods. There are two factors of production, labor and capital. It is assumed that there is no factor intensity reversal for any pair of commodities. Denote the labor and capital endowments of the home country by L and K, respectively. The set of commodities are indexed in ascending order of capital intensity. The following conditions are imposed on the production technology.

ASSUMPTION A1. The production technologies of the two countries are identical. There is no joint production. The production function for each good is concave and exhibits constant returns to scale.

Let w, r and $\omega \equiv w/r$ be the wage, rental and the wage–rental ratio, respectively. Denote the capital and labor used for producing one unit of good j by $a_{Kj}(\omega)$ and $a_{Lj}(\omega)$.

ASSUMPTION A2. The input coefficients $a_{Kj}(\omega)$ and $a_{Lj}(\omega)$ are continuously differentiable in j and ω. Moreover, $0 < a_{Kj}(\omega)/a_{Lj}(\omega) < \infty$, $\lim_{\omega \to 0} a_{Kj}(\omega)/a_{Lj}(\omega) = 0$ and $\lim_{\omega \to \infty} a_{Kj}(\omega)/a_{Lj}(\omega) = \infty$ for all $\omega > 0$ and all $j \in [0, 1]$.

ASSUMPTION A3. (No Factor Intensities Reversal): $a_{Kj}(\omega)/a_{Lj}(\omega) < a_{Ki}(\omega)/a_{Li}(\omega)$ for any $i > j$ and all $\omega \in R_{++}$.

The consumption space is assumed to be the positive cone $C^{++}[0, 1] = \{x \in C[0, 1] : x(j) > 0, \forall j \in [0, 1]\}$ with the sup norm $\|x\| = \sup_{j \in [0,1]} |x_j|$.

Let $f : C^{++}[0,1] \times R_{+} \to C^{++}[0,1]$ be the Marshallian demand function derived from utility maximization subject to the budget constraint $pf(p,M) \equiv \int_0^1 p_j f_j(p,M)\mathrm{d}j = M$, where p and M are commodity prices and income, respectively.

Assumption B1. (Identical and Homothetic Preferences): For all $(p,M) \in C^{++}[0,1] \times R_{+}$, $f(p,M) = f^{*}(p,M)$ and $f(p,\delta M) = \delta f(p,M)$ for any $\delta > 0$.

Assumption B2. The demand function f is continuously differentiable.[2]

The derivative $Df(p,M) : C[0,1] \times R \to C[0,1]$ can be written as

$$Df(p,M)(g,m) = \frac{\partial f(p,M)}{\partial p}(g) + \frac{\partial f(p,M)}{\partial M}(m).$$

For convenience, the price and quantity of good j are written as p_j and x_j instead of $p(j)$ and $x(j)$. Consider the demand for good j as a function $f_j : C^{++}[0,1] \times R_{+} \to R_{+}$ defined by $f_j(p,M) = f(p,M)(j)$. Lemma 1 shows that $Df(p,M)$ has a convenient form.

Lemma 1. *Under Assumption* B2, f_j *is continuously differentiable in* (p, M) *for all* $j \in [0,1]$. *Moreover, for all* $(g,m) \in C[0,1] \times R$,

$$\frac{\partial f(p,M)}{\partial p}(g)(j) = \frac{\partial f_j(p,M)}{\partial p}(g)$$

and

$$\frac{\partial f(p,M)}{\partial M}(m)(j) = \frac{\partial f_j(p,M)}{\partial M}(m).$$

The substitution effect is defined by a function $s(p,M) : C[0,1] \to [0,1]$ such that:

$$s(p,M)(g) \equiv \frac{\partial f(p,M)}{\partial p}(g) + \frac{\partial f(p,M)}{\partial M}\int_0^1 g(j) f_j(p,M)\mathrm{d}j.$$

By Lemma 1, I can rewrite the substitution effect on the demand for good j as a function $s_j(p,M) : C[0,1] \to R$ such that

$$s_j(p,M)(g) \equiv \frac{\partial f_j(p,M)}{\partial p}(g) + \frac{\partial f_j(p,M)}{\partial M}\int_0^1 g(j) f_j(p,M)\mathrm{d}j. \tag{1}$$

[2] See the appendix for the definition of the Frechet derivative. In infinite dimensional space, a demand function may not be differentiable or even not well defined, as shown by Araujo (1988). Chichilnisky and Zhou (1998), however, showed that if the utility function is additively separable and the consumption and price sets are $C^{++}(T, R^n)$, where T is any compact manifold, the excess demand function is well defined and differentiable.

Similar to the finite-commodity case, for homothetic preferences, the Marshallian demand satisfies the "law of demand" so that the price and demand change in the opposite direction on average.

LEMMA 2. *Under Assumption* B1-2,

$$\int_0^1 g(j)\frac{\partial f_j(p,M)}{\partial p}(g)\mathrm{d}j \leq 0, \text{for all } g \in C[0,1].$$

The law of demand ensures that the derived demand for factors are well behaved in an integrated world equilibrium. In the absence of FPE, however, the factor demand functions can still exhibit irregularities. Two more conditions on the compensated demand are needed.

ASSUMPTION B3. (Net substitutability): For $p, p' \in C^{++}[0,1]$, if $p'_j \geq p_j$ for all $j \in [0,1]$ or $p'_j \leq p_j$ for all $j \in [0,1]$, then $[p'_i - p_i]$ $[f_j(p', p'f(p,M)) - f_j(p,M)] > 0$ for $p'_i \neq p_i$ and $p'_j = p_j$.

ASSUMPTION B4. Let $h, i \in [0,1]$ with $i < h$ and $p, p' \in C^{++}[0,1]$. If $p'_j \geq p_j$ for all $j > h$ and $p'_j = p_j$ for all $j \leq h$, then

$$\frac{f_h(p', p'f(p,M))}{f_h(p,M)} \geq \frac{f_i(p', p'f(p,M))}{f_i(p,M)}.$$

If $p'_j \geq p_j$ for all $j < i$ and $p'_j = p_j$ for all $j \geq i$, then

$$\frac{f_h(p', p'f(p,M))}{f_h(p,M)} \leq \frac{f_i(p', p'f(p,M))}{f_i(p,M)}.$$

Assumption B3 implies that $s_j(p,M)(g) \geq 0$ for $g \in C^{+}[0,1]$, with $g(j) = 0$. Assumption B4 means that goods closer together in the factor intensities ranking are better substitutes than goods farther apart. One interpretation for this condition is that the index set [0,1] indicates the quality of a good, which is determined by the production technique. For example, higher input of physical or human capital is needed in production of higher quality product. Naturally, the substitutability between any two commodities depends on the difference in their qualities.[3]

The world economy is parameterized in the following way. The sizes of the countries are determined by two parameters $(\alpha, \beta) \in (0,1] \times (0,1]$, while the factor proportions are determined by some fixed $(\bar{K}, \bar{L})$ and $(\bar{K}^*, \bar{L}^*)$ such that the factor endowments equal $(\alpha\bar{K}, \alpha\bar{L}, \beta\bar{K}^*, \beta\bar{L}^*)$.[4]

[3] Falvey (1981) analyzed a similar continuum–good model and also interpreted it in terms of quality differentiation. Its comparative statics results, however, are not based on the properties of the commodity–demand functions.

[4] Note that the trading economy is not well defined for $\alpha = 0$ or $\beta = 0$. In Section 4, the domain of α is extended to [0,1]. When $\alpha = 0$, ω^* is equal to the autarkic factor price ratio of the foreign country.

Without loss in generality, assume that $\bar{K}/\bar{L}<\bar{K}^*/\bar{L}^*$. These countries trade goods only and factors are immobile across countries. When $\alpha=\beta=1$, the equilibrium is just the trading equilibrium of the world economy with endowments $\left(\bar{K},\bar{L},\bar{K}^*,\bar{L}^*\right)$. When $\beta=1$ and $\alpha\rightarrow 0$, ω^* approaches the factor price ratio of the foreign country in autarky. Similarly, when $\alpha=1$ and $\beta\rightarrow 0$, ω converges to the autarkic factor price ratio of the home country. The factor price ratios of these equilibria will be compared to see whether international factor price differentials decrease under free trade.

3. *An integrated world equilibrium*

I will first consider the benchmark case where FPE holds. Fix $\beta=1$ and allow α to vary. It is possible that FPE holds for some $\alpha<1$ even though FPE does not hold when $\alpha=1$. When FPE occurs, the trading equilibrium is identical to an integrated world equilibrium, which can be characterized by the market-clearing conditions of the two factors. By Walras law, one of the two equilibrium equations is redundant. Denote the equilibrium wage, rental and wage–rental ratio in the integrated world economy by $\bar{w},\bar{r}$ and $\bar{\omega}$, respectively. The integrated world equilibrium is characterized by:

$$G(\bar{\omega},\alpha)=\ln\frac{\int_0^1 a_{Kj}(\bar{\omega})f_j(p,M+M^*)\mathrm{d}j}{\int_0^1 a_{Lj}(\bar{\omega})f_j(p,M+M^*)\mathrm{d}j}-\ln\frac{\alpha\bar{K}+\bar{K}^*}{\alpha\bar{L}+\bar{L}^*}=0 \tag{2}$$

where

$$p_j=\bar{w}a_{lj}(\bar{\omega})+\bar{r}a_{kj}(\bar{\omega}),\quad \forall\, j\in[0,1], \tag{3}$$

$$M=\alpha[\bar{w}\bar{L}+\bar{r}\bar{K}] \tag{4}$$

and

$$M^*=\bar{w}\bar{L}^*+\bar{r}\bar{K}^* \tag{5}$$

Let good n be the numeraire where n is implicitly determined by $a_{Kn}(\bar{\omega})/a_{Ln}(\bar{\omega})=(\alpha\bar{K}+\bar{K}^*)/\alpha\bar{L}+\bar{L}^*$. Some simple algebraic manipulation yields

$$\frac{\partial p_j}{\partial\bar{\omega}}=\frac{[\alpha\bar{K}+\bar{K}^*]a_{Ln}(\bar{\omega})}{[\bar{\omega}a_{Ln}(\bar{\omega})+a_{Kn}(\bar{\omega})]^2}\left[\frac{a_{Lj}(\bar{\omega})}{\alpha\bar{L}+\bar{L}^*}-\frac{a_{Kj}(\bar{\omega})}{\alpha\bar{K}+\bar{K}^*}\right]. \tag{6}$$

Thus $(\partial p_j/\partial\bar{\omega})>0$ if and only if $a_{Lj}(\bar{\omega})/a_{Kj}(\bar{\omega})>(\alpha\bar{L}+\bar{L}^*)/(\alpha\bar{K}+\bar{K}^*)$. Differentiate (2) and use (6) to get

$$\frac{\partial G}{\partial\bar{\omega}}=\int_0^1\left[\frac{1}{\alpha\bar{K}+\bar{K}^*}\frac{\partial a_{Kj}(\bar{\omega})}{\partial\bar{\omega}}-\frac{1}{\alpha\bar{L}+\bar{L}^*}\frac{\partial a_{Lj}(\bar{\omega})}{\partial\bar{\omega}}\right]f_j(p,M+M^*)\mathrm{d}j$$
$$-\frac{[\bar{\omega}a_{Ln}(\bar{\omega})+a_{Kn}(\bar{\omega})]^2}{\left[\alpha\bar{K}+\bar{K}^*\right]a_{Ln}(\bar{\omega})}\int_0^1\frac{\partial p_j}{\partial\bar{\omega}}\frac{\partial f_j(p,M+M^*)}{\partial p}\left(\frac{\partial p}{\partial\bar{\omega}}\right)\mathrm{d}j$$
$$+\int_0^1\left[\frac{a_{Kj}(\bar{\omega})}{\alpha\bar{K}+\bar{K}^*}-\frac{a_{Lj}(\bar{\omega})}{\alpha\bar{L}+\bar{L}^*}\right]\frac{\partial f_j(p,M+M^*)}{\partial M}\left(\frac{\partial(M+M^*)}{\partial\bar{\omega}}\right)\mathrm{d}j \quad (7)$$

$$\frac{\partial G}{\partial\alpha}=\frac{\bar{L}}{\alpha\bar{L}+\bar{L}^*}-\frac{\bar{K}}{\alpha\bar{K}+\bar{K}^*}>0.$$

The first term on the RHS in (7) is the factor substitution effect and the last two terms constitute the output effects. Obviously, the factor substitution effect is positive. By homotheticity, $\partial f_j(p,M+M^*)/\partial M = f_j(p,M+M^*)/(M+M^*)$ and the third term in (7) is zero. By Lemma 2, the second term is positive. In words, a rise in $\bar{\omega}$ raises the relative prices of the labor-intensive goods and consumers will buy more capital-intensive goods. Thus, $(\partial G/\partial\bar{\omega})>0$ and by the implicit function theorem, $\bar{\omega}$ is locally a function of α and

$$\frac{d\bar{\omega}}{d\alpha}=-\frac{(\partial G/\partial\alpha)}{(\partial G/\partial\bar{\omega})}<0. \quad (8)$$

Similarly, the effect of a change in β on $\bar{\omega}$ can be shown:

$$\frac{d\bar{\omega}}{d\beta}>0. \quad (9)$$

4. Trading equilibrium without FPE

When trade in consumption goods does not equalize factor prices of the two countries, the zero profit conditions and the trade balance would determine the pattern of specialization. Choose $r=1$. The equilibrium prices must satisfy the following competitiveness condition

$$p_j=\min\{\omega a_{Lj}(\omega)+a_{Kj}(\omega),r^*[\omega a_{Lj}(\omega^*)+a_{Kj}(\omega^*)]\},\quad \forall j\in[0,1].$$

Given the factor prices, the competitive margin $z\in[0,1]$ is determined by

$$p_z=\omega a_{Lz}(\omega)+a_{Kz}(\omega)=w^*a_{Lz}(\omega^*)+r^*a_{Kz}(\omega^*), \quad (10)$$

since $K/L<K^*/L^*$, $\omega<\omega^*$ and

$$w^*a_{Lj}(\omega^*)+r^*a_{Kj}(\omega^*)>p_j=\omega a_{Lj}(\omega)+a_{Kj}(\omega),\quad \forall\, j<z \quad (11)$$

$$\omega a_{Lj}(\omega) + a_{Kj}(\omega) > p_j = w^* a_{Lj}(\omega^*) + r^* a_{Kj}(\omega^*), \quad \forall\, j > z. \tag{12}$$

Use (10) to solve for r^*, p, M and M^*:

$$r^* = \frac{\omega a_{Lz}(\omega) + a_{Kz}(\omega)}{\omega^* a_{Lz}(\omega^*) + a_{Kz}(\omega^*)}, \tag{13}$$

$$p_j = \left\{ \begin{array}{c} \omega a_{Lj}(\omega) + a_{Kj}(\omega), \quad \forall j \in [0, z] \\ \dfrac{\omega a_{Lz}(\omega) + a_{Kz}(\omega)}{\omega^* a_{Lz}(\omega^*) + a_{Kz}(\omega^*)} \left[\omega^* a_{Lj}(\omega^*) + a_{Kj}(\omega^*)\right], \quad \forall j \in [0, z] \end{array} \right\}, \tag{14}$$

$$M = \omega L + K \tag{15}$$

and

$$M^* = \frac{\omega a_{Lz}(\omega) + a_{Kz}(\omega)}{\omega^* a_{Lz}(\omega^*) + a_{Kz}(\omega^*)} [\omega^* L^* + K^*]. \tag{16}$$

Let $V \equiv (\alpha\bar{L}, \alpha\bar{K}, \beta\bar{L}^*, \beta\bar{K}^*)$. When ω, ω^*, z and (α,β) are given, p, M and M^* are also uniquely determined. Following Dornbusch *et al.* (1980), I use the derived factor demand and the trade balance to characterize the equilibrium.[5]

$$E(\omega, \omega^*, z, V) = \ln \frac{\int_0^z a_{Kj}(\omega) f_j(p, M + M^*)\mathrm{d}j}{\int_0^z a_{Lj}(\omega) f_j(p, M + M^*)\mathrm{d}j} - \ln \frac{K}{L} = 0 \tag{17}$$

$$E^*(\omega, \omega^*, z, V) = \ln \frac{\int_z^1 a_{Kj}(\omega^*) f_j(p, M + M^*)\mathrm{d}j}{\int_z^1 a_{Lj}(\omega^*) f_j(p, M + M^*)\mathrm{d}j} - \ln \frac{K^*}{L^*} = 0 \tag{18}$$

$$B(\omega, \omega^*, z, V) = \int_0^z p_j f_j(p, M^*)\mathrm{d}j - \int_z^1 p_j f_j(p, M)\mathrm{d}j = 0, \tag{19}$$

where p, M and M^* are determined by Equations (14)–(16).

4.1. Specialization effects

A rise in z affects the derived factor demand and trade balance in two ways. The factor demand in the home country increases directly from the expansion of the range of commodities produced. In addition, this change is compatible with production efficiency only when the cost of production in the foreign country rises. Consider an increase in the competitive margin

[5] Alternatively, the equilibrium can be defined by zero excess demand for factors in the trading world economy as in Helpman (1976) and Kehoe (1984). It can be easily shown that these market-clearing conditions are equivalent to (17)–(19).

from z to z' for given ω and ω^*. By Equations (10)–(16), $\hat{p}_j = \hat{M}^* = \hat{r}^* = \hat{w}^* > \hat{p}_i = \hat{M} = 0$ for all $j \in [z', 1]$ and all $i \in [0, z]$, where the hat notation "^" signifies the proportional change of the variable underneath. The changes in prices and income in turn affect the derived factor demand. Obviously, given prices and income, an increase in z raises the value of both E and E^* since the goods ranged from z to z' are capital-intensive in the home country but labor-intensive in the foreign country. This is still true even when the changes in prices and income are taken into account.

Lemma 3. Under Assumptions A1-3 and B1-4,

(i) if $B(\omega, \omega^*, z, V) = 0$, then $[z'-z]B(\omega, \omega^*, z', V) > 0$ for any $z' \neq z$,
(ii) E and E^* are increasing in z.

Let $\tilde{z}$ be the competitive margin satisfying $B(\omega, \omega^*, \tilde{z}, V) = 0$. By Lemma 3, $\tilde{z}$ is uniquely determined by (19) and is a function of ω, ω^* and V. A rise in ω signifies an improvement in the terms of trade for the home country since the home country exports labor-intensive goods. By contrast, a rise in ω^* worsens the foreign country's terms of trade because its exports are capital-intensive. By homotheticity and net substitutability of preferences, an improvement in the home country's terms of trade worsen its trade balance. This should be offset by an expansion of the range of commodities produced in the home country.[6] Figure 1 illustrates the adjustment required to keep trade balance in equilibrium. The curves U_j and U_j' are the unit-value curves for industry j before and after the change, respectively. Initially the home country's production ranges from good 0 to good $\tilde{z}$. A rise in $\tilde{z}$ is indicated by the shift in initial unit-value isocost line from I_1 to I_2. The prices of the goods produced in the foreign country also increase, but in a smaller proportion, indicated by the unit-value isocost line I_2^*. At the initial competitive margin $\tilde{z}$, the home country has trade balance deficit and has to produce a larger range of goods to restore trade balance equilibrium. This is only possible if the cost of production in the foreign country increases further. This shifts the unit-value isocost line of the foreign country to I_3^*, and raises the competitive margin to $\tilde{z}'$.

For the formal comparative static analysis, differentiability has to be assured.[7] I impose the following innocuous condition.

Assumption C1. E, E^* and B are twice continuously differentiable functions and $(\partial B/\partial z) \neq 0$.

---

[6] Similar conditions were used in Hahn (1959) in the analysis of the effect of devaluation on balance of payment.

[7] In general, p is not differentiable in z. To see this, let i be the initial equilibrium competitive margin. While $(\partial p_j/\partial z) = 0$ for all $j \in (i, 1]$, there is $\varepsilon > 0$ such that $(\partial p_j/\partial z) = (p_j/\theta)(\partial\theta/\partial z) > \varepsilon > 0$ for all $j \in [0, i)$, where $\theta = [\omega a_{Lz}(\omega) + a_{Kz}(\omega)]/[\omega^* a_{Lz}(\omega^*) + a_{Kz}(\omega^*)]$.

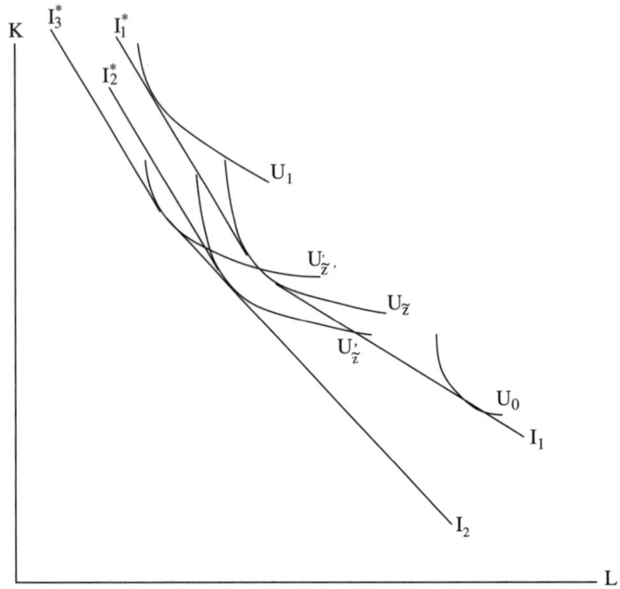

Fig. 1. ***The relationship between*** α **and** z**.**

By Lemma 3 and Assumption C1, $(\partial E/\partial z) \geq 0$ and $(\partial E^*/\partial z) \geq 0$. Moreover, $\tilde{z}$ is locally a differentiable function of ω and ω^* and $(\partial \tilde{z}/\partial \omega) = -(\partial B/\partial \omega)/(\partial B/\partial z)$ and $(\partial \tilde{z}/\partial \omega^*) = -(\partial B/\partial \omega^*)/(\partial B/\partial z)$.

Lemma 4. *Under Assumptions* A1-3, B1-4 *and* C1, $(\partial \tilde{z}/\partial \omega) > 0$ *and* $(\partial \tilde{z}/\partial \omega^*) > 0$.

Substitute $\tilde{z}$ into (17) and (18) and rewrite the equilibrium conditions as:

$$\tilde{E}(\omega, \omega^*, V) = \ln \frac{\int_0^{\tilde{z}} a_{Kj}(\omega) f_j(p, M + M^*) \mathrm{d}j}{\int_0^{\tilde{z}} a_{Lj}(\omega) f_j(p, M + M^*) \mathrm{d}j} - \ln \frac{K}{L} = 0 \tag{20}$$

$$\tilde{E}^*(\omega, \omega^*, V) = \ln \frac{\int_{\tilde{z}}^1 a_{Kj}(\omega^*) f_j(p, M + M^*) \mathrm{d}j}{\int_{\tilde{z}}^1 a_{Lj}(\omega^*) f_j(p, M + M^*) \mathrm{d}j} - \ln \frac{K^*}{L^*} = 0. \tag{21}$$

The effects of a change in ω and ω^* on the values of $\tilde{E}$ and $\tilde{E}^*$ through the change in $\tilde{z}$ are referred to as the specialization effect. When the competitive margin rises from $\tilde{z}$ to $\tilde{z}'$, the capital–labor ratios of the derived factor demand in both countries rise because the goods ranged from $\tilde{z}$ and $\tilde{z}'$ are capital-intensive in the home country but labor-intensive in the foreign country. Moreover, as discussed above, an increase in $\tilde{z}$ will raise the prices of the goods produced in the foreign country. Consequently, the home country faces a higher demand for its production while the opposite happens in the foreign country.

4.2. Local comparative statics

Consider the effect of a change in α on the factor price ratios. Differentiate (20) and (21) totally to get:

$$\begin{bmatrix} \frac{\partial \tilde{E}}{\partial \omega} & \frac{\partial \tilde{E}}{\partial \omega^*} \\ \frac{\partial \tilde{E}^*}{\partial \omega} & \frac{\partial \tilde{E}^*}{\partial \omega^*} \end{bmatrix} \begin{bmatrix} \frac{d\omega}{d\alpha} \\ \frac{d\omega^*}{d\alpha} \end{bmatrix} = \begin{bmatrix} -\frac{\partial \tilde{E}}{\partial \alpha} \\ -\frac{\partial \tilde{E}^*}{\partial \alpha} \end{bmatrix} \tag{22}$$

Denote the 2×2 matrix on the LHS of (22) by Δ. The term $\partial \tilde{E}/\partial \omega$ can be written as follows:

$$\begin{aligned} \frac{\partial \tilde{E}}{\partial \omega} &= \frac{\partial E}{\partial z}\frac{\partial \tilde{z}}{\partial \omega} + \frac{\partial E}{\partial \omega} \\ &= \frac{\partial E}{\partial z}\frac{\partial \tilde{z}}{\partial \omega} + \int_0^{\tilde{z}} \left[\frac{1}{K}\frac{\partial a_{Kj}(\omega)}{\partial \omega} - \frac{1}{L}\frac{\partial a_{Lj}(\omega)}{\partial \omega}\right] f_j(p, M + M^*)\mathrm{d}j \\ &\quad + \int_0^{\tilde{z}} \left[\frac{a_{Kj}(\omega)}{K} - \frac{a_{Lj}(\omega)}{L}\right] \frac{\partial f_j(p, M + M^*)}{\partial p}\left(\frac{\partial p}{\partial \omega}\right)\mathrm{d}j \\ &\quad - \int_0^{\tilde{z}} \left[\frac{a_{Kj}(\omega) f_j(p, M^*)}{K} - \frac{a_{Lj}(\omega) f_j(p, M^*)}{L}\right] \frac{1}{M}\frac{\partial M}{\partial \omega}\mathrm{d}j. \end{aligned} \tag{23}$$

The first and the second terms on the RHS in (23) are the specialization effect and the factor substitution effect, respectively. The output effect comprises the last two terms, which show the change in the derived factor demand induced by changes in prices and income. Obviously, the factor substitution effect is positive. As shown in the previous section, the specialization effect is also positive. By homotheticity,

$$\frac{M}{f_j(p, M)}\frac{\partial f_j(p, M)}{\partial M} = 1 \quad \text{for all } j \in [0, 1].$$

Thus the output effect induced by changes in income vanishes. The other terms in the matrix Δ can also be written as:

$$\begin{aligned} \frac{\partial \tilde{E}^*}{\partial \omega^*} &= \frac{\partial E^*}{\partial z}\frac{\partial \tilde{z}}{\partial \omega^*} + \int_{\tilde{z}}^{1} \left[\frac{1}{K^*}\frac{\partial a_{Kj}(\omega^*)}{\partial \omega^*} - \frac{1}{L^*}\frac{\partial a_{Lj}(\omega^*)}{\partial \omega^*}\right] f_j(p, M + M^*)\mathrm{d}j \\ &\quad + \int_{\tilde{z}}^{1} \left[\frac{a_{Kj}(\omega^*)}{K^*} - \frac{a_{Lj}(\omega^*)}{L^*}\right] \frac{\partial f_j(p, M + M^*)}{\partial p}\left(\frac{\partial p}{\partial \omega^*}\right)\mathrm{d}j \\ \frac{\partial \tilde{E}}{\partial \omega^*} &= \frac{\partial E}{\partial z}\frac{\partial \tilde{z}}{\partial \omega^*} + \int_0^{\tilde{z}} \left[\frac{a_{Kj}(\omega)}{K} - \frac{a_{Lj}(\omega)}{L}\right] \frac{\partial f_j(p, M + M^*)}{\partial p}\left(\frac{\partial p}{\partial \omega^*}\right)\mathrm{d}j \\ \frac{\partial \tilde{E}^*}{\partial \omega} &= \frac{\partial E^*}{\partial z}\frac{\partial \tilde{z}}{\partial \omega} + \int_{\tilde{z}}^{1} \left[\frac{a_{Kj}(\omega^*)}{K^*} - \frac{a_{Lj}(\omega^*)}{L^*}\right] \frac{\partial f_j(p, M + M^*)}{\partial p}\left(\frac{\partial p}{\partial \omega}\right)\mathrm{d}j. \end{aligned}$$

The following result concerns the signs of the output effects caused by a change in commodity prices.

LEMMA 5. *Under Assumptions* A1–3 and B1–4, *(i) the output effects in* $\partial\tilde{E}/\partial\omega$ *and* $\partial\tilde{E}^*/\partial\omega^*$ *comprise a positive own price effect and a non-positive cross price effect and (ii)* $(\partial E^*/\partial\omega) \leq 0$ *and* $(\partial E/\partial\omega^*) \leq 0$.

Although the sign of $\partial E/\partial\omega$ may be ambiguous, there is a presumption that it is positive because both the factor substitution effect and the own price output effect are positive. The case $(\partial E/\partial\omega)<0$, which only arises when the cross price effect is very strong, can be considered as unusual. For example, if the preferences are additively separable and homothetic (i.e., CES utility function), the cross price effect will become zero and $(\partial E/\partial\omega)>0$. To see this, for additively separable preferences, the cross price effect for each good is proportional to the income effect and the income effect vanishes by homotheticity.

ASSUMPTION B5. $\dfrac{\partial E}{\partial\omega}>0, \quad \dfrac{\partial E^*}{\partial\omega^*}>0.$

Under Assumption B1, it can be shown that $|\Delta|\geq 0$ if $(\partial\tilde{E}/\partial\omega)>0$. Hence the following result.

LEMMA 6. *Under Assumptions* A1–3, B1–5 *and* C1, $|\Delta|\geq 0$.

An increase in α raises the income of the home country but this has no effect on E and E^* as preferences are homothetic. On the other hand, the higher income of the home country has to be offset by an increase in $\tilde{z}$ to keep the trade balance in equilibrium.

$$\frac{\partial\tilde{E}}{\partial\alpha}=\frac{\partial E}{\partial z}\frac{\partial\tilde{z}}{\partial\alpha}=\frac{\partial E}{\partial z}\frac{\int_{\tilde{z}}^{1} p_j((\partial f_j(p,M))/\partial M)(\partial M/\partial\alpha)\mathrm{d}j}{\partial B/\partial\tilde{z}}>0 \tag{24}$$

$$\frac{\partial\tilde{E}^*}{\partial\alpha}=\frac{\partial E^*}{\partial z}\frac{\partial\tilde{z}}{\partial\alpha}=\frac{\partial E^*}{\partial z}\frac{\int_{\tilde{z}}^{1} p_j((\partial f_j(p,M))/\partial M)(\partial M/\partial\alpha)\mathrm{d}j}{\partial B/\partial\tilde{z}}>0. \tag{25}$$

LEMMA 7. *Under Assumptions* A1–3, B1–5 *and* C1, $(d\omega^*/d\alpha)<0$ *and* $(d\omega/d\beta)>0$.

5. Global analysis

The previous sections only deal with small changes in the parameters. For finite change in α or β from 0 to 1, I need to fill in some details of the global equilibrium structure. For the moment, assume the factor prices of the two countries remain unequal for all $\alpha \in (0, 1]$ and all $\beta \in (0, 1]$. Let (ω^a, ω^{*a}) and (ω^t, ω^{*t}) be the equilibrium factor price ratios under autarky and free trade, respectively. Obviously, setting $\alpha = \beta = 1$ yields the trading equilibrium. To get the autarky equilibrium, the domains of the functions

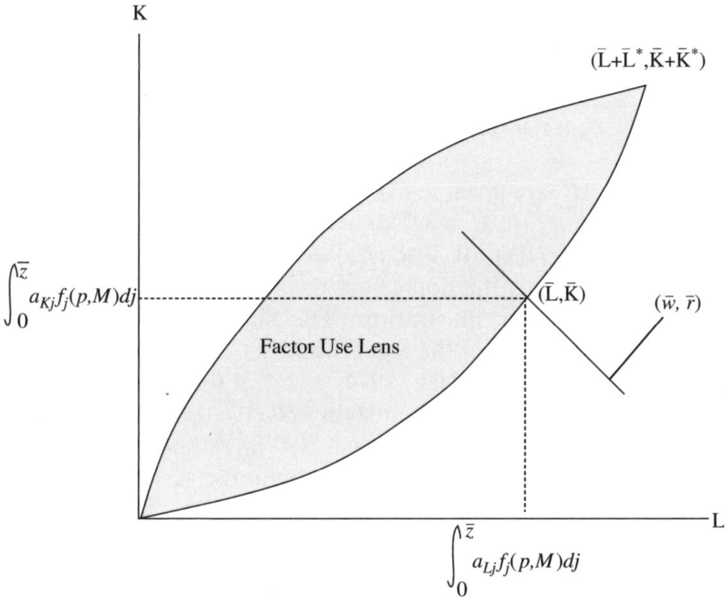

Fig. 2. FPE with complete specialization.

E and E^* have to be extended to encompass the cases of $\alpha = 0$ and $\beta = 0$. If ω and ω^* are differentiable functions of α and β, $\lim_{\alpha \to 0} \omega^* = \omega^{*a}$ and $\lim_{\beta \to 0} \omega = \omega^a$, then by Lemma 7, commodity trade would partially equalize factor prices of the two trading countries.

THEOREM 1. *Under Assumptions* A1–3, B1–5, *and* C1, *if the equilibrium factor price ratios of two countries are different for all* $\alpha \in (0, 1]$ *and all* $\beta \in (0, 1]$, *then* $\omega^{*a} > \omega^{*t} > \omega^t > \omega^a$.

To strengthen the result, the possibility of a regime change between an equilibrium with FPE and one without FPE has to be considered. Figure 2 depicts the FPE region of the economy. A point on the lower boundary of this lens-shape area indicates the total factor uses from sectors 0 to j in the integrated world equilibrium. FPE occurs if and only if the endowment point lies in this area.[8] As α changes, both the endowment point and the FPE area move. There is no guarantee that the endowment stay outside the region throughout the change of α from 0 to 1. A regime change occurs when the endowment point crosses the border of the FPE region as point $(\bar{L}, \bar{K})$ in the diagram. To see how likely this happen, define a function

[8] The analysis of the factor use lens in the finite-good model, see Deardorff (1994).

H:[0,1]$\rightarrow R$ such that

$$H(\alpha) = \ln \frac{\int_{\bar{z}}^{1} a_{Kj}(\bar{\omega}^{*}) f_j(p, M + M^{*}) \mathrm{d}j}{\int_{\bar{z}}^{1} a_{Lj}(\bar{\omega}^{*}) f_j(p, M + M^{*}) \mathrm{d}j} - \ln \frac{\bar{K}^{*}}{\bar{L}^{*}}, \tag{26}$$

where p, M and M^* are given in (3), (4) and (5), $\bar{\omega}$ is implicitly determined by (2) and $\bar{z}$ by $\int_{\bar{z}}^{1} p_j f_j(p, M + M^*)\mathrm{d}j - M^* = 0$. Given $\bar{K}/\bar{L} < \bar{K}^*/\bar{L}^*$, FPE holds if and only if $H(\alpha) \leq 0$. For $H(\alpha) = 0$, FPE holds and yet countries specialize, in particular, the home country produces good j if and only if $j \leq \bar{z}$. See Figure 2 for illustration. The sign of $\partial H/\partial\alpha$ is crucial in determining the structure of the equilibrium set. By the preimage theorem (see, e.g., Guillemin and Pollack, 1974, p. 21), if 0 is a regular value of H, i.e. $(\partial H/\partial\alpha) \neq 0$, for all $\alpha \in [0, 1]$ satisfying $H(\alpha) = 0$, $H^{-1}(0)$ will be a zero-dimensional manifold in the compact set [0,1] and thus a finite set. Unfortunately, the sign of $\partial H/\partial\alpha$ is ambiguous. A rise in α raises the income of the home country and this needs to be offset by a larger $\bar{z}$ and the value of H is raised. On the other hand, $\bar{\omega}$ falls due to a lower world capital–labor ratio. The production techniques become more labor-intensive and the relative prices of the labor-intensive goods also fall. These changes reduce the value of H. However, it can be shown that for almost all distribution of endowments, such change in regime can only happen for a finite number of times as α or β changes from 0 to 1.[9] Accordingly, it is unrestrictive to make the following assumption.

Assumption C2. When α or β changes from 0 to 1, the switches from an equilibrium with FPE to one without FPE or vice versa occur finite times only.

Under Assumption C2, the equilibrium set is the graph of a continuous and piecewise smooth function and the main result follows.

Theorem 2. *Under Assumptions* A1, A2, B1–5 *and* C1-2, $\omega^{*a} > \omega^{*t} \geq \omega^{t} > \omega^{a}$.

6. Concluding remarks

In this chapter, I examine whether partial FPE holds in a multi-commodity, two-factor model. Under the assumption of identical and homothetic preferences, the problem can be considered as the comparative

---

[9] By the transversality theorem, it can be shown that 0 is a regular value of H and its preimage is finite for almost all distribution of endowments. That is to say, a small perturbation in the factor endowments can always restore the regularity of H. For the transversality theorem, see Guillemin and Pollack (1974), for example.

statics for endowment changes. When goods closer together in the factor intensities ranking are better substitutes than goods farther apart, international trade reduces the international factor price differentials. In this chapter, the continuum good model is used to ensure that the derived factor demand is differentiable. Ideally, it can be considered as an approximation to a finite-good model but there is a caveat. When the number of goods is small, the finite-good model may possess very different comparative statics properties.[10] For example, consider a three-good case, in which goods again are indexed in ascending order of capital intensity. Assume FPE does not hold, and the labor-abundant home country produces goods 1 and 2 and the foreign country produces goods 2 and 3. As shown in Jones (1998), a rise in the labor endowment of the home country can raise the wage–rental ratio of the foreign country. Since good 2 is capital-intensive in the home country, a labor endowment increase raises its excess demand and its relative price. But good 2 is labor-intensive in the foreign country and thus the wage–rental ratio there rises. By contrast, a similar endowment change tends to lower the wage–rental ratio of the foreign country in the continuum good model if $(\partial \tilde{E}^* / \partial \omega) \leq 0$, which seems plausible under Assumption B4. Further study on the relationship between the finite-good and the continuum good models should be desirable.

Acknowledgement

This research is supported by the grant under Program 985 for regional economics from the Social Science Foundation at Nankai University.

Appendix

Frechet derivative: Let $(X, \|\|_X)$ and $(Y, \|\|_Y)$ be real normed spaces. Let S be a nonempty open subset of X. Given a mapping $\psi : S \rightarrow Y$ and an element $x \in S$. If there is a continuous linear mapping $D\psi(x) : X \rightarrow Y$ satisfying

$$\lim_{\|g\|_X \rightarrow 0} \frac{\left\| \psi(x+g) - \psi(x) - D\psi(x)(g) \right\|_Y}{\|g\|_X} = 0,$$

then $D\psi(x)$ is called the Frechet derivative of ψ at x.

---

[10] I thank Ronald Jones for reminding me the difference between the continuum good model and the finite-good model some years ago.

Proof of Lemma 1. Consider $\phi_j : C[0,1] \to R$ defined by $\phi_j(g) = g(j)$. Since $\phi_j(\alpha g) = \alpha g(j) = \alpha\phi_j(g)$ and $\phi_j(g+g') = (g+g')(j) = g(j) + g'(j) = \phi_j(g) + \phi_j(g')$, both ϕ_j and $\phi_j \circ Df(p, M)$ are linear. Since f is differentiable, for all $g \in C[0, 1]$.

$$\begin{aligned}
&\lim_{||g||\to 0} \frac{\left|f_j(p+g, M) - f_j(p, M) - \phi_j((\partial f(p, M))/(\partial p))(g)\right|}{||g||} \\
&\quad \leq \lim_{||g||\to 0} \frac{\sup_j \left|f_j(p+g, M) - f_j(p, M) - ((\partial f(p, M))/(\partial p))(g)(j)\right|}{||g||} \\
&\quad = \lim_{||g||\to 0} \frac{\left\|f(p+g, M) - f(p, M) - Df(p, M)(g)\right\|}{||g||} \\
&\quad = 0.
\end{aligned}$$

Hence

$$\phi_j\left(\frac{\partial f(p, M)}{\partial p}(g)\right) = \frac{\partial f_j(p, M)}{\partial p} \quad \text{for all } j.$$

The result follows as the Frechet derivative is unique.

Proof of Lemma 2. First I show that $\int_0^1 g(j)s_j(p, M)(g)\mathrm{d}j \leq 0$ for all $g \in C[0, 1]$. Given any $p, p' \in C^{++}[0, 1]$, $p' \neq tp$ for any $t > 0$, let $g = p' - p$, $p(\theta) = \theta p' + (1-\theta)p$, $0 \leq \theta \leq 1$ and $M(\theta) = p(\theta)f(p, M)$. By the weak axiom of revealed preference,

$$\frac{[p(\theta) - p][f(p(\theta), M(\theta)) - f(p, M)]}{\theta} = \frac{M - pf(p(\theta), M(\theta))}{\theta} < 0.$$

Thus,

$$\begin{aligned}
&\lim_{\theta\to 0} \frac{[p(\theta) - p][f(p(\theta), M(\theta)) - f(p, M)]}{\theta} \\
&\quad = \int_0^1 g(j) \lim_{\theta\to 0} \frac{f_j(p(\theta), M(\theta)) - f_j(p, M)}{\theta} \mathrm{d}j \\
&\quad = \int_0^1 g(j)s_j(p, M)(g)\mathrm{d}j \leq 0.
\end{aligned}$$

By homotheticity, $(\partial f_j(p, M))/(\partial M) = (f_j(p, M))/M$ for all $j \in [0, 1]$. Therefore,

$$\begin{aligned}
\int_0^1 g(j)\frac{\partial f_j(p, M)}{\partial p}(g)\mathrm{d}j &= \int_0^1 g(j)s_j(p, M)(g)\mathrm{d}j \\
&\quad - \int_0^1 g(j) \int_0^1 g(i)f_i(p, M)\mathrm{d}i \frac{\partial f_j(p, M)}{\partial M} \mathrm{d}j \\
&= \int_0^1 g(j)s_j(p, M)(g)\mathrm{d}j - \frac{\left[\int_0^1 g(j)f_j(p, M)\mathrm{d}j\right]^2}{M} \\
&< 0.
\end{aligned}$$

PROOF OF LEMMA 3.

(i) Consider z, z' satisfying $B(\omega, \omega^*, z, V) = 0$ and $z' > z$. The balance of payment of the home country is equal to:

$$B(\omega, \omega^*, z, V) = \int_0^z p_j f_j(p, M + M^*)\mathrm{d}j - M. \tag{27}$$

Let p',M' and $M^{*\prime}$ be the corresponding prices and incomes at z'. By (14)–(16), $M^{*\prime}/M^* = p_i'/p_i > p_j'/p_j > p_h'/p_h = M'/M = 1$, for all $i \in [z'1], j \in (z, z')$ and $h \in [0, z]$. Thus,

$$\begin{aligned} M + M^{*\prime} &= \int_0^z p_j f_j(p, M + M^*)\mathrm{d}j + \frac{M^{*\prime}}{M^*}\int_z^1 p_j f_j(p, M + M^*)\mathrm{d}j \\ &> p' f(p, M + M^*). \end{aligned} \tag{28}$$

Using Assumption B3 and (28), I obtain

$$\begin{aligned} &B(\omega,\omega^*,z',V) - B(\omega,\omega^*,z,V) \\ &= \int_0^{z'} p_j' f_j\big(p', M + M^{*\prime}\big)\mathrm{d}j + \int_0^z p_j f_j\big(p, M + M^*\big)\mathrm{d}j \quad (\text{by}\,(27)) \\ &\geq \int_0^z p_j \big[f_j\big(p', p'f(p, M + M^*)\big) - f_j\big(p, pf(p, M + M^*)\big)\big]\mathrm{d}j \;(\text{by}\,(28)) \\ &\geq 0 \quad (\text{by Assumption B3}). \end{aligned}$$

(ii) For any $z' > z$,

$$\begin{aligned} &\frac{\int_0^{z'} a_{Kj}(\omega) f_j(p', M + M^{*\prime})\mathrm{d}j}{\int_0^{z'} a_{Lj}(\omega) f_j(p', M + M^{*\prime})\mathrm{d}j} \\ &\quad > \frac{\int_0^z a_{Kj}(\omega) f_j(p', M + M^{*\prime})\mathrm{d}j}{\int_0^z a_{Lj}(\omega) f_j(p', M + M^{*\prime})\mathrm{d}j} \\ &\quad = \frac{\int_0^z a_{Kj}(\omega) f_j\big(p', p'f(p, M + M^*)\big)\mathrm{d}j}{\int_0^z a_{Lj}(\omega) f_j\big(p', p'f(p, M + M^*)\big)\mathrm{d}j} \quad (\text{by homotheticity}) \\ &\quad > \frac{\int_0^z a_{Kj}(\omega) f_j(p, M + M^*)\mathrm{d}j}{\int_0^z a_{Lj}(\omega) f_j(p, M + M^*)\mathrm{d}j} \quad (\text{by Assumption B4}). \end{aligned}$$

Thus E is increasing in z. Similarly, $\tilde{E}^*$ is increasing in z.

PROOF OF LEMMA 4. By Lemma 3, $\partial B/\partial z > 0$. Locally $\tilde{z}$ is a continuously differentiable function of (ω, ω^*, α) and $(\partial\tilde{z}/\partial\omega) = -(\partial B/\partial\omega)/(\partial B/\partial z)$, where

$$\begin{aligned} \frac{\partial B}{\partial \omega} &= \int_0^{\tilde{z}} \frac{\partial p_j}{\partial \omega} f_j(p, M^*)\mathrm{d}j + \int_0^{\tilde{z}} p_j \left\{\frac{\partial f_j(p, M)}{\partial p}\left(\frac{\partial p}{\partial \omega}\right) + \frac{\partial f_j(p, M^*)}{\partial M^*}\frac{\partial M^*}{\partial \omega}\right\}\mathrm{d}j \\ &\quad - \int_{\tilde{z}}^1 \frac{\partial p_j}{\partial \omega} f_j(p, M)\mathrm{d}j + \int_{\tilde{z}}^1 \left\{\frac{\partial f_j(p, M)}{\partial p}\left(\frac{\partial p}{\partial \omega}\right) + \frac{\partial f_j(p, M)}{\partial M}\frac{\partial M}{\partial \omega}\right\}\mathrm{d}j. \end{aligned} \tag{29}$$

By Assumption B1, the following equations hold:

$$\int_0^{\tilde{z}} p_j \frac{\partial f_j(p, M)}{\partial M} \mathrm{d}j = 1 - \int_{\tilde{z}}^1 p_j \frac{\partial f_j(p, M)}{\partial M} \mathrm{d}j \tag{30}$$

$$\int_0^1 p_j s_j(p, M) \left(\frac{\partial p}{\partial \omega} \right) \mathrm{d}j = 0 \tag{31}$$

$$p_j \frac{\partial f_j(p, M)}{\partial M} = p_j \frac{\partial f_j(p, M^*)}{\partial M}, \quad \forall j. \tag{32}$$

Substitute (1), (30), (31) and (32) into (29) to obtain

$$\begin{aligned} \frac{\partial B}{\partial \omega} = & \int_{\tilde{z}}^1 p_j s_j(p, M + M^*) \left(\frac{\partial p}{\partial \omega} \right) \mathrm{d}j \\ & + \left[\int_0^{\tilde{z}} \frac{\partial p_i}{\partial \omega} f_i(p, M + M^*) \mathrm{d}i - \frac{\partial M}{\partial \omega} \right] \int_0^{\tilde{z}} p_j \frac{\partial f_j(p, M)}{\partial M} \mathrm{d}j \\ & + \left[\int_{\tilde{z}}^1 \frac{\partial p_i}{\partial \omega} f_i(p, M + M^*) \mathrm{d}i - \frac{\partial M^*}{\partial \omega} \right] \left[\int_0^{\tilde{z}} p_j \frac{\partial f_j(p, M)}{\partial M} \mathrm{d}j - 1 \right]. \end{aligned} \tag{33}$$

Let $y(p)$ be the outputs of the home country at p. By the zero profit condition and the envelope theorem,

$$\frac{\partial M}{\partial \omega} = \int_0^1 \frac{\partial p_i}{\partial \omega} y_i(p) \mathrm{d}i = \int_0^{\tilde{z}} \frac{\partial p_i}{\partial \omega} f_i(p, M + M^*) \mathrm{d}i \tag{34}$$

$$\frac{\partial M^*}{\partial \omega} = \int_0^1 \frac{\partial p_i}{\partial \omega} y_i^*(p) \mathrm{d}i = \int_{\tilde{z}}^1 \frac{\partial p_i}{\partial \omega} f_i(p, M + M^*) \mathrm{d}i. \tag{35}$$

Substitute (34) and (35) into (33) to obtain

$$\frac{\partial B}{\partial \omega} = \int_{\tilde{z}}^1 p_j s_j(p, M + M^*) \left(\frac{\partial p}{\partial \omega} \right) \mathrm{d}j.$$

As $(\omega/p_j)(\partial p_j/\partial \omega) \geq (\omega/p_i)(\partial p_i/\partial \omega) = (\omega/p_h)(\partial p_h/\partial \omega)$ for any $j \in [0, \tilde{z}]$ and $h, i \in [\tilde{z}, 1]$, $(\partial B/\partial \omega) \leq 0$ by Assumption B3. Thus $(\partial \tilde{z}/\partial \omega) \geq 0$. Similarly, $(\partial \tilde{z}/\partial \omega^*) \geq 0$.

Proof of Lemma 5.

(i) Consider two sequences $\{g^n\}, \{h^n\}$ in $C[0,1]$ defined by

$$g^n(j) = \left\{ \begin{array}{c} \dfrac{\partial p(j)}{\partial \omega} + \varphi, \quad j \in [0, \tilde{z}] \\ \left[1 - \dfrac{n[j - \tilde{z}]}{\varepsilon} \right] \left[\dfrac{\partial p(j)}{\partial \omega} + \varphi \right], \quad j \in \left[\tilde{z}, \tilde{z} + \dfrac{\varepsilon}{n} \right] \\ 0, \quad j \in \left[\tilde{z} + \dfrac{\varepsilon}{n}, 1 \right] \end{array} \right\} \tag{36}$$

and

$$h^n \equiv \frac{\partial p}{\partial \omega} + \varphi - g^n, \tag{37}$$

where $\varepsilon > 0$ and $\varphi : [0,1] \to R$ such that $\varphi(j) = -p_j(1/M)(\partial M/\partial \omega) = -p_j/(\omega + K/L)$. Since f is homogenous of degree zero, a change in the prices and income in the direction of φ would not change the demand. The output effect in (23) can be written as

$$\int_0^{\tilde{z}} \left\{ \frac{a_{Kj}(\omega)}{K} - \frac{a_{Lj}(\omega)}{L} \right\} \frac{\partial f_j(p, M + M^*)}{\partial p} \left(\frac{\partial p}{\partial \omega} + \varphi \right) \mathrm{d}j. \tag{38}$$

Substitute (37) into (38) to get

$$\begin{aligned} &\int_0^{\tilde{z}} \left[\frac{a_{Kj}(\omega) f_j(p, M + M^*)}{K} - \frac{a_{Lj}(\omega) f_j(p, M + M^*)}{L} \right] \\ &\quad \times \frac{1}{f_j(p, M + M^*)} \frac{\partial f_j(p, M + M^*)}{\partial p} (h^n) \mathrm{d}j \\ &\quad - \frac{KL}{\omega + K/L} \int_0^1 g^n(j) \frac{\partial f_j(p, M + M^*)}{\partial p} (g^n) dj \\ &\quad + \frac{KL}{\omega + K/L} \int_{\tilde{z}}^1 g^n(j) \frac{\partial f_j(p, M + M^*)}{\partial p} (g^n) \mathrm{d}j. \end{aligned} \tag{39}$$

The limits of the first and the second terms in (39) are the cross and own price effect respectively. The former is negative by Assumption B4 and the latter is positive by Lemma 2. The last term in (39) converges to zero. Since $(\partial f(p, M + M^*)/\partial p)$ is continuous and linear, there exists some $b \geq 0$ such that $\|(\partial f(p, M + M^*)/\partial p)(g)\| \leq b\|g\|$ for any $g \in C[0,1]$. Also $\|g^n\| \leq \|(\partial p/\partial \omega) + \varphi\|$ for all n. Thus there is some constant $c \geq 0$, $|(\partial f(p, M + M^*)/\partial p)(g^n)| < c$ for all n and all j. Hence,

$$\lim_{n \to 0} \int_{\tilde{z}}^1 \left| g^n(j) \frac{\partial f(p, M + M^*)}{\partial p} (g^n) \right| dj \leq c \lim_{n \to 0} \int_{\tilde{z}}^1 |g^n(j)| dj = 0.$$

The decomposition of $\partial E^*/\partial \omega^*$ is similar and the details are omitted.

(ii) Change the price proportionally to make good z as the numeraire. When ω increases, p_j rises for $j < z$ while p_j remains constant for $j \geq z$. By Assumption B4, $(\partial E^*/\partial \omega) \leq 0$. Similarly, $(\partial E/\partial \omega^*) \leq 0$.

Proof of Lemma 6. The world economy can be considered as a closed economy by treating the factors of the two countries as different factors. Let $\gamma \equiv (w, r, w^*, r^*)$. Under Assumption B1, the factor prices and the factor endowments change in the opposite direction (see Dixit and Norman, 1980, Chapter 4). Thus for, $V' - V = (1, -\omega, 0, 0)$,

$$[\gamma' - \gamma][V' - V] = w' - w - [r' - r]\omega < 0, \tag{40}$$

which implies $\omega' < \omega$. Let ρ signify the change in V in the direction $(1, -\omega, 0, 0)$. Given the initial prices, income does not change and thus $(\partial\tilde{E}^*/\partial\rho) = 0$ and $(\partial\tilde{E}/\partial\rho) > 0$. The inequality in (40) implies

$$\frac{d\omega}{d\rho} = -|\Delta|^{-1}\begin{vmatrix} \dfrac{\partial\tilde{E}}{\partial\rho} & \dfrac{\partial\tilde{E}}{\partial\omega^*} \\ \dfrac{\partial\tilde{E}^*}{\partial\rho} & \dfrac{\partial\tilde{E}^*}{\partial\omega^*} \end{vmatrix} = -|\Delta|^{-1}\frac{\partial\tilde{E}^*}{\partial\omega^*}\frac{\partial\tilde{E}}{\partial\rho} \leq 0.$$

By Assumption B5, $(\partial\tilde{E}^*/\partial\omega^*) \geq 0$. Thus $|\Delta| \geq 0$.

Proof of Lemma 7. Under Assumptions B4 and B5, $\partial E/\partial\omega$ is positive and $\partial E^*/\partial\omega$ is negative. By Lemma 6, $|\Delta|$ is positive (strictly positive sign assumed). By (22), (24), and (25),

$$\begin{aligned}\frac{d\omega^*}{d\alpha} &= -|\Delta|^{-1}\left[\left(\frac{\partial E}{\partial z}\frac{\partial\tilde{z}}{\partial\omega^*} + \frac{\partial E}{\partial\omega}\right)\frac{\partial E^*}{\partial z} - \left(\frac{\partial E^*}{\partial z}\frac{\partial\tilde{z}}{\partial\omega^*} + \frac{\partial E^*}{\partial\omega}\right)\frac{\partial E}{\partial z}\right]\frac{\partial\tilde{z}}{\partial\alpha} \\ &= -|\Delta|^{-1}\left[\frac{\partial E}{\partial\omega}\frac{\partial E^*}{\partial z} - \frac{\partial E^*}{\partial\omega}\frac{\partial E}{\partial z}\right]\frac{\partial z}{\partial\alpha} < 0.\end{aligned}$$

Similar derivation shows

$$\frac{d\omega}{d\beta} = -|\Delta|^{-1}\left[\frac{\partial E^*}{\partial\omega}\frac{\partial E}{\partial z} - \frac{\partial E}{\partial\omega^*}\frac{\partial E^*}{\partial z}\right]\frac{\partial\tilde{z}}{\partial\beta} > 0.$$

Proof of Theorem 1. Under Assumption B5, the equilibrium set $S \equiv \{(\omega, \omega^*, \alpha) : \tilde{E}(\omega, \omega^*, \alpha) = \tilde{E}^*(\omega, \omega^*, \alpha) = 0\}$ is a one-dimensional C^1 manifold by the preimage theorem. Let $\pi : S \to (0, 1]$ be a projection map such that $\pi(\omega, \omega^*, \alpha) = \alpha$. By Assumption B5 and Lemma 6, Δ is a P-matrix (Gale and Nikaido, 1965) and thus given any $\alpha \in (0, 1]$, the (ω, ω^*) satisfying (20) and (21) is unique. Therefore π is one-to-one. Obviously, π is onto and smooth. By the implicit function theorem, (ω, ω^*) is locally a smooth function of α for any $\alpha \in (0, 1]$. So π^{-1} is also smooth. This shows that S is diffeomorphic to (0,1] and ω and ω^* are differentiable functions of α.

The domain of ω^* can be extended to [0,1] if ω^* is uniformly continuous in α. Let $O(a,b)$ be an open interval with centre a and radius b. Since ω^* is continuous and decreasing, given $\alpha \in (0, 1)$ and $\varepsilon > 0$, $\omega^{*-1}(O(\omega^*(\alpha),\varepsilon))$ is either equal to (c,d) for $d \leq 1$ or $(c, d]$ for $d = 1$. Let $\delta(\alpha, \varepsilon) = \min\{\alpha - c, d - \alpha\}$. Suppose ω^* is not uniformly continuous. There exists an $\varepsilon' > 0$ and a sequence $\{\alpha_n\}$ in (0,1) such that $\delta(\alpha_n,\varepsilon') \to 0$. Since [0,1] is compact, there is a subsequence $\{\alpha_m\}$ converging to some $\bar{\alpha} \in [0, 1]$. By Assumption A2, the set $\omega^*((0, 1])$ is bounded. There exists some $\tilde{\alpha} \in (0, 1]$ such that for all $\alpha, \alpha' \in (0, \tilde{\alpha}]$, $|\omega^*(\alpha) - \omega^*(\alpha')| < \varepsilon'$.

Thus $\bar{\alpha} \in (0, 1]$. There is a sub subsequence $\{\alpha_q\}$ and a $t \in \{1, -1\}$ such that

$$\lim_{q\to\infty} \frac{|\omega^*(\alpha_q + t\delta(\alpha_q, \varepsilon')) - \omega^*(\alpha_q)|}{\delta(\alpha_q, \varepsilon')} = \infty.$$

This is a contradiction because ω^* is differentiable at $\bar{\alpha}$. Thus ω^* is uniformly continuous and can be continuously extended to [0,1].

As $\alpha \to 0$, both z and M converge to 0, and f is continuous in the sup norm,

$$\lim_{\alpha\to 0} \ln \frac{\int_z^1 a_{Kj}(\omega^*(\alpha)) f_j(p, M + M^*) dj}{\int_z^1 a_{Lj}(\omega^*(\alpha)) f_j(p, M + M^{*\prime}) dj} - \ln \frac{\bar{K}^*}{\bar{L}^*}$$
$$= \ln \frac{\int_0^1 a_{Kj}(\omega^*(0)) f_j(p, M^*) dj}{\int_0^1 a_{Lj}(\omega^*(0)) f_j(p, M^*) dj} - \ln \frac{\bar{K}^*}{\bar{L}^*} = 0.$$

Thus $\omega^*(0) = \omega^{*a}$. As $(d\omega^*/d\alpha) < 0$ for all $\alpha \in (0, 1]$, $\omega^{*t} < \omega^{*a}$. Similarly, $\omega^t > \omega^a$.

Proof of Theorem 2. Let $A \equiv \{\alpha \in [0, 1 : h(\alpha) = 0]\}$. If $A = \varnothing$, Theorem 1 applies. Suppose $A \neq \varnothing$ and write $A = \{\alpha_1, \ldots, \beta_N\}$ where $\alpha_n < \alpha_{n+1}$ for all $n = 1, \ldots, N-1$. If FPE does not hold for $(0, \alpha_1]$, it can be shown that ω^* is a differentiable function of $\alpha \in (0, \alpha_1]$ and $\lim_{\alpha\to 0} \omega^*(\alpha) = \omega^{*a}$. The proof is similar to that of Theorem 1. If FPE holds for $(0, \alpha_1]$, then Equation (2) characterizes the equilibrium. Since the equilibrium is unique and $(\partial G/\partial\bar{\omega}) > 0$, ω^* is a differentiable function of α and $\omega^*(0) = \omega^{*a}$. Similarly, for each of the intervals $[\alpha_N, 1]$ and $[\alpha_n, \alpha_{n+1}], n = 1, \ldots, N-1$, ω^* is a differentiable function of α. Since the equilibrium is unique for all $\alpha \in (0, 1]$ and both Equations (20), (21) and (2) hold at α_n, there cannot be any discontinuous change in ω^* at α_n. Hence $\omega^*(\alpha)$ is single-valued, continuous in α and differentiable except for the set A. By Lemma 7 and (8), $(\partial\omega^*/\partial\alpha) < 0$ for all $\alpha \notin A$. Therefore, $\omega^{*a} > \omega^{*t}$. The proof for $\omega^t > \omega^a$ is analogous.

References

Araujo, A. (1988), The non-existence of smooth demand in general banach spaces. *Journal of Mathematical Economics* 17, 309–319.

Chichilnisky, G., Zhou, Y. (1998), Smooth infinite economies. *Journal of Mathematical Economics* 29, 27–42.

Deardorff, A. (1986), Firless firwoes: how preferences can interfere with the theorems of international trade. *Journal of International Economics* 20, 131–142.

Deardorff, A. (1994), The possibilities of FPE revisited. *Journal of International Economics* 36, 167–175.

Dixit, A., Norman, V. (1980), *Theory of International Trade*. Cambridge University Press, Cambridge.

Dornbusch, R., Fischer, S., Samuelson, P.A. (1980), Heckscher-Ohlin trade theory with a continuum of goods. *Quarterly Journal of Economics* 94, 203–224.

Falvey, R. (1981), Commercial policy and intra-industry trade. *Journal of International Economics* 11, 495–511.

Falvey, R. (1999), Trade liberalization and factor price convergence. *Journal of International Economics* 49, 195–210.

Gale, D., Nikaido, H. (1965), The Jacobian matrix and global univalence of mapping. *Mathematische Annalen* 159, 81–93.

Guillemin, V., Pollack, A. (1974), *Differential Topology*. Prentice-Hall, New Jersey.

Hahn, F. (1959), The balance of payments in a monetary economy. *Review of Economic Studies* 26, 110–125.

Helpman, E. (1976), Solutions of general equilibrium problems for a trading world. *Econometrica* 44, 547–559.

Jones, R.W. (1998), Comment on J. Bhagwati "Trade and wages: a malign relationship". In: Collins, S. (Ed.), *Imports, Exports and American Worker*. Brookings Institution Press, Washington, DC.

Jones, R.W. (2002), Trade theory and factor intensities: an interpretive essay. *Review of International Economics* 10 (4), 581–603.

Kehoe, T.J. (1984), Computing all of the equilibria of economies with two factors of production. *Journal of Mathematical Economics* 13, 207–223.

McKenzie, L. (1955), Equality of factor prices in world trade. *Econometrica* 23, 239–257.

Ohlin, B. (1952), *Interregional and International Trade*. Harvard University Press, Cambridge, MA.

Pearce, I.F. (1970), *International Trade*. Norton, New York.

Samuelson, P.A. (1953), Prices of factors and goods in general equilibrium. *Review of Economic Studies* 21, 1–20.

Uzawa, H. (1959), Prices of the factors of production in international trade. *Econometrica* 27, 448–468.

Wilson, C. (1980), On the general structure of ricardian models with a continuum of goods: applications to growth, tariff theory, and technical change. *Econometrica* 48, 1675–1702.

Xu, Y. (1993), A General model of comparative advantage with two factors and a continuum of goods. *International Economic Review* 34, 365–380.

SECTION IV

Dynamic Issues

CHAPTER 9

Distortions in the Two-Sector Dynamic General Equilibrium Model

Eric W. Bond and Robert A. Driskill

Department of Economics, Vanderbilt University, VU Station B #351819, 2301 Vanderbilt Place, Nashville, TN 37235, USA
E-mail addresses: eric.bond@vanderbilt.edu; robert.a.driskill@vanderbilt.edu

Abstract
We extend the Jones (1971) analysis of the effects of distortions in 2×2 trade models to the case of a two-sector dynamic general equilibrium model of a small open economy with capital accumulation. We do a comparative steady state analysis for the effect of policy changes on factor prices and the capital stock, and examine the dynamics of the system in the neighborhood of the steady state. We also show that the system will have multiple equilibria when value and physical factor intensity rankings of the sectors do not agree.

Keywords: Factor market distortions, two sector model, policy issues

JEL classifications: F11, C02

1. Introduction

The static two-sector model with factor market differentials has been used to examine a number of issues, including the incidence of the corporate income tax, the effect of union/non-union wage differentials, and the rural/urban dichotomy. In an important paper, Jones (1971) emphasized the importance of the distinction between the measurement of the capital intensity of a sector on the basis of its value intensity (share of capital costs in total costs) and its physical intensity (capital per unit labor) in understanding the comparative static results. He showed that the determination of the direction of changes in factor prices in response to a change in output prices was determined by which sector was capital intensive in the value ranking, whereas the direction in change of outputs in response to a change in factor endowments depended on which sector was capital intensive in the physical ranking. Furthermore, he showed that

Frontiers of Economics and Globalization
Volume 4 ISSN: 1574-8715
DOI: 10.1016/S1574-8715(08)04009-8

paradoxical comparative statics results could arise in the case in which the value intensity ranking of sectors differed from the physical intensity ranking. These paradoxes include the possibility that an increase in the relative price of a good results in a decrease in its supply and the possibility that a tax imposed on the earnings of a factor in one sector results in an increase in the output of that sector.[1]

The purpose of this chapter is to extend the static analysis of factor market distortions to a dynamic two-sector model in which capital is accumulating. We will examine the effect of factor market distortions on the steady state levels of relative prices and output levels, as well as on the dynamics in the neighborhood of the steady state. These questions are of interest because the two-sector model with factor accumulation and factor market distortions has been used to examine a number of policy issues. For example, it has been used to study the long-run effects of income and factor taxation (e.g. Rebelo (1991); Bond *et al.* (1996); and Milesi-Ferretti and Roubini (1998) for models with endogenous growth). In addition, models with constant returns to scale and factor market distortions have been used to generate the possibility of dynamic indeterminacy (Benhabib and Nishimura (1998) and Meng and Velasco (2004) in models with steady states, Bond *et al.* (1996) and Benhabib et al. (2000) for models with endogenous growth).

In this chapter we focus on the case of a small open economy in which one sector produces a traded consumption good and the other sector produces a non-traded investment good, so that the economy will exhibit a steady state.[2] We show that this dynamic model can be characterized by adding an intertemporal arbitrage condition and a capital accumulation equation to the full employment and zero profit conditions of the static model. This model allows us to contrast the short-run and long-run effects of distortions and to characterize the local dynamics in the neighborhood of the steady state for a small open economy in a particularly simple way.

One question we address is the impact of changes in factor market distortions on the long-run return to factors of production and the steady state capital stock. In the static model, the direction of the impact of factor market distortions on factor prices depends critically on whether the taxes

---

[1] A number of other possible paradoxical outcomes arise in the presence of factor market distortions, such as the possibility that the transformation schedule is convex to the origin and the possibility that trade liberalization reduces welfare for a small country. However, these outcomes are not identically linked to the reversal of value and physical intensities. Magee (1973) provides a survey of results on factor market distortions.

[2] The production structure we adopt is similar to that of Meng and Velasco (2004), although we generalize their assumption of Cobb Douglas production functions. We also consider distortions arising from factor taxation, rather than externalities as in their model. We show below (footnote 4) that the Meng and Velasco model has an equivalent interpretation using factor taxes.

are imposed on the capital-intensive or labor-intensive sector (when measured in the value sense). In the steady state of the dynamic model, in contrast, the impact on the return to capital of taxes imposed on factors in the investment good sector is the same regardless of whether the investment good sector is capital intensive or labor intensive. The reason for this is that in the steady state, the return to capital is tied to the price of the investment good through an intertemporal arbitrage condition. A similar lack of linkage between factor intensities arises when considering the impact of factor taxes on the steady state capital stock, because all factor taxes except a tax on labor in the consumption good sector will reduce the steady state capital stock. Physical and value intensity rankings do not play a role in the comparative statics for steady state capital because of its link to the output of the investment good.

A second question concerns the characteristics of the dynamic system in the neighborhood of the stead state. We first show that the dynamic system will have a saddle path if the ranking of the sectors on value and physical intensity are the same. In the cases where the physical and value intensity ranking differ, the system will not have a saddle path. If the investment good sector is capital intensive in the value sense and labor intensive in the physical sense, the system will exhibit local indeterminacy in that there will be a continuum of paths converging to the (unique) steady state. If the investment good sector is labor intensive in the value sense and capital intensive in the physical sense, then the steady state will be unstable.

We also extend the analysis of the dynamics to consider the possibility that the economy is completely specialized. In the case where the physical and value intensity rankings agree, there will be a unique production equilibrium that satisfies equilibrium in factor markets for a given capital/labor ratio. In this case the regions of the phase plane that are consistent with complete specialization are bounded away from the steady state, so specialization will only be observed in cases where the endowment ratios are sufficiently far from the steady state. Transitions between complete specialization and incomplete specialization in production can only occur at the boundary of the region where the economy is incompletely specialized. However, we show that in the case where the physical and value rankings differ, any capital labor ratio for which there is a production equilibrium with incomplete specialization also has equilibria with specialization in production of each of the goods. The existence of multiple equilibria in the region of specialization leads to the possibility that the economy can have dynamic paths in which the economy switches between patterns of specialization at any point in the region of incomplete specialization (including any neighborhood of the steady state).

This model also generates some surprising results concerning the factor price equalization property of international trade. Since the model has two factors of production and only one traded good, one would not expect that international trade would equalize factor prices between countries with different levels capital per worker. However, we show that in the case where the investment good is labor intensive in both the physical and value senses, factor prices will be equalized between countries with the same level of distortions as long as their endowments are contained within the interval associated with incomplete specialization. The equalization of factor prices results from the intertemporal arbitrage condition, which requires that the price of the investment good be constant along the saddle path that converges to the steady state capital stock in the region of incomplete specialization. Thus, all countries whose factor supplies are contained in this range will have the same price of the non-traded investment good and the same factor prices. However, the case of indeterminacy (the investment good is capital intensive in the value sense but labor intensive in the physical sense) creates a situation where two economies with identical factor supplies and factor market distortions might have different factor prices. The existence of indeterminacy means that there is a continuum of paths converging to the steady state from an initial capital stock, so factor price equalization could fail if identical countries select different convergent paths to the steady state.

Section 2 of the chapter outlines the model and shows that the dynamic model can be characterized by adding an intertemporal arbitrage condition and a capital accumulation equation to the full employment and zero profit conditions of the static model. Section 3 analyzes the static equilibrium and establishes the conditions for a unique steady state equilibrium to exist with incomplete specialization. Comparative steady state results for changes in factor market distortions are also derived. Section 4 analyzes the dynamics in the region of the phase plane where there is specialization in production, and discusses the implications of the multiplicity of equilibria that arise when value and physical intensity rankings differ.

2. *A dynamic open economy model with factor market distortions*

We consider a two-factor, two-good dynamic model of an open economy in which sector 1 produces a traded consumption good and sector 2 produces a non-traded investment good. We assume that factor market distortions take the form of sector-specific taxes on the incomes from factors located in that sector, so that the mobility of factors will equalize the after tax returns to factors. Although we refer to these distortions as taxes, an equivalent formulation could be given in which these barriers represent sector-specific externalities from factor usage. Our purpose in this section is to derive the system of differential equations that describe the competitive equilibrium in this model, and to illustrate how the behavior of the system varies between the regions in which the economy is incompletely specialized and the region in which it is completely specialized. In particular, we illustrate the possibility that there are regions of the state space in which there are multiple equilibria in the case in which the factor market distortions are sufficiently large.

We begin with a characterization of the optimization problem for a representative household. Household preferences are given by $U = \int_0^\infty u(C(t))e^{-\rho t}dt$, where $C(t)$ denotes household consumption at time t. It will be assumed households earn income from their stock of labor (exogenously given) and accumulated capital, with w and r denoting the after tax returns to the respective factor. Units of the capital good, which depreciate at an exogenously given rate δ, can be purchased from the investment good sector at a relative price p in terms of the consumption good. In addition, households have access to an international bond market where they can lend or borrow at a rate equal to the household discount rate, ρ. The household budget constraint at time t will be $C(t) = w(t)L + r(t)K(t) + \rho B(t) - \dot{B} - p(t)\dot{K}(t) + \delta K(t))$, where B is the stock of bonds. Households choose the time path of C, $\dot{B}$, and $\dot{K}$ to maximize utility, given the time path of w, r, and p.

It is straightforward to show that under these assumptions households will have a constant level of consumption, with decisions on capital accumulation made to maximize the present value of income and bond holdings used to smooth consumption. The necessary conditions for the household optimization problem also yield the requirement that the after tax return to holding a unit of capital equal be equal to the return that can be earned on the international bond, which can be expressed as

$$\frac{r + \dot{p}}{p} - \delta = \rho \tag{1}$$

This condition must hold at all points in time in order for households to be willing to hold the domestic capital stock.[3]

We now turn to the determination of factor rewards and output levels from the production side of the economy. Each good is produced under conditions of constant returns to scale and perfect competition using labor and capital, with factors being exchanged in competitive factor market. We denote the production function in sector i by $F_i(K_i, L_i) = f_i(k_i)L_i$, where $k_i \equiv K_i/L_i$ and f is strictly concave. The mobility of capital and labor between sectors means that the after tax returns to factors will be equated across sectors, and the factor market distortions result from the fact that factors returns may be subject to different rates of tax

[3] Since there is only one consumption good, the focus here is on intertemporal trade. Trade based on comparative advantage could be introduced by allowing there to be many traded goods that exchange at fixed world prices. The consumption good could then be thought of as a composite of the traded goods. The unit isoquant in the production technology would then represent the factor combinations required to produce a unit of value of traded goods at given world prices.

across sectors. The pretax cost of the respective factors in sector i will be $w_i = w/(1-t_{Li})$ and $r_i = r/(1-t_{Ki})$, where t_{ji} is the tax rate on income from factor j in sector i.

Following the elegant approach of Jones (1965, 1971), we can solve for the equilibrium factor prices, (w, r), and output levels, (X_1, X_2), in the presence of factor market distortions using the competitive profit conditions and the full employment conditions. Letting $T_{ji} = 1/(1-t_{ji})$, the competitive profit conditions in sector i require that

$$p_i \leq c^i(wT_{Li}, rT_{Ki}) \tag{2}$$

with strict equality holding if good i is produced.[4] The full employment conditions require that

$$\begin{aligned} c^1_{w_1}(wT_{L1}, rT_{K1})X_1 + c^2_{w_2}(wT_{L2}, rT_{K2})X_2 &= L \\ c^1_{r_1}(wT_{L1}, rT_{K1})X_1 + c^2_{r_2}(wT_{L2}, rT_{K2})X_2 &= K \end{aligned} \tag{3}$$

The solutions to (2) and (3) can be summarized by the equilibrium relations $\{w^e(p,K,T), r^e(p,K,T), X_i(p,K,T)\}$ for $i = 1, 2$. The properties of these relations, and the possibility that these relationships may be correspondences rather than functions, will be discussed in detail below. For now it is sufficient to note that the equilibria may be of two types. An equilibrium with *incomplete specialization* will exist if the competitive profit conditions hold with equality in each sector and the full employment conditions are satisfied with $X_1,\ X_2 > 0$. An equilibrium with *specialization in good i* will exist if the competitive profit condition in sector i holds with equality and the full employment conditions are satisfied with $X_j = 0$ for $j \neq i$.

Since the investment good is assumed to be non-traded, the evolution of the capital stock will be determined by the output of good 2,

$$\dot{K} = X_2 - \delta K \tag{4}$$

Given the solutions $\{w^e(p, K, T), r^e(p, K, T), X_i(p, K, T)\}$ for factor prices and output levels from (2) and (3), equations (1) and (4) yield a system of differential equations in p and K. In the remainder of this section we derive the properties of the equilibrium solutions.

---

[4] Meng and Velasco (2004) analyze a case in which the sectoral production function takes the form $X_i = L_i^{\alpha_i} K_i^{\beta_i} \bar{K}^{1-\alpha_i-\beta_i}$, where $\alpha_i > 0, \beta_i > 0, 1 - \alpha_i - \beta_i \geq 0$, and $\bar{K}_i$, denotes the industry capital stock. The distortion in this case arises from the externality from capital, which firms ignore in making decisions on the level of capital. In this case the loci of factor prices that are consistent with factor market equilibrium (i.e. the equating of private marginal products to the factor price) will have the form $w_i = p_i\alpha_i(r_i/\beta_i)^{(\alpha_i-1)/\alpha_i}$. These conditions yield equilibrium conditions analogous to those in (1), where the social factor shares α_i and $(1-\alpha_i)$ play the role of the value shares and determine the impact of goods price changes on factor prices. The capital labor ratios, however, are determined by the private factor shares α_i and β_i.

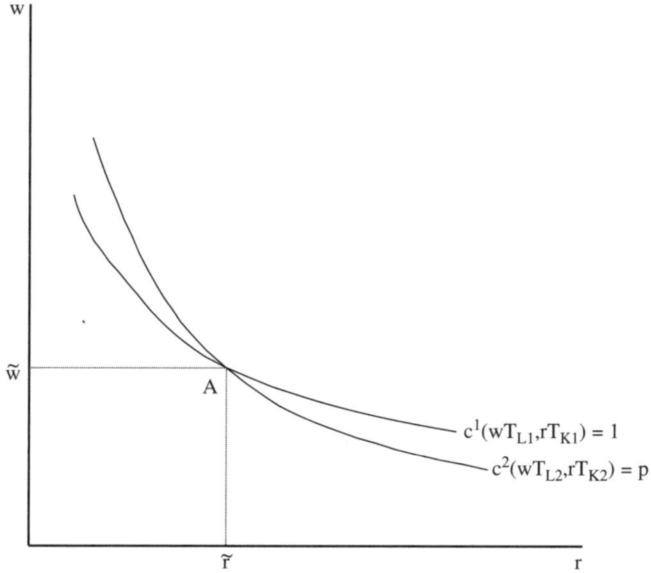

Fig. 1. Unit cost curves and equilibrium factor prices.

2.1. Complete and incomplete specialization equilibria

We begin by showing how the state space (p, K) can be divided into three regions: one consistent with incomplete specialization and one associated with specialization in each of the two sectors. Our main result is to show that if the factor market distortions are sufficiently small that the capital intensity rankings of the two sectors on the value and physical measures agree these three regions are disjoint. However, if the distortions are such that the physical and value intensity rankings differ, the region of the state space consistent with incomplete specialization is contained in the regions of specialization for each of the two sectors.

The determination of factor prices consistent with incomplete specialization is illustrated in Figure 1, which shows the unit cost functions in (w, r) space for a given level of p and T. The intersection of these curves will determine the factor prices $(\tilde{w}, \tilde{r})$ that are consistent with incomplete specialization.[5] Letting $k_i \equiv c^i_{r_i}/c^i_{w_i}$ denote the cost-minimizing capital labor ratio in sector i and $k \equiv K/L$, there will exist an equilibrium with incomplete specialization if $k \in (\min_i k_i(\tilde{w}/\tilde{r}), \max_i k_i(\tilde{w}/\tilde{r}))$. This defines the familiar cone of diversification from the Heckscher–Ohlin model of international trade, although in this case the cone depends on the factor market distortions as well as on world prices.

[5] It will be assumed that this equilibrium point is unique. A sufficient condition for uniqueness is that the elasticity of substitution be the same across sectors.

An equilibrium with complete specialization in good i will exist if there are factor prices (w, r) such that $c^i_{r_i}(wT_{Li}, rT_{Ki})/c^i_{w_i}(wT_{Li}, rT_{Ki}) = k, c^i(wT_{Li}, rT_{Ki}) = p_i$, and $c^j(wT_{Lj}, rT_{Kj}) \geq p_j$ for $j \neq i$. Referring to Figure 1, for any (w, r) such that $w/r > \tilde{w}/\tilde{r}$ and $c^2(wT_{L2}, rT_{K2}) = p_2$, we have $c^1(wT_{L1}, rT_{K1}) > 1$. These factor prices will be consistent with complete specialization in good 2 for $k = c^2_{r_2}/c^2_{w_2}$. A similar argument establishes that for $w/r < \tilde{w}/\tilde{r}$, there will be an equilibrium with complete specialization in good with $k = c^1_{r_1}/c^1_{w_1}$.

The factor price frontier for the economy will be the upper envelope of the unit cost curves in Figure 1. The determination of which sector the economy will specialize in for $w/r > \tilde{w}/\tilde{r}$ is determined by the relative slopes of the unit cost curves at $(\tilde{w}, \tilde{r})$. Since the slope of the unit cost function for sector i in Figure 1 will be $-T_{Ki}k_i/T_{Li}$, the unit cost curve for sector 2 will be steeper than that for sector 1 at an intersection point iff sector 2 is capital intensive in the value sense, $\theta_{K2} > \theta_{K1}$, where $\theta_{Ki} \equiv w_i c^i_{w_i}/p_i$. At high wage/rental ratios the economy specializes in the good that is capital intensive in the value sense. In the absence of factor market distortions, the slopes of these curves will equal the physical factor intensities, k_i, and the equilibrium factor prices can be obtained by finding a tangency between a line with slope $-k$ and the factor price frontier.

With factor market distortions, the slope of the unit cost curve equals $-k_i$ iff there is the same degree of factor market distortion for each factor in that sector. The slope of the unit cost curve in Figure 1 will be steeper than $-k_i$ when there is a relatively greater tax on capital. Note in particular that if the distortion on capital is relatively larger in sector 2, it is possible that sector 2 is capital intensive in the value sense even though $k_2 < k_1$. We refer to this case as one where the ranking of industries by value intensity differs from the ranking by physical intensity. If sector i is capital intensive in the physical sense, then it will also be capital intensive in the value sense as long as $k_i/k_j > (T_{Li}/T_{Ki})/(T_{Lj}/T_{kj})$. This means that a necessary condition for a reversal of the value and physical rankings is that the distortion on labor relative to capital be higher in the physically capital-intensive sector. It should be emphasized that when we are making the comparison of value and physical intensities, the physical capital intensity ranking is made for the given factor market distortions. Thus, it says nothing about the ranking of the sectors in the absence of factor market distortions. For example, it is possible that sector 2 is capital intensive in both the value and physical sense in a distorted economy (i.e. there is no reversal of sectoral rankings in our measure), even though sector 2 might be labor intensive if all distortions were removed.[6]

[6] Suppose that the sector 2 is has a CES production technology with $\sigma_2 > 1$ and is capital intensive in the absence of factor taxation. The capital intensity of sector 2 in both the physical and value sense will be decreasing in T_{K2}, so there will be a value of T_{K2} sufficiently large that sector 2 will become labor intensive in both the physical and value sense for given w/r.

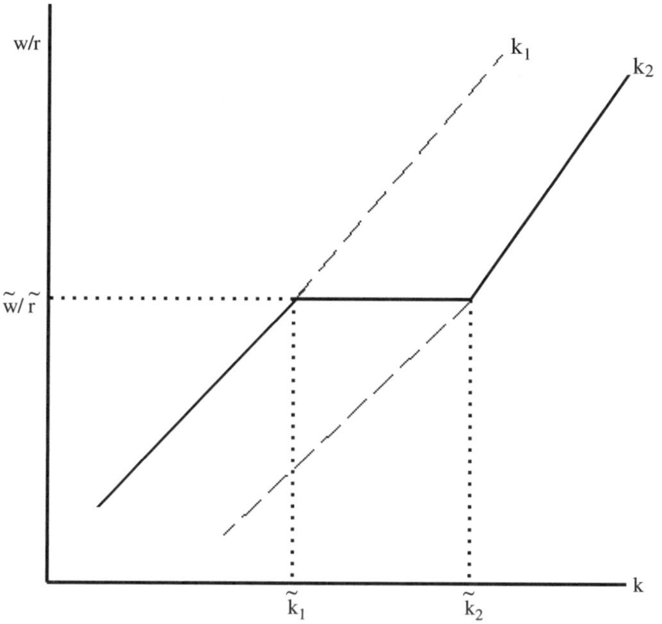

Fig. 2. Physical and value intensity rankings the same: $\theta_{K2} > \theta_{K1}$ and $k_2 > k_1$.

Figure 2 illustrates the relationship between the level of endowments and the value of w/r consistent with equilibrium in factor markets. The $k_i(w/r)$ loci show capital/labor ratios chosen in sector i as a function of factor prices, given the level of distortions. When sector 2 is capital intensive in both the physical and value sense, as shown in Figure 2, there will be a unique equilibrium for each k. The above argument shows that for $w/r > \tilde{w}/\tilde{r}$ and $c^2(wT_{L2}, rT_{K2}) = p_2$, there will be an equilibrium with complete specialization in good 2 for $k \geq k_2(\tilde{w}/\tilde{r})$. Similarly, for $w/r < \tilde{w}/\tilde{r}$ and $c^1(wT_{L1}, rT_{K1}) = 1$ there will be an equilibrium with complete specialization in good 1 with $k = k_1(w/r)$. Hence, for all $k \leq k_1(\tilde{w}/\tilde{r})$ there will be an equilibrium with specialization in good 1. The remaining interval, $\big(k_1(\tilde{w}/\tilde{r}), k_2(\tilde{w}/\tilde{r})\big)$, has a unique equilibrium with incomplete specialization. Since this argument does not depend on features of the consumption and investment good sectors, a similar conclusion is reached in the case where sector 1 is capital intensive in both physical and value sense. An equilibrium with specialization in the capital intensive good arises when k is sufficiently high, and an equilibrium with specialization in the labor intensive good when k is sufficiently low. In the intermediate range, there is incomplete specialization.

In contrast, the model generates a region of endowments associated with multiple equilibria when physical and value intensity rankings differ as illustrated in Figure 3. The reversal of factor intensity rankings means that $k_1(\tilde{w}/\tilde{r}) > k_2(\tilde{w}/\tilde{r})$. In this case the region in which there is complete

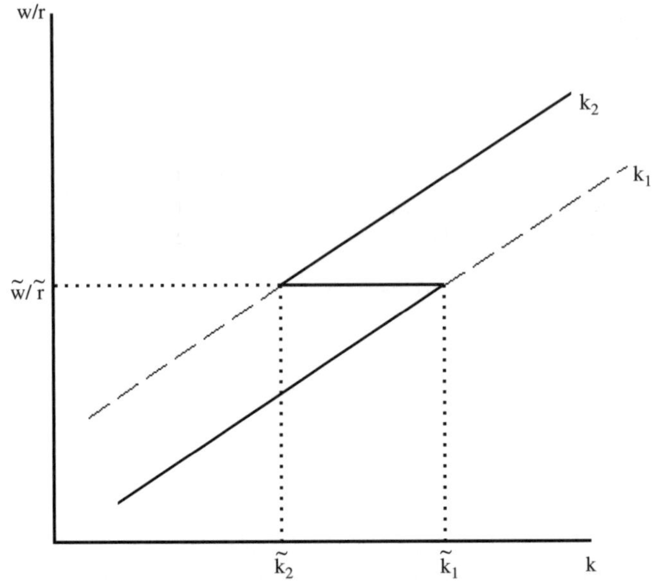

Fig. 3. Physical and value intensities differ: $\theta_{K2} > \theta_{K1}$ and $k_1 > k_2$.

specialization in good 1, $k \leq k_1(\tilde{w}/\tilde{r})$, overlaps with the region in which there is complete specialization in good 2, $k \geq k_2(\tilde{w}/\tilde{r})$. Furthermore, the region of overlap also contains the regions of incomplete specialization. The interval $(k_2(\tilde{w}/\tilde{r}), k_1(\tilde{w}/\tilde{r}))$ will therefore be associated with three potential equilibria to the static model. The multiplicity arises because an increase in w/r $\tilde{w}/\tilde{r}$ has two conflicting effects on the demand for capital. One effect is to induce substitution of capital for labor in each sector of the economy. The second effect is to result in the shutdown of sector 1 (labor intensive in the value sense), which reduces the demand for capital when $k_1(\tilde{w}/\tilde{r}) > k_2(\tilde{w}/\tilde{r})$. The value of w/r at which these two effects exactly offset will also be an equilibrium of the static model. A similar argument applies for reductions in w/r in the neighborhood of $\tilde{w}/\tilde{r}$.[7]

[7] Although there is an extensive literature on factor market distortions, the possibility of multiple production equilibria when value and physical intensities differ has received relatively little attention in the literature. Magee (1973) discusses the possibility of conflicts between value and physical intensities, but focuses on the comparison between the ranking of industries in the absence of distortions with that which occurs in distorted equilibria. Neary (1978) appends an adjustment process to the static model and shows that the interior equilibria are unstable under this adjustment process when value and physical intensity rankings differ (see the discussion in Section 3). He then argues that the economy will move either to another equilibrium where value and physical rankings coincide or to an equilibrium with specialization. Figure 3 shows that the specialization equilibria will exist for any equilibrium with incomplete specialization. For another equilibrium with incomplete specialization to exist, there must be a value factor intensity reversal in Figure 1 so that there is more than one intersection of the unit cost curves.

2.2. Comparative statics for the production model

The previous section established the relationship between the state variables $\{p, k\}$ of the dynamic system (for given T) and the pattern of production. In this section we derive comparative statics results for the effect of changes in $\{p, k, T\}$ on factor prices and output levels in the respective production regions. These results will be useful for analyzing the dynamics of the model and for contrasting the long-run effects of changes in factor prices in the dynamic model with those obtained in the static model.

We begin by summarizing the comparative statics results when there is incomplete specialization, which are due to Jones (1971). The impact of goods prices and factor taxes on factor prices with incomplete specialization can be obtained by total differentiation of (2), which yields

$$\hat{r} = \left(\frac{\theta_{L1}\hat{p} + \theta_{L1}\theta_{L2}(\hat{T}_{L1} - \hat{T}_{L2}) + \theta_{K1}\theta_{L2}\hat{T}_{K1} - \theta_{L1}\theta_{K2}\hat{T}_{K2}}{\theta_{K2} - \theta_{K1}}\right)$$

$$\hat{w} = -\left(\frac{\theta_{K1}\hat{p} + \theta_{K1}\theta_{K2}(\hat{T}_{K1} - \hat{T}_{K2}) + \theta_{K2}\theta_{L1}\hat{T}_{L1} - \theta_{K1}\theta_{L2}\hat{T}_{L2}}{\theta_{K2} - \theta_{K1}}\right) \tag{5}$$

where a "^" over a variable denotes a percentage change. The first term in each expression captures the Stolper–Samuelson result: a factor will experience a more than proportional increase in its return from an increase in the price of the good in which it is used intensively. A factor's return decreases in response to an increase in the price of the good in which it is not used intensively. The relevant factor intensity for determining the effect of price changes on factor incomes is the value intensity. The remaining terms show that a factor loses from an increase in taxes on any factor in the sector in which it is used intensively, and benefits from taxes on factors in the other sector. Thus it is the sector in which taxes are imposed, and not the identity of the factor being taxed, that determines the impact on after tax returns in the short run at fixed output prices.

The comparative statics for output changes with fixed factor supplies can be derived using (3). Letting λ_{ij} denote the share of factor $i\ \varepsilon\{L, K\}$ employed in sector $j\ \varepsilon\{1, 2\}$ and $\gamma_{Li} \equiv -w_i c^i_{w_i w_i}/c^i_{w_i}$ $(\gamma_{Ki} \equiv -r_i c^i_{r_i r_i}/c^i_{r_i})$ the own price elasticity of demand for labor (capital) in sector i,[8] we have

$$\begin{pmatrix} \lambda_{L1} & \lambda_{L2} \\ \lambda_{K1} & \lambda_{K2} \end{pmatrix}\begin{pmatrix} \hat{X}_1 \\ \hat{X}_2 \end{pmatrix} = \begin{pmatrix} \hat{L} + \sum_{i=1}^{2} \lambda_{Li}\gamma_{Li}(\hat{w} - \hat{r} + \hat{T}_{Li} - \hat{T}_{Ki}) \\ \hat{K} - \sum_{i=1}^{2} \lambda_{Ki}\gamma_{Ki}(\hat{w} - \hat{r} + \hat{T}_{Li} - \hat{T}_{Ki}) \end{pmatrix} \tag{6}$$

[8] The elasticity of substitution in sector i will be $\sigma_i \equiv \gamma_{Li} + \gamma_{Ki}$. The symmetry of the substitution matrix implies that $\gamma_{Li} = \theta_{Ki}\sigma_i$.

The terms on the right hand side of (6) show that at constant factor prices, an increase in T_{Li}/T_{Ki} will increase the demand for capital and reduce the demand for labor. This can be thought of as the "factor demand" effect of factor taxation, because its impact depends on which factor is being taxed. It follows from (5) that there will also be an indirect effect of factor taxation, since changes in factor taxes on the capital (labor) intensive sector will raise (lower) w/r. This latter effect can be described as the "output tax" effect of factor taxation, since its impact depends on the sector in which the tax is imposed.

Substituting from (5) into (6) and solving yields

$$\hat{X}_1 = \frac{\lambda_{K2}\hat{L} - \lambda_{L2}\hat{K}}{\lambda_{K2} - \lambda_{L2}} - \frac{\alpha_1\hat{p} + \sum_{j\in\{K,L\}} \beta_{j1}(\hat{T}_{j1} - \hat{T}_{j2})}{(\theta_{K2} - \theta_{K1})(\lambda_{K2} - \lambda_{L2})}$$

$$\hat{X}_2 = \frac{\lambda_{L1}\hat{K} - \lambda_{K1}\hat{L}}{\lambda_{K2} - \lambda_{L2}} + \frac{\alpha_1\hat{p} + \sum_{j\in\{L,K\}} \beta_{j2}(\hat{T}_{j1} - \hat{T}_{j2})}{(\theta_{K2} - \theta_{K1})(\lambda_{K2} - \lambda_{L2})} \quad (7)$$

where $\alpha_i \equiv \lambda_{Km}(\sum_{j=1}^{2}\lambda_{Lj}\gamma_{Lj}) + \lambda_{Lm}(\sum_{j=1}^{2}\lambda_{Kj}\gamma_{Kj}) > 0$ for $i,\ m \in \{1,\ 2\},\ m \neq i$ and $\beta_{ji} \equiv \lambda_{Km}(\lambda_{L1}\gamma_{L1}\theta_{j2} + \lambda_{L2}\gamma_{L2}\theta_{j1}) + \lambda_{Lm}(\lambda_{K1}\gamma_{K1}\theta_{j2} + \lambda_{K2}\gamma_{K2}\theta_{j1}) > 0$ *for* $j \in \{K, L\};\ i, m \in \{1, 2\}, m \neq i$. The first term in each expression is the Rybczynski effect, which shows that an increase in the stock of a factor of production will increase the output of the good that uses that factor intensively (in the physical sense) and decrease the output of the other good. It is the physical factor intensities that are relevant for the Rybczynski effect with factor market distortions.

The second term in each expression shows that an increase in the relative price of good 2 will raise the output of good 1 and reduce the output of good 2 iff the value and physical factor intensities agree. The remaining terms in (7) show that a tax on factors in one sector will raise the output of that sector and decrease output in the other sector when the value and factor intensities agree. The "output tax" effect dominates the "factor demand" effect, because a tax on labor or capital in sector i will reduce the output of good i regardless of which factor is used intensively in sector i. As in the case of output price changes, a counter-intuitive result is obtained when the value and factor intensity rankings differ.

In the complete specialization equilibria, factor prices will be determined by the requirement that all factors be employed in the operative sector. The full employment conditions (3) require that $\hat{K} - \hat{L} = \sigma_i(\hat{w} - \hat{r} + \hat{T}_{Li} - \hat{T}_{Ki})$, while the zero profit condition for sector i requires $\theta_{Li}(\hat{w} + \hat{T}_{Li}) + \theta_{Ki}(\hat{r} + \hat{T}_{Ki}) = \hat{p}_i$. Combining these expressions yields

$$\hat{r} = \hat{p} - \hat{T}_{Ki} - \frac{\theta_{Li}}{\sigma_i}\hat{K},\ \ \hat{w} = \hat{p} - \hat{T}_{Li} + \frac{\theta_{Ki}}{\sigma_i}\hat{K},\ \ \hat{X}_i = \theta_{Ki}\hat{K} \quad (8)$$

With specialization, factors do not have an alternative employment opportunity in response to changes in returns. As a result, an increase in factor taxes will result in a proportional decline in the return to the taxed factor. An increase in the supply of capital will require substitution along the isoquant in the active sector to fully employ the increment of capital, which requires an increase in w and a decline in r, with the magnitude of the change being inversely related to the elasticity of substitution between factors in the sector.

3. Steady state

In this section we use the properties of the production equilibrium relations derived above to analyze the steady state of the system of differential equations given by (1) and (4). We first obtain results on existence and uniqueness of the steady state, and show that this steady state will be characterized by incomplete specialization. We then examine the local stability of this steady state, since the steady state will only be observed if there is an equilibrium path to the steady state for initial capital stocks in the neighborhood of the steady state. Finally, we derive results for the effects of changes in distortions on the steady state relative price and capital stock.

3.1. Existence and uniqueness of the steady state

The conditions for a steady state equilibrium can be obtained from (1) and (4) as

$$\left(\frac{r}{p}\right)^{SS} = \rho + \delta$$

$$k^{SS} = X_2/(\delta L) \tag{9}$$

We first establish the conditions under which there will be a steady state equilibrium (p^{SS}, K^{SS}) with incomplete specialization satisfying (9). Since $\tilde{r}(p)/p$ is a monotone function of p for all factor intensity rankings by (5), there can be at most one value of p^{SS} that is consistent with incomplete specialization. The existence of a steady state output price p^{SS} is ensured if $\min_p r(p)/p \leq \rho + \delta \leq \max_p r(p)/p$. Note that this condition imposes restrictions on both the technology and the level of distortions. Since $r/p = f'_2(k)/T_{K2}$, a necessary condition for this to hold is $\lim_{k-0} f_2'(k) > (\rho + \delta)T_{K2} > \lim_{k-\infty} f_2'(k)$. If there is a finite upper bound on the marginal product of capital, there will also be a finite upper bound on T_{K2}.

With incomplete specialization, the steady state capital labor ratio will be the value $k^{SS} \equiv K^{SS}/L$ that solves $E(k) = X_2^e(p^{SS}, k)/L - \delta k = 0$, where X_2^e is obtained from (7). The function $E(k)$ will be linear in k with $E(\tilde{k}_1) < 0$ by the factor price equalization property, so a unique value of k^{SS} consistent with incomplete specialization will exist if it can be shown that

$E(\tilde{k}_2)>0$. Utilizing (9) and the competitive profit conditions we have $E(k^{SS}) = (\rho+\delta)T_{K2}k^{SS} + w^{SS}T_{L2} - \delta k^{SS}$. A sufficient condition for $E(\tilde{k}_2)>0$ is that $T_{K2} > \delta/(\rho+\delta)$, so that a steady state with incomplete specialization will exist as long as the subsidy to capital in the investment good sector is not too large.

We next show that there can be no steady state with complete specialization. A steady state with specialization in good 1 and $K > 0$ is clearly not possible because $\dot{K} = -\delta K$. A steady state with specialization in good 2 requires $f_2'(\bar{k}_2) = (\delta + \rho)T_{K2}$, where $\bar{k}$ is the minimum value of k satisfying $f(k) - \delta k = 0$. However, this marginal product condition cannot occur for $T_{K2} > \delta/(\rho+\delta)$ because $f_2'(\bar{k}_2) \leq \delta$ by the concavity of f.

3.2. Local dynamics of the steady state

Linearizing the system of differential equations (1) and (4) in the neighborhood of the steady state and using the comparative statics results (5) and (7) yields

$$\begin{pmatrix} d\dot{p} \\ d\dot{K} \end{pmatrix} = \begin{pmatrix} A & 0 \\ B & \Gamma \end{pmatrix} \begin{pmatrix} p - p^{SS} \\ K - K^{SS} \end{pmatrix}$$

$$A \equiv \frac{-(\rho+\delta)(1-\theta_{K2})}{\theta_{K2} - \theta_{K1}} \qquad B \equiv \frac{X_2\alpha_2}{(\theta_{K2} - \theta_{K1})(\lambda_{K2} - \lambda_{L2})}$$

$$\Gamma \equiv \frac{\delta(1-\lambda_{K2})}{\lambda_{K2} - \lambda_{L2}} \tag{10}$$

The sign of the coefficient A is determined by the Stolper–Samuelson effect from (5), and will be negative *iff* industry 2 is capital intensive in the value sense. Similarly, the sign of Γ is determined by the Rybczynski effect and will be positive *iff* good 2 is capital intensive in the physical sense. Due to the block recursive structure of the system, the diagonal elements of this matrix will be the eigenvalues. The system will exhibit saddle path stability if the eigenvalues have opposite signs, and it is clear from the definitions of the terms that the eigenvalues will have opposite signs if the value and physical intensities agree. The system will be locally indeterminate if the diagonal terms are negative, which will occur if $\theta_{K2}>\theta_{K1}$ and $\lambda_{K2}<\lambda_{L2}$. Finally, the system is locally unstable if the diagonal elements are both positive, which arises if $\theta_{K2}<\theta_{K1}$ and $\lambda_{K2}>\lambda_{L2}$. Since the dynamics of the system will differ substantially across the various cases, we consider each case in turn.[9]

---

[9] The coefficient B will be positive iff the physical and value intensities agree. It is this element which reflects the perverse output-price responses when physical and value intensity rankings differ. In the dynamic process studied here this term has no impact on the local stability of the system.

We begin with the two cases in which sector 2 is capital intensive in the value sense. With $\theta_{K2} > \theta_{K1}$, an increase in the price of good 2 raises the rental on capital more than proportionally by the Stolper–Samuelson theorem. This will require a reduction in the capital gain on investment goods to restore the net return on capital to ρ, which results in a stable price adjustment process for good 2 ($A < 0$). If the physical intensity ranking agrees with the value ranking, (i.e. $\lambda_{K2} > \lambda_{L2}$), the adjustment process of capital (at fixed p) is unstable ($\Gamma > 0$) because an increase in the capital stock will raise the output of the investment good more than proportionately. The fact that the diagonal elements of the matrix have opposite signs ensures that the system will have a saddle path. The dynamic adjustment process when sector 2 is capital intensive in both physical and value sense is illustrated in the phase diagram in Figure 4. Let $\tilde{k}_i(p) = k(\tilde{w}(p)/\tilde{r}(p))$ be the capital labor ratio in sector i at incomplete specialization at p. Using (5) and the definition of the elasticity of substitution in sector i,

$$\frac{\hat{p}}{\hat{k}}\bigg|_{\tilde{k}_i} = \frac{\theta_{K1} - \theta_{K2}}{\sigma_i} \tag{11}$$

These loci will be downward-sloping in this case, because w/r is a decreasing function of p. The results of Section 2 ensure that incomplete specialization will be the unique equilibrium for $k \in \left(\tilde{k}_1(p), \tilde{k}_2(p)\right)$. The $\dot{p} = 0$ locus will be horizontal at p^{SS}, with $\dot{p} < 0$ for $p > p^{SS}$. The $\dot{k} = 0$ locus will have a slope of Γ/B, which will be negative in the neighborhood of the steady state. The existence result above ensures that these curves

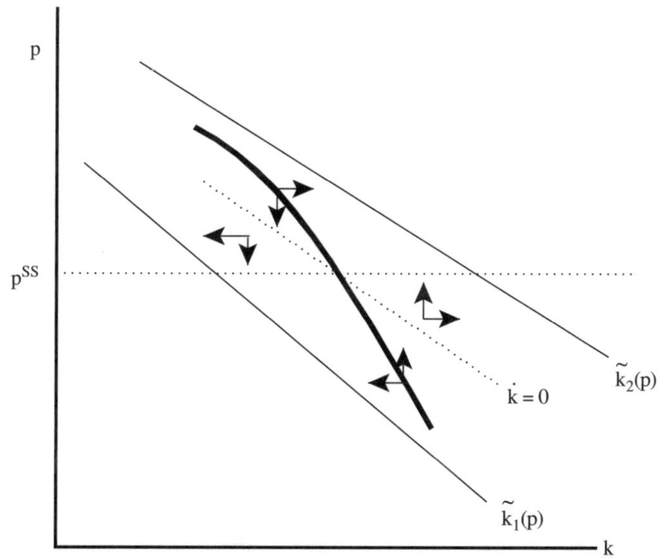

Fig. 4. Saddle paths with $\theta_{K2} > \theta_{K1}$ and $\lambda_{K2} > \lambda_{L2}$.

intersect in the region of incomplete specialization. Along the saddle path, the price of the investment good will decline (increase) as capital accumulates (decumulates) toward the steady state level. The adjustment of the price is such that it stabilizes the adjustment process of capital. It can also be seen that factor price equalization would not hold along the adjustment path to the steady state between two countries with the same factor market distortions but different capital stocks, because the relative price of the investment good varies with the level of the capital stock. The absence of factor price equalization along the transition path is not surprising, since there are two non-traded factors of production and only one traded good in this model.

If sector 2 is capital intensive in the value sense but labor intensive in the physical sense, the capital adjustment process will be stable at fixed p ($\Gamma < 0$). This case is illustrated in Figure 5, which differs from Figure 4 in that $\tilde{k}_1(p) > \tilde{k}_2(p)$. The dynamics differ in this case because $\dot{k}$ is decreasing in k and $\dot{p}$ is decreasing in p, so the motion of the system will be in the direction of the steady state in each region between the $\dot{k} = 0$ and $\dot{p} = 0$ loci. The system will exhibit local indeterminacy because there will be a continuum of p values for which the system will converge to the (unique) steady state from an initial k. When the roots A and Γ are unequal, this convergence will be tangent to a line through the steady state for all but one of the paths (Takayama, 1993).

We next consider the two cases in which sector 2 is labor intensive in the value sense. In these cases the price adjustment process is unstable, because an increase in p reduces the return to capital and requires an increase in the

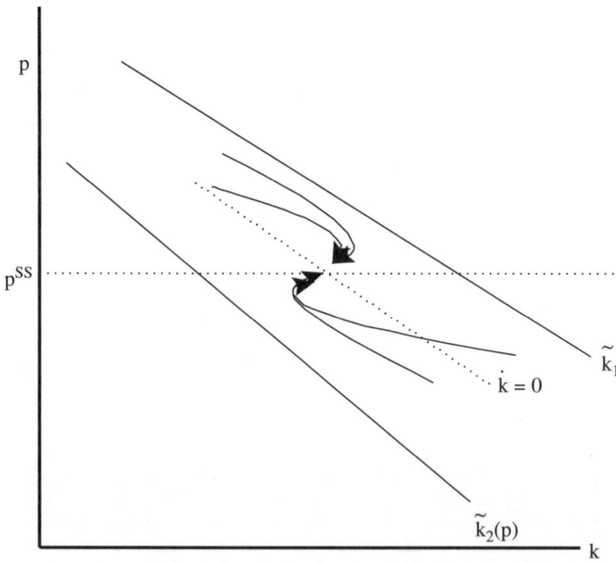

Fig. 5. ***Local indeterminacy with $\theta_{K2} > \theta_{K1}$ and $\lambda_{K2} < \lambda_{L2}$.***

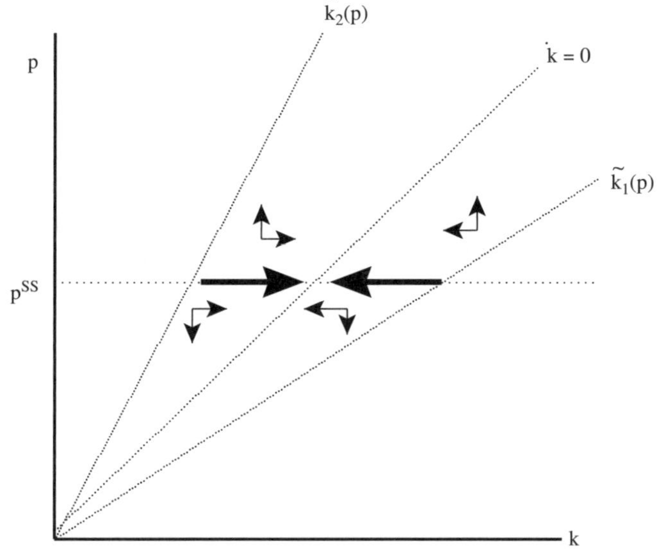

***Fig. 6.* Saddle path with $\theta_{K2} < \theta_{K1}$ and $\lambda_{K2} < \lambda_{L2}$.**

rate of capital gain to satisfy the intertemporal arbitrage condition. Figure 6 shows the adjustment process for the case with $\theta_{K2} < \theta_{K1}$ and $\lambda_{K2} < \lambda_{L2}$, in which sector 2 is labor intensive in both the physical and value sense. The slope of the $\tilde{k}_i(p)$ loci is reversed from Figure 4, because a higher p results in a higher w/r when $\theta_{K2} < \theta_{K1}$. The slope of the $\dot{k} = 0$ locus is also reversed, since an increase in k will reduce the output of the investment goods sector more than proportionally. This requires an increase in p to restore $\dot{k} = 0$. With an unstable price adjustment process, the saddle path must be characterized by a constant value of p at the steady state level. The capital stock will converge to the steady state level with a constant price in this case because increases in the capital stock result in a decrease in the output of the investment good (i.e. $\Gamma < 0$). In this case factor price equalization would also hold along the adjustment path to the steady state for countries with identical factor market distortions.

In the remaining case in which sector 2 is labor intensive in the value sense but capital intensive in the physical sense, the steady state is locally unstable. Since the price process is unstable in this case, the only possible path to the steady state is along the $\dot{p} = 0$ locus. However, the adjustment for k at fixed p is unstable when sector 2 is capital intensive in the physical sense. Therefore, there can be no path to the steady state with incomplete specialization in this case.[10]

[10] The results on instability and indeterminacy for this case are obtained by Meng and Velasco (2004).

It is useful to compare the results of this analysis with those obtained by Neary (1978), who examined the stability of the static two-sector model with factor market distortions. He used an adjustment process in which the stock of labor (capital) employed in sector 2 will be increasing iff the after tax return to labor (capital) in sector 2 exceeds that in sector 1. In the case of a small open economy with both goods traded, he showed that the adjustment process is unstable in any case in which value and physical intensities differ between sectors. In our setting, the adjustment process arises out of an explicitly dynamic optimization process with capital accumulation. Local instability of the steady state will arise in only one of the two cases where value and physical rankings differ.

3.3. Steady state effects of factor taxation

For all of the cases in which the steady state is locally stable, we can do a comparative statics analysis to determine how p^{SS} and k^{SS} are affected by changes in tax rates. The determination of the steady state factor rewards can be obtained by substituting the real return for capital in the steady state from (9) into the competitive profit condition for good 2, which yields $c^2(w^{SS}T_{L2}, r^{SS}T_{K2}) = r^{SS}/(\rho+\delta)$. Since the unit cost function is homogeneous of degree 1 in factor prices, it follows that the steady state wage/rental ratio will be determined by the factor taxes in sector 2 alone. Differentiating this condition yields

$$\hat{w}^{SS} - \hat{r}^{SS} = -\hat{T}_{L2} - \frac{\theta_{K2}}{\theta_{L2}}\hat{T}_{K2} \tag{12}$$

The steady state wage/rental ratio will be decreasing in taxes on factors located in sector 2. Any tax on factors in sector 2 will raise the cost of production, which must reduce w^{SS}/r^{SS} in order to keep r^{SS}/p^{SS} constant. Combining (12) with the competitive profit condition from sector 1 yields the solutions for the impact of taxes on the respective factor returns

$$\begin{aligned}\hat{r}^{SS} &= \hat{p}^{SS} = \theta_{L1}(\hat{T}_{L2} - \hat{T}_{L1}) + \theta_{L1}\theta_{K2}\hat{T}_{K2}/\theta_{L2} - \theta_{K1}\hat{T}_{K1}\\ \hat{w}^{SS} &= -\theta_{L1}\hat{T}_{L1} - \theta_{K1}\hat{T}_{K1} - \theta_{K1}\hat{T}_{L2} - \theta_{K1}\theta_{K2}\hat{T}_{K2}/\theta_{L2}\end{aligned} \tag{13}$$

The steady state relative price of investment goods, and hence the steady state return to capital, will be increasing in the factor taxes on the investment good sector and decreasing in the taxes on the consumption good sector. The steady state return to labor is decreasing in all of the tax rates, reflecting the shifting of taxes onto the inelastically supplied factor in the long run. A proportional increase in all taxes will raise the cost of the investment good iff the investment good sector is capital intensive in the value sense. Since steady state prices are independent of factor supplies, this model will generate factor price equalization in the steady state for all countries with the same level of factor market distortions.

Equations (12) and (13) illustrate two differences important between the impact of factor taxes on factor returns between instantaneous and steady state effects. The first is that the direction of the impact of factor taxes on factor returns in the steady state does not depend on which sector is the capital-intensive sector, because the return on capital is tied to the relative price of the investment good in the steady state. A second difference is that a proportional increase in all taxes will reduce the steady state wage/rental ratio, whereas in the static model there was no effect on the wage rental ratio. Increasing the tax on all factors reduces the attractiveness of investments in capital, and will thus raise the relative cost of capital services in the steady state.

The effects of factor taxes on the steady state capital stock are obtained by solving the system (10) using $\hat{X}_2 = \hat{K}$ and substituting for $\hat{w} - \hat{r}$ from (12). This yields

$$\hat{K}^{SS} = \lambda_{L1}(\gamma_{L1} + \gamma_{K1})(\hat{T}_{L1} - \hat{T}_{K1} - \hat{T}_{L2} - \frac{\theta_{K2}}{\theta_{L2}}\hat{T}_{K2}) - \frac{\lambda_{L1}\lambda_{K2}\gamma_{K2} + \lambda_{K1}\lambda_{L2}\gamma_{L2}}{\theta_{L2}\lambda_{K1}}\hat{T}_{K2} \tag{14}$$

The first set of terms in (14) reflect substitution effects in sector 1 from parameter changes. Factor taxes on sector 2 raise the relative cost of capital in sector 1 as shown in (13), leading to substitution of labor for capital. Taxes on factors in sector 1 will not affect $(w/r)^{SS}$, but will cause substitution between factors in sector 1. An increase in the tax on labor (capital) in sector 1 will result in substitution away from labor (capital) leading to an increase (decrease) in the steady state capital stock. The remaining terms in (14) capture substitution effects in sector 2. The change in the relative factor cost in sector 2 is given by the change in $T_{L2}w^{SS}/(T_{K2}r^{SS})$. This relative factor cost is independent of T_{L2} but decreasing in T_{K2} from (12), so only the tax on capital creates substitution of capital for labor in sector 2.

Equation (14) shows that the effect of changes in factor taxes on the capital stock (and hence the output of the investment good) does not depend on which sector is capital intensive, or on whether the value and physical intensities agree. This stands in sharp contrast to the static results in (7). Value intensities played a role in the static output effect of tax changes because they determined the direction of change in the wage/rental ratio. However, the direction of the change in the steady state wage rental ratio in response to a tax change does not depend on the value intensity of the sectors as shown in (12). The relative physical intensities of the sectors do not matter because capital must be adjusted to match the output of sector 2 in the steady state (i.e. the determinant of the matrix on the left hand side of (6) is simply $-\lambda_{K1}$ when $\hat{X}_2 = \hat{K}$).

4. Dynamics in the region of complete specialization

We conclude with an analysis of the dynamics in the region in which the economy is completely specialized. The results of Section 2 identified the region of the phase plane in which the economy is specialized in production. In this section we characterize the properties of the system of differential equations (1) and (4) when the economy is specialized, which yields an autonomous system that is defined in the respective regions of complete specialization. We then combine these with the results on dynamics with incomplete specialization to show how the economy could move between regions of specialization and incomplete specialization.

We begin by examining the region of the phase plane where the economy is specialized in good 1, which we refer to as region I. We can substitute the equilibrium conditions for specialization in good 1 into (1) and (4) to obtain the dynamic system for region I,

$$\dot{p} = p(\rho + \delta) - f_1'(k)/T_{K1}$$
$$\dot{k} = -\delta k \tag{15}$$

Equations (15) comprise an autonomous coupled system of differential equations so that one and only one integral curve passes through each point in region I. These integral curves describe the path of p and k satisfying (15) starting from a point in region I, and can be described by the implicit function $\Psi_1(k, C_1)$, where C_1 is a constant of integration. One question of interest is whether any of the integral curves in the region of complete specialization will enter the region of incomplete specialization and connect to a path that converges to the steady state.

The capital stock must be decreasing in the region of the phase plane associated with complete specialization in the consumption good. The change in price of good 2 is increasing in p and increasing in k, so the locus of values consistent with $\dot{p} = 0$ will be negatively sloped in the phase plane in region I. Since $\hat{p} = \hat{r}$ along the $\dot{p}_{\mathrm{I}} = 0$ locus, we have from (8) that

$$\left.\frac{\hat{p}}{\hat{k}}\right|_{\dot{p}_{\mathrm{I}}=0} = -\frac{\theta_{L1}}{\sigma_1} \tag{16}$$

Note in particular that the point $(p^{\mathrm{SS}}, \tilde{k}_1(p^{\mathrm{SS}}))$ will lie on this locus.

We refer to the region in which the economy is specialized in the investment good as region II. If the economy is specialized in the investment good,

$$\frac{\dot{p}}{p} = (\rho + \delta) - f_2'(k)/T_{K2}$$
$$\dot{k} = f_2(k) - \delta k \tag{17}$$

As in the case of (15), these equations derive a set of integral curves that can be defined by the implicit function $\psi_{\mathrm{II}}(k, C_2)$, where C_2 is a constant of integration. Changes in the price of good 2 generate a proportional increase in w and r when the economy is specialized in good 2, which affects the costs and benefits of holding the investment good by the same proportion. Therefore, there will be a unique value of k at which $\dot{p} = 0$, and it can be seen from (6) that this value will be $\tilde{k}_2(p^{SS})$. Similarly, there is a unique value $\bar{k}_2$ at which $\dot{k} = 0$, by the strict concavity of f. Assuming $T_K > \delta/(\delta + \rho)$, we must also have $\bar{k}_2 > \tilde{k}(p^{SS})$.

These results establish that region II can be divided into three segments base on the initial capital stock. For $k < \tilde{k}_2(p^{SS})$, the capital stock will be rising and the price of the investment good falling. For $k \in (\tilde{k}_2(p^{SS}), \bar{k}_2)$, the capital stock is still rising but the marginal product of capital is sufficiently low that the value of a unit of capital is rising. For $k > \bar{k}_2$, the stock of capital is falling and the value of a unit of capital is rising.

4.1. Dynamics in regions of specialization when value and physical intensities agree

If the physical and value intensity rankings agree, specialization in the labor (capital) intensive good will occur for values of k below (above) the capital intensity $\tilde{k}(p)$ associated with that good at current prices. The region of complete specialization will be bounded away from the steady state in this case, so specialization will not be observed in the neighborhood of the steady state. However, complete specialization could be observed if the initial capital stocks are sufficiently far from the steady state and there is an integral curve in the region of specialization that is part of a path leading to the steady state.

Figure 7 illustrates the dynamics for the case in which good 2 is capital intensive in both the value and physical senses. Specialization in good 1 will occur for (p, k) combinations to the left of the $\tilde{k}_1(p)$ locus. The locus of values in region I at which p is constant is denoted by $\dot{p}_{\mathrm{I}} = 0$. By comparing (11) and (16), it can be seen that this locus must be steeper than the $\tilde{k}_1(p)$ at their intersection point, $\tilde{k}_1(p^{SS})$. To the left of the $\dot{p}_{\mathrm{I}} = 0$ locus, the rental on capital is sufficiently high that price of the investment good is declining. Initial values of (p, k) in this region of the phase plane could not be consistent with a path that converged to the steady state, since the dynamics of (p, k) do not allow the economy to escape specialization in good 1. To the right of $\dot{p}_{\mathrm{I}} = 0$ locus, the capital stock is declining and the price of the investment good is rising. A path starting in this region could be part of a convergent path to the steady state, since the dynamics allow the path to enter the region of incomplete specialization.

Specialization in good 2 holds for values to the right of the $\tilde{k}_2(p)$ locus in Figure 7. A path starting in region II could never converge to the steady state for $k > \tilde{k}_2(p^{SS})$, because the price of the investment good is increasing

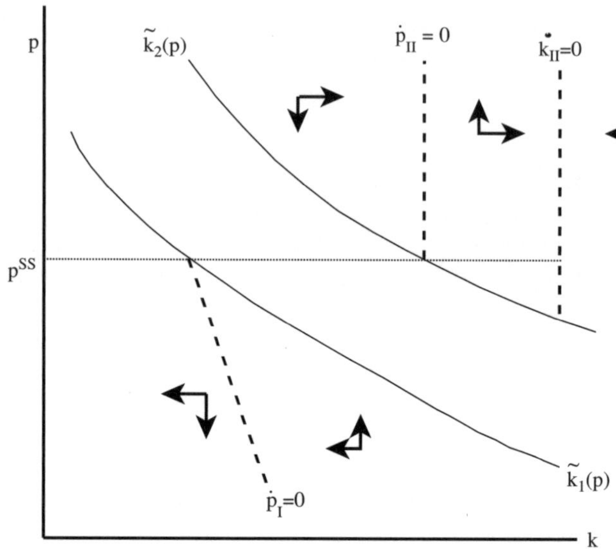

Fig. 7. Phase plane in regions of specialization for $\theta_{K2} > \theta_{K1}$ and $\lambda_{K2} > \lambda_{L2}$.

and the path will be asymptotic to the $\dot{k}_{II} = 0$ line. For $k < \tilde{k}_2(p^{SS})$, the price of the investment good is decreasing and the capital stock is increasing. A path starting in this region could enter the region of incomplete specialization, and could converge to the steady state if it intersects the saddle path shown in Figure 7 at the boundary of the region of incomplete specialization.

A similar result is illustrated in Figure 8, which shows the dynamics in the regions of specialization when good 2 is labor intensive in the both the physical and value sense. Complete specialization in good 1 (good 2) occurs for initial values to the right of the $\tilde{k}_1(p)$ locus (left of the $\tilde{k}_2(p)$ locus). The characterization of paths that begin in the region of complete specialization and converge to the steady state is straightforward in this case, since the saddle path corresponds to $p = p^{SS}$ in the region of incomplete specialization as illustrated in Figure 8. Since there is an integral curve going through each point in region I, there will be a path that goes through the point $(p^{SS}, \tilde{k}_1(p^{SS}))$. It is clear from the phase diagram that this path must lie to the left of the $\dot{p}_I = 0$ locus. This path will then be part of the saddle path that converges to the steady state. A similar argument establishes that there will be a path in region II lying to the right of the $\dot{p}_{II} = 0$ locus that converges to the point $(p^{SS}, \tilde{k}_1(p^{SS}))$.

These results show that when the value and physical intensity rankings agree, the saddle path to the steady state may start in the region with specialization in the consumption good if the initial capital stock is sufficiently high. Similarly, the saddle path may start in the region with

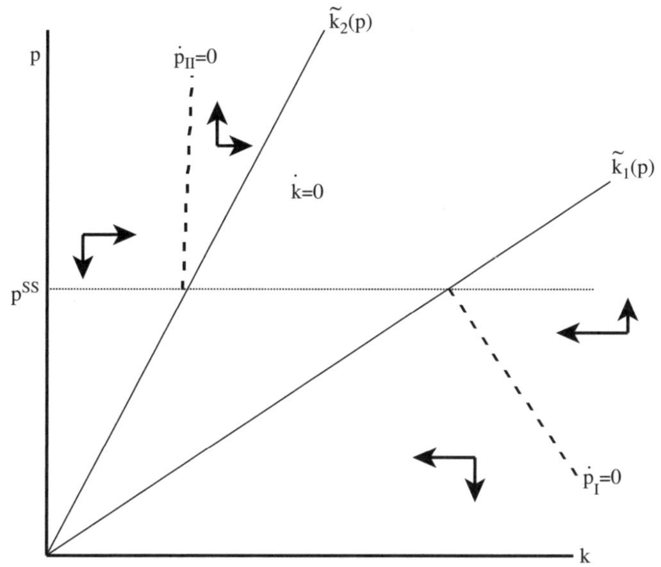

Fig. 8. Phase plane in regions of specialization for $\theta_{K2} < \theta_{K1}$ **and** $\lambda_{K2} < \lambda_{L2}$.

specialization in the investment good if the initial capital stock is sufficiently low.

4.2. Dynamics in the region of specialization when value and physical intensities differ

In the case where physical and value intensities differ, regions I and II will both overlap the region of incomplete specialization. Figure 9 illustrates this point for the case where sector 2 is capital intensive in the value sense but labor intensive in the physical sense. Region I lies to the right of the $\tilde{k}_1(p)$ locus and region II lies to the left of the $\tilde{k}_2(p)$ locus. The dynamics in the respective regions are the same as illustrated in Figure 5. The difference is that in this case there are three autonomous systems that describe the dynamics in the region of specialization: one associated with incomplete specialization and one associated with complete specialization in each of the goods. The dynamic system for the case of complete specialization exhibits local indeterminacy as illustrated in Figure 5. For the portion of region I contained between the $\tilde{k}_2(p)$ and $\tilde{k}_1(p)$ loci, the capital stock is decreasing and the price is decreasing (increasing) to the left (right) of the $\dot{p}_{\mathrm{I}} = 0$ locus. The arrows for this case are shown as dotted in Figure 7, to distinguish them from the ones associated with region II. For the portion of region II contained between the $\tilde{k}_2(p)$ and $\tilde{k}_1(p)$ loci for which $k < \tilde{k}_2$, the stock is increasing and the price is increasing (decreasing) to the left (right) of the $\dot{p}_{\mathrm{II}} = 0$ locus.

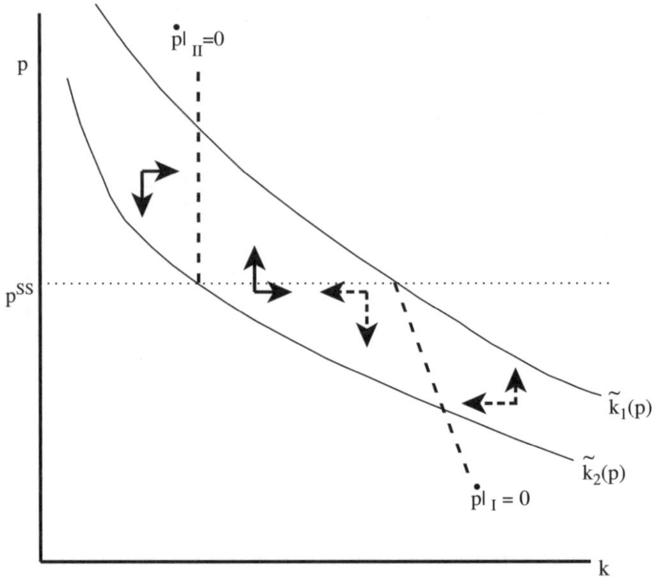

Fig. 9. Phase plane in regions of specialization for $\theta_{K2} > \theta_{K1}$ **and** $\lambda_{K2} < \lambda_{L2}$.

In the case in which the regions of specialization and incomplete specialization are non-intersection, any movement between production patterns must occur at the boundary of the region of incomplete specialization and must involve transitions between specialization and incomplete specialization. In the case where regions I and II overlap the region of incomplete specialization, we have the possibility that there are transitions between production regimes in the interior of the region of specialization. For example, suppose that the production pattern is one of complete specialization in good 1 from 0 to T_1 at which time the pair $(p(T_1), k(T_1))$ is contained in the region of incomplete specialization. Since production with specialization in good 2 or production with incomplete specialization is also an equilibrium at $(p(T_1), k(T_1))$, then there will also be an integral curve starting at that point associated with each of these alternative production patterns. A switch from specialization in good 1 to one of the other production patterns at T_1 would be consistent with a competitive equilibrium if it follows a path from T_1 onward that satisfies the transversality conditions. For example, transition at T_1 to one of the continuum of paths with incomplete specialization that converges to the steady state would be such a path. However, there could also potentially be paths that cycle within the region of incomplete specialization without converging to the paths. We examine "compound paths" of this type in more detail in Bond and Driskill (2006), and also extend the analysis to the locally unstable case in which the investment good sector is labor intensive in the value ranking but capital intensive in the physical ranking.

5. Conclusions

In this chapter we have examined the impact of distortions in a dynamic open economy model of capital accumulation. As in the analysis of the static model analyzed by Jones, the potential for divergence between the capital intensity ranking of sectors by the value and physical measures is a source of paradoxes. In particular, this divergence has two effects on the dynamics of the system. The first is that it can lead to either local instability or local indeterminacy in the neighborhood of the steady state. The second is that it generates a multiplicity of static equilibria for the range of factor supplies consistent with incomplete specialization. The latter result also creates the possibility of an additional source of multiplicity, which is due to the possibility of paths that switch between patterns of specialization. Interestingly, however, the value and physical intensities do not play a role in determining the direction of changes in fact or market distortions on the return to factors of production and the level of the steady state capital stock. The direction of these changes is determined by the sectors in which taxes are imposed.

The open economy model we have examined here emphasizes the role of the production structure. Extensions of the analysis to the case of a closed economy model, or to an endogenous growth model with physical and human capital accumulation remain an area for future research.

Acknowledgements

We thank participants at the conference at City University of Hong Kong for comments on an earlier draft.

References

Benhabib, J., Meng, Q., Nishimura, K. (2000), Indeterminacy under constant returns to scale in multisector economies. *Econometrica* 68, 1541–1548.

Benhabib, J., Nishimura, K. (1998), Indeterminacy and sunspots with constant returns. *Journal of Economic Theory* 81, 58–96.

Bond, E.W., Driskill, R.A. (2006), Indeterminacy in two sector models with factor market distortions: the importance of VIPIRS. Working paper 0626, Department of Economics, Vanderbilt University, Nashville, TN.

Bond, E.W., Wang, P., Yip, C.K. (1996), A general two-sector model of endogenous growth with human and physical capital: balanced growth and transitional dynamics. *Journal of Economic Theory* 68, 149–173.

Jones, R.W. (1965), The structure of simple general equilibrium models. *Journal of Political Economy* 73, 557–572.

Jones, R.W. (1971), Distortions in factor markets and the general equilibrium model of production. *Journal of Political Economy* 79, 437–495.

Magee, S.P. (1973), Factor market distortions, production, and trade: a survey. *Oxford Economic Papers* 25, 1–43.

Meng, Q., Velasco, A. (2004), Market Imperfections and Instability in Open Economies. *Journal of International Economics* 64, 503–519.

Milesi-Ferretti, G.M., Roubini, N. (1998), On the taxation of human and physical capital in models of endogenous growth. *Journal of Public Economics* 70, 237–254.

Neary, P.J. (1978), Dynamic stability and the theory of factor market distortions. *American Economic Review* 68, 671–682.

Rebelo, S. (1991), Long-run policy analysis and long-run growth. *Journal of Political Economy* 99, 500–521.

Takayama, A. (1993), *Analytical Methods in Economics*. University of Michigan Press, Ann Arbor.

CHAPTER 10

Specific Factor Models and Dynamics in International Trade

Yunfang Hu[a], Kazuo Nishimura[b] and Koji Shimomura[c]

[a]*Graduate School of International Cultural Studies, Tohoku University, Japan*
E-mail address: yhu@intcul.tohoku.ac.jp
[b]*Institute of Economic Research, Kyoto University, Japan*
E-mail address: nishimura@kier.kyoto-u.ac.jp
[c]*Research Institute for Economics & Business Administration, Kobe University, Japan*

Abstract

Based on the Jones (1971) model, we construct two dynamic models of international trade in which the rate of time preference is either constant or time-varying. The main purpose is to study whether and under what conditions the results derived in the Jones model still hold in the dynamic framework. It is shown that the results of dynamic models may be similar or different to those obtained in the static model. For example, it is possible that, in both static and dynamic models, an increase in the commodity price raises this commodity's output and the return to the specific factor in this sector. However, the effects on the wage rate may be different due to the factor accumulation impact in the dynamic framework.

Keywords: Dynamics, international trade, specific-factor model

JEL classifications: D90, F11

1. Introduction

In the seminal 1971 paper, Ronald W. Jones developed a specific factor model which is regarded to as one of the basic general equilibrium models of international trade. Subsequently, this three-factor model has been developed in many ways. For example, it has been used intensively in discussing the short-run issues of international trade.[1] Though this literature is large, there are few studies, to our knowledge, examining

[1] Among others, see Mayer (1974), Mussa (1974) and Neary (1978), for example.

Frontiers of Economics and Globalization
Volume 4 ISSN: 1574-8715
DOI: 10.1016/S1574-8715(08)04010-4

the dynamic property of the above general equilibrium model. To extend the Jones model to the dynamic framework, in the present chapter we assume that the general production factor is accumulable and households allocate their income intertemporally. The main purpose is to study whether and under what conditions the results derived from the Jones model still hold in the dynamic frameworks.

The reason we investigate the specific factor model in a dynamic framework is that there exist some production factors that cannot move across sectors even in the long run. This can happen either because of a large transportation cost, or because of differences in the factors they use in production processes. For example, if specifying the two industries as agriculture and manufacturing, and their productions need labor–land and labor–capital as production factors, respectively, then in this case labor is the mobile factor while capital and land are not.

The Jones model can be extended in different ways. To obtain a dynamic counterpart to the Jones model, we specify the mobile factor as human capital, which can be promoted by education. The human capital literature tells us that there are two components in the education-related expenditure, investment and consumption (Schultz, 1963). That is, households' education expenditure can, on the one hand, raise the level of human capital, and, on the other, it can augment the households' utility through consumption of the education service directly.

Two dynamic models will be presented here. In the first one, we extend directly the Jones model to a dynamic framework by assuming an accumulable general factor and a constant rate of time preference. This model is refined in the second model by assuming that the rate of time preference depends on the utility level. This kind of variable rate of time preference is originally considered by Uzawa (1968) and its relevance in improving economic models has been proved by empirical studies.[2] In both models, we prove the existence, uniqueness and saddle-point stability of the steady state. Next, we conduct comparative statics with respect to the commodity prices. Then we compare the results with those obtained in the static framework. The welfare effect in the first dynamic model is also investigated.

The rest of the chapter is arranged as follows. Section 2 reconstructs the Jones model. Section 3 presents a dynamic version of the Jones model in which the rate of the time preference is constant. This model is modified in Section 4 by endogenizing the rate of time preference and we conclude the chapter in Section 5. The proofs of the main results can be found in the Appendix.

---

[2] A recent paper by Guest and McDonald (2001) shows how the Uzawa preference improves the simulations properties of the small open economy world.

2. The Jones model

In this section, we reformulate the Jones model with duality. Following the convention, we consider a world economy consisting of a large number of countries. Each country is small in the sense that it takes the world price as given. Produced commodities are internationally tradable, while production factors are not.

There are two production sectors in which two internationally tradable goods, goods 1 and 2, are produced. Good 1 is a pure consumption good with price p, while good 2 is a consumable capital good which serves as the numeraire. Good i ($i = 1, 2$) is produced by using a sector-specific factor of production L_i and a general factor, K. While L_i is given and constant over time, K is the accumulated good 2. As we mentioned in the introduction, the general factor K is human capital and sector 2 is the education sector. Households' education expenditure can, on the one hand, increase productivity through human capital accumulation, and, on the other, provide utility to households by consuming those services directly.

Following the Jones model, we assume neoclassical production technologies in both sectors. Let us denote the production function of good i by $Y_i = F^i(K_i, L_i)$. Denote the wage to the general factor K, and the returns to the sector-i specific factors L_i as w, r_i, respectively. Then market competition makes each factor's marginal production equal to its rate of return. That is, $w = pF_1^1 = F_1^2$, $r_1 = pF_2^1$ and $r_2 = F_2^2$.

For given aggregate amounts of general factor K and specific forces L_1, L_2, we have the GDP function

$$\begin{aligned} G(p, K, L_1, L_2) &\equiv \max_{K_i}\{pF^1(K_1, L_1) + F^2(K_2, L_2) | K_1 + K_2 \leq K\} \\ &= pF^1(K_1(p, K, L_1, L_2), L_1) + F^2(K_2(p, K, L_1, L_2), L_2), \end{aligned}$$

where $(K_1(p, K, L_1, L_2), K_2(p, K, L_1, L_2))$ is the optimal solution. From the constant return-to-scale property of the production functions, the GDP function has the following properties:[3]

$$\begin{aligned} &G_p = F^1, G_K = pF_1^1 = F_1^2 = w, G_{L_1} = pF_2^1 = r_1, G_{L_2} = F_2^2 = r_2, \\ &G_{pp} > 0, G_{Kp} = G_{pK} > 0, G_{KK} < 0, \text{and} \\ &G_{L_1p} > 0, G_{L_2p} < 0, G_{L_1K} > 0, G_{L_2K} > 0. \end{aligned}$$

That is, GDP function's partial derivative with respect to the commodity price p is equal to the output of this good; its partial derivatives with respect to the factor endowments are the same as the value of these factors' marginal productivity in each sector.

We define the representative household's momentary utility function as, $u = U(c_1, c_2)$, where c_i is the consumption of good i. We assume that the

[3] See Appendix (1) for the proof.

utility function satisfies the standard properties and also homotheticity. That is, $U(c_1,c_2)$ can be rewritten as the composite function of a strictly increasing function $g(v)$ and a linearly homogeneous function $v(c_1,c_2)$: $U(c_1,c_2) \equiv g(v(c_1,c_2))$.

LEMMA 1. *$g(v)$ is strictly concave if and only if $U(c_1,c_2)$ is strictly concave.*

PROOF. See Appendix (2). ∎

For given preference level u, the representative household's expenditure function is

$$E(p,u) \equiv \min_{c_i}\{pc_1 + c_2 | u \leq U(c_1,c_2) \equiv g(v(c_1,c_2))\}.$$

From the homothetic property of the utility function, the following results can be obtained.

LEMMA 2. *If the momentary utility function $U(c_1,c_2)$ is homothetic, then the expenditure function is multiplicatively separable,*

$$E(p,u) \equiv e(p)\phi(u),$$

where $e(p)$ is increasing and concave in p, while $\phi(u)$, the inverse function of $g(v)$, is increasing and convex in u. That is,

$$e' > 0, e'' < 0, \phi' > 0, \phi'' > 0.$$

PROOF. See Appendix (3). ∎

The household's decision problem is

$$\max_u \ e(p)\phi(u) \text{ subject to } e(p)\phi(u) \leqq wK + r_1L_1 + r_2L_2,$$

where w, r_1, r_2 (and p) are given. In the original Jones model, factor endowments, K, and L_i ($i = 1, 2$) are fixed. The equilibrium consumptions, hence the maximum level u for given p, K and L_i ($i = 1, 2$), are obtained from

$$\max_{c_1,c_2} U(c_1,c_2)$$

subject to

$$pc_1 + c_2 = G(p,K,L_1,L_2)$$

or equivalently

$$e(p)\phi(u) = G(p,K,L_1,L_2). \tag{1}$$

The equilibrium factor prices are then given by $w = G_K$, $r_1 = G_{L_1}, r_2 = G_{L_2}$. Any imbalance between domestic consumption (c_1,c_2) and domestic production (Y_1,Y_2) is resolved, since the prices of these commodities is fixed by imports and/or exports of these goods.

For given K, L_i ($i = 1, 2$), the effects of a change in commodity price p upon outputs and factor prices are shown as

$$\frac{\partial Y_1}{\partial p} = \frac{\partial}{\partial p} G_p = G_{pp} > 0, \tag{2a}$$

$$\frac{\partial w}{\partial p} = \frac{\partial}{\partial p} G_K = G_{Kp} > 0 \tag{2b}$$

and

$$\frac{\partial r_1}{\partial p} = \frac{\partial}{\partial p} G_{L_1} = G_{L_1 p} > 0. \tag{2c}$$

The relations in (2) make clear that the effects of price change upon outputs and factor prices. It is shown that a price increase of good 1 can raise all the factor prices in that sector. Notice also that, preference parameters do not affect those comparative static results that rely solely on the production side of the economy.

As in Jones (1971), we can derive the following factor price/commodity price relation by using the properties of the GDP function (see Appendix (4) for the proof):

$$\frac{\mathrm{d}r_1}{r_1} > \frac{\mathrm{d}p}{p} > \frac{\mathrm{d}w}{w} > 0 > \frac{\mathrm{d}r_2}{r_2}. \tag{3}$$

That is, there is no *magnification effect* for the mobile factor.

To obtain the welfare effect of a change in p, let us totally differentiate (1) with respect to p and u, then

$$e\phi' \mathrm{d}u = \left[G_p - e'(p)\phi(u)\right] \mathrm{d}p. \tag{4}$$

We find that whether a rise in p makes the community better-off or worse-off depends on trade patterns. Equation (4) shows that if the pure consumption good is imported (resp. exported), a rise in the price of this good makes the representative household worse-off (better-off). For tractability, in the following, we will concentrate on the case where the economy is approximately in autarky.

3. Dynamic model with a constant rate of time preference

When capital is accumulable, households shall maximize their aggregate utility intertemporally. The representative household's optimization problem is

$$\max_{u(t)} \int_0^{+\infty} u(t) e^{-\rho t} \mathrm{d}t$$

subject to

$$\dot{K}(t) = w(t)K(t) + r_1(t)L_1 + r_2(t)L_2 - e(p)\phi(u(t)),$$

where the factor prices $w(t)$, $r_1(t)$, $r_2(t)$ are given for t in $[0,+\infty)$.

The Hamiltonian is

$$H(u(t), \lambda(t), K(t); p, L_1, L_2) \equiv u(t) + \lambda(t)[G(p, K(t), L_1, L_2) - e(p)\phi(u(t))]$$

and at the interior solutions, the first-order conditions are

$$\frac{\partial H}{\partial u} = 1 - \lambda(t)e(p)\phi'(u(t)) = 0,$$
$$\dot{\lambda}(t) = \lambda(t)[\rho - w(t)].$$

The dynamic equilibrium is obtained here by adjustment of the trajectories of factor prices $w(t)$, $r_1(t)$, $r_2(t)$ so that demands for inputs are equal to the supplies of these inputs $K(t)$, L_1, L_2. In equilibrium one will have for any t in $[0,+\infty)$:

$$w(t)K(t) + r_1(t)L_1 + r_2(t)L_2 \equiv G(p, K(t), L_1, L_2)$$

and $w(t) = G_K$, $r_1(t) = G_{L_1}$, $r_2(t) = G_{L_2}$. By plugging these relations into the first-order conditions of the household, one gets the dynamic system

$$\dot{K} = G(p, K, L_1, L_2) - e(p)\phi(u), \tag{5}$$

$$\dot{\lambda} = \lambda[\rho - G_K(p, K, L_1, L_2)] \tag{6}$$

and

$$0 = 1 - \lambda e(p)\phi'(u). \tag{7}$$

The steady-state conditions are

$$G(p, K, L_1, L_2) = e(p)\phi(u) \tag{8}$$

and

$$G_K(p, K, L_1, L_2) = \rho. \tag{9}$$

Recall that, in the static formulation, K is fixed and u is determined by (8). The basic difference is that in the dynamic case, the steady-state K is determined by (9). All potential differences in comparative statics in the two cases come from this added equation exclusively.

PROPOSITION 1. *There is one and only one steady state in this economy which is locally saddle-point stable.*

PROOF. See Appendix (5). ■

Furthermore, the relation in (9) implies that a constant wage rate must be realized at the steady state.

3.1. Comparative statics

Let us consider how an exogenous change in the commodity price affects the outputs and factor prices. Since K is an endogenous variable, we have, from (9)

$$G_{KK}\mathrm{d}K = -G_{Kp}\mathrm{d}p. \tag{10}$$

By the properties of the GDP function, a price increase in the consumption goods lowers the level of the general factor in the long run.

Using the above analysis, we obtain the following comparative static results with respect to production:

$$\frac{\partial Y_1}{\partial p} = \frac{\partial G_p}{\partial p} + \frac{\partial G_p}{\partial K}\frac{\mathrm{d}K}{\mathrm{d}p} = G_{pp} - \frac{(G_{Kp})^2}{G_{KK}} > 0, \tag{11a}$$

$$\frac{\partial w}{\partial p} = 0 \tag{11b}$$

and

$$\frac{\partial r_1}{\partial p} = \frac{\partial G_{L_1}}{\partial p} + \frac{\partial G_{L_1}}{\partial K}\frac{\mathrm{d}K}{\mathrm{d}p} = G_{L_1p} - G_{L_1K}\frac{G_{Kp}}{G_{KK}} > 0 \tag{11c}$$

We find that: (i) as in the static model, an increase in commodity price p raises the output and the rate of returns to the specific factor in this sector; (ii) unlike the static model, the steady-state wage rate is restrained to the constant rate of time preference. This result will be modified in the second dynamic model.

3.2. Welfare effect

For given L_1, L_2, total differentiation of the two sides of the steady-state conditions (8) and (9) with respect to K, u and p yields

$$e\phi'\mathrm{d}u = \left\{[G_p - e'(p)\phi(u)] - \frac{G_{Kp}G_K}{G_{KK}}\right\}\mathrm{d}p. \tag{12}$$

It follows that the welfare effect of p now depends not only on the steady-state trade pattern but also the factor accumulation effect shown by the positive term $(-G_{Kp}G_K/G_{KK})$ on the right-hand side of (12).

PROPOSITION 2 (Long-run welfare effect). *When the country exports (imports) the (pure) consumption good, an increase in the price of this good always makes the country better-off (worse-off).*

In the present dynamic framework, in addition to the above effect (12), there is an additional welfare effect of this commodity price change along the transitional path. From (5), along the equilibrium paths it holds that

$$\dot{K}_p(t,p) = G_K(K,p)K_p(t,p) - e(p)\phi'(u)u_p(t,p) + \left[G_p(K,p) - e'(p)\phi(u)\right].$$

Hence the total welfare effect on time t is

$$u_p(t,p) = \lambda\left\{\left[G_p(K,p) - e'(p)\phi(u)\right] + G_K(K,p)K_p(t,p) - \dot{K}_p(t,p)\right\},$$

where the first-order condition $\lambda = (1/e(p)\phi'(u))$ has been used. Notice that, the total welfare effects of a change in the commodity price p contains three parts which are respectively the effect through the statical trade pattern $[G_p(K, p) - e'(p)\phi(u)]$, the long-run capital accumulation effect $G_K(K, p)K_p(t, p)$ and the transitional effect from the old steady state to the new steady state $\dot{K}_p(t, p)$.

Denote the indirect lifetime utility as $W = \int_0^{+\infty} ue^{-\rho t}\mathrm{d}t$, then the aggregate welfare effect of a change in p is

$$\begin{aligned}\frac{\partial W}{\partial p} &= \int_0^{+\infty} u_p(t,p)e^{-\rho t}\mathrm{d}t \\ &= \int_0^{+\infty} \lambda\left\{\left[G_p(K,p) - e'(p)\phi(u)\right] + G_K(K,p)K_p(t,p) - \dot{K}_p(t,p)\right\}e^{-\rho t}\mathrm{d}t\end{aligned}$$

Since the negative transitional effect

$$\begin{aligned}\int_0^{+\infty} \dot{K}_p(t,p)\lambda e^{-\rho t}\mathrm{d}t &= \lambda e^{-\rho t}K_p(t,p)\Big|_0^{+\infty} - \int_0^{+\infty} K_p(t,p)\left(\dot{\lambda} - \rho\lambda\right)e^{-\rho t}\mathrm{d}t \\ &= \int_0^{+\infty} K_p(t,p)G_K(K,p)e^{-\rho t}\mathrm{d}t\end{aligned}$$

can be canceled out by the positive long-run capital accumulation effect $G_K(K, p)K_p(t, p)$, then, as a whole, like in the static Jones model, the aggregate welfare effect of p's change is determined by the trade pattern solely. That is,

$$\frac{\partial W}{\partial p} = \int_0^{+\infty} \frac{1}{e(p)\phi'(u)}[G_p - e'(p)\phi(u)]e^{-\rho t}\mathrm{d}t,$$

where $G_p - e'(p)\phi(u)$ is the excess supply of the pure consumption good.[4]

4. *Dynamic model with a variable rate of time preference*

We have seen in the preceding section that, when the rate of time preference is constant, the rate of return to the general factor is fixed. Hence, any change in the commodity price will not affect the wage rate.

[4] Alternatively one can apply the dynamic envelop theorem, see Caputo (1990), directly to do the comparative dynamics. We appreciate the referee for pointing out this. His comments also helped us to simplify the proofs.

Furthermore, households' preference parameters do not affect the output and factor prices in the case of a commodity price change. We will show in the following that these results can be modified by introducing a variable rate of time preference.[5]

Following Uzawa (1968), we assume the rate of time preference ρ is a positive, increasing and convex function of the instantaneous utility level u. That is, for all $u>0$:

$$\rho(u)>0, \quad \rho'(u)>0, \quad \rho''(u)>0, \quad \rho(u)-u\rho'(u)>0$$

and $\rho(0)>0$. If $X(t)=e^{-\rho(u)t}$, then we have the discount term X satisfying $\dot{X}=-\rho(u)X$ and $X(0)=1$. Therefore, the representative household's decision problem is for $K(0)$ given

$$\max_{u(t)} \int_0^{+\infty} u(t)X(t)\mathrm{d}t$$

subject to

$$\dot{K}(t)=w(t)K(t)+r_1(t)L_1+r_2(t)L_2-e(p)\phi(u(t)),$$
$$\dot{X}=-\rho(u)X, \quad X(0)=1,$$

where the factor prices $w(t)$, $r_1(t)$, $r_2(t)$ are given for t in $[0, +\infty)$.

The current value Hamiltonian of the above optimization problem is

$$H\equiv u(t)X(t)+\lambda(t)[w(t)K(t)+r_1(t)L_1+r_2(t)L_2-e(p)\phi(u(t))] - \theta(t)\rho(u(t))X(t),$$

where $\lambda(t)$ and $\theta(t)$ are the co-state variables related to the human capital $K(t)$ and the discount term $X(t)$. At interior solutions, the necessary conditions for optimization are

$$\dot{K}=G(p,K,L_1,L_2)-e(p)\phi(u),$$
$$\dot{X}=-\rho(u)X,$$
$$\dot{\lambda}=-\lambda G_K(p,K,L_1,L_2),$$
$$\dot{\theta}=-u+\theta\rho(u) \text{ and}$$
$$0=X-\lambda e(p)\phi'(u)-\theta\rho'(u)X,$$

where we have taken into consideration the factor prices adjustment process, which equalizes the supplies of inputs to the supplies of these inputs $K(t)$, L_1, L_2, and the equilibrium condition $w(t)K(t)+r_1(t)L_1+r_2(t)L_2\equiv G(p, K, L_1, L_2)$.

Notice that the right-hand side of the last equation is linearly homogeneous in λ and X. Defining a new variable $\xi\equiv\lambda/X$, we can rewrite

[5] A recent paper by Chen *et al.* (2004) used a variable rate of time preference in order to pin down a unique steady state.

the above system as

$$\dot{K} = G(p, K, L_1, L_2) - e(p)\phi(u), \tag{13}$$

$$\dot{\xi} = \xi\rho[(u) - G_K(p, K, L_1, L_2)], \tag{14}$$

$$\dot{\theta} = -u + \theta\rho(u) \tag{15}$$

and

$$0 = 1 - \xi e(p)\phi'(u) - \theta\rho'(u). \tag{16}$$

The steady-state conditions for K and u are

$$G(p, K, L_1, L_2) = e(p)\phi(u) \tag{17}$$

and

$$G_K(p, K, L_1, L_2) = \rho(u) \tag{18}$$

and the steady-state value of θ is determined by $u = \theta\rho(u)$.

Recall that, in the static formulation, K is fixed and u is determined by (8), and in the dynamic model with constant rate of time preference, the steady-state K is determined by (9). However, in the present dynamic model with variable rate of time preference, the steady-state K and u are determined simultaneously by (17) and (18), which will lead to new results in the following comparative statics.

Proposition 3. *There is one and only one steady state satisfying* (17) *and* (18)*, which is locally saddle-point stable.*

Proof. See Appendix (6). ■

4.1. Comparative statics

For given specific factor endowments, totally differentiate the two sides of (17) and (18) with respect to K, p and u to yield K,

$$\left[e\phi' - \frac{G_K}{G_{KK}}\rho'\right]\mathrm{d}K = \left\{[G_p - e'(p)\phi(u)]\frac{\rho'}{G_{KK}} - \frac{G_{Kp}}{G_{KK}}e\phi'\right\}\mathrm{d}p. \tag{19}$$

Notice that, the varying effect of the rate of time preference ρ' enters the two sides of (19), which makes the trade pattern affect on the general factor K when commodity price p changes. For given K, a worsening of the terms of trade lowers the welfare level, which in turn leads to a smaller rate of time preference. That is, households in this case is more patient and will accumulate more capital.

It is clear that an increase in p raises K when the country imports the consumption goods. Otherwise, if the country exports the consumption goods, generally there is no clear-cut result since the two terms on the right-hand side of the above expression have opposite signs.

PROPOSITION 4. *When the country imports the pure consumption good (i.e.,* $G_p - e'(p)\phi(u) < 0$*), or exports this good in a small amount (i.e.,* $G_p - e'(p)\phi(u)$ *is close to 0), then a price increase in this good will increase the accumulation of the general factor K.*

Based on the above result, we can derive the effects of commodity price change upon outputs and factor prices:

$$\frac{\partial Y_1}{\partial p} = G_{pp} + G_{Kp}\frac{\mathrm{d}K}{\mathrm{d}p} > 0, \tag{20a}$$

$$\frac{\partial w}{\partial p} = G_{Kp} + G_{KK}\frac{\mathrm{d}K}{\mathrm{d}p} \tag{20b}$$

and

$$\frac{\partial r_1}{\partial p} = G_{L_1p} + G_{L_1K}\frac{dK}{dp} > 0. \tag{20c}$$

Notice that, similar to the preceding models, an increase in commodity price p raises (conditionally) the output and the rate of return to the specific factor of this sector. As for the effect of this price change on the wage rate, the result is generally ambiguous. On the one hand, an increase in p raises the wage rate directly, as in the Jones model; on the other, however, an increase in p has an indirect decreasing effect on the wage rate through its impact on K. Depending on the relative scales of these two effects, an increase in p can raise or lower the wage rate in the long run. However, unlike the static model, the magnification effect of commodity price on factor prices does not necessarily hold in our dynamic setting.

5. *Conclusion*

In this chapter, we extended the Jones (1971) model to two dynamic frameworks with constant and variable rates of time preference. We found that, when households face a constant rate of time preference, comparative static results similar to those in the static model can be obtained. When households' rate of time preference is time-varying, as long as the country imports the consumption good or exports the consumption good in a small volume, we can still obtain results similar to those in the Jones model.

Acknowledgments

This chapter is an extended version of the paper by Hu *et al.* (2006). The third author, Koji Shimomura, passed away on February 24, 2007, shortly before this chapter was completed. We want to express our deepest sorrow for the loss of a close friend and an excellent economist, from whom we have learned much over the years. We also thank Jean-Michel Grandmont and an anonymous referee for helpful comments on the earlier version of this chapter. This chapter is dedicated to and in memory of the late Professor Koji Shimomura, a prolific economist, a dedicated teacher and a truthful friend.

Appendix

(1) Properties of the GDP function $G(p, K, L_1, L_2)$

Let $\mathcal{L} \equiv pF^1(K_1, L_1) + F^2(K_2, L_2) + \lambda(K - K_1 - K_2)$, then at the interior points

$$\frac{\partial \mathcal{L}}{\partial K_1} = pF_1^1 - \lambda = 0; \quad \frac{\partial \mathcal{L}}{\partial K_2} = F_1^2 - \lambda = 0; \quad K_1 + K_2 = K$$

or

$$pF_1^1 = F_1^2 (= \lambda) \quad \text{and} \quad K_1 + K_2 = K$$

from which we obtain the optimal solution $K_1 = K_1(p, K, L_1, L_2)$, $K_2 = K_2(p, K, L_1, L_2)$. Notice that at the optimal point

$$pF_1^1(K_1(p, K, L_1, L_2), L_1) = F_1^2(K - K_1(p, K, L_1, L_2), L_2)$$

always holds. Hence,

$$F_1^1 \mathrm{d}p + p\left(F_{11}^1 \mathrm{d}K_1 + F_{12}^1 \mathrm{d}L_1\right) = F_{11}^2(\mathrm{d}K - \mathrm{d}K_1) + F_{12}^2 \mathrm{d}L_2.$$

Therefore,

$$\begin{aligned} \frac{\partial K_1}{\partial p} &= \frac{-F_1^1}{pF_{11}^1 + F_{11}^2}, \quad \frac{\partial K_1}{\partial K} = \frac{F_{11}^2}{pF_{11}^1 + F_{11}^2} \\ \frac{\partial K_1}{\partial L_1} &= \frac{-F_{12}^1}{pF_{11}^1 + F_{11}^2}, \quad \frac{\partial K_1}{\partial L_2} = \frac{F_{12}^2}{pF_{11}^1 + F_{11}^2}. \end{aligned} \tag{21}$$

Since $G(p, K, L_1, L_2) = pF^1(K_1(p, K, L_1, L_2), L_1) + F^2(K_2(p, K, L_1, L_2), L_2)$, then

$$\begin{aligned} G_p &= F^1(p, K, L_1, L_2) + pF_1^1 \frac{\partial K_1}{\partial p} + F_1^2 \frac{\partial K_2}{\partial p} \\ &= F^1(p, K, L_1, L_2) + \lambda\left(\frac{\partial K_1}{\partial p} + \frac{\partial K_2}{\partial p}\right). \end{aligned}$$

Notice that $K_1(p, K, L_1, L_2) + K_2(p, K, L_1, L_2) = K$ and K is given, thus $((\partial K_1/\partial p) + (\partial K_2/\partial p)) = 0$, which means $G_p = Y_1$.

Similarly,

$$G_K = pF_1^1 = F_1^2 = w, \quad G_{L_1} = pF_2^1 = r_1, \quad G_{L_2} = F_2^2 = r_2.$$

Combining these relations with (21), we obtain

$$G_{pp} = -\frac{(F_1^1)^2}{pF_{11}^1 + F_{11}^2}, \quad G_{KK} = \frac{pF_{11}^1 F_{11}^2}{pF_{11}^1 + F_{11}^2},$$

$$G_{Kp} = G_{pK} = \frac{F_1^1 F_{11}^2}{pF_{11}^1 + F_{11}^2},$$

$$G_{L_1p} = F_2^1 - \frac{pF_{21}^1 F_1^1}{pF_{11}^1 + F_{11}^2}, \quad G_{L_2p} = \frac{F_{21}^2 F_1^1}{pF_{11}^1 + F_{11}^2},$$

$$G_{L_1K} = \frac{pF_{21}^1 F_{11}^2}{pF_{11}^1 + F_{11}^2}, \quad G_{L_2K} = \frac{F_{21}^2 F_{11}^2}{pF_{11}^1 + F_{11}^2}.$$

(2) Proof of Lemma 1

If $U(c_1, c_2)$ is a quasi-concave function and satisfies $U_1>0$, $U_2>0$, then

$$U_{11}U_2^2 + U_1^2 U_{22} - 2U_1U_2U_{12} < 0.$$

Using this result and the monotonicity of $g(v)$, it is straightforward that $v(c_1, c_2)$ satisfies

$$v_{11}v_2^2 + v_1^2 v_{22} - 2v_1v_2v_{12} = \frac{1}{(g')^3}\left(U_{11}U_2^2 + U_1^2U_{22} - 2U_1U_2U_{12}\right) < 0$$

that is, $v(c_1, c_2)$ is a quasi-concave function too. Since, in addition, it is linearly homogenous, then $v(c_1, c_2)$ satisfies $v_{11} \le 0$, $v_{22} \le 0$ and $v_{11}v_{22} - (v_{12})^2 = 0$.

Since

$$\begin{aligned} U_{11} &= g''(v)v_1^2 + g'(v)v_{11}, U_{22} \\ U_{12} = U_{21} &= g''(v)v_1v_2 + g'(v)v_{12}, \\ U_{11}U_{22} - U_{12}U_{21} &= g'(v)g''(v)\left(v_{11}v_2^2 + v_1^2v_{22} - 2v_1v_2v_{12}\right) \\ &\quad + [g'(v)]^2\left[v_{11}v_{22} - (v_{12})^2\right], \end{aligned}$$

then $g''(\cdot)<0$ if $U(c_1,c_2)$ satisfies $U_{11}U_{22}-U_{12}U_{21}>0$, and $U_{11}U_{22}-U_{12}U_{21}>0$, $U_{11}<0$, $U_{22}<0$ if $g''(\cdot)<0$. That is, $g(v)$ is strictly concave if and only if $U(c_1,c_2)$ is strictly concave.

(3) Proof of Lemma 2

From the definition of the expenditure function

$$E(p, u) \equiv \min_{c_i}\left\{pc_1 + c_2 \middle| u \le U(c_1, c_2) \equiv g(v(c_1, c_2))\right\},$$

we have the optimal c_i which satisfies

$$p = \frac{v_1(c_1, c_2)}{v_2(c_1, c_2)}.$$

Remember that $v(c_1,c_2)$ is linearly homogenous, then the above relation can be rewritten as

$$\frac{c_1}{c_2} = \psi(p).$$

Substitute this relation into $u = U(c_1, c_2)$, that is, $g^{-1}(u) = v(c_1, c_2)$ to obtain $g^{-1}(u) = c_2 v(\psi(p), 1)$, or

$$c_2 = \frac{g^{-1}(u)}{v(\psi(p), 1)}.$$

Notice that, at the optimal point,

$$\frac{\partial c_1}{\partial p} = \frac{g' v_2}{v_2^2 v_{11} - 2v_1 v_2 v_{12} + v_1^2 v_{22}} < 0.$$

For the optimal $c_1(p, u)$, $c_2(p, u)$

$$\begin{aligned} E(p,u) &= pc_1(p,u) + c_2(p,u) = [p\psi(p) + 1]\frac{g^{-1}(u)}{v(\psi(p), 1)} \\ &\equiv e(p)\phi(u), \end{aligned}$$

where $e(p) = [p\psi(p)+1]/v(\psi(p),\ 1)$ and $\phi(u) = g^{-1}(u)$. Notice that, since $E_p(p, u) = c_1(p, u)$ and $\partial c_1/\partial p<0$, $e(p)$ is increasing and concave. And $\phi(u)$, the inverse function of $g(v)$, is increasing and convex in u. That is,

$$e' > 0,\ e'' < 0,\ \phi' > 0,\ \phi'' > 0.$$

(4) Proof of the factor price/commodity price relationship in (3)
From

$$G_{L_1} - pG_{L_1 p} = pF_2^1 - p\left(F_2^1 - \frac{pF_{21}^1 F_1^1}{pF_{11}^1 + F_{11}^2}\right) < 0$$

$$G_K - pG_{pK} = F_1^2 - p\frac{F_1^1 F_{11}^2}{pF_{11}^1 + F_{11}^2} = \frac{pF_1^2 F_{11}^1}{pF_{11}^1 + F_{11}^2} > 0$$

we have $\mathrm{d}r_1/r_1 > \mathrm{d}p/p > \mathrm{d}w/w$ if $\mathrm{d}p/p > 0$. While $G_{Kp} > 0$ and $G_{L2p} < 0$ mean $\partial w/\partial p > 0$ and $\partial r_2/\partial p < 0$, respectively, which mean in turn that $\mathrm{d}w/w > 0$ and $\mathrm{d}r_2/r_2 < 0$ if $\mathrm{d}p/p > 0$, then the relation in (3) is obtained.

(5) Proof of Proposition 1
At the steady state, (8) and (9) hold. As G_K is monotonic in K, given p, L_1, L_2 and ρ, (9) determines a unique steady state of K. Substitute K's

steady-state value into (8), a unique steady-state value of u can be derived.

To examine the stability of the above steady state, from the dynamic system, we have

$$\begin{aligned}\dot{K}_p(t,p) &= G_K(K,p)K_p(t,p) - e(p)\phi'(u)u_p(t,p)\\ &\quad + \left[G_p(K,p) - e_p(p)\phi(u)\right]\\ \dot{\lambda}_p(t,p) &= -\lambda G_{KK}(K,p)K_p(t,p) - \lambda G_{Kp}(K,p)\\ 0 &= -e(p)\phi'(u)\lambda_p(t,p) - \lambda e(p)\phi''(u)u_p(t,p) - \lambda e_p(p)\phi'(u).\end{aligned}$$

Therefore the eigen equation of the dynamic system is

$$\begin{aligned}\Psi(x) &= \begin{vmatrix} G_K - x & 0 & -e\phi' \\ -\lambda G_{KK} & -x & 0 \\ 0 & -e\phi' & -\lambda e\phi'' \end{vmatrix}\\ &= -\lambda e\phi'' x^2 + G_K \lambda e\phi'' x - \lambda G_{KK}(e\phi')^2,\end{aligned}$$

which has a positive and a negative root, respectively. Since the dynamic system of the model is constituted by a state variable K and a control variable λ, then the unique steady state in this economy is locally saddle-point stable.

(6) Proof of Proposition 3

For a given price and labor endowments, (17) reveals a positive relation between the steady-state values of K and u, i.e., $\partial u/\partial K > 0$. Since K is indispensable in production and ϕ is increasing in u, then a smaller human–capital stock level K should correspond to a lower utility level u. However, from (18), $\partial u/\partial K > 0$. Since a smaller K corresponds a higher level of G_K, and ρ is increasing in u, therefore a sufficiently small K will now lead to a large u. The above two relations together determine a unique steady state.

Linearizing the dynamic system (13)–(16) around the above steady state, the following characteristic equation of the linear system is obtained.

$$\Gamma(x) \equiv \begin{vmatrix} G_K - x & 0 & 0 & -e\phi' \\ -\xi G_{KK} & -x & 0 & \xi\rho' \\ 0 & 0 & \rho - x & -1 + \theta\rho' \\ 0 & -e\phi' & -\rho' & \Delta \end{vmatrix} = 0,$$

where $\Delta \equiv -\xi e\phi'' - \theta\rho'' < 0$. Since $-\xi e\phi' = -1 + \theta\rho'$ and at the steady state, $G_K = \rho$, therefore

$$\Gamma(x) = \begin{vmatrix} \rho - x & 0 & 0 & -e\phi' \\ -\xi G_{KK} & -x & 0 & \xi\rho' \\ 0 & 0 & \rho - x & -\xi e\phi' \\ 0 & -e\phi' & -\rho' & \Delta \end{vmatrix}$$

$$= \begin{vmatrix} \rho - x & 0 & 0 & -e\phi' \\ 0 & -x & 0 & -\frac{\xi G_{KK}}{\rho - x} e\phi' + \xi\rho' \\ 0 & 0 & \rho - x & -\xi e\phi' \\ 0 & -e\phi' & -\rho' & \Delta \end{vmatrix}$$

$$= \begin{vmatrix} -x(\rho - x) & 0 & \xi\rho'(\rho - x) - \xi G_{KK} e\phi' \\ 0 & \rho - x & -\xi e\phi' \\ -e\phi' & -\rho' & \Delta \end{vmatrix}$$

$$= (\rho - x)\{-x(\rho - x)\Delta + x\rho'\xi e\phi' + e\phi'\xi[\rho'(\rho - x) - G_{KK} e\phi']\}$$

$$= (\rho - x)[\Delta x^2 - \rho\Delta x + e\phi'\xi(\rho'\rho - G_{KK} e\phi')].$$

Note that $\delta < 0$ and $e\phi'\xi(\rho'\rho - G_{KK} e\phi') > 0$. Hence, the linearized dynamic system has one stable and two unstable eigenvalues, which mean the steady state is saddle-point stable. The stable eigenvalue is

$$x_B = \frac{1}{2\Delta}\left[\rho\Delta + \sqrt{(\rho\Delta)^2 - 4\Delta e\phi'\xi(\rho'\rho - G_{KK} e\phi')}\right].$$

References

Caputo, M.R. (1990), Comparative dynamics via envelope methods in variational calculations. *Review of Economic Studies* 57, 689–697.

Chen, B.-L., Nishimura, K., Shimomura, K. (2004), An Uzawa-Oniki-Uzawa dynamic two-country model of international trade: back to Heckscher and Ohlin. Mimeo, Kobe University.

Guest, R.S., McDonald, I.M. (2001), How Uzawa preferences improve the simulation properties of the small open economy model. *Journal of Macroeconomics* 23 (3), 417–440.

Hu, Y., Nishimura, K., Shimomura, K. (2006), Dynamic three-factor models of international trade. *Asia-Pacific Journal of Accounting and Economics* 13 (2), 73–85.

Jones, R.W. (1971), A three-sector model in theory, trade, and history. In: Bhagwati, J., Vanek, J. (Eds.), *Trade, Balance of Payments and Growth*. North-Holland, Amsterdam.

Mayer, W. (1974), Short-run and long-run equilibrium for a small open economy. *Journal of Political Economy* 82 (5), 955–967.

Mussa, M. (1974), Tariffs and the distribution of income: the importance of factor specificity, substitutability, and intensity in the short and long run. *Journal of Political Economy* 82, 1191–1204.

Neary, P. (1978), Short-run capital specificity and the pure theory of international trade. *Economic Journal* 88, 488–512.

Schultz, T.W. (1963), *The Economic Value of Education*. Columbia University Press, New York.

Uzawa, H. (1968), Time preferences, the consumption function and optimal asset holdings. In: Wolfe, J.N. (Ed.), *Value, Capital, and Growth: Papers in Honour of Sir John Hicks*. Chicago, Aldine, pp. 458–504.

SECTION V

Trade and the Developing Economy

CHAPTER 11

Skill Formation and Income Distribution in a Three Class Small Developing Economy

Sugata Marjit

Centre for Studies in Social Sciences, R-1, Baishnabghata Patuli Township, Kolkata-700094, India
E-mail address: smarjit@hotmail.com

Abstract
This chapter builds up a simple general equilibrium trade model where, in the absence of a credit market for human capital formation, initial distribution of capital endowment and relevant factor prices determine the size of the three income classes. The poor, with little capital, invests in traditional manufacturing, the middle-income group invests solely in human capital and the rich invests in both. Chances are that such an economy will export both high- and low-skilled goods, importing the middle one. Conventional wisdom suggests that greater skill premium encourages skill formation. In contrast, we show that higher unskilled wage and lower degree of income inequality are consistent with greater skill formation. We also show that protection discourages skill formation and may aggravate inequality.

Keywords: Asset distribution, income distribution, international trade, skill formation

JEL classifications: D31, D33, F16, J31

1. Introduction

The purpose of this chapter is to develop a simple general equilibrium model of production and trade to discuss issues such as skill formation in a credit-constrained economy and its implication for pattern of trade and income distribution among three income classes, the poor, the middle and the rich. A small body of theoretical literature has developed analyzing issues related to trade and wage inequality in the developing countries. Interested readers may look at Marjit and Acharyya (2003), Feenstra (2003), Acemoglu (2003), Jones and Marjit (2003), Marjit *et al.* (2004), Zhu and Trefler (2005), etc. Starting from the classic work of Findlay and

Frontiers of Economics and Globalization
Volume 4 ISSN: 1574-8715
DOI: 10.1016/S1574-8715(08)04011-6

Kierzkowski (1983) and continuing with the recent papers by Das (2001), Ranjan (2000) and Eicher (1999) another line of work has emphasized the role of credit market imperfection in skill formation in open developing economies in dynamic context. This literature is also related to Galor and Zeira (1993) and Banerjee and Newman (1993). The present chapter assimilates these two different areas of research in terms of a neo-classical Heckscher–Ohlin–Samuelson type structure providing further insights and new results. In particular we show:

As our severely credit-constrained economy opens up for trade, it may export both "high"-skill-intensive and "low"-skill-intensive goods, importing the "middle" one.

If unskilled wage increases through the removal protection, thus reducing the so-called skill premium, skill formation is still encouraged through a decline in cost of capital.

Since people provide labor and own capital, one can distinguish between wage and income distribution in this framework. Also instead of the conventional two-tier comparison of the rich and the poor, our framework allows for a comparison with the middle class. With liberal trade policies in place both the poor and the rich can gain relative to the middle class.

Removal of protection and movement towards free trade has the potential to increase inequality between the skilled and the unskilled. But in our model such a move increases human capital formation and can definitely reduce inequality. This underscores the point that lack of skill formation in a poor economy is the main cause behind rising inequality following a shift in the trade regime. Hence trade as such should not be blamed for rising inequality.

The literature on credit market imperfection and poverty trap builds up a supply side story in which cost of acquiring skill or human capital becomes relatively expensive for poor people without much of inherited wealth. Typically, higher is the unskilled wage, lower seems to be the incentive to acquire human capital. We can clearly assert from our set-up that higher unskilled wage will, in general, reduce the return to physical capital inducing people to allocate more of it for acquiring skill. Hence, there is potentially interesting relationship between occupational wage distribution and skill formation.

Typically in a dynamic framework initial inequality in the distribution of assets coupled with an imperfect credit market lead to either high or low levels of income. In the present work our emphasis is not on the dynamic story. In the static general equilibrium model we use, there will emerge three classes of people in terms of their attitude towards skill formation. Trade affects local prices in our small economy, factor returns, skill formation and income distribution for very poor, middle class and the rich. We can determine a large variety of inter- and intra-class distributional consequence, thus relating our work to the recent literature on trade and inequality in poor economy. The classic dynamic model of Findlay and Kierzkowski (1983) asserts that with trade the skill abundant north will have further incentive to acquire skill and the south will be even more disinterested in skill formation as the Stolper–Samuelson result predicts a rise in the relative income of the abundant factor in each country.

In relation to this literature our attempted contribution is as follows:

We derive the positive relationship between unskilled wage and skill formation in a much simpler framework. We highlight the possibility that an economy can exhibit a pattern of trade whereby it exports both a primitive as well as a skill-intensive product. In other words, as trade expands it is quite possible that traditional manufacturing gives way simultaneously to more primitive and more sophisticated products. This has natural implication for trade and wage distribution in poor countries.[1] We use a three-good model to capture a latent complementarity between sectors.[2] The pattern of trade that may emerge corroborates the observations made in Jones *et al.* (1999).

The model that we construct suggests that quite complex issues such as trade and skill formation can be tackled in a very simple static framework, a framework that builds on a standard simple general equilibrium model. We argue that if investing in human capital is relatively costly in terms of alternative return from physical capital, poor people will choose not to be educated. In that case higher skilled to unskilled wage does not generate adequate incentive for human capital formation. We also explore the relationship between protection, skill formation and income distribution. We argue that protection is likely to aggravate inequality.

One could be curious regarding the use of a "static" model to capture the idea of skill formation, which is essentially a dynamic concept. We try to imagine a world where each period is characterized by a distribution of endowment of capital, which can be put to use either for production or skill formation. Each period is self-sustained in the sense that there is no "bequest" across periods so that the endogenous evolution of the distributional pattern is ignored. But the division of the work force between the skilled and unskilled is decided within a period. At the end of each period world collapses, capital stock vanishes and people cease to exist. The world is newborn next period with a set of initial conditions. Since our world is that of a small open economy we can imagine the "rest-of-the world" to remain active all through. Whether our world exists or transforms does not affect world prices anyway. Hence, what is allowed to change across time is a subset of "parameters" characterizing the initial

---

[1] For some recent work in this area which uses simple general equilibrium framework one may look at Jones and Marjit (2003) and Marjit and Kar (2005).

[2] For results related to the "complementarity" in trade models, refer to Marjit and Beladi (1999), Marjit (2003) and Marjit (2005).

conditions. Such a change allows us to compare two alternative states of the same world or two adjacent generations. One of the parameters is the condition of the global markets, as reflected in the world prices. The small open economy assumption is made to abstract from the general equilibrium consequence of price changes. But exogenously given prices provides an important avenue through which relative income between the skilled and unskilled change. The model is meant for considering income inequality rather than wage inequality as individuals earn income through the ownership of capital as well. This type of a model building exercise is an essential step between the straightjacket applications of the Heckscher–Ohlin–Samuelson framework and explicit dynamic models.

The plan of the chapter is as follows: Section 2 deals with the basic model and describes the underlying general equilibrium mechanism, Section 3 considers interesting comparative static experiments and Section 4 concludes.

2. *The foundation*

Our small open economy produces three goods X, Y and S. X is the primitive good, which uses only unskilled labor, Y the traditional manufacturing product made of capital and labor with neo-classical technology and S the skilled product produced only with skilled labor where "skill" is acquired through the investment of capital.

Two primary factors of production are capital and unskilled labor. Population is born unskilled, each owning one unit of labor and some capital. $f(z)$ is the density of population indexed on a continuum $z \in [0,1]$, such that total population is $\int_0^1 (z)\mathrm{d}z$. Each class of people is born with $k(z)$ amount of capital. Capital serves dual purpose. It can be employed in producing Y or can be used for acquiring education or skill. Credit market does not exist reflecting a scenario of extreme imperfection in credit market. While imperfection is a natural catalyst in Galor and Zeira (1993) or Banerjee and Newman (1993), we retain such a stronger assumption because in the developing world credit market is hardly tapped for generating resources for human capital formation. Also we do away with the assumption of the "indivisibility" in costs for acquiring human capital, a standard technique followed in the current literature. There is no threshold level of capital required for education. We add a distributional assumption i.e., $k'(z) > 0$ and $f'(z) < 0$. Higher values of z denote richer people. Capital allocated for education and labor-acquiring skill cannot be allocated to the production of Y and X. Given the set of prices and endowment such allocations are decided. We assume competitive markets and full employment of resources.

Competitive price conditions look like

$$wa_{lx} = P_x \tag{1}$$

$$wa_{ly} + ra_{ky} = P_y \tag{2}$$

$$w_s a_s(k) = P_s, \tag{3}$$

where w, w_s are unskilled and skilled wages. r is the return to capital in manufacturing a_{ij}s are input–output coefficients, Ps are commodity prices given exogenously to this small open economy. $a_s(k)$ is the productivity in the skilled sector and $a_s'(k)<0$ i.e., greater amount of capital put into education leads to higher skilled wage.

Now,

$$w_s(k) = \frac{P_s}{a_s(k)}. \tag{4}$$

We assume the following: $\lim_{k\to 0} a_s(k) = \propto$, $\lim_{k\to \propto} a_s(k) = \bar{a}$ and $w_s'(k)>0$, $w_s''(k)<0$, i.e., there is diminishing marginal return from skill acquisition.

Decision to acquire skill depends on w, r and $w_s[k(z)]$ for the individual belonging to the zth group. Note that given P_x, P_y ($\equiv 1$, we choose Y as the numeriare), w and r will be determined and given P_s and $a_s[k(z)]$, $w_s[k(z)]$ will also be determined. Also note that skill attainment is instantaneous since we are focusing on a single period. Let us now turn to the quantity system. For any individual belonging to the zth group, the earning from "unskilled" occupation is w and the associated capital income $rk(z)$. Since $\lim_{k\to 0} w_s(k) = 0$, there will exist a "$\underline{k}$" such that w_s

$$w_s(\underline{k}) = w + r\underline{k}. \tag{5}$$

Note that at $k = 0$, $w > w_s(k = 0) = 0$.

Such k, however, may not be unique as depicted in Figure 1.

Let $\underline{k}$ denote the smaller of these values and $\underline{z}$ the cut-off group such that $k(\underline{z}) = \underline{k}$. Let us consider the subset $[\underline{z},1]$ function which people will have endowments greater than $\underline{k}$. The typical agent belonging to this set

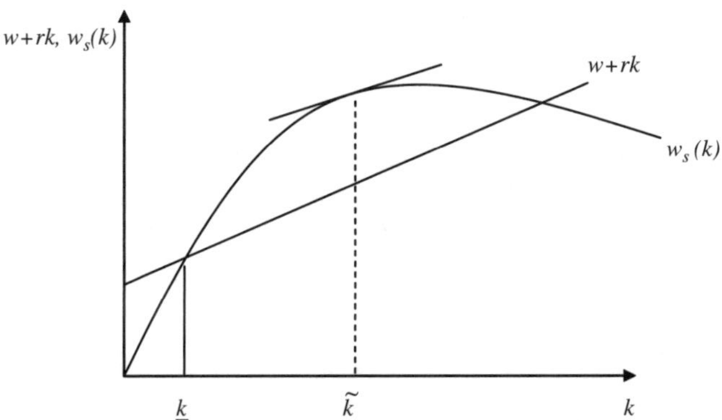

Fig. 1. Asset level and skill acquisition.

will solve the following maximization problem:

$$\max_k w_s + r[k(z) - k] \tag{6}$$

$$\text{FOC} \;\; w_s'(\tilde{k}) = r \tag{7}$$

(SOC is automatically satisfied with $w_s'' < 0$).

Let $\tilde{V}(\tilde{k}, r, z)$ denote the maximum value function of the maximization problem (6). We retain $\tilde{k}$ explicitly for reference although $\tilde{k}$ is itself determined by r.

People will get skilled as long as

$$\tilde{V}(\tilde{k}, r, z) > w + rk(z). \tag{8}$$

Note that no one will employ more than $\tilde{k}$ for acquiring skill (from (7)).

Consider z such that $k(z) > \tilde{k}$.

$$\tilde{V}(\tilde{k}, r, z) = w_s(\tilde{k}) + r\left[k(z) - \tilde{k}\right].$$

Now,

$$\begin{aligned} \tilde{V} - [w + rk(z)] &= w_s(\tilde{k}) + \mathrm{r}\left(k(z) - \tilde{k}\right) - w - rk(z) \\ &= w_s(\tilde{k}) - (r\tilde{k} + w) \\ &= w_s(\tilde{k}) - w_s(\underline{k}) - r(\tilde{k} - \underline{k}) \end{aligned} \tag{9}$$

[(9) > 0 as $w_s'(\underline{k}) > r$.]

Let us consider $k(z) \in [\underline{k}, \tilde{k}]$.

Note that now $\tilde{V}(\tilde{k}, r, z) = w_s(\tilde{k})$ as $\tilde{k} \geq k(z)$.

Hence,

$$\tilde{V} - [w + rk(z)] = w_s(k(z)) - [w + rk(z)]. \tag{10}$$

Follow the previous argument to show that (10) > 0.

Also we know $\tilde{V} - [w + rk(z)] = 0$ for $k(\underline{z}) = \underline{k}$.

Therefore, $\forall z \in [\underline{z}, \tilde{z}]$. (10) ≥ 0.

We can now write down the following proposition:

PROPOSITION 1. *Given the distribution of capital stock, there will emerge three classes of agents. The poorest $z \in [0, \underline{z}]$ will work as unskilled and allocate their capital to manufacturing. The middle class $z \in [\underline{z}, \tilde{z}]$ will acquire skill and will have nothing left to invest in production. The richest $z \in [\tilde{z}, 1]$ will allocate $\tilde{k}$ to skill formation and invest the rest in production.*

PROOF. See the discussion above. QED

Incidentally therefore, given (w, r) and the distribution of endowment, resources available for production of X and Y are also determined.

Total capital available for producing Y is given by

$$K_y \equiv \int_0^{z} k(z)f(z)\mathrm{d}z + \int_{\tilde{z}}^{1} (k(z) - \tilde{k})f(z)\mathrm{d}z. \tag{11}$$

Similarly, total labor force available for producing X and Y is given by

$$L_x + L_y \equiv \int_0^{z} f(z)\mathrm{d}z. \tag{12}$$

Consider Equations (1) and (2) which determine w and r and therefore factor proportion, i.e., capital–labor ratio in Y. Let us denote it by $\Phi_y(w/r)$.

Therefore,

$$L_y = \Phi_y\left(\frac{w}{r}\right) \cdot k_y, \tag{13}$$

where K_y is already known from (11).

As (13) determines L_y, we know X from (14):

$$a_{lx} \cdot X = L_y = \int_0^{z} f(z)\mathrm{d}z - L_y. \tag{14}$$

Since a_{ky} is already determined through a given w/r. We determine Y in the following manner:

$$a_{ky} Y = K_y. \tag{15}$$

One can crosscheck that for X to be produced in this economy (14) must yield $L_x > 0$. In other words following must hold.

$$\int_0^{z} f(z)\mathrm{d}z > L_y. \tag{16}$$

From (13) and (16),

$$\frac{a_{lx}}{a_{kx}} > \frac{\int_0^{z} f(z)\mathrm{d}z}{k_y} > \frac{a_{ly}}{a_{ky}}. \tag{17}$$

Note that $a_{kx} = 0$, hence the left inequality is trivially satisfied. The right inequality has to be satisfied for $X > 0$. (17) is the very familiar and well-known "cone of diversification" condition in trade theory, i.e., the relative endowment of labor to capital must be trapped by the respective intensities for incomplete specialization in production. This completes the characterization of variables in general equilibrium.

3. Comparative statics

The interpretation of comparative static experiments in this model is as follows. We can study unrelated generations in terms of their reactions to the altered set of parameters they face. If we consider the effect of a rise in the P_x on the endogenous variables of the system, it will essentially mean a comparison between how a generation facing a higher P_x decides on their choices and a generation that does not experience any such change.

In the standard modals of human capital accumulation higher unskilled wage is a deterrent towards skill formation. In our model this is not necessarily the case.

PROPOSITION 2. *A higher P_x must increase the degree of skill formation provided $\underline{k} > a_{ky}/a_{ly}$.*

PROOF. Note that it is sufficient to check whether $\mathrm{d}\underline{k}/\mathrm{d}P_x < 0$. Lower value of $\underline{k}$ will mean more people getting educated now than before.

We know, $w_s(\underline{k}) = w + r\underline{k}$.
Hence,

$$\frac{\mathrm{d}\underline{k}}{\mathrm{d}P_x} = \frac{(\mathrm{d}w/\mathrm{d}P_x) + (\mathrm{d}r/\mathrm{d}w)\,(\mathrm{d}w/\mathrm{d}P_x)\,\underline{k}}{w_s'(\underline{k}) - r}.$$

We know $w_s'(\underline{k}) > r$, $(\mathrm{d}w/\mathrm{d}P_x) = (1/a_{1x})$ and $(\mathrm{d}r/\mathrm{d}w) = -(a_{ly}/a_{ky})$ (from (2)).
Therefore,

$$\frac{\mathrm{d}\underline{k}}{\mathrm{d}P_x} = \frac{(1/a_{lx})\big(1 - (a_{ly}/a_{ky})\,\underline{k}\big)}{w_s'(\underline{k}) - r},$$

$$\frac{\mathrm{d}\underline{k}}{\mathrm{d}P_x} < 0 \ \text{iff} \ \underline{k} > \frac{a_{ky}}{a_{ly}} \quad \text{QED.}$$

Higher P_x means higher w and hence lower r. The borderline group $\underline{z}$ earning $w + r\underline{k}$ will experience a decline in their income if $\underline{k} > a_{ky}/a_{ly}$ and therefore skill accumulation will appear to be mare attractive now pulling down $\underline{k}$. Since everyone is endowed with one unit of labor, $\underline{k}$ represents the capital intensity of endowment, i.e., relative capital abundance at an individual level. The condition in Proposition 2 boils down to a comparison between endowment intensity and capital intensity in manufacturing. Higher value of a_{ky}/a_{ly} will mean smaller decline in r following an increase in w, and higher values of $\underline{k}$ will mean stronger adverse impact of that fall on personal income. If $\underline{k}$ is low increase in w will prevail and a decline in r will not adversely affect the personal income of the inframarginal group.

PROPOSITION 3. *An increase in P_x must increase total allocation of capital towards skill formation provided $\underline{k} > a_{ky}/a_{ly}$.*

PROOF. We have already shown that a rise in P_x will reduce $\underline{k}$ under the stipulated condition reducing capital available for manufacturing to that extent. Think of $z \in (\underline{z}, 1)$. Since $w_s'(\tilde{k}) = r$.

$$\frac{d\tilde{k}}{dP_x} = -\frac{1}{w_s''(\tilde{k})}\frac{dr}{dP_x} > 0.$$

Therefore, $[k(z) - \tilde{k})$ must fall $\forall z \in (\tilde{z}, 1)$. Since for $z \in (\underline{z}, \tilde{z})$ people cannot increase their allocation of capital towards skill formation, they will remain neutral. So $\underline{z}$ will fall and $\{k(z) - \underline{k}\}$ will fall, implying a decline in K_y. QED

Output changes are straightforward to infer. As K_y goes down Y will go down and X will go up. Skilled output must expand as $\underline{z}$ goes down.

$$S \equiv \text{Total skilled output} = \int_{\underline{z}}^{\tilde{z}} \frac{1}{a_s[k(z)]} f(z)\mathrm{d}z + \int_{\tilde{z}}^{1} \frac{1}{a_s(\tilde{k})} f(z)\mathrm{d}z. \tag{18}$$

S must go up as $\underline{z}$ falls and $\tilde{z}$ goes up (see the Appendix).

Note the complementarity between X and S. An increase in P_x not only increases X but also increases S. It is easy to check that an increase in P_s will also increase X. Such complementarity between S and X adds to a set of results such as in Marjit and Beladi (1999).

Let us now consider the impact of an increase in P_x on the degree of income inequality. To streamline our query let us define the following:

$$y_1 \equiv y(z_1) \equiv w + rk(z_1) \quad \text{for} \quad z_1 \in [0, \underline{z}],$$

$$y_2 \equiv y(z_2) \equiv w_s[k(z_1)] \quad \text{for} \quad z_2 \in [\underline{z}, \tilde{z}],$$

$$y_3 \equiv y(z_3) \equiv w_s(\tilde{k}) + r\left[k(z_1) - \tilde{k}\right] \quad \text{for} \quad z_3 \in [\tilde{z}, 1].$$

PROPOSITION 4. *$\ni \bar{z}_1$ such that (a) $\forall z_1 < \bar{z}_1$, y_1/y_2 and y_1/y_3 increase following an increase in w, i.e., inequality decreases. (b) $\forall z_1 \geq \bar{z}_1 (y_1/y_2)$ goes down or remains the same and y_1/y_3 may go up or down, i.e., the degree of income inequality can move either way.*

PROOF. Earlier results show that $(\mathrm{d}y_1/\mathrm{d}w) \leq\ \geq 0$ iff $k(z_1) \geq\ \leq (a_{ky}/a_{1y})$.

Since, $k(0) = 0$ and $k' > 0$, $\exists \bar{z}_1$ such that $k(\bar{z}_1) = (a_{ky}/a_{1y})$. Therefore, $(\mathrm{d}y_1/\mathrm{d}w) > 0\ \forall z_1 < \bar{z}_1$. Also we have proved that for $z_2 \in [\underline{z}, \tilde{z}]$, $w_s[k(z_2)]$ does not change as w goes up or r goes down. Hence, (y_1/y_2) must go up for $z_1 < \bar{z}_1$. This completes the proof of (a).

Since, $(\mathrm{d}y_1/\mathrm{d}w) < 0\ \forall z_1 < \bar{z}_1$, $z_1 \in [0, \underline{z}]$ and y_2 does not change, y_1/y_2 must go down for the relevant range and for the borderline case of $z_1 = \bar{z}_1$, $(\mathrm{d}y_1/\mathrm{d}w) = 0$, hence y_1/y_2 dose not change.

Now,

$$\frac{d(y_1/y_3)}{dw} = \left[1 - \frac{a_{ly}}{a_{ky}} k(z_1)\right] y_3 + y_1 \frac{a_{ly}}{a_{y_3}} \left[k(z_3) - \tilde{k}\right].$$

Therefore,

$$\frac{d(y_1/y_3)}{dw} > \; = \; <0 \quad \text{iff } y_3 + y_1 \frac{a_{ly}}{a_{ky}} \left[k(z_3)y_1 - k(z_1)y_3 - y_1\tilde{k}\right] > \; = \; <0.$$

This completes the proof of (b). QED

While comparing the income level between the poorest and the rich, one should note that the absolute income level of the rich must go down as r drops since the rich is net supplier of capital to the manufacturing. Any increase in w_s through an increase in $\tilde{k}$ has a neutral effect due to the familiar "envelope" condition. The absolute income of the poor $[z_1 > \bar{z}_1]$ will fall also. However, the relative strength of these two effects will be determined by the relative endowments. Higher is $\{k(z) - \tilde{k}\}$, more severe will be the negative impact on y_3 following the drop in r. Slight manipulation of the above condition will yield

$$\frac{d(y_1/y_3)}{dw} < 0 \quad \text{iff } \frac{y_1}{y_3} < \frac{1 + (dr/dw)k(z_1)}{(dr/dw)\left[k(z_3) - \tilde{k}\right]}. \tag{19}$$

Higher is y_1 or y_3, the absolute impact of a decline in r would be more severe. But lower is y_1 relative to y_3, the relative impact of such a change will be more severe for the poor people, hence inequality is likely to grow. What (19) and Proposition 4 suggest is that between the poor and the middle or rich, absolute and relative income will move in favor of the poor following an increase in w. Between not-so-poor and the middle or rich, the not-so-poor is likely to suffer in absolute and relative terms. Those nearing the middle class will have a decline in absolute income but vis-à-vis the richest; they are likely to experience an increase in their relative income. Relatively, the middle lose vis-à-vis the poor, gains vis-à-vis the not-so-poor and the rich.

Typically closer is the wage gap between the skilled and the unskilled, weaker is the incentive for thc unskilled to acquire skill. This is the standard outcome in the literature with an exception where people talk about higher unskilled wage leading to greater savings and hence greater accumulation of human capital. Note that in our model it is possible that an increase in the degree of skill formation, i.e., lowering of $\underline{z}$ is consistent with the poor getting better relative to the middle and the rich. Even if $\underline{z}$ goes up so that the number of people acquiring skill falls, one can have greater amount of capital being allocated to S as r goes down.

This may not be an egalitarian outcome in the sense that the rich accumulates greater skill. But does that mean inequality grow? No. Since the rich is a net supplier of capital to manufacturing, a decline in r, even if

$\tilde{k}$ adjusts accordingly, will have an income reducing impact. What we emphasize is that in a general equilibrium setting an increase in w, the unskilled wage, is also associated with a decline in r and therefore in a world with two types of assets there is a tendency for people to switch to the other type, i.e., human capital. Hence higher w, lower $\underline{z}$, higher $\tilde{k}$ these are all consistent outcomes. Somehow this is not highlighted in the literature.

So far we have not derived the pattern of trade endogenously since there are three goods and comparative advantage is difficult to determine.[3] But it is clear from our analysis that if the possibility of trade increases P_x, w must increase and through a drop in r it may also increase the output of the skilled sector. Hence, one can easily confront a situation where X and skilled product will be exported and Y will be imported. The squeezing of unskilled manufacturing output leads to such a pattern of trade, a possibility that is ruled out in the two-good model.

Suppose the economy under consideration imports Y and initially has levied a tariff on its imports. Let us explore the consequence of a drop in such a tariff rate, which effectively reduces the price of Y in the local market. Note that such a drop in price reduces r, but leaves w unchanged as P_x is held fixed. But it alters $\underline{k}$ and $\tilde{k}$ and hence the size of the skilled sector. This leads us to the following proposition:

PROPOSITION 5. *A decline in degree of protection must promote skill formation by reducing* $\underline{k}$ *and increasing* $\tilde{k}$. *Also income distribution between the poorest and the richest must move in favor of the former.*

PROOF. $w + r\underline{k} = w_s(\underline{k})$

$$\left[w_s'(\underline{k}) - r\right]\left(\frac{\mathrm{d}\underline{k}}{\mathrm{d}r}\right) - \underline{k} = 0.$$

Since $w_s'(\underline{k}) - r, \quad (\mathrm{d}\underline{k}/\mathrm{d}r) > 0$.

Hence, as r drops $\underline{k}$ falls inducing more people to go for skill formation.

It is straightforward to argue that $\tilde{k}$ will go up as r drops since net marginal benefit of investing in skill increases. This implies everyone having $k > \tilde{k}$ will reallocate his or her capital towards skill formation and away from Y.

As in Proposition 4, we look at y_1/y_3.

$$\frac{\mathrm{d}(y_1/y_3)}{\mathrm{d}r} < 0 \quad \text{iff} \quad \frac{k_3 - \tilde{k}}{k_1} > \frac{w_s(\tilde{k})}{W}.$$

Note that for very rich $k_3 - \tilde{k}$ is very high and for very poor k_1 is close to zero. Therefore, between the richest and the poorest as r drops, income distribution moves in favor of the "poorest". QED

[3] How trade can limit the adverse consequence of credit market imperfection is suggested briefly in Jones and Marjit (2001).

Since it is a small economy lower tariff raises "welfare" in the standard trade-theoretic sense. But here we also have distributional concern. Interestingly, liberal trade policy can lead to distributive justice as well.

4. Conclusion

We have demonstrated that a suitably constructed simple general equilibrium model can address several aspects of the literature on imperfect credit market, skill formation, trade and income distribution. In particular, we have proved that higher unskilled wage and more even income distribution is perfectly consistent with the idea of skill formation. Protection increases the attractiveness of physical capital, deters skill formation and can worsen the distribution of income.

Two extensions are straightforward.

First, one can bring in land as a specific factor of production and transform the "only labor" sector into one that also uses land. The commodity price–factor price relationship will change. But our major results will go through. An interesting corollary will be that a country having large stock of land will mean a depressed r and possibly greater skill formation. In this context one fruitful exercise will be to consider a case where one does allow some borrowing or lending, but does not allow free movement of capital across various sectors. It is also straightforward to show that with an overlapping generations framework the dynamic version of the model leads to poverty traps and in the long run one would expect either a "rich" or a "poor" equilibrium. The middle segment will vanish.

Acknowledgments

This chapter has benefited immensely from presentations at the Indian Statistical Institute, Universities of McGill and Rochester. Discussions with Amiya Bagchi, Mark Bils, Maitreesh Ghatak, Ronald Jones, Ngo Van Long, Indrajit Mallick and Lin Zhou have been quite rewarding. The usual disclaimer applies.

Appendix. Effects of an increase in P_x on S

$$S \equiv \int_{\underline{z}}^{\tilde{z}} \frac{1}{a_s[k(z)]} f(z)\mathrm{d}z + \int_{\tilde{z}}^{1} \frac{1}{a_s\tilde{k}} f(z)\mathrm{d}z$$

$$\begin{aligned}\frac{\mathrm{d}S}{\underline{z}} = & -\frac{1}{a_s[k(\underline{z})]} f(\underline{z}) + \frac{1}{a_s[k(\tilde{z})]} f(\tilde{z}) \frac{\mathrm{d}\tilde{z}}{\mathrm{d}\,\underline{z}} \\ & - \frac{1}{a_s\tilde{k}} f(\tilde{z}) \frac{\mathrm{d}\tilde{z}}{\mathrm{d}\,\underline{z}} \left[\frac{a_s'(\tilde{k})}{[a_s(\tilde{k})]^2} \int_{\tilde{z}}^{1} f(z)\mathrm{d}z \right] \frac{\mathrm{d}\tilde{k}}{\mathrm{d}\,\underline{z}}.\end{aligned}$$

Since

$$a_s(\tilde{k}) < 0 \frac{\mathrm{d}\tilde{z}}{\mathrm{d}\underline{z}} = \frac{\mathrm{d}\tilde{k}}{\mathrm{d}r}\frac{\mathrm{d}r}{\mathrm{d}\underline{z}} < 0, \quad \frac{\mathrm{d}s}{\mathrm{d}\underline{z}} < 0.$$

As $\underline{z}$ goes down, total skilled output must go up.

References

Acemoglu, D.K. (2003), Patterns of skill – premia. *Review of Economic Studies* 70, 199–230.

Banerjee, A.V., Newman, A. (1993), Occupational choice and the process of development. *Journal of Political Economy* 101, 274–298.

Das, S.P. (2001). Trade, skill acquisition and distribution. Mimeo, ISI, Delhi.

Eicher, T. (1999), Trade, development and converging growth rates: gains from trade redistributed. *Journal of International Economics* 48, 179–198.

Feenstra, R. (2003), *Advanced International Trade: Theory and Evidence*. Princeton University Press, Princeton, NJ.

Findlay, R., Kierzkowski, H. (1983), International trade and human capital: a simple general equilibrium model. *Journal of Political Economy* 91, 957–978.

Galor, E., Zeira, J. (1993), Income distribution and macroeconomics. *Review of Economic Studies* 60, 35–52.

Jones, R.W., Beladi, H., Marjit, S. (1999), Three faces of factor intensities. *Journal of International Economics* 48, 413–420.

Jones, R.W., Marjit, S. (2001), Role of international fragmentation in the process of development. *American Economic Review* 91 (2), 363–366.

Jones, R.W., Marjit, S. (2003), Economic development, trade and wages. *German Economic Review* 4 (1), 1–17.

Marjit, S. (2003), Economic reform and informal wage – a general equilibrium analysis. *Journal of Development Economics* 72 (1), 371–378.

Marjit, S. (2005), Complementarity and international trade – on some recent developments in structural general equilibrium models. In: Lahiri, S, Maiti, P. (Eds.), *Economic Theory in a Changing World*. Oxford University Press, New Delhi.

Marjit, S., Acharyya, R. (2003), *International Trade, Wage Inequality and the Developing Economy – A General Equilibrium Approach*. Physica/Springer, Heidelberg, NY.

Marjit, S., Beladi, H. (1999), Complementarity between import competition and import promotion. *Journal of Economic Theory* 86, 280–285.

Marjit, S., Beladi, H., Chakraborti, A. (2004), Trade and wage inequality in developing countries. *Economic Inquiry* 42 (2), 295–303.

Marjit, S., Kar, S. (2005), Emigration and inequality. *Economics Letters* 87 (3), 141–145.

Ranjan, P. (2000), Dynamic evolution of income distribution and credit-constrained human capital investment in open economies. *Journal of International Economics* 55 (2), 329–358.

Zhu, S.C., Trefler, D. (2005), Trade and inequality in developing countries – a general equilibrium framework. *Journal of International Economics* 65, 21–48.

CHAPTER 12

Foreign Capital and Skilled–Unskilled Wage Inequality in a Developing Economy with Non-Traded Goods

Sarbajit Chaudhuri[a] and Shigemi Yabuuchi[b]

[a]*Department of Economics, University of Calcutta, Kolkata 700 050, India*
E-mail addresses: sceco@caluniv.ac.in; sarbajitch@yahoo.com
[b]*Department of Economics, Nagoya City University, Yamanohata, Mizuho, Nagoya 467-8501, Japan*
E-mail address: yabuuchi@econ.nagoya-cu.ac.jp

Abstract

The existing theoretical literature does not adequately take into consideration the existence of non-traded goods and the nature of capital mobility between the traded and the non-traded sectors in analyzing the consequences of liberalized investment policies on the relative wage inequality in the developing countries. The present chapter purports to fill in this gap by using two four-sector general equilibrium models reasonable for a developing economy. We have examined the outcome of foreign capital inflows on wage inequality when non-traded goods are intermediate inputs and final goods. Appropriate policy recommendations for improving the wage inequality have also been made.

Keywords: Skilled labour, unskilled labour, wage inequality, foreign capital inflows, non-traded goods, intersectoral capital mobility, labour market imperfection

JEL classifications: F13, J31

1. Introduction

Developing countries have chosen free trade as their development strategy and been vigorously implementing liberalized trade and investment policies for the last two decades or so. Radical measures for reducing tariff barriers and completely doing away with non-tariff barriers to ensure freer global trade have been undertaken in manufacturing commodities. FDI norms have liberalized considerably and several sectors, hitherto protected, have been opened up to foreign capitalists so that inflows of foreign capital take place in abundance in order to facilitate economic growth. It is important to mention that the developing countries have been able to attract a substantial amount of foreign capital during the period of economic reforms.[1]

The new development approach has not so far been an unmixed blessing. In their endeavour in implementing liberalized economic policies the developing countries have been facing some adjustment costs. Increasing skilled–unskilled wage inequality[2] and unemployment of unskilled labour are two major exacerbating problems of the developing world in the post-reform era. It is quite perplexing as to why the relative wage inequality has deteriorated, especially when as per the baseline $2 \times 2 \times 2$ Heckscher–Ohlin–Samuelson trade model, economic liberalization was expected to improve the wage inequality in the developing economies following increases in the prices of the export commodities as these are generally exporters of commodities that are intensive in the use of unskilled labour.

There is a growing theoretical literature on trade and development that explains the deteriorating wage inequality in the developing countries in the liberalized regime. Marjit *et al.* (2000), Marjit and Acharyya (2003, 2006), Chaudhuri and Yabuuchi (2007) and Yabuuchi and Chaudhuri (2007) have shown how trade liberalization, international migration of labour, inflows of foreign capital and inadequate educational opportunities and infrastructure might produce unfavourable effects on the wage inequality in the South given the specific structural characteristics of the less-developed countries, such as features of labour markets, structures of production, nature of capital mobility, etc. Two other important works in this area are those of Zhu and Trefler (2005) and Xiang (2007). Using a model that includes both Ricardian and endowments-based comparative advantage Zhu and Trefler (2005) have shown how technological catch-up and shifting of export shares towards more skill-intensive goods can worsen the wage inequality in the Southern countries. Xiang (2007), however, has shown how the introduction of new goods in the developed nations can lead to deterioration in wage inequality in the developing economies with the help of a setup of two-cone Heckscher–Ohlin model with CES preferences and a continuum of goods.

As per the empirical literature, growth in foreign direct investment which is positively correlated with the relative demand for skilled labour has been one of the prime factors[3] responsible for the growing incidence of

---

[1] As per the UNCTAD Report (2005), FDI inflows to developing countries increased from 8,455 millions of dollars in 1980 to 2,33,227 millions of dollars in 2004. FDI inward stocks in the corresponding years were 1,32,044 and 22,32,868 millions of dollars, respectively.

[2] See Robbins (1994, 1995, 1996), Wood (1997), Khan (1998) and Tendulkar *et al.* (1996) among others.

[3] See Harrison and Hanson (1999), Hanson and Harrison (1999), Currie and Harrison (1997), and Beyer *et al.* (1999) in this context.

wage inequality in the South. The paper of Feenstra and Hanson (1996) is based on the famous Dornbusch–Fischer–Samuelson continuum-of-goods framework. According to them, inflows of foreign capital induced greater production of skilled-intensive commodities in Mexico, thereby leading to a relative decrease in the demand for unskilled labour. Marjit *et al.* (2004) have analyzed how diverse trade pattern and market fragmentation in world trade can adversely affect the skilled–unskilled wage inequality in the developing countries. They have also studied the consequences of an improvement of terms of trade and inflows of foreign capital on wage inequality with or without trade fragmentation. Their paper shows that without trade fragmentation improvements in terms of trade and/or inflows of foreign capital may worsen wage inequality if the vertically integrated skilled export sector is more capital-intensive vis-à-vis the import-competing sector. But, with trade fragmentation the consequences on the relative wage inequality might be different.[4] However, in these papers all input markets have been assumed to be perfect and therefore labour market imperfection especially that of unskilled labour has not been taken care of. Furthermore, none of these papers takes into consideration the existence of non-traded goods and the nature of capital mobility between the traded and the non-traded sectors in analyzing the consequence of foreign capital inflows on the relative wage inequality.

The existence of non-traded goods, the prices of which are determined domestically by demand–supply forces, is an essential feature of a developing economy. Liberalized economic policies are supposed to move resources away from the non-traded sectors to the traded sectors of the economy. The importance of non-traded goods has been recognized by Marjit and Acharyya (2003) who have used a four-sector general equilibrium model to study the consequences of an import liberalization and an increase in world price of agricultural exports on the relative wage inequality in the developing countries. Interestingly, if the non-traded good is produced in a formal sector an import liberalization accentuates the inequality while an increase in the price of exportable, either agricultural or manufacturing, is likely to improve the relative wage inequality. The worsening effect of trade liberalization is magnified if the non-traded good is produced in an informal sector. However, Marjit and Acharyya (2003) have neither examined the consequence of an inflow of foreign capital in the presence of non-traded goods nor they have taken into consideration the nature of capital mobility that may exist between

[4] An inflow of foreign capital may worsen the wage inequality even with trade fragmentation if the traded intermediate good sector is capital-intensive relative to the import-competing sector.

the traded and the non-traded sectors which are exceedingly important from policy perspective.

Non-traded goods may be either inputs or final commodities. A non-traded sector that produces an intermediate good for a traded sector lives or dies with the latter. On the contrary, a final good-producing non-traded sector expands or contracts with an increase or a decrease in the purchasing power of the people who consume the commodity. Hence how the prices of non-traded goods change in response to policy changes plays a crucial role in determining the direction of relative wage movements. Furthermore, capital mobility between the traded and the non-traded sectors may be of different types. If the non-traded sector produces an agricultural commodity there should be capital mobility between the non-traded sector and the primary export sector while capital is likely to flow freely between the non-traded, low-skill manufacturing and the high-skill sectors if the non-traded sector produces a manufacturing good. The outcomes of any policy changes on the relative wages should depend on the type of non-traded good and the nature of capital mobility between the traded and the non-traded sectors.

Keeping all these into consideration the present chapter seeks to analyze the consequence of an inflow of foreign capital on the skilled–unskilled wage inequality in a developing economy in the presence of non-traded goods. Two four-sector general equilibrium models[5] have been used for the analytical purpose. First, the case of non-traded input is taken up where one of the four sectors produces an intermediate good for another sector. Both these sectors use unskilled labour, and capital flows freely between them. There is also capital mobility between these two sectors and the high-skill sector whereas in the latter skilled labour is a specific input. We then deal with the case of final commodity where capital[6] is mobile only between the primary export sector and the non-traded sector. These two sectors, however, cannot receive capital from the other sectors, i.e. the low-skill manufacturing and the high-skill sectors. There is imperfection in the market for unskilled labour in the low-skill sector (formal sector) where unskilled workers receive a high unionized wage whereas their counterparts in the other two sectors receive only a low competitive wage. The capital endowment of the economy consists of both domestic capital and foreign capital and these are perfect substitutes.[7]

---

[5] One should ideally make use of a four-sector general equilibrium for capturing simultaneously both non-traded goods and imperfections in the market for unskilled labour.

[6] These two sectors use land which is one type of capital in a wider sense. To avoid confusion, however, we can call this input land-capital which is broadly conceived to include durable capital equipments of all kinds. See Bardhan (1973) and Chaudhuri (2007) in this context.

[7] This assumption has been widely used in the theoretical literature on foreign capital and welfare. See, Brecher and Alejandro (1977), Chandra and Khan (1993), Yabuuchi (1982) and Chaudhuri (2007) among others.

The inflow of foreign capital is conceptualized in the form of exogenous capital flows.[8]

This theoretical analysis leads to some interesting results. When the non-traded sector produces an intermediate input, inflows of foreign capital improve the wage inequality if the low-skill manufacturing sector is capital-intensive (in a special sense) relative to the high-skill sector. On the contrary, relative wages may move against unskilled labour when the high-skill sector is capital-intensive and the low-skill sector employs only a very small proportion of unskilled workforce. But, in the case of the non-traded final commodity skilled–unskilled wage inequality worsens (improves) if the primary export sector is land-capital-intensive (unskilled labour-intensive) relative to the non-traded sector whereas the high-skill (low-skill) sector is capital-intensive vis-à-vis the low-skill (high-skill) sector and the low-skill sector employs only a very small proportion of the unskilled workforce. The wage inequality, however, improves if the high-skill sector is capital-intensive and the non-traded sector is land-intensive. The wage inequality also improves if the low-skill sector is capital-intensive and the primary export sector is land-capital-intensive. A wage subsidy policy and/ or a capital subsidy policy should be undertaken under different circumstances so as to make wages move in favour of unskilled workers.

2. *The model with non-traded intermediate input*

Let us consider a small open economy with four sectors. Sector 1 is the primary export sector that produces an agricultural commodity using unskilled labour and land-capital. The input 'land-capital' is broadly conceived to include durable capital equipments of all kinds.[9] Sector 2 produces a non-traded input for the low-skill manufacturing sector (sector 3) with the help of unskilled labour and capital. Sector 3, however, uses unskilled labour and capital apart from the non-traded input to produce a final manufacturing commodity. The per-unit requirement of the intermediate input, a_{23}, is assumed to be technologically fixed.[10] Sector 3 is the

[8] Although the mobility of capital has increased considerably across countries owing to the liberalized investment policies, it is still far from being complete. In the developing countries like India, the FDI proposals are considered and approved on a case-to-case basis. Hence, due to incomplete and restricted mobility of capital the world rate of return and the domestic rate of return to capital do not get equalized. We should note that if capital were perfectly mobile internationally a large capital inflow would have brought down the domestic return to capital thereby lowering the wage rates unambiguously.

[9] See footnote 6 in this context.

[10] It rules out the possibility of substitution between the non-traded input and other factors of production in sector 3. Although this is a simplifying assumption, it is not totally unrealistic. In industries like shoe making and garments, large formal sector firms farm out their production to small informal sector firms under the system of subcontracting. So the production is done in the informal sector while labeling, packaging and marketing are done

import-competing sector of the economy. Finally, sector 4, another export sector, produces a high-skill product using skilled labour and capital. So land-capital and skilled labour are specific factors in sectors 1 and 4, respectively. Capital is perfectly mobile between the non-traded, low-skill and high-skill sectors. Unskilled workers employed in the low-skill sector (sector 3) earn a unionized wage, W^*, while their counterparts in the other two sectors earn a competitive wage, W with $W^* > W$. Production functions exhibit constant returns to scale with diminishing marginal productivity to each factor. Perfect competition prevails in all markets, except the unskilled labour market in sector 3. The prices of the traded commodities are given by the small open economy assumption. But, the price of the non-traded input is determined domestically. The diverse trade pattern of the economy is reflected in the fact that it exports both the primary agricultural and the high-skill commodities while it is a net importer of the low-skill manufacturing commodity. A developing country which fits this type of comparative advantage is India.[11] Commodity 1 is chosen as the numeraire.

The following symbols will be used in the equations.

a_{Ki} = capital–output ratio in the ith sector, $i = 2,3,4$;
a_{N1} = land-capital–output ratio in sector 1;
a_{Li} = unskilled labour–output ratio in the ith sector, $i = 1,2,3$;
a_{S4} = skilled labour–output ratio in sector 4;
P_i = internationally given price[12] of the ith commodity, $i = 1,3,4$;
P_2 = domestically determined price of commodity 2;
X_i = level of output of the ith sector, $i = 1,2,3,4$;
W_S = wage rate of skilled labour;
W^* = institutionally determined (or unionized) unskilled wage rate in sector 3;
W = competitive wage rate of unskilled labour;
R = return to land-capital;
r = return to capital;

---

by the formal sector firms. One pair of shoes produced in the informal sector does not change in quantity when it is marketed by the formal sector as a final commodity. Thus, there remains a fixed proportion between the use of the intermediate good and the quantity of the final commodity produced and marketed by the formal sector.However, if sector 2 produces an agricultural product like sugarcane or cotton, there might exist a fixed proportion between the quantity of input used and the quantity of output produced in the sugar mills/textile firms. It may be noted that papers like Chaudhuri (2003), Marjit (2003) and Chaudhuri *et al.* (2006) have also made this assumption for different reasons.

[11] It may be mentioned that besides primary agricultural commodities, India is also a large exporter of high-skill products like computer software. However, one may also consider alternative trade patterns as results of this chapter do not depend on the pattern of trade of the economy.

[12] Commodity 1 is chosen as the numeraire here. So, these are relative prices as well.

U,α = parameters denoting the extent of bargaining power of the trade unions;
L = endowment of unskilled labour;
S = endowment of skilled labour;
N = endowment of land-capital;
K = endowment of capital of the economy (domestic plus foreign);
θ_{ji} = distributive share of the jth input in the ith sector for $j = L,S,N,K$ and $i =$ 1, 2, 3,4;
λ_{ji} = proportion of the jth input employed in the ith sector for $j = L,K$ and $i = 1,2,3,4$;
$W_A = (\lambda_{L1}W + \lambda_{L3}W^*) =$ average unskilled wage;
S_{ji}^k = the degree of substitution between factors j and i in the kth sector, $j, i = L, N, S, K$; and, $k =$ 1,2,3. For example,
$S_{LN}^1 \equiv (R/a_{L1})(\partial a_{L1}/\partial R)$, $S_{LL}^1 \equiv (W/a_{L1})(\partial a_{L1}/\partial W)$, etc. $S_{ji}^k > 0$ for $j \neq i$; and, $S_{jj}^k < 0$;
'$\wedge$' = proportional change.

Given the assumption of perfectly competitive markets the usual price–unit cost equality conditions relating to the four sectors of the economy are given by the following four equations, respectively.

$$Wa_{L1} + Ra_{N1} = 1 \tag{1}$$

$$Wa_{L2} + ra_{N2} = P_2 \tag{2}$$

$$W^*(W, U)a_{L3} + ra_{K3} + P_2a_{23} = P_3 \tag{3}$$

$$W_Sa_{S4} + ra_{K4} = P_4 \tag{4}$$

The formal sector faces a unionized labour market. The relationship for the unionized wage rate is specified as:[13]

$$W^* = W^*(W, U) \text{ with } W^* = W \text{ for } U = 0, W^* > W \text{ for } U > 0$$

where U denotes the bargaining strength of the trade unions. This relationship states that in the absence of any bargaining power[14] of the trade unions, i.e. when $U = 0$, the wage rates are equal in different sectors. However, the unionized wage rate in sector 3, $W*$, exceeds the competitive wage rate, W, when there is at least some power to the trade unions. The

[13] Assuming that each formal sector firm has a separate trade union, the unionized wage function may be derived as a solution to the Nash bargaining game between the representative firm and the representative union in the formal sector. For detailed derivation see Chaudhuri (2003).

[14] The union power, denoted by U, is amenable to policy measures. If the government undertakes labour market reform measures, e.g. partial or complete ban on resorting to strikes by the trade unions, reformation of employment security laws to curb union power, U takes a lower value.

unionized wage is scaled upward as the competitive wage rate rises. Also with an increase in the bargaining power, the unions bargain for a higher wage.

For the sake of analytical simplicity we consider the following specific algebraic form of the unionized wage function.

$$W^* = \alpha W \text{ with } \alpha > 1 \tag{5}$$

Here α captures the degree of imperfection in the market for unskilled labour.[15] When the mark-up of the wage over the alternative (informal sector) wage is higher, the higher is the union power, the lower is the product market competitiveness and the lower is the labour intensity. Thus the mark-up depends on the rents coming from product market power and the quasi-rents coming from fixed capital – together with the power of the union to appropriate these rents. In the present competitive product market structure the rent coming from the product market is zero. During the time of recession when the alternative income is low the unions are prepared to accept a lower wage.[16]

Using (3), Equation (5) can be rewritten as follows.

$$\alpha W a_{L3} + r a_{K3} + P_2 a_{23} = P_3 \tag{6}$$

Full-employment conditions for unskilled labour, capital, land-capital and skilled labour are as follows, respectively.

$$a_{L1}X_1 + a_{L2}X_2 + a_{L3}X_3 = L \tag{7}$$

$$a_{K2}X_2 + a_{K3}X_3 + a_{K4}X_4 = K \tag{8}$$

$$a_{N1}X_1 = N \tag{9}$$

$$a_{S4}X_4 = S \tag{10}$$

The output of sector 2, X_2, is used entirely for producing X_3, so that the supply of X_2 is circumscribed by its total demand by sector 3. The demand–supply equality condition is given by

$$X_2^D = a_{23}X_3 = X_2 \tag{11}$$

There are nine endogenous variables in the system: W, W_S, R, r, P_2, X_1, X_2, X_3 and X_4; and, nine independent equations, namely, Equations (1), (2), (6), (4) and (7)–(11). This is an indecomposable production system. Hence, factor prices depend on both commodity prices and factor endowments. Using Equations (9) and (10), (7) and (8) can be rewritten

[15] One may alternatively consider $\alpha = (1+\alpha_0)$ where α_0 includes the institutional characteristics of the formal sector labour market.

[16] See Layard *et al.* (2005) for details.

as follows, respectively.

$$(a_{L1}N/a_{N1}) + \tilde{a}_{L3}X_3 = L \tag{12}$$

$$(a_{K4}S/a_{S4}) + \tilde{a}_{K3}X_3 = K \tag{13}$$

where $\tilde{a}_{L3} = a_{L2}a_{23} + a_{L3}$ and $\tilde{a}_{K3} = a_{K2}a_{23} + a_{K3}$. Note that $\tilde{a}_{L3}$ and $\tilde{a}_{K3}$ are the both direct and indirect uses of unskilled labour and capital in sector 3, respectively. The indirect uses take place through the application of the non-traded input.

The working of the general equilibrium model is as follows. The five input prices, W, W_S, r, R and P_2 and X_3 are determined by solving Equations (1), (2), (6), (4), (12) and (13) simultaneously. Once the factor prices are known the factor coefficients, a_{ji} s, are also known. X_1, X_4 and X_2 are obtained from Equations (9), (10) and (11), respectively.

Unskilled workers in this economy earn two different wages – either the unionized wage, W^*, in sector 3 or the competitive wage, W, in sectors 1 and 2. The average wage for unskilled labour must be a weighted average of the two wage rates and is given by

$$W_A \equiv (W(\lambda_{L1} + \lambda_{L2}) + W^*\lambda_{L3})$$

and using (5) it can be rewritten as follows.

$$W_A = W[1 + (\alpha - 1)\lambda_{L3}] \tag{14}$$

where λ_{Li} denotes the proportion of unskilled labour employed in sector i, $i = 1, 2, 3$. In this case, the skilled–unskilled wage gap improves (worsens) in absolute terms if the gap between W_S and W_A falls (rises), that is, $d(W_S - W_A) = (dW_S - dW_A) < (>) 0$. However, the wage inequality improves (deteriorates) both in absolute and relative terms if $d(W_S/W_A) < (>) 0$, or equivalently, $(\hat{W}_S - \hat{W}_A) < (>) 0$.

Differentiating Equations (1), (2), (6), (4), (12) and (13) the following expression can be derived.[17]

$$(\hat{W}_S - \hat{W}_A) = \left(\frac{\hat{K}}{\Delta}\right)\Bigg[(\theta_{N1}\lambda_L)\Bigg\{(\theta_{K4}\tilde{\theta}_{L3} - \theta_{S4}\tilde{\theta}_{K3}) - \left\{\frac{W\lambda_{L3}\theta_{S4}}{W_A}(\alpha - 1)\right\}\lambda_{L1}\tilde{\theta}_{K3}(S^1_{LN} + S^1_{NL}) + \theta_{N1}(S^2_{LK} - S^3_{LK})\lambda_{L2}\Bigg\}\Bigg] \tag{15}$$

where $\tilde{\theta}_{L3} = \theta_{L2}\theta_{23} + \theta_{L3}$ and $\tilde{\theta}_{K3} = \theta_{K2}\theta_{23} + \theta_{K3}$. The expression for Δ has been presented in Appendix I and it can be noted that

$$\Delta > 0 \tag{16}$$

From (15) it is evident that $(\hat{W}_S - \hat{W}_A) < 0$ when $\hat{K} > 0$, if (i)$S^2_{LK} \geq S^3_{LK}$ and (ii) $(\theta_{K4}/\theta_{S4}) < (\tilde{\theta}_{K3}/\tilde{\theta}_{L3})$. On the contrary, $(\hat{W}_S - \hat{W}_A) > 0$ when $\hat{K} > 0$,

[17] See Appendix I for detailed derivation of this expression.

if (i) $\lambda_{L3} \cong 0$ and (ii) $(\theta_{K4}/\theta_{S4}) > (\tilde{\theta}_{K3}/\tilde{\theta}_{L3})$. This establishes the following proposition.

PROPOSITION 1. *When the non-traded informal sector produces an input for the low-skill manufacturing sector an inflow of foreign capital improves the skilled–unskilled wage inequality if* (i) *the vertically integrated low-skill formal sector is capital-intensive (in a special sense)*[18] *and* (ii) $S^2_{LK} \geq S^3_{LK}$. *The relative wage inequality, however, deteriorates if the proportion of unskilled labour employed in the low-skill formal sector is significantly low and the high-skill sector is capital-intensive.*

Proposition 1 can be intuitively explained as follows. As the system does not satisfy the decomposition property factor prices depend on both final commodity prices and factor endowments. An inflow of foreign capital lowers the return to capital, r, as the supply rises given the demand. All the three capital-using sectors expand. Sector 2 expands because sector 3 uses the output of the former as input in fixed proportion. The demand for skilled labour rises in sector 4 and that of unskilled labour increases in both sectors 2 and 3. Consequently, W_S and W increase. An increase in W implies an increase in the unionized unskilled wage, W^*. What happens to the average unskilled wage, W_A, depends crucially on the change in the proportion of unskilled labour employed in the high wage-paying sector (sector 3), i.e. λ_{L3}. As the (W^*/r) has increased producers in sector 3 would substitute unskilled labour by capital. This lowers the labour-output ratio in sector 3, a_{L3}. But, as sector 3 has expanded the aggregate employment of unskilled labour (and hence λ_{L3}) increases if $S^2_{LK} \geq S^3_{LK}$.[19] Under this sufficient condition W_A also rises. The outcome of foreign capital inflows on the skilled–unskilled wage inequality crucially depends on the rates of increase in W_S and W_A. Our analysis shows that if the vertically integrated low-skill manufacturing sector is capital-intensive relative to the high-skill sector relative wages move in favour of unskilled labour. However, when the low-skill formal sector employs a very small proportion of the unskilled workforce,[20] an expansion of sector 3 cannot produce any

---

[18] Here sectors 3 and 4 use two different types of labour. However, there is one intersectorally mobile input which is capital. So, these two industries cannot be classified in terms of factor intensities which is usually done in the Heckscher–Ohlin–Samuelson model. Despite this, a special type of factor intensity classification in terms of the relative distributive shares of the mobile factor, i.e. capital, may be used for analytical purposes. The industry in which this share is higher relative to the other may be considered as capital-intensive in a special sense. See Jones and Neary (1984) for details.

[19] See Appendix I.

[20] As per NSS estimates the proportion of workforce engaged in unorganized sector in 1999–2000 in India was as high as 93%. The unorganized sector, commonly known as the informal sector, comprises mainly of unskilled workers. Hence, the percentage of workforce engaged in the formal sector in 1999–2000 was quite low and this share is continuously declining over time with economic reforms. See Bhalotra (2002) in this context.

significant positive effect on λ_{L3} and W_A. The direction of relative wage movements now entirely depends on the rates of increases in the competitive unskilled wage and the skilled wage. Relative wages move against unskilled labour if the vertically integrated low-skill sector is less capital-intensive vis-à-vis the high-skill sector.

3. *The modified system with non-traded final commodity*

In this section, we propose to modify the model of Section 2 in two directions. First, sector 2 now produces a non-traded final commodity using unskilled labour and land-capital as two inputs. Thus, sectors 1 and 2 constitute a miniature Heckscher–Ohlin Subsystem (HOSS). Second, we introduce land-capital in the non-traded sector as well as in the primary export sector. Capital flows perfectly freely between the low-skill manufacturing sector (sector 3) and the high-skill sector (sector 4). But, there is no capital mobility between the high-skill (or low-skill) sector and the non-traded sector. This setup fits well to developing countries that still have a dual structure with rural and urban areas.

In addition to the symbols that we have been used in Section 2 we shall here use the following symbols as well.[21]

a_{N2} = land-capital–output ratio in sector 2;
Y = national income at domestic prices[21];
K_D = domestic capital stock;
D_2 = demand for the non-traded final commodity;
E_P = own price elasticity of demand good 2;
E_Y = income elasticity of demand for good 2.

The usual zero-profit conditions for the four sectors are as follows.

$$Wa_{L1} + Ra_{N1} = 1 \tag{17}$$

$$Wa_{L2} + Ra_{N2} = P_2 \tag{18}$$

$$\alpha Wa_{L3} + ra_{K3} = P_3 \tag{19}$$

$$W_S a_{S4} + ra_{K4} = P_4 \tag{20}$$

The demand for the non-traded final commodity is given by the following.

$$D_2 = D_2(P_2, Y) \tag{21}$$

where, Y, is national income at domestic prices and is given by

$$Y = WL + (W^* - W)a_{L3}X_3 + RN + rK_D + W_S S \tag{22}$$

---

[21] As there are no tariffs or subsidies national income at domestic prices and national income at world prices are the same in this model.

In Equation (22), $(WL + (W^* - W)a_{L3}X_3)$ gives the aggregate wage income of the unskilled workers employed in the three sectors of the economy. RN is the rental income from land-capital while $W_S S$ is the wage income of skilled labour. Finally, rK_D is the domestic capital income. Income from foreign capital is fully repatriated.[22] Hence, it is not included in Equation (22).

The demand for commodity 2 is a positive function of Y and a decreasing function of P_2. So we have: $(\partial D_2/\partial Y)>0; (\partial D_2/\partial P_2)<0$. The market for commodity 2 must clear domestically. So in equilibrium we have

$$D_2(P_2, Y) = X_2 \tag{23}$$

Full-employment conditions for resources are as follows.

$$a_{N1}X_1 + a_{N2}X_2 = N \tag{24}$$

$$a_{L1}X_1 + a_{L2}X_2 + a_{L3}X_3 = L \tag{25}$$

$$a_{K3}X_3 + a_{K4}X_4 = K_D + K_F = K \tag{26}$$

$$a_{S4}X_4 = S \tag{27}$$

The modified model comprises of 11 equations (namely, Equations (17)–(27)) and exactly the same number of endogenous variables; namely, W, W_S, R, r, P_2, X_1, X_2, X_3, X_4, D_2 and Y. The four unknown factor prices are solved from Equations (17)–(20) as functions of P_2. As a_{ji}s are functions of factor prices these are automatically obtained. Then from (24)–(27) X_is are found as functions of P_2. Finally, using (22) P_2 is solved from (23). Once P_2 is obtained the values of all endogenous variables are obtained.

The average unskilled wage is again given by

$$W_A = W[1 + (\alpha - 1)\lambda_{L3}] \tag{28}$$

Differentiating (17)–(20), (22)–(27) and (28) the following expression can be obtained.[23]

$$(\hat{W}_S - \hat{W}_A) = -\left(\frac{\theta_{N1}\hat{K}}{\Omega}\right)|\lambda^*|\left[(\theta_{K4} - \theta_{K3}) - (\alpha - 1)\lambda_{L3}(\theta_{S4}\theta_{K3} - S^3_{LK})\right] - \left[W(\alpha - 1)\left(\frac{\lambda_{L3}}{W_A}\right)\hat{X}_3\right] \tag{29}$$

---

[22] This is the standard assumption made in the literature on foreign capital and welfare. See, for example, Brecher and Alejandro (1977), Khan (1982) and Chao and Yu (1994).

[23] See Appendices II–IV for mathematical derivation of this expression.

where,

$$\left.\begin{aligned} |\lambda^*| &= [(\lambda_{L2}\lambda_{N1} - \lambda_{N2}\lambda_{L1})B_{13} + \lambda_{N1}\lambda_{L3}]; \text{ and,} \\ B_{13} &= [(E_Y/Y)(\alpha - 1)Wa_{L3}X_3] > 0 \end{aligned}\right\} \quad (30)$$

The expression for Ω has been presented in Appendix II and using the static stability condition in the market for the non-traded commodity[24] it can be shown that in the stable equilibrium we must have:[25]

$$\Omega < 0; \quad \text{and,} \quad \hat{X}_3 > 0 \quad \text{when} \quad \hat{K} > 0 \quad (31)$$

Note that relative factor intensities between the sectors, $|\lambda| = \lambda_{K3}(\lambda_{N1}\lambda_{L2} - \lambda_{N2}\lambda_{L1})$ and $(\theta_{K4} - \theta_{K3})$ play extremely crucial roles in determining the consequence of foreign capital inflows ($\hat{K} > 0$) on the relative wage inequality, $(\hat{W}_S - \hat{W}_A)$. Note that the factor intensity between sectors 3 and 4 is defined in terms of the relative distributive shares. This is not identical with the usual (physical) factor intensity since the sectors use two different types of labour. Thus, it is possible that the low-skilled manufacturing sector 3 is capital-intensive in this sense, i.e., $\theta_{K3} > \theta_{K4}$, or equivalently, $(\theta_{K3}/\theta_{L3}) > (\theta_{K4}/\theta_{S4})$ even when sector 4 is capital-intensive in the usual (physical) sense, i.e., $(a_{K3}/a_{L3}) < (a_{K4}/a_{S4})$ if W_S (then θ_{S4}) is sufficiently large.[26] Our results are summarized in Table 1.

From the results one can now establish the following proposition.

Proposition 2. *Inflows of foreign capital are likely to improve the skilled–unskilled wage inequality if the low-skill manufacturing sector is capital-intensive and employs a significant proportion of the unskilled workforce and the primary export sector is land-intensive. On the contrary, when the low-skill sector employs only a very small proportion of unskilled labour the wage inequality improves if the primary export sector is land-capital-intensive (or unskilled labour-intensive) and the low-skill manufacturing sector (or high-skill sector) is capital-intensive. Otherwise, the relative wage inequality deteriorates.*

We explain Proposition 2 in the following fashion. Here the non-traded sector and the primary export sector use the same two inputs – unskilled labour and land-capital, and together form an HOSS. We have already stated that the factor prices come out from the price system as functions of the price of the non-traded good, P_2, and that P_2 is determined by its demand and supply forces. Besides, an inflow of foreign capital leads to expansion of both sector 3 and sector 4. As sector 3 expands more (less) unskilled workers are now employed in the higher (lower) wage-paying

---

[24] The stability condition has been derived in Appendix V.

[25] Mathematical proofs of the two results have been provided in Appendices V and VI, respectively.

[26] See also footnote 18.

Table 1. The effects on wage inequality

$\lambda_{L3} > 0$	$\lvert\lambda\rvert > 0$ (or $\lvert\lambda\rvert < 0$ but $\lvert\lambda *\rvert > 0$)	$\theta_{K3} \geq \theta_{K4}$	$\theta_{S4}\theta_{K3} \geq S^3_{LK}$	(Inequality) Improves
$\lambda_{L3} \cong 0$	$\lvert\lambda\rvert > 0$	$\theta_{K3} > \theta_{K4}$		Improves
		$\theta_{K3} < \theta_{K4}$		Deteriorates
	$\lvert\lambda\rvert < 0$	$\theta_{K3} < \theta_{K4}$		Improves
		$\theta_{K3} > \theta_{K4}$		Deteriorates

sector (sectors). This raises the aggregate unskilled wage income. This we call the unskilled labour reallocation effect, which produces a positive effect on the aggregate factor income, Y, and raises the demand for the non-traded good (good 2). As sector 3 draws unskilled labour from the HOSS a Rybczynski-type effect takes place that results in a contraction of the unskilled labour-intensive sector and an expansion of the other.

If sector 1 is land-capital-intensive, it expands while sector 2 contracts. P_2 rises[27] as its supply has fallen while the demand has increased. This in turn produces a Stolper–Samuelson effect in the HOSS and raises the competitive unskilled wage, W, as sector 2 is labour-intensive. The unionized unskilled wage, W^*, also rises. To satisfy the zero-profit condition for sector 3 the return to capital, r, falls. Saving on capital input raises the skilled wage, W_S, in sector 4. As producers in sector 3 substitute unskilled labour by capital, a_{L3} falls. Despite this, the proportion of unskilled labour employed in the higher wage-paying sector 3 (i.e. λ_{L3}) rises if $\theta_{K3} \geq S^3_{LK}$.[28] We, therefore, find that the average unskilled wage increases due to (i) an increase in W; (ii) an increase in W^* and (iii) an increase in the proportion of unskilled labour employed in the higher wage-paying sector if $\theta_{K3} \geq S^3_{LK}$. Consequently, the average unskilled wage, W_A, rises in this case under the sufficient condition as stated above. What happens to the skilled–unskilled wage inequality depends on the rates of increase in W_S and W_A. If $(\theta_{K3}/\theta_{L3}) > (=) (\theta_{K2}/\theta_{S2})$ the saving on capital input in sector 3 is more than (equal to) that in sector 4, which in turn implies that the rate of increase of the unionized unskilled wage, W^*, is greater than (equal to) that of the skilled wage, W_S. But, there are two other factors working positively on the average unskilled wage.[29] Thus, the wage inequality gets better following inflows of foreign capital under the two sufficient conditions as mentioned above. However, if the proportion

[27] See Appendix III.

[28] This has been shown in Appendix IV.

[29] These have already been discussed under (i) and (iii).

of unskilled labour employed in the high wage-paying sector is considerably small (i.e. $\lambda_{L3} \cong 0$), W_A increases following an inflow of foreign capital as the competitive unskilled wage, W, rises. If $\theta_{K3} > (<) \theta_{K4}$ saving on capital cost will be higher (lower) in the low-skill sector than that in the high-skill sector. Consequently, the wage inequality improves (worsens).

If sector 1 (sector2) is unskilled labour-intensive (land-capital-intensive) the supply of the non-traded good rises following a Rybczynski-type effect. The larger is the proportion of unskilled labour employed in the low-skill sector, the higher would be the magnitude of the Rybczynski-type effect in the HOSS. Although both the demand and the supply of the non-traded good increase, the Rybczynski-type effect of a sufficiently high magnitude (consequence of a high λ_{L3}) will make the expansionary supply side effect of the non-traded good stronger than the demand side effect. The price of the non-traded good, P_2, falls which in turn raises W following the Stolper–Samuelson effect as sector 1 is now unskilled labour-intensive. The qualitative effects on $W^*, r, W_S, \lambda_{L3}$ and W_A would exactly be the same as in the earlier case. Consequently, the skilled–unskilled wage inequality improves under the same set of sufficient conditions.

Finally, if sector 1 (sector 2) is unskilled labour-intensive (land-capital-intensive) but the proportion of the unskilled workforce employed in the low-skill sector is significantly low (i.e. $\lambda_{L3} \cong 0$), the magnitude of the Rybczynski-type effect in the HOSS would be very small and consequently the supply of good 2 rises only by a small magnitude. P_2 increases in this case as the demand side effect dominates over the supply side effect. The competitive unskilled wage, W, decreases following the Stolper–Samuelson effect as sector 2 is land-capital-intensive.[30] The return to capital rises despite an increase in the endowment of capital as sector 3 expands and the allocative share of capital in this sector is sufficiently high. Sector 4 contracts for want of capital[31] and the skilled wage, W_S, falls as its demand falls. As $\lambda_{L3} \cong 0$, the average unskilled wage, W_A, decreases as W falls. If $\theta_{K4} > (<) \theta_{K3}$ increase on, capital cost will be higher (lower) in the high-skill sector vis-à-vis the low-skill sector. Consequently, the wage inequality improves (worsens).

4. *Policy implications and concluding remarks*

Growth in foreign direct investment, positively correlated with the relative demand for skilled labour, has been one of the prime factors responsible

---

[30] The return to land-capital rises.

[31] This has been shown in Appendix VII.

for widening of wage inequality in the Latin American countries like Mexico. But, foreign capital may not be held accountable for the growing incidence of wage inequality in other developing economies like India. It is extremely important to judge the consequences of foreign capital in the light of the typical structural characteristics of these economies, e.g. presence of non-traded goods, imperfections in the market for unskilled labour and type of intersectoral capital mobility. This has been carried out in this chapter using two four-sector specific factors general equilibrium models.

We have found that barring a few special cases inflows of foreign capital in general improve the wage inequality when the low-skill sector is capital-intensive. But, the relative wage gap may widen if the high-skill sector is capital-intensive. A capital subsidy policy to the low-skill manufacturing sector should be undertaken so as to increase the capital-intensity of production in this sector. However, when the non-traded sector produces a final commodity wage inequality worsens if the low-skill sector is capital-intensive and employs only a very small proportion of the unskilled workforce and if the primary export sector is unskilled labour-intensive. In such a case, the policy prescription should be there to provide a wage subsidy to the low-skill sector.[32] A wage subsidy would help in increasing the proportion of employment of unskilled labour in the low-skill sector. This would also lend a hand in raising the competitive unskilled wage. If these policies are followed whenever necessary abundant inflows of foreign capital might be a solution to deteriorating skilled–unskilled wage in the developing nations during the liberalized regime.

Acknowledgement

We wish to thank an anonymous referee for many helpful comments and suggestions on an earlier version of the chapter. The usual disclaimer, however, applies. Yabuuchi's research was financially supported by the Japan Economic Research Foundation and the Grants-in-Aid for Scientific Research (c-19530210) from the Japan Society for the Promotion of Science.

[32] This is, of course, not a WTO-compliant policy. In fact, the developing countries have been advised to remove all tariffs, quotas, subsidies and other impediments to free trade so as to completely reap the harvests of economic reforms. However, in a developing country with high degree of income and wealth inequalities, the distributional and growth aspects are equally important for economic development. These economies, therefore, need not follow all the WTO recommendations so as to protect the interest of the poorer section of the working population.

Appendix I

Differentiating totally Equations (1), (2), (6), (4) and (7)–(11) and arranging in a matrix notation one gets:

$$\begin{pmatrix} \theta_{L1} & \theta_{N1} & 0 & 0 & 0 & 0 \\ \theta_{L2} & 0 & \theta_{K2} & 0 & -1 & 0 \\ \theta_{L3} & 0 & \theta_{K3} & 0 & \theta_{23} & 0 \\ 0 & 0 & \theta_{K4} & \theta_{S4} & 0 & 0 \\ -A_1 & A_2 & A_3 & 0 & 0 & \lambda_L \\ A_4 & 0 & -A_5 & A_6 & 0 & \lambda_K \end{pmatrix} \begin{pmatrix} \hat{W} \\ \hat{R} \\ \hat{r} \\ \hat{W}_S \\ \hat{P}_2 \\ \hat{X}_3 \end{pmatrix} = \begin{pmatrix} 0 \\ 0 \\ 0 \\ 0 \\ 0 \\ \hat{K} \end{pmatrix} \tag{A.1}$$

where:

$$\left.\begin{aligned} &A_1 = (\lambda_{L1}S^1_{LN} + \lambda_{L2}S^2_{LK} + \lambda_{L3}S^3_{LK} + \lambda_{L1}S^1_{NL}) > 0; \\ &A_2 = \lambda_{L1}(S^1_{LN} + S^1_{LN}) > 0; A_3 = (\lambda_{L2}S^2_{LK} + \lambda_{L3}S^3_{LK}) > 0; \\ &A_4 = (\lambda_{K2}S^2_{KL} + \lambda_{K3}S^3_{KL}) > 0; \\ &A_5 = (\lambda_{K2}S^2_{KL} + \lambda_{K3}S^3_{KL} + \lambda_{K4}S^4_{KS} + \lambda_{K4}S^4_{SK}) > 0; \\ &A_6 = \lambda_{K4}(S^4_{KS} + S^4_{SK}) > 0; \\ &\lambda_L = (\lambda_{L2} + \lambda_{L3}) > 0; \lambda_K = (\lambda_{K2} + \lambda_{K3}) > 0. \end{aligned}\right\} \tag{A.2}$$

and,

$$\begin{aligned} \Delta = \theta_{L1}\theta_{S4}A_2\lambda_K(\theta_{23}\theta_{K2} + \theta_{K3}) + \theta_{N1}[\theta_{S4}(\theta_{23}\theta_{K2} + \theta_{K3})(A_1\lambda_K + A_4\lambda_L) \\ + (\theta_{23}\theta_{L2} + \theta_{L3})\{\theta_{K4}A_6\lambda_L + \theta_{S4}(A_3\lambda_K + A_5\lambda_L)\}] > 0. \end{aligned} \tag{A.3}$$

As commodity 2 is internationally non-traded its market must clear domestically through adjustments in its price, P_2. The stability condition in the market for commodity 2 requires that $(d(X_2^D - X_2)/dP_2) < 0$. This implies around equilibrium, initially, $X_2^D = X_2$. Thus, $((\hat{X}_2^D/\hat{P}_2) - (\hat{X}_2/\hat{P}_2)) < 0$. This requires that $\Delta > 0$. In this case, of course, the stability condition is automatically satisfied. This is because from (A.2) and (A.3) it follows that Δ is unconditionally positive.

Solving (A.1) by Cramer's rule the following expressions are obtained.

$$\hat{W} = (\theta_{N1}\theta_{S4}\lambda_L\tilde{\theta}_{K3})\hat{K}/\Delta \tag{A.4}$$

$$\hat{W}_S = (\theta_{N1}\theta_{K4}\lambda_L\theta_{L3})\hat{K}/\Delta \tag{A.5}$$

$$\hat{r} = -(\theta_{N1}\theta_{S4}\lambda_L\theta_{L3})\hat{K}/\Delta \tag{A.6}$$

$$\hat{X}_3 = \theta_{S4}[\tilde{\theta}_{K3}(\theta_{L1}A_2 + \theta_{N1}A_1) + \theta_{N1}\tilde{\theta}_{L3})A_3]\hat{K}/\Delta \tag{A.7}$$

$$\hat{P}_2 = (\theta_{N1}\theta_{S4}\lambda_L)(\theta_{L2}\theta_{K3} - \theta_{L3}\theta_{K2})\hat{K}/\Delta \tag{A.8}$$

where $\tilde{\theta}_{L3} = \theta_{L2}\theta_{23} + \theta_{L3}$ and $\tilde{\theta}_{K3} = \theta_{K2}\theta_{23} + \theta_{K3}$. Differentiating (14), using (A.4), (A.6) and (A.7) and simplifying one can derive the following expression.

$$\hat{W}_{\mathrm{A}} = \left(\frac{W\hat{W}}{W_{\mathrm{A}}}\right)[1 + (\alpha - 1)\lambda_{L3}] + \frac{W}{W_{\mathrm{A}}}(\alpha - 1)\lambda_{L3}\theta_{S4}\frac{\hat{K}}{\Delta}\left[\lambda_{L1}\tilde{\theta}_{K3}(S^1_{LN} + S^1_{NL}) + \theta_{N1}(S^2_{LK} - S^3_{LK})\lambda_{L2}\right] \quad (A.9)$$

Using (A.2) and (A.3) and from (A.4)–(A.9) the following results are obtained.

When $\hat{K}>0$, (i) $\hat{W}>0$; (ii) $\hat{W}_{\mathrm{S}}>0$; (iii) $\hat{r}<0$; (iv) $\hat{X}_3>0$; (v) $\hat{W}_{\mathrm{A}}>0$ if $S^2_{LK} \geq S^3_{LK}$; and, (vi) $\hat{P}_2>0$ (as $\theta_{L2}\theta_{K3}>\theta_{L3}\theta_{K2}$, i.e. sector 3 is more capital-intensive vis-à-vis sector 2 with respect to unskilled labour).

Appendix II

Total differentials of (17)–(20) yield the following expressions, respectively.

$$\theta_{L1}\hat{W} + \theta_{N1}\hat{R} = 0 \quad (A.10)$$

$$\theta_{L2}\hat{W} + \theta_{N2}\hat{R} - \hat{P}_2 = 0 \quad (A.11)$$

$$\theta_{L3}\hat{W} + \theta_{K3}\hat{r} = 0 \quad (A.12)$$

$$\theta_{S4}\hat{W}_{\mathrm{S}} + \theta_{K4}\hat{r} = 0 \quad (A.13)$$

Using Equation (27), (26) may be rewritten as follows.

$$a_{K3}X_3 + (a_{K4}S/a_{S4}) = K \quad (A.14)$$

Differentiating totally Equations (24), (25) and (26) one gets, respectively.

$$B_1\hat{W} - B_2\hat{R} + \lambda_{N1}\hat{X}_1 + \lambda_{N2}\hat{X}_2 = 0 \quad (A.15)$$

$$-B_3\hat{W} + B_4\hat{R} + B_5\hat{r} + \lambda_{L1}\hat{X}_1 + \lambda_{L2}\hat{X}_2 + \lambda_{L3}\hat{X}_3 = 0 \quad (A.16)$$

$$B_6\hat{W} - B_7\hat{r} + B_8\hat{W}_{\mathrm{S}} + \lambda_{K3}\hat{X}_3 = \hat{K} \quad (A.17)$$

Also differentiating (22) and (23) one gets:

$$B_9\hat{W} + B_{10}\hat{R} + B_{11}\hat{r} + B_{12}\hat{r} + B_{13}\hat{X}_3 + E_P\hat{P}_2 - \hat{X}_2 + B_{13}\hat{X}_3 = 0 \quad (A.18)$$

where,

$$\left.\begin{aligned}
&B_1 = B_2 = (\lambda_{N1}S^1_{NL} + \lambda_{N2}S^2_{NL}) > 0;\\
&B_3 = (\lambda_{L1}S^1_{LN} + \lambda_{L2}S^2_{LN} + \lambda_{L3}S^3_{LK}) > 0;\\
&B_4 = (\lambda_{L1}S^1_{LN} + \lambda_{L2}S^2_{LN}) > 0;\ B_5 = (\lambda_{L3}S^3_{LK}) > 0;\ B_6 = (\lambda_{K3}S^3_{KL}) > 0;\\
&B_7 = (\lambda_{K3}S^3_{KL} + \lambda_{K4}(S^4_{KS} + S^4_{SK})) > 0;\ B_8 = \lambda_{K4}(S^4_{KS} + S^4_{SK})) > 0;\\
&B_9 = (E_Y W/Y)[L + (\alpha - 1)a_{L3}X_3(1 - S^3_{LK})];\ B_{10} = (E_Y RN/Y) > 0;\\
&B_{11} = (E_Y/Y)[rK_D + (\alpha - 1)Wa_{L3}X_3S^3_{LK}] > 0;\\
&B_{12} = (E_Y W_S S/Y) > 0 \text{ and},\\
&B_{13} = [(E_Y/Y)(\alpha - 1)Wa_{L3}X_3] > 0
\end{aligned}\right\} \tag{A.19}$$

Arranging (A.10)–(A.13), (A.15)–(A.17) and (A.18) in a matrix notation one gets the following.

$$\begin{pmatrix}
\theta_{L1} & \theta_{N1} & 0 & 0 & 0 & 0 & 0 & 0\\
\theta_{L2} & \theta_{N2} & 0 & 0 & -1 & 0 & 0 & 0\\
\theta_{L3} & 0 & \theta_{K3} & 0 & 0 & 0 & 0 & 0\\
0 & 0 & \theta_{K4} & \theta_{S4} & 0 & 0 & 0 & 0\\
B_1 & -B_2 & 0 & 0 & 0 & \lambda_{N1} & \lambda_{N2} & 0\\
-B_3 & B_4 & B_5 & 0 & 0 & \lambda_{L1} & \lambda_{L2} & \lambda_{L3}\\
B_6 & 0 & -B_7 & B_8 & 0 & 0 & 0 & \lambda_{K3}\\
B_9 & B_{10} & B_{11} & B_{12} & E_P & 0 & -1 & B_{13}
\end{pmatrix}
\begin{pmatrix}\hat{W}\\ \hat{R}\\ \hat{r}\\ \hat{W}_S\\ \hat{P}_2\\ \hat{X}_1\\ \hat{X}_2\\ \hat{X}_3\end{pmatrix}
=
\begin{pmatrix}0\\0\\0\\0\\0\\0\\ \hat{K}\\0\end{pmatrix} \tag{A.20}$$

where:

$$\begin{aligned}
\Omega = &- [(|\theta||\lambda|E_P) - \{(B_9\theta_{N1}\theta_{K3}\theta_{S4}|\lambda|)\\
&- (B_{10}\theta_{L1}\theta_{K3}\theta_{S4}|\lambda|) - (B_{11}\theta_{N1}\theta_{L3}\theta_{S4}|\lambda|)\\
&+ (B_{12}\theta_{N1}\theta_{L3}\theta_{K4}|\lambda|)\\
&- B_{13}(\lambda_{L2}\lambda_{N1} - \lambda_{N2}\lambda_{L1})\theta_{N1}(\theta_{K3}\theta_{S4}B_6 + \theta_{L3}\theta_{K4}B_8 + \theta_{L3}\theta_{S4}B_7)\\
&- (\theta_{N1}\theta_{K3}\theta_{S4})(\lambda_{N1}\lambda_{K3}B_3 + \lambda_{N1}\lambda_{L3}B_6 + \lambda_{L1}\lambda_{K3}B_1)\\
&- (\lambda_{K3}\theta_{K3}\theta_{S4}\theta_{L1})(B_2\lambda_{L1} + B_4\lambda_{N1})\\
&- (\lambda_{N1}\theta_{N1}\theta_{L3}\theta_{S4})(B_5\lambda_{K3} + B_7\lambda_{L3})\\
&- (\lambda_{N1}\lambda_{L3}\theta_{N1}\theta_{L3}\theta_{K4}B_8)\}]
\end{aligned} \tag{A.21}$$

$$|\theta| = \theta_{K3}\theta_{S4}(\theta_{L1}\theta_{N2} - \theta_{N1}\theta_{L2});\ \text{and}, \tag{A.22}$$

$$|\lambda| = \lambda_{K3}(\lambda_{N1}\lambda_{L2} - \lambda_{N2}\lambda_{L1}) \tag{A.23}$$

So, we always have:

$$|\theta||\lambda| < 0 \tag{A.24}$$

Using the stability condition in the market for commodity 2 (see Appendix V) it can be shown that: $\Omega < 0$.

Appendix III

Solving (A.20) by Cramer's rule the following expressions are obtained.

$$\hat{W} = -(\theta_{N1}\theta_{K3}\theta_{S4}|\lambda^*|\hat{K}/\Omega) \tag{A.25}$$

$$\hat{W}_S = -(\theta_{N1}\theta_{L3}\theta_{K4}|\lambda^*|\hat{K}/\Omega) \tag{A.26}$$

$$\hat{r} = (\theta_{N1}\theta_{L3}\theta_{S4}|\lambda^*|\hat{K}/\Omega) \tag{A.27}$$

$$\hat{P}_2 = (\theta_{K3}\theta_{S4}|\lambda^*|\hat{K}/\Omega)(\theta_{L1}\theta_{N2} - \theta_{N1}\theta_{L2}) \tag{A.28}$$

where,

$$|\lambda^*| = [(\lambda_{L2}\lambda_{N1} - \lambda_{N2}\lambda_{L1})B_{13} + \lambda_{N1}\lambda_{L3}] \tag{A.29}$$

$\hat{X}_3$ also can be solved in the same manner. The final expression for $\hat{X}_3$ has been derived in Appendix VI. Using the stability condition in the market for commodity 2 it can be shown that: $\hat{X}_3 > 0$ when $\hat{K} > 0$.

From Equations (A.25)–(A.28) the following results can be obtained.

1. If sector 1 is more land-capital-intensive vis-à-vis sector 2 with respect to unskilled labour (i.e. $|\lambda|, |\lambda^*| > 0$; $|\theta| < 0$) when $\hat{K} > 0$ (i) $\hat{W} > 0$; (ii) $\hat{W}_S > 0$; (iii) $\hat{r} < 0$; (iv) $\hat{P}_2 > 0$.
2. If sector 1 is more labour-intensive (but not sufficiently labour-intensive) than sector 2 (i.e. $|\lambda| < 0$; $|\lambda^*|$, $|\theta| > 0$) when $\hat{K} > 0$ (i) $\hat{W} > 0$; (ii) $\hat{W}_S > 0$; (iii) $\hat{r} < 0$; (iv) $\hat{P}_2 < 0$.
3. If sector 1 is sufficiently labour-intensive (i.e. $|\lambda|$, $|\lambda^*| < 0$; $|\theta| > 0$) when $\hat{K} > 0$ (i) $\hat{W} < 0$; (ii) $\hat{W}_S < 0$; (iii) $\hat{r} > 0$; (iv) $\hat{P}_2 > 0$.

Appendix IV

Differentiating (28) one gets:

$$\hat{W}_A = \left(\frac{W\hat{W}}{W_A}\right)[1 + (\alpha - 1)\lambda_{L3}(1 - S^3_{LK})] + W(\alpha - 1)\left(\frac{\lambda_{L3}S^3_{LK}}{W_A}\right)\hat{r} + W(\alpha - 1)\left(\frac{\lambda_{L3}}{W_A}\right)\hat{X}_3$$

Using (A.25) and (A.27) the above expression may be simplified to

$$\hat{W}_{\mathrm{A}} = \left(\frac{W\hat{K}}{\Omega W_{\mathrm{A}}}\right)[(\theta_{N1}\theta_{S4}|\lambda^*|)\{(\alpha-1)\lambda_{L3}(S^3_{LK}-\theta_{K3})-\theta_{K3}\} + \left(\frac{W}{W_{\mathrm{A}}}(\alpha-1)\lambda_{L3}\right)\hat{X}_3 \quad \text{(A.30)}$$

From (A.30) it is evident that

1. When $\hat{K}>0$, $\hat{W}_{\mathrm{A}}>0$ if (i) ($|\lambda|>0$ and $\lambda_{L3}>0 \Rightarrow |\lambda^*|>0$)/($|\lambda|<0$ (and $\lambda_{L3}>0$ such that $|\lambda^*|>0$); and, (ii) $\theta_{K3} \geq S^3_{LK}$.
2. When $\hat{K}>0$, $\hat{W}_{\mathrm{A}}<0$ if (i) $|\lambda|<0$ and $\lambda_{L3} \cong 0$ so that $|\lambda^*|<0$.

Subtracting (A.30) from (A.26), using (A.25) and (A.27) and simplifying we get:

$$(\hat{W}_{\mathrm{S}}-\hat{W}_{\mathrm{A}}) = -\left(\frac{\theta_{N1}\hat{K}}{\Omega}\right)[(\lambda_{L2}\lambda_{N1}-\lambda_{N2}\lambda_{L1})B_{13}+\lambda_{N1}\lambda_{L3}][(\theta_{K4}-\theta_{K3}) -(\alpha-1)\lambda_{L3}(\theta_{S4}\theta_{K3}-S^3_{LK})] - \frac{W(\alpha-1)\lambda_{L3}\hat{X}_3}{W_{\mathrm{A}}} \quad \text{(A.31)}$$

For the sake of analytical convenience we rewrite (A.31) to obtain Equation (29) as follows

$$(\hat{W}_{\mathrm{S}}-\hat{W}_{\mathrm{A}}) = -\left(\frac{\theta_{N1}\hat{K}}{\Omega}\right)|\lambda^*|[(\theta_{K4}-\theta_{K3}) -(\alpha-1)\lambda_{L3}(\theta_{S4}\theta_{K3}-S^3_{LK})] - \frac{W(\alpha-1)\lambda_{L3}\hat{X}_3}{W_{\mathrm{A}}}$$

The notation, $|\lambda^*|$, has already been defined in (A.29).

Appendix V: Stability condition of the market for commodity 2

As commodity 2 is internationally non-traded its market must clear domestically through adjustments in its price, P_2. The stability condition of the market for commodity 2 requires that $(d(D_2-X_2)/dP_2)<0$. This implies around equilibrium, initially, $D_2 = X_2$. Thus,

$$\left((\hat{D}_2/\hat{P}_2)-(\hat{X}_2/\hat{P}_2)\right)<0. \quad \text{(A.32)}$$

Totally differentiating Equations (17)–(20) and solving one can find out the following expressions.

$$(\hat{W}/\hat{P}_2) = -(\theta_{N1}\theta_{K3}\theta_{S4}/|\theta|); \quad \text{(A.33)}$$

$$(\hat{R}/\hat{P}_2) = (\theta_{L1}\theta_{K3}\theta_{S4}/|\theta|); \tag{A.34}$$

$$(\hat{r}/\hat{P}_2) = (\theta_{N1}\theta_{L3}\theta_{S4}/|\theta|) \text{ and,} \tag{A.35}$$

$$(\hat{W}_S/\hat{P}_2) = -(\theta_{N1}\theta_{L3}\theta_{K4}/|\theta|) \tag{A.36}$$

Then differentiating Equations (24)–(27), using (A.33)–(A.36), putting $\hat{K} = 0$ and solving by Cramer's rule the following expressions may be obtained.

$$\begin{aligned}\hat{X}_2 = \left(\frac{-\hat{P}_2}{|\theta||\lambda|}\right)&[(\lambda_{N1}\lambda_{K3}B_3 + \lambda_{N1}\lambda_{L3}B_6 \\ &+ \lambda_{L1}\lambda_{K3}B_1)(\theta_{N1}\theta_{K3}\theta_{S4}) + (\lambda_{N1}B_4 + \lambda_{L1}B_2)\lambda_{K3}(\theta_{K3}\theta_{S4}\theta_{L1}) \\ &+\lambda_{N1}(\lambda_{K3}B_5 + \lambda_{L3}B_7)(\theta_{N1}\theta_{L3}\theta_{S4}) + \lambda_{N1}\lambda_{L3}B_8\theta_{N1}\theta_{L3}\theta_{K4}]\end{aligned} \tag{A.37}$$

$$\hat{X}_3 = -\left(\frac{\hat{P}_2}{|\lambda||\theta|}\right)[(\lambda_{N2}\lambda_{L1} - \lambda_{N1}\lambda_{L2})(\theta_{K3}B_6 + \theta_{L3}B_7 + \theta_{L3}B_8)\theta_{N1}\theta_{S4}] \tag{A.38}$$

Differentiating Equations (21) and (22) and considering $\hat{K} = 0$ one can derive

$$\hat{D}_2 = E_P\hat{P}_2 + B_9\hat{W} + B_{10}\hat{R} + B_{11}\hat{r} + B_{12}\hat{W}_S + B_{13}\hat{X}_3 \tag{A.39}$$

Using Equations (A.33)–(A.36) and (A.38), (A.39) may be rewritten as follows

$$\begin{aligned}\hat{D}_2 = (\hat{P}_2)\Bigg[E_P - \left(\frac{1}{|\theta|}\right)&\{B_9\theta_{N1}\theta_{K3}\theta_{S4} \\ &- B_{10}\theta_{K3}\theta_{S4}\theta_{L1} - B_{11}\theta_{N1}\theta_{L3}\theta_{S4} + B_{12}\theta_{N1}\theta_{L3}\theta_{K4} \\ &-(B_{13}/|\lambda|)(\lambda_{N1}\lambda_{L2} - \lambda_{N2}\lambda_{L1})\theta_{N1}(\theta_{K3}\theta_{S4}B_6 + \theta_{L3}\theta_{S4}B_7 \\ &+\theta_{L3}\theta_{S4}B_8)\}\Bigg]\end{aligned} \tag{A.40}$$

Substituting the expressions for $(\hat{D}_2/\hat{P}_2)$ and $(\hat{X}_2/\hat{P}_2)$ from (A.40) and (A.37) into (A.32) and simplifying one obtains

$$\begin{aligned}\Bigg[E_P - \left(\frac{1}{|\lambda||\theta|}\right)&\{|\lambda|(B_9\theta_{N1}\theta_{K3}\theta_{S4} \\ &- B_{10}\theta_{K3}\theta_{S4}\theta_{L1} - B_{11}\theta_{N1}\theta_{L3}\theta_{S4} + B_{12}\theta_{N1}\theta_{L3}\theta_{K4}) \\ &- (B_{13}\theta_{N1})(\lambda_{N1}\lambda_{L2} - \lambda_{N2}\lambda_{L1})(\theta_{K3}\theta_{S4}B_6 + \theta_{L3}\theta_{S4}B_7 + \theta_{L3}\theta_{S4}B_8) \\ &- (\theta_{N1}\theta_{K3}\theta_{S4})(\lambda_{N1}\lambda_{K3}B_3 + \lambda_{N1}\lambda_{L3}B_6 + \lambda_{L1}\lambda_{K3}B_1) \\ &- (\lambda_{K3}\theta_{K3}\theta_{S4}\theta_{L1})(\lambda_{N1}B_4 + \lambda_{L1}B_2) \\ &-(\lambda_{N1}\theta_{N1}\theta_{L3}\theta_{S4})(\lambda_{K3}B_5 + \lambda_{L3}B_7) - (\lambda_{N1}\lambda_{L3}B_8\theta_{N1}\theta_{L3}\theta_{K4})\}\Bigg] < 0\end{aligned} \tag{A.41}$$

Thus, the stability condition in the market for commodity 2 is given by (A.41).

Using (A.24) and (A.41) from (A.21) it now trivially follows that

$$\Omega < 0 \tag{A.42}$$

Appendix VI: Derivation of expression for $\hat{X}_3$

Solving (A.20) we can find the following expression.

$$\begin{aligned}\hat{X}_3 = & -\left(\frac{\hat{K}}{\Omega\lambda_{K3}}\right)[|\theta||\lambda|E_P - \{\theta_{K3}\theta_{S4}(\theta_{N1}B_9 - \theta_{L1}B_{10}) \\ & + \theta_{N1}\theta_{L3}(\theta_{K4}B_{12} - \theta_{S4}B_{11})\}|\lambda| \\ & + \theta_{S4}\lambda_{K3}\{\theta_{N1}\theta_{K3}(\lambda_{N1}B_3 + \lambda_{L1}B_1) \\ & + \theta_{K3}\theta_{L1}(B_2\lambda_{L1} + B_4\lambda_{N1}) + \lambda_{N1}\theta_{N1}\theta_{L3}B_5\}]\end{aligned} \tag{A.43}$$

It may be noted that:

$$\left.\begin{aligned} W_S S &= \theta_{P4}X_4;\ Wa_{L3} = (P_3\theta_{L3}/\alpha); \\ rK_D &= (\theta_{K3}P_3X_3 + \theta_{K4}P_4X_4 - rK_F); \\ (\theta_{N1}WL - \theta_{L1}RN) &= [P_2X_2(\theta_{N1}\theta_{L2} - \theta_{L1}\theta_{N2}) + \theta_{N1}\theta_{L3}P_3X_3]; \\ (\theta_{K4}W_S S - \theta_{S4}rK_D) &= \theta_{S4}(rK_F - \theta_{K3}P_3X_3) \end{aligned}\right\} \tag{A.44}$$

Inserting the values of B_is from (A.19), using (A.44) and simplifying it is easily seen that

$$\begin{aligned}&\{\theta_{K3}\theta_{S4}(\theta_{N1}B_9 - \theta_{L1}B_{10}) + \theta_{N1}\theta_{L3}(\theta_{K4}B_{12} - \theta_{S4}B_{11})\} \\ &\quad = \left(\frac{E_Y}{Y}\right)\{\theta_{N1}\theta_{S4}W(\alpha - 1)a_{L3}X_3(\theta_{K3} - S_{LK}^3) \\ &\qquad + \theta_{N1}\theta_{S4}\theta_{L3}rK_F - |\theta|P_2X_2\}\end{aligned} \tag{A.45}$$

Using (A.45) and simplifying, from (A.43) the following expression can be easily obtained.

$$\begin{aligned}\hat{X}_3 = & -\left(\frac{\hat{K}}{\lambda_{K3}\Omega}\right)\left[|\theta||\lambda|\left(E_P + \frac{E_Y P_2 X_2}{Y}\right)\right. \\ & - |\lambda|\left(\frac{E_Y\theta_{N1}\theta_{S4}\theta_{L3}}{Y}\right)\left\{\left(\frac{\alpha - 1}{\alpha}\right)P_3X_3(\theta_{K3} - S_{LK}^3) + rK_F\right\} \\ & + \theta_{S4}\lambda_{K3}\{\theta_{N1}\theta_{K3}(\lambda_{N1}B_3 + \lambda_{L1}B_1) \\ & + \theta_{L1}\theta_{K3}(\lambda_{L1}B_2 + \lambda_{N1}B_4) + \lambda_{N1}\theta_{N1}\theta_{L3}B_5\}]\end{aligned} \tag{A.46}$$

Using (A.19) and (A.41) and comparing terms we can check that the sign of the square-bracketed term in (A.46) is positive. As $\Omega < 0$, from (A.46) it now follows that: $\hat{X}_3 > 0$ when $\hat{K} > 0$.

Appendix VII: Derivation of expression for $\hat{X}_4$

Differentiating Equation (27) one gets:

$$\hat{X}_4 = -\hat{a}_{S4} = S^4_{SK}(\hat{W}_S - \hat{r}) \quad \text{(A.47)}$$

Inserting the values of $\hat{W}_S$ and $\hat{r}$ from (A.26) and (A.27) into (A.47) and simplifying the following expression is finally obtained.

$$\hat{X}_4 = -\left(\frac{S^4_{SK}\theta_{N1}\theta_{L3}|\lambda^*|\hat{K}}{\Omega}\right) \quad \text{(A.48)}$$

From (A.48) the following results can be stated.

1. If sector 1 is land-capital-intensive/unskilled labour-intensive (but not sufficiently enough) (i.e. $|\lambda^*| > 0$), $\hat{X}_4 > 0$ when $\hat{K} > 0$.
2. If sector 1 is sufficiently unskilled labour-intensive (i.e. $|\lambda^*| < 0$), $\hat{X}_4 < 0$ when $\hat{K} > 0$.

References

Bardhan, P.K. (1973), A model of growth of capitalism in a dual agrarian economy. In: Bhagwati, J.M., Eckaus, R.S. (Eds.), *Development and Planning: Essays in Honour of Paul Rosenstein-Rodan*. MIT Press, USA.

Beyer, H., Rojas, P., Vergara, R. (1999), Trade liberalization and wage inequality. *Journal of Development Economics* 59, 103–123.

Bhalotra, S. (2002), *The Impact of Economic Liberalization on Employment and Wages in India*. ILO, Geneva.

Brecher, R.A., Diaz Alejandro, C.F. (1977), Tariffs, foreign capital and immiserizing growth. *Journal of International Economics* 7, 317–322.

Chandra, V., Khan, M.A. (1993), Foreign investment in the presence of an informal sector. *Economica* 60, 79–103.

Chao, C.C., Yu, E.S.H. (1994), Foreign capital inflow and welfare in an economy with imperfect competition. *Journal of Development Economics* 45, 141–154.

Chaudhuri, S. (2003), How and how far to liberalize a developing economy with informal sector and factor market distortions. *Journal of International Trade and Economic Development* 12, 403–428.

Chaudhuri, S. (2007), Foreign capital, welfare and unemployment in the presence of agricultural dualism. *Japan and the World Economy* 19, 149–165.

Chaudhuri, S., Yabuuchi, S. (2007), Economic liberalization and wage inequality in the presence of labour market imperfection. *International Review of Economics and Finance* 16, 592–603.

Chaudhuri, S., Yabuuchi, S., Mukhopadhyay, U. (2006), Inflow of foreign capital and trade liberalization in a model with an informal sector and urban unemployment. *Pacific Economic Review* 11, 87–103.

Currie, J., Harrison, A. (1997), Sharing the costs: the impact of trade reform on capital and labor in Morocco. *Journal of Labour Economics* 15, S44–S71.

Feenstra, R.C., Hanson, G.H. (1996), Foreign investment, outsourcing and relative wages. In: Feenstra, R., Grossman, G., Irwin, D. (Eds.), *Political Economy of Trade Policies: Essays in Honor of J. N. Bhagwati*. MIT Press, Cambridge, MA.

Hanson, G.H., Harrison, A. (1999), Trade liberalization and wage inequality in Mexico. *Industrial and Labour Relations Review* 52, 271–288.

Harrison, A., Hanson, G. (1999), Who gains from trade reform? Some remaining puzzles. *Journal of Development Economics* 59, 125–154.

Jones, R.W., Neary, P. (1984), Positive theory of international trade. In: Jones, R.W., Kenen, P.B. (Eds.), *Handbook of Development Economics*, vol. 1, Elsevier, North-Holland, pp. 1–62.

Khan, A.R. (1982), Tariffs, foreign capital and immiserizing growth with urban unemployment and specific factors of production. *Journal of Development Economics* 10, 245–256.

Khan, A.R. (1998), The impact of globalization in South Asia. In: Bhalla, A.S. (Ed.), *Globalization, Growth and Marginalization*. Macmillan, New Delhi.

Layard, R., Nickell, S., Jackman, R. (2005), *Unemployment: Macroeconomic Performance and the Labour Market*. Oxford University Press, New York.

Marjit, S. (2003), Economic reform and informal wage – a general equilibrium analysis. *Journal of Development Economics* 72, 371–378.

Marjit, S., Acharyya, R. (2003), *International Trade, Wage Inequality and the Developing Countries: A General Equilibrium Approach*. Physica/Springer Verlag, Heidelberg.

Marjit, S., Acharyya, R. (2006), Trade liberalization, skill-linked intermediate production and the two-sided wage gap. *Journal of Economic Policy Reform* 9, 203–217.

Marjit, S., Broll, U., Sengupta, S. (2000), Trade and wage-gap in poor countries: the role of the informal sector. In: Bose, A., et al. (Eds), *Macroeconomics, Trade and Institutions: Essays in Honour of M.K. Rakshit*. Oxford University Press, Kolkata.

Marjit, S., Beladi, H., Chakrabarti, A. (2004), Trade and wage inequality in developing countries. *Economic Inquiry* 42, 295–303.

Robbins, D. (1994), *Malaysian Wage Structure and its Causes*. Harvard Institute for International Development (HIID), Harvard University, Cambridge.

Robbins, D. (1995), *Trade, Trade Liberalization and Inequality in Latin America and East Asia: Synthesis of Seven Country Studies*. HIID, Harvard University, Cambridge.

Robbins, D. (1996), *HOS Hits Facts: Facts Win: Evidence on Trade and Wages in Developing World*. HIID, Harvard University, Cambridge.

Tendulkar, S., Sundaram, D.K., Jain, L.R. (1996), *Macroeconomic Policies and Poverty in India 1966–67 to 1993–94, manuscript*. ILO, New Delhi.

UNCTAD Report. (2005), http://stats.unctad.org/fdi/ReportFolders/ReportFolders.aspx

Wood, A. (1997), Openness and wage inequality in developing countries: the Latin American challenge to East Asian conventional wisdom. *World Bank Research Observer* 11, 33–57.

Xiang, C. (2007), New goods and the skill premium. *Journal of International Economics* 71, 133–147.

Yabuuchi, S. (1982), A note on tariff-induced capital inflow and immiserization in the presence of taxation of foreign profits. *Journal of International Economics* 12, 183–189.

Yabuuchi, S., Chaudhuri, S. (2007), International migration of labour and skilled–unskilled wage inequality in a developing economy. *Economic Modelling* 24, 128–137.

Zhu, S.C., Trefler, D. (2005), Trade and inequality in developing countries: a general equilibrium analysis. *Journal of International Economics* 65, 21–48.

CHAPTER 13

Trade, Wage Inequality and the Vent for Surplus

Brati Sankar Chakraborty and Abhirup Sarkar

Economics Research Unit, Indian Statistical Institute, 203, B. T. Road, Kolkata-700108, India
E-mail addresses: brati@isical.ac.in; abhirup@isical.ac.in

Abstract

Most models attempting to give an account of trade-induced symmetric increase in wage inequality have abandoned the factor price equalization (FPE) framework. The present chapter retains the FPE framework and identifies a plausible route through which trade might increase wage inequality in all trading countries. A two-sector model with one constant returns sector producing basic goods and another increasing returns to scale sector producing fancy goods is developed. A quasi-linear utility function is used to capture the divide between basic and fancy goods. There are two types of productive factors, skilled and unskilled labour, and they differ with respect to their occupational options. Skilled labour can work both in the skill using fancy goods sector and in the unskilled labour using basic good producing sector, whereas unskilled labour is tied down to unskilled job. The model holds possibilities of multiple equilibria and under reasonable parameterization skill premium increases in all countries following trade.

Keywords: Factor price equalization, increasing returns to scale, wage inequality

JEL classifications: F12, F15, F16

1. Introduction

This chapter is yet another attempt at theoretically reconciling the empirical observation that wage premium has increased across board: both in skill-scarce and skill-abundant countries. We propose a very simple model of trade with a constant and an increasing returns to scale (IRS)

DOI: 10.1016/S1574-8715(08)04013-X

sector and with goods differing in their income elasticities. We depart from the usual trade theoretic mode of treating skilled and unskilled labour as substitutible factors. In a very stylized way we introduce the notion that skilled labour has a larger spectrum of occupational options than unskilled labour in the sense that skilled labour can work both in skilled and unskilled jobs, deciding what they do by the rewards that are held by the two options, whereas unskilled labour is necessarily tied down to an unskilled job, a presumption that we do not think needs any intellectual labour to defend. As we show, this feature interacting with IRS gives rise to myriad possibilities of multiple equilibria, and very naturally renders an avenue through which skill premium can rise in *all* countries following trade. Notably, we show this in a factor price equalization (FPE) framework.

Symmetric movements in wage gap is not consistent with 2×2 Heckscher–Ohlin–Samuelson (HOS) model, which would predict relative skill wages to go up in the skill-abundant country and come down in the skill-scarce one following trade.

Jones (1999) in a reconciliatory move proposes an interesting variant of the HOS model with 3 goods and 2 factors (skilled and unskilled labour) with the goods uniquely ranked in terms of intensities. The good with middle ranked intensity is produced in both the countries and one with the highest and lowest skill intensity are produced in the developed North and the less developed South respectively. The South exports the good with middle intensity. Trade liberalization by North leads to an improvement in terms of trade for the South leading to a rise in demand for skilled labour in the South and in the North, lower import tariff reduces the domestic price of the middle good and which in turn is the unskilled labour-intensive good for the North. Consequently unskilled wage rate in the North goes down, leading to a rise in the wage gap. This model, thus can account for the symmetric movement in the wage gap. But also note that if the North were to export the middle-intensive good and the South reduced tariff on the middle-intensive good, wage inequality would fall in both the countries. Though once again relative wage movements are symmetric, whether inequality rises or falls crucially depends on the trade pattern. Interesting variants on similar theme have been worked out in several other papers. Feenstra and Hanson (1996) in an oft cited paper redesigns the Dornbusch *et al.* (1980) model by adding a third factor, capital. In their model a single manufacturing output is assembled from a continuum of intermediate inputs. Such inputs are produced by skilled labour, unskilled labour and capital. In equilibrium the South produces and exports a range of inputs and the North does the rest. A rise in the stock of capital in the South shifts the intermediate intensity goods from the developed North to the underdeveloped South raising relative demand for skilled labour in both countries, thus symmetrically increasing the wage gap. What is also crucial to note is that most of these models abandon the

FPE framework. Trefler and Zhu (2001) closely builds up on the Feenstra, Hanson insight. In their model, similar product shifting from North to South is initiated by technological catch up in the South. Marjit and Acharyya (2003) in an interesting contribution suggests yet another route, namely intermediate goods trade, through which trade might symmetrically increase the skill premium. They consider a world where North exports a skill-intensive intermediate good to the South on which South imposes a tariff. This intermediate good in turn along with skilled labour is used to produce a final good. A cut in tariff by the South increases the international price of the intermediate good raising skill rewards in the North. Assuming there is no Metzler Paradox, domestic price of intermediates fall in the South and thus it is cheaper to produce the final good. Since this sector uses skilled labour, competition tends to push up the demand for them and skill wage goes up in South as well.

These models, are essentially stepped in the tradition of standard competitive markets and constant returns to scale (CRS) technology. Returns to scale, it seems, is a natural point to depart from these models. Krugman (1981) has shown that trade under IRS might lead to co-movements in absolute factor prices, antithetically to the Stolper–Samuelson theorem. But even then in Krugman (1981), the relative factor prices follow the same pattern as HOS model would predict. Similarly in Ethier (1982), for a small open economy Stolper–Samuelson theorem remains valid, even with IRS in production, to the extent the equilibrium is Marshall stable. These models thus cannot account for symmetric movements in the wage gap across countries.

We explore the potential of IRS in giving a very plausible explanation of rising wage inequality. The basic insight is very simple and as follows. If demand conditions are such that skilled labour cannot be fully employed in the skill-using IRS sector then part of the skilled labour force goes to join the unskilled job and hence skilled labour in general can merely earn the unskilled wage. Trade via intermediate goods can generate sufficient external economies such that supply prices in the IRS sector falls significantly and is then accommodated by the demand to operate at a level that fully utilizes skill labour in the skill-using sector. Thus skill and unskilled wage rates diverge. Trade thus allows to fully utilize hitherto *underutilized* skilled labour. This we identify to be closely in the spirit of the thesis proposed by Hla Myint (1958) several decades back. Myint in a somewhat different context identified trade as *vent for surplus*, the idea being that trade opened a vent or an outlet for a resource that had been previously underutilized. This was an apt description of the trajectory of development driven by agricultural exports in the second half of the 19th century that transformed the economies of Canada and the United States. Our context is surely different. We show that when the size of the market limits the scale of operation of a skill intensive sector, trade, through external economies, can sufficiently reduce average costs so that a scale of production that fully utilizes the available skilled labour, can be accommodated by the demand. Hence trade opens up the opportunity of fully utilizing skilled resources that has till then remained underutilized.

The model uses the Dixit–Stiglitz specification to formalize the IRS sector and is like any other standard two-sector model except for the fact that we explicitly introduce the notion that skilled and unskilled labour faces differential employment options in that skilled labour can work both in skilled and unskilled job whereas unskilled labour is tied down to the unskilled job. This apparently innocent looking assumption, as we will see, gives rise to myriad possibilities of multiple equilibria.

In what follows, Section 2 lays down the model, Section 3 solves for the autarky, Section 4 is a digression on the trade equilibrium and the last section concludes the chapter.

2. *Model*

2.1. The economy: Basic description

The economy is populated with two distinct types of agents. We choose to call them skilled and unskilled labour. Each type of labour is endowed with one unit of labour time, which they supply inelastically. Total amount of skilled and unskilled labour endowment in the economy is given by $\bar{H}$ and $\bar{L}$ respectively. We depart from the usual trade theoretic mode of characterizing skilled and unskilled labour where they enter into the production function as substitutible inputs just as capital and labour enters into an usual production function (see Jones, 1999; Feenstra and Hanson, 1996; Marjit and Acharyya, 2003). In our model we assume that skilled labour can perform both unskilled and skilled job and they choose the one which holds higher reward. Unskilled labour, on the other hand, is tied down to the unskilled job and is not suited for the skilled work. This assumption, we believe, captures in a very stylized manner a real life situation and that this is real life, we believe, does not require much persuasion. This otherwise innocent looking assumption, as we will see, has serious implications for our model. If the skilled wage rate w_s falls below the unskilled wage rate w_u all skilled workers join the unskilled labour force so it must be true that $w_s \geq w_u$.

2.2. Production

The economy produces two goods: 1 and 2, where X_1 and X_2 are the outputs respectively. Good 1 is produced using unskilled labour under CRS technology. We choose units such that one unit of unskilled labour is required to produce one unit of good 1. Thus the price of good 1 equals the unskilled wage rate w_u. We also choose good 1 to be the numeraire.

This implies that w_u is equal to unity. Good 2 on the other hand is produced using differentiated intermediate inputs. The production technology for X_2 follows Dixit and Stiglitz (1977) specification and is given by

$$X_2 = \left[\sum_{i=1}^{n} y_i^{\rho}\right]^{1/\rho} \quad \text{where } 0<\rho<1 \tag{1}$$

where y_i is the input of intermediate good i. Intermediate goods are imperfect substitutes. ρ measures the degree of differentiation of intermediate inputs. Given the number of intermediate inputs the production function (1) exhibits CRS but there is increasing returns to higher degree of specialization as measured by the number of intermediate varieties n. These economies are external to the firm but internal to the industry i.e. X_2 producers take n as given. As in Ethier (1982), we assume that all intermediate goods have identical cost functions. The cost of producing the quantity x of a given variety of intermediate input is $C_x = (a + bx)w_s$, where a and b are the fixed and marginal requirements of skilled labour respectively. The presence of fixed cost gives rise to internal economies of scale at the firm level. An individual producer of X_2 maximizes profits subject to the production function considering n to be parametrically given. This gives rise to the inverse input demand function for each intermediate input (see Helpman and Krugman, 1985)

$$y_i = \frac{(q_i)^{-\sigma} \sum_{i=1}^{n} q_i y_i}{\sum_{i=1}^{n} q_i^{1-\sigma}} \tag{2}$$

where q_i is the price of the ith intermediate input and $\sigma = 1/(1-\rho)$ is the elasticity of substitution between any pair of intermediate inputs. Assuming large number of intermediate good producers, such that strategic behaviour is ruled out on their part, it can be easily shown that σ is the elasticity of demand faced by the intermediate producers.

Thus each producer of intermediate inputs equate marginal revenue to marginal cost

$$q_i\left(1 - \frac{1}{\sigma}\right) = bw_s$$

Taking note of the fact that $\sigma = 1/(1-\rho)$ we may write

$$q_i = \frac{bw_s}{\rho} \tag{3}$$

Thus prices of intermediate goods are a constant mark up over the marginal cost. With identical technology all firms charge the same price for intermediate goods i.e. $q_i = q \ \forall i$. Free entry in the production of intermediate inputs drives down profits to zero (the Chamberlinian large group case). Thus the operating surplus must be just enough to cover the fixed cost

$$\frac{q}{\sigma}x_i = aw_s \tag{4}$$

This also implies that output x_i is the same for all producers, i.e. $x_i = x \ \forall i$. Dividing Equation (4) by (3) we get,

$$x = \frac{a\rho}{b(1-\rho)} \tag{5}$$

The symmetry in output choice across firms, i.e. $x_i = x$ and demand supply equilibrium in intermediate goods market implying $y_i = x \ \forall i$, taken together, would allow us to express Equation (1) as

$$X_2 = n^{\alpha}x \tag{6}$$

where $\alpha \equiv (1/\rho) > 1$. Further, note that Equation (5) implies output per firm (x) is a constant. Thus Equation (6) implies that any expansion of X_2 would be in terms of increased n, and this, as has already been noted, implies IRS at the industry level in X_2 production.

If in equilibrium n is the effective number of produced varieties, then the total amount of skilled labour used in the production of intermediate goods is given by

$$H = n(a + bx) \tag{7}$$

Note that x is a constant which in turn implies that all changes in n and thereby in the output of X_2 are brought about singularly by changes in H.

2.3. Preferences

All agents share the same quasi-linear utility function given by

$$U = C_1^{\beta} + C_2 \quad \text{where } 0<\beta<1 \tag{8}$$

The quasi-linear form notionally captures the idea that agents might even go without good 2. And in this sense this good is not a basic one. As we will see we might have an equilibrium where sector 2 production does not come into being.

First order conditions for utility maximization imply

$$\beta C_1^{\beta-1} = \lambda \tag{9}$$

$$1 = \lambda p \tag{10}$$

where p is the relative price of good 2 and λ the associated Lagrange multiplier.

Equations (8) and (9) imply

$$p = \frac{1}{\beta} C_1^{1-\beta} \tag{11}$$

3. Autarky

3.1. The general equilibrium supply curve

Noting that zero profit condition prevails in the production of final output X_2 we have

$$pX_2 = nqx \tag{12}$$

where the left hand side is the total revenue and the right hand side is the total cost.

Substituting for X_2 from Equation (6), Equation (12) boils down to

$$p = n^{1-\alpha} q \tag{13}$$

Using Equations (3), (5) and (7), Equation (13) can be rewritten as

$$p = ZH^{1-\alpha} w_s \tag{14}$$

where

$$Z \equiv \left[\frac{1-\rho}{a}\right]^{1-\alpha} \frac{b}{\rho}$$

Equation (14) is nothing but the price and average cost equality. This is our fundamental supply side equation and it essentially follows Ethier (1982). But we intend to tailor this equation bit differently for the purpose of our model.

Let us now focus on the factor market. Note that until the moment the whole of skilled labour has been absorbed in intermediate goods sector, skilled labour can be employed in this sector at the wage rate of unity (i.e. $w_s = 1$, the wage rate prevailing in sector 1). Simply because the residual skilled labour remains employed in sector 1 and earn the unskilled wage rate unity. This therefore implies that in this relevant regime Equation (14) holds with $w_s = 1$ so that

$$p = ZH^{1-\alpha} \tag{15}$$

The moment skilled labour has been completely employed in the intermediate goods sector, Equation (14) reduces to

$$p = Z\bar{H}^{1-\alpha} w_s \tag{16}$$

where $\bar{H}$ is the total amount of skilled labour available in the economy.

In Equation (15) w_s remains frozen at unity and H, thereby the output of good 2, adjusts to bring the price and average cost to equality. Increase in H increases the output of good 2 and there being IRS, depresses the average cost and therefore the price. In Equation (16) H remains frozen at $\bar{H}$ and output of good 2 does not change and any increase in price translates into an increase in skilled wages.

The two regimes corresponding to Equation (14) are depicted as the curve SUM in Figure 1. The downward sloping section SU of this curve depicts Equation (15). Here w_s remain fixed at unity and any increase in H depresses p. It can readily be checked that this section of the curve is asymptotic to the p axis and is also convex. To see this note that in Equation (15) as $H \to 0, p \to \infty$. Furthermore from Equation (15),

$$\frac{\mathrm{d}p}{\mathrm{d}H} = (1 - \alpha)ZH^{-\alpha} < 0 \tag{17}$$

and

$$\frac{\mathrm{d}^2p}{\mathrm{d}H^2} = -\alpha(1 - \alpha)ZH^{-(\alpha+1)} > 0 \tag{18}$$

Note that point U corresponds to a price $p = Z\bar{H}^{(1-\alpha)}$. This is the minimum price at which good 2 can be sold. At U skilled labour is employed at the wage rate unity and total amount of skilled labour $\bar{H}$ has been absorbed in intermediate goods production so the output of good 2 is at its maximum and noting that there being IRS this imply that average cost of production and hence price of good 2 is at its minimum. On the

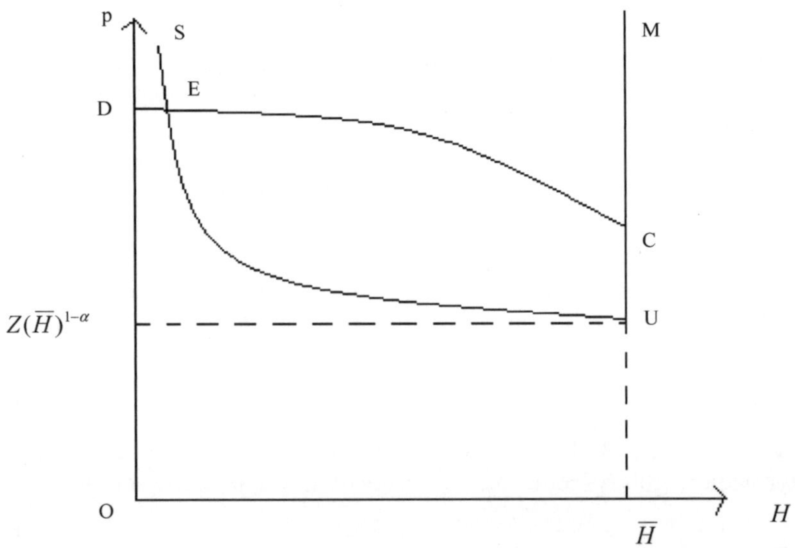

Fig. 1. ***The case where skilled labour can get fully utilized under autarky.***

other hand, to the left of U on the segment SU, though the skilled wage is at unity, skilled labour employed (H) in sector 2 is less than $\bar{H}$ and therefore output of good 2 is less than that at U. Hence average cost and thereby price of good 2 on this segment is higher than that at U. On the segment UM which corresponds to Equation (16) skilled labour has been completely absorbed in intermediate production so output of good 2 is at its maximum and there cannot be any further expansion of the same. Any rise in p is therefore translated into a rise in w_s to bring average cost in line with p, as can be seen from Equation (16). Thus on the segment UM $w_s \geq 1$ with $w_s = 1$ at U and $w_s > 1$ at all other points.

3.2. The general equilibrium demand curve

On the demand side Equation (11) can be integrated with the factor market equilibrium to arrive at an expression for the general equilibrium demand. First note that for all $H < \bar{H}$ skilled wage $w_s = 1$. Thus with both skilled and unskilled wage equal to unity all agents skilled and unskilled should consume the same amount of good 1 at any given p, given the fact that the utility is quasi-linear and good one is the basic good. Thus $C_1 = (\bar{L} + (\bar{H} - H))/(\bar{L} + \bar{H})$ where the numerator is the total production of good 1, and the denominator gives the total number of people consuming good 1. To see that the numerator is the total amount of good 1 produced in the economy, note that with H being the amount of skilled labour employed in the intermediate goods sector, $(\bar{H} - H)$ is left to work in sector 1 over and above $\bar{L}$ unskilled labour who can only work in sector 1. Thus noting that production of one unit of good 1 requires one unit of labour, $(\bar{L} + (\bar{H} - H))$is the total amount of good 1 produced in the economy. Inserting this expression of C_1 in Equation (11) we arrive at

$$p = \frac{1}{\beta}\left(\frac{\bar{L} + \bar{H} - H}{\bar{L} + \bar{H}}\right)^{1-\beta} \tag{19}$$

This demand expression can thus be depicted on the p, H plane as shown by the curve DC in Figure 1. Now note that the argument we rendered to derive this curve was premised on the assumption $H < \bar{H}$, which implied $w_s = w_u = 1$. We now argue that the same demand relation (Equation (19)) remains valid at $H = \bar{H}$ or to put it otherwise the terminal point C on the curve DC which from Equation (19) corresponds to the demand price $p = (1/\beta)/[\bar{L}/(\bar{L} + \bar{H})]^{(1-\beta)}$ is truly the demand price at $H = \bar{H}$. Note that at $H = \bar{H}$ skilled wage w_s can either be equal to or greater than unity. If it is unity then both skilled and unskilled labour consumes same amount of good 1 and the above argument goes through and Equation (19) remains valid at $H = \bar{H}$. We now argue that even if $w_s > 1$ Equation (19) remains valid. To see this first note that at $H = \bar{H}$ all skilled people are working in the intermediate goods sector, but given the quasi-linear utility they must be consuming good 1. This entails that unskilled labour trades some of its good 1. Carrying the argument little further this would imply that unskilled labour consumes some of good 2, or to put it differently is saturated in consumption of good 1. Now, given the quasi-linear structure of the utility, if unskilled labour is saturated in consumption of good 1 then at any common price it must be true that skilled labour with higher wages must also be saturated in consumption of good 1 and their consumption levels of good 1 must be the same. With this in view the previous argument follows and Equation (19) remains valid at $H = \bar{H}$.

It can readily be checked that $\mathrm{d}p/\mathrm{d}H$ and $\mathrm{d}^2p/\mathrm{d}H^2$ are both negative.

$$\frac{\mathrm{d}p}{\mathrm{d}H} = -\frac{(1-\beta)}{\beta(\bar{L}+\bar{H})}\left[\frac{\bar{L}+\bar{H}-H}{\bar{L}+\bar{H}}\right]^{-\beta} < 0 \tag{20}$$

$$\frac{\mathrm{d}^2p}{\mathrm{d}H^2} = -\frac{(1-\beta)}{(\bar{L}+\bar{H})^2}\left[\frac{\bar{L}+\bar{H}-H}{\bar{L}+\bar{H}}\right]^{-(1+\beta)} < 0 \tag{21}$$

Hence the curve DC in Figure 1 is concave and downward sloping.

3.3. Autarkic equilibrium

We now have all the resources to determine the autarkic equilibrium. The supply side curve SUM and the demand side curve DC determines the equilibrium of the economy. Three alternative possibilities can arise as shown in Figures 1, 2 and 3.

In Figures 1 and 2 the economy exhibits multiple equilibria at points D, E and C and at D, E and V respectively. Under reasonable presumptions of Marshallian adjustment (as is customary to assume in the IRS literature (see Ethier, 1982) one can see that point E is an unstable equilibrium in both these cases with the demand curve intersecting the supply curve from below. So in Figure 1, D and C and in Figure 2, D and V are the two stable equilibria. At D in both figures sector 2 production never takes off and in the vicinity of point D supply price exceeds demand price. Thus under Marshallian adjustment, small attempts at increasing production of good 2 (which is the same as increasing H) would not work. With supply price exceeding the demand price the economy comes back to point D.

At C in Figure 1 and at V in Figure 2, sector 2 is operative. But as is evident there is a crucial point of difference in the two cases shown in Figures 1 and 2. At the stable equilibrium C in Figure 1, skilled labour has been completely employed in the skill using intermediate goods sector and noting that the segment UM of the supply curve corresponds to $w_s > 1$, skilled wage is greater than the unskilled wage. On the other hand, at V in Figure 2 though the skill using sector 2 is operative, skilled labour has not

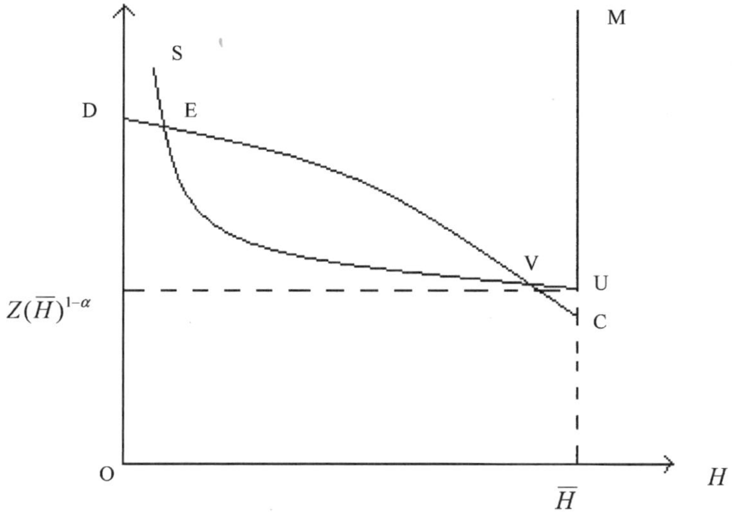

Fig. 2. The case where the skill using sector can take off under autarky, but skilled labour remains under-utilized.

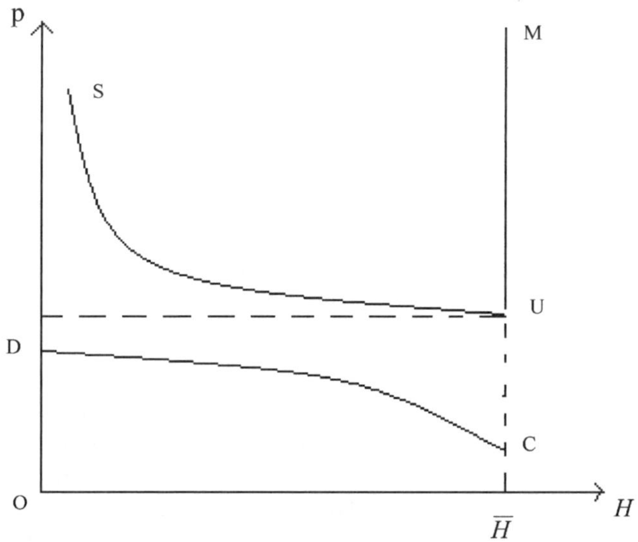

Fig. 3. The case where the skill using sector can never take off under autarky.

been completely absorbed in intermediate goods production and noting that the segment SU corresponds to $w_s = 1$, both skilled and unskilled wages are equal. And no wonder this happens. With skilled labour not being completely absorbed in intermediate goods sector some of the skilled workers remain working in the unskilled job in sector 1 earning a wage of unity, consequently the economy wide skilled wages are tied down to the level of unskilled wages at unity. We choose to call an equilibrium of this kind as shown by point V in Figure 2, an *underutilization equilibrium*. This we believe has a semblance to the argument put forward by Myint, where he was making a case in favour of international trade as a *vent for surplus*. As we will show later, international trade can deliver a country from such an *underutilization equilibrium* to full utilization of its skilled labour.

It is straightforward to see that the difference in the two cases shown in Figures 1 and 2 lies in the fact that in Figure 1 the demand curve intersect the supply curve stretch UM at $H = \bar{H}$ and in Figure 2 the demand curve lies below the UM stretch at $H = \bar{H}$. Alternatively in Figure 1 (Figure 2) the demand price at $H = \bar{H}$ which from Equation (19) is given by $1/\beta[\bar{L}/(\bar{L} + \bar{H})]^{(1-\beta)}$, is greater (less) than the minimum supply price of good 2 at $H = \bar{H}$ (which corresponds to the point U), which from Equation (16) is given by $Z\bar{H}^{1-\alpha}$. Thus strong scale economies or high α favours the case shown in Figure 1. In Figure 2, which corresponds to a case of low α, the supply price, even at the largest possible scale of operation of sector 2 ($H = \bar{H}$) is not sufficiently low as to be matched by a corresponding demand price (see that point U lies above C), consequently the economy cannot fully absorb the skilled work force in the skill using sector.

Figure 3 corresponds to a case where the supply price is uniformly higher than the demand price. Hence the unique equilibrium is given by point D. This would be the case if the strength scale economies or which is the same as α, is sufficiently low.

In such a case sector 1 is the only operative sector. And all wages, skilled and unskilled would be unity.

The observations made above are summarized in the following manner:

The economy exhibits multiple equilibria. The following three situations exhaust all the possibilities:

(a) The economy has two stable equilibria (D and C, as shown in Figure 1). One in which sector 2 is non-operative and skilled wage is equal to unskilled wage and another with an operative sector 2 with skilled labour completely absorbed in that sector and with skilled wage higher than the unskilled wage. It is evident that a necessary and sufficient condition for such a situation to arise is given by

$$\frac{1}{\beta}\left[\frac{\bar{L}}{\bar{L}+\bar{H}}\right]^{(1-\beta)} > Z\bar{H}^{1-\alpha}$$

(b) The economy has two stable equilibria (D and V, as shown in Figure 2): one in which sector 2 is non-operative and skilled wage is equal to unskilled wage and another with an operative sector 2 with skilled labour partially absorbed in that sector and with skilled wage remaining equal to the unskilled wage. Necessary and a sufficient condition for such a situation to arise is given by

$$\exists H, 0 < H < \bar{H}$$

such that

$$\frac{1}{\beta}\left[\frac{\bar{L}+\bar{H}-H}{\bar{L}+\bar{H}}\right]^{(1-\beta)} > ZH^{1-\alpha} \text{ and } \frac{1}{\beta}\left[\frac{\bar{L}}{\bar{L}+\bar{H}}\right]^{(1-\beta)} < Z\bar{H}^{1-\alpha}$$

(c) The economy has a unique equilibrium in which sector 2 production never takes off (point D, as shown in Figure 3). All skilled and unskilled workers are employed in sector 1 and they earn the same wage unity. Necessary and a sufficient condition for such a situation to arise is given by

$$\frac{1}{\beta}\left[\frac{\bar{L}+\bar{H}-H}{\bar{L}+\bar{H}}\right]^{(1-\beta)} < ZH^{1-\alpha} \ \forall H \in (0, \bar{H}]$$

From the above findings we arrive at the following three propositions.

PROPOSITION 1. *Under autarky three types of equilibria are possible:* (i) *where sector 2 production never takes off,* (ii) *where sector 2 production takes off but is unable to absorb the entire skilled labour force,* (iii) *sector 2 employs the entire skilled labour force. In situations* (i) *and* (ii) *there is no inequality of income between skilled and unskilled labour* ($w_s = 1$) *while* (iii) *represents an equilibrium exhibiting wage inequality* ($w_s > 1$).[1]

PROPOSITION 2. *A necessary condition for wage inequality to exist in autarky equilibrium is given by*

$$\frac{1}{\beta}\left[\frac{\bar{L}}{\bar{L}+\bar{H}}\right]^{1-\beta} > Z\bar{H}^{1-\alpha}$$

PROPOSITION 3. *A sufficient condition for no inequality to hold in autarky equilibrium is given by*

$$\frac{1}{\beta}\left[\frac{\bar{L}}{\bar{L}+\bar{H}}\right]^{1-\beta} < Z\bar{H}^{1-\alpha}$$

---

[1] There is a pathological case where the demand curve intersects the supply curve at the supply curve's lowest point where it is kinked. In this case, the entire skilled labour force is just employed in sector 2 but $w_s = 1$. We are ignoring this case.

The inequality in Proposition 2 needs to be interpreted. First, an increase in the *proportion* of unskilled labour in the economy increases the LHS and hence makes wage inequality more likely. This effect works through the demand side. More unskilled labour relative to skilled labour expands relative production of sector 1 creating more income in that sector. This, in turn, increases demand for the product produced by sector 2 leading to its expansion. Second, an increase in the *absolute* endowment of skilled labour reduces the LHS (recall that $\alpha > 1$) making wage inequality more likely. This is a pure supply side effect working through increasing returns. An increase in skilled labour endowment reduces the minimum price at which the entire skilled labour force is employed in sector 2 and hence increases the chance of full utilization of skilled labour.

Finally, note that the case where sector 2 fails to take off exhibits a coordination failure or a lack of demand. Here at zero level of production of sector 2, the price at which the first unit can be supplied is arbitrarily high while the price at which the first unit is demanded remains finite. Hence production never takes off. If production could be started, both the demand price and the supply price would fall and some other equilibrium with positive production in sector 2 could have been reached. There is of course the other possibility that the demand price lies below the supply price for all levels of H and so the only possible equilibrium is the no take-off equilibrium.

An important point needs clarification here. In an equilibrium with underutilization of skilled labour, both skilled and unskilled labour fetches the same reward. It might then be, not unreasonably, claimed that if skill accumulation were to be costly, labourers would not acquire skill at all. We should make here clear the purpose of our model building exercise. We are beginning with a given stock of skilled labour, that might be considered to be historically given, or might be thought of as a distribution of innate abilities. Given that stock, we explore the conditions under which that gets fully utilized or otherwise. This helps us to capture meaningfully Myint's notion of underutilization of resources, and show, as we do in the subsequent section, how trade can possibly help to come out of such a situation, though of course with adverse distributional consequences. In a follow up exercise (Chakraborty and Sarkar, 2007), we have explored the consequences of having purposive accumulation in a similar model, where we do not any more have an equilibrium with underutilization of skilled labour, but the story of trade driven wage inequality survives.

4. Trade

Let two countries having the above structure engage in commodity trade. We call them home and foreign (whenever needed, we denote them by h and f respectively). Countries are similar preference and technology wise but can possibly differ in their quantities of factor endowments.

We assume all goods (final goods 1 and 2, and also the intermediate goods) to be freely tradable.

With commodity trade equalizing good 1 prices in home and foreign, it must be the case that unskilled wages are equalized in both the countries.

Now let us focus on the market clearing conditions for intermediate goods.

$$x^{\mathrm{h}} = y^{\mathrm{h}}_{\mathrm{h}} + y^{\mathrm{h}}_{\mathrm{f}} \tag{22a}$$

$$x^{\mathrm{f}} = y^{\mathrm{f}}_{\mathrm{h}} + y^{\mathrm{f}}_{\mathrm{f}} \tag{22b}$$

where x^{h} and x^{f} are the supplies of a representative brand of intermediate input of home and foreign country, respectively, and y^j_i denotes the amount of intermediate input produced in the jth country and used by the ith country producers of good 2. Thus the LHS in Equations (22a–b) denotes the total world supply and the RHS denotes the total world demand of intermediate inputs respectively.

Now from the demand Equation (2) and noting that zero profit condition prevails in the production of good 2, and that trade equalizes price of commodity 2 in both the countries, the set of Equations (22) reduces to

$$x^{\mathrm{h}} = \frac{(q^{\mathrm{h}})^{-\sigma} p X^{\mathrm{h}}_2}{n^{\mathrm{h}}(q^{\mathrm{h}})^{1-\sigma} + n^{\mathrm{f}}(q^{\mathrm{f}})^{1-\sigma}} + \frac{(q^{\mathrm{h}})^{-\sigma} p X^{\mathrm{f}}_2}{n^{\mathrm{h}}(q^{\mathrm{h}})^{1-\sigma} + n^{\mathrm{f}}(q^{\mathrm{f}})^{1-\sigma}} \tag{23a}$$

$$x^{\mathrm{f}} = \frac{(q^{\mathrm{f}})^{-\sigma} p X^{\mathrm{h}}_2}{n^{\mathrm{h}}(q^{\mathrm{h}})^{1-\sigma} + n^{\mathrm{f}}(q^{\mathrm{f}})^{1-\sigma}} + \frac{(q^{\mathrm{f}})^{-\sigma} p X^{\mathrm{f}}_2}{n^{\mathrm{h}}(q^{\mathrm{h}})^{1-\sigma} + n^{\mathrm{f}}(q^{\mathrm{f}})^{1-\sigma}} \tag{23b}$$

where q^j now denotes the price of a representative brand of intermediate input produced in the jth country, X^j_2 is the output of good 2 produced in the jth country and n^j the number of varieties produced in the jth country.

It is clear from Equation (5) that with identical technology, $x^{\mathrm{h}} = x^{\mathrm{f}}$. Therefore the set of Equations (23) imply $q^{\mathrm{h}} = q^{\mathrm{f}}$. Now noting that intermediate good prices are set as a constant mark-up over skilled wages (see Equation (3)), skilled wages are also equalized across countries.

Therefore the following proposition is immediate.

Proposition 4. *Free trade in final and intermediate goods equalizes skilled and unskilled wages in both the countries.*

With price of intermediate goods produced in both the countries now equal (i.e. $q^{\mathrm{h}} = q^{\mathrm{f}}$), it must be true that a country will be using the same amount of each brand of intermediate input whether produced at home or foreign, in the production of final good 2. Which imply

$y_h^h = y_h^f$ and $y_f^f = y_f^h$

Now with zero profit condition prevailing in the final good 2 production

$$pX_2^j = n^h q^h y_j^h + n^f q^f y_j^f : j = h, f \tag{24}$$

Recalling that $q^h = q^f$ and $y_j^h = y_j^f : j = h, f$, and using the production function given in Equation (1), Equation (24) reduces to

$$p = (n^h + n^f)^{1-\alpha} q^h \tag{25}$$

This is evidently the trade counterpart of Equation (13).

As in Equation (14), Equation (25) reduces to

$$p = Z(H^h + H^f)^{1-\alpha} w_s \tag{26}$$

where H^h and H^f are the amount of skilled labour employed in intermediate goods production in the home and in the foreign country, respectively. Comparing Equations (13) and (25) it is clear that trade in intermediate goods by making available a larger number of varieties of intermediate inputs have depressed the supply price of good 2 for any given q.

With factor prices equalized through trade, the trading equilibrium can be solved just as was done under autarky, but now by considering the world as an integrated economy.

Thus on the demand side we have the counterpart of Equation (19)

$$p = \frac{1}{\beta}\left(\frac{\bar{L}^w + \bar{H}^w - H^w}{\bar{L}^w + \bar{H}^w}\right)^{1-\beta} \tag{27}$$

where $\bar{L}^w = \bar{L}^h + \bar{L}^f$, $\bar{H}^w = \bar{H}^h + \bar{H}^f$ and $H^w = H^h + H^f$.

Equation (26) is now the supply side relation depicted by the SUM curve and Equation (27) is the demand side relation depicted as the DC curve in Figures 4, 5 and 6. As under autarky, these two relations determine the trade equilibrium.[2]

4.1. Trade, vent for surplus and wage inequality

Let us start with the most straightforward case in which trade leads to an increase in skill premium in both the countries. And in this, we will also try

[2] Note that in the stable equilibrium shown by point V in Figure 5 the total amount of skilled labour employed in the intermediate goods sector worldwide (H^w) is determined. But it is important to note that the amount of skilled labour devoted to intermediate goods production for each country (H^h and H^f) separately remain indeterminate. Any allocation of H^h and H^f is consistent with this equilibrium as long as $H^w = H^h + H^f$.

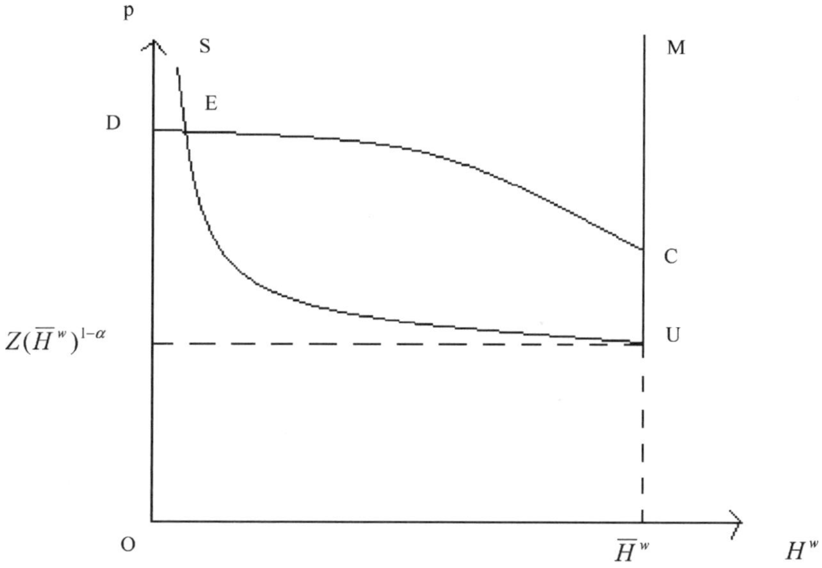

Fig. 4. The case where skilled labour can get fully utilized under trade.

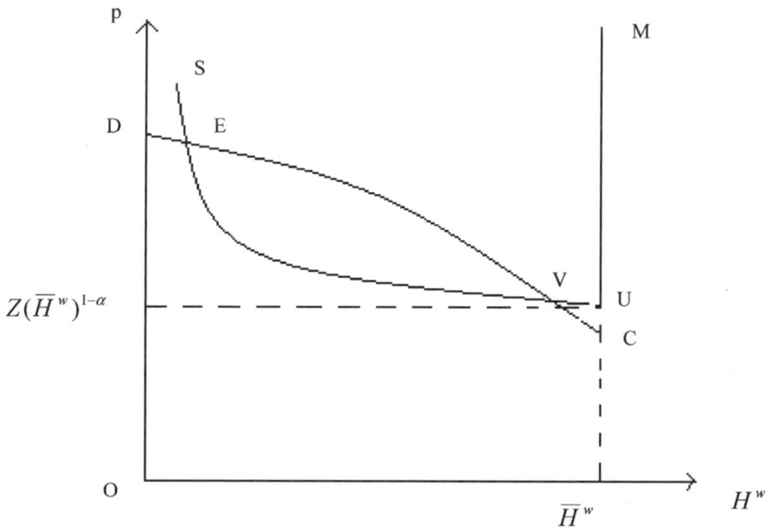

Fig. 5. The case where the skill using sector can take off under trade, but skilled labour remains under-utilized.

to argue that trade plays a role of a *vent for surplus* in the spirit of the thesis proposed by Hla Myint.

Let us assume that the parameters of the model are such that both the economies, home and foreign, begin from a situation where the autarkic

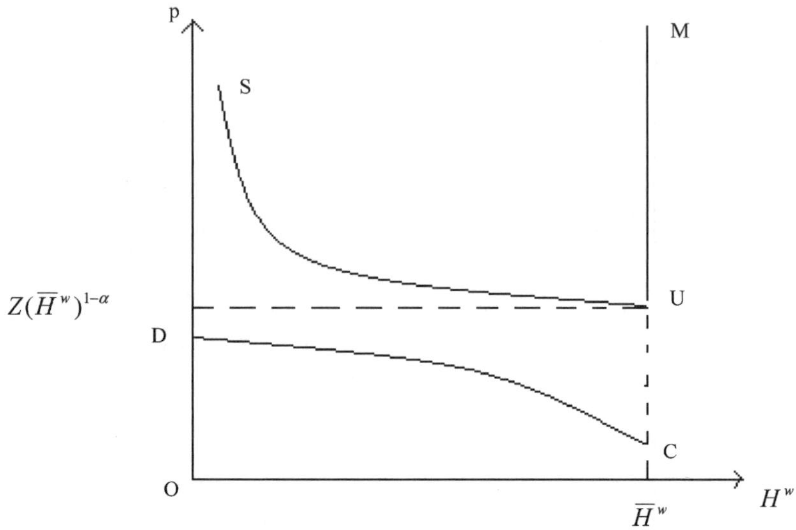

Fig. 6. The case where the skill using sector can never take off under trade.

equilibrium is of the kind depicted by point V in Figure 2. That is to say, both the countries have an operative sector 2 but skilled labour remains *underutilized*. And thereby in both the countries skilled and unskilled wages are equal to unity. A situation of this order is evidently characterized by

$$\frac{1}{\beta}\left[\frac{\bar{L}^i}{\bar{L}^i + \bar{H}^i}\right]^{(1-\beta)} < Z(\bar{H}^i)^{1-\alpha}$$

and there exists H^i, $0 < H^i < \bar{H}^i$ such that

$$\frac{1}{\beta}\left[\frac{\bar{L}^i + \bar{H}^i - H^i}{\bar{L}^i + \bar{H}^i}\right]^{(1-\beta)} > Z(H^i)^{1-\alpha}; \quad i = \mathrm{h, f} \tag{28}$$

Now with opening up of trade it can always be possible that the trading equilibrium is of the kind depicted as point C in Figure 4. Clearly such an equilibrium ensures a higher wage for skilled workers than unskilled workers.

Note that under trade the minimum supply price, which corresponds to point U in Figures 4, 5 and 6, is given by

$$p = Z(\bar{H}^{\mathrm{h}} + \bar{H}^{\mathrm{f}})^{1-\alpha} \tag{29}$$

Thus the minimum supply price under autarky in both the countries, as given by the RHS of the first inequality in (28) is greater than what would be achieved under trade, given by Equation (29).

For the trade equilibrium to be of the kind depicted as point C in Figure 4, the demand price given by Equation (27) evaluated at $H^w = \bar{H}^w$, has to be greater than the minimum supply price given by Equation (29). Putting the arguments together, the following proposition follows:

PROPOSITION 5. *Ignoring the case of total coordination failure, opening up of trade leads to a symmetric rise in wage inequality if the following two conditions hold*:

$$\frac{1}{\beta}\left[\frac{\bar{L}^i}{\bar{L}^i + \bar{H}^i}\right]^{(1-\beta)} < Z(\bar{H}^i)^{1-\alpha}, \quad i = \mathrm{h, f}$$

$$\frac{1}{\beta}\left[\frac{\bar{L}^w}{\bar{L}^w + \bar{H}^w}\right]^{1-\beta} > Z(\bar{H}^w)^{1-\alpha}$$

Thus we have a very plausible theory of trade-led rise in skill premium in both the trading countries. The mechanism is intuitively pretty clear. Trade in intermediate goods, generate externalities which reduces average cost of producing good 2 in both the countries. If to begin with the autarky, the minimum average cost (which corresponds to the full utilization of skilled labour in the intermediate goods sector and skilled wage of unity) of producing good 2 is higher than the demand price evaluated at full absorption of skilled labour in the skill using intermediate goods sector, skilled labour cannot be fully absorbed in the skill-using sector. Part of the skilled work force therefore remains engaged in sector 1. Skilled wage thus remains tied down to the level of unskilled wage. Trade by bringing down the minimum average cost to a level that can be accommodated by the demand price, helps absorb skilled labour in the skill-using sector fully. Thereby skilled and unskilled wages diverge. What is crucial in the mechanism involved is that trade helps utilize fully, hitherto underutilized skilled labour. Noticeably we can show here a case of trade-induced rise in skill premium, symmetrically incident on both the countries, remaining within the FPE framework which most of the models in this genre of the literature abandon.

Yet another case could be, both countries having an equilibrium of the kind depicted as point C in Figure 1 in autarky and the trade equilibrium is of the kind depicted as point C in Figure 4. Thus both under autarky and trade these countries are fully utilizing the skilled labour in the skill-using sector. Even under such a situation inequality could rise in both the countries following trade. To see this note that skilled wage under autarky in this situation can be solved from Equation (16) and Equation (19) evaluated at $H = \bar{H}$. Yielding

$$w_s^i = \frac{\frac{1}{\beta}\left[\frac{\bar{L}^i}{\bar{L}^i + \bar{H}^i}\right]^{1-\beta}}{Z(\bar{H}^i)^{1-\alpha}}; \quad i = \mathrm{h, f} \tag{30}$$

where w_s^i denotes the autarkic skilled wage in the *i*th country.

Similarly the solution for skilled wage under trade for an equilibrium like point C in Figure 4 would be given by solving Equations (26) and (27) evaluated at $H^h = \bar{H}^h$, $H^h = \bar{H}^h$ and $H^w = \bar{H}^w$. Thus

$$w_{sT} = \frac{\frac{1}{\beta}\left[\frac{\bar{L}^w}{\bar{L}^w + \bar{H}^w}\right]^{1-\beta}}{Z(\bar{H}^h + \bar{H}^f)^{1-\alpha}} \tag{31}$$

where w_{sT} denotes the skilled wage under trade.

Comparing Equations (30) and (31), we can see that on count of the denominator (which captures the external economies generated through intermediate goods trade) trade pushes up skilled wages in both the countries. But noting that the numerator in Equation (31) is increasing in $\bar{L}/\bar{H}$, and that $\bar{L}^w/\bar{H}^w$ lies between $\bar{L}^h/\bar{H}^h$ and $\bar{L}^f/\bar{H}^f$ skilled wage in a country relatively scarce in skilled labour (i.e. higher $\bar{L}/\bar{H}$) can potentially suffer a fall in skilled wages. And for a skilled labour abundant country both on the numerator and the denominator count trade pushes up skilled wage. Thus if strength of external economies generated through trade is strong enough to outweigh the fall in skilled wage due to factor endowment difference in a skill scarce country, wage inequality will rise in both the countries. These points are summarized in the following proposition.

PROPOSITION 6. *If both the countries operate at the full utilization equilibrium under autarky and under free trade and if* $(\bar{L}^h/\bar{H}^h) > (\bar{L}^f/\bar{H}^f)$ *then a necessary and sufficient condition for trade to increase wage inequality in both the countries is given by*

$$\frac{\left[\frac{\bar{L}^h}{\bar{L}^h + \bar{H}^h}\right]^{1-\beta}}{(\bar{H}^h)^{1-\alpha}} < \frac{\left[\frac{\bar{L}^w}{\bar{L}^w + \bar{H}^w}\right]^{1-\beta}}{(\bar{H}^h + \bar{H}^f)^{1-\alpha}}.$$

The argument presented above can be straightforwardly extended to a multi-country framework. Let there be k countries indexed by $j = 1, 2, \ldots, k$, engaged in trade, with the above structure and differing among themselves possibly only in terms of $\bar{L}^j/\bar{H}^j$ ratio. Under the trading equilibrium it readily follows that intermediate goods price has to be equalized i.e. $q^j = q \; \forall j$. Which in turn implies equalization of skilled wage across the trading countries. And absolutely similar arguments as above will allow us to write the supply and demand relationships of the trading world as in Equations (26) and (27), with $\bar{H}^w = \sum_{j=1}^{k} \bar{H}^j$, $\bar{L}^w = \sum_{j=1}^{k} \bar{L}^j$ and $H^w = \sum_{j=1}^{k} H^j$.

Suppose we begin with a situation where each country in autarky has $(1/\beta)[\bar{L}^j/(\bar{L}^j + \bar{H}^j)]^{(1-\beta)} < Z(\bar{H}^j)^{1-\alpha}$ i.e. each country is in underutilization equilibrium with $w_s = 1$. Now if similar countries (i.e. having same $\bar{L}^j/\bar{H}^j$) start opening up to trade, then in the trading equilibrium the lowest point of the demand curve is given by $(1/\beta)[\bar{L}^w/(\bar{L}^w + \bar{H}^w)]^{(1-\beta)}$, which remains the same as in the LHS of the above inequality, as all the entrants in the trading world have same $\bar{L}^j/\bar{H}^j$ and the RHS, which is the minimum point of the supply curve, goes down. As entry of these similar countries continue the inequality gets reversed to $(1/\beta)[\bar{L}^w/(\bar{L}^w + \bar{H}^w)]^{(1-\beta)} > Z(\bar{H}^w)^{1-\alpha}$ in the trading world (assuming $\bar{H}^w$ and/or the strength of the scale economy (α) is sufficiently high). Thus all such similar countries in the trading equilibrium will end up having $w_S > 1$. Next, let the sequence of entry be such that countries with higher $\bar{L}^j/\bar{H}^j$ (those which can reasonably be identified as labour abundant developing countries) start entering the trading world, with countries having higher $\bar{L}^j/\bar{H}^j$ entering later. Then it evidently follows that the minimum point of the demand curve moves up even further with each successive entry, as the LHS of the inequality is increasing in $\bar{L}^j/\bar{H}^j$ and the minimum point of the supply curve shifts down. This necessarily entails that the skilled wages of the countries already in the trading world goes up even further and at any stage of entry, for the last of the entrants which had $w_S = 1$ in autarky (being in an underutilization equilibrium), skilled wages moves above unity. Thus for such a sequence of trade liberalization, skill premium goes on increasing across the trading globe. The following proposition puts the above argument formally.

PROPOSITION 7. *Let all the countries (typical country indexed by j) in autarky be in underutilization equilibrium with* $(1/\beta)[\bar{L}^j/(\bar{L}^j + \bar{H}^j)]^{(1-\beta)} < Z(\bar{H}^j)^{1-\alpha}$ *and let trade liberalization follow sequentially with countries having equal or higher* $\bar{L}^j/\bar{H}^j$ *entering later. Then if it is such that on entry of the k*th country $(1/\beta)[\bar{L}^w/(\bar{L}^w + \bar{H}^w)]^{(1-\beta)} > Z(\bar{H}^w)^{1-\alpha}$ *then for all successive entries following k, skill premium will increase for all the countries engaged in trade.*

5. Conclusion

We develop a simple two-sector (with a constant and an IRS sector), two-factor trade model explicitly introducing the notion that skilled and unskilled labour faces differential employment options, in that skilled labour can work both in skilled and unskilled job whereas unskilled labour is tied down to the unskilled job. The demand pattern is generated out of a quasi-linear utility function. Thus one of the good is basic in the sense that it is always consumed in positive quantities for any positive income. The other good may not be consumed at all. We show that such a model can, in an intuitively appealing way, account for trade-driven wage inequality. Remaining within the FPE framework (which most of the models in the relevant literature abandon) we are able to show that trade can symmetrically raise wage inequality in both the trading countries. The model holds interesting possibilities of multiple equilibria. Of which an equilibrium can be either characterized by a non-operative skill using IRS sector or an operative IRS sector but not fully absorbing the available skilled labour or an operative IRS sector fully absorbing the available skilled labour.

If to begin with at the autarky, the minimum average cost (which corresponds to the full utilization of skilled labour in the IRS sector and with skilled wage equal to the unskilled wage) of producing the IRS good is higher than the demand price, skilled labour cannot be fully absorbed in the skill-using IRS sector. Part of the skilled work force remains engaged in the CRS sector, which uses unskilled labour. Skilled wage thus remains tied down to the level of unskilled wage.

Trade by bringing down the minimum average cost to a level that can be accommodated by the demand price, helps absorb skilled labour in the skill-using sector fully. Thereby skilled and unskilled wages diverge. What is crucial in the mechanism involved is that trade helps full utilization of hitherto underutilized skilled labour.

References

Chakraborty, B.S., Sarkar, A. (2007), Wage inequality with endogenous skill formation. Mimeo, Indian Statistical Institute, Calcutta.

Dixit, A., Stiglitz, J.E. (1977), Monopolistic competition and optimum product diversity. *American Economic Review* 67, 297–308.

Dornbusch, R., Fischer, S., Samuelson, P.A. (1980), Heckscher–Ohlin trade theory with a continuum of goods. *Quarterly Journal of Economics* 95, 203–224.

Ethier, W.J. (1982), National and international returns to scale in the modern theory of international trade. *American Economic Review* 72, 389–405.

Feenstra, R., Hanson, G. (1996), Foreign investment, outsourcing and relative wages. In: Feenstra, R., Grossman, G., Irwin, D. (Eds.), *Political Economy of Trade Policy: Papers in Honour of Jagadish Bhagawati*. MIT Press, Cambridge, MA.

Helpman, E., Krugman, P. (1985), *Market Structure and International Trade*. MIT Press, Cambridge, MA.

Jones, R.W. (1999), Heckscher–Ohlin trade models for the new century. Mimeo, University of Rochester.

Krugman, P. (1981), Intra-industry specialization and the gains from trade. *Journal of Political Economy* 89, 959–973.

Marjit, S., Acharyya, R. (2003), *International Trade, Wage Inequality and the Developing Economy: A General Equilibrium Approach*. Physica-Verlag, Heidelberg.

Myint, H. (1958), The "classical theory" of international trade and the underdeveloped countries. *Economic Journal* 68, 317–337.

Trefler, D., Zhu, S.C. (2001), Ginis in general equilibrium: trade, technology and southern inequality. NBER Working Paper No. 8446.

CHAPTER 14

Informed Buyers and Trade Sanction against Child Labour: Does It Work?

Rajat Acharyya

Department of Economics, Jadavpur University, Kolkata 700032, India
E-mail address: racharya@cal2.vsnl.net.in

Abstract
With product labelling has already been in vogue in the developed countries to distinguish products produced by child labour from those that are "child labour free" to influence the buyers' choice, one might be tempted to suggest that such labels should contain more information regarding the extent to which child labour has been used in a product. But, as this chapter shows, if labels contain such information and the buyers react to this by offering increasingly lower prices for the varieties containing more child labour per unit of output, it may do more harm than helping the cause. That is, a trade sanction against child labour content of a good exported by developing countries may not be a good idea since it may, in fact, raise the incidence of child labour in those countries. This result is established in a simple general equilibrium framework where parents are altruist.

Keywords: Child labour, trade sanction, schooling

JEL classifications: F11, F13, J13

1. Introduction

Despite innumerable legislative, policy and social actions, child labour continues to be widespread in most of the developing and poor nations. Such actions against employing child labour have ranged from legislature in the developing countries imposing fines on the employing firms and formal trade sanctions against import of such goods by the developed

Frontiers of Economics and Globalization
Volume 4 ISSN: 1574-8715
DOI: 10.1016/S1574-8715(08)04014-1

nations to social boycotting of products by the concerned buyers.[1] One primary reason why such wide range of actions could not reduce the incidence of child labour is that these actions have targeted the demand side of the problem when it was necessary to address the supply side factors or the causes of the incidence of child labour.

It is an undeniable fact that abject poverty is the major cause of child labour. It is hard to find middle and high-income parents in the developing countries sending their children to work. But the low-income parents often send their children to work in order to achieve a subsistence level of consumption, and evidence towards such a cause of child labour is growing[2] (Grootaert and Patrinos, 1999; Edmonds, 2005; Edmonds and Pavcnik, 2005a, 2005b). Once this is understood, it may not appear too surprising why legislative, policy and social actions have not worked to the extent they were expected to, and at worst, in some cases may actually have aggravated the problem. Edmonds and Pavcnik (2005a, 2005b) have observed that an increase in the domestic price of rice exports in Vietnam to the level of the world price after the Vietnamese government had relaxed the export quota has lowered the incidence of child labour there. Their finding may suggest that trade sanctions against exports produced by child labour (which should lower the world and the domestic price) may induce more parents to send their children to work. Theoretical possibility of such perverse effect of a fine on firms has been explored by Basu (2004), and of trade sanctions (or product boycotting) by Basu and Zarghamee (2005), Ranjan (2001) and Jafarey and Lahiri (2002). In Basu (2004) and Basu and Zarghamee (2005), the declining adult and household incomes as a consequence of trade sanctions induce more children being sent to work by their parents. In Jafarey and Lahiri (2002), however, the parents, despite being altruist, send more children to work after trade sanction because their lack of access to credit markets makes the cost of borrowing to smooth out consumption during the period of a child's education high for them. Trade sanctions may also hurt the children when they have very little alternatives and opportunities (Edmonds, 2003). Without simultaneously improving the income of the households and thereby lowering the opportunity cost of schooling, such sanctions only shift the working children to the non-traded production activities and services like small restaurants, road-side tea shops, motor garages and, worst of all, to

[1] For example, by the Child Labour (Prohibition and Regulation) Act, 1986, the Government of India can fine a person or a firm employing children in contravention of the provisions of the Act.

[2] In Bangladesh, India and Pakistan most of the children work under compulsion from their parents. A sizeable proportion of them, at least 15 million among the 70–80 million working children in India across all age groups by the most conservative estimate of Human Rights Watch (1996), work as bonded child labour in order to pay off debts of their parents. In all the cases, the creditor-employer offers loans to the destitute parents to secure labour of a child that is even cheaper under bondage.

prostitution, the incidence of which among the girl children is alarmingly on the rise in many Asian countries.

This chapter demonstrates similar perverse effect of a worldwide trade sanction against child labour content (or intensity) of a product. More precisely, we show that if a worldwide trade sanction lowers the world demand and consequently the world price by a greater margin when a good is relatively more intensive in child labour than when it is relatively less intensive in child labour, the parents send their children to work for longer hours. Consequently, the incidence of child labour rises in the exporting country. The theoretical relevance of this result lies in the fact that this perverse effect of a trade sanction (against child labour content) may arise even when the inter-linkage of credit market (imperfect or perfect) and labour market is not considered, and the supply curve for child labour is not backward bending. Of course, the purpose of this chapter is not to contest these alternative explanations but to provide another plausible theoretical explanation to make a point in case for the possible perverse effect of a trade sanction.

There is also a policy implication of this result. Product labelling has already been in vogue to distinguish products produced by child labour from those that are "child labour free" to influence the buyers' choice. Carpets produced in India are labeled by RUGMARK and KALEEN for exports to Germany and USA. The certificates for fair labour standards and child labour-free produce is provided by STEP in Switzerland for manufacturing goods imported from India, Nepal and Pakistan and ABRINQ in Brazil labels goods produced and sold locally. Soccer balls produced in Pakistan are also labeled for exports to USA. The other labelling organizations for goods produced in India, Kenya and Nepal include CARE and FARE, and DIP. These product labels, setting aside the issue of false labelling and the associated moral hazard problem as discussed in Basu et al. (2006), enable the buyers to get product-specific information instead of relying solely upon their country-of-origin perception when they buy such goods. But if labels are also used to provide information regarding the intensity of child labour employment and the buyers react to this by offering increasingly lower prices for varieties containing more child labour per unit of output, it may do more harm than helping the cause.[3] This result is in contrast to Basu et al. (2006) who demonstrate in a North–South trade framework with price premium for the products with social labels over those without labels that a trade sanction against unlabeled products has no effect on the child labour employment. The difference arises due to the perverse response of parents

---

[3] Of late, Davies (2005) has demonstrated that under Bertrand competition among firms producing goods with and without child labour, social labeling is unlikely to drive out child labour products even when consumers prefer child labour free products.

to the trade sanction against the magnitude of the child labour content in our case.

In a static general equilibrium framework of a small open economy developed here, the children are assumed to work part time. A child is more productive when he spends more time in school. The parents decide about the allocation of the available time unit over schooling and work for their children, along with the levels of the household consumption of the two goods by maximizing the household utility. Children are employed only in the export sector along with the adult workers. Suppose the same export good is also produced and exported using child labour by other *similar* small open economies. Now, consider a worldwide trade sanction on the import of goods produced by child labour, regardless of the country-of-origin, by which all the informed foreign buyers pay increasingly less for products that use more child labour-intensive production techniques.[4] More work for a child now means a fall in the world price of the good since by the consequent (adverse) productivity effect more child labour time per unit of output is needed making the product relatively more child labour-intensive. But this means that as a consumer a parent has to pay less for the good and there will thus be utility gains. Thus, a worldwide trade sanction against child labour content paradoxically raises the marginal benefit for a parent from sending his child to work for a higher fraction of the time unit, and this raises the supply of child labour.

The demand for child labour, however, declines as expected, but the magnitude of such decline varies inversely with the pre-sanction school time. If initially the parents send their children to school for a sufficiently high time fraction, the favourable demand effect is small and is outweighed by the perverse supply effect. A trade sanction against child labour content, in such a case, raises the incidence of child labour at the new equilibrium.

The rest of the chapter is organized as follows. In Section 2 we present the basic analytical framework with altruist parents. Section 3 formalizes the perverse effect of a trade sanction against the child labour content by the informed buyers. In Section 4 we consider how does a trade sanction affect the decision of poor parents. Finally, concluding remarks are made in Section 5.

---

[4] With product boycotting still being an informal arrangement or at best a social or moral action, not all buyers refrain from buying such products. There is, of course, what Basu and Zarghamee (2005) calls a guilt feeling from such an act which gets reflected in a lower willingness-to-pay for such products. Our assumed demand behaviour can be interpreted as a generalization of such a guilt factor to the intensity of child labour in the production processes.

2. A formal argument

2.1. The analytical framework

Consider a small open economy with $\bar{K}$ number of capitalists each endowed with one unit of physical capital stock (K) and n number of adult workers (L). The economy produces two traded goods: an exportable good X and an importable good Y. The world prices of these goods are exogenously given to this small open economy. We take good Y as the numeraire and set its world price as unity by suitable choice of unit. We assume that all capitalists send their children to school for the entire time unit. As we will show later, this follows from either high (interest) income of the capitalist parents and/or their high preference for schooling of a child.

Each adult worker has one child and they together comprise a household. A child and an adult (or parent) are each endowed with one unit of time. Whereas each parent as adult worker works full time for a wage W (measured in terms of good Y) per unit of time, i.e., inelastically supplies its labour as in Basu and Van (1998), a child's time is allocated over schooling (Z) and work ($1-Z$). Thus, each child in this economy works for ($1-Z$) unit of time $T=1$ and earns a wage W_C (once again measured in terms of good Y) per unit of time, where $Z\in[0, 1]$. At an interior equilibrium, each child works part time. An adult worker and a child worker are imperfect substitutes in production and their wages are determined separately by competitive forces. A child's productivity, however, improves with the time spent in school and accordingly a child worker with higher school time earns a higher wage than the one with lower school time. However, with all parents assumed to be identical, the optimal allocation of time over schooling and work decided by the parents will be the same for each child and, therefore, at equilibrium all children will earn the same wage W_C. But by the favourable productivity effect of schooling they will all earn a higher wage if a higher fraction of their available time is allocated to schooling by their parents. All adult workers, however, are endowed with the same given level of skill and have no scope of improving upon it through schooling. Thus they earn the same wage, W, as well.

A parent is the sole decision maker in a household. Each parent decides about the levels of household consumption of the two goods, C_X and C_Y, and about the allocation of the child's unit time over schooling and work. Parents are altruist in the sense that they derive utility not only from the household consumption levels, but also from a child's school time (Z). We assume a Cobb-Douglas utility function for a representative parent, defined over all non-negative consumption levels and for all $Z\in[0, 1]$:

$$U = C_X^{\alpha} C_Y^{1-\alpha} Z^{\rho}, \quad 0<\alpha<1, \quad \rho>0, \tag{1}$$

ρ, which is a positive constant, is the proportional change in utility level of a parent (or a household) brought about by a proportional change in the time fraction spent in school by a child at the margin. This is assumed to be the same for all parents. Thus, instead of warm glow preferences of parents as in Galor and Zeira (1993) and Chiu (1998), we assume that parents directly care for their children's education. With no savings and borrowing, and full appropriation of a child's income by his parent, each parent has the following budget constraint:

$$P_X^* C_X + C_Y = W + (1 - Z)W_C, \tag{2}$$

where, P_X^* is the (relative) world price of the export good X.

Each parent maximizes the utility defined in (1) by choosing C_X, C_Y and Z subject to the budget constraint (2). The optimal consumption choices, and the supply of child labour time $(1-Z)$ will depend on the wages, the relative commodity price and on α and ρ. Since all parents are identical, the choices will also be the same. Thus, for any such choice of work time for a child, the aggregate child labour (time) will be endogenously determined:

$$C = (1 - Z)n. \tag{3}$$

Let us now turn to the production side and the demand for child labour. There are plenty of examples of child labour working together with adult workers to produce labour-intensive manufacturing export products of the developing countries, besides agricultural export production (mostly in the form of family farming). Carpet and diamond cutting and finishing in India, production of soccer balls in Pakistan, gem mining and wood furniture in Indonesia, and garments and footwear productions in Bangladesh, India, Pakistan and Indonesia, are a few specific instances. In keeping with these observations, we assume that the exportable good X is produced by child labour (C) and adult labour (L). We also assume a Leontief or fixed-coefficient production technology. Of course, by this we do not mean that child labour is essential for producing the export good, and in fact the nimble-hand argument does not seem to be a plausible hypothesis for child labour employment in many of the above-mentioned production activities. The fixed-coefficient production function serves a purely analytical convenience than anything else as will be made clear later. Under this assumption, the per unit requirement of adult and child labour (times) in production of the export good X, denoted by a_{LX} and a_{CX}, respectively, are exogenously given independent of the relative wage, $\mu_X \equiv W_C/W$. However, by the productivity effect of schooling, the per unit requirement of child labour (time) in production, a_{CX}, declines if the child spends higher fraction of time unit in school. In particular,

$$a_{CX} = a_{CX}(Z), \quad \frac{\partial a_{CX}}{\partial Z} < 0, \quad \frac{\partial^2 a_{CX}}{\partial Z^2} < 0. \tag{4}$$

By the assumption of diminishing returns from education the second partial derivative is negative. Note that under these assumptions as the parents send their children to school for a greater fraction of the unit time the child labour intensity (or the child labour content per unit of output) of the export good declines, for any (and all) μ_X.

However, the import-competing good Y, which is a perfect substitute of the imported good, is produced by adult labour and domestic capital, under a constant-returns-to-scale technology with diminishing marginal productivities. Denoting the (adult) wage-rental ratio as $\mu_Y \equiv W/r$, the least-cost choices of inputs in the import-competing sectors are given as:

$$a_{iY} = a_{iY}(\mu_Y), \quad i = L,\ K, \tag{5}$$

where, a_{iY} is the per unit requirement of factor i in the production of good Y.

Given these production structures, perfect competition in all markets mean the following zero-profit conditions:

$$P_X^* = a_{LX}W + a_{CX}(Z)W_C \quad \text{and} \tag{6}$$

$$1 = a_{LY}W + a_{KY}r, \tag{7}$$

where, r is the (real) rate of return to domestic capital.

We close the model with the following full employment conditions:

$$\bar{K} = a_{KY}Y, \tag{8}$$

$$n = a_{LX}X + a_{LY}Y \tag{9}$$

$$C = a_{CX}(Z)X, \tag{10}$$

where, $\bar{K}$ is the stock of domestic capital, and X and Y denote output levels of good X and Y, respectively.

Note, for any given parental allocation of a child's unit time over schooling and work, the production structure of our small open economy displays the property of a specific-factor model a la Jones (1971).

2.2. Incidence of child labour under no trade sanction

Consider an initial situation where the buyers in the importing advanced countries have neither any product-specific information nor any country-of-origin perception regarding child labour employment. Thus, they pay the same price for the imported good X regardless of the child labour content (as well as of its country-of-origin):

$$P_X^* = P. \tag{11}$$

For this world price, which is exogenously given to our small open economy, it should be immediate from the framework as described earlier, the parental decision regarding a child's work time $(1-Z)$, and the wages required to maintain full employment of all factors of production are *interdependent*. This means, given the fixed number of child (n), the incidence of child labour, $(1-Z)n$ and the (relative) wage of a child, μ_X, are to be determined simultaneously.

2.2.1. Parental allocation of a child's time

For any given set of world prices of the goods, the productivity effect of schooling raises the wage that a child earns and enables the household to consume more. The resulting utility (or real income) gain constitutes the incentive for a parent to send his child to school for a larger fraction of time. At the same time, more schooling time means smaller income for a child worker for any given child wage. This constitutes the opportunity cost of an additional schooling time. The optimal allocation of time is thus the one for which these marginal benefit and cost are equal.

Formally, the parental decision regarding a child's work time $(1-Z)$ is determined from maximization of utility subject to the budget constraint as defined above in (1) and (2) respectively. It is straightforward to check that, for $P_X^* = P$, the *optimal* schooling (work) time varies inversely (positively) with the relative wage μ_X:

$$Z = \frac{\rho}{1+\rho}\left[\frac{1}{\mu_X} + 1\right]. \qquad (12)$$

The supply of child labour time is illustrated in Figure 1 by the downward sloping, convex to the origin curve labeled $Z(\mu_X)$ in the (Z, μ_X) space. Since $\rho/(1+\rho)<1$, an increase in μ_X lowers the schooling time less than proportionately. The bounds on the $Z(\mu_X)$-curve follow from the fact that $Z \rightarrow \rho/(1+\rho)$ as $\mu_X \rightarrow \infty$ and $Z = 1$ when $\mu_X = \rho$. These properties of

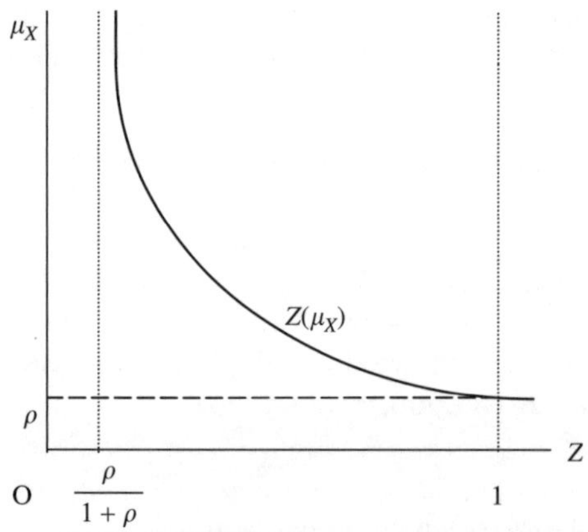

Fig. 1. Supply of child labour.

the child labour supply function have two implications. First, at any *equilibrium*, (all) children will always be sent to school for some positive time fraction. That is, *full time work can never be an equilibrium outcome for a child in this model* when buyers do not have the information regarding the child labour content of the good. Second, when the relative adult wage $1/\mu_X$ is sufficiently high (i.e., $\mu_X \leq \rho$), children are not sent to work. This is similar to what has been shown by Basu and Van (1998) and Basu (2004) under the subsistence-income motive of parents in sending their children to work.

Note that if we work out a similar time allocation problem for a capitalist-parent with (interest) income r and the preference parameter β, the utility maximizing schooling time would have been equal to $Z^K = [\beta/(1+\beta)][(r/W)(1/\mu_X)+1]$. Thus, as long as a capitalist-parent's income is higher than a worker-parent, $r > W$, and/or his preference for his child's schooling is higher, $\beta > \rho$, he sends his child to school for a higher fraction of time than a worker-parent. Since, typically the incidence of child labour is not to be seen in middle and high-income households, we assume that the preference parameter is high enough for each child born to a capitalist-parent to be sent to full-time school.

2.2.2. *Factor market equilibrium and Wages*

For any given allocation of a child's unit time over schooling and work, the equation system (4)–(11) specifying the factor and product market equilibrium conditions, determines the market-clearing wages along with the (real) rate of return to capital. Clearly, any change in the schooling time (Z), and consequently the supply of child labour (time) by (3), should change the market-clearing relative wage, μ_X, for any given world relative price of the traded goods. Thus,

$$\mu_X = \mu_X(Z). \tag{13}$$

The nature of such a relationship between the market-clearing relative wage and the school time can be traced out as follows. Consider a ceteris paribus increase in the school time, Z. As evident from the zero-profit condition (6), this raises the child wage in two ways. First, the productivity effect of an increase in schooling time raises the child wage by the amount $\varepsilon\hat{Z}$, where $\varepsilon \equiv -a_{CX}\partial Z/Z\partial a_{CX}$ is the (absolute) schooling-elasticity of a child's productivity, and $\hat{Z} \equiv \mathrm{d}Z/Z$ is the proportional change in the school time. Second, a larger school time affects the child wage by changing the adult wage: the child wage falls (rises) if the adult wage rises (falls). The direction of the change in the adult wage, however, depends on whether the export production expands or contracts consequent upon an increase in the school time.

Since each child now requires less time to complete a part of the production job, the productivity effect of an increase in the school time creates scope for an expansion of export production. At the same time, as each child spends a larger fraction of his available time in school, each child devotes less time in work place. Given the n number of children, this means a fall in the total supply (or endowment) of child labour (time), which lowers the production of export good by the amount $\gamma\hat{Z}$, where $\gamma \equiv Z/(1-Z)$ is the ratio of schooling to work time. Thus, production of the export good (X) falls if the endowment effect is larger than the productivity effect ($\gamma > \varepsilon$), and rises otherwise. This can also be verified from (10):

$$\hat{X} = (\varepsilon - \gamma)\hat{Z}.$$

A fall in the export production releases adult labour and thus lowers the adult wage. This, in turn, encourages the producers of the import-competing good (Y) to raise the demand for adult labour for two reasons. First, a lower adult wage induces the producers to adopt relatively more (adult) labour-intensive production techniques. Second, since capital is used only in the import-competing sector, less capital used per unit of output creates scope for an expansion of production there and thus raises the demand for adult labour further. That is, by the technique and consequent scale effects, the demand for labour in the import-competing sector rises. This moderates the initial decline in the adult wage, the extent of which depends, among others, on the factor substitution elasticity, σ_Y. Consequent upon this fall in the adult wage (W), the child wage rises further over and above the initial increase due to the (direct) productivity effect. For $\gamma<\varepsilon$, however, the export production expands, which raises the adult labour demand and its wage. This triggers similar technique and scale effects in the import-competing sector, which, however, now work in the opposite direction to release some adult labour. Once again the value of σ_Y determines the extent to which such release of labour from the import-competing sector moderates the initial rise in the adult wage. Now, this rise in the adult wage puts a downward drag on the child wage. The child wage can still, however, rise if the initial productivity effect was sufficiently large.

Formally, as shown in the appendix,

$$\hat{W} = -\frac{\lambda_{LX}(\gamma - \varepsilon)}{\lambda_{LY}\frac{1}{\theta_{KY}}\sigma_Y}\hat{Z}<0 \qquad \text{if } \gamma>\varepsilon \quad \text{and} \tag{14}$$

$$\hat{W}_C = \left[\varepsilon + \frac{\lambda_{LX}\theta_{LX}(\gamma-\varepsilon)}{\lambda_{LY}\sigma_Y\frac{\theta_{CX}}{\theta_{KY}}}\right]\hat{Z}, \tag{15}$$

where, $\lambda_{LX}\equiv a_{LX}X/L$ and $\lambda_{LY}\equiv a_{LY}Y/L$ are respectively the shares of the export sector and import-competing sector in total employment of adult workers; $\theta_{CX} \equiv a_{CX}W/P_X^*$ is the share of child labour in unit cost of production of good X; θ_{LX} and θ_{KY} are similarly defined; and $\sigma_Y \equiv (\hat{a}_{KY} - \hat{a}_{LY})/(\hat{W} - \hat{r})$ is the factor substitution elasticity in the import-competing sector.

Combining (14) and (15) we arrive at the relationship between the market-clearing relative wage and the schooling time (and consequent supply of child labour) as:

$$\hat{\mu}_X = \frac{\lambda_{LY}\dfrac{\theta_{CX}}{\theta_{KY}}\sigma_Y\varepsilon + \lambda_{LX}(\gamma - \varepsilon)}{\lambda_{LY}\dfrac{\theta_{CX}}{\theta_{KY}}\sigma_Y}\hat{Z}. \tag{16}$$

Once again a stronger endowment effect ensures that an increase in schooling time raises the *relative* child wage to clear all the markets. Of course, the relative wage can rise even for a weaker endowment effect. However, to reduce the multiplicity of cases, *as a sufficient condition* for the relative wage to increase for a larger school time (which ensures stability of equilibrium as well as we see shortly), we assume that the endowment effect is stronger than the productivity effect ($\gamma > \varepsilon$) in rest of our analysis.

The positive relationship between the supply of child labour and the market-clearing relative wage is shown in the Figure 2 by the positively sloped curve labeled $\mu_X(Z)$. Though this curve is drawn as a straight line, this need not be the case. However, the shape of this curve does not really matter for the desirable properties of the equilibrium allocation of a child's time as long as the market-clearing relative wage is *monotonically* increasing in the schooling time, as implied by the assumption made in (14).

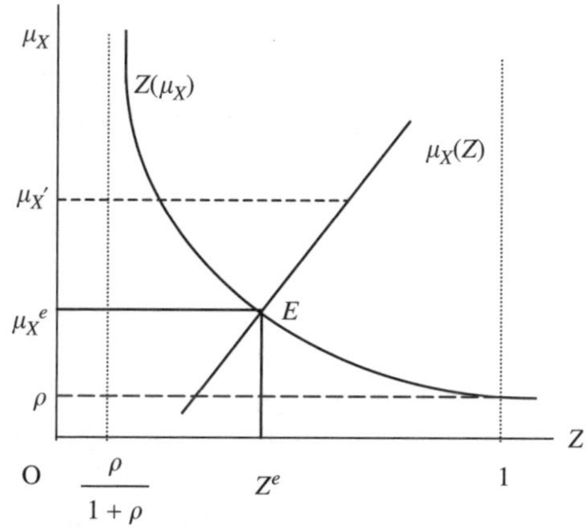

Fig. 2. Equilibrium school time.

2.2.3. Equilibrium wage and supply of child labour

The equilibrium schooling time and the market-clearing relative wage correspond to the intersection point E between the $Z(\mu_X)$ and $\mu_X(Z)$ curves. Recall that $Z(\mu_X)$ curve gives us the optimal parental choice of a child's schooling time for any particular relative wage, whereas $\mu_X(Z)$ curve gives us market-clearing wage for any choice of schooling time. Thus, the domestic markets are cleared and parents' plans are realized only at point E.

A few comments are warranted at this point. First, if such an equilibrium exists, by $\gamma > \varepsilon$ it will be unique. This follows from the fact that under such an assumption the market-clearing relative wage μ_X is monotonically increasing in Z (along the $\mu_X(Z)$ curve), whereas by (12) the optimal parental choice of Z is monotonically decreasing in μ_X. Second, the equilibrium pair of schooling time and relative wage is stable. This follows from the monotonic property of $Z(\mu_X)$ and $\mu_X(Z)$ functions. To check this, consider any relative wage higher than μ_X^e, such as μ'_X. Let $(1 - Z')n$ be the supply of child labour for which the markets clear at such wage. Since market clearing means supply of child labour should equal the demand for child labour as described in (10) above, $(1-Z')n$ can alternatively be taken as the demand for child labour corresponding to the market-clearing wage μ'_X. Now for any $\mu'_X > \mu_X^e$, by (12), (14) and (16), $Z(\mu'_X) < Z'$. This means the supply of child labour, $(1-Z')n$, exceeds the demand for child labour, $[1-Z(\mu'_X)]n$, at that relative wage. The relative wage, thus, should fall. By similar logic, for any $\mu''_X < \mu_X^e$, the supply of child labour is lower than the demand for child labour. The relative wage then should rise. Therefore, the equilibrium relative wage μ_X^e is stable.

Having specified the incidence of child labour at such a unique and stable equilibrium (if it exists) under the assumption in (14), we now proceed to examine the effect of a trade sanction.

3. Product labelling, trade sanction and the incidence of child labour

Suppose there are other economies similar to our small open economy producing and exporting the same good X using child labour. This is not an unreasonable assumption because the incidence of child labour is not confined to any particular developing country but is widespread in Asia let alone the developing countries in other continents. Also suppose the buyers in the importing advanced countries are informed through product labelling about whether and in what intensity child labour is used in producing the good. Given such product-specific information, consider a worldwide trade sanction by which all buyers in all the importing countries offer increasingly lower prices than P for the imported product X

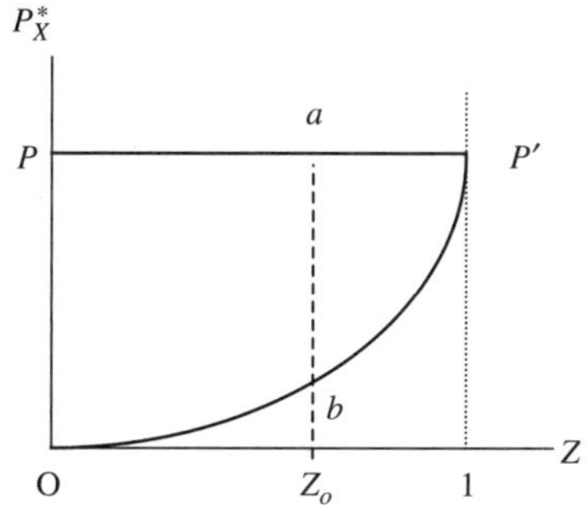

Fig. 3. The world price schedule.

produced by more intensive use of child labour regardless of the country-of-origin.[5]

Given our assumption of fixed-coefficient production function for good X, for any given schooling time (Z), and decline in the child labour intensity of the good with the increase in the time spent by a child in the school, the world price of exports under such a worldwide trade sanction against child labour content can be specified as:

$$P_{XS}^* = PZ^{\delta}, \quad \delta \geq 0. \tag{17}$$

Note that as long as $\delta > 0$, $P_{XS}^* < P_X^* \; \forall \; 0 < Z < 1$. Thus a trade sanction lowers the world price of exports regardless of the child labour content, though the rate of decline in the price, $\delta PZ^{\delta-1}$, increases with the child labour content. Now it should be clear why did we assume fixed input coefficients in the production of the export good, for any given Z. In case of flexible coefficient, an increase in the child labour content (a_{CX}) would result from a fall in either μ_X or Z. Since the price offer made by the foreign buyers actually vary inversely with a_{CX}, by assuming fixed coefficients for any given Z, we establish a one-to-one relationship between the child labour content and the schooling time and accordingly define the foreign buyers' willingness-to-pay to vary directly with the schooling time. A flexible coefficient technology would have only complicated the algebra without any qualitative difference in the results obtained below.

The world price schedule is shown in Figure 3. A trade sanction against child labour content means the foreign buyers pay for their imports according to the OP' schedule. Thus, if initially $Z = Z_o$, after the trade

[5] Alternatively, we can conceive of the worldwide trade sanction resulting in lower world demand and consequently lower world price for the child labour produced good X, with such declines being larger for varieties that have used child labour more intensively in production.

sanction the world price of good X falls from aZ_o to bZ_o, with such declines being higher for smaller values of Z.

Algebraically, the decline in the world price equals,

$$\hat{P}_X^* = \frac{PZ^\delta - P}{P} = -(1 - Z^\delta) < 0. \tag{18}$$

Now, it is straightforward to check that for the world price schedule (17) the parental choice leads to,

$$Z(\delta) = \frac{\rho - \alpha\delta}{1 + \rho - \alpha\delta}\left[\frac{1}{\mu_X} + 1\right]. \tag{19}$$

Thus now a parent may not send his child to school at all. We, however, rule out such a case by assuming ρ to be sufficiently large:

$$\rho > \alpha\delta. \tag{20}$$

For one percent increase in the schooling time for a child, his parents' utility rises by ρ and declines by $\alpha\delta$ percent. By the world price schedule (17), the world price rises by δ percent, whereas every one percent rise in the price and corresponding fall in the consumption of good X cause utility loss of α percent. With ρ, α and δ being constant, if condition (20) is not satisfied, utility losses will always dominate the utility gain from any reallocation of the unit time towards schooling. Since schooling implies a loss of household income for any given set of wages, there will thus be no incentive for the worker-parents to send their children for schooling. Thus, condition (20) is necessary for children being sent to school for some positive fraction of time under the trade sanction.

It is immediate from comparing (19) with (12) that for any given relative wage, $Z(\delta) < Z$. That is, a trade sanction lowers the schooling time of children and hence increases the supply of child labour at any given relative wage. The reason is simple. More work for a child now means a fall in the world price of the good since by the productivity effect the child labour content of the good increases. But this means that as a consumer a parent has to pay less for the good and there will thus be utility gains. Thus, trade sanction against child labour content raises the marginal benefit for a parent from sending his child to work for a higher fraction of the time unit, and this raises the supply of child labour. In Figure 1, the supply curve shift to the left and the magnitude of such shift equals, given $\delta = 0$ initially (so that $d\delta = \delta$):[6]

$$dZ = \frac{-\alpha\delta}{(1 + \rho - \alpha\delta)^2}\left[\frac{1}{\mu_X} + 1\right]. \tag{21}$$

[6] Comparing (11) and (17) it is immediate that $\delta = 0$ means no trade sanction, which is the initial situation for our thought experiment.

The trade sanction also shifts the $\mu_X(Z)$ curve. For any given schooling time (Z) and corresponding supply of child labour since our economy displays the properties of the Specific-Factor model a la Jones (1971), the relative wage (μ_X) falls as a consequence of the trade sanction induced decline in the world price:

$$\hat{r} > 0 > \hat{W} > \hat{P}_X^* > \hat{W}_C.$$

By the property of the specific-factor model, for any given Z, the child workers being specific to the export sector loses unambiguously as the world price of exports declines. The capitalists gain unambiguously being specific to the import-competing sector. The return to the adult workers, who are sectorally mobile, however, declines in terms of the import-competing good but rises in terms of the export good. Thus, the $\mu_X(Z)$ curve shifts down as a consequence of the trade sanction.

Alternatively, for any given μ_X, a decline in the world price of exports require a proportionate decline in the child labour content, or more precisely in a_{CX}, to enable the export producers to break-even at the new world price. Thus, the demand for child labour with greater schooling time increases since only that way in this model the producers can lower their unit cost of production. Given the requirement of full employment, this necessitates a decline in the supply of child labour through greater schooling time. Formally, as shown in the appendix, the required increase in Z (and corresponding decline in the supply of child labour) to clear all the domestic markets at the new world price of exports should be equal to:

$$\mathrm{d}Z = \frac{1}{\theta_{CX}}(1 - Z)(1 - Z^{\delta}) > 0. \tag{22}$$

This increase in the schooling time at any given μ_X specifies the (rightward) shift of the $\mu_X(Z)$ curve. Note that this favourable demand effect is small if the initial (or pre-trade sanction) schooling time is high. This is not surprising because if initially children go to school for a longer duration, by the productivity effect they are used less intensively in the export production. Consequently, trade sanction lowers the world price of exports by a smaller margin than when initially children are sent to school for smaller duration of time.

Thus, whereas a trade sanction raises the supply of child labour, it lowers the demand for child labour. The relative wage as a consequence falls unambiguously at the new equilibrium. The change in the incidence of child labour, however, is ambiguous as it depends on the magnitudes of changes in the demand for and supply of child labour (time) and on the decline in the relative wage. More precisely, the (proportional) change in the schooling time at the new equilibrium can be worked out as (see appendix):

$$\hat{Z} = \frac{\lambda_{LY}\dfrac{1}{\theta_{KY}}\sigma_Y}{\left(\lambda_{LY}\dfrac{\theta_{CX}}{\theta_{KY}}\sigma_Y - \lambda_{LX}\right)\varepsilon + \lambda_{LX}\gamma + (\mu_X + 1)} \times \left[\left(1 - Z^{\delta}\right) - \frac{\theta_{CX}(\mu_X + 1)\alpha\delta}{(\rho - \alpha\delta)(1 + \rho - \alpha\delta)}\right]. \tag{23}$$

Since $0 < \left(1 - Z^{\delta}\right) \forall \delta > 0$, so $\hat{Z} < 0$ if,

$$\frac{\theta_{CX}(\mu_X + 1)\alpha\delta}{(\rho - \alpha\delta)(1 + \rho - \alpha\delta)} > 1. \tag{24}$$

Otherwise, for all values of Z at the pre-trade sanction equilibrium higher than $\tilde{Z}$, where $\tilde{Z}$ equals,

$$\tilde{Z} = \left[1 - \frac{\theta_{CX}(\mu_X + 1)\alpha\delta}{(\rho - \alpha\delta)(1 + \rho - \alpha\delta)}\right]^{1/\delta}, \tag{25}$$

a trade sanction against child labour content make children work for a greater fraction of time. $\tilde{Z}$ is the schooling time for which the favourable demand effect and the perverse supply effect of a trade sanction cancel out each other at the margin. Since for high initial Z (i.e., for low incidence of child labour), the demand effect is small (see (22)), for all $Z > \tilde{Z}$, it is outweighed by the perverse supply effect. Therefore,

Proposition 1. *If the parametric configuration satisfies* (24), *a trade sanction against child labour content raises the incidence of child labour. Otherwise, the children spend less time in school for all initial schooling time greater than $\tilde{Z}$ as defined in* (25).

Proof. Follows from the above discussion.

What the above proposition tells us is that a worldwide trade sanction that lowers the world price of the child labour produced goods to the extent defined in (18) may actually raise the incidence of child labour. And, interestingly, this is more likely in an economy where the incidence of child labour is not too high initially. Thus, attempts to influence buyers price offer through additional information provided in a product label regarding the extent to which children have been used in a production process may actually force the children to work more.

4. *Trade sanction and decision of poor* parents

So far we have assumed that the worker-parents decide about allocation of a child's time over schooling and work by maximizing utility of the household. In a sense, there is an altruistic motive on part of the parents in sending their child to school. But even when parents have pecuniary motives to send their children to work, we get similar perverse effect of a trade sanction imposed by our informed buyers. This essentially extends the perverse effect demonstrated by Basu and Zarghamee (2005) to the case of trade sanction against child labour content by the informed buyers.

Let I denote the income level (measured in terms of good Y) of a household that is required for bare subsistence. Following Basu and Van (1998) and Basu and Zarghamee (2005), suppose if the adult wage W is at least equal to this subsistence-income, a child is not sent to work at all. But for all $W < I$, the child is sent to work for hours just sufficient to cover the income shortfall. Thus, the child's work time, $(1-Z)$, varies inversely with the child wage, W_C. Formally, the child labour supply function can be specified as follows:

$$(1-Z) = \begin{cases} 0 \ \forall \ W \geq I \\ \min\left(1, \ \left(\dfrac{I-W}{W_C}\right) \forall \ W < I\right) \end{cases}. \tag{26}$$

Note that since each child is endowed with one unit of time, the work time for each child $(1-Z)$ cannot exceed one. Let $\underline{W}$ denote the adult wage for which the income shortfall, for any given W_C, can be covered only if the child works full time, i.e., $Z = 0$. From (26) it is immediate that this critical adult wage should equal,

$$\underline{W} = I - W_C. \tag{27}$$

Given these specifications, the supply of child labour time is shown in Figure 4 by the upward sloping curve labeled $Z(W)$ in (Z, W)-space with slope equal to $1/W_C$. This curve rotates upward along the wage-axis if the child wage falls, because by (26), for any given $W < I$, the work time for a

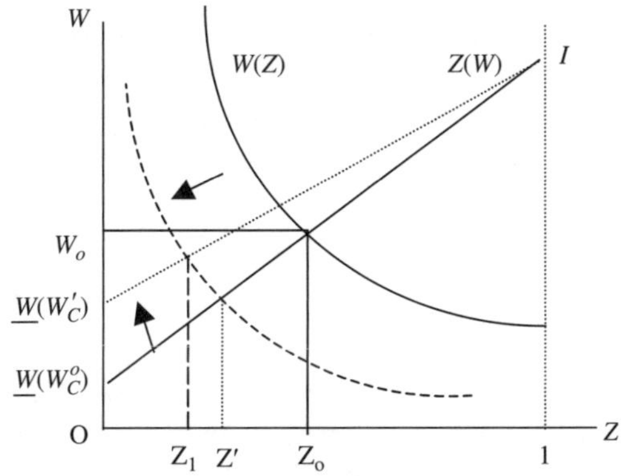

Fig. 4. Subsistence-income and child labour.

child, $(1-Z)$, increases as W_C falls. The downward sloping curve labeled $W(Z)$, however, is the locus of different combinations of the adult wage and the supply of child labour time for which the domestic markets clear. The negative slope of this curve follows from (14) under the assumption that the endowment effect of an increase in schooling time (or decrease in work time), γ, is larger than its productivity effect, ε. Let the pre-trade sanction equilibrium allocation be Z_o corresponding to the intersection point of the bold $Z(W)$ and $W(Z)$ curves.

As we have spelled out earlier, for any given Z, a trade sanction lowers both the adult and child wage by the price-magnification effect. Parents, therefore, make their children work longer to compensate for the loss of household income. In Figure 4, the $W(Z)$ curve shifts down whereas the $Z(W)$ curve rotates upward thereby lowering Z from Z_o to Z_1. This increase in child labour time in turn affects the wages. As spelled out earlier, on the assumption that the consequent supply (or endowment) effect is stronger than the productivity effect, the adult wage rises (which is the movement up along the broken $W(Z)$ curve to the new equilibrium in Figure 4) and the child wage falls. The latter moderates the initial decline in child wage and thus the parent's incentive for sending him to work for longer fraction of time to some extent.

5. *Conclusion*

This chapter establishes that a trade sanction against child labour content of a good exported by a developing country may induce the parents, even if they are altruist, to send their children to work for a larger fraction of time. This perverse effect of trade sanctions by the informed buyers works through a fall in the marginal benefit for a parent of an additional time spent in the school by a child relative to that of an additional fraction of work time.

Thus, if the product labels, which have already been used in the developed countries to distinguish products produced by child labour, contain more information regarding the extent to which child labour has been used in a product to further influence the buyers' choice, it may not help the cause.

Acknowledgements

Earlier versions of this chapter have been presented at the conference on Disparity and Development organized by the Department of Economics, University of Calcutta, and seminars at the Centre for Studies in Social Science, Calcutta, and Department of Economics, University of Kent at Canterbury. I wish to thank Sugata Marjit, Kalyan K. Sanyal, Mathan

Satchi and other participants for helpful comments. The usual disclaimer applies, however.

Appendix

I. Slope of the $\mu_X(Z)$ curve

From the full employment conditions (8)–(10) in the text, following equations of change can be obtained:

$$\hat{K} = 0 = \hat{a}_{KY} + \hat{Y}, \tag{A.1}$$

$$\hat{L} = 0 = \lambda_{LY}(\hat{a}_{LY} + \hat{Y}) + \lambda_{LX}\hat{X} \quad \text{and} \tag{A.2}$$

$$\hat{C} \equiv \hat{n} - \gamma\hat{Z} = -\varepsilon\hat{Z} + \hat{X}. \tag{A.3}$$

Given the total number children, n, substitution of values for $\hat{X}$ and $\hat{Y}$ from (A.1) and (A.2) in (A.3) yields,

$$\lambda_{LY}(\hat{a}_{LY} - \hat{a}_{SY}) - \lambda_{LX}(\gamma - \varepsilon)\hat{Z} = 0.$$

Defining the factor substitution elasticity in the import-competing sectors as

$$\sigma_Y = \frac{\hat{a}_{LY} - \hat{a}_{SY}}{\hat{W}_S - \hat{W}},$$

the above expression boils down to:

$$\lambda_{LY}\sigma_Y(\hat{r} - \hat{W}) - \lambda_{LX}(\gamma - \varepsilon)\hat{Z} = 0. \tag{A.4}$$

However, from the zero-profit conditions, we obtain:

$$\hat{W}_C = \frac{1}{\theta_{CX}}\hat{P}_X^* + \varepsilon\hat{Z} - \frac{\theta_{LX}}{\theta_{CX}}\hat{W} \quad \text{and} \tag{A.5}$$

$$\hat{r} = -\frac{\theta_{LY}}{\theta_{KY}}\hat{W}. \tag{A.6}$$

Substitution of (A.6) in (A.4) yields the change in the adult unskilled wage as stated in Equation (14) in the text,

$$\hat{W} = -\frac{\lambda_{LX}(\gamma - \varepsilon)}{\lambda_{LY}\sigma_Y(1/\theta_{KY})}\hat{Z}.$$

Hence, the change in child wage equals:

$$\hat{W}_C = \frac{1}{\theta_{CX}}\hat{P}_X^* + \left[\varepsilon + \frac{\theta_{LX}}{\theta_{CX}}\frac{\lambda_{LX}(\gamma - \varepsilon)}{\lambda_{LY}\sigma_Y(1/\theta_{KY})}\right]\hat{Z}. \tag{A.7}$$

For no change in the world price of good X (the pre-sanction case), this boils down to the expression in Equation (15) in the text. Finally, using the definition of the relative wage we arrive at,

$$\hat{\mu}_X = \frac{1}{\theta_{CX}}\hat{P}_X^* + \frac{(\lambda_{LY}(\theta_{CX}/\theta_{KY})\sigma_Y - \lambda_{LX})\varepsilon + \lambda_{LX}\gamma}{\lambda_{LY}(\theta_{CX}/\theta_{KY})\sigma_Y}\hat{Z}. \tag{A.8}$$

Thus, as stated in the text, the $\mu_X(Z)$ curve slopes upward under the parametric configuration specified in (14).

II. Perverse effect of trade sanction

For any given wages, the change in Z necessitated to make the export producers break-even after the trade sanction can be obtained from (A.5) as

$$\hat{Z} = -\frac{1}{\theta_{CX}\varepsilon}\hat{P}_X^* = \frac{1}{\theta_{CX}\varepsilon}(1 - Z^{\delta}). \tag{A.9}$$

The consequent change in demand for child labour then equals:

$$\hat{C}^d = -\varepsilon\hat{Z} + \hat{X}.$$

But, given the specific-factor production structure, since output levels cannot change without changes in wages, by (A.9) this boils down to

$$\hat{C}^d = -\frac{1}{\theta_{CX}}(1 - Z^{\delta}) < 0.$$

Since the supply of child labour should decline proportionately to clear the market, and for any given number of children, n, supply of child labour declines when Z increases, so the required change in Z to clear the market at the same wages after the trade sanction is given as,

$$\hat{C} \equiv -\gamma\hat{Z} = -\frac{1}{\theta_{CX}}(1 - Z^{\delta})$$

$$\text{i.e.,}\quad dZ = \frac{1}{\theta_{CX}}(1 - Z)(1 - Z^{\delta}) > 0.$$

This is the magnitude of the shift in the $\mu_X(Z)$ curve as specified in the text.

The change in the incidence of child labour, however, can be arrived at only after taking into account the change in relative wage. Total differentiation of the relationship between parental allocation of a child's time to schooling and the relative wage as specified in (19), with $d\delta = \delta$ because initially $\delta = 0$, yields,

$$\hat{Z} = -\frac{1}{(\mu_X + 1)}\hat{\mu}_X - \frac{\alpha\delta}{(\rho - \alpha\delta)(1 + \rho - \alpha\delta)}. \tag{A.10}$$

Equations (A.8) and (A.10) constitute the equation system which simultaneously solve for the change in relative wage and the schooling time as:

$$\hat{\mu}_X = -\frac{(\mu_X + 1)}{D + \theta_{CX}(\mu_X + 1)}\left[\left(1 - Z^{\delta}\right) + \frac{D\alpha\delta}{(\rho - \alpha\delta)(1 + \rho - \alpha\delta)}\right] \quad \text{and}$$

$$\hat{Z} = \frac{\lambda_{LY}\dfrac{1}{\theta_{KY}}\sigma_Y}{D + (\mu_X + 1)}\left[\left(1 - Z^{\delta}\right) - \frac{\theta_{CX}(\mu_X + 1)\alpha\delta}{(\rho - \alpha\delta)(1 + \rho - \alpha\delta)}\right],$$

where $D \equiv \left(\lambda_{LY}\dfrac{\theta_{CX}}{\theta_{KY}}\sigma_Y - \lambda_{LX}\right)\varepsilon + \lambda_{LX}\gamma$.

References

Basu, K. (2004). Child labour and the law. Notes on possible pathologies. Discussion Paper # 2052, Harvard Institute of Economic Research, Harvard University, Cambridge, MA.

Basu, K., Van, P.H. (1998), The economics of child labour. *American Economic Review* 88, 412–427.

Basu, K., Zarghamee, H. (2005). Is product boycott a good idea for controlling child labour? Mimeo, Cornell University.

Basu, A., Chau, N.H., Grote, U. (2006), Guaranteed manufactured without child labour: the economics of consumer boycotts, social labeling and trade sanctions. *Review of Development Economics* 10 (3), 466–491.

Chiu, W.H. (1998), Income inequality, human capital accumulation, and economic performance. *Economic Journal* 108, 44–59.

Davies, R.B. (2005), Abstinence from child labour and profit seeking. *Journal of Development Economics* 76, 251–263.

Edmonds, E.V. (2003), Should we boycott child labour? *Ethics and Economics* 1 (December).

Edmonds, E.V. (2005), Does child labour decline with improvements in economic status? *Journal of Human Resources* 40 (1), 77–99.

Edmonds, E.V., Pavcnik, N. (2005a), The effect of trade liberalization on child labour. *Journal of International Economics* 65, 401–419.

Edmonds, E.V., Pavcnik, N. (2005b), Child labour in the global economy. *Journal of Economic Perspectives* 18, 199–220.

Galor, O., Zeira, J. (1993), Income distribution and macroeconomics. *Review of Economic Studies* 60 (1), 35–52.

Grootaert, C., Patrinos, H. (1999), *The Policy Analysis of Child Labour*. St. Martin's Press, New York.

Human Rights Watch. (1996). The small hands of slavery: bonded child labour in India. Human Rights Watch Children's Rights Project.

Jafarey, S., Lahiri, S. (2002), Will trade sanctions reduce child labour? The role of credit markets. *Journal of Development Economics* 68, 137–156.

Ranjan, P. (2001), Credit constraints and the phenomenon of child labour. *Journal of Development Economics* 68, 81–102.

CHAPTER 15

Public Inputs, Urban Development, and Welfare in a Developing Economy

Chi-Chur Chao[a], Jean-Pierre Laffargue[b] and Eden S.H. Yu[c]

[a]*Department of Economics, Chinese University of Hong Kong, 9/F, Esther Lee Building, Chung Chi Campus, Shatin, Hong Kong*
E-mail address: ccchao@cuhk.edu.hk
[b]*University of Paris I (Pantheon-Sorbonne) and CEPREMAP, 48 Boulevard Jourdan, 750143 Paris, France*
E-mail address: jean-pierre.laffargue@orange.fr
[c]*Department of Economics and Finance, City University of Hong Kong, 83 Tat Chee Avenue, Kowloon Tong, Hong Kong*
E-mail address: efedenyu@cityu.edu.hk

Abstract
This chapter examines the impact of urban development through the government provision of public inputs in a developing economy. When a financing constraint is taken into account, an increase in public inputs may worsen urban unemployment and hence reduce welfare of the economy. Further, the optimal level of public-input provision is larger (smaller) than that under full employment, if there exits a positive (negative) employment effect. The theoretical results are confirmed by numerical simulations.

Keywords: Public input, urban development, employment effect

JEL classifications: F11, O18

1. Introduction

Public investment in infrastructure, education, technical and vocational trainings, health facilities, and R&D can be a key factor in generating and promoting economic growth. Due to their public-goods attributes, most of these activities are provided or financed by governments, especially in developing countries. The ramifications of investment in public inputs have been examined in the literature. Barro (1991) delineates two types of government spending, consumption expenditure vs. productive spending,

Frontiers of Economics and Globalization
Volume 4 ISSN: 1574-8715
DOI: 10.1016/S1574-8715(08)04015-3

with opposite effects on the economy.[1] Similarly, Krueger and Orsmond (1993, Chapter 14), consider two kinds of government activities: growth promoting by investing in infrastructure, etc., vs. wasteful spending due to political and bureaucratic motives. It is customarily assumed that financing of public inputs is carried out by lump-sum taxation,[2] while in reality the financing can come from various types of taxes that can result in distortions in an economy.[3]

Despite increasing trade liberalization, virtually all countries have imposed trade barriers, such as import quotas and tariffs, for the purpose of generating government revenue as well as for protecting domestic import-competing industries. For developing nations in particular, trade taxes constitute a main source of government revenue.[4] A standard assumption in the literature is that revenue from trade taxes is completely redistributed to consumers in the form of lump-sum transfers. However, in the present chapter we shall consider a case that the government will appropriate a certain portion of revenue from trade taxes for the provision of public inputs. Consequently, any change in expenditures on public inputs will alter, dollar for dollar, revenues available for consumers, thereby affecting the demand side of the economy besides its direct effect on the supply side. This will trigger further repercussions on domestic goods prices, urban employment, and national welfare.

This chapter considers a dual developing economy characterized by a high-wage urban area co-existing with a low-wage rural area. The interregional wage differential leads to rural–urban migration, and the institutionally set high rigid wage causes unemployment in the urban sector. This is the well-known Harris–Todaro economy, which has been validated in a work by Todaro (1976) for developing nations and studies by Suits (1985) and Partridge and Rickman (1997) for a developed economy, USA. We maintain the key assumptions of the Harris–Todaro (1970) model but extend it by introducing government attempts to aid the urban sector in the form of providing public inputs. When the financing constraint of public inputs is taken into account, however, urban development through public investment may worsen the problem of urban unemployment and as a result, reduce welfare in the economy. What is

---

[1] Krueger and Orsmond (1993) also provide an empirical estimation on direct and indirect government effects on per capita output growth in 26 nations. See also the citations there.

[2] See Chambers and Lopez (1993) for an example.

[3] The marginal deadweight loss of taxation in the United States estimated by Fullerton (1991) is \$0.24 per dollar of tax revenue raised.

[4] Feehan (1992) reports that more than 60 developing countries raised at least 20% of their tax revenues from trade duties in 1987. Vanek (1971), Boadway *et al.* (1973), and Feehan (1992) suggest that trade taxes may be a main source of financing public goods in developing countries. Choi and Lapan (1991) adopt this financing constraint in examining optimal trade policies for developing nations.

then the optimal level of provision of public inputs for a dual economy? This chapter examines this issue.

The remainder of the chapter is structured as follows. A two-region general-equilibrium framework depicting the dual economy with public-input provision in the urban sector is developed in Section 2. Some comparative static results regarding the direct and the indirect effects of public inputs are worked out in Section 3. While the price and the employment impacts of a change in public inputs are examined in Section 4, the welfare implications are explored in Section 5. Section 6 provides simulations of the model and Section 7 contains some concluding remarks.

2. *Public inputs in a dual economy*

At the outset, we develop a general-equilibrium, dual-economy framework based on Harris and Todaro (1970), incorporating public inputs, such as infrastructure, technical and vocational training, or R&D.[5] The production side of the economy consists of two activities: agriculture (X_1), which takes place in the rural area, and manufacturing (X_2), which is found in the urban area. The primary factors, labor (L) and capital (K), are used to produce X_1 and X_2 with constant returns to scale technologies; each factor exhibits positive but diminishing marginal productivity. A novel feature of the present model is that the output of X_2 in the urban region depends upon the level of public inputs in addition to the use of the two factors. Thus, the production functions can be expressed as

$$X_1 = F_1(L_1,\ K_1), \tag{1}$$

$$X_2 = g(R)F_2(L_2,\ K_2), \tag{2}$$

where L_i and K_i denote the ith sector's employment of labor and capital, $i = 1, 2$, and R is the level of public inputs.[6] It is noticed that F_i represents the "kernel" production function and is homogenous of degree one in factors. The variations of technology for X_2 are described by a function, g, which is strictly concave in R. The impact of public inputs available in the urban region on the manufacturing output can be captured by the output elasticity:

$$e = \left(\frac{\mathrm{d}g}{\mathrm{d}R}\right)\left(\frac{R}{g}\right) > 0. \tag{3}$$

It is noticed that the traditional case prevails when $g(R) = 1$. The assumption that public inputs are available only in the urban region is because the productivity of public inputs is higher in urban manufacturing.

---

[5] For a simple interregional wage differential model, see Yu (1979) and Beladi and Ingene (1994). For recent studies on the Harris and Todaro (1970) model, see Khan (1982), Beladi (1988), Feldmann (1989), Chao and Yu (1990, 1994), and Hazari and Sgro (1991).

[6] See Abe (1990) for an exposition on the modeling of public inputs.

It is commonly observed that indigenous equipment, skill, and technology available in most developing countries characterized by a dual economy are not mature enough for carrying out public-input production. We thus assume that the production of them is conducted by utilizing mainly foreign equipment, skill or technology, K^*, in addition to domestic labor, L_3, in the urban area. It is assumed that there is a single activity for producing public inputs and its production function is

$$R = R(L_3,\ K^*), \tag{4}$$

where the return to K^*, denoted by r^*, is exogenously given in the world market. It is further assumed that one unit of K^*, along with one unit of L_3, is utilized to "produce" one unit of R. Thus, the public expenditures can be expressed by $(w_2+r^*)R$, where w_2 represents the wage rate paid to urban workers.

We assume that the dual developing economy exports agricultural product X_1 and imports manufacturing good X_2. There are no restrictions on the trade of the exportable product. However, the economy imposes quotas (Q) on the imports of manufacturing.[7] Let p be the domestic price of the manufacturing good (in terms of the agricultural product) and p^* be its world price. The imposition of quotas raises the domestic manufacturing price so that $p>p^*$, and hence quota rents collected by the government is $(p–p^*)Q$. The government appropriates a certain percentage of quota rents, say k, to finance the provision of public inputs. The financing constraint relating public-input expenditure to government revenue is expressed by

$$(w_2 + r^*)R = k(p - p^*)Q, \tag{5}$$

where $0<k<1$.[8]

Consider now the equilibrium condition for the labor market. Rural–urban migration occurs when the rural wage rate, w_1, differs from the expected urban wage rate, which is the product of the institutionally set urban wage rate w_2 and the probability of employment in the urban area. Restoration of the labor market equilibrium requires the following condition:

$$w_2 = w_1(1 + \lambda), \tag{6}$$

where λ [$= L_u/(L_2+L_3)$] is the urban unemployment ratio and $1/(1+\lambda)$ serves as an index for the probability of finding an urban job. Here, L_u represents the level of urban unemployment.

---

[7] We consider quotas on imports in this study, because the price-induced effect of public inputs can be obtained when protection exists in the form of non-tariff barriers. In addition, quotas rather tariffs have become the more important trade barriers in recent years.

[8] Other sources for funding public inputs are income tax, sales tax and tariff revenue, which are not considered in this chapter. The share of the quota rent, which is not spent on the provision of public inputs is distributed as a lump-sum transfer to households or may be grabbed by corrupted bureaucrats.

Assuming perfect competition, labor and capital in both rural and urban areas are paid according to the value of the marginal product:

$$w_1 = \frac{\partial X_1}{\partial L_1}, \tag{7}$$

$$w_2 = p\left(\frac{\partial X_2}{\partial L_2}\right), \tag{8}$$

$$r = \frac{\partial X_1}{\partial K_1} = p\left(\frac{\partial X_2}{\partial K_2}\right), \tag{9}$$

where r denotes the rental rate of domestic capital in both rural and urban regions.

It is enlightening to describe the productions in two regions by using the unit cost functions. The unit cost function for the rural agriculture is $C^1(w_1, r)$, while the unit cost function for the urban manufacturing is expressed as[9]

$$C^2(w_2, r, R) = \frac{\tilde{C}^2(w_2, r)}{g(R)}, \tag{10}$$

which depends on R. The cost functions are quasi-concave and homogenous of degree one in factor prices. By Shephard's lemma, the labor and capital demand in sector i are $L_i C^i_w X_i$ and $K_i = C^i_r X_i$, respectively, where the subscript in the unit cost function denotes the partial derivative.

Equations (11) and (12) below show that in competitive equilibrium, unit cost in each sector equals its output price. Denoting the endowments of labor and capital by L and K, the employment conditions of labor and capital are presented in (13) and (14). Equation (15) is the demand for foreign capital based on a one-to-one fixed-coefficient production function of R:

$$C^1(w_1, r) = 1, \tag{11}$$

$$C^2(w_2, r, R) = p, \tag{12}$$

$$C^1_w(w_1, r)X_1 + (1+\lambda)[C^2_w(w_2, r, R)X_2 + R] = L, \tag{13}$$

$$C^1_r(w_1, r)X_1 + C^2_r(w_2, r, R)X_2 = K, \tag{14}$$

$$K^* = R. \tag{15}$$

[9] See Abe (1990) for a related discussion.

The supply side of the dual economy can be described by (5), (6), and (11) through (15). There are seven equations encompassing seven endogenous variables: w_1, r, λ, X_1, X_2, K^*, and k, with one policy variable R and a parameter w_2. By treating the domestic goods price p as given, we can solve for the endogenous variables in terms of the public-input provision R. Note that p will be determined later in a complete model, consisting of the above supply-side information coupled with the demand-side conditions.

3. *Effects of public inputs*

To set the stage for our analysis, we carry out some comparative statics exercises. To gain insight concerning the role played by the domestic goods price, it is useful to separate the total effect of changes in public inputs into two partial effects: the direct effect evaluated at a constant goods price and the indirect price-induced effect. Thus, for example, the effect of changes in public inputs on the urban unemployment ratio can be expressed as

$$\lambda = \lambda(R,\ p). \tag{16}$$

Since p can be solved as a function of R (shown below), (16) can be written as[10]

$$\lambda = \lambda(R(p),\ p). \tag{17}$$

Differentiating (17) with respect to R yields

$$\frac{\mathrm{d}\lambda}{\mathrm{d}R} = \frac{\partial\lambda}{\partial R} + \left(\frac{\partial\lambda}{\partial p}\right)\left(\frac{\mathrm{d}p}{\mathrm{d}R}\right). \tag{18}$$

The first term on the right-hand side of (18) captures the direct effect of public inputs on the urban unemployment ratio with a constant goods price, while the second term shows the price-induced effect of changes in public inputs.

The partial derivatives in (18) can be solved by differentiating (6) and (11) through (15). Letting "^" over the variable denote the percentage change, the results of changes in p or R on the endogenous variables are summarized as follows (see Appendix):

$$\hat{w}_1/\hat{p}<0,\ \hat{\lambda}/\hat{p}>0,\ \hat{r}/\hat{p}>0,\ \hat{X}_1/\hat{p}<0,\ \hat{X}_2/\hat{p}>0,$$
$$\hat{w}_1/\hat{R}<0,\ \hat{\lambda}/\hat{R}>0,\ \hat{r}/\hat{R}>0,\ \hat{X}_1/\hat{R}<0,\ \hat{X}_2/\hat{R}>0. \tag{19}$$

By imposing the stability conditions that X_2 is capital-intensive relative to X_1, the output responses to the goods price in (19) are normal

[10] This decomposition technique is well known in the trade literature; see, for example, Batra and Scully (1971).

($\hat{X}_1/\hat{p}<0$ and $\hat{X}_2/\hat{p}>0$). It is noteworthy that $\hat{\lambda}/\hat{p}>0$, indicating that a higher manufacturing price results in a larger urban unemployment ratio. There is an explanation for this somewhat surprising result. Consistent with the Stolper–Samuelson result, an increase in p raises the urban rental rate ($\hat{r}/\hat{p}>0$), inducing capital to move out of the rural into the urban area. The capital outflow causes a rise in the rural capital productivity and a concomitant drop in the labor productivity, thereby triggering a fall in w_1. The resulting widening in the interregional wage differential induces workers to migrate from rural to urban areas. Given that w_2 is set institutionally, to maintain equilibrium in the labor market, a fall in w_1 implies a rise in λ.[11] The direct effects of changes in public inputs are similar to those of the domestic goods price. An increase in R lowers the unit cost for urban manufacturing. At given w_2 and p, the rental rate r must rise to maintain zero profits for urban manufacturing (i.e., $\hat{r}/\hat{R}>0$). Hence, the reasoning for the effects of changes in p as stated in (19) can then be applied to the present case of R. It may be noted that $\hat{X}_1/\hat{R}<0$ and $\hat{X}_2/\hat{R}>0$ $\hat{X}_2/\hat{R}$ are reminiscent of the ultra-biased output effect of technical progress.

4. Public inputs, goods prices, and urban unemployment

To determine the impact of public inputs on the domestic goods price, we need to specify the demand-side model, which can be represented by an expenditure function:

$$E(p,\ u) = \min\ \{C_1 + pC_2\}, \tag{20}$$

by minimizing the value of the consumption of the two final goods, C_1 and C_2, subject to a strictly quasi-concave utility function $U(C_1,\ C_2) = u$. The economy's budget constraint is thus given by

$$\begin{aligned} E(p,\ u) &= X_1 + pX_2 + [(w_2 + r^*)R - r^*K^*] + (1-k)(p-p^*)Q \\ &= X_1 + pX_2 + w_2L_3 + (1-k)(p-p^*)Q, \end{aligned} \tag{21}$$

where $p>p^*$ due to the quota restriction. The first three terms on the right side of (21) are equivalent to the income paid to the domestic labor and capital for their production, and the last term is the quota rents distributed to consumers.[12] Equation (21) simply states that consumer expenditures equal their total income. Let us turn to the goods-market equilibrium condition, which requires that the demand for good X_2 equals the domestic production of X_2 plus the imports Q:

---

[11] Equivalently, $E(p, u) = w_1L_1 + w_2(L_2 + L_3) + r(K_1 + K_2) + (1-k)(p-p^*)Q$.

[12] This can be seen by noting that the return to capital in manufacturing is $r_2 = r_2(R, p)$. The change in r_2 due to a change in R is $(R/r_2)(\mathrm{d}r_2/\mathrm{d}R) = (e + \hat{p}/\hat{R})/\theta_{K_2}$, which is negative if $-\hat{p}/\hat{R}>e$.

$$E_p(p,\ u) = X_2 + Q, \tag{22}$$

where, by Shephard's lemma, $E_p\ (= \partial E(p, u)/\partial p) = C_2$.

We can now solve for the impacts of public inputs on the domestic goods price p. Totally differentiating the budget constraint in (21), and then utilizing the goods–market equilibrium in (22) gives:

$$E_u \mathrm{d}u = \mathrm{d}X_1 + p\mathrm{d}X_2 + w_2\mathrm{d}L_3 - kQ\mathrm{d}p - (p - p^*)Q\mathrm{d}k \tag{23}$$

where $E_u\ (= \partial E/\partial u) > 0$, being the inverse of marginal utility of income. The first three terms on the right-hand side of (23) can be further simplified. Differentiating (1), (2), (6), and (13), and combining the results yields

$$\mathrm{d}X_1 + p\mathrm{d}X_2 + w_2\mathrm{d}L_3 = ve\mathrm{d}R - w_1(L_2 + L_3)\mathrm{d}\lambda, \tag{24}$$

where $v = pX_2/R$ denotes the value ratio of the manufacturing good to public inputs, and e, as defined in (3), captures the spillover effect of public inputs on urban manufacturing.

Differentiating next the government financing constraint in (5), we have

$$kQ\mathrm{d}p + (p - p^*)Q\mathrm{d}k = (w_2 + r^*)\mathrm{d}R. \tag{25}$$

Apparently, changes in the expenses of public inputs can be attributed to changes in either p and/or k. Note that from (25), we have $\partial k/\partial p = -k/(p{-}p^*) < 0$ and $\partial k/\partial R = (w_2 + r^*)/Q(p{-}p^*) > 0$. An increase in the urban manufacturing price reduces the appropriation ratio for financing public inputs, while an increase in public-input expenditure raises the ratio. By utilizing (24) and (25), we can rewrite (23) as

$$E_u \mathrm{d}u = (ve - w_2 - r^*)\mathrm{d}R - w_1(L_2 + L_3)\mathrm{d}\lambda. \tag{26}$$

Recalling (18), λ is a function of R and p, and $\mathrm{d}\lambda = (\partial\lambda/\partial R)\mathrm{d}R + (\partial\lambda/\partial p)\mathrm{d}p$ with $\partial\lambda/\partial R > 0$ and $\partial\lambda/\partial p > 0$ as shown in (19).

Next, totally differentiating (22) yields

$$E_{pu}\mathrm{d}u - (c + s)(Q/p)\mathrm{d}p = (\partial X_2/\partial R)\mathrm{d}R, \tag{27}$$

where $E_{pu}\ (= \partial E_p/\partial u) = \partial C_2/\partial u > 0$. Note that $c = -(p/Q)(\partial E_p/\partial p) > 0$ describes the consumption substitution for a given utility in response to a change in p, and $s = (p/Q)(\partial X_2/\partial p) > 0$ represents the substitution in production of good X_2 in response to p. Here, from (19), $\partial X_2/\partial R > 0$.

Using (26) and (27), the effect of public inputs on the domestic price of urban manufacturing can be obtained as

$$\frac{\mathrm{d}p}{\mathrm{d}R} = \frac{\{-p(\partial X_2/\partial R) + m[(ve - w_2 - r^*) - w_1(L_2 + L_3)(\partial\lambda/\partial R)]\}}{\Delta}, \tag{28}$$

where $m = pE_{pu}/E_u$ and $\Delta = Q(c + s) + mw_1(L_2 + L_3)(\partial\lambda/\partial p)$. Since the expenditure function $E(p, u)$ is homogeneous of degree one in goods prices, m expresses the marginal propensity to consume X_2 and lies in (0, 1), assuming that both goods are normal. Since $\partial\lambda/\partial p > 0$ in (19), we have $\Delta > 0$. The numerator of (28) consists of two parts. The first part denotes the price effect of the supply response to public inputs; the increase in public inputs raises the domestic supply, thereby exerting a negative pressure on the relative goods price of X_2. The second part represents the price effect of the demand response to public inputs through the marginal propensity to consume X_2. We can obtain the direct income effect by differentiating $I = X_1 + pX_2 + w_2L_3 + (1-k)(p-p^*)Q$ with respect to R: $\partial I/\partial R = (ve-w_2-r^*) - w_1(L_2 + L_3)(\partial\lambda/\partial R)$. The sign of $\partial I/\partial R$ is therefore ambiguous. Although the demand response to public inputs is indeterminate, the overall effect is definite. This can be seen by simplifying (28) as

$$\frac{\mathrm{d}p}{\mathrm{d}R} = \frac{-\{v(\hat{X}_2/\hat{R} - em) + m[w_2 + r^* + w_1(L_2 + L_3)(\partial\lambda/\partial R)]\}}{\Delta}, \tag{29}$$

where, as shown in the Appendix, $\hat{X}_2/\hat{R} > e$. Given $m < 1$ and $\hat{X}_2/\hat{R} > em$, thus $\mathrm{d}p/\mathrm{d}R < 0$. Stated in words, for the dual economy, an increase in public inputs in the urban area always lowers the relative price of the manufacturing good.

The present model allows for the existence of urban unemployment. The effect of public inputs on the urban unemployment ratio can be easily deduced. Recalling (18),

$$\frac{\mathrm{d}\lambda}{\mathrm{d}R} = \frac{\partial\lambda}{\partial R} + \left(\frac{\partial\lambda}{\partial p}\right)\left(\frac{\mathrm{d}p}{\mathrm{d}R}\right), \tag{30}$$

where $\partial\lambda/\partial R > 0$, $\partial\lambda/\partial p > 0$ and $\mathrm{d}p/\mathrm{d}R < 0$. It is clear from (18) and (29) that $\mathrm{d}\lambda/\mathrm{d}R < (>)\ 0$ according to $-\hat{p}/\hat{R} > (<) e$. Thus, we may state the following proposition:

PROPOSITION 1. *For the dual economy, an increase in public inputs in the urban areas results in a lower (higher) urban unemployment ratio, if the price elasticity of public inputs dominates (is outweighed by) the output elasticity.*

The rationale for this proposition is as follows. If urban development through the government provision of public inputs substantially lowers p, the return to capital in manufacturing falls.[13] As a result, capital moves out from the urban to the rural areas, thereby raising the rural wage rate. This discourages migration from the rural to the urban areas, and hence the urban unemployment ratio declines. It is also clear from the labor market equilibrium condition in (6) that a rise in w_1 necessarily implies a drop in λ.

[13] The constraints that $p > p^*$, $X_1 > C_1$ and $C_2 > X_2$ are satisfied. The stability condition (given in the Appendix) is also satisfied, i.e., $K_2/K - [(L_2 + L_3 + Lu)/L]\{[L_2 + (K_2/K)L_3]/(L_2 + L_3)\} = 0.1884 > 0$.

5. Urban development and national welfare

We are now ready to examine the welfare effect of urban development on domestic welfare. Denoting the change in welfare by $\mathrm{d}W = E_u \mathrm{d}u$, (26) can be used to identify the welfare consequence of an increase in public inputs:

$$\frac{\mathrm{d}W}{\mathrm{d}R} = (ve - w_2 - r^*) - w_1(L_2 + L_3)\left(\frac{\mathrm{d}\lambda}{\mathrm{d}R}\right). \tag{31}$$

Consider first the full-employment economy (i.e., $\lambda = 0$ and hence $\mathrm{d}\lambda/\mathrm{d}R = 0$), a special case of the present model. Then (31) reduces to

$$\frac{\mathrm{d}W}{\mathrm{d}R} = ve - (w_2 + r^*), \tag{32}$$

which shows the first-order welfare effect of urban development. Note that ve is the marginal gain from each additional unit of R and $w_2 + r^*$ the marginal cost of an additional unit of R, as the quota rents available for consumers must be reduced by this amount. It is clear that urban development through the provision of public inputs will improve welfare if $ve > w_2 + r^*$. Conversely, urban development will reduce welfare if $ve < w_2 + r^*$.

When the financing constraint of public inputs is taken into account, urban development through public inputs can actually reduce welfare for the dual economy, which is simply a special case of the framework. Of course, for a very small level of public inputs, i.e., $R \to 0$ and $v \to \infty$, the society will always benefit from urban development. Thus, urban development through public inputs can reduce welfare for the dual economy. The intuition behind this is straightforward. The financing of public inputs competes for the limited resources of an economy. Consider a hypothetical case in which all resources are put into public inputs so that no resources are available to produce goods. As a result, national income declines to zero. Thus, public inputs can be "excessive" and become socially suboptimal, regardless of whether unemployment exists or not in the economy.

In the present model, public inputs generate a second-order effect on welfare via the induced shift between urban employment and unemployment. The second term on the right-hand side of (31) indicates such an employment effect. As can be seen from (30), the employment effect may display any sign. If $\mathrm{d}\lambda/\mathrm{d}R < 0$, the induced employment effect either reinforces the first-order welfare gain or mitigate the welfare loss. Conversely, if $\mathrm{d}\lambda/\mathrm{d}R > 0$, the induced unemployment effect either offsets the direct welfare gain or worsens the welfare loss. So, we may state the following proposition:

PROPOSITION 2. *Urban development through the government provision of public inputs can reduce welfare for a small dual economy with or without full employment.*

Bhagwati (1971) shows that growth in the presence of a distortion can reduce welfare of a small economy. Khan (1982) argues that growth cannot be immiserizing despite the presence of the dual distortions of a Harris–Todaro economy. Our result obtained in a framework of the Harris–Todaro economy with public inputs shows that urban development can still reduce welfare once the financing aspect is taken into consideration.

What then is the optimal level of public inputs? Setting (31) equal to zero, we obtain:

$$ve = w_2 + r^* + w_1(L_2 + L_3)\left(\frac{d\lambda}{dR}\right), \tag{33}$$

which implicitly defines the optimal level. The intuition for (33) is simple. The level of public inputs is optimal when the direct marginal gain (cost) of public inputs is exactly offset by the marginal loss (gain). Note that if the economy is under full employment ($d\lambda/dR = 0$), the optimal level of public inputs is determined when $ve = w_2 + r^*$. However, when urban unemployment exists, the optimal level of public inputs is identified by: $ve = w_2 + r^* + w_1(L_2 + L_3)(d\lambda/dR)$. Given the concavity of the spillover function $g(R)$, the optimal level of public inputs is larger (smaller) if $d\lambda/dR < (>)\ 0$. We have the following proposition:

PROPOSITION 3. *In a dual economy suffering from urban unemployment, the optimal level of public inputs is larger (smaller) than that under full employment, if there exists a positive (negative) employment effect.*

6. Simulations

Based on the above theoretical model, we calibrate in this section the results of the various effects of public inputs on the dual economy. For purpose of calibrations, the key equations in the model are rewritten in specific functional forms.

6.1. Specifications

The production functions of the agricultural and the manufacturing good, X_1 and X_2, are assumed to exhibit the Cobb–Douglas form:

$$X_1 = AL_1^{\alpha}K_1^{1-\alpha}, \tag{34}$$

$$X_2 = BL_2^{\beta}K_2^{1-\beta}R^e, \tag{35}$$

where $0 < \alpha < 1$ and $0 < \beta < 1$, and A and B are the technology parameters. In addition, the production function of public inputs R is expressed in a Leontief form:

$$R = \min\ \{L_3, K^*\}. \tag{36}$$

Total employments of labor and domestic capital in the economy are respectively: $L - L_u = L_1 + L_2 + L_3$ and $K = K_1 + K_2$. Given the goods price, wage rates and capital rentals, profit maximization yields the equilibrium allocation of labor and demand for capital:

$$w_1 = aX_1/L_1, \tag{37}$$

$$w_2 = p\beta X_2/L_2, \tag{38}$$

$$r = (1-\alpha)X_1/K_1 = p(1-\beta)X_2/K_2. \tag{39}$$

The equilibrium condition on the labor market is: $\lambda = w_2/w_1 - 1$, and hence $L_u = \lambda(L_2 + L_3)$.

On the demand side of the economy, we assume a Cobb–Douglas utility function:

$$U(C_1,\ C_2) = C_1^{\gamma} C_2^{1-\gamma} \tag{40}$$

where $0 < \gamma < 1$. Utility maximization gives the following demand relation between agricultural and manufacturing goods:

$$C_1 = p\gamma C_2/(1-\gamma). \tag{41}$$

The market-clearing condition for the manufacturing good is:

$$C_2 = X_2 + Q. \tag{42}$$

Finally, the budget constraints of the government and the economy are:

$$(w_2 + r^*)R = k(p - p^*)Q, \tag{43}$$

$$C_1 + pC_2 = X_1 + pX_2 + w_2 L_3 + (1-k)(p-p^*)Q. \tag{44}$$

These yield the condition of balance of payments: $X_1 - C_1 = p^*(C_2 - X_2) + r^* K^*$.

We proceed to solve the above system recursively. For a given p, we can compute the equilibrium values of the supply side of the model. Equation (36) determine the amounts of L_3 and K^* used in the production of public inputs: $R = L_3 = K^*$, and then (43) gives the percentage of the quota rents (k) appropriated for financing public inputs. Further, w_1 and r can be obtained from (34), (35), and (37–39), and with given w_2, we can then compute λ. Note that the labor and capital constraints can be rewritten as: $L_1 + (1+\lambda)(L_2 + L_3) = L$ and $[(1-\alpha)/\alpha]w_1 L_1 + [(1-\beta)/\beta]w_2 L_2 = rK$. From these two equations, we can solve for L_1 and L_2, and hence X_1 and X_2 by (37) and (38). Next, by adding the demand-side information into the model, (42) and (44) determine the values of C_2 and C_1, while p can be deduced from (41). Finally, welfare U is obtained from (40).

6.2. Calibrations

We start by setting the values of the main endogenous variables of the reference equilibrium of the model: $X_1 = 8$, $X_2 = 3$, $L_1 = 8$, $L_2 = 2$, $L_3 = 1$, $r^* = 0.1$, $r = 0.1$, $p = 1$, $C_1 = 4.8$, and $C_2 = 7.8$, and the values of the elasticity parameters: $\alpha = 0.8$, $\beta = 0.6$, and $e = 0.1$. Then, we compute the values of the other endogenous or exogenous variables: $K_1 = 16$, $K_2 = 12$, $K = 28$, $w_1 = 0.8$, $w_2 = 0.9$, $R = 1$, $K^* = 1$, $\lambda = 0.125$, $L_u = 0.375$, $L = 11.375$, $Q = 4.8$, $p^* = 0.6458$, $k = 0.5882$, and $U = 6.4829$, and the values of the other parameters: $A = 0.8706$, $B = 0.7325$, and $\gamma = 0.3810$.

First, we consider the supply-side impact of changes in R for various goods prices p. The results, presented in Table 1, are: (i) w_1 is decreasing with p and R, and hence λ is increasing with p and R; (ii) r is increasing with p and R; and (iii) X_1 is decreasing with p and R, while X_2 is increasing with them. These simulations confirm the theoretical results derived in (19).

Table 1. Simulations of the supply side of the model

w_1			R	
		0.8	1	1.2
	0.95	0.8377	0.8261	0.8167
p	1	0.8112	0.8	0.7909
	1.1	0.7643	0.7537	0.7452
λ			R	
		0.8	1	1.2
	0.95	0.0744	0.0895	0.1020
p	1	0.1094	0.125	0.1379
	1.1	0.1775	0.1941	0.2077
r			R	
		0.8	1	1.2
	0.95	0.0832	0.0880	0.0921
p	1	0.0946	0.1	0.1047
	1.1	0.12	0.1269	0.1328
X_1			R	
		0.8	1	1.2
	0.95	10.6287	9.6039	8.6863
p	1	9.0714	8	7.0421
	1.1	5.8666	4.6874	3.6360
X_2			R	
		0.8	1	1.2
	0.95	0.5359	1.4270	2.2121
p	1	2.0845	3	3.8054
	1.1	4.9710	5.9452	6.7997

Next, we simulate the whole model by increasing R from 0 to some high value. The main results, illustrated in Figure 1, are as follows:

i. The output of the agricultural good falls while the production of the manufacturing rises.
ii. The proportion k of the quota rents appropriated for financing the production of public inputs rises from almost 0 to 1, when R increases from a little above 0–1.5.

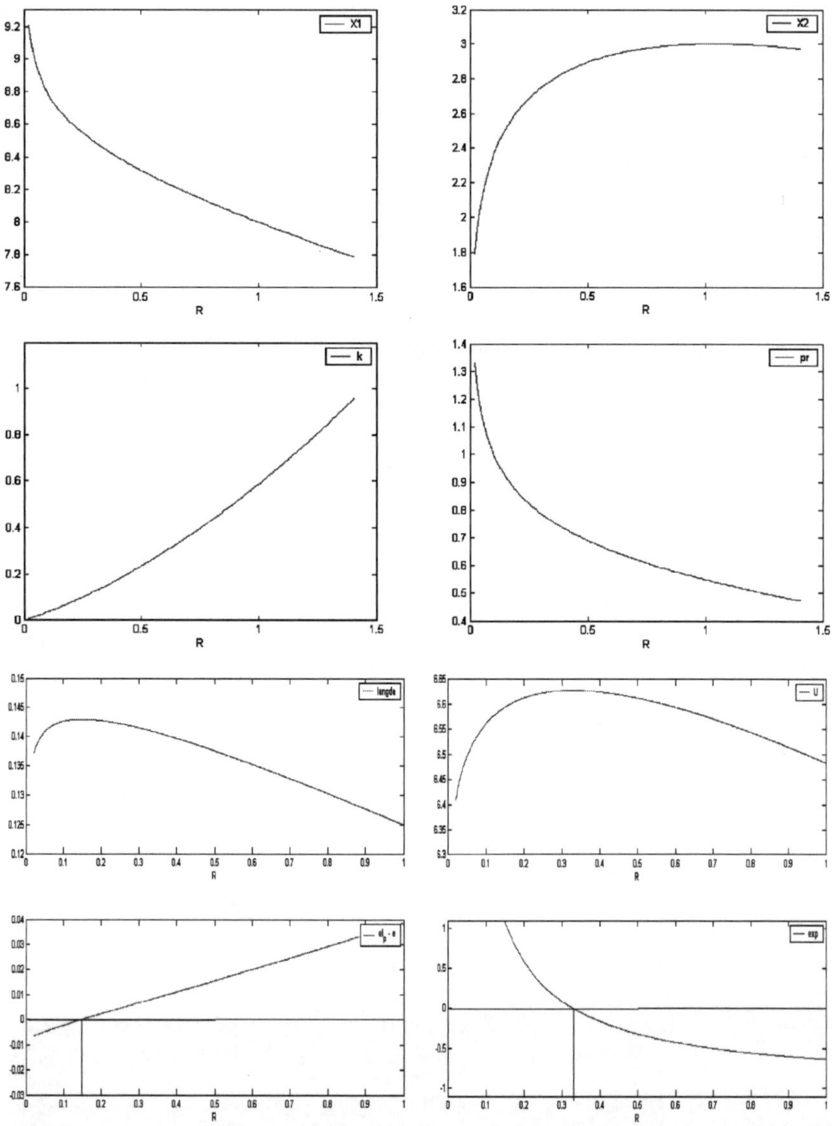

Fig. 1. Profiles of changes in key variables.

iii. The relative excess of the domestic manufacturing price on the world price, $pr = p/p^{*}-1$, falls with increases of public inputs R. As p^{*} is set to 0.6458, p also decreases with R. This result is consistent with (29).
iv. The urban unemployment ratio λ first increases and then decreases with public inputs R, and λ reaches its maximum for $R = 0.149$. Note that $-\hat{p}/\hat{R} - e$ ($\equiv el_p - e$) is first negative then positive, while the zero value is reached for $R = 0.149$. These results agree with (30).
v. The utility of households U first increases and then decreases with public inputs R, and U reaches its maximum for $R = 0.329$. The expression, $exp = ve - w_2 - r^{*} - w_1(L_2 + L_3)(\mathrm{d}\lambda/\mathrm{d}R)$, is positive for low values of R and negative for high values of R, and its value reaches zero for $R = 0.329$. This is the value for which U is maximum. These results agree with (33).

7. Concluding remarks

We have examined theoretically and numerically the impacts of urban development through the government provision of public inputs in a dual developing economy. An increase in public inputs promotes the output of urban manufacturing at the expense of that of the rural agricultural sector. These changes in sectoral outputs lead to a fall in rural wage and a rise in the urban unemployment ratio. Hence, taking into account of the financing constraint of public inputs, urban development can reduce the welfare of the dual developing economy.

Several tasks remain for future research. First, public inputs in this chapter affect only urban production. The analysis can be extended to the case in which public inputs also affect agricultural activities. Second, as noted earlier, the public-input activities referred to in this chapter are financed through quota rents. It may be of interest to examine the optimal appropriation of the quota rents for financing public inputs. The implications of other financing schemes, such as tariffs or income taxes, may also be explored in this framework. As is well known, urban development generates intertemporal gains and also exhibits irreversibilities. It seems desirable to consider these aspects of urban development in a dynamic setting. We will attempt to address these issues in the future.

Acknowledgement

We thank Ronald Jones, Ali Khan, Sugata Marjit and the participants of the APJAE Symposium on International Trade in Honor of Professor Ronald Jones at City University of Hong Kong on May 19–20, 2006, and Biswajit Mandol, the referee, for useful comments.

Appendix

1. *Comparative statics*

Let $\theta_{L_i} = w_i C_w^i / C^i$ and $\theta_{K_i} = rC_r^i / C^i$ be the distributive shares of labor and capital in sector i, and $\lambda_{L_i} = C_w^i X_i / L$ and $\lambda_{K_i} = C_r^i X_i / K$ be the fractions of labor and capital employed in sector i, respectively.

The comparative statics results can be solved by differentiating the system of the equations (6) and (11)–(15), as

$$\hat{r}/\hat{p} = 1/\theta_{K_2} > 0,$$

$$\hat{w}_1/\hat{p} = -\theta_{K_1}/\theta_{L_1}\theta_{K_2} < 0,$$

$$\hat{\lambda}/\hat{p} = -[(1+\lambda)/\lambda](\hat{w}_1/\hat{p}) > 0,$$

$$\begin{aligned}\hat{X}_1/\hat{p} = &- \{\theta_{L_1}\lambda_{L_2}(1+\lambda)(s_{K_1}+s_{K_2}) + \theta_{L_1}\lambda_{K_2}[s_{L_1}+s_{L_2}(1+\lambda)] \\ &+ \theta_{L_2}\lambda_{L_2}s_{K_1}(1+\lambda) \\ &+ \theta_{K_1}\lambda_{K_2}[s_{L_1}+(1+\lambda)(\lambda_{L_2}+\lambda_{L_3})]\}/D < 0,\end{aligned}$$

$$\begin{aligned}\hat{X}_2/\hat{p} = &\{\theta_{L_1}\lambda_{L_1}(s_{K_1}+s_{K_2}) + \theta_{L_1}\lambda_{K_1}[s_{L_1}+s_{L_2}(1+\lambda)] + \theta_{K_1}\lambda_{L_1}s_{K_1} \\ &+ \theta_{K_1}\lambda_{K_1}[s_{L_1}+(1+\lambda)(\lambda_{L_2}+\lambda_{L_3})]\}/D > 0,\end{aligned}$$

$$\hat{r}/\hat{R} = e/\theta_{K_2} > 0,$$

$$\hat{w}_1/\hat{R} = -e\theta_{K_1}/\theta_{L_1}\theta_{K_2} < 0,$$

$$\hat{\lambda}/\hat{R} = -[(1+\lambda)/\lambda](\hat{w}_1/\hat{R}) > 0,$$

$$\hat{X}_1/\hat{R} = e(\hat{X}_1/\hat{p}) - \lambda_{K_2}\lambda_{L_3}\theta_{L_1}\theta_{K_2}(1+\lambda)/D < 0,$$

$$\hat{X}_2/\hat{p} = e + e(\hat{X}_2/\hat{p}) + \lambda_{K_1}\lambda_{L_3}\theta_{L_1}\theta_{K_2}(1+\lambda)/D > 0,$$

where $s_{L_i} = \sigma_i\lambda_{L_i}\theta_{K_i}$, $s_{K_i} = \sigma_i\lambda_{K_i}\theta_{L_i}$, $D = \theta_{L_1}\theta_{K_2}[\lambda_{L_1}\lambda_{K_2} - (1+\lambda)\lambda_{K_1}\lambda_{L_2}]$ and σ_i denotes the factor substitution in sector i. Note that D can be rewritten as: $D = \theta_{L_1}\theta_{K_2}[\lambda_{K_2} - \lambda_{L_2}(1+\lambda) - \lambda_{K_2}\lambda_{L_3}(1+\lambda)]$. The stability condition requires $D > 0$, i.e., $\lambda_{K_2} > (1+\lambda)(\lambda_{L_2} + \lambda_{K_2}\lambda_{L_3})$. It may be interesting to note that this condition is stronger than that found in the two-sector Harris–Todaro model (see Khan, 1980; Neary, 1981). Under a special case $\lambda_{L_3} = 0$, the Khan–Neary stability condition is recovered.

2. *Stability*

Following Dei (1985), the adjustment process for goods market is

$$\dot{p} = aZ(p),$$

where the dot is the time derivative, a a positive constant, and $Z = E_p(p, u)-(X_2+Q)$ the excess demand for the importable good. From (21), we can obtain that u is a function of p. By keeping Q constant, we can take a linear approximation of the above adjustment process around the equilibrium point p^e as

$$\dot{p} = a\left(\frac{\mathrm{d}Z}{\mathrm{d}p}\right)(p - p^e).$$

Hence, the necessary and sufficient condition for stability of the system is $\mathrm{d}Z/\mathrm{d}p<0$. From (26) and (27), we obtain $\mathrm{d}p/\mathrm{d}Z = -p/\Delta$, where $\Delta = Q(c+s)+mw_1(L_2+L_3)(\partial\lambda/\partial p)$. Since $c = -(p/Q)(\partial E_p/\partial p)>0$ and $\partial\lambda/\partial p>0$, a sufficient condition for $\Delta>0$ as $s=(p/Q)(\partial X_2/\partial p)>0$, which requires $D>0$ in the above comparative statics. That is, the normal price–output response assures stability of the system.

References

Abe, K. (1990), A public input as a determinant of trade. *Canadian Journal of Economics* 23, 400–407.

Barro, R.J. (1991), Economic growth in a cross section of countries. *Quarterly Journal of Economics* 106, 407–443.

Batra, R.N., Scully, G.W. (1971), The theory of wage differentials: welfare and immerizing growth. *Journal of International Economics* 1, 241–247.

Beladi, H. (1988), Variable returns to scale, urban unemployment and welfare. *Southern Economic Journal* 55, 412–423.

Beladi, H., Ingene, C.A. (1994), A general equilibrium analysis of rural-urban migration under uncertainty. *Journal of Regional Science* 34, 91–103.

Bhagwati, J.N. (1971), The generalized theory of distortions and welfare. In: Bhagwati, J.N., Jones, R.W, Mundell, R.A., Vanek, J. (Eds.), *Trade, Balance of Payments, and Growth*. North Holland, Amsterdam.

Boadway, R., Maital, S., Prachowny, M. (1973), Optimal tariffs, optimal taxes and public goods. *Journal of Public Economics* 2, 391–403.

Chambers, R.G., Lopez, R. (1993), Public investment and real-price supports. *Journal of Public Economics* 52, 73–82.

Chao, C.C., Yu, E.S.H. (1990), Urban unemployment, terms of trade and welfare. *Southern Economic Journal* 56, 743–751.

Chao, C.C., Yu, E.S.H. (1994), Foreign capital inflows and welfare in an economy with imperfect competition. *Journal of Development Economics* 45, 141–154.

Choi, E.K., Lapan, H.E. (1991), Optimal trade policies for developing countries under uncertainty. *Journal of Developing Economics* 35, 243–260.

Dei, F. (1985), Voluntary export restraints and foreign investment. *Journal of International Economics* 19, 305–312.

Feehan, J.P. (1992), The optimal revenue tariff for public input provision. *Journal of Development Economics* 25, 155–164.

Feldmann, D.H. (1989), The trade-off between GNP and unemployment in a dual economy. *Southern Economic Journal* 56, 46–55.

Fullerton, D. (1991), Reconciling recent estimates of the marginal welfare cost of taxation. *American Economic Review* 81, 302–308.

Harris, J.R., Todaro, M. (1970), Migration, unemployment and development: a two-sector analysis. *American Economic Review* 60, 126–142.

Hazari, B.R., Sgro, P.M. (1991), Urban-rural structural adjustment, urban unemployment with traded and non-traded goods. *Journal of Development Economics* 35, 187–196.

Khan, M.A. (1980), Dynamic stability, wage subsidies and generalized Harris-Todaro model. *Pakistan Development Review* 19, 1–24.

Khan, M.A. (1982), Social opportunity costs and immiserizing growth: some observations on the long run versus the short. *Quarterly Journal of Economics* 97, 353–362.

Krueger, A.O., Orsmond, D.W.H. (1993), Impact of government on growth and trade. In: Ethier, W.J., Helpman, E., Neary, J.P. (Eds.), *Theory, Policy and Dynamics in International Trade*. Cambridge University Press, Cambridge.

Neary, J.P. (1981), On the Harris-Todaro model with intersectoral capital mobility. *Economica* 48, 219–234.

Partridge, M.D., Rickman, D.S. (1997), Has the wage curve nullified the Harris-Todaro model? Further U.S. evidence. *Economics Letters* 54, 277–282.

Suits, D.B. (1985), US Farm migration: an application of the Harris-Todaro model. *Economic Development and Cultural Change* 34, 815–828.

Todaro, M.P. (1976), *Internal Migration in Developing Countries*. International Labor Office, Geneva.

Vanek, J. (1971), Tariffs, economic welfare and development potential. *Economic Journal* 81, 904–913.

Yu, E.S.H. (1979), On the theory of interregional wage differential and technical change. *Journal of Regional Science* 19, 245–256.

SECTION VI

International Factor Mobility

CHAPTER 16

Moving People or Jobs? A New Perspective on Immigration and International Outsourcing

Hamid Beladi[a] and Avik Chakrabarti[b]

[a]*Department of Economics, College of Business, University of Texas at San Antonio, One UTSA Circle, San Antonio, Texas 78249-0633*
E-mail address: hamid.beladi@utsa.edu
[b]*Department of Economics, 816 Bolton Hall, College of Letters and Science, University of Wisconsin-Milwaukee, P.O. Box 413, Wisconsin 53201*
E-mail address: chakra@uwm.edu

Abstract

We present a model that allows us to compare the effects that frictions involved in immigration and international outsourcing have on the skilled–unskilled wage inequality. We show that, for any given level of contractual friction in the production of intermediate goods, the wedge between the wages of the skilled and unskilled workers widens as the frictions in immigration wear out. The skilled–unskilled wage gap, for any given level of friction in immigration, is sensitive to variations in contractual frictions in intermediates that affect international outsourcing.

Keywords: Wage inequality, immigration, outsourcing, contract theory

JEL classifications: F1, F3, F33

> *Although immigration and international outsourcing do differ in the manner in which local wage rates (or employment levels) are affected, the current scare scenarios need to be placed in context.*
>
> R. W. Jones (2005)

1. Introduction

The forces of immigration to and outsourcing from the United States continue to draw increasing attention of those in the media and academics. On the one hand, U.S. legal and illegal immigration combined averages over 1.5 million a year. Most immigrants to the United States are unskilled and originate in developing countries. According to the Bureau of Labor Statistics, between 2002 and 2012, the U.S. economy is expected to create

56 million new jobs, half of which will require no more than a high school education. More than 75 million baby boomers will retire in that period and declining native-born fertility rates will be approaching replacement level. Native-born workers, meanwhile, are becoming more educated with every decade. While in the 1960s, half of all Americans dropped out of high school to look for unskilled work, less than 10% do so now.[1] On the other hand, no economist would dispute Gregory Mankiw's[2] observation that outsourcing has become America's "new way of doing international trade" which makes it "a good thing" but a group of politicians, journalists[3] and consulting agencies continue to warn against "export of jobs" to countries like India, Brazil and China. While academic interest in international migration dates back to the early 20th century, the literature on outsourcing has far outpaced that on immigration.[4] With this backdrop, in this chapter, we offer a new perspective on the labor market effects of immigration by embedding it in a model of outsourcing subject to contractual incompleteness.

The rest of the chapter is organized as follows. In the next section, we provide a brief review of the relevant literature. In Section 3, we present our model and propositions. We draw our conclusion in Section 4.

2. Literature

Academic interest in identifying the forces behind international migration dates back to Jerome (1926). However, in the early 1990s the absence of a coherent theory of immigration began to trouble several researchers[5] as conflicts between key empirical regularities and the predictions of existing theories of immigration were becoming increasingly conspicuous. Stark (1994) remarked that one of the least satisfactory features of theories of immigration, available at that time, was their lack of ability to predict a corpus of stylized facts rather than provide an *ad hoc* analytical rationale

[1] See Jacoby (2006).

[2] At the time of this quote, Gregory Mankiw was the head of President George W. Bush's Council of Economic Advisors.

[3] CNN's Lou Dobbs routinely harangues U.S. companies engaged in offshore outsourcing in his *Exporting America* series. Many IT executives have themselves contributed to this perception. When IBM announced plans to outsource 3000 jobs overseas this year, one of its executives said, "[Globalization] means shifting a lot of jobs, opening a lot of locations in places we had never dreamt of before, going where there's low-cost labor, low-cost competition, shifting jobs offshore." Nandan Nilekani, the chief executive of the India-based Infosys Technologies, said at this year's World Economic Forum, "Everything you can send down a wire is up for grabs." In January testimony before Congress, Hewlett-Packard chief Carly Fiorina warned that "there is no job that is America's God-given right anymore."

[4] In a thought-provoking article on the labor market effects of U.S. immigration and outsourcing, Jones (2005) pointed out the significance of substitutability/complementarity between immigration and outsourcing.

[5] See Massey *et al.* (1993).

for an isolated observation. Chiswick (2000) offered a variant of the human capital investment model of migration where an individual computes the gross benefit to migration, based on the wage difference in the source and the destination, and compares it with the cost of migration, which could include both foregone earnings and direct costs. Hendricks (2001) developed a model of immigration with positive assortative matching under incomplete information in which worker skills are complementary in production and only imperfectly observable by firms.

The phenomenon of outsourcing is certainly not new. Yet it has appeared more frequently in the recent literature on international trade. Several authors, including Jones and Engerman (1996), Jones and Kierzkowski (1998, 2001), Arndt (1998), Deardorff (1998), Harris (1998), Grossman and Helpman (1999), Jones (2000), Jones and Marjit (2001), Marjit *et al.* (2004), Kohler (2004), Wan (2005), Long (2005) and Jones *et al.* (2005) have captured distinct dimensions of outsourcing through parsimonious yet meaningful modifications of the traditional structure of general equilibrium models of international trade.

The traditional theories of trade and their refinements have had much to offer in terms of explaining the phenomenon and consequences of outsourcing (Jones, 2000). Still continued attempts at understanding the complex organizational arrangements encompassed by the process of transnational production sharing, have given birth to a growing body of literature beyond traditional trade theories that treated the choice of a firm's organizational form as exogenous by focusing on the production and sale of final goods and/or on arms-length transactions while incorporating trade in intermediate goods. Some notable contributions include Grossman and Helpman (2002, 2003, 2005), Antràs (2003, 2005), Antràs and Helpman (2004), Grossman *et al.* (2005) and Acemoglu *et al.* (2007).

We hope to complement these contributions by embedding immigration in a model of outsourcing subject to contractual incompleteness.

3. Model and propositions

Consider[6] a world that has three countries (indexed by $j = 0, 1, 2$) and ends in two periods (indexed by $t = 0, 1$). In the initial period, each country is endowed with only unskilled labor (L_u^{j0}) that produces only one non-traded homogeneous agricultural good (X) using constant-returns-to-scale

[6] From an analytical perspective, our model incorporates the possibility of international migration in Antràs' (2005) structure to compare the effects of immigration and outsourcing on the skilled–unskilled wage inequality. Antràs (2005) combined incomplete international outsourcing contracts with a model North–South trade to explain the development of product cycles in which new goods are initially designed and produced in the North, with later production moving to the South. For ease of comparison, we preserve his notations to the fullest extent possible.

technology. Each unskilled worker is rewarded w_u^{jt}. We assume that unskilled workers live for two periods and $w_u^{00} > w_u^{10} = w_u^{20}$. In the final period, the amount of unskilled labor remains unchanged (i.e., $L_u^{j1} = L_u^{j0}$) but country 0 (the home country where the research center is located) is endowed with an additional pool of skilled workers (L_s^{01}) who live for one period. Each skilled worker in country 0 is rewarded w_s^{01}.

Country 1 is the origin of exogenous immigration flows of unskilled labor to country 0 and country 2 is the destination for outsourcing from country 0. Let μ represent the premium, due to friction in immigration, necessary to induce a worker to move from country 1 to country 0, i.e. the wage of an unskilled worker in the home country 0 is $w_u^{01} = (1+\mu)w_u^{11}$.

In the final period, a single firm produces a brand of a differentiated product (Y), for which it faces an iso-elastic demand function:[7]

$$y = \lambda p^{1/(\alpha-1)} \quad \alpha \in (0,1) \tag{1}$$

where p is the price of the good. Production of good Y is characterized by:

$$y = \xi_z x_h^{1-z} x_1^z \quad z \in (0,1) \tag{2}$$

The revenue generated is:

$$R = \lambda^{1-\alpha} \xi_z^\alpha x_h^{\alpha(1-z)} x_1^{\alpha z} \quad \alpha \in (0,1) \quad z \in (0,1) \tag{3}$$

Here $\xi_z = z^{-z}(1-z)^{-(1-z)}$, x_h is a high-tech intermediate good (e.g., research and development, marketing, etc.) and x_l is a low-tech intermediate good (e.g., manufacturing, assembly, etc.). The skilled–unskilled wage-ratio (ω), in general equilibrium, for the home country is

$$\omega = \frac{w_u^{01}}{w_s^{01}} = \left(\frac{2}{\alpha \int_{\bar{z}}^1 z f(z) \mathrm{d}z} - 1 \right) \frac{L_u^{01}}{L_s^{01}} \tag{4}$$

where $f(z)$ is the probability density function associated with the fraction of manufacturing plants employing native unskilled workers (Figure 1).

Each intermediate, $x_i (i = h,l)$, can be of high- or low quality. If either of the two intermediates is of low quality, the output of the final good is zero. If both intermediates are of high quality, production of the final good requires no additional inputs. In country 0, production of one unit of a good-quality high-tech intermediate requires the employment of one unit of skilled labor. Since country 0 alone is endowed with skilled workers x_h is produced exclusively in country 0. Production of the high-quality low-tech intermediate requires unskilled labor and the unit input requirement is assumed to be equal to 1.

---

[7] This form of demand results from constant elasticity-of-substitution preferences for brands of a differentiated product.

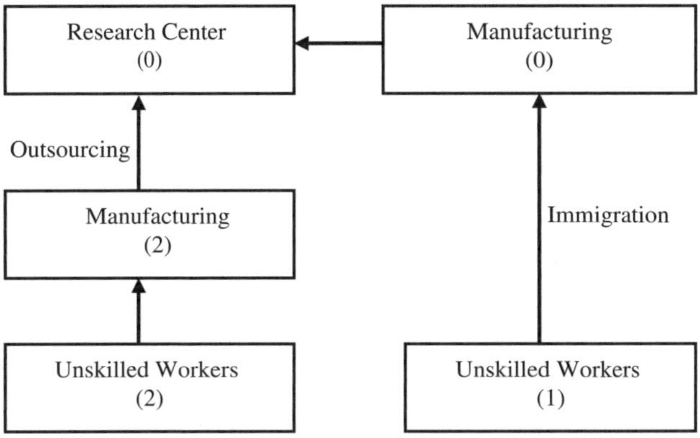

Fig. 1. Organizing production: immigration from (1) vs. outsourcing to (2).

The sequence of events is as follows. At $t = 1$, a research center located in the home country, decides whether to produce the high-tech intermediate and, if so, whether to obtain the low-tech intermediate from an independent manufacturing plant in country 0 that hires unskilled immigrant workers from country 1 or from a manufacturing plant in country 2 to maximize its *ex ante* profits. Upon entry, the manufacturer makes a lump-sum transfer T to the research center. Because of the existence of a large number of identical potential manufacturers of the final good, competition among them will make T adjust so as to exhaust the manufacturer's profits. The source of contractual incompleteness arises from international production sharing:[8] the manager of the research center in country 0 and that of a manufacturing plant cannot sign an enforceable contract specifying the purchase of a certain type of intermediate input for a certain price. Otherwise, the party receiving a positive payment would have an incentive to produce the low-quality intermediate at a negligible cost. The parties cannot write contracts contingent on the volume of sale revenues obtained when the final good is sold. The only contractible *ex ante* is the transfer between the parties.

For simplicity in the exposition of the proofs of our propositions, let

$$A(z) = \frac{1}{1+\mu}\left(\frac{2(1-\alpha)^{(1-\alpha)/\alpha}}{(1-(\alpha/2))^{(1-\alpha)/\alpha}}\right)^{1/z}$$

PROPOSITION 1. *As the friction in immigration falls (rises), the skilled–unskilled wage gap rises (falls) in the home country.*

[8] See Antràs (2005) for a more detailed discussion.

PROOF. Consider first the decision of the research center in country 0 to transact with an independent manufacturer located in country 0 that hires unskilled workers migrating from country 1 to country 0. This leaves no room for *ex post* renegotiation between the research center and the manufacturer since the two parties can write an *ex ante* quality-contingent contract. Using backward induction, the research center's problem is to

$$\underset{\{x_h, x_l\}}{\text{Maximize}}: \Pi^0 = R - w_s^{01} x_h - (1+\mu) w_u^{11} x_l$$

The *ex ante* profits, with immigration (IMM), for the research center boils down to

$$\Pi_R|_{\text{IMM}} = \lambda(1-\alpha)\left(\frac{((1+\mu)w_u^{11})^x (w_s^{01})^{1-x}}{\alpha}\right)^{\alpha/(\alpha-1)} \tag{5}$$

Consider next the decision of the research center in country 0 to transact with an independent manufacturer that is located in country 2 and employs unskilled workers located in country 2. In this case, the initial contract between the research center and the manufacturer stipulates only the transfer (T). The research center chooses x_{hz} and the manufacturer chooses x_s, simultaneously. The research center and the manufacturer play a simultaneous game in the initial stage. The problem of the research center is to

$$\underset{\{x_h\}}{\text{Maximize}}: \Pi^0 = \frac{1}{2} R - w_s^{01} x_h$$

The problem of the manufacturer is to

$$\underset{\{x_l\}}{\text{Maximize}}: \Pi^2 = \frac{1}{2} R - w_u^{21} x_l$$

The *ex ante* profits, with outsourcing (OUT), for the research center boils down to

$$\Pi_R|_{\text{OUT}} = \lambda\left(1-\frac{\alpha}{2}\right)\left(\frac{2\left(w_u^{21}\right)^x \left(w_s^{01}\right)^{1-x}}{\alpha}\right)^{\alpha/(\alpha-1)} \tag{6}$$

Therefore, the research center is indifferent between transacting with an independent manufacturer located in country 0 that hires unskilled immigrants from country 1 and outsourcing to an independent manufacturer located in country 2 if $\Pi_R|_{\text{IMM}} = \Pi_R|_{\text{OUT}}$ which implies $(w_u^{11}/w_u^{21}) = A(z)$. $\Pi_R|_{\text{IMM}} > \Pi_R|_{\text{OUT}}$ if $(w_u^{11}/w_u^{21}) < A(z)$ and $\Pi_R|_{\text{IMM}} < \Pi_R|_{\text{OUT}}$ if $(w_u^{11}/w_u^{21}) > A(z)$. Since $(\partial A/\partial \mu) < 0$ and $\lim_{\mu \to 0} A = \infty$, a decline in μ below a threshold will support immigration raising the skilled–unskilled wage gap in country 0. [QED]

Let us now allow variations in the degree of contractual frictions, á la Acemoglu *et al.* (2007). We assume that the low-tech intermediate input is produced with a set of activities, indexed by points on an interval [0, 1], subject to a Cobb–Douglas technology:

$$x_l = e^{\int_0^1 \log x_l(k)\mathrm{d}k} \tag{7}$$

where $x_l(k)$ represents the manufacturer's input-specific investment in activity k that can be used only to produce the input for which it is designed. The activities in the range [0, β] are subject to contractual incompleteness, i.e. the characteristics of these activities cannot be fully specified in advance in an enforceable *ex ante* contract.

PROPOSITION 2. *As contractual frictions in the low-tech intermediate decline (rise), for any given level of friction in immigration, the skilled–unskilled wage inequality falls (rises) in the home country.*

PROOF. With immigration, the research center's problem is to

$$\underset{\{x_h,\{x_l(k)\}_{k=0}^{\beta}\}}{\text{Maximize}}: \Pi^0 = R - w_s^{01}x_h - (1+\mu)w_u^{11}\int_0^{\beta} x_l(k)\mathrm{d}k$$

The *ex ante* profits the research center is

$$\Pi_R|_{\text{IMM}} = \lambda(1-\alpha)\left(\frac{((1+\mu)\beta w_{\text{u}}^{11})^x (w_{\text{s}}^{01})^{1-x}}{\alpha}\right)^{\alpha/(\alpha-1)} \tag{8}$$

With outsourcing, the problem of the research center is to

$$\underset{\{x_h\}}{\text{Maximize}}: \Pi^0 = \frac{1}{2}R - w_s^{01}x_h$$

The problem of the manufacturer is to

$$\underset{\{\{x_l(k)\}_{k=0}^{\beta}\}}{\text{Maximize}}: \Pi^2 = \frac{1}{2}R - w_u^{21}\int_0^{\beta} x_1(k)\mathrm{d}k$$

The *ex ante* profits for the research center is

$$\Pi_R|_{\text{OUT}} = \lambda\left(1-\frac{\alpha}{2}\right)\left(\frac{2(\beta w_u^{21})^x (w_s^{01})^{1-x}}{\alpha}\right)^{\alpha/(\alpha-1)} \tag{9}$$

Therefore, $\Pi_R|_{\text{IMM}} > \Pi_R|_{\text{OUT}}$ if $(w_u^{11}/w_u^{21}) < \beta A(z)$ and $\Pi_R|_{\text{IMM}} < \Pi_R|_{\text{OUT}}$ if $(w_u^{11}/w_u^{21}) > \beta A(z)$. A decline in β, for any given level of μ, below a threshold will support outsourcing that will lower the skilled–unskilled wage gap in country 0. [QED]

Finally we allow the degree of contractual frictions to vary in both the intermediates (low-tech and high-tech), i.e. each intermediate is produced with a set of activities subject to a Cobb–Douglas technology:

$$x_i = e^{\int_0^1 \log x_i(k)\mathrm{d}k} \quad (i = h, l) \tag{10}$$

where $x_i(k)$ represents input-specific investments in activity k. The activities in the range $[0,\beta_i]$ are subject to contractual incompleteness.

PROPOSITION 3. *As contractual frictions in the high-tech intermediate decline (rise)* relative *to the frictions in low-tech intermediate the skilled–unskilled wage inequality rises (declines) in the home country.*

PROOF. With immigration, the research center's problem is to

$$\underset{\{\{x_h(k)\}_{k=0}^{\beta_h},\{x_l(k)\}_{k=0}^{\beta_l}\}}{\text{Maximize}:}\quad \Pi^0 = R - w_s^{01}\int_0^{\beta_h} x_h(k)\mathrm{d}k - (1+\mu)w_u^{11}\int_0^{\beta_l} x_l(k)\mathrm{d}k$$

The *ex ante* profits the research center is

$$\Pi_R|_{\text{IMM}} = \lambda(1-\alpha)\left(\frac{\left((1+\mu)\beta_1 w_u^{11}\right)^x\left(\beta_h w_s^{01}\right)^{1-x}}{\alpha}\right)^{\alpha/(\alpha-1)} \tag{11}$$

With outsourcing, the problem of the research center is to

$$\underset{\{\{x_h(k)\}_{k=0}^{\beta_h}\}}{\text{Maximize}}:\ \Pi^0 = \frac{1}{2}R - w_s^{01}\int_0^{\beta_h} x_h(k)\mathrm{d}k$$

The problem of the manufacturer is to

$$\underset{\{\{x_l(k)\}_{k=0}^{\beta}\}}{\text{Maximize}}:\ \Pi^2 = \frac{1}{2}R - w_u^{21}\int_0^{\beta_l} x_l(k)\mathrm{d}k$$

The *ex ante* profits for the research center is

$$\Pi_R|_{\text{OUT}} = \lambda\left(1-\frac{\alpha}{2}\right)\left(\frac{2(\beta_1 w_u^{21})^x(\beta_h w_s^{01})^{1-x}}{\alpha}\right)^{\alpha/(\alpha-1)} \tag{12}$$

Therefore, $\Pi_R|_{\text{IMM}} > \Pi_R|_{\text{OUT}}$ if $(w_u^{11}/w_u^{21}) < (\beta_l/\beta_h)A(z)$ and $\Pi_R|_{\text{IMM}} < \Pi_R|_{\text{OUT}}$ if $(w_u^{11}/w_u^{21}) > (\beta_l/\beta_h)A(z)$. A decline in β_h, all else equal, below a threshold will support immigration raising the skilled–unskilled wage gap in country 0. [QED]

In sum, for any given level of contractual friction in the production of intermediate goods, the wedge between the wages of the skilled and unskilled workers widens as the frictions in immigration wear out. The skilled–unskilled wage gap, for any given level of friction in immigration, can widen or shrink depending on the contractual frictions in intermediates that affect international outsourcing.

4. Conclusion

We have presented a model of immigration in the presence of the possibility of offshore outsourcing where we demonstrate how interactions between the frictions involved in immigration and outsourcing can affect the skilled–unskilled wage inequality. We have shown that the skilled–unskilled wage inequality, while affected by frictions in immigration, is sensitive to variations in contractual frictions in intermediates that affect international outsourcing. In particular, we predict that a fall in the friction involved in immigration will cause the skilled–unskilled wage gap to widen while the gap would be dampened by a decline in the contractual frictions in the low-tech intermediates. A decline in the contractual frictions in the high-tech intermediate relative to the frictions in low-tech intermediate will increase the wage gap. A natural extension, we are currently working on, of our model is to integrate it with the structure of Antràs and Helpman (2007) allowing cross-country variations in the degrees of contractual frictions. Since this is an emerging area of research, we hope that future researchers will extend our work within the structure of general equilibrium models.

Acknowledgement

We wish to thank anonymous referee(s) for insightful comments and suggestions on an earlier version of this paper. The usual disclaimer applies.

References

Acemoglu, D., Antràs, P., Helpman, E. (2007), Contracts and technology adoption. *American Economic Review* 97, 916–943.

Antràs, P. (2003), Firms, contracts, and trade structure. *Quarterly Journal of Economics* 118, 1375–1418.

Antràs, P. (2005), Incomplete contracts and the product cycle. *American Economic Review* 95, 1054–1073.

Antràs, P., Helpman, E. (2004), Global sourcing. *Journal of Political Economy* 112, 552–580.

Antràs, P., Helpman, E. (2007), Contractual frictions and global sourcing. C.E.P.R. Discussion Paper No. 6033.

Arndt, S.W. (1998), Globalization and the gains from trade. In: Koch, K., Jaeger, K. (Eds.), *Trade, Growth, and Economic Policy in Open Economies*. Springer-Verlag, New York, pp. 3–12.

Chiswick, B.R. (2000), Are immigrants favorably self-selected? An economic analysis. In: Brettell, C.D., Hollifield, J.F. (Eds.), *Migration Theory: Talking Across Disciplines*. Routledge, New York, pp. 61–76.

Deardorff, A.V. (1998), Technology, trade, and increasing inequality: does the cause matter for the cure? *Journal of International Economic Law* 1, 353–376.

Grossman, G.M., Helpman, E. (1999), *The Internationalization of Economic Activity*. National Science Foundation Grant.

Grossman, G.M., Helpman, E. (2002), Integration versus outsourcing in industry equilibrium. *Quarterly Journal of Economics* 117, 85–120.

Grossman, G.M., Helpman, E. (2003), Outsourcing versus FDI in industry equilibrium. *Journal of the European Economic Association* 1, 317–327.

Grossman, G.M., Helpman, E. (2005), Outsourcing in a global economy. *Review of Economic Studies* 72, 135–159.

Grossman, G.M., Helpman, E., Szeidl, A. (2005), Complementarities between outsourcing and foreign sourcing. *American Economic Review* 95, 19–24.

Harris, R. (1998). A communications based model of global fragmentation, *mimeo*, Simon Fraser University Press.

Hendricks, L. (2001), The economic performance of immigrants: a theory of assortative matching. *International Economic Review* 42, 417–449.

Jacoby, T. (2006), Immigration nation. *Foreign Affairs* 85, New York.

Jerome, H. (1926), *Migration and Business Cycles*. National Bureau of Economic Research, New York.

Jones, R.W. (2000), *Globalization and the Theory of Input Trade*. The MIT Press, Cambridge, MA.

Jones, R.W. (2005), Immigration vs. outsourcing: effects on labor markets. *International Review of Economics and Finance* 14, 105–114.

Jones, R.W., Engerman, S.L. (1996), Trade, technology, and wages: A tale of two countries. *American Economic Review* 86, 35–40.

Jones, R.W., Kierzkowski, H. (1998), Globalization and the consequences of international fragmentation. In: Calvo, G., Obstfeld, M., Dornbusch, R. (Eds.), *The Festschrift in Honor of Robert A. Mundell*. MIT Press, Cambridge, MA.

Jones, R.W., Kierzkowski, H. (2001), A framework for fragmentation, in Jones. In: Arndt, S.W., Kierzkowski, H. (Eds.), *Fragmentation: New Production Patterns in the World Economy*. Oxford University Press, Oxford and New York, pp. 17–34.

Jones, R.W., Kierzkowski, H., Lurong, C. (2005), What does evidence tell us about fragmentation and outsourcing. *International Review of Economics and Finance* 14, 305–316.

Jones, R.W., Marjit, S. (2001), The role of international fragmentation in the development process. *American Economic Review* 91, 363–366.

Kohler, W. (2004), International outsourcing and factor prices with multistage production. *Economic Journal* 114, 166–185.

Long, N.V. (2005), Outsourcing and technology spillovers. *International Review of Economics and Finance* 14, 297–304.

Marjit, S., Beladi, H., Chakrabarti, A. (2004), Trade and wage inequality in developing countries. *Economic Inquiry* 42, 295–303.

Massey, D.S., Arango, J., Hugo, G., Kouaouci, A.L., Pellegrino, A.D., Taylor, J.E. (1993), Theories of international migration: A review and appraisal. *Population and Development Review* 19, 431–466.

Stark, O. (1994), Market environment, trade technology, and migrants' performance. *Institut fur Weltwirtschaft an der Universitat Kiel Symposia and Conference Series* 59–68.

Wan, H. (2005), Fragmented trade and manufacturing services: examples for a non-convex general equilibrium. *International Review of Economics and Finance* 14, 273–295.

CHAPTER 17

Commodity Demand, Capital Mobility, and International Trade: A Ricardian Approach[☆]

Morihiro Yomogida[a]

[a]*Department of Economics, Sophia University, Japan*
E-mail address: m-yomogi@sophia.ac.jp

Abstract
In this chapter, I explore the impacts of international capital movements on income distribution within countries and the value of trade in goods. Jones (1980) introduces sector-specific capital into a simple Ricardian setting and examines the role of comparative and absolute advantage in determining the allocation of capital between countries. I introduce a simple structure of the demand for commodities into Jones (1980) so that commodity prices are determined endogenously in commodity markets. This extension allows us to show how the pattern of demand plays a crucial role in the effects of capital movements on income distribution and goods trade.

Keywords: The Ricardian model of trade, capital movements, income distribution

JEL classifications: F11, F21

1. Introduction

In the recent wave of globalization, production factors such as capital and skilled or unskilled workers are gradually allowed to move internationally. The movement of production factors clearly affects income distribution within as well as across nations. As a result, economists and policy makers have paid more attention to the distributional effects of factor movements.[1] How does the movement of production factors affect trade flows?

[☆] This chapter is an extended version of Yomogida (2006).

[1] In an article of *New York Times*, Charles Schumer (the senior Senator from New York state) and Paul Craig Roberts (2004) state, "American jobs are being lost not to competition from foreign companies, but multinational corporations, often with American roots, that are cutting costs by shifting operations to low-wage countries."

Frontiers of Economics and Globalization
Volume 4 ISSN: 1574-8715
DOI: 10.1016/S1574-8715(08)04017-7

What is the impact of factor movements on income distribution within nations? For the investigation of these issues, I use a simple general equilibrium model.

If production factors are trapped within countries, the principle of comparative advantage predicts the pattern of trade. If some of production factors are mobile internationally, absolute advantage as well as comparative advantage plays a role in determining the pattern of trade in goods and factors. Using a two-country and two-good Ricardian model with sector-specific capital, I explore the impact of capital movements on the value of trade in goods and the distribution of income within nations.

There is extensive theoretical work on trade and capital mobility, including Mundell (1957), Purvis (1972), Uekawa (1972), Jones and Ruffin (1975), Markusen (1983), Jones and Dei (1983), Ohyama (1989), Suzuki (1989), Neary (1995), and Jones (2000) among others.[2] In particular, this chapter is related to Jones (1980, 1994). He extends a two-country and two-good Ricardian model to a setting in which one sector requires sector-specific capital in addition to labor. Using this extended model, he shows that comparative advantage as well as absolute advantage plays a role in the determination of capital allocation in a world economy. In his work, commodity prices are treated as exogenously given parameters. In this chapter, I explicitly consider a simple structure of the demand for commodities so that commodity prices are determined endogenously in commodity markets. This extension allows us to analyze some issues that are not investigated in Jones (1980, 1994).

First, I examine the role of the demand structure in determining the direction of international capital movements. The demand side as well as the supply side plays a role in determining the allocation of capital between countries. I show that the direction of capital movements crucially depends on the size of the relative demand for a commodity.

Second, I analyze who gains and who loses from international capital movements. Capital flows affect the relative price of a commodity, which leads to a change in income distribution within countries. I examine whether or not the owners of capital and workers gain from capital flows relative to a free trade baseline.

Finally, I investigate the effects of international capital movements on the pattern and value of goods trade. Capital flows affect the production pattern of each country, which may induce a change in the pattern of trade in goods. Given that the owners of capital do not move with capital across borders, I examine whether capital movements raise or reduce the value of trade in goods.

---

[2] See Jones (2000) for recent developments in this topic.

The rest of this chapter is organized as follows. In Section 2, I develop the model. In Section 3, I examine free trade equilibrium in a regime in which capital is not allowed to move between countries. In Section 4, I allow capital to move internationally and examine how the direction of capital movements depends on the size of the relative demand for a commodity. I also analyze the effect of capital movements on income distribution within countries, and the pattern and value of trade in goods. In Section 5, I close this chapter with conclusions.

2. *The model*

Let us consider a simple Ricardian setting. There are two sectors, X and Y. Sector X requires capital as well as labor in production. Sector Y uses labor only. Since only sector X uses capital, capital is a sector-specific input. Labor moves between these two sectors since it is required in both sectors. There are two countries, Home and Foreign. Each country is endowed with fixed units of labor and capital. Let L denote the supply of labor at Home. The full employment constraint states

$$a_{LX}X + a_{LY}Y \leqq L, \tag{1}$$

where a_{Lj} units of labor are required to produce one unit of good j ($j = X, Y$), and $X(Y)$ is the output of sector $X(Y)$ at Home. If capital is not allowed to move between countries, there is another constraint,

$$a_{KX}X \leqq K, \tag{2}$$

where a_{KX} units of capital are required to produce one unit of good X, and K units of capital exist at Home. The demand for capital must be equal to or less than the Home supply of capital. If there is plenty of capital at Home, the capital constraint may not matter at all for production patterns. To avoid this situation, we assume that the following condition holds,

$$K < \frac{a_{KX}}{a_{LX}} L \equiv K_{\mathrm{M}}, \tag{3}$$

where K_{M} is the maximum capacity for the use of capital at Home. This condition implies that the capital constraint determines the maximum capacity for the output of X. Similarly, we can derive labor and capital market constraints for Foreign,

$$a^*_{LX}X^* + a^*_{LY}Y^* \leqq L^*, \tag{4}$$

$$a^*_{KX}X^* \leqq K^*, \tag{5}$$

where asterisks denote variables associated with Foreign. We assume that Foreign is endowed with capital, the amount of which is smaller than the maximum capacity for the use of capital at Foreign,

$$K^* < \frac{a^*_{KX}}{a^*_{LX}} L^* \equiv K^*_{\mathrm{M}}. \tag{6}$$

Using these labor and capital constraints, we can illustrate a production possibility frontier for each country. In Figure 1(a), the solid line shows the

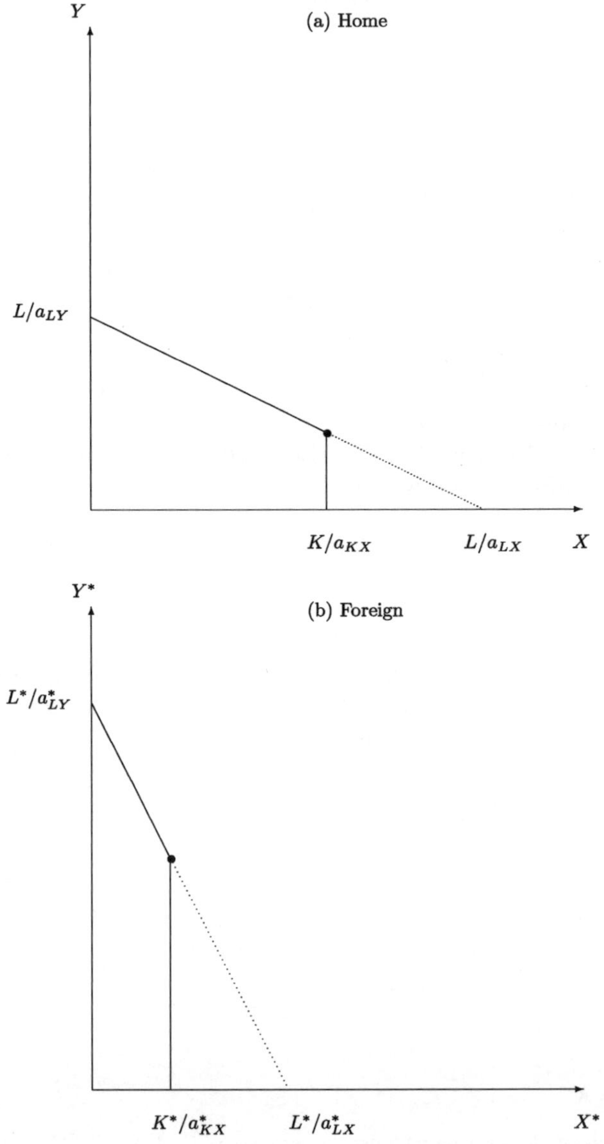

Fig. 1. Home PPF and Foreign PPF.

production possibility frontier for Home.[3,4] The maximum output of X is equal to K/a_{KX}. Figure 1(b) shows the production possibility frontier for Foreign. Notice that the slope of the labor constraint of Home is flatter than that of Foreign. This reflects that Home has a comparative advantage in producing X in terms of labor productivity,

$$\frac{a_{LX}}{a_{LY}} < \frac{a^*_{LX}}{a^*_{LY}}. \tag{A1}$$

We assume that this condition holds in the following analysis. In addition to the labor constraint, the capital constraint does matter for production patterns. This implies that absolute capital productivity as well as comparative labor productivity plays an important role in the determination of production structures. It is possible to consider two different scenarios. First, Home has a comparative advantage in X in terms of labor productivity, but Foreign has an absolute advantage in X in terms of capital productivity. Second, Home has an absolute advantage in terms of capital productivity as well as a comparative advantage in terms of labor productivity in producing X. We shall focus on the first scenario since it is more interesting.[5] Thus, we assume that

$$a^*_{KX} < a_{KX}. \tag{A2}$$

In Figure 1, the maximum output of X at Foreign is smaller than that at Home. This implies that Home has the larger amount of capital than Foreign, and as a result, it has the greater capacity for X even though it has an absolute capital disadvantage in X.

Since markets are perfectly competitive, the following competitive conditions must be satisfied at equilibrium,

$$p_X \leqq wa_{LX} + ra_{KX}, \tag{7}$$

$$p_Y \leqq wa_{LY}, \tag{8}$$

where p_j is the price of good j ($j = X, Y$), w the home wage rate, and r is the return to capital at Home. If both goods are produced at equilibrium, the competitive conditions (7) and (8) hold with equality, and the following

---

[3] Figures 1 through 5 are all drawn with the following parameters: Home $L = 50$, $K = 30$, $a_{LX} = 5$, $a_{KX} = 5$, $a_{LY} = 10$. Foreign $L^* = 50$, $K^* = 5$, $a^*_{LX} = 10$, $a^*_{KX} = 2.5$, $a^*_{LY} = 5$.

[4] In this numerical example, we assume that $K^*_M < K + K^* < K_M$ holds. This assumption implies that only Home can "absorb" all of capital existing in the world if international capital mobility is allowed. It is also possible to consider other cases, (1) $K^*_M < K + K^*, K_M < K + K^*$, and $K + K^* < K_M + K^*_M$ and (2) $K^*_M > K + K^*, K_M > K + K^*$. These alternative assumptions do not affect qualitatively most of results obtained in the following analysis.

[5] In the second scenario, Home would necessarily import capital from Foreign. However, in the first scenario, this is not true.

equation is derived,

$$\frac{p_X}{p_Y} = \frac{a_{LX}}{a_{LY}} + a_{KX}\frac{r}{p_Y}. \qquad \text{(AH)}$$

The relative cost of good X is decomposed into two parts. On the RHS, the first term represents the relative labor productivity and the second term represents the capital cost in terms of good Y. This implies that absolute capital productivity as well as comparative labor productivity plays an important role in the determination of the production cost. Similarly, we can derive competitive conditions for Foreign,

$$p_X \leqq w^* a^*_{LX} + r^* a^*_{KX}, \qquad (9)$$

$$p_Y \leqq w^* a^*_{LY}, \qquad (10)$$

If Foreign produces both goods at equilibrium, the following equation is obtained as well,

$$\frac{p_X}{p_Y} = \frac{a^*_{LX}}{a^*_{LY}} + a^*_{KX}\frac{r^*}{p_Y}. \qquad \text{(AF)}$$

In Figure 2, the two conditions (AH) and (AF) are illustrated in the space of the return to capital in terms of good Y and the relative price of good X. The slope of each line is determined by the absolute productivity of capital. The intercept at the vertical axis is determined by the comparative labor productivity, i.e., $\mathrm{OA} = a_{LX}/a_{LY}$ and $\mathrm{OA}^* = a^*_{LX}/a^*_{LY}$. I have assumed that Home has the higher comparative labor productivity in X but Foreign has the higher absolute capital productivity in X. Under this assumption, (AH) has a steeper slope but lower intercept than (AF), and thus the two lines intersect with each other in the first quadrant. Solving (AH) and (AF) simultaneously for p_X/p_Y, we can obtain

$$\mathrm{OB} = \frac{a^*_{LX}}{a^*_{LY}} + \left[\frac{a^*_{KX}}{a_{KX} - a^*_{KX}}\right]\left[\frac{a^*_{LX}}{a^*_{LY}} - \frac{a_{LX}}{a_{LY}}\right]. \qquad (11)$$

Figure 2 shows that Home can offer the higher return to capital than Foreign when p_X/p_Y is smaller than OB. This suggests that comparative as well as absolute advantage plays a role in determining the direction of capital movements.

Finally, let us turn to preferences of consumers. Home and Foreign are assumed to have identical preferences that are represented by a Cobb–Douglas utility function,

$$u = C_X^{\alpha} C_Y^{1-\alpha}, \; 0 < \alpha < 1, \qquad (12)$$

where C_j denotes the consumption quantity of good $j(j = X, Y)$ at Home.

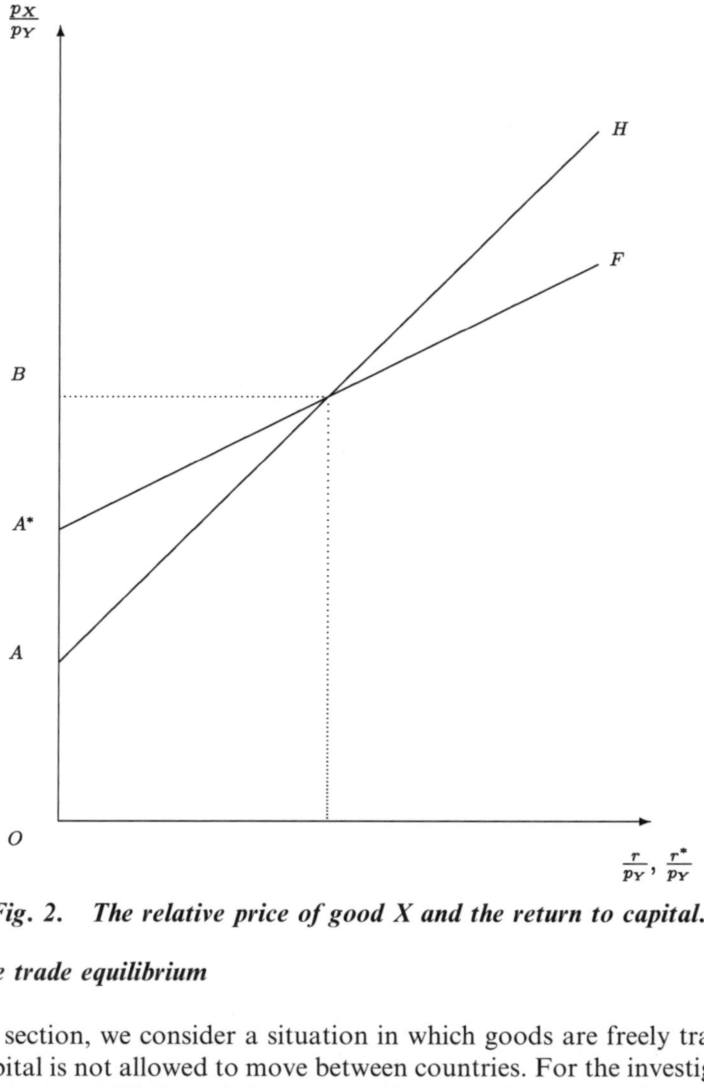

Fig. 2. The relative price of good X and the return to capital.

3. Free trade equilibrium

In this section, we consider a situation in which goods are freely tradable but capital is not allowed to move between countries. For the investigation of free trade equilibrium, it is useful to illustrate the relative demand and supply curves. In Figure 3, RS1 is the relative supply curve of the world. When p_X/p_Y is smaller than $\mathrm{OA} = a_{LX}/a_{LY}$, both countries specialize in producing good Y. As p_X/p_Y rises, Home starts producing good X due to its comparative labor advantage. If $\mathrm{OA} < p_X/p_Y < \mathrm{OA}^*$, then Home produces both goods, but Foreign still specializes in producing good Y. Further increases in p_X/p_Y induce either country to produce good X. When $p_X/p_Y > \mathrm{OA}^*$, Home and Foreign produce both goods. Unlike the standard Ricardian model, the countries do not specialize in producing good X. This is because the capital constraint does bind at each country before all of labor supplies are absorbed in sector X.

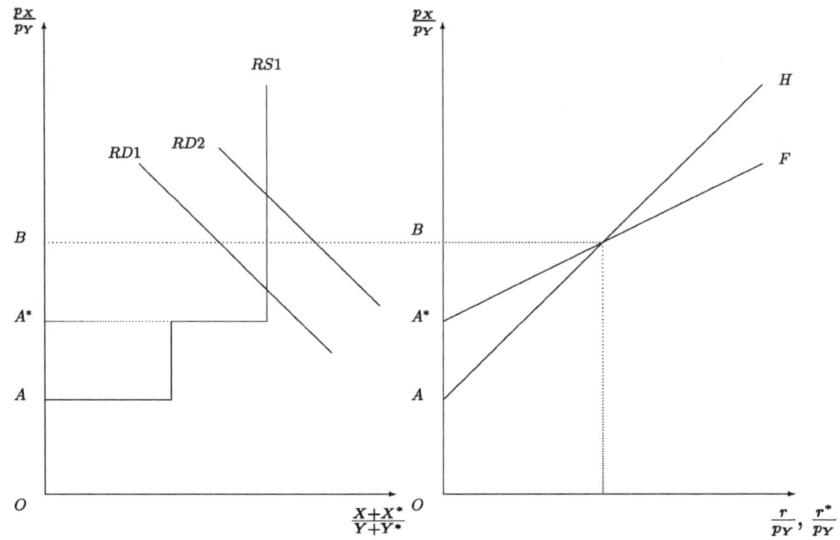

Fig. 3. The equilibrium without international capital mobility.

Let us turn to the demand side. Given the utility function (12), the relative demand for good X in the world is represented by

$$\frac{C_X + C_X^*}{C_Y + C_Y^*} = \left(\frac{\alpha}{1-\alpha}\right)\left(\frac{p_Y}{p_X}\right). \tag{13}$$

We shall focus on a case in which countries are incompletely specialized in production. There are two types of equilibria. First, suppose that the expenditure share of good X is small and the relative demand curve of the world is given by RD1 in Figure 3. Then, in the free trade equilibrium at which RS1 intersects with RD1, the countries produce both goods, and Home offers the higher return to capital than Foreign. This implies that capital would flow into Home from Foreign under free capital mobility. Second, suppose that the share of expenditure on good X is large and the relative demand curve of the world is given by RD2 in Figure 3. Then, in contrast to the previous case, Foreign offers the higher return to capital than Home at the free trade equilibrium, which implies that capital would flow into Foreign from Home.

4. Capital movements

In this section, I shall consider a situation in which capital mobility as well as goods trade is allowed between countries. As we have shown in Figure 3, the direction of capital movements crucially depends on the size of the relative demand. If the expenditure share of good X is small and the

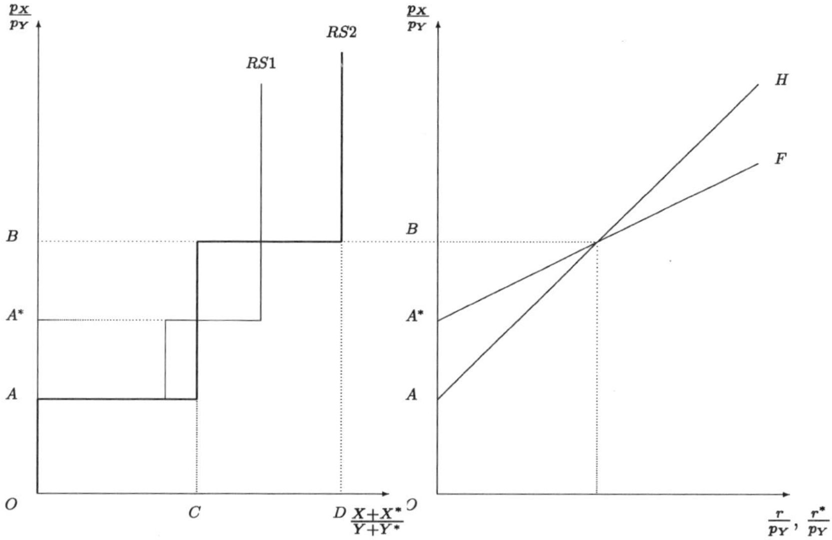

Fig. 4. RS2 is the relative supply curve under capital movements.

relative demand curve is given by RD1, then Foreign would export capital to Home. On the other hand, if the share of expenditure on good X is sufficiently large and the relative demand curve is given by RD2, then Home would export capital to Foreign.

First, let us consider how international capital movements affect the shape of the relative supply curve. In Figure 4, the relative supply curve under capital mobility is drawn as RS2. The direction of capital movements depends on the relative price of good X. If $\mathrm{OA} < p_X/p_Y < \mathrm{OB}$, Home offers the higher return, and thus it attracts capital from Foreign. Eventually, all of capital moves to Home since it has the sufficiently large capacity.[6] Then, the relative supply of good X in the world is

$$\mathrm{OC} = \frac{(K+K^*)/a_{KX}}{L/a_{LY} - a_{LX}(K+K^*)/a_{KX}a_{LY} + L^*/a^*_{LY}}. \tag{14}$$

The production of good X concentrates at Home, and Foreign is driven to specialize in producing good Y. On the other hand, if the relative price of good X is sufficiently high, then the direction of capital flows is reversed. When p_X/p_Y is greater than OB, capital flows into Foreign. Since Foreign does not have the sufficiently large capacity, some of capital

[6] Remember that $K + K < K_{\mathrm{M}}$.

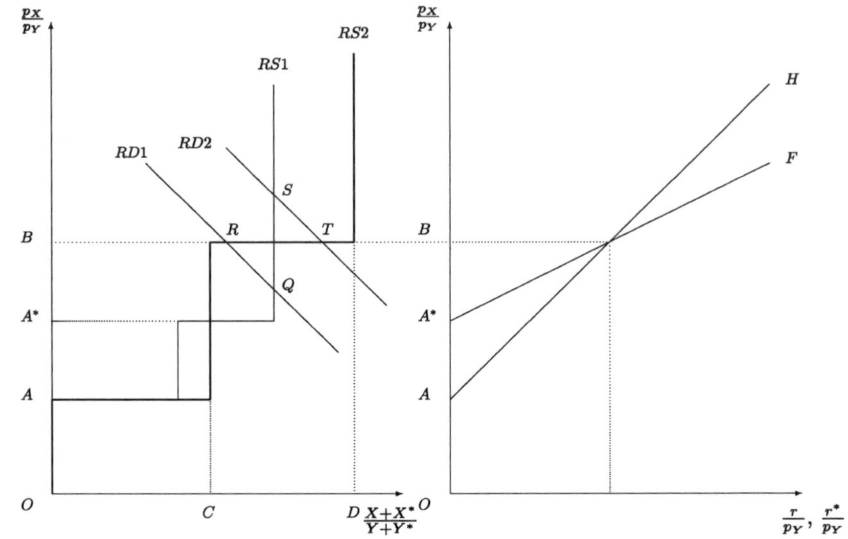

Fig. 5. The equilibrium with capital mobility.

remains at Home.[7] Then, the relative supply of good X is

$$\mathrm{OD} = \frac{(K + K^* - a^*_{KX}L^*/a^*_{LX})/a_{KX} + L^*/a^*_{LX}}{L/a_{LY} - a_{LX}(K + K^* - a^*_{KX}L^*/a^*_{LX})/a_{KX}a_{LY}}. \tag{15}$$

Foreign is driven to specialize in producing good X, and Home produces both good X and Y.[8] Finally, when p_X/p_Y equals OB, both countries offer the same return to capital. Then, the world relative supply curve becomes horizontal at OB and incomplete specialization can occur at either country. When the relative output of good X equals OC in Figure 4, all of capital is located at Home and Foreign produces good Y only. As capital moves to Foreign from Home, the relative output of good X expands, and eventually, Foreign specializes in producing good X at point D in Figure 4.[9]

Now, we are ready to show free trade equilibrium with capital mobility. Figure 5 shows how equilibrium changes due to capital movements. Let us first consider a case in which the relative demand curve is given by RD1. When the countries trade goods only, the relative supply curve is illustrated as RS1 and thus the equilibrium is point Q. At the equilibrium,

---

[7] Recall that $K + K^* > K^*_M$.

[8] It is easy to show that OD > OC given (A1) and (A2).

[9] The movement of capital from Home to Foreign raises the world output of good X because Foreign has the higher productivity of capital than Home. At the same time, the production of good Y shifts to Home from Foreign, but this reduces the world output of good Y since Home has a comparative disadvantage in producing good Y.

the return to capital is higher at Home than at Foreign. Thus, if capital markets are opened up, Home imports capital from Foreign. Under capital mobility, the relative supply curve is drawn as RS2, and thus the equilibrium turns out to be point R. Clearly, due to capital movements, the relative price of good X rises, which leads to an increase in the return to capital at both countries.

Next, suppose that the relative demand curve is given by RD2. Before capital markets are opened up, the equilibrium is point S, and Foreign offers the higher return to capital than Home. When capital mobility is allowed, Foreign imports capital from Home. The relative supply curve is illustrated as RS2, and thus the equilibrium turns out to be point T. Clearly, capital movements reduce the relative price of good X, which results in a fall in the return to capital at either country.

4.1. The effect of capital movements on income distribution

It is easy to show how capital movements affect income distribution within the countries. Suppose that good Y is numeraire, and thus $p_Y = 1$. Since both countries are incompletely specialized before and after capital movements, the wage rate for labor is fixed by the labor productivity of good Y,

$$w = \frac{1}{a_{LY}}, \quad w^* = \frac{1}{a^*_{LY}}. \tag{16}$$

The competitive conditions for good X, (7) and (9), hold with equality as well. Let θ_{iX} denote the distributive share of factor i ($i = K, L$) in good X, where $\theta_{LX} = wa_{LX}/p_X$ and $\theta_{KX} = ra_{KX}/p_X$. Then, with (7), we can derive

$$\hat{p}_X = \theta_{LX}\hat{w} + \theta_{KX}\hat{r}, \tag{17}$$

where $\hat{z}$ denotes dz/z, a relative change in a variable z. When the expenditure share of good X is small and the relative demand curve for good X is given by RD1, we can show that $\hat{p}_X > \hat{w} = 0$ due to capital movements. Given this result, (17) implies that $\hat{r} > \hat{p}_X > \hat{w} = 0$.[10] Thus, if the demand for the capital-intensive good is weak, the owners of capital gain but workers lose due to the liberalization of international capital movements.

Next, suppose that the share of expenditure on good X is large and the relative demand curve is given by RD2. Since the relative price of good X falls due to capital flows, workers at either country gain. However, the owners of capital lose since (17) implies that $\hat{r} < \hat{p}_X < \hat{w} = 0$.[11] Therefore, if

[10] Similarly, we can show that $\hat{r}^* > \hat{p}_X > \hat{w}^* = 0$ by using (9).

[11] We can also show that $\hat{r}^* < \hat{p}_X < \hat{w}^* = 0$.

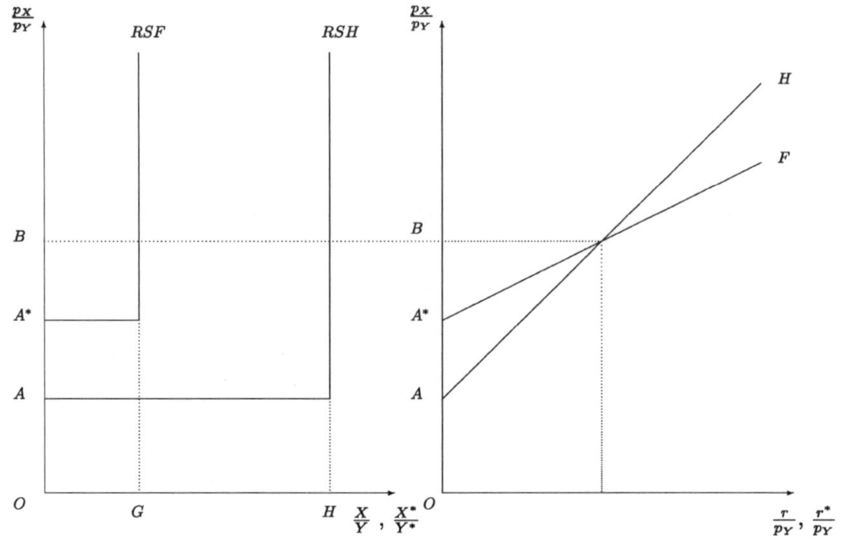

Fig. 6. The relative supply curve of each country.

the demand for the capital-intensive good is strong, capital movements hurt the owners of capital but benefit workers at either country.

4.2. The effect of capital movements on the pattern and value of goods trade

We can also examine how capital movements affect trade patterns.[12] Before capital markets are opened up, Home has the greater capacity of good X than Foreign because the initial amount of capital located at Home is large enough to overcome its absolute capital disadvantage (see Figure 1). This implies that Home exports good X for the import of good Y before capital mobility is allowed. Figure 6 shows the relative supply curve of each country under the initial allocation of capital between countries. *RSH* and *RSF* denote the the relative supply curve of Home and that of Foreign, respectively. We can show that Home's maximum relative output of good X is

$$\mathrm{OH} = \left(\frac{a_{LY}}{a_{LX}}\right)\left(\frac{K}{K_{\mathrm{M}} - K}\right).$$

Similarly, Foreign's counterpart is

$$\mathrm{OG} = \left(\frac{a^*_{LY}}{a^*_{LX}}\right)\left(\frac{K^*}{K^*_{\mathrm{M}} - K^*}\right).$$

[12] Here we assume that capitalists, the owners of capital, do not move together with capital.

Figure 6 shows that OH > OG, which implies that Home exports good X and imports good Y before capital mobility is allowed. The import value of good Y at Home is

$$VT = (1-\alpha)(wL + rK) - \left(\frac{a_{LX}}{a_{LY}}\right)\left(\frac{K_M - K}{a_{KX}}\right) \tag{18}$$

If we allow capital mobility across borders, the direction of capital flows is determined according to the pattern of the demand for goods. As before, we can consider the two cases. First, suppose that the share of expenditure on good X is small and the relative demand curve is given by RD1 in Figure 5. Then, before capital mobility is allowed, the equilibrium relative price of good X is lower than OB because the equilibrium is determined at point Q. Since Home offers the higher return to capital than Foreign, capital flows into Home from Foreign, which induces a change in the production structure of each country. By importing capital, Home expands the production of good X, which is shown by the rightward shift of the vertical portion of *RSH* in Figure 6. The vertical portion of *RSF* moves leftward since capital outflows drive Foreign to reduce the production of good X. As a result, the production patterns become more dissimilar between countries. We can also show that capital movements positively affect the value of trade in goods. Since capital allocated to Home increases and its return rises, (18) implies that capital movements raise the value of home import of good Y.[13]

The value of home export of good X also increases since the import of capital expands the production of good X. Therefore, if the expenditure share of the capital-intensive good is small, then capital movements would raise the value of trade in goods.

Next, suppose that the share of expenditure on good X is large and the relative demand curve is given by RD2 in Figure 5. Before capital mobility is allowed, the equilibrium is determined at point S in Figure 5, and the equilibrium relative price of good X is higher than OB. When the capital markets are opened up, capital flows into Foreign from Home. As a result, the production patterns become more similar between countries since *RSH* moves leftward and *RSF* moves rightward in Figure 6. The trade pattern in goods may not change when OH is greater than OG, i.e., Home exports capital and good X and imports good Y. Suppose this trade pattern is preserved at the equilibrium with capital mobility. Since capital allocated to Home decreases and its return falls, (18) implies that the value of home import of good Y declines. The value of home export of good X falls as

[13] Let VT′ denote the value of home import of good Y at the equilibrium with capital movements. Then, we have $VT' = (1-\alpha)(wL + r'K) - (a_{LX}/a_{LY})(K_M - K'/a_{KX})$, where r' is the equilibrium return and K' is the equilibrium amount of capital allocated to the production of good X at Home. We can show that $VT' - VT = (1-\alpha)(r'-r)K + (a_{LX}/a_{LY})(K'-K)/a_{KX} > 0$ because $r' > r$ and $K' > K$.

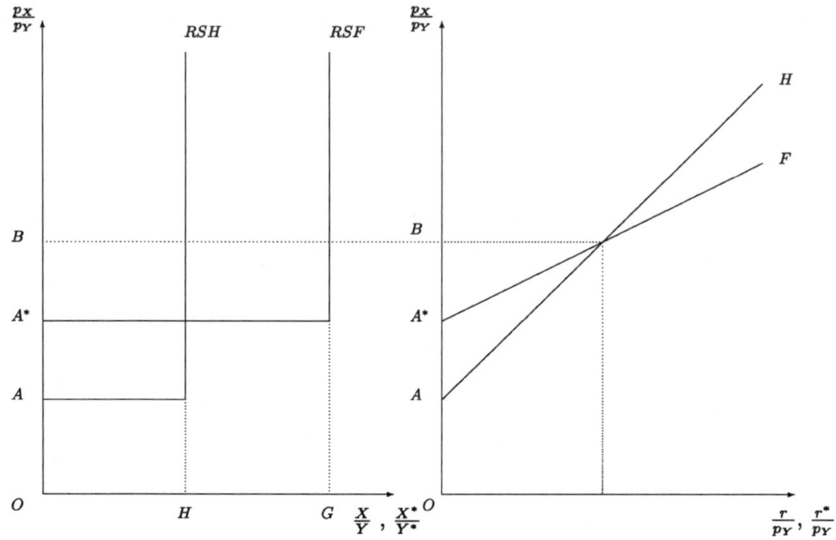

Fig. 7. Capital movements can cause a situation in which the maximum relative output of good X at home becomes smaller than that at foreign.

well since the production of good *X* declines at Home. This result suggests that capital movements reduce the value of trade in goods when the share of expenditure on the capital-intensive good is large.

However, the above result may not hold when the pattern of trade is reversed. As a result of capital movements, veridical portion of *RSH* may coincide with that of *RSF*. Then, Home exports capital but imports both good *X* and *Y*. Further increases in the volume of capital movements may cause the reversal of the trade pattern in goods. If the vertical portion of *RSH* moves to the left of that of *RSF* (see Figure 7), the trade pattern in goods may be reversed, i.e., Home may export capital and good *Y* for the import of good *X*. Under this trade pattern, an increase in the home export of capital raises the value of home export of good *Y*. Therefore, if the relative demand for the capital-intensive good is high, it can be ambiguous whether capital movements raise or reduce the value of goods trade.

5. *Conclusions*

I have incorporated the structure of goods demand into the simple Ricardian framework developed by Jones (1980). This allows us to examine when international capital movements benefit or hurt the owners of capital and workers at countries that trade goods and capital with each other. If both countries are incompletely specialized in production and the world demand for the capital-intensive good is strong, capital flows into the country having the higher capital productivity and the world production of the capital-intensive good expands. As a result, the capital-intensive good becomes less expensive, which benefits workers but hurts the owners of capital. However, if the demand for the capital-intensive good is weak, the direction of capital movements is reversed, and the effects on income distribution are totally opposite.

It is also possible to examine the effect of capital flows on the pattern and value of trade in goods. When capital mobility is not allowed, the country with the absolute capital disadvantage exports the capital-intensive good due to its overwhelmingly large amount of capital. If the relative demand for the capital-intensive good is low, this trade pattern is preserved at the equilibrium with capital mobility. Then, the value of goods trade increases due to capital movements. On the other hand, if the demand for the capital-intensive good is high, the country having the absolute capital advantage imports capital and expands the production of the capital-intensive good. Then, the country with the absolute capital disadvantage, which initially exports the capital-intensive good, may eventually import it at the equilibrium with capital mobility. When such a reversal in the pattern of trade arises, it is ambiguous whether capital movements raise or reduce the value of goods trade.

Acknowledgements

I am grateful to Prof. Ronald Jones for his valuable comments on the earlier draft of this chapter. I would also like to thank the participants of APJAE Symposium on International Trade in Honor of Prof. Ronald Jones at City University of Hong Kong, and seminar participants at Hitotsubashi University and Kwansei Gakuin University for helpful discussions. All remaining errors are my own.

References

Jones, R. (1980), Comparative and absolute advantage. *Swiss Journal of Economics* 116, 235–260.

Jones, R. (1994), Trade and capital mobility: a Ricardian setting. *Nagasaki Prefectural University Review* 28, 77–89.

Jones, R. (2000), *Globalization and the Theory of Input Trade*. The MIT Press, Cambridge, MA.

Jones, R., Dei, F. (1983), International trade and foreign investment: a simple model. *Economic Inquiry* 21, 449–464.

Jones, R., Ruffin, R. (1975), Trade patterns and capital mobility. In: Parkin, M., Nobay, A.R. (Eds.), *Current Economic Problems*. Cambridge University Press, New York, pp. 307–332.

Markusen, J. (1983), Factor movements and commodity trade as complements. *Journal of International Economics* 19, 341–356.

Mundell, R. (1957), International trade and factor mobility. *American Economic Review* 47, 321–335.

Neary, J.P. (1995), Factor mobility and international trade. *Canadian Journal of Economics* 28, S4–S23.

Ohyama, M. (1989), Factor endowments and the pattern of commodity and factor trade. *Keio Economic Studies* 23, 57–60.

Purvis, D. (1972), Technology, trade, and factor mobility. *Economic Journal* 82, 991–999.

Schumer, C., Roberts, P.C. (2004), Second thoughts on free trade. *New York Times* January 6.

Suzuki, K. (1989), Choice between international capital and labor mobility for diversified economies. *Journal of International Economics* 27, 347–361.

Uekawa, Y. (1972), On the existence of incomplete specialization in international trade with capital mobility. *Journal of International Economics* 2, 1–24.

Yomogida, M. (2006), International capital movements: who gains and who loses? *Asia-Pacific Journal of Accounting and Economics* 13, 123–134.

CHAPTER 18

International Outsourcing Under Monopolistic Competition: Winners and Losers

Viet Do and Ngo Van Long

Department of Economics, McGill University, 855 Rue Sherbrooke West, Montréal, Québec, H3A 2T7, Canada
E-mail addresses: viet.do@mail.mcgill.ca; ngo.long@mcgill.ca

Abstract
We show that, even with flexible domestic wages, international outsourcing may worsen the welfare of the home country and reduce the profits of all firms. If wages are rigid, outsourcing is welfare-improving if and only if the sum of the "trade creation" effect and the "exploitation effect" exceeds the "trade diversion" effect. A wage subsidy may improve welfare. We also extend the model to a two-period framework. Delaying outsourcing can be gainful because the fixed cost of outsourcing may fall over time. A social planner would choose a different speed of outsourcing than that achieved under laissez-faire.

Keywords: International outsourcing, monopolistic competition, welfare-improving, outsourcing

JEL classifications: F12, F13, F16

1. Introduction

International outsourcing has become an increasingly common phenomenon in advanced economies. Sinn (2004) reports that no fewer than 60% of German small and medium enterprises (SMEs) have established plants outside the old EU. He argues that outsourcing and offshoring have gone too far. Firms that relocate all or parts of their production in low-wage economies have contributed to a rising pool of unemployed workers. Due to wage inflexibility, globalization "creates unemployment instead of gains from trade" (Sinn, 2004, p. 117). The main losers are obviously the low-skilled manufacturing workers in advanced economies. What can be said about the winners? In popular discussions, many people would think that the winners of globalization are owners of firms that outsource.

Frontiers of Economics and Globalization
Volume 4 ISSN: 1574-8715
DOI: 10.1016/S1574-8715(08)04018-9

This view, however, is implicitly based on the assumption that either outsourcing does not involve a fixed cost, or the outsourcing firm is a monopolist. When outsourcing firms have rivals, and fixed costs of outsourcing are non-negligible, it is not clear that the firms always come out as winners.

In this chapter, using a model of outsourcing by monopolistically competitive firms, we show that, even in the case of flexible domestic wages, international outsourcing (and/or relocation of plants to a low-wage economy) by home firms may worsen the welfare of the home country and reduce the profits of all firms in the industry, even though it is individually rational for each firm to choose to outsource. If a social planner for the home country can choose the extent of international outsourcing, his optimal choice will not coincide with the equilibrium outcome under laissez-faire. A wage subsidy may reduce the extent of outsourcing and improve welfare. This confirms Sinn's perception that "Wage subsidies make the state into a partner. They do not establish minimum wage demands and create the very flexibility in wage setting that is required for reaping the gains from trade" (Sinn, 2004, p. 119).

When the wage in the home country is rigid we show that outsourcing is welfare-improving for the home country if and only if the sum of the "trade creation" effect and the "exploitation" effect exceeds the "trade diversion" effect of the access to the low-wage labour in the foreign country.

We also extend the model to a two-period framework, where each domestic firm faces the choice between beginning outsourcing (or relocation) in the first period, or in the second period. Delaying outsourcing can be gainful because the fixed cost of outsourcing may fall over time. However, delaying means the firm's variable production cost in period 1 will be higher than that of rivals who are outsourcing. The equilibrium of this two-period game may involve some firms outsourcing in period 1, while others will outsource in period 2, even though ex ante they are identical firms. Under monopolistic competition with homogeneous costs, in equilibrium, the sum of discounted profits is identical for all firms. Again, a social planner for the home country may choose a different speed of outsourcing than the speed achieved by an industry under laissez-faire.

Before proceeding, we would like to make some remarks on the literature on international outsourcing. The impacts of outsourcing on wages and profits have been subjected to empirical studies (Feenstra and Hansen, 1999; Kimura, 2002; Görzig and Stephen, 2002; Görg and Hanley, 2004), as well as theoretical analysis (see, for example, Glass and Saggi, 2001; Grossman and Helpman, 2002, 2003, 2005; Grossman and Rossi-Hansberg, 2006a, 2006b; Jones, 2004; Long, 2005; and a special issue of the *International Review of Economics and Finance* 2005). A related literature is the theory of fragmentation, see Jones and Kierzkowski (1990, 2001a, 2001b), Long *et al.* (2005).

2. *The model*

2.1. The basic assumptions

This is basically a partial equilibrium model. We are concerned with international outsourcing decisions of firms in an advanced economy (called the home country, or H for short), and their impact on wages, profits, consumers surplus, and social welfare. We also want to find out if the gainers in H can compensate the losers in H, and how such compensation may take place.

The structure of the economy of H is simple. There are two industries, producing two goods. The numeraire good is produced by a perfectly competitive industry. The second good is a differentiated good, which consists of many varieties. It is produced by an imperfectly competitive industry consisting of a continuum of monopolistically competitive firms, indexed by z, where $z \in [0,1]$. Each of these firms produces a unique variety. The varieties are imperfect substitutes. The price of a unit of variety z is denoted by $p(z)$. Each firm has a constant marginal cost of production and has incurred a fixed cost (e.g., it bought the patent for the variety it produces). We take the number of firms as fixed, because we wish to focus on the short run issues. (In this respect, we follow the approach of Obstfeld and Rogoff, 1995.)

The foreign country is a low-wage economy. It does not have any differentiated-product firms of its own. Any variety produced in the foreign country is made possible only by a firm in H that sets up a factory abroad to take advantage of the low wage. Thus we do not treat the two countries symmetrically, in contrast to the standard literature on trade under monopolistic competition, as exemplified by the work of Helpman and Krugman (1985), Venables (1987) and others.

2.1.1. Consumers

Let $c(z)$ be the quantity of variety z consumed by the representative consumer. The sub-utility obtained from consuming the differentiated good is assumed to be:

$$C \equiv \left[\int_0^1 c(z)^{\frac{\theta-1}{\theta}} \mathrm{d}z\right]^{\frac{\theta}{\theta-1}}$$

where $\theta > 1$.

For any given sub-utility level $C \geq 0$, the consumer chooses the amounts $c(z)$ to minimize the cost of achieving C. It is as if she solved the problem

$$\min \int_0^1 p(z)c(z)\mathrm{d}z$$

subject to

$$\left[\int_0^1 c(z)^{\frac{\theta-1}{\theta}} \mathrm{d}z\right]^{\frac{\theta}{\theta-1}} = C$$

The solution to this problem is

$$c(z) = \left[\frac{p(z)}{P}\right]^{-\theta} C \tag{1}$$

where P is defined by

$$P \equiv \left[\int_0^1 p(z)^{1-\theta} \mathrm{d}z\right]^{\frac{1}{1-\theta}}$$

We call P the price index for the differentiated good. It is the cost of achieving one unit of sub-utility. The utility function of the representative consumer is assumed to be quasi-linear: $U = v(C) + X$ where X is her consumption of the numeraire good. We assume that $v(C)$ is a strictly concave function, with $v(0) = 0$ and $v'(0) > 0$.

$$C^* \equiv v'^{-1}(P) \tag{2}$$

We assume that there are two types of workers: skilled workers and unskilled workers. The population consists of a continuum of individuals, indexed by $i \in [0,1]$. This continuum is the union of two continuums, $[0,n)$ and $[n,1]$, where $n < 1$ is the fraction of population that is unskilled. Skilled workers work only in the numeraire good sector. They earn a fixed wage W_s (for example, their marginal product is a constant). Unskilled workers work only in the differentiated-good sector. Their wage rate is denoted by W. Each unskilled worker is willing to offer $\bar{L}$ units of labour time, as long as the wage rate W exceeds their reservation wage $W_r = \gamma$. If $W = \gamma$ then they are indifferent between offering $\bar{L}$ or zero unit of labour (or any $L_u \in (0, \bar{L})$). We may interpret γ as the disutility of work. This labour supply behaviour may be rationalized by postulating the following overall utility function of the unskilled worker,

$$\hat{U}(C_u, X_u, L_u) = v(C_u) + X_u - \gamma L_u \quad \text{where} \quad 0 \leq L_u \leq \bar{L}$$

where $\bar{L}$ is his fixed endowment of labour. The total supply of unskilled labour in this economy is then $n\bar{L}$. The disposable income of an unskilled worker that supplies L_u units of labour is $Y_u = WL_u + T_u$, where T_u is the real transfer from the government. We assume that $Y_u > PC^*(P)$ so that all individuals consume the same quantity of differentiated good.

The welfare of the unskilled worker is calculated as follows. Given P, his demand for the differentiated good is $C^*(P)$. The excess of Y_u over $PC^*(P)$ is used to buy the numeraire good: $X_u = Y_u - PC^*(P)$. His welfare level is therefore $\hat{U}_u = v(PC^*(P)) + [Y_u - PC^*(P)] - \gamma L_u$ where $L_u = \bar{L}$ as long as $W > \gamma$.

2.1.2. Firms

Let $q(z)$ denote the output of firm z. We define the aggregate output of the differentiated-good industry by

$$Q \equiv \left[\int_0^1 q(z)^{\frac{\theta-1}{\theta}} \mathrm{d}z\right]^{\frac{\theta}{\theta-1}} \quad \text{where } \theta > 1$$

Each firm z faces the demand function

$$q(z) = \left[\frac{p(z)}{P}\right]^{-\theta} c^*(P)$$

The firm that produces variety z takes P and $C^*(P)$ as given, and thus perceives the following demand function $q(z) = p(z)^{-\theta} P^{\theta} C^*(P) = p(z)^{-\theta} P^{\theta} v'^{-1}(P)$. The perceived elasticity of demand for firm zs output is θ. The perceived marginal revenue is $p(z)(\theta-1)/\theta$. Suppose the firm uses unskilled labour as the only input, and each additional unit of output requires 1 unit of unskilled labour. Then marginal cost is W. Equating MR to MC, the firm sets its price at $\hat{p}(z) = (\theta/\theta - 1)W \equiv \mu W$ where $\mu > 1$.

The profits of firms are redistributed to individuals who are their owners. We denote by Π the aggregate profit of the differentiated-good sector. We assume for simplicity that only skilled workers are owners of firms. The disposable income of the representative skilled worker is then $Y_s = W_s \bar{L}_s + (1-n)\Pi + T_s$ and her welfare level is $\hat{U}_s = v(C^*(P)) + \left[Y_s - PC^*(P)\right] - \gamma_s L_s$.

2.2. Equilibrium output and equilibrium profit

In what follows, we assume that $v(C_i) = (1/\alpha)C_i^{\alpha}$ where $0 < \alpha < 1$. Then

$$C_i = v'^{-1}(P) = P^{-\beta} \quad \text{where} \quad 1 < \beta \equiv \frac{1}{1-\alpha} < \theta$$

The demand function for variety z is then $q(z) = p(z)^{-\theta} P^{\theta-\beta} \equiv q(p(z),P)$. The firm maximizes $\pi(z) = (p(z) - W)q(z)$.

From the firm's first-order condition, we obtain a useful relationship between its equilibrium output, $q(z)$, and its equilibrium profit, $\pi(z)$.

$$\begin{aligned}\hat{\pi}(z) &= \frac{\hat{p}(z)}{\theta}\hat{q}(z) = \frac{\mu W}{\theta}\hat{q}(z) = \frac{W}{\theta-1}\hat{q}(z) = (\mu-1)W\hat{q}(z) \\ &= \left(\frac{\hat{p}(z)}{\theta}\right)\hat{p}(z)^{-\theta} P^{\theta-\beta} = \frac{P^{\theta-\beta}}{\theta \hat{p}(z)^{\theta-1}}\end{aligned} \tag{3}$$

This implies that for a given $\hat{p}(z)$, the higher is the industry price index P, the higher is firm zs equilibrium profit. When all firms charge the same price, equilibrium profit is

$$\hat{\pi}(z) = \frac{1}{\theta}\hat{p}(z)^{1-\beta} = \frac{1}{\theta}[\mu W]^{1-\beta} \quad \text{where} \quad \beta > 1 \tag{4}$$

2.3. The closed economy: Equilibrium and welfare

Suppose the supply of unskilled labour is fixed at nL. If the wage is flexible, the output of the differentiated-product sector is $\bar{Q} = \bar{C} = n\bar{L}$ and the equilibrium price is $\bar{P} = (n\bar{L})^{\alpha-1}$. Note that, in our model with no fixed cost, output and price under monopolistic competition are identical to those under perfect competition. The wage rate under monopolistic competition is lower than that under perfect competition. The equilibrium wage rate is

$$W = \bar{W} = \frac{\bar{P}}{\mu} = \frac{(n\bar{L})^{\alpha-1}}{\mu}$$

As long as $\bar{W} > \gamma$, the total employment of unskilled workers is $n\bar{L}$.

Consumer surplus is

$$CS = \int_0^{\bar{Q}} v'(Q)\mathrm{d}Q - \overline{PQ} = v(\bar{Q}) - \overline{PQ} = \frac{(1-\alpha)(n\bar{L})^{\alpha}}{\alpha}$$

The aggregate profit of the differentiated-good industry is $\Pi = (\bar{P} - \bar{W})\bar{Q}$. Aggregate unskilled workers' surplus, denoted by ω, is $(\bar{W} - \gamma)\bar{Q}$. Social welfare in the closed economy is then

$$\begin{aligned}\bar{\Omega} &= CS + \Pi + \omega = [v(\bar{Q}) - \bar{P}\bar{Q}] + [(\bar{P} - \bar{W})\bar{Q}] + [(\bar{W} - \gamma)n\bar{L}] \\ &= v(\bar{Q}) - \gamma n\bar{L}\end{aligned}$$

The overall utility of the representative unskilled worker is

$$\hat{U}_{\mathrm{u}} = v(\bar{Q}) + \left[Y_{\mathrm{u}} - \bar{P}\bar{Q}\right] - \gamma L_{\mathrm{u}} = v(\bar{Q}) - \bar{P}\bar{Q} + \left[\bar{W} - \gamma\right]L_{\mathrm{u}} + T_{\mathrm{u}}$$

3. International outsourcing: The case of zero fixed cost of outsourcing

Now let us open the economy to trade. To focus on outsourcing, we assume that the foreign country is a low-wage economy, with surplus labour available at the wage $W^{\mathrm{f}} < W$. Assume residents of the low-wage economy consume only the numeraire good. In this section, we assume that home firms can relocate their plants to the low-wage economy costlessly. The outputs of relocated differentiated-good firms are exported back to the home country (H), where they are sold at the price p^{f} per unit, where $p^f = \mu W^f$. Let s be the fraction of home firms that are relocated to the low-wage economy, and let $\hat{q}^f$ be the equilibrium output of the representative relocated firm. By assumption, all the outputs are re-exported to home. The value of exports from the low-wage economy (foreign) to home is then $sp^f\hat{q}^f = s\mu W^f\hat{q}^f$. The profits of the relocated firms, $s(\mu - 1)W^f\hat{q}^f$, are repatriated to home. The difference between the foreign country's export revenue and the repatriated profit is $sW^f\hat{q}^f$, which is used to buy the numeraire good from home. The current account of each country is therefore balanced. It is as if the relocated firms themselves ship the quantity $sW^f\hat{q}^f$ of the numeraire good to pay labour in foreign and ship their output back to H.

We now consider the simplest scenario, where outsourcing does not involve any fixed cost. Under this scenario, all firms would want to relocate, unless the wage rate in home falls to W^f.

3.1. Case 1: Flexible wage in the home country

Assume $\bar{W} > W^f \geq \gamma$. All firms would want to relocate to the low-wage economy, unless the wage rate in H falls to W^f. In this sub-section, we assume that the threat of relocation and hence of unemployment in H is sufficient to cause the wage rate in H to fall to W^f. The price falls to $P^f = \mu W^f < \mu\bar{W} = v'(\bar{Q})$. So output of the differentiated good expands to $\tilde{Q} > \bar{Q}$, where $v'(\tilde{Q}) = P^f$. Of the total output $\tilde{Q}$, the quantity $\bar{Q}$ is produced in home. The difference $\tilde{Q} - \bar{Q}$ is produced in the low-wage country. Home's social welfare is then $\Omega^1 = v(\tilde{Q}) - W^f L^f - \gamma\bar{Q}$.

Proposition 1. *If the wage rate in the home country is flexible, outsourcing will expand industry output, lower the price, and increase H's aggregate welfare.*

Proof. From the strict concavity of the function $v(Q)$,

$$v(\tilde{Q}) - v(\bar{Q}) > v'(\tilde{Q})[\tilde{Q} - \bar{Q}]$$

Define

$$R(\tilde{Q}, \bar{Q}) \equiv v(\tilde{Q}) - v(\bar{Q}) - v'(\tilde{Q})[\tilde{Q} - \bar{Q}] > 0$$

The change in welfare is then

$$\begin{aligned}\Omega^1 - \bar{\Omega} &= v(\tilde{Q}) - v(\bar{Q}) - W^f L^f \\ &= R(\tilde{Q}, \bar{Q}) + v'(\tilde{Q})[\tilde{Q} - \bar{Q}] - W^f L^f \\ &= R(\tilde{Q}, \bar{Q}) + (\mu W^f)[\tilde{Q} - \bar{Q}] - W^f L^f \\ &= R(\tilde{Q}, \bar{Q}) + (\mu - 1)W^f L^f > 0\end{aligned}$$

where $R(\tilde{Q}, \bar{Q}) > 0$ because of the strict concavity of $v(Q)$.

Of course, home unskilled workers receive a lower wage income. Their gains in consumer surplus may not be sufficient to offset the fall in wage income. But the gainers (the capitalists and the consumers) can compensate the losers.

3.2. Case 2: Wage rigidity in the home country

Consider now the opposite extreme where unskilled wage is fixed at $\bar{W} > W^{\mathrm{f}}$. All workers in H will become unemployed, even though individually each would be willing to work at any wage $W \geq \gamma$. All the differentiated-product firms relocate to the low-wage country, and since their prices are now $p^{\mathrm{f}} = \mu W^{\mathrm{f}}$, the industry output is $\tilde{Q}$, where $v'(\tilde{Q}) = \mu W^{\mathrm{f}}$. Firms employ L^{f} units of foreign labour, where$L^{\mathrm{f}} = \tilde{Q}$. Who gain and who lose?

Under outsourcing, consumer's surplus is $CS = v(\tilde{Q}) - p^{\mathrm{f}}\tilde{Q}$. Firms' aggregate profits are

$$\Pi = [p^{\mathrm{f}} - W^{\mathrm{f}}]\tilde{Q} = \frac{1}{\theta}(\mu\bar{W})^{1-\beta} \text{ as } \beta > 1$$

Since the unskilled workers are now unemployed, they lose all their worker's surplus. The social welfare of the home country under outsourcing is thus

$$\Omega^2 = CS + \Pi = v(\tilde{Q}) - W^{\mathrm{f}}\tilde{L}^{\mathrm{f}} = v(\tilde{Q}) - W^{\mathrm{f}}\tilde{Q} = v(\tilde{Q})\frac{1}{\mu}v'(\tilde{Q})\tilde{Q}$$

The change in welfare is

$$\begin{aligned}
\Omega^2 - \bar{\Omega} &= [v(\tilde{Q}) - v(\bar{Q})] - \left\{\frac{v'(\tilde{Q})}{\mu}\tilde{Q} - \gamma\bar{Q}\right\} \\
&= [v(\tilde{Q}) - v(\bar{Q})] - W^{\mathrm{f}}[\tilde{Q} - \bar{Q}] - \{W^{\mathrm{f}}\bar{Q} - \gamma\bar{Q}\} \\
&= v(\tilde{Q}) - v(\bar{Q}) - \mu W^{\mathrm{f}}[\tilde{Q} - \bar{Q}] - \{W^{\mathrm{f}}\bar{Q} - \gamma\bar{Q}\} \\
&\quad + (\mu - 1)W^{\mathrm{f}}[\tilde{Q} - \bar{Q}] \qquad (5)
\end{aligned}$$

The first term, $[v(\tilde{Q}) - v(\bar{Q})] - \mu W^{\mathrm{f}}[\tilde{Q} - \bar{Q}]$, which is positive, may be called the "*trade creation*" effect of the access to low-wage foreign labour: consumers in H buy more of the differentiated good, because the price is now lower. This term is can be represented by the familiar Harberger triangle (see Figure 1). The second term, $W^{\mathrm{f}}\bar{Q} - \gamma\bar{Q}$, may be called "*trade diversion*" effect: home producers are diverted to the foreign labour market because of the lower wage there. But from the point of view of home's welfare, the true cost of Hs labour is only γ per unit, not the fixed wage$\bar{W} > W^{\mathrm{f}}$. The expression $W^{\mathrm{f}}\bar{Q} - \gamma\bar{Q}$ is positive if the reservation wage γ in H is lower than the foreign wage W^{f}. The third term, $(\mu - 1)W^{\mathrm{f}}[\tilde{Q} - \bar{Q}]$ is called the "*exploitation*" effect: foreign labour is paid

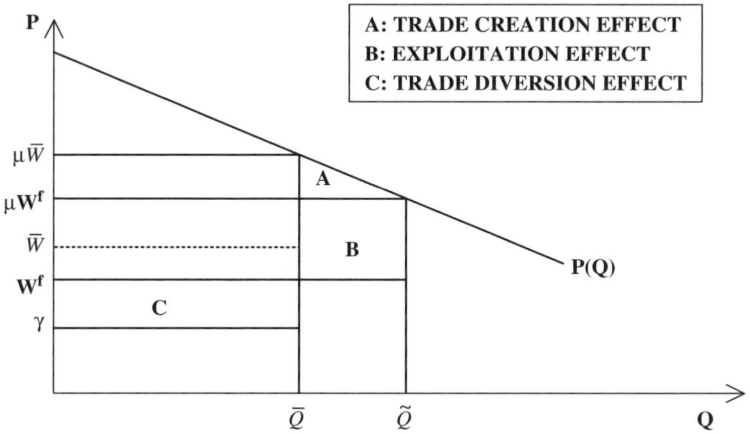

Fig. 1. Decomposition of gains and losses.

W^f but the price of what they produce is μW^f. The change in social welfare of the home country is therefore *ambiguous*; it is positive if the sum of the trade creation effect and the exploitation effect exceeds the adverse trade diversion effect. A (overly) sufficient condition for this is $\gamma \geq W^f$.

PROPOSITION 2. *If the wage rate in the home country does not fall to the foreign level W^f, unemployment will result, and the effect of outsourcing on social welfare of the home country is ambiguous, depending on whether the sum of the "trade creation" effect and the "exploitation" effect dominates the "trade diversion" effect.*

COROLLARY 2 (*Welfare-enhancing Wage Subsidies*). Assume $W^f > \gamma$. To avoid the "trade diversion" effect, the government of the Home country can introduce a wage-subsidy scheme: for each unit of home labour employed, the firms need to pay only W^f, and the government pays the difference, $\bar{W} - W^f$. In our model, this subsidy is non-distorting. Under this wage-subsidy scheme, social welfare is higher, because the "trade diversion" effect of outsourcing is avoided.

EXAMPLE 1. Outsourcing resulting in a decrease in welfare.

Let $\alpha = 1/3$, and $\theta = 2$. Then $\mu = 2$ and $\beta = 1.5$. Assume $n\bar{L} = 1/(2\sqrt{2})$. Then full employment output is $\bar{Q} = 1/(2\sqrt{2})$, and thus $\bar{P} = 2$ and $\bar{W} = 1$. Assume wage rigidity: the home wage is fixed at $\bar{W} = 1$ both before and after outsourcing. The reservation wage in the home country is $\gamma = 0.1$ and foreign wage is $W^f = 0.9$. The price levels before and after outsourcing are $\bar{P} = \mu\bar{W} = 2$ and $P^f = \mu W^f = 1.8$, respectively. Since $Q = v'^{-1}(P) = P^{(1/\alpha - 1)}$, we have $\bar{Q} = 2^{-1.5}$ and $\tilde{Q} = 1.8^{-1.5}$. The change in welfare, from Equation (5), is $\Omega^2 - \bar{\Omega} = -0.22257 < 0$. The "trade diversion" effect in this example dominates the sum of the "trade creation" effect and the "exploitation" effect. As the result, the net change in welfare is negative, i.e., a welfare reduction. The intuition is clear: when the foreign wage falls bellow the home wage, all firms have the incentive to outsource in order to maximize their profits. However, if the wage difference between the foreign country and home country is small, and the reservation wage at home is low, the social welfare will fall. This is because the increase in firm's profits and the increase in consumer's surplus are not large enough to compensate for the loss in worker's surplus at home.

While outsourcing may result in lower welfare, it remains true that, *given that outsourcing takes place*, a lower W^{f} always increases welfare.

PROPOSITION 3. *Given that outsourcing takes place and there is no fixed cost, a lower W^f always increases welfare.*

PROOF.

$$\frac{\mathrm{d}\Omega^2}{\mathrm{d}W^f} = \left[v'(\tilde{Q}) - \frac{v'(\tilde{Q})}{\mu} - \frac{\tilde{Q}}{\mu}v''(\tilde{Q})\right]\frac{\mathrm{d}\tilde{Q}}{\mathrm{d}W^{\mathrm{f}}} < 0$$

4. *Outsourcing with homogeneous fixed costs*

Now suppose that outsourcing involves a fixed cost $F(z) > 0$ for firm z. In this section, we assume $F(z) = F$ for all $z \in [0,1]$. In a later section, we will allow for heterogeneity in $F(z)$ across firms. A firm will choose to outsource only if the gain in gross profit (relative to keeping production in H) is sufficient to compensate for the fixed cost of outsourcing that must be incurred.

4.1. Equilibrium profit under outsourcing

Suppose that only a faction δ of firms outsource. Suppose that wage in home is rigid and fixed at some level W^{h} (for example, $W^{\mathrm{h}} = \bar{W}$, the equilibrium wage before outsourcing takes place). Foreign wage is $W^{\mathrm{f}} < W^{\mathrm{h}}$. The price of the varieties produced at home is $p^{\mathrm{h}} = \mu W^{\mathrm{h}}$ and the price of the varieties that are outsourced is $p^{\mathrm{f}} = \mu W^{\mathrm{f}} < p^{\mathrm{h}}$. The price index becomes

$$P = [(1-\delta)(\mu W^{\mathrm{h}})^{1-\theta} + \delta(\mu W^{\mathrm{f}})^{1-\theta}]^{1/1-\theta} \equiv P(\delta, W^{\mathrm{f}}, W^{\mathrm{h}})$$

Let $K \equiv [(1-\delta)(\mu W^{\mathrm{h}})^{1-\theta} + \delta(\mu W^{\mathrm{f}})^{1-\theta}]$. Clearly, the price index $P(\delta, W^{\mathrm{f}}, W^{\mathrm{h}})$ falls as the fraction δ rises:

$$\frac{\mathrm{d}P}{\mathrm{d}\delta} = \frac{1}{1-\theta}P^{\theta}\left[\frac{1}{(\mu W^{\mathrm{f}})^{\theta-1}} - \frac{1}{(\mu W^{\mathrm{h}})^{\theta-1}}\right] < 0$$

The equilibrium output of a home-produced variety is $q^{\mathrm{h}} = (\mu W^{\mathrm{h}})^{-\theta}P^{\theta-\beta}$, while that of an outsourced variety is $q^{\mathrm{f}} = (\mu W^{\mathrm{f}})^{-\theta}P^{\theta-\beta}$. The gross profit of the non-outsourcing firm is

$$\pi^{h} = q^{h}[\mu - 1]W^{h} = \frac{1}{\theta(\mu W^{h})^{\theta-1}} P^{\theta-\beta} \tag{6}$$

and that of the outsourcing firm is

$$\pi^{f} = \frac{1}{\theta(\mu W^{f})^{\theta-1}} P^{\theta-\beta}$$

Given the outsourcing fraction δ, the gain in *gross profit* by an outsourcing firm (as compared with the alternative of producing in H) is

$$g(\delta) \equiv \pi^{h} - \pi^{f} = \frac{1}{\theta}\left[\frac{1}{(\mu W^{f})^{\theta-1}} - \frac{1}{(\mu W^{h})^{\theta-1}}\right]\left[P(\delta; W^{f}; W^{h})\right]^{\theta-\beta} > 0$$

Clearly $g(\delta)$ is a decreasing function of δ.

Suppose there exists a number $\delta^{*} \in (0,1)$ that satisfies the equation

$$F = \frac{1}{\theta}\left[\frac{1}{(\mu W^{f})^{\theta-1}} - \frac{1}{(\mu W^{h})^{\theta-1}}\right]\left[P(\delta; W^{f}; W^{h})\right]^{\theta-\beta} \tag{7}$$

Then in equilibrium, δ^{*} is the fraction of the industry that chooses to outsource. At the price $P(\delta^{*}; W^{f}; W^{h})$, any individual firm is indifferent between remaining in the home country, and relocating to the low-wage economy.

The RHS of Equation (7) is a positive and decreasing function of δ and the LHS is a positive constant. If F is neither too large nor too small, the Equation (7) will identify a unique $\delta^{*} \in (0,1)$ which is the equilibrium fraction of the industry that choose to outsource. We now determine exactly the range (F_{L}, F_{H}) that F must belong to in order to generate an equilibrium with fractional outsourcing of the industry. We define

$$F_{L} = \frac{1}{\theta}\left[\frac{1}{(\mu W^{f})^{\theta-1}} - \frac{1}{(\mu W^{h})^{\theta-1}}\right]\left[P(1; W^{f}; W^{h})\right]^{\theta-\beta} = g(1) < g(\delta)$$

If the fixed cost F of outsourcing is lower than F_{L}, every firm will find that outsourcing is better than keeping production in H, regardless of how many firms it thinks will outsource (i.e., regardless of its conjectured δ value). Next define

$$F_{H} = \frac{1}{\theta}\left[\frac{1}{(\mu W^{f})^{\theta-1}} - \frac{1}{(\mu W^{h})^{\theta-1}}\right]\left[P(0; W^{f}; W^{h})\right]^{\theta-\beta} = g(0) > g(\delta)$$

With $F > F_{H}$, every firm will find that outsourcing is inferior to keeping production in H, regardless of how many firms it thinks will outsource. Note that the upper and lower threshold levels F_{L} and F_{H} are functions of the parameters (W^{h}, W^{f}).

EXAMPLE 2. Upper and lower threshold levels of fixed cost.

Assume $n\bar{L} = 1/(2\sqrt{2})$, $\theta = 2$ and $\alpha = 1/3$. Assume the wage rate at home is $W^{\mathrm{h}} = 1$ and $W^{\mathrm{f}} = 0.7$. When every firm chooses to outsource, i.e., $\delta = 1$, the price index will only include foreign prices and $P_{\delta=1} = \mu W^{\mathrm{f}} = 1.4$. Similarly, when every firm chooses keep production at home, i.e., $\delta = 0$, the price index only include home prices and $P_{\delta=0} = \mu W^{\mathrm{h}} = 2$. Then, the upper and lower threshold levels of fixed cost that generate an equilibrium with fractional outsourcing of the industry are $F_{\mathrm{L}} = 0.12677$ and $F_{\mathrm{H}} = 0.15152$. Therefore, when $0.12677 < F < 0.15152$, a positive fraction of firm will choose to relocate to the foreign country where cheap labour is available. For example, when $F = 0.14$, $\delta^* = 0.4$. As the foreign wage rate falls, both threshold levels of fixed cost increase and the gap between them widens. For example, when $W^{\mathrm{f}} = 0.5$, $F_{\mathrm{L}} = 0.25$, and $F_{\mathrm{H}} = 0.35355$.

Is it possible that the net profit under outsourcing is smaller than the net profit when outsourcing is not an available option? The answer is yes.

PROPOSITION 4. *If the fixed cost F of outsourcing is within the range (F_L, F_H), in equilibrium only a fraction $\delta^* \in (0,1)$ will outsource. The outsourcing firms and the non-outsourcing firms earn the same profit in equilibrium. This profit may be lower than what firms earn when outsourcing is not available. It is definitely lower, if $W^{\mathrm{h}} = \bar{W}$.*

PROOF. Suppose $W^{\mathrm{h}} = \bar{W}$, and assume that $F \in (F_{\mathrm{L}}, F_{\mathrm{H}})$. Then a positive fraction δ of the industry will outsource, and the remaining fraction, $1-\delta$, will keep production at home. Since no individual firm has any influence on industry price and output, and firms do not differ in cost characteristics, at the equilibrium, the net profit of an outsourcing firm is equal to that of a non-outsourcing firm. Now, since the price index P falls (relative to the closed economy level) with outsourcing, while p^{h} remains at $\mu\bar{W}$, the demand q^{h} is now lower, and the profit π^{h} is also lower (as compared with the closed economy case), see Equation (6). From this result, and the fact that at the outsourcing equilibrium with $\delta \in (0,1)$, all firms earn the same profit level, irrespective of their outsourcing status, it follows that all firms earn less profit when a fraction of the industry outsource in equilibrium. By continuity, if W^{h} is marginally lower than $\bar{W}$, outsourcing can reduce the profits of all firms.

EXAMPLE 3. Reduced profit under complete outsourcing.

Assume $n\bar{L} = 1/(2\sqrt{2})$, $\theta = 2$ and $\alpha = 1/3$. Assume that both before and after outsourcing, the home wage is fixed at $\bar{W} = 1$. In the closed economy, the price is $\bar{P} = \mu\bar{W} = 2$, and the profit of each firm is, from Equation (4)

$$\hat{\pi}_{\text{closed}} = \frac{1}{\theta} p(z)^{1-\beta} = \frac{1}{\theta} [\mu\bar{W}]^{1-\beta} = \frac{1}{2\sqrt{2}}$$

Suppose now outsourcing is available at some wage $W^{\mathrm{f}} < 1$. Suppose that the fixed cost is F_{L} so that every firm finds that outsourcing is better than keeping production at H, regardless of how many firms it believes to choose to outsource. Therefore all firms will outsource, and the gross profit under outsourcing is

$$\hat{\pi}_{\text{out}} = \frac{1}{\theta}[\mu W^{\mathrm{f}}]^{1-\beta} = \frac{1}{2\sqrt{2W^{\mathrm{f}}}} > \frac{1}{2\sqrt{2}} > 0$$

The net profit from outsourcing is

$$\hat{\pi}_{\text{out}}^{\text{net}} = \hat{\pi}_{\text{out}} - F_{\mathrm{L}} = \frac{1}{2\sqrt{2W^{\mathrm{f}}}}[1 - (1 - W^{\mathrm{f}})] > 0$$

Clearly, since $W^{\mathrm{f}} < \sqrt{W^{\mathrm{f}}}$ when W^{f}, the following inequality holds: $\hat{\pi}_{\text{out}}^{\text{net}} < \hat{\pi}_{\text{closed}}$. It follows that, given $F = F_{\mathrm{L}}$, the net profit from outsourcing is smaller than the profit that each firm makes when outsourcing is not available.

Corollary 4. If $W^{\mathrm{h}} = \bar{W}$, and fractional outsourcing takes place (i.e., $\delta \in (0,1)$), then employment in H will fall.

Proof. Since q^{h} falls relative to the output of the representative firm in the closed economy case, the total employment in H falls from $n\bar{L}$ to δq^{h}.

Remark 1. Let us consider a given $F > 0$. At the initial closed economy equilibrium, the output is $\bar{Q} \equiv n\bar{L}$, the price is $\bar{P} = (n\bar{L})^{1-\beta}$, and the wage rate is $\bar{W} = \bar{P}/\mu$. If W^{h} is just marginally lower than $\bar{W}$, there will be no outsourcing, because the saving in variable cost is not sufficient to outweigh the fixed cost of outsourcing. Outsourcing begins only when W^{f} falls below the critical threshold value W^{fc} (which is a function of F and $\bar{W}$) defined by

$$F = \frac{1}{\theta}\left[\frac{1}{(\mu W^{\mathrm{fc}})^{\theta-1}} - \frac{1}{(\mu \bar{W})^{\theta-1}}\right][P(0; W^{\mathrm{fc}}; \bar{W})]^{\theta-\beta}$$

i.e.,

$$\mu W^{\mathrm{fc}} = \left[\frac{(\mu \bar{W})^{\theta-\beta}}{\theta F + (\mu \bar{W})^{1-\beta}}\right]^{\frac{1}{\theta-1}}$$

Further falls in W^{f} will lead to a positive δ. If W^{h} remains fixed at $\bar{W}$ due to institutional wage rigidity, the employment level in H will fall, as described in Corollary 4 above.

Example 4. Critical level of foreign wage, given fixed cost of outsourcing.

Assume the parameters take the same values as in Example 1, except now there is a fixed cost of outsourcing, $F = 0.3$. Given this fixed cost, firms will relocate only if the foreign wage falls bellow a critical level W^{fc}

which satisfies

$$\mu W^{\mathrm{fc}} = \left[\frac{(\mu \bar{W})^{\theta-\beta}}{\theta F + (\mu \bar{W})^{1-\beta}} \right]^{\frac{1}{\theta-1}}$$

Thus $W^{\mathrm{fc}} = 0.54097$. As the fixed cost becomes larger, say $F = 1.0$, this critical level of foreign wage falls to $W^{\mathrm{fc}} = 0.2612$. The fall in foreign wage is necessary to compensate for a large cost of relocating production facilities.

REMARK 2. (*On the simultaneous determination of the extent of outsourcing and post-outsourcing domestic wage*).

Now assume W^{h} is *flexible*. Then it will fall to preserve full employment in H. In that case, we have the following two conditions that simultaneously determine the equilibrium value of δ and W^{h}, denoted by δ^* and $W^{\mathrm{h}*}$:

$$(1-\delta)q^{\mathrm{h}} = n\bar{L} \tag{8}$$

and

$$F = \frac{1}{\theta}\left[\frac{1}{(\mu W^{\mathrm{f}})^{\theta-1}} - \frac{1}{(\mu W^{\mathrm{h}*})^{\theta-1}}\right][P(\delta;\, W^{\mathrm{f}};\, W^{\mathrm{h}*})]^{\theta-\beta} \tag{9}$$

where $q^{\mathrm{h}} = (\mu W^{\mathrm{h}*})^{-\theta}[P(\delta;\, W^{\mathrm{f}};\, W^{\mathrm{h}*})]^{\theta-\beta}$. We can then compute the gains in consumer surplus, the loss in worker's surplus, the gains (or losses) in net profits, the net welfare gains, etc., associated with a given pair (F, W^{f}) where W^{f} is assumed to be below the *critical* threshold value W^{fc}.

4.2. Possibility of welfare loss under outsourcing with fixed cost, with or without domestic wage flexibility

We know that if (i) the fixed cost is zero, and (ii) $\gamma = W^{\mathrm{f}}$, then the socially optimal extent of outsourcing is $\delta^{\mathrm{so}} = 1$, and this coincides with the equilibrium extent of outsourcing. However, with positive fixed cost of outsourcing, it is possible to construct numerical examples where the gains from increased consumer surplus is not enough to compensate for the reduction in profits caused by outsourcing.

REMARK 3. (*On consumer's surplus under fractional outsourcing and flexible domestic wage*). Before outsourcing, the consumer's surplus is

$$\overline{CS} = \frac{1}{\alpha}(\bar{Q})^{\alpha} - (\bar{Q})^{\alpha} = (\bar{Q})^{\alpha}\left[\frac{1}{\alpha} - 1\right] = (\mu \bar{W})^{-\alpha\beta}\left(\frac{1-\alpha}{\alpha}\right)$$

After outsourcing, with δ^* being the fraction of firms that outsource, the price level is $P(\delta^*; W^{\mathrm{f}}; W^{\mathrm{h}*})$ and the associated consumption index is

$$\hat{Q} = \left[P(\delta^*;\, W^{\mathrm{f}};\, W^{\mathrm{h}*})\right]^{-\beta} \tag{10}$$

The CS after outsourcing is

$$\widehat{CS}(=\hat{Q})^{\alpha}\left[\frac{1}{\alpha}-1\right]=\left[P(\delta^*;W^{\rm f};W^{\rm h*})\right]^{-\alpha\beta}\left(\frac{1-\alpha}{\alpha}\right)$$

EXAMPLE 5. Welfare loss under fractional outsourcing with fixed cost and flexible domestic wage.

As before, we assume $n\bar{L}=1/(2\sqrt{2}), \theta=2$ and $\alpha=(1/3)$. The home wage rate before outsourcing is $\bar{W}=1$. The fixed cost of production relocation is $F=0.3$. As shown in Example 4, the critical value of foreign wage is $W^{\rm fc}=0.54097$. As the foreign wage falls bellow this critical level, a fraction of firm will choose to outsource their production. Assume foreign wage is $W^{\rm f}=0.5$. We first calculate the level of consumer's surplus before outsourcing. This quantity is given by

$$\overline{CS}=\frac{1}{\alpha}(\bar{Q})^{\alpha}-(\bar{Q})^{\alpha}=(\bar{Q})^{\alpha}\left[\frac{1}{\alpha}-1\right]=(\mu\bar{W})^{-\alpha\beta}\left(\frac{1-\alpha}{\alpha}\right)=1.4142$$

The profit and worker surplus (assuming $\gamma=0$) in the closed economy case are $\pi_{\rm closed}=0.35355$ and $\omega_{\rm closed}=0.35355$. Assume that the home wage rate is **flexible**, then $W^{\rm h}$ will fall bellow $\bar{W}$ to preserve full employment in home country. The equilibrium values δ^* and $W^{\rm h*}$ can be obtained from the systems of Equation (8) and (9):

$$(1-\delta^*)q^{\rm h}=n\bar{L}=\bar{Q}=(\mu\bar{W})^{-\beta}$$
$$F=\frac{1}{\theta}\left[\frac{1}{(\mu W^{\rm f})^{\theta-1}}-\frac{1}{(\mu W^{\rm h*})^{\theta-1}}\right][P(\delta^*;W^{\rm f};W^{\rm h*})]^{\theta-\beta}$$

where

$$q^{\rm h}=(\mu W^{\rm h*})^{-\theta}[P(\delta^*;W^{\rm f};W^{\rm h*})]^{\theta-\beta}$$
$$P(\delta^*;W^{\rm f};W^{\rm h*})=[(1-\delta^*)(\mu W^{\rm h*})^{1-\theta}+\delta^*(\mu W^{\rm f})^{1-\theta}]^{\frac{1}{1-\theta}}$$

Substitute the parameter values in the above equations and solve for equilibrium values, we have $\delta^*=0.084504$ and $W^{\rm h*}=0.9215$. The price level after outsourcing is $P(\delta^*;W^{\rm f};W^{\rm h*})=1.7204$ and the associated consumption index is $\hat{Q}=[P(\delta^*;W^{\rm f};W^{\rm h*})]^{-\beta}=0.44316$. Therefore, the CS after outsourcing is $\widehat{CS}=1.5248$. The profit and worker surplus (assuming $\gamma=0$) in the fractional outsourcing case are $\pi_{\rm out}=0.0683$ and $\omega_{\rm out}=0.32580$. This example shows a net fall in welfare (by the amount 0.2033) when outsourcing takes place.

5. *Outsourcing under heterogeneous fixed costs*

Assume that firms differ with respect to fixed cost of outsourcing. Rang them in the increasing order of fixed costs, and assume that $F(0)=0$ and

$F(1) = \infty$. We now determine the equilibrium fraction of firms that choose to outsource when fixed costs differ across firms.

5.1. Equilibrium fractional outsourcing: The pivot firm

Suppose that only a fraction δ of firms outsource. Suppose the wage in home is rather rigid and is *fixed* at W^{h}. Taking into account the fixed cost of outsourcing, there is a "pivot firm", say firm z^*, that is indifferent between outsourcing and keeping production at home; clearly z^* satisfies the equation

$$F(z) = \frac{1}{\theta}\left[\frac{1}{(\mu W^{\mathrm{f}})^{\theta-1}} - \frac{1}{(\mu W^{\mathrm{h}})^{\theta-1}}\right][P(z;\, W^{\mathrm{f}};\, W^{\mathrm{h}})]^{\theta-\beta} \tag{11}$$

Assume $\theta > \beta$. Then the RHS of Equation (11) is a positive and decreasing function of z^* and the LHS is increasing in z^*. Since $F(z^*)$ is increasing in z^*, there is a unique z^* (which depends on the fixed W^{h} and W^{f}).

Lemma 1. Given $(W^{\mathrm{h}}, W^{\mathrm{f}})$, the equilibrium fraction of firms that choose to outsource is unique, and satisfies Equation (11).

Comparative statics. For a fixed W^{h}, a decrease in W^{f} will shift the RHS of Equation (11) up, leading to a larger z^*, as expected. More formally, define

$$\psi(z^*, W^{\mathrm{f}}) = F(z^*) - \frac{1}{\theta}\left[\frac{1}{(\mu W^{\mathrm{f}})^{\theta-1}} - \frac{1}{(\mu W^{\mathrm{h}})^{\theta-1}}\right]\left[P(z^*;\, W^{\mathrm{f}};\, W^{\mathrm{h}})\right]^{\theta-\beta} = 0$$

We want to show that

$$\frac{dz^*}{dW^{\mathrm{f}}} = \frac{[\partial\psi/\partial W^{\mathrm{f}}]}{[-\partial\psi/\partial z]} < 0$$

where

$$P(z^*;\, W^{\mathrm{f}};\, W^{\mathrm{h}}) = [(1 - z^*)(\mu W^{\mathrm{h}})^{1-\theta} + z^*(\mu W^{\mathrm{f}})^{1-\theta}]^{\frac{1}{1-\theta}}$$

The denominator $[-(\partial\psi/\partial z)]$ is negative, because $F' > 0$ and $(\partial P(z^*;\, W^{\mathrm{f}};\, W^{\mathrm{h}})/\partial z) < 0$ for $W^{\mathrm{f}} < W^{\mathrm{h}}$. The numerator is positive because $0 < ((\partial P(z^*;\, W^{\mathrm{f}})/\partial W^{\mathrm{f}})(W^{\mathrm{f}}/P)) < 1$.

Lemma 2. An increase in W^{f} will reduce z^*.

Suppose the wage in H is fixed at W^{h}. Does outsourcing decrease employment at home? After outsourcing, employment at home is

$$(1 - z^*)q^{\mathrm{h}} = (1 - z^*)(\mu W^{\mathrm{h}})^{-\theta}[P(z^*;\, W^{\mathrm{f}};\, W^{\mathrm{h}})]^{\theta-\beta} \tag{12}$$

The RHS of Equation (12) is decreasing in z^*. So employment falls, if W^{h} is fixed at $\bar{W}$. The quantity of foreign labour employed by firms that outsource abroad is $L^{\mathrm{f}} = z^*(\mu W^{\mathrm{f}})^{-\theta}[P(z^*)]^{\theta-\beta}$. Assume all workers prefer being employed at wage W^{h} to being unemployed with assistance payment W_{A}. Then the labour market allocates the fixed number of jobs at random.

5.2. Welfare under heterogeneous fixed costs

Social welfare consists of the utility of consuming the quantity Q (all output are consumed at home) minus (i) the effort cost of home labour, $\gamma(nL_{\mathrm{u}})$, where $nL_{\mathrm{u}} = (1-z^*)q^{\mathrm{h}} \leq n\bar{L}$, and (ii) the value of all payments to foreign factors of production. Note that (ii) is the sum of fixed costs and variable costs:

$$\int_0^{z^*} F(z)\mathrm{d}z + W^{\mathrm{f}}[z^* q^{\mathrm{f}}] = \Phi(z^*) + z^* W^{\mathrm{f}}(\mu W^{\mathrm{f}})^{-\theta}[P(z^*; W^{\mathrm{f}}; \bar{W})]^{\theta-\beta}$$

Welfare under outsourcing is

$$\begin{aligned}\hat{\Omega} = {} & v(\hat{Q}) - \gamma(1-z^*)(\mu W^{\mathrm{h}})^{-\theta}[P(z^*; W^{\mathrm{f}}; \bar{W})]^{\theta-\beta} \\ & -\Phi(z^*) - z^* W^{\mathrm{f}}(\mu W^{\mathrm{f}})^{-\theta}[P(z^*; W^{\mathrm{f}}; \bar{W})]^{\theta-\beta}\end{aligned}$$

where, using a modified version of Equation (10),

$$\hat{Q} = [P(z^*; W^{\mathrm{f}}; \bar{W})]^{-\beta} \tag{13}$$

The net gain (or loss) due to outsourcing is

$$\hat{\Omega} - \bar{\Omega} = [v(\hat{Q}) - v(\bar{Q})] - \{\gamma(1-z^*)q^{\mathrm{h}} + z^* W^{\mathrm{f}} q^{\mathrm{f}} - \gamma\bar{Q}\} - \Phi(z^*)$$

Again, this expression is ambiguous in sign. It can be negative if $W^{\mathrm{f}} - \gamma$ is sufficiently large.

Example 6. Heterogeneous fixed cost and negative welfare change.

Assume the same set of parameter values, i.e., $\theta = 2$ and $\alpha = 1/3$, then $\mu = 2$ and $\beta = 1.5$. The home wage rate is assumed to be fixed at $W^{\mathrm{h}} = \bar{W} = 5$, the foreign wage is $W^{\mathrm{f}} = 4$ and the reservation wage at home is $\gamma = 0.2$. Assume the "pivot firm" has the fixed cost of outsourcing $F(z^*) = 0.0355$. By substituting $F(z^*)$ into $F(z^*) = \frac{1}{\theta}[((1/(\mu W^{\mathrm{f}})^{\theta-1}) - (1/(\mu W^{\mathrm{h}})^{\theta-1}))][P(z^*; W^{\mathrm{f}}; W^{\mathrm{h}})]^{\theta-\beta}$, we can calculate the value of $z^* = 0.95933$. Given the value of z^*, the price index is $P(z^*; W^{\mathrm{h}}, W^{\mathrm{f}}) = 8.0656$. The price index before outsourcing is $P(0, W^{\mathrm{h}}, W^{\mathrm{f}}) = 10$. Using the above quantities, we calculate the change in welfare when outsourcing is allowed, given heterogeneous fixed costs of relocation: $\hat{\Omega} - \bar{\Omega} = [0.10765] - [0.16419] - \Phi(z^*) < 0$.

6. Optimal outsourcing vs. equilibrium outsourcing

Suppose the government can influence the fraction of firms that outsource, e.g., by subsidizing the fixed costs of outsourcing. What is the optimal z? This depends on whether W^h is fixed (which implies an increase in unemployment when there is an increase in outsourcing), or W^h is flexible (so that full employment is maintained at home). Let us consider the case where the wage rate in H is rigid. Social welfare consists of gross consumer surplus, minus the payments of fixed costs (to foreigners), minus the disutility of work of home workers.

Let z^{so} be the socially optimal fraction of the industry to outsource. Then z^{so} satisfies the equation:

$$F(z^{so}) = P^{\theta-\beta}\frac{\beta}{\theta-1}\left[\frac{1}{(\mu W^f)^{\theta-1}} - \frac{1}{(\mu W^h)^{\theta-1}}\right] - W^f[(\mu W^f)^{-\theta}P^{\theta-\beta}] - W^f z^{so}\frac{dq^f}{dz} \tag{14}$$

Equation (14) can be re-written as

$$\frac{1}{P^{\theta-\beta}}F(z^{so}) = \frac{\beta}{\theta-1}\left[\frac{1}{(\mu W^f)^{\theta-1}} - \frac{1}{(\mu W^h)^{\theta-1}}\right] - W^f(\mu W^f)^{-\theta}\left\{1 - z^{so}\frac{(\theta-\beta)}{(1-\theta)}P^{\theta-1}\left[\frac{1}{(\mu W^f)^{\theta-1}} - \frac{1}{(\mu W^h)^{\theta-1}}\right]\right\} \tag{15}$$

However, under laissez-faire, the equilibrium fraction of firms that outsource, denoted by z^*, satisfies the equation

$$\frac{1}{P^{\theta-\beta}}F(z^*) = \frac{1}{\theta}\left[\frac{1}{(\mu W^f)^{\theta-1}} - \frac{1}{(\mu W^h)^{\theta-1}}\right] \tag{16}$$

Thus we can have $z^{so} = z^*$ if and only if

$$\left[\frac{1}{(\mu W^f)^{\theta-1}} - \frac{1}{(\mu W^h)^{\theta-1}}\right]\left\{\left(\frac{\beta\theta-\theta+1}{\theta}\right)\mu^{\theta}(W^f)^{\theta-1} - (\theta-\beta)z^*P^{\theta-1}\right\} = 1 \tag{17}$$

PROPOSITION 5. *In general, the equilibrium extent of outsourcing, z^*, does not coincide with the socially optimal extent, z^{so}. A necessary and sufficient condition for the two values to coincide is that the equality* (17) *holds.*

Since z^* depends on the function $F(.)$, while condition (17) does not, we conclude that generically $z^{so} \neq z^*$.

7. *A two-period model*

Now consider a two-period framework. Assume that any firm that outsources incurs the fixed cost only once. We suppose that $F_1 > F_2$. By delaying outsourcing to the second period, a firm can save on the fixed cost, but at the same time, it cannot take advantage of the low wage in period 1. There are three strategies that a firm can adopt. We denote by (f, f) the strategy of outsourcing in both periods (and thus incurring the fixed cost in period 1). The strategy (h, f) means producing in H in period 1, and outsourcing in period 2. Finally, the strategy (h, h) means to keep production in H in both periods. Consider the case where firms are ex ante identical, i.e., the fixed cost of outsourcing is the same for all. Let F_t be the fixed cost that a firm must pay if it begins outsourcing in period t. Let z_1 denote the measure of firms that choose (f, f), $z_2 - z_1$ denote the measure of firms that choose (h, f), and $1 - z_2$ denote the measure of firms that choose (h, h). Let W^{f} be the wage in the foreign country, which we assume to be the same in both periods. Let $\bar{W}$ be the fixed wage in H.

The price index for the differentiated good in period 1 is

$$P_1 \equiv P(z_1; W^{\mathrm{f}}; \bar{W}) = [(1 - z_1)(\mu W^{\mathrm{h}})^{1-\theta} + z_1(\mu W^{\mathrm{f}})^{1-\theta}]^{\frac{1}{1-\theta}} \tag{18}$$

and for period 2,

$$P_2 \equiv P(z_2; W^{\mathrm{f}}; \bar{W}) = [(1 - z_2)(\mu W^{\mathrm{h}})^{1-\theta} + z_2(\mu W^{\mathrm{f}})^{1-\theta}]^{\frac{1}{1-\theta}} < P_1 \tag{19}$$

The period 1 demand and period 2 demand for the output of the firm that chooses (f, f) are $q_1(f,f) = (\mu W^{\mathrm{f}})^{-\theta}[P(z_1; W^{\mathrm{f}}; \bar{W})]^{\theta-\beta}$ and $q_2(f,f) = (\mu W^{\mathrm{f}})^{-\theta}[P(z_2; W^{\mathrm{f}}; \bar{W})]^{\theta-\beta}$. Similarly, $q_1(h,f) = (\mu \bar{W})^{-\theta}[P(z_1; W^{\mathrm{f}}; \bar{W})]^{\theta-\beta}$ and $q_2(h,f) = (\mu W^{\mathrm{f}})^{-\theta}[P(z_2; W^{\mathrm{f}}; \bar{W})]^{\theta-\beta} = q_2(f,f)$ and so on.

Let $r > 0$ denote the interest rate. Define $R = (1 + r)$. The present value of net profits of a representative firm of type (f, f) is

$$\begin{aligned} V(f,f) = {} & \frac{1}{\theta}(\mu W^{\mathrm{f}})^{1-\theta}[P(z_1; W^{\mathrm{f}}; \bar{W})]^{\theta-\beta} \\ & - F_1 + \frac{1}{\theta} R^{-1}(\mu W^{\mathrm{f}})^{-\theta}[P(z_2; W^{\mathrm{f}}; \bar{W})]^{\theta-\beta} \end{aligned} \tag{20}$$

That of a representative firm of type (h, f) is

$$\begin{aligned} V(h,f) = {} & \frac{1}{\theta}(\mu \bar{W})^{1-\theta}[P(z_1; W^{\mathrm{f}}; \bar{W})]^{\theta-\beta} - R^{-1}F_2 \\ & + \frac{1}{\theta} R^{-1}(\mu W^{\mathrm{f}})^{-\theta}[P(z_2; W^{\mathrm{f}}; \bar{W})]^{\theta-\beta} \end{aligned} \tag{21}$$

and that of a representative firm of type (h, h) is

$$V(h,f) = \frac{1}{\theta}(\mu \bar{W})^{1-\theta}[P(z_1; W^{\mathrm{f}}; \bar{W})]^{\theta-\beta} + \frac{1}{\theta} R^{-1}(\mu \bar{W})^{-\theta}[P(z_2; W^{\mathrm{f}}; \bar{W})]^{\theta-\beta} \tag{22}$$

All three types of firms co-exist in equilibrium if and only if there are values $z_1^* \in (0,1)$ and $z_2^* \in (z_1^*, 1)$ that satisfy the following pair of equations: $V(f,f) = V(h,f)$ and $V(f,f) = V(h,h)$. In this case, all firms earn the same present value of net profits, and they all make less profit than in the closed economy equilibrium. (Of course, lower profits do not necessarily mean lower welfare; the gain in consumer's surplus may dominate the fall in profits.)

EXAMPLE 7. Fractional outsourcing in a two-period model.

We assume $\theta = 2$ and $\alpha = 1/3$. Assume the home wage rate is rigid, $\bar{W} = 1$, and $W^{\mathrm{f}} = 0.5$. Let $F_1 = 0.55$. If they wait until period 2, the fixed cost of outsourcing falls to $F_2 = 0.27$. Assume a discount rate $r = 0.1$. It is easy to verify that the equilibrium values are $z_1^* = 0.34771$ and $z_2^* = 0.71468$.

8. Concluding remarks

We have developed a theoretical model to evaluate the effects of outsourcing on consumer surplus, profits, worker's surplus and welfare. One of the conclusions is that outsourcing is not necessarily profit-enhancing in equilibrium, even though it is individually rational for each firm to choose to outsource. This is because firms do not internalize the effect of their outsourcing decision on the industry price level. With a sufficiently large fall in price, the benefits of the low wage in the foreign country turns out to be a curse. Another source of welfare loss from outsourcing is the "trade diversion" effect of access to the foreign labour pool. Firms prefer foreign labour to domestic labour because of the low foreign wage rate. However, from the perspective of social welfare of the advanced economy, the true labour cost in the home country is not the high wage there, but only the disutility of work. In general, outsourcing need not be welfare-improving.

We have also indicated that the extent and the speed of outsourcing in a laissez-faire equilibrium may not be socially optimal. Under certain conditions, a slowing down of the speed of outsourcing can improve welfare.

Acknowledgements

We would like to thank Peter Debaere, Rod Falvey, Elhanan Helpman, Kim Long, Oliver Lorz, Peter Neary, Martin Richardson, Peter Robertson, Frank Stähler, Juuso Välimäki, Hans-Werner Sinn and participants at the Helsinki Workshop on International Outsourcing (June 1–2, 2007), and University of Otago Workshop on International Trade for comments and discussions. The financial support of SSHRC and FQRSC are gratefully acknowledged.

References

Feenstra, R., Hansen, G. (1999), The impact of outsourcing and high-technology capital on wages: estimates for the United States 1979–1990. *Quarterly Journal of Economics* 114, 907–940.

Glass, A., Saggi, K. (2001), Innovation and wage effects of international outsourcing. *European Economic Review* 45, 67–86.

Görg, H., Hanley, A. (2004), Does outsourcing increase profitability? *Economic and Social Review* 35, 367–387.

Görzig, B., Stephen, A. (2002), Outsourcing and firm-level performance. Discussion Paper 309, German Institute for Economic Research (DIW), Berlin.

Grossman, G.M., Helpman, E. (2002), Integration versus outsourcing in industry equilibrium. *Quarterly Journal of Economics* 117, 58–119.

Grossman, G.M., Helpman, E. (2003), Outsourcing versus FDI in industry Equilibrium. *Journal of the European Economic Association* 1, 317–327.

Grossman, G.M., Helpman, E. (2005), Outsourcing in a global economy. *Review of Economic Studies* 72, 135–159.

Grossman, G.M., Rossi-Hansberg, E. (2006a), *Trading Tasks: A Simple Theory of Offshoring*. Manuscript, Princeton University, Princeton, NJ.

Grossman, G.M., Rossi-Hansberg, E. (2006b), *The Rise of Offshoring: It's Not Wine for Cloth Anymore*. Manuscript, Princeton University, Princeton, NJ.

Helpman, E., Krugman, P. (1985), *Increasing Returns, Imperfect Competition and International Trade*. MIT Press, Cambridge, MA.

Jones, R.W. (2004), *Immigration versus Outsourcing: Effects on Labor Markets*. Unpublished manuscript, University of Rochester, Rochester, NY.

Jones, R.W., Kierzkowski, H. (1990), The role of services in production and international trade: a theoretical framework. In: Jones, R.W., Krueger, A. (Eds.), *The Political Economy of International Trade*. Blackwell, Cambridge, MA, pp. 31–48.

Jones, R.W., Kierzkowski, H. (2001a), Globalization and the consequence of international fragmentation. In: Calvo, G.A., Dornbush, R., Obstfeld, M. (Eds.), *Money, Capital Mobility, and Trade: Essays in Honor of Robert Mundell*. MIT Press, Cambridge, MA, pp. 365–387.

Jones, R.W., Kierzkowski, H. (2001b), A framework for fragmentation. In: Arndt, S., Kierzkowski, H. (Eds.), *Fragmentation and International Trade*. Oxford University Press, Oxford, UK, pp. 17–34.

Kimura, F. (2002), Subcontracting and the performance of small and medium firms in Japan. *Small Business Economics* 18, 1049–1065.

Long, N.V. (2005), Outsourcing and technology spillovers. *International Review of Economics and Finance* 16 (1), 137–152.

Long, N.V., Riezman, R., Soubeyran, A. (2005), Fragmentation and services. *North American Journal of Economics and Finance* 16 (1), 137–152.

Obstfeld, M., Rogoff, K. (1995), Exchange rate dynamics redux. *Journal of Political Economy* 103, 624–660.

Sinn, H.-W. (2004), The dilemma of globalisation: a German perspective. *Economie Internationale* 100, 111–120.

Venables, A.J. (1987), Trade and trade policy with differentiated products: a Chamberlinian–Ricardian model. *Economic Journal* 97, 700–717.

CHAPTER 19

The Effect of New Environment on Foreign Direct Investment in an Oligopolistic Heckscher–Ohlin Model

Sajal Lahiri[a] and Yoshiyasu Ono[b]

[a]*Department of Economics, Southern Illinois University Carbondale, MC 4515, 1000 Faner Drive, Carbondale, IL, 62901, USA*
E-mail address: lahiri@siu.edu
[b]*Institute of Social and Economic Research, Osaka University, Osaka 567-0047, Japan*
E-mail address: ono@iser.osaka-u.ac.jp

Abstract
We develop a $2 \times 2 \times 2$ model of international trade in which one of the sectors is oligopolistic. The oligopolistic sector consists of a given number of *a priori* identical firms belonging to one of the two countries, but some deciding to locate in the other country so as to realize higher profits. If a firm locates in the foreign country, its technological capability is assumed to go down due to the alien environment. In this framework we examine the effect of the environment on the level of foreign direct investment and on factor prices in the two countries.

Keywords: FDI, oligopoly, Heckscher–Ohlin

JEL classifications: F12, F23

1. *Introduction*

Professor Ron Jones's contributions to the Theory of International Trade in general and to the development of the well-known Heckscher–Ohlin (HO) model in particular cannot be overstated. His early contributions to the HO model has helped several generations of international trade theorists to understand the intricate working of trade models.[1] This chapter – on HO model in an imperfectly competitive framework – is our way of expressing our gratitude to this great economist.

---

[1] See Jones (1956). For one of his more recent writing on this model see Jones (2004).

Frontiers of Economics and Globalization
Volume 4 ISSN: 1574-8715
DOI: 10.1016/S1574-8715(08)04019-0

The HO model is one of the cornerstones of the modern international trade theory. In recent years, this model has been extended to allow for oligopolistic interdependence. Many researchers have examined if the traditional HO results carry over in the presence of oligopolistic interdependence. Markusen (1981) considered international duopoly as the basis of the interdependence and found that most of the traditional results may not hold in the extended HO model. In sharp contrast, Lahiri and Ono (1995) allowed free entry and exit of firms in the oligopolistic sector in each of the two countries and found that most of the traditional HO results go through in the new framework.[2]

There is an independent theoretical literature on foreign direct investment (FDI) which also uses imperfect competition – Cournot oligopoly or monopolistic competition – as the framework of analysis.[3]

In this chapter, we combine the above two strands in the literature to analyze a FDI equilibrium where factor prices are endogenous and in fact play a crucial role in establishing the equilibrium. Furthermore, we examine an aspect of FDI that is somewhat neglected in the theoretical literature. This aspect is about an alien 'environment' that foreign firms often face in a host country. In the empirical literature it is often found that if a firm locates in a foreign country, its technological capability goes down due to the alien environment such as different working practices, language difficulties, and other cultural differences. For example, Pothukuchi *et al.* (2002) find that cultural differences between the management of foreign firms located in India and their local partners have a significant negative impact on the productivity of the foreign firms. Hajkova *et al.* (2006) focus on 'business environment' including tax rates in the OECD countries and their effect on the profitability of foreign firms, but they also examine the effects of certain unobservable attributes representing cultural and other social differences in the host countries via fixed effects in their panel-data analysis.

In order to examine the effect of new environment on factor prices and the location of firms, we develop a two-country, two-good, two-factor HO model in which one of the two sectors is oligopolistic. All the firms in that industry belong to one of the countries (called the home country), but some of them locate themselves in the other country (called the foreign country). This division of all the firms between the two countries are endogenously determined so that profits are equated in the two countries. This equilibrium is achieved because of the flexibility of the factor prices, i.e., the factor prices work as the equilibrating force. We assume that the

---

[2] See also, among others, Shimomura (1998) and Fujiwara and Shimomura (2005) for contributions to this field.

[3] See, for example, Helpman (1984), Ethier (1986), Ethier and Horn (1990), Horstmann and Markusen (1992), Lahiri and Ono (1998), and Glass and Saggi (1999). There is also a substantial literature on foreign investment in a competitive trade model. For this, see, for example, Jones *et al.* (1983) and Ruffin (1984).

firms located in the foreign country have lower productivity than the firms located in the home country. The productivity differences are parametrized, and we examine the effect of changes in the parameter on the equilibrium factor prices in the two countries and on the incidence of FDI.

The layout of the chapter is as follows. The next section describes the model. Section 3 establishes the factor-price equalization result for our model when there are no productivity differences between the two countries. Comparative static exercises with respect to the productivity-difference parameter is carried out in Section 4. Finally, some concluding remarks are made in Section 5.

2. An H–O model of FDI

In our model there are two countries called the home and the foreign country. Each country has two sectors: one is competitive and the other is Cournot oligopolistic. Both the competitive and the oligopolistic goods are homogeneous and their international markets are fully integrated. In the oligopolistic sector, there are N firms in all belonging to the home country; n of them are located in the home country and $N-n$ in the foreign country. $N-n$ is therefore the incidence of FDI. The allocation of the N firms between the two countries is endogenously determined. Both commodities are produced from two factors, labor L and capital K, using constant-returns-to-scale technologies.

The production technology in the competitive sector is the same across the two countries and is given by

$$A = L_{\mathrm{a}}f(k_{\mathrm{a}}), \tag{1}$$

$$A^* = L_{\mathrm{a}}^*f(k_{\mathrm{a}}^*), \tag{2}$$

where

$$k_{\mathrm{a}} = K_{\mathrm{a}}/L_{\mathrm{a}} \quad \text{and} \quad k_{\mathrm{a}}^* = K_{\mathrm{a}}^*/L_{\mathrm{a}}^* .$$

Variables with superscript $*$ denote those for the foreign country.

The production technologies of oligopolistic firms in the two countries are characterized by the following production functions:

$$x = L_{\mathrm{o}}g(k_{\mathrm{o}}), \tag{3}$$

$$x^* = L_{\mathrm{o}}^*\theta g(k_{\mathrm{o}}^*), \tag{4}$$

where

$$k_{\mathrm{o}} = K_{\mathrm{o}}/L_{\mathrm{o}}, \quad \text{and} \quad k_{\mathrm{o}}^* = K_{\mathrm{o}}^*/L_{\mathrm{o}}^*,$$

and θ (≤ 1) is a parameter representing environmental factors facing the home firms in the foreign country that reduces the productivity of each home firm located in the foreign country in a Hicks-neutral fashion.

Cost-minimizing behavior in the two sectors gives

$$\omega(= w/r) = f(k_a)/f'(k_a) - k_a = g(k_o)/g'(k_o) - k_o, \tag{5}$$

$$\omega^*(= w^*/r^*) = f(k_a^*)/f'(k_a^*) - k_a^* = g(k_o^*)/g'(k_o^*) - k_o^*, \tag{6}$$

where w and r are the wage rate and the capital rent, respectively. Equations (5) and (6) yield the following functions:

$$k_a = k_a(\omega), \quad k_o = k_o(\omega), \tag{7}$$

$$k_a^* = k_a(\omega^*), \quad k_o^* = k_o(\omega^*), \quad \text{with} \quad k_a' > 0, \quad k_o' > 0. \tag{8}$$

Without loss of any generality, we assume that the marginal cost (price) equals unity in the competitive sector. Therefore,

$$f(k_a(\omega)) = r(\omega + k_a(\omega)), \tag{9}$$

$$f(k_a(\omega^*)) = r^*(\omega^* + k_a(\omega^*)), \tag{10}$$

which yield $w = w(r)$, $w^* = w(r^*)$ that satisfy

$$w'(r) = -k_a(\omega) < 0, \quad w'(r^*) = -k_a(\omega^*) < 0.$$

Each oligopolist has the following marginal cost c (c^*):

$$c = r(\omega + k_o(\omega))/g(k_o(\omega)) = c(w, r), \tag{11}$$

$$c^* = r^*(\omega^* + k_o(\omega^*))/(\theta g(k_o(\omega^*))) = c^*(w^*, r^*) = c(w^*, r^*)/\theta, \tag{12}$$

and maximizes profit π (π^*): [4]

$$\pi = (p - c)x, \tag{13}$$

$$\pi^* = (p - c^*)x^*, \tag{14}$$

where p is the price of the good in the oligopolistic sector.

Under free trade the inverse demand function for the good produced in the oligopolistic sector is

$$p = p(D + D^*, Y, Y^*), \tag{15}$$

where Y and Y^* are national income, and D and D^* the demand for the oligopoly good, in the two countries. Since the good market is assumed to

---

[4] We ignore fixed costs here for avoiding added complications. However, following the analysis in Lahiri and Ono (1995), these costs can easily be included without affecting any of our results.

be fully integrated, we have

$$D + D^* = nx + (N - n)x^*. \tag{16}$$

Given the demand function, the first-order profit maximizing conditions for the Cournot-oligopolistic firms are given by

$$p + p_X x = c, \tag{17}$$

$$p + p_X x^* = c^*, \tag{18}$$

where $p_X = \partial p(X, Y, Y^*)/\partial X < 0$. Since the N oligopolistic firms freely move between the two countries so as to realize higher profits, equilibrium profits in the two countries – π and π^*– are the same:

$$\pi = \pi^*. \tag{19}$$

We shall call this the FDI equilibrium.

Substituting (17) and (18) into (13) and (14) respectively and using (19) yields

$$\pi = -p_X x^2 = -p_X x^{*2} = \pi^*,$$

which implies that $x = x^*$ for any value of θ. Furthermore, by applying this property to (17) and (18) we find that $c = c^*$. Formally,

LEMMA 1. *For all values of* θ*,*

$$x = x^*, \quad c = c^*,$$

i.e., the marginal costs and output levels of all oligopolistic firms are the same in the FDI equilibrium.

Since the oligopolistic firms can move freely between the two countries and the oligopolistic-good markets in the two countries are fully integrated, if they are located in the country with higher marginal costs, they move to the other country. It will, in turn, affect the factor prices in the two countries and bring the marginal cost levels closer to each other. It is thus the free international movement of the oligopolistic firms that works as the equilibrating force in our model.

All the oligopolistic firms are assumed to be owned by nationals of the home country and the two countries realize the following national income levels:

$$Y = w\bar{L} + r\bar{K} + N\pi, \tag{20}$$

$$Y^* = w^*\bar{L}^* + r^*\bar{K}^*, \tag{21}$$

where $(\bar{L}, \bar{K})$ and $(\bar{L}^*, \bar{K}^*)$ are factor endowments in the two countries. The equilibrium conditions of the factor markets are

$$L_a + nL_o = \bar{L}, \tag{22}$$

$$L_a^* + (N-n)L_o^* = \bar{L}^*, \tag{23}$$

$$L_a k_a(\omega) + nL_o k_o(\omega) = \bar{K}, \tag{24}$$

$$L_a^* k_a(\omega^*) + (N-n)L_o^* k_o(\omega^*) = \bar{K}^*. \tag{25}$$

Since we consider labor-cost motivated FDIs, in the following argument we assume that the oligopolistic sector is labor intensive. Additionally, following the HO tradition, we assume away the possibility of factor-intensity reversal and require the factor endowments of both countries to be located in the cone of diversification. Formally,

Assumption A1.

$$k_a(\omega) > \bar{K}/\bar{L} > k_o(\omega), \text{ and } k_a(\omega^*) > \bar{K}^*/\bar{L}^* > k_o(\omega^*).$$

This completes the description of the model structure.

3. *Factor-price equalization with $\theta = 1$*

In this section, we assume that technologies in the two countries are the same so that $\theta = 1$, and then explore the property of the equilibrium. In the next section, we shall take this equilibrium as the benchmark and consider the effect of a change in θ on some of the key endogenous variables, starting from the equilibrium where $\theta = 1$.

From (11), (12) and lemma 1, we find

$$c(w(r), r) = c(w(r^*), r^*) \quad \text{when} \quad \theta = 1.$$

Furthermore, totally differentiating (11) and using (15) yields

$$\frac{dc}{dr} = -\frac{k_a - k_o}{g},$$

which is negative under assumption A1. Thus, the values of r and r^* satisfying $c(w(r), r) = c(w(r^*), r^*)$ must be the same since the functional forms of the functions $c(\cdot)$ and $w(\cdot)$ are the same in the two countries. Since there is a one-to-one relationship between w and r, the values of w and w^* must also be the same. Then from (7) and (8) it follows that the capital–labor ratios in the two countries are the same for each sector. Therefore, from (3), (4) and lemma 1, the amount of labor employed by each oligopolistic firm is also the same, i.e., $L_o = L_o^*$, when $\theta = 1$. Formally,

Proposition 1 *(Factor-price equalization theorem). Under assumption* A1, *and when $\theta = 1$, free trade leads to factor-price equalization in an HO world where one of the two sectors is a Cournot oligopoly sector and the* *oligopolistic firms can move freely between the two countries. The amount of labor employed by each oligopolistic firm is also the same internationally.*

It is to be noted that Markusen (1981) has shown factor-price equalization to be invalid in a model of international duopoly. In contrast, Lahiri and Ono (1995) found that introducing free entry and exist of oligopolistic firms in the two countries restores the factor-price equalization property of the HO model. Proposition 1 states that even when the total number of firms in the oligopoly sector is fixed, their free mobility between the two countries allows the factor-price equalization theorem to hold.

4. New environment and FDI

In this section, we examine the effect of new environment on factor prices and on the incidence of FDI. As mentioned earlier, by new environment we mean a reduction of θ that occurs when θ is initially 1.

Differentiating (11) and (12) yields

$$\mathrm{d}c = -\frac{[k_\mathrm{o}(\omega) - k_\mathrm{a}(\omega)]r}{g(k_\mathrm{o}(\omega))[\omega + k_\mathrm{a}(\omega)]} \cdot \mathrm{d}\omega, \tag{26}$$

$$\mathrm{d}c^* = -\frac{[k_\mathrm{o}(\omega^*) - k_\mathrm{a}(\omega^*)]r^*}{\theta g(k_\mathrm{o}(\omega^*))[\omega^* + k_\mathrm{a}(\omega^*)]} \cdot \mathrm{d}\omega^* - \frac{[\omega^* + k_\mathrm{o}(\omega^*)]r^*}{\theta^2 g(k_\mathrm{o}(\omega^*))} \cdot \mathrm{d}\theta. \tag{27}$$

Since lemma 1 implies that $c = c^*$ for all values of θ, equating Equations (26) and (27) under assumption A1 leads to

$$\left.\frac{\mathrm{d}\omega}{\mathrm{d}\theta}\right|_{\theta=1} - \left.\frac{\mathrm{d}\omega^*}{\mathrm{d}\theta}\right|_{\theta=1} = \frac{[\omega + k_\mathrm{a}(\omega)][\omega + k_\mathrm{o}(\omega)]}{k_\mathrm{o} - k_\mathrm{a}} < 0. \tag{28}$$

It implies that $\omega > \omega^*$ in the new equilibrium since initially ω was equal to ω^* (when $\theta = 1$, see proposition 1).

From Equations (22) to (25), we obtain

$$nL_\mathrm{o} = \frac{\bar{K} - k_\mathrm{a}(\omega)\bar{L}}{k_\mathrm{o}(\omega) - k_\mathrm{a}(\omega)}, \tag{29}$$

$$(N - n)L_\mathrm{o}^* = \frac{\bar{K}^* - k_\mathrm{a}(\omega^*)\bar{L}^*}{k_\mathrm{o}(\omega^*) - k_\mathrm{a}(\omega^*)}. \tag{30}$$

Since $x = x^*$ from lemma 1, Equations (3) and (4) yield

$$L_\mathrm{o}^* = \frac{g(k_\mathrm{o}(\omega))L_\mathrm{o}}{\theta g(k_\mathrm{o}(\omega^*))}. \tag{31}$$

By substituting n given by (29) and L_o^* given by (31) into (30) and applying (3) to the result we obtain

$$\begin{aligned}&\left[k_o(\omega^*) - k_a(\omega^*)\right] Nx[k_o(\omega) - k_a(\omega)]\\&\quad - \left[k_o(\omega^*) - k_a(\omega^*)\right] g(k_o(\omega))\left[\bar{K} - k_a(\omega)\bar{L}\right]\\&= \theta g\left(k_o(\omega^*)\right)\left[\bar{K}^* - k_a(\omega^*)\bar{L}^*\right][k_o(\omega) - k_a(\omega)].\end{aligned} \quad (32)$$

For the remaining analysis, for simplicity, we assume the demand function for the oligopoly good to be linear in price alone and thus the entire income effect to fall on the numeraire good.[5] That is,

$$p = \alpha - \beta(D + D^*).$$

Since $x = x^*$ for any value of θ, as stated in lemma 1, substituting this function into (17) and (18) solves x and x^* as follows:

$$x = x^* = \frac{\alpha - c}{(N+1)\beta}. \quad (33)$$

Differentiating (32) and (33) and then solving them along with (28) leads to

$$\begin{aligned}\Delta \frac{d\omega}{d\theta}\bigg|_{\theta=1} &= -(\omega + k_a)\left[(\omega + k_a)k_a' L_a^* + (\omega + k_a)k_o'(N - n)L_o^*\right]\\&\quad - (N - n)L_o(k_o - k_a)^2 < 0,\end{aligned} \quad (34)$$

$$\begin{aligned}\Delta \frac{d\omega^*}{d\theta}\bigg|_{\theta=1} &= -(N - n)L_o(k_o - k_a)^2 + \frac{(k_o - k_a)^2 Nr(\omega + k_o)}{g^2\beta(N+1)}\\&\quad + k_a' L_a(\omega + k_o)(\omega + k_a)\\&\quad - k_o'(\omega + k_a)L_o[N(\omega + k_o) - n(\omega + k_a)],\end{aligned} \quad (35)$$

where

$$\Delta = \frac{k_o'(k_a - k_o)^2 NL_o}{\omega + k_o} + \frac{(k_a - k_o)^3 Nr}{g^2\beta(N+1)(\omega + k_a)} + k_a'(k_a - k_o)(L_a + L_a^*) > 0.$$

From (34) and (35), a decrease in θ increases ω whereas the direction of the change in ω^* is ambiguous. However, as noted later in (28), $\omega > \omega^*$ in the new equilibrium (after a decrease in θ). These results are explained intuitively as follows. A decrease in θ lowers the profitability of the oligopolistic firms in the foreign country. This would, *ceteris paribus*, involve a flow of firms into the home country increasing the demand for labor (relative to that for capital) since the oligopolistic sector is assumed to be more labor intensive (assumption A1), raising the value of ω.

[5] See Lahiri and Ono (2004, chapter1), for example, for the exact specification of the underlying preferences.

There are two opposing effects on ω^*. The direct effect would lower ω^*, but the increase in ω indirectly raises it, and thus the net effect is ambiguous. Note that a higher value of ω implies a higher value of w and a lower value of r.

Having examined the effect of new environment on factor prices, we now examine the effect on the FDI incidence represented by the level of $N-n$. From Equations (29) to (31) we find

$$\left(\frac{n}{N-n}\right)\left(\frac{\theta g(k_o(\omega^*))}{g(k_o(\omega))}\right) = \left(\frac{\bar{K} - k_a(\omega)\bar{L}}{\bar{K}^* - k_a(\omega^*)\bar{L}^*}\right)\left(\frac{k_o(\omega^*) - k_a(\omega^*)}{k_o(\omega) - k_a(\omega)}\right). \tag{36}$$

Differentiating (36) yields

$$\begin{aligned}\frac{N(k_a - k_o)}{n(N-n)} \cdot \left.\frac{dn}{d\theta}\right|_{\theta=1} &= -(k_a - k_o) + \left[\frac{(\omega + k_a)k_o'}{\omega + k_o} + \frac{\bar{K}/\bar{L} - k_o}{k_a - \bar{K}/\bar{L}}k_a'\right]\frac{d\omega}{d\theta} \\ &\quad - \left[\frac{(\omega + k_a)k_o'}{\omega + k_o} + \frac{\bar{K}^*/\bar{L}^* - k_o}{k_a - \bar{K}^*/\bar{L}^*}k_a'\right]\frac{d\omega^*}{d\theta}.\end{aligned} \tag{37}$$

Substituting (28) into (37) and using (22)–(25) leads to

$$\begin{aligned}\frac{N(k_a - k_o)}{n(N-n)} \cdot \left.\frac{dn}{d\theta}\right|_{\theta=1} &= -(k_a - k_o) \\ &\quad - \left[\frac{(\omega + k_a)k_o'}{\omega + k_o} + \frac{\bar{K}^*/\bar{L}^* - k_o}{k_a - \bar{K}^*/\bar{L}^*}k_a'\right]\frac{(\omega + k_a)(\omega + k_o)}{(k_a - k_o)} \\ &\quad + \frac{k_a'(k_a - k_o)\left[(N-n)\bar{L} - n\bar{L}^*\right]}{n(k_a\bar{L}^* - \bar{K}^*)} \cdot \frac{d\omega}{d\theta}.\end{aligned} \tag{38}$$

From assumption A1, (34) and (38) it follows that

$$(N-n)\bar{L} - n\bar{L}^* > 0 \Rightarrow \left.\frac{dn}{d\theta}\right|_{\theta=1} < 0. \tag{39}$$

When $\theta = 1$ (36) reduces to

$$\frac{n}{N-n} = \frac{\bar{K} - k_a\bar{L}}{\bar{K}^* - k_a\bar{L}^*}.$$

Therefore, under assumption A1 we have

$$\frac{\bar{K}^*}{\bar{L}^*} \geq \frac{\bar{K}}{\bar{L}} \Leftrightarrow (N-n)\bar{L} - n\bar{L}^* > 0.$$

By applying the above property to (36) we obtain

$$\frac{\bar{K}^*}{\bar{L}^*} \geq \frac{\bar{K}}{\bar{L}} \Rightarrow \left.\frac{dn}{d\theta}\right|_{\theta=1} < 0,$$

i.e., if the home country is more labor-abundant, a reduction in θ leads to more oligopolistic firms – which are more labor intensive than the firms in the competitive sector – to locate in the home country.

The above results are summarized as follows:

PROPOSITION 2. *Under assumption* A1, *a reduction in new environment parameter θ from its initial value $\theta = 1$, will unambiguously lower the rental rate of capital, and increase the wage rate, in the home country and will decrease the incidence of FDI in the foreign country $(N-n)$ if the home country is more labor-abundant than the foreign country. After such a reduction in θ, the new equilibrium value of ω will be higher than that of ω^*.*

5. Conclusion

Direct investment in a foreign country may make the investors face a completely new business, social, and cultural environment and hence cause them to incur some additional costs. Their daily dealing with the workforce who possibly speaks a completely different language, with the government officials who follow a completely different protocol than their domestic counterparts, etc., can add up to a significant loss of productivity. This has been corroborated by empirical studies in different parts of the world. In this chapter we develop a two-country, two-good, two-factor HO model of FDI in which adjustments in factor prices allow an interior solution of a FDI equilibrium. The sector in which FDI takes place is Cournot oligopolistic. In this framework we examine the effect of a productivity loss in FDI due to new environment on factor prices and on the incidence of FDI.

We find that the loss of FDI productivity expands the international difference in the price of the factor that is used more intensively in the oligopolistic sector. We also find that, under certain conditions, it reduces the incidence of FDI.

Acknowledgement

Ono's research is financially supported by the Grants-in-Aid for Scientific Research, JSPS.

References

Ethier, W.J. (1986), The multinational firm. *Quarterly Journal of Economics* 101, 805–833.

Ethier, W.J., Horn, H. (1990), Managerial control of international firms and the pattern of direct investment. *Journal of International Economics* 28, 25–45.

Fujiwara, K., Shimomura, K. (2005), A factor endowment theory of international trade under imperfect competition and increasing returns. *Canadian Journal of Economics* 38, 273–289.

Glass, A.J., Saggi, K. (1999), FDI policies under shared factor markets. *Journal of International Economics* 49, 309–332.

Hajkova, D., Nicoletti, G., Vartia, L., Yoo, K.-Y. (2006), Taxation, business environment and FDI location in OECD countries. OECD Working Paper No. 502.

Helpman, E. (1984), A simple theory of international trade with multinational corporations. *Journal of Political Economy* 92, 451–471.

Horstmann, I., Markusen, J. (1992), Endogenous market structures in international trade (natura facit saltum). *Journal of International Economics* 32, 109–129.

Jones, R.W. (1956), Factor proportions and the Heckscher–Ohlin theorem. *The Review of Economic Studies* 24, 1–10.

Jones, R.W. (2004), Eli Heckscher and the Holy Trinity. Mimeo, Department of Economics, University of Rochester.

Jones, R.W., Neary, P.J., Ruanne, F. (1983), Two way capital flows: cross-hauling in a model of foreign investment. *Journal of International Economics* 14, 357–366.

Lahiri, S., Ono, Y. (1995), The role of free entry in an oligopolistic Heckscher–Ohlin model. *International Economic Review* 36, 609–624.

Lahiri, S., Ono, Y. (1998), Foreign direct investment, local content requirement, and profit taxation. *Economic Journal* 108, 444–457.

Lahiri, S., Ono, Y. (2004), *Trade and Industrial Policy under International Oligopoly*. Cambridge University Press, Cambridge.

Markusen, J.R. (1981), Trade and gains from trade with imperfect competition. *Journal of International Economics* 11, 531–551.

Pothukuchi, P., Damanpour, F., Choi, J., Chen, C.C., Park, S.H. (2002), National and organizational culture differences and international joint venture performance. *Journal of International Business Studies* 33, 243–265.

Ruffin, R.J. (1984), International factor movements. In: Jones, R.W., Kenen, P.B. (Eds.), *Handbook of International Economics*, vol. 1. North-Holland, Amsterdam, pp. 237–288.

Shimomura, K. (1998), Factor income function and an oligopolistic Heckscher–Ohlin model of international trade. *Economics Letters* 61, 91–100.

SECTION VII

International Trade Policy

CHAPTER 20

International Trade Agreements

Wilfred J. Ethier

Department of Economics, University of Pennsylvania, Philadelphia, PA 19104-6297, USA
E-mail address: ethier@econ.upenn.edu

Abstract
Over the last 60 years, multilateral trade liberalization has reduced tariffs to historically low levels. The dominant theory of multilateral trade agreements, based solely on terms-of-trade externalities between national governments, is the conventional wisdom among international trade theorists. But it features two defects that render it inconsistent with reality. This chapter proposes a simple formulation of the political economy of protection that dispenses with terms-of-trade externalities, predicts the properties that empirical work has confirmed, and is free of the counterfactual implications of the dominant approach. The model is applied to trade agreements.

Keywords: Trade agreements, the received theory, the terms-of-trade puzzle, the export-subsidy-transfer puzzle

JEL classifications: F02, F13

A prominent twentieth-century accomplishment of international trade theory was its theory of international trade policy and trade agreements. Building on Harry Johnson's classic paper (Johnson, 1953/1954), scores of contributions developed and elaborated what can be called the "Received Theory." The deservedly influential work of Bagwell and Staiger (1999, 2002) has triumphantly completed the research agenda implied by Johnson nearly half a century earlier. The multilateral trade liberalization of the previous six decades may well be the most successful deliberate exercise of economic policy in human history, so one could argue that understanding it is the most important task of applied economic theory.

Another aspect[1] of the Received Theory, emphasizing political economy, emerged in the 1980s. Grossman and Helpman (1994, 1995,

[1] See Hillman (1982, 1990), Hillman *et al.* (1995), and Hillman and Moser (1996). Surveys of the literature on the political economy of trade policy may be found in Hillman (1989), Magee (1994), Nelson (1988), and Rodrik (1995).

Frontiers of Economics and Globalization
Volume 4 ISSN: 1574-8715
DOI: 10.1016/S1574-8715(08)04020-7

2002) expound its most widely used component. The current state of the Received Theory is therefore conveniently described in two recent books by Bagwell and Staiger (2002) and Grossman and Helpman (2002).

However, the Received Theory is dramatically inconsistent with reality.[2] Thus, despite a half-century of work, we still lack a satisfactory framework for analyzing history's most significant example of deliberate economic policymaking.

1. Introduction

The central premise of the Received Theory is that trade agreements arise *solely* because countries with market power are concerned, to at least *some* degree, with the fact that trade barriers, imposed for *whatever* reason, can move the terms of trade in their favor, shifting real income there from the rest of the world.

As pointed out in Ethier (2004), this is inconsistent with actual multilateral trade agreements, which do *not* prevent countries from trying to influence their terms of trade. I refer to this discrepancy as the *Terms-of-Trade Puzzle*.

Nothing in the GATT prevents a country from implementing export taxes. In their negotiated concessions, countries have bound their import taxes: They have *not*, with very rare exception, bound export taxes. If the EU, for example, were to decide, for *whatever* reason, to impose aggressively a set of export taxes to improve its terms of trade, outstanding multilateral trade obligations would *not* prevent it from doing so.[3]

More realistic contributions to the Received Theory – notably Bagwell and Staiger (1999, 2002) – allow governments to care about any number of internal or political-economy objectives that relate to the domestic relative price of imports in terms of exports. This price can be manipulated unilaterally with trade policy, but, if a country has market power, such manipulation will impact the terms of trade, creating an international externality that shifts part of the cost of the policy onto the rest of the world. Dealing with this terms-of-trade externality is the *sole* reason for trade agreements in these models.[4] For six decades, successive GATT rounds have produced trade agreements that do not prevent

---

[2] See Ethier (2006, 2007).

[3] The United States is prevented by its Constitution from taxing exports. So here the puzzle is why the United States is willing to sign trade agreements that prevent only itself from terms-of-trade manipulation.

[4] Although the Received Theory assigns the central role to terms-of-trade considerations, they are ignored virtually without exception by trade lawyers and policymakers. See Regan (2004) for an argument that neither the public rhetoric of trade, nor the specific provisions of trade agreements, nor the full range of policy behavior of countries, is well explained by terms-of-trade considerations.

terms-of-trade manipulation while trade theorists have produced theories of trade agreements in which such prevention is the sole object.

To summarize, the Terms-of-Trade Puzzle has two aspects:

> (i) Trade agreements do not prevent countries from manipulating their terms of trade with export taxes; (ii) Countries nevertheless usually do not implement such taxes.

If the interests of owners of factors specific to export sectors are sufficiently important, governments will not wish to tax exports, so the Export-Tax Puzzle disappears. But this just introduces a new problem: the Export-Subsidy-Transfer Puzzle:

> In equilibrium, exporting nations will (i) offer large export subsidies, which will (ii) be incompletely countervailed by importing nations, who (iii) would decline to implement actual countervailing-duty laws, which lead to complete countervailing.

Thus the Received Theory necessarily implies equilibria that are dramatically counterfactual. Furthermore, the source of these counterfactual predictions is exactly the distinguishing feature of the Received Theory: the central role played by the terms of trade and/or by trade-tax revenue (Ethier, 2006, 2007).

The Grossman–Helpman variant (2002) of the Received Theory has received considerable empirical attention (Goldberg and Maggi, 1999; Gawande and Bandyopadhyay, 2000; Mitra *et al.*, 2002; McCallum, 2004). These papers have been uniformly supportive of the theory, but in a highly selective way. They have not investigated the predictions that reflect the central presumptions of the Received Theory (import subsidies for all politically unorganized import-competing sectors and export taxes for all politically unorganized export sectors). But they have given powerful evidence that, in politically organized import-competing sectors, protection is negatively related to the import penetration ratio, presumably reflecting the conflict between sectoral special interests and consumer surplus central to most political-economy approaches to trade policy. In such sectors, protection appears to be negatively related to the domestic elasticity of import demand. Furthermore, this literature argues persuasively that distinguishing between politically organized and unorganized sectors is crucial to understanding this dependence.

This chapter takes seriously both the theoretical argument that the Received Theory generates dramatically counterfactual predictions, because of its central presumption, and the empirical evidence that the conflict between sectoral interests and consumer surplus matters for policy, and that political organization determines how it matters. I construct a model on this basis and then investigate the role of trade agreements in such a context. I do not attempt a microeconomic explanation of this basis.

The chapter proceeds as follows. The next section describes an economic model, simplified for transparency,[5] and the following section adds a model of lobbying. I then describe a non-cooperative equilibrium in trade-policy setting, and investigate the potential role of a trade agreement.

2. *The Model: Economics*

Assume two countries (*H*ome and *F*oreign), two factors (*K*apital and *L*abor), and $N+1$ traded goods (0, 1,..., *N*). Good 0 is a numeráire good, produced by labor alone. Goods 1 to *N* are produced by capital and labor, with capital specific to each of these sectors. *H* imports goods 1 to *n* and exports goods $n+1$ to *N*.

Ownership of each specific factor is distributed uniformly over a fraction α_i of the population (labor force), with each individual owning some of the specific factors. Normalize so that $L = 1 = \alpha_1 + \cdots + \alpha_N$. Choose units so that a unit of good 0 is produced by a unit of labor. Thus, assuming good 0 is actually produced, the wage $w = 1$.

Each individual in each country has preferences summarized by the utility function $U = c_0 + u_1(c_1) + \cdots + u_N(c_N)$, where c_i denotes consumption of good *i*. This implies individual demand functions $d_i = d_i(Q_i)$, $i = 1,\ldots, N$, where Q_i denotes the relative price of good *i* in terms of good 0. Residual income is all spent on the numeráire good 0. I assume that endowments in both countries are such that each produces and consumes good 0.

Each country may tax or subsidize either imports or exports. For *H*, let Q_i and P_i denote, respectively, the domestic and international relative price (in terms of the numeráire) of good *i*, and τ_i one plus the *ad-valorem* trade tax t_i. Thus $Q_i = \tau_i P_i$, for $i = 1,\ldots, n$, and $Q_j = \tau_j / P_j$, for $j = n+1,\ldots, N$. Analogous *F* variables will be distinguished by asterisks.

2.1. International trade

Equilibrium in the world market for good *i*, $i = 1,\ldots, n$, is represented by $M_i(\tau_i P_i) = X_i^*(P_i/\tau_i^*)$, where M_i and X_1^*, respectively denote *H* import demand and *F* export supply. *H*'s import tax and *F*'s export tax thus determine P_i, independently of other sectors. This in turn implies the following:

$$\frac{\tau_i}{P_i}\frac{\mathrm{d}P_i}{\mathrm{d}t_i} = -\frac{e_i}{e_i + f_i^*}$$

[5] The attentive reader will have observed that I have followed the research strategy described in Jones (1977).

and

$$\frac{\tau_i}{Q_i}\frac{\mathrm{d}Q_i}{\mathrm{d}t_i} = \frac{\tau_i}{P_i}\frac{\mathrm{d}P_i}{\mathrm{d}t_i} + 1 = \frac{f_i^*}{e_i + f_i^*},$$

where $e_i \equiv -(\tau_i P_i M_i')/M_i > 0$ and $f_i^* \equiv P_i X_i' X^*/\tau_i^* X_i^* > 0$.

Similarly, equilibrium in the world market for goods $n+1$ to N can be represented by $M_j^*(\tau_j^* P_j) = X_j(P_j/\tau_j)$. Thus,

$$\frac{\tau_i}{P_i}\frac{\mathrm{d}P_i}{\mathrm{d}t_i} = -\frac{f_i}{f_i + e_i^*}$$

and

$$\frac{\tau_j}{Q_j}\frac{\mathrm{d}Q_j}{\mathrm{d}t_j} = \frac{\tau_j}{P_j}\frac{\mathrm{d}P_j}{\mathrm{d}t_j} - 1 = -\frac{e_j^*}{f_j + e_j^*}.$$

H imports of goods 1, ..., *n* need not equal in value *H* exports of goods $n+1$, ..., *N*: Trade balance is reached with a net echange of good 0.

3. *The model: Policy formation*

I now introduce the political-economy side of my model. My intent is to present a reduced-form model of policy formation consistent with what we have learned, as discussed above.

3.1. Lobbies

I assume that the owners α_i of each specific factor *i* potentially organize a lobby to bargain with the government over t_i. Nobody lobbies for policy regarding the numeráire good. The sectors differ in the abilities of the associated factor owners to organize as well as in the abilities of those that do organize to bring pressure to bear on the government (Olson, 1965).

If a sector does not organize, and so does not lobby, the government leaves trade policy unchanged at its existing level, which, for convenience, I assume to be free trade. Organized sectors elicit a government response. In this response, the government wishes to increase the specific-factor income $\pi_i(Q_i)$ of the associated lobby, but is also reluctant to reduce the consumer surplus $S_i\ (Q_i) \equiv u_i(c_i\ (Q_i)) - Q_i\ d_i(Q_i)$.

W_i denotes the objective function of the government if in that sector the α_i group is organized, and, thus, does lobby.

$$W_i(t_i) = (\delta_i - 1)\pi_i(Q_i) + s_i(Q_i) \quad (1)$$

Here, $\delta_i \geq 0$ denotes the importance the government attaches to the welfare of the α_i lobby. The government wishes to drive W_i as high as possible, but it is constrained in this by a desire not to drive consumer surplus too low;

$$S_i(Q) \geq \frac{1}{\varepsilon_i}. \tag{2}$$

The parameters δ_i and ε_i both reflect the political influence of the i lobby: higher values imply more influence. For simplicity I assume that they are always consistent in the sense that,

$$\delta_i > \delta_j \text{ if and only if } \in_i > \in_j. \tag{A1}$$

Number each country's imports in decreasing order of political influence, and likewise for each country's exports.

3.2. Policy choice

Differentiating (1) yields, for each import-competing sector (the sector subscript i is omitted):

$$\frac{t}{Q}\frac{\mathrm{d}W}{\mathrm{d}t} = \left[\delta\frac{x}{M} - 1\right] M\frac{f^*}{e + f^*}, \tag{3}$$

where x denotes domestic production. If the term in brackets on the right-hand side is positive, a tariff is called for. This will be more likely the greater the degree δ of political influence possessed by that sector's lobby. For a given degree of influence, this will be more likely the smaller the import penetration ratio M/x. If the term in brackets is negative, the sector's organized interest group lacks the power to influence policy: thus it will not lobby and the government will not depart from free trade.

If $\mathrm{d}W/\mathrm{d}t$ is indeed positive, the government will impose a tariff. Doing so will both increase x and reduce M: $\mathrm{d}W/\mathrm{d}t$ will remain positive. Thus the government will raise t until (2) binds. Thus, other things equal, the greater the degree ε of political influence, the greater the tariff t and the lower the import penetration ratio M/x.

Next, from (2),

$$\frac{\varepsilon}{t}\frac{\mathrm{d}t}{\mathrm{d}\varepsilon} = \frac{d}{S}\frac{f^*}{e + f^*}$$

More political influence ε implies a higher tariff t, but how much higher is negatively related to the import elasticity e.

Proposition 1. *A sectoral import-competing interest group is more likely to lobby the lower the import penetration ratio. For those that lobby, the tariff will positively relate to the degree of political influence, and negatively correlate with the import penetration ratio and to the elasticity of import demand.*

REMARK 1. *This simple model predicts just those properties that empirical investigations of the Grossman–Helpman model have supported.*

Turning to export sectors, we have

$$\frac{t}{Q}\frac{\mathrm{d}W}{\mathrm{d}t} = \left[-\delta\frac{x}{X} - 1\right]X\frac{e^*}{e^* + f} < 0. \tag{4}$$

Thus the government will wish to subsidize the exports of all politically organized sectors. If it does so, the resulting increase in the domestic relative price will reduce domestic demand, so that X/x will rise with the subsidy. From (2),

$$\frac{\varepsilon}{d}\frac{\mathrm{d}t}{\mathrm{d}\varepsilon} = -\frac{d}{S}\frac{e^*}{e^* + f}$$

Thus an increase in sectoral influence will increase the subsidy the government is willing to offer, and it will increase it more the smaller is the domestic export elasticity f.

PROPOSITION 2. *The government will be willing to subsidize the exports of all organized export sectors. The government's desired subsidy will be positively related to the degree of political influence, and negatively related to the export-production ratio and to the elasticity of export demand.*

4. The non-cooperative equilibrium

Next, consider the non-cooperative, trade-policy equilibrium between H and F. Because of the partial-equilibrium structure of the model, the various sectors can be analyzed independently. So look at good 1, which H imports and F exports, and whose respective specific-factor owners are organized and sufficiently potent to influence policy in each country. Then by Propositions 1 and 2, the H government wishes to tax imports of good 1, and the F government wishes to subsidize its export. Figure 1 shows the relevant policy plane.

4.1. Best responses

Let Q_1^A solve $S_1(Q_1^A) = 1/\varepsilon_1$. In Figure 1, A shows the value of τ_1 that will cause $Q_1 = Q_1^A$ when $\tau_1^* = 1$, that is, it denotes H's best response to $\tau_1^* = 1$. In like manner, B denotes F's best response to $\tau_1 = 1$.

The ϕ locus depicts all those combinations of τ_1 and τ_1^* implying the same value of Q_1 as at A. Thus ϕ is the locus of solutions to

$$M_1(Q_1^A) = X_1^*\left(\frac{Q_1^A}{\tau_1\tau_1^*}\right),$$

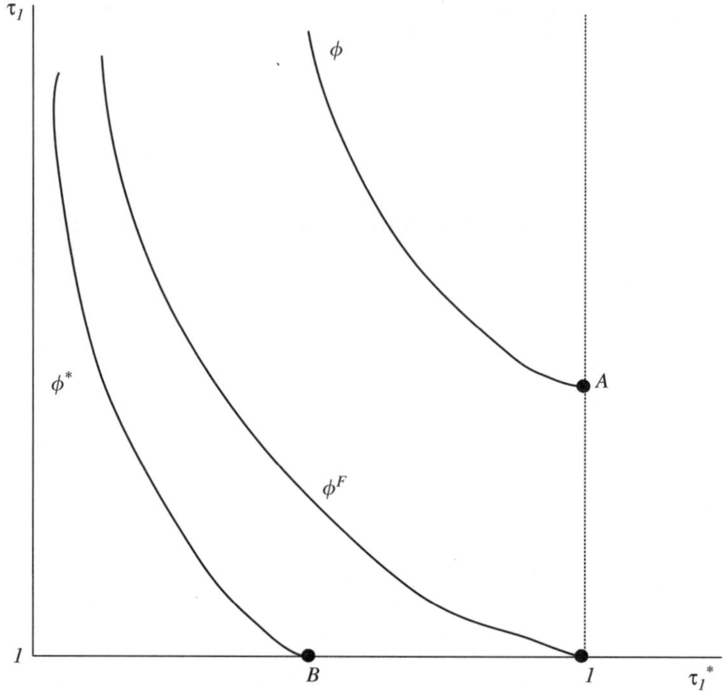

Fig. 1. Non-cooperation.

so that ϕ is a rectangular hyperbola. Since Q_1^* is uniquely related to Q_1 via the market-clearing condition for good 1, it too is constant along ϕ.

Now, suppose *F* departs from A by imposing an export subsidy $dt_1^* < 0$. Then an increase in the *H* tariff of $dt_1 = -\tau_1 dt_1^*$ will hold Q_1 and Q_1^* unchanged: We move upwards and to the left along ϕ. This will maintain the initial situation except that *F* pays an export subsidy which *H* taxes away with an equivalent increase in its tariff. This countervailing increase in its tariff constitutes a beneficial *H* response to *F*'s adoption of an export subsidy.

4.2. Equilibrium

In like manner, ϕ^F depicts the iso-domestic-price locus corresponding to free trade ($\tau_1\tau_1^* = 1$), and ϕ^* , which is *F*'s best-response curve, that corresponding to B. Since these three loci (all rectangular hyperbolae) correspond to different values of the domestic prices, they cannot intersect. Moving northwest along any one of these loci leaves all demands and supplies unchanged: The only effect is to shift trade-tax revenue from *F* to *H*.

As ϕ and ϕ^* are distinct rectangular hyperbolae, they do not intersect. There is no Nash equilibrium in t_1 and t_1^* alone!

An equilibrium can be obtained if we slightly enlarge each country's set of policy instruments. Suppose that, in addition to setting its trade taxes or subsidies, each country can decide whether to implement, or not, a countervailing-duty law. Such a law would mandate that imports of goods receiving a foreign export subsidy would be subject to a matching tariff, in addition to whatever trade tax or subsidy the importing country might otherwise wish to implement.

If H, for example, were to implement such a law and also to set τ equal to the value that would cause $Q_1 = Q_1^{\mathrm{A}}$ when $\tau_1^* = 1$, those actions would credibly commit H to be on ϕ. Then F's best response, assuming it does not want simply to give government revenue to H, would be A.

Proposition 3. *There is a non-cooperative equilibrium in trade policy. Each country adopts a countervailing-duty law, and employs neither export taxes nor export subsidies. Import-competing sectors with sufficient political influence receive protection and those without do not. Such tariffs will be higher the degree of political influence, and lower the import penetration ratio and the elasticity of import demand.*

Remark 2. *Countervailing-duty laws emerge here as the result of non-cooperative choices by the two governments,* not *as a result of a trade agreement.*

In reality it is true that Article XVI of the GATT attempts to curtail the use of export subsidies and also provides a code of conduct regarding countervailing-duty laws for WTO members. But such laws were in existence *long* before the GATT. Another implication of the endogenous introduction of countervailing duty laws is the following:

Remark 3. *Each government is powerless to offer its export lobby anything in Nash equilibrium.*

This will be the essential reason for trade agreements of the sort actually observed. This environment is *not* assumed: It's a direct consequence of the requirements for a non-cooperative equilibrium given the political climate of policy described here.

Remark 4. *Proposition 3 displays those predictions of the Grossman–Helpman approach that have found empirical support, and does not display those predictions that appear to be counterfactual.*

5. *Trade agreements*

Now suppose that the H and F governments can undertake negotiations for a trade agreement that would stipulate trade taxes or subsidies. In the event of such negotiations, each interest group would lobby its government about the taxes in the agreement that pertain directly to it. I inquire whether there is a basis for such negotiations.

5.1. The exchange of market access

A large literature insists that trade agreements seek to *exchange market access*: I'll grant your exporters increased access to my market in exchange for increased access to your market for my exporters. For an institutional approach, see Hauser (1986), Finger (1988, 1991), and Moser (1990); for a more formal approach, see Hillman *et al.* (1995), and Hillman and Moser (1996). Bagwell and Staiger use similar terminology. For example, they state (2002, pp. 28–29), "we may interpret 'cost shifting,' 'terms-of-trade gain,' and 'market-access restriction' as three phrases that describe ... [a] single economic experience." The earlier literature, it seems clear, had "something else" in mind. But drawing an analytical distinction has proved elusive, largely because the earlier literature, when it expressed its ideas in formal terms, did so in models that, as Bagwell and Staiger (2002, p. 20) correctly observe, were very often special cases of their own. Given the Received Theory, Bagwell and Staiger's interpretation is convincing.

The present analysis provides a formal basis to define trade agreements based on the exchange of market access and to distinguish them from those that are not. The basic idea behind the exchange of market access seems to be that each country, for whatever reason, agrees to allow increased imports of a particular good in exchange for increased exports of another particular good. That is, such trade agreements are necessarily *inter-sectoral*.

My model features extensive separability: Equilibrium policies in each sector are determined independently of those in the other sector. This has so far been a matter of expositional convenience, but now it serves another purpose as well. With policies in each sector determined independently, there could be an incentive for independent sector-by-sector international negotiations not involving inter-sectoral trade-offs, such as the 1965 US–Canada automobile agreement. In such an *intra-sectoral* negotiation the governments would bargain over t_1 and t_1^*, with any implied change in $M_1 = X_1^*$ settled by a change in the trade volume of the numeráire good.

I can now pose the following question. With policy determination in each sector independent of that in the other sector, is it *necessary* for trade negotiations to serve a useful purpose that they address inter-sectoral trade-offs? If so, I regard the negotiations as motivated by a desire to exchange market access.

DEFINITION. *Trade agreements are said to be based on the exchange of market access if and only if there is no reason for sector-by-sector negotiations.*

Note that this definition requires the necessity of inter-sectoral negotiations. Since in this model agents ignore cross-sectional effects, negotiations addressing those effects could well be useful, as would national policymaking addressing those effects. So defining the exchange of market access on the *sufficiency* of inter-sectoral negotiations would not be a useful discriminatory device.

5.2. Trade agreements to exchange market access

The equilibrium described in Proposition 3 offers no opportunity for an intra-sectoral trade agreement. In sector 1, for example, F is implementing no policy and so can offer H nothing in return for a lower tariff. Thus any trade agreement must be based on the exchange of market access.

To focus on such an exchange in the sharpest possible way, consider a simple trade agreement involving only goods 1 and $n+1$. Since these constitute each country's most politically powerful import-competing sector, suppose for simplicity that the two tariffs called for by Proposition 3 are both prohibitive.

The motive for a trade agreement based on the exchange of market access would be to enable each government to offer its export sector something while taking something less from its import-competing sector. It is true that, with the non-cooperative equilibrium, each government is powerless to offer its export sector something in any other way. But it is not clear that it will be tempted to use this way. The reason is that, since retreating from the t_1 would impose a first-order cost on H, doing so would be tempting to H only if the implied negotiated benefit for good $n+1$ is large enough. It is not clear that a trade agreement can be found that would do this for both countries simultaneously.

Now consider a hypothetical trade agreement stipulating $\mathrm{d}t_1 < 0$ and $\mathrm{d}t^*_{n+1} = \alpha \mathrm{d}t_1$ for some parameter negotiated α. Such an agreement would raise the joint surplus in each country, and so be perceived as beneficial by each government, if and only if the following holds:

$$\frac{\partial W_1}{\partial t_1} + \alpha \frac{\partial W_{n+1}}{\partial t^*_{n+1}} > 0$$

$$\frac{\partial W^*_1}{\partial t_1} + \alpha \frac{\partial W^*_{n+1}}{\partial t^*_{n+1}} > 0.$$

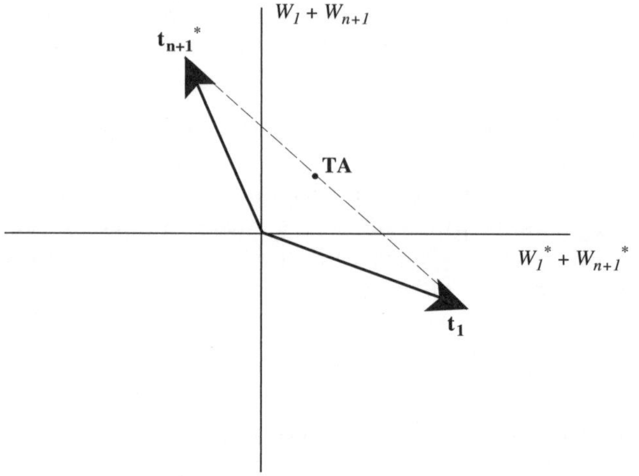

Fig. 2. Mutually beneficial exchange of market access.

This will in turn be possible for some choice of $\alpha > 0$ if and only if the following condition is met:

$$\left(\frac{\partial W_1^*}{\partial t_1}\right)\left(\frac{\partial W_{n+1}}{\partial t_{n+1}^*}\right)\left(\frac{\partial W_{n+1}^*}{\partial t_{n+1}^*}\right)\left(\frac{\partial W_1}{\partial t_1}\right). \tag{5}$$

Figure 2 illustrates how satisfaction of (5) is equivalent to the existence of a mutually beneficial trade agreement. The vectors labeled $\mathbf{t_1}$ and $\mathbf{t_{n+1}}^*$ depict the effects of reductions in the respective tariffs on the two joint surpluses. When these vectors have the relative slopes illustrated, reflecting (5), an appropriate linear combination, such as at point **TA**, will be mutually beneficial.[6]

Condition (5) in effect requires that, at the margin, tariffs have relatively greater impact on export lobbies than on import lobbies. This is intuitively understandable, and, since in Nash equilibrium the tariffs were set with exclusive reliance on the effects on the latter lobbies, unlikely to be demanding. So we have the following result:

PROPOSITION 4. *With (5) a mutually beneficial trade agreement is feasible. This agreement is based on the exchange of market access, and it need not constrain export taxes.*

Recall that we have chosen this pair of goods arbitrarily. The existence of a trade agreement based on the exchange of market access requires only that the analog of (5) hold for some set of goods from both countries. So,

---

[6] The still-attentive reader will recognize this logic as that behind the familiar Hawkins-Simon (1949) condition for the feasibility of an input–output system.

the model can deliver trade agreements resembling those that actually exist.

6. Concluding remarks

The Received Theory of international trade agreements, the result of half a century of research, suffers from fundamental puzzles that call into question its relevance to reality.

- If terms-of-trade motives dominate, each government will (counter-factually) employ both import tariffs and export taxes in Nash equilibrium. Any trade agreement would presumably wish to address export taxes (the Terms-of-Trade Puzzle). If political-support effects dominate, each government will tax imports but not exports, but, again counter-factually, neither country will implement a countervailing-duty law, and each will, with an export subsidy only partly countervailed by its partner, "bribe" the other government into allowing more imports than it otherwise would (the Export-Subsidy-Transfer Puzzle).
- But several empirical papers have given powerful evidence that, in politically organized import-competing sectors, protection is negatively related to the import penetration ratio and is negatively related to the domestic elasticity of import demand, and that distinguishing between politically organized and unorganized sectors is crucial to understanding this dependence.
- This chapter has utilized a simple formulation of the political economy of protection based directly on a trade-off between the income of special interests and consumer surplus. The model delivers the predictions that appear to be supported by the empirical evidence, but is free of the puzzles exhibited by the Received Theory.
- Neither government can unilaterally deliver anything to its export lobby, nor can sector-by-sector negotiations achieve anything. The two governments have an incentive to negotiate a trade agreement to exchange market access, and such an agreement would resolve the puzzles.

References

Bagwell, K., Staiger, R.W. (1999), An economic theory of GATT. *American Economic Review* 89, 215–248.

Bagwell, K., Staiger, R.W. (2002), *The Economics of the World Trading System*. The MIT Press, Cambridge, MA.

Ethier, W.J. (2004), Political externalities, nondiscrimination, and a multilateral world. *Review of International Economics* 12 (3), 303–320.

Ethier, W.J. (2006), Selling "protection for sale". *Asia-Pacific Journal of Accounting & Economics* 13, 153–162.

Ethier, W.J. (2007), The theory of trade policy and trade agreements: a critique. *European Journal of Political Economy* 23, 605–623.

Finger, J.M. (1988), Protectionist rules and internationalist discretion in the making of national trade policy. In: Vosgerau, H.-J. (Ed.), *New Institutional Arrangements for the World Economy*. Springer-Verlag, Heidelberg, pp. 310–323.

Finger, J.M. (1991), The GATT as an international discipline over trade restrictions. In: Vaubel, R., Willett, T.D. (Eds.), *The Political Economy of International Organizations*. Westview Press, Boulder, pp. 125–141.

Gawande, K., Bandyopadhyay, U. (2000), Is protection for sale? Evidence on the Grossman-Helpman theory of endogenous protection. *Review of Economics and Statistics* 82, 139–152.

Goldberg, P.K., Maggi, G. (1999), Protection for sale: an empirical investigation. *American Economic Review* 84, 1135–1155.

Grossman, G., Helpman, E. (1994), Protection for sale. *American Economic Review* 89, 833–850.

Grossman, G., Helpman, E. (1995), Trade wars and trade talks. *Journal of Political Economy* 85, 667–690.

Grossman, G., Helpman, E. (2002), *Interest Groups and Trade Policy*. Princeton University Press, Princeton.

Hauser, H. (1986), Domestic policy foundation and domestic policy function of international trade rules. *Aussenwirtschaft* 41, 171–184.

Hawkins, D., Simon, H. (1949), Some conditions of macroeconomic stability. *Econometrica* 17, 245–248.

Hillman, A.L. (1982), Declining industries and political-support protectionist motives. *American Economic Review* 72, 1180–1190.

Hillman, A.L. (1989), *The Political Economy of Protection*. Harwood Academic Publishers, Chur.

Hillman, A.L. (1990), Protectionist policies as the regulation of international industry. *Public Choice* 67, 101–110.

Hillman, A.L., Moser, P. (1996), Trade liberalization as politically optimal exchange of market access. In: Canzoneri, M., Ethier, W.J., Grilli, V. (Eds.), *The New Transatlantic Economy*. Cambridge University Press, Cambridge, pp. 295–312.

Hillman, A.L., Long, N.V., Moser, P. (1995), Modeling reciprocal trade liberalization: the political-economy and national-welfare perspectives. *Swiss Journal of Economics and Statistics* 131, 503–515.

Johnson, H.G. (1953–1954), Optimum tariffs and retaliation. *Review of Economic Studies* 21, 142–153.

Jones, R. W. (1977), Two-Ness in trade theory: costs and benefits. Special Papers in International Economics 12. International Finance Section, Princeton University.

Magee, S.P. (1994), Endogenous protection: a survey. In: Mueller, D.C. (Ed.), *Handbook of Public Choice*. Basil Blackwell, Cambridge, MA.

McCallum, P. (2004), Protection for sale and trade liberalization: an empirical investigation. *Review of International Economics* 12, 81–94.

Mitra, D., Thomakos, D.D., Ulubaşoğlu, M.A. (2002), "Protection for sale" in a developing country: democracy vs. dictatorship. *Review of Economics and Statistics* 84, 497–508.

Moser, P. (1990), *The Political Economy of the GATT*. Verlag Ruegger, Grüsch.

Nelson, D. (1988), Endogenous tariff theory: a critical survey. *American Journal of Political Science* 32, 796–837.

Olson, M. (1965), *The Logic of Collective Action*. Harvard University Press, Cambridge, MA.

Regan, D. H. (2004), Why do we have trade agreements? And why does it matter? – A lawyer's view of some economic theory. Unpublished manuscript. University of Michigan.

Rodrik, D. (1995), Political economy of trade policy. In: Grossman, G., Rogoff, K. (Eds.), *Handbook of International Economics*. North-Holland, Amsterdam, pp. 1457–1495.

CHAPTER 21

Competition Policy as a Substitute for Tariff Policy

Rika Takahashi[a], Jin Kenzaki[b] and Makoto Yano[c]

[a]*Faculty of Business Administration, Hosei University, 2-17-1 Fujimi, Chiyoda-ku, Tokyo 102-8160, Japan.*
E-mail address: rika@hosei.ac.jp
[b]*Economic and Market Analysis, Nikko Citigroup Limited, Shin-Marunouchi Building 1-5-1 Marunouchi, Chiyoda-ku, Tokyo 100-6520, Japan.*
E-mail address: jin.kenzaki@nikkociti.com
[c]*Kyoto Institute of Economic Research, Kyoto University, Yoshida-Honmachi, Sakyo-ku, Kyoto 606-8501, Japan.*
E-mail address: yano@kier.kyoto-u.ac.jp

Abstract
In the real world, developed countries are permitted to impose tariffs only on a small range of imports (partial tariff). For this reason, tariff policies have been replaced in many countries by other policy devices such as a competition policy. This study compares a competition policy with a partial tariff policy. It demonstrates that if a country can impose a tariff on only a small part of the imports and at sufficiently low tariff rates, optimal partial tariff policy may not create as large a protective effect as optimal competition policy.

Keywords: Tariffs, competition policy, protective effect

JEL classifications: F11, F13, L13, L42

1. Introduction

In the post-WWII international trade regime, the role of a tariff as a commercial policy has diminished significantly. Developed countries are permitted to impose tariffs only on a small range of imports, and tariff rates that are tolerated are fairly low. Perhaps for this reason, tariff policies have been replaced in many countries by other policy devices such as voluntary export restraints (VERs).[1] In particular, Yano (2001) and

[1] See Yano (1989) for an analysis of VERs from such a viewpoint.

Frontiers of Economics and Globalization
Volume 4 ISSN: 1574-8715
DOI: 10.1016/S1574-8715(08)04021-9

Yano and Dei (2003) point out the possibility that tariff policies may have been substituted by competition policies imposed on a country's non-tradable sector. Those studies, however, follows the existing literature on tariff by comparing a competition policy with a tariff policy imposed uniformly on a country's entire imports.

The purpose of this study is to extend the work of Yano (2001) and Yano and Dei (2003) by introducing the possibility that a country may impose a tariff only on part of the entire imports (a partial tariff policy). It compares the protective effect of a competition policy with that of a partial tariff policy. For this purpose, it changes the ratio between imports protected by a tariff and country's entire imports.

The main results of this study are (1) that a country achieves a higher welfare level by optimal competition policy than by optimal partial tariff policy if a tariff is imposed on a small range of imports, and (2) that a tariff must be imposed on only a few percents of total import volume in order to keep optimal tariff at rates usually adopted by various developed countries.[2] These results imply that if a country is permitted to impose a tariff on only a small part of the imports and at sufficiently low tariff rates, optimal partial tariff policy may not be as effective a policy tool for creating a welfare gain as optimal competition policy.

In a framework of Yano and Dei's vertical production model, an increasing number of existing studies has examined the role of competition policy as a tariff substitute.[3] In particular, Yano, Takahashi, and Kenzaki (2006) is closely related to the present study in the sense to compare competition policy and partial tariff policy. They adopt one case which reflects the current Japanese situation in which a tariff is imposed on 36 percent of total import volume and demonstrate that a country increases its own welfare level by using optimal competition policy to just about the same extent as optimal partial tariff policy in that case. The present study, however, compares welfare effects of two policies when the fraction of tariff imposition in the total import volume is adjusted from 0 to 100 percent. In this case, optimal partial tariff policy is less protective to increase its own utility than optimal competition policy, if a tariff is imposed on a small range of imports.

The model of this study is closely related to the highly influential model of Sanyal and Jones (1982), in which consumables are assumed to be non-tradables produced from tradable middle products. Yano and Dei (2003) extend their model into a model of vertical production chain, in which the retail sector's services are necessary to convert tradable middle products

---

[2] It is well-known that an imposition of tariff on an entire tradable market can be the first best trade policy creating the protective effect.

[3] See Yano and Dei (1998, 2000), Yano (2004), Ma (2005), Honryo and Yano (2006) and Ota (2006) for related studies. See also Takahashi (2005), who compares welfare effects between the optimal competition policy and the real world tariff policy in which a standard rate of a tariff in the real world is imposed.

into consumables. They investigate the effect of competition policy on the retail sector in that setting. This study is also related to the study of Yano and Dei (2001), in terms of the relationship between competition policy and tariff policy in a general equilibrium trade model. That study demonstrates a Nash equilibrium in the vertical production model of Yano and Dei (2003), when two countries retaliate against each other by adopting competition policy instead of tariff policy.

The rest of this chapter is organized as follows. Section 2 introduces the basic model, characterizes optimal partial tariff policy and optimal competition policy and adopts specified functional forms. Section 3 compares the extent of welfare effects between optimal partial tariff policy and optimal competition policy and calculates optimal tariff rate, by using numerical examples of parameters.

2. Basic structure

This section sets up our model by extending the Yano–Dei model. The optimal partial tariff policy is characterized in Section 2.1, and the optimal competition policy in Section 2.2. Functional specification is introduced into the basic structure in Section 2.3. In the model, three tradable middle products are produced upstream and transformed into non-tradable final consumption goods downstream. Middle product A is produced in the home country, and middle products B and C are produced in the foreign country. The home country exports product A to the foreign country and imports products B and C from the foreign country. These middle products are produced upstream by using only labor with a Ricardian technology. A final consumption good, which is non-tradable, is produced downstream by using three middle products A, B and C, and labor in each country. The total labor endowment that each country initially holds is distributed to leisure and labor to produce middle products in the upstream sector and final consumption goods in the downstream sector.

2.1. Partial tariff policy

In this subsection, it is assumed that the home country adopts partial tariff policy but not competition policy and that the foreign country adopts neither. The home government imposes a tariff on one import, the middle product B, but not on another middle product C. Let t be a tariff rate imposed upon product B. The world prices of products B and C are denoted by p_B^* and p_C^*, respectively. The basic structure is characterized in the following seven equations:

$$1 = wa_{LA}, \tag{1}$$

$$p_F = c(1, p_B, p_C, w), \tag{2}$$

$$p_F x_F(p_F, w, u) + w x_L(p_F, w, u) = wL + tp_B^* a_{BF}(1, p_B, p_C, w) x_F(p_F, w, u), \tag{3}$$

$$[p_B^* a_{BF}(1, p_B, p_C, w) + p_C^* a_{CF}(1, p_B, p_C, w)] x_F(p_F, w, u) = M^*(p_B^*), \tag{4}$$

$$p_B = (1 + t)p_B^*, \tag{5}$$

$$p_C = p_C^*, \tag{6}$$

$$p_B^*/a_{LB}^* = p_C^*/a_{LC}^*. \tag{7}$$

Equation (1) is the zero profit condition in the home upstream sector. The middle products are produced by the Ricardian technology of labor under perfect competition. It is assumed that product A is the numeraire good and that the amount of labor required to produce one unit of product A, a_{LA}, is constant. The wage rate w is therefore fixed.

Equation (2) is the zero profit condition in the home downstream sector with $p_A = 1$, where p_F and c are the price and unit cost, respectively, of the final goods F. From the cost minimization, the unit cost c, which is equivalent to the marginal cost, depends on the wage rate w and the prices of middle products $p_A = 1$, p_B and p_C.

Equation (3) implies the representative consumer's budget constraint in the home country. The representative consumer's utility u depends on the consumption levels of final good F, x_F and leisure, x_L, i.e., $u(x_F, x_L)$. The compensated demand functions for the final goods and leisure in the home country can therefore be written as $x_F = x_F(p_F, w, u)$ and $x_L = x_L(p_F, w, u)$, respectively. Since the representative consumer in the home country initially holds the total labor endowment L and receives the tariff revenue from home imported goods B, $tp_B^* a_{BF} x_F$, we obtain (3).

Equation (4) states the trade balance between two countries. The left-hand side in (4) shows the total volume of imports in the home country. The amount of middle product input to produce one unit of final goods is denoted by a_{iF}, where $i = A$, B, C and L. From the cost minimization, a_{iF} depends on four input prices, $p_A = 1$, p_B, p_C and w. The right-hand side of (4) shows the foreign imports volume M^* depends solely on p_B^*.[4]

[4] Foreign variables are denoted by an asterisk. Because the foreign country imports product A, the foreign import volume M^* is written as $M^* = a_{AF}^*(1, p_B, p_C, w) x_F^*(p_F^*, w^*, u^*)$. From the foreign upstream market conditions given by $p_B^* = w^* a_{LB}^*$ and $p_C^* = w^* a_{LC}^*$, we can obtain w^* and p_C^* as functions of p_B^*, because a_{LB}^* and a_{LC}^* are constant. Since the foreign country adopts neither policy, the market condition on the foreign final consumption good is written as $p_F^* = c^*(1, p_B^*, p_C^*, w^*) = c^*(p_B^*)$, and the foreign consumer's budget is written as $p_F^* x_F^*(p_F^*, w^*, u^*) + w^* x_L^*(p_F^*, w^*, u^*) = w^* L^*$. From these expressions, the foreign import volume M^* is a function of p_B^*.

Equation (5) determines the price deference of product B between two countries at the rate of tariff t. Equation (6) shows the price relationship of product C between two countries.

Equation (7) is the zero profit conditions in the foreign upstream sector. Because products B and C are respectively produced by the Ricardian technology of labor, equilibrium conditions under perfect competition are written as $w^*a^*_{LB} = p^*_B$ and $w^*a^*_{LC} = p^*_C$, where w^* is the wage rate in the foreign country, and constants of a^*_{LB} and a^*_{LC} are the amounts of labor required to produce one unit of products B and C, respectively.

The home government maximizes the level of utility in the home country u by controlling tariff rate t. By solving (1)–(7) with respect to seven variables, u, p_F, w, p_B, p^*_B, p_C and p^*_C, we obtain utility u as a function of tariff rate t. The first order condition given by $\mathrm{d}u/\mathrm{d}t = 0$ determines the optimal level of tariff rate t^{opt} (see Appendix A).[5] By setting the tariff rate optimally, the home country can achieve its own maximum utility under the partial tariff policy, u_t^{opt}.

2.2. Competition policy

It is assumed that the home government adopts competition policy for the downstream sector but not tariff policy for imported middle products B and C and that the foreign government adopts neither policy. The basic structure is characterized by the following five equations:

$$1 = wa_{LA}, \tag{8}$$

$$(1 - \rho)p_F = c(1, p_B, p_C, w), \tag{9}$$

$$p_F x_F(p_F, w, u) + wx_L(p_F, w, u) = wL + \rho p_F x_F(p_F, w, u), \tag{10}$$

$$[p_B a_{BF}(1, p_B, p_C, w) + p_C a_{CF}(1, p_B, p_C, w)]x_F(p_F, w, u) = M^*(p_B), \tag{11}$$

$$p_B/a^*_{LB} = p_C/a^*_{LC}. \tag{12}$$

Equation (8) is the zero profit conditions in the home upstream sector; (9) is the $MR = MC$ condition in the home downstream sector. It is assumed that the identical firms of the final goods in the home country behave in a Cournot–Nash fashion. Given constant returns to scale, the profit maximization condition in the home downstream sector is $(1 - (1/n\varepsilon))p_F = c$, where n is the number of the final goods firms, and ε the perceived elasticity of aggregate demand for the final goods. Using the

[5] Unlike the case of the optimal competition policy, the optimal level of tariff rate which the first order condition $\mathrm{d}u/\mathrm{d}t = 0$ determines is too complicated to formulate if we do not specify functional forms of the utility and cost functions. In order to overcome this difficulty, we show the optimal tariff formula when we adopt the special functional forms in Section 2.3.

Lerner index $\rho \equiv 1/n\varepsilon$, we obtain (9); (10) implies the representative consumer's budget constraint in the home country. The second term on the right-hand side shows the profit from the oligopoly; (11) states the trade balance between two countries; (12) is the zero profit conditions in the foreign upstream sector.

Maximizing welfare in the home country, which is represented by the consumer's utility function u, the home government can control the number of firms in the downstream sector n. Because n is not explicitly determined in the model, however, we use the Lerner index $\rho = 1/n\varepsilon$ instead as a policy instrument.[6]

The home government maximizes the level of utility in the home country u by controlling the Lerner index ρ. By solving (8)–(12) with respect to five variables, u, p_F, w, p_B and p_C, we obtain utility u as a function of the Lerner index ρ. The first order condition given by $\mathrm{d}u/\mathrm{d}\rho = 0$ determines the optimal level of the Lerner index (see Appendix B)

$$\rho^{\mathrm{opt}} = \frac{\zeta}{\zeta + e + (n^* - 1)}, \tag{13}$$

where ζ, e, η^* are defined as follows:

$$\zeta \equiv \frac{p_B a_{BF} + p_C a_{CF}}{c},$$

$$e \equiv -\left[\frac{p_B}{\left(a_{BF} + \frac{a^*_{LC}}{a^*_{LB}} a_{CF}\right)}\left(\frac{\partial a_{BF}}{\partial p_B} + \frac{a^*_{LC}}{a^*_{LB}}\frac{\partial a_{CF}}{\partial p_B}\right) + \frac{p_C}{\left(a_{BF} + \frac{a^*_{LC}}{a^*_{LB}} a_{CF}\right)}\left(\frac{\partial a_{BF}}{\partial p_C} + \frac{a^*_{LC}}{a^*_{LB}}\frac{\partial a_{CF}}{\partial p_C}\right)\right],$$

$$\eta^* \equiv \frac{\mathrm{d}M^*}{\mathrm{d}p_B}\frac{p_B}{M^*}.$$

By setting the Lerner index optimally, the home country can achieve its own maximum utility of the competition policy u_ρ^{opt}.

2.3. Functional specification

To quantify the welfare effects of optimal partial tariff policy and optimal competition policy, we adopt specific functional forms. We introduce the Stone–Geary utility functions and the Cobb–Douglas production

[6] The perceived elasticity of aggregate demand ε is dealt with as the constant variable. This is because it is too complicated to analyze the influence of the elasticity on the equilibrium system, although, in fact, ε depends on various variables.

functions. And then, based on the functional forms, the optimal partial tariff policy and the competition policy are characterized.

Assume that utility functions are of the Stone–Geary form. The functions in the home and foreign countries can be written as follows:

$$u = \mu\, log(x_F + \gamma) + (1 - \mu)\, \log x_L, \tag{14}$$

$$u^* = \mu^* \log(x_F^* + \gamma^*) + (1 - \mu^*) \log x_L^*, \tag{15}$$

where $0 < \mu < 1, x_F + \gamma > 0, 0 < \mu^* < 1$ and $x_F^* + \gamma^* > 0$.

Assume that the unit production functions in both countries are of the Cobb–Douglas form, $1 = (a_{AF})^{\psi}((a_{BF}/\alpha)^{\alpha}(a_{CF}/(1-a))^{1-\alpha})^{\theta}(a_{LF})^{\lambda}$ and $1 = (a_{AF}^*)^{\psi*}((a_{BF}^*/\alpha^*)^{\alpha^*}(a_{CF}^*/(1-\alpha^*))^{1-\alpha^*})^{\theta^*}(a_{LF}^*)^{\lambda^*}$, respectively. The unit cost functions in both countries are written as

$$c = \left(\frac{1}{\psi}\right)^{\psi}\left(\frac{(p_B)^{\alpha}(p_C)^{1-\alpha}}{\theta}\right)^{\theta}\left(\frac{w}{\lambda}\right)^{\lambda}, \tag{16}$$

$$c^* = \left(\frac{1}{\psi^*}\right)^{\psi^*}\left(\frac{p_B^*}{\theta^*}\right)^{\theta^*}\left(\frac{w^*}{\lambda^*}\right)^{\lambda^*}, \tag{17}$$

where parameters are non-negative and satisfy $\psi + \theta + \lambda = 1, \alpha \leq 1$, $\psi^* + \theta^* + \lambda^* = 1$. For simplicity, by assuming $a_{LB}^* = a_{LC}^*$, the price relationship between products B and C can be written as $p_B^* = p_C^*$ from (7) in the case of partial tariff policy and $p_B = p_C$ from (12) in the case of competition policy.[7]

These functional specifications determine the optimal tariff rate. The optimal tariff rate in the special functional case satisfies the following equation (see Appendix C1):

$$(2\alpha\theta - 1)(1-\alpha)\eta^*(t^{\text{opt}})^2 + [(2\alpha\theta - 1)\eta^* - (2\theta - 1)]t^{\text{opt}} - (2\theta - 1) = 0. \tag{18}$$

Let $\Theta = p_B^* a_{BF}/(p_B^* a_{BF} + p_C^* a_{CF})$, which is the ratio between the value of imports on which a tariff is imposed and the total value of imports. We call this ratio, Θ, the rate of tariff coverage. In equilibrium, the rate of tariff coverage is determined as

$$\Theta = \frac{\alpha}{\alpha + (1-\alpha)(1+t)}. \tag{19}$$

The model we adopt is constructed in such a way that if the rate of tariff coverage Θ is set, parameter α is determined by (19) under the optimal tariff rate t^{opt}.

[7] Under the assumption $a_{LB}^* = a_{LC}^*$, when the home government adopts competition policy, the home unit cost function is written as $c = (1/\psi)^{\psi}(p_B/\theta)^{\theta}(w/\lambda)^{\lambda}$. The model characterizing competition policy is independent of parameter α.

Setting the ratio Θ, we calculate tariff rates measured in terms of the ratio between the tariff revenue and the total value of imports under optimal tariff rate t^{opt}. We call T^{opt} an effective tariff rate. That is, the effective tariff rate is given by

$$T^{opt} = \frac{t^{opt} p_B^* a_{BF} x_F}{(p_B^* a_{BF} + p_C^* a_{CF}) x_F}.$$

Similarly, the functional specifications determine the optimal Lerner index formula (13) as follows (see Appendix D1):

$$\rho^{opt} = \frac{\theta}{\eta^*}. \tag{20}$$

3. Quantitative analysis

In this section, we compare the extent of welfare effects between tariff policy and competition policy and quantify the effective tariff rate numerically when a tariff is imposed on a part of entire imported goods by adopting numerical examples of parameters.

We first compare the extent of the welfare effect between optimal partial tariff policy and optimal competition policy when the rate of tariff coverage Θ is set at different levels. Although the extent of optimal competition policy is independent of Θ, that of optimal partial tariff policy depends on Θ. The rate of a GDP increase by a protection policy is measured by the Laspeyres quantity index, which we call a protection rate. By using this method, the protection rate of optimal partial tariff policy is given by

$$R_t(\Theta) \equiv \frac{p_F x_F^t(\Theta) + w x_L^t(\Theta) - (p_F x_F + w x_L)}{p_F x_F + w x_L}, \tag{21}$$

where $x_F^t(\Theta)$ and $x_L^t(\Theta)$ are respectively the demand for final good and that for leisure by optimal partial tariff policy with Θ, x_F and x_L are respectively those by no policies, and p_F and w are the price of good F and wage rate by no policies ($\rho = t = 0$). Similarly, the protection rate of optimal competition policy is given by

$$R_\rho \equiv \frac{p_F x_F^\rho + w x_L^\rho - (p_F x_F + w x_L)}{p_F x_F + w x_L}, \tag{22}$$

where x_F^ρ and x_L^ρ are respectively the demand for the final good and that for leisure by optimal competition policy.

We adopt the following values to special functional parameters:

$$\mu = 0.4, \psi = 0.2, \theta = 0.2, \lambda = 0.6, L = 24, a_{LA} = 6, \gamma = 1,$$

$$\mu^* = 0.4, \psi^* = 0.2, \theta^* = r^* = 0.1, \lambda^* = 0.6, L^* = 24, a_{LB}^* = a_{LC}^* = 6, \gamma^* = 1.$$

We call these the basic parameter values.

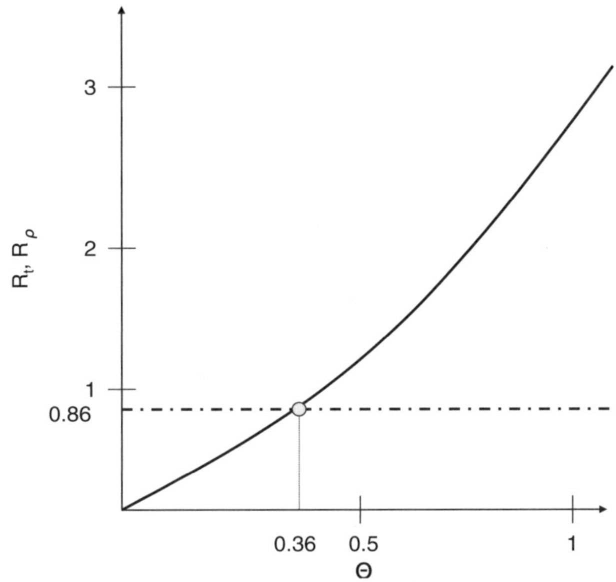

***Fig. 1. The rate of tariff coverage* (Θ) *and the protective effects* (R_t(Θ) *and* R_ρ)*. x-axis,* Θ*; y-axis, optimal partial tariff policy,* R_t(Θ) (*solid line*) *and optimal competition policy,* R_ρ (*dashed line*)*; intersection,* (Θ, *R*) = (*0.36, 0.86*).**

Figure 1 illustrates that the protection rate of optimal partial tariff policy, $R_t(\Theta)$, for the rate of tariff coverage, Θ, and that of optimal competition policy, R_ρ, for the basic parameter values. The solid line indicates $R_t(\Theta)$, and the dashed line indicates R_ρ. Figure 1 shows that although R_ρ is constant with Θ, $R_t(\Theta)$ declines with decreasing Θ. Two lines intersect at $R_t(\Theta) = R_\rho = 0.86$ with $\Theta = 0.36$. The point of intersection, surprisingly, reflects the relative magnitude of imports on which the Japanese government actually imposes tariffs; Japan imposes tariffs on some 36 percent of the imports.[8]

Next, we calculate the effective tariff rate when the rate of tariff coverage Θ is set at different levels. Figure 2 illustrates the relationship between the effective tariff rate, T^{opt}, and the rate of tariff coverage, Θ for the basic parameter values. The solid line in Figure 2 shows that T^{opt} sharply declines as a rate of tariff coverage Θ decreases. These results imply that as a beggar-thy-neighbor policy, tariff policy may not be as effective as competition policy if tariffs are permitted to be imposed only

[8] According to Ministry of Finance (2005), the ratio between the value of imported goods on which tariffs are imposed and the total value of imports in fiscal years 2003 and 2004 is 0.351 and 0.371, respectively, in Japan.

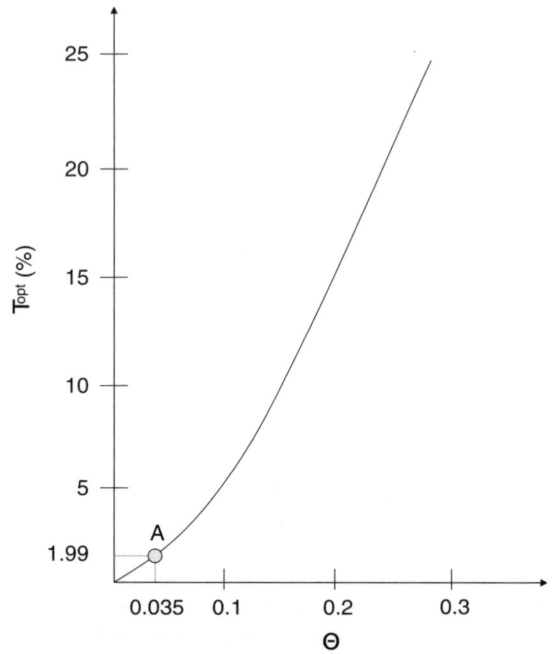

Fig. 2. ***The rate of tariff coverage (Θ) and the effective tariff rate (T^{opt}). x-axis, Θ; y-axis, T^{opt} (%); Point A, (Θ,T^{opt}) = (0.035, 1.99).***

on selected imports and at sufficiently low tariff rates. For example, in Japan, a ratio between tariff revenue and value of total import is about 2 percent.[9] The point A in Figure 2 shows that the rate of tariff coverage given by Θ must be about 3.5 percent in order to keep the 2 percent of the tariff be optimum. This result imply that if the effective tariff rate in Japan is optimal, a tariff should be imposed on less than 4 percent of total import volume. Comparing the protection rate between optimal partial tariff policy and optimal competition policy with $\Theta = 0.035$ and $t^{opt} = 0.02$, we demonstrate that the latter protection rate, R_ρ, is much larger than the former protection rate, R_t (0.035). Under the international political climates which restrict countries to impose tariffs on some selected imports and at fairly low tariff rates, optimal competition policy may play an important role as a substitute for optimal partial tariff policy.

REMARK. To examine the robustness of the above results, we calculate the protection rate of optimal partial tariff policy and optimal competition

[9] According to Ministry of Finance (2005), the ratio between the tariff revenue and the total import value in fiscal years 2003 and 2004 is 1.9% and 1.7%, respectively.

***Table 1.* Comparison of protective effects: optimal partial tariff policy ($R_t^{opt}(\Theta)$), optimal competition policy (R_ρ)**

μ	R_t (1)	R_t (0.36)	R_t (0.035)	R_ρ
0.2	1.07	0.21	0.017	0.32
0.4	3.35	0.86	0.076	0.86
0.6	6.49	1.55	0.118	1.04
0.8	12.23	2.20	0.164	0.79
L	R_t (1)	R_t (0.36)	R_t (0.035)	R_ρ
12	2.07	0.57	0.045	0.75
24	3.35	0.86	0.076	0.86
48	4.32	1.06	0.081	0.89
120	5.19	1.23	0.085	0.90
a_{LA}	R_t (1)	R_t (0.36)	R_t (0.035)	R_ρ
1	4.42	1.06	0.081	0.92
6	3.35	0.86	0.076	0.86
12	2.89	0.77	0.060	0.82
18	2.60	0.71	0.056	0.79
γ^*	R_t (1)	R_t (0.36)	R_t (0.035)	R_ρ
0.1	5.15	1.08	0.081	1.02
1	3.35	0.86	0.076	0.86
3	0.80	0.26	0.023	0.32
6	0.006	0.002	0	0.003

policy and the effective tariff rate with respect to four various parameters: μ, L, a_{LA} and γ^*, which are main determinants of the home country's economic structure in the present model.[10] For quantitative analysis, we set the rate of tariff coverage in three cases:

Case 1: $\Theta = 1$,
Case 2: $\Theta = 0.36$,
Case 3: $\Theta = 0.035$.

A tariff is imposed on entire imported items in Case 1, and on 36 percent of entire imports in Case 2 and on 3.5 percent in Case 3.

In Table 1, $R_t(\Theta)$ and R_ρ are compared in Cases 1, 2 and 3, for the various sets of parameters through numerical examples. Even if a parameter value changes, the basic nature of the above results does not

[10] The home country's marginal propensity to consume final good F, μ determines the shape of the home country's utility function. The total labor endowment L determines the shape of the home country's production possibility frontier. The labor input coefficient in the home upstream sector, a_{LA} determines the home country's wage rate, w. The foreign subsistence level of good F, γ^* determines the shape of the foreign offer curve.

Table 2. Effective tariff rates in Cases 1, 2 and 3

μ	T^{opt}	L	T^{opt}	a_{LA}	T^{opt}	γ^*	T^{opt}
Case 1: Effective tariff rates, with $\Theta = 1$ (%)							
0.2	387.4	12	435.9	1	922.0	0.1	5880.9
0.4	583.5	24	583.5	6	583.5	1	583.5
0.6	689.1	48	724.8	12	477.6	3	86.2
0.8	736.3	120	920.2	18	421.2	6	4.9
Case 2: Effective tariff rates, with $\Theta = 0.36$ (%)							
0.2	30.41	12	31.08	1	34.55	0.1	37.48
0.4	32.65	24	32.65	6	32.65	1	32.65
0.6	33.39	48	33.63	12	31.59	3	16.45
0.8	33.80	120	34.53	18	30.83	6	1.25
Case 3: Effective tariff rates, with $\Theta = 0.035$ (%)							
0.2	1.90	12	1.93	1	2.07	0.1	2.18
0.4	1.99	24	1.99	6	1.99	1	1.99
0.6	2.02	48	2.03	12	1.95	3	1.20
0.8	2.04	120	2.07	18	1.92	6	0.11

change. For all parameter values, the protection rate of optimal partial tariff policy is much larger than in the case of $\Theta = 1$, almost the same as in the case of $\Theta = 0.36$, and much smaller than the protection rate of optimal competition policy in the case of $\Theta = 0.035$.

Table 2 reports effective tariff rates T^{opt} in Cases 1, 2 and 3 under the various examples of parameter values. Even if parameter values change, the basic characteristic under the basic example of parameter values does not change: if a tariff is imposed on entire imported items with $\Theta = 1$, the effective tariff rate, which is equivalent to optimal tariff rate t^{opt}, exceeds 300 percent in all parameter examples excluding $\gamma^* = 3$ and 6, as is reported in Takahashi (2005). If a tariff is imposed on a part of imports, the effective tariff rate T^{opt} with $\Theta = 0.36$ exceeds 30 percent in all parameter examples excluding $\gamma^* = 3$ and 6, and that with $\Theta = 0.035$ is no more than 2.18 percent.

Appendix

Appendices here explain the process of derivations of optimal tariff rate and optimal Lerner index in the extended Yano and Dei's model with three middle products. Appendix A shows the derivations of optimal tariff rate in the extended Yano–Dei model without functional forms specified; Appendix B shows those of optimal Lerner index in that model; Appendices C1 and C2 show the derivations of optimal tariff rate, trade balance equation and elasticity of foreign import demand in the optimal partial tariff policy under the special functional forms; Appendices D1 and D2 show those of optimal Lerner index, trade balance equation and elasticity of foreign import demand in the optimal competition policy under the special functional forms.

Appendix A. Optimal partial tariff policy

Equations (1)–(7) except for (5) are totally differentiated with respect to $p_F, p_B, p_B^*, p_C, p_B^*, w$ and u by using the relationship of $tp_B^* = (p_B - p_B^*)$. Since $\mathrm{d}w = 0$ from (1), the other equations are differentiated as

$$\mathrm{d}p_F = \frac{\partial c}{\partial p_B}\mathrm{d}p_B + \frac{\partial c}{\partial p_C}\mathrm{d}p_C, \tag{A.1}$$

$$\begin{aligned}
&\left[p_F\frac{\partial x_F}{\partial p_F} + w\frac{\partial x_L}{\partial p_F} + x_F - (p_B - p_B^*)a_{BF}\frac{\partial x_F}{\partial p_F}\right]\mathrm{d}p_F \\
&\quad + \left(p_F\frac{\partial x_F}{\partial u} + w\frac{\partial x_L}{\partial u} - (p_B - p_B^*)a_{BF}\frac{\partial x_F}{\partial u}\right)\mathrm{d}u \\
&\quad = \left[a_{BF}x_F + (p_B - p_B^*)\frac{\partial a_{BF}}{\partial p_B}x_F\right]\mathrm{d}p_B \\
&\quad + (p_B - p_B^*)x_F\frac{\partial a_{BF}}{\partial p_C}\mathrm{d}p_C - a_{BF}x_F\mathrm{d}p_B^*,
\end{aligned} \tag{A.2}$$

$$\begin{aligned}
&[p_B^*a_{BF} + p_C^*a_{CF}]\frac{\partial x_F}{\partial p_F}\mathrm{d}p_F + [p_B^*a_{BF} + p_C^*a_{CF}]\frac{\partial x_F}{\partial u}\mathrm{d}u + a_{BF}x_F\mathrm{d}p_B^* \\
&\quad + a_{CF}x_F\mathrm{d}p_C^* + \left(p_B^*\frac{\partial a_{BF}}{\partial p_B} + p_C^*\frac{\partial a_{CF}}{\partial p_B}\right)x_F\mathrm{d}p_B \\
&\quad + \left(p_B^*\frac{\partial a_{BF}}{\partial p_C} + p_C^*\frac{\partial a_{CF}}{\partial p_C}\right)x_F\mathrm{d}p_C \\
&\quad = \frac{\mathrm{d}M^*}{\mathrm{d}p_B^*}\mathrm{d}p_B^*,
\end{aligned} \tag{A.3}$$

$$\mathrm{d}p_C = \mathrm{d}p_C^*, \tag{A.4}$$

$$\mathrm{d}p_B^*/a_{LB}^* = \mathrm{d}p_C^*/a_{LC}^*. \tag{A.5}$$

To derive the optimal tariff rate formula, we use three relationships: $p_F(\partial x_F/\partial p_F)\mathrm{d}p_F + w(\partial x_L/\partial p_F)\mathrm{d}p_F = 0, \partial c/\partial p_B = a_{BF}$ and $\partial c/\partial p_C = a_{CF}$. The first relationship is derived by Shephard's Lemma applied to the consumer's expenditure function, and the second and the third ones are derived by that applied to the cost function in the downstream sector. Substitute the first relationship into (A.2) and the second and the third ones into (A.1). By eliminating $\mathrm{d}p_F$, $\mathrm{d}p_C^*$ amd $\mathrm{d}p_C$ from (A.1)–(A.5), Equations (A.2) and (A.3) are transformed as follows:

$$\begin{aligned}
&\left(p_F\frac{\partial x_F}{\partial u}+w\frac{\partial x_L}{\partial u}-(p_B-p_B^*)a_{BF}\frac{\partial x_F}{\partial u}\right)\frac{\mathrm{d}u}{\mathrm{d}p_B^*}\\
&\quad=\left[(p_B-p_B^*)\left(\frac{\partial a_{BF}}{\partial p_B}x_F+a_{BF}a_{BF}\frac{\partial x_F}{\partial p_F}\right)\right]\frac{\mathrm{d}p_B}{\mathrm{d}p_B^*}\\
&\qquad-\left[\left(a_{BF}+\frac{a_{LC}^*}{a_{LB}^*}a_{CF}\right)x_F-\frac{a_{LC}^*}{a_{LB}^*}(p_B-p_B^*)\right.\\
&\qquad\left.\left(\frac{\partial a_{BF}}{\partial p_C}x_F+a_{CF}a_{BF}\frac{\partial x_F}{\partial p_F}\right)\right], \qquad\qquad (\mathrm{A}.2')
\end{aligned}$$

$$\begin{aligned}
&\left[p_B^*a_{BF}+p_C^*a_{CF}\right]\frac{\partial x_F}{\partial u}\frac{\mathrm{d}u}{\mathrm{d}p_B^*}\\
&\quad=-\left[p_B^*\left(\frac{\partial a_{BF}}{\partial p_B}x_F+a_{BF}a_{BF}\frac{\partial x_F}{\partial p_F}\right)+p_C^*\left(\frac{\partial a_{CF}}{\partial p_B}x_F+a_{CF}a_{BF}\frac{\partial x_F}{\partial p_F}\right)\right]\frac{\mathrm{d}p_B}{\mathrm{d}p_B^*}\\
&\qquad-\left[\left(a_{BF}+\frac{a_{LC}^*}{a_{LB}^*}a_{CF}\right)x_F+\frac{a_{LC}^*}{a_{LB}^*}\left(p_B^*\left(\frac{\partial a_{BF}}{\partial p_C}x_F+a_{CF}a_{BF}\frac{\partial x_F}{\partial p_F}\right)\right.\right.\\
&\qquad\left.\left.+p_C^*\left(\frac{\partial a_{CF}}{\partial p_C}x_F+a_{CF}a_{CF}\frac{\partial x_F}{\partial p_F}\right)\right)-\frac{\mathrm{d}M^*}{\mathrm{d}p_B^*}\right]. \qquad\qquad (\mathrm{A}.3')
\end{aligned}$$

Although the optimal tariff rate is determined when the home government maximizes u by controlling t, it has the same effect to maximize u by controlling p_B^* because $\mathrm{d}p_B^*/\mathrm{d}t\neq 0$. The left-hand side of two equations above is zero, that is, $\mathrm{d}u/\mathrm{d}p_B^*=0$. Substituting $p_B-p_B^*=tp_B^*$ into Equations (A.2′) and (A.3′), we have simultaneous equations with respect to $\mathrm{d}p_B/\mathrm{d}p_B^*$ and t. By solving these equations, the optimal tariff rate t^{opt} can be determined.

The optimal tariff formula is simple if a tariff is imposed on all imports. In contrast, it is not as simple if a tariff is imposed on a part of imports. In the former case, because imported middle product C on which a tariff is not imposed is ignored, i.e., $a_{CF}=0$ and $\partial a_{CF}/\partial p_B=\partial a_{CF}/\partial p_C=\partial a_{BF}/\partial p_C=0$, (A.2′) and (A.3′) are respectively written as $tp_B^*\,((\partial a_{BF}/\partial p_B)x_F+a_{BF}a_{BF}(\partial x_F/\partial p_F))(\mathrm{d}p_B/\mathrm{d}p_B^*)=a_{BF}x_F$ and $p_B^*((\partial a_{BF}/\partial p_B)x_F+a_{BF}a_{BF}(\partial x_F/\partial p_F))(\mathrm{d}p_B/\mathrm{d}p_B^*)=(\mathrm{d}M^*/\mathrm{d}p_B^*)-a_{BF}x_F$.

By eliminating $\mathrm{d}p_B/\mathrm{d}p_B^*$ from these equations, the optimal tariff rate is formulated as $t^{\mathrm{opt}}=(1/(\eta^*-1))$, where $\eta^*=(\mathrm{d}M^*/\mathrm{d}p_B^*)(p_B^*/M^*)$.

Appendix B. Optimal competition policy

Equations (8)–(12) are totally differentiated with respect to p_F, p_B, p_C, w, u and ρ.

Since $\mathrm{d}w = 0$ from (8), the other equations are differentiated as follows:

$$(1-\rho)\mathrm{d}p_F - p_F\mathrm{d}\rho - \frac{\partial c}{\partial p_B}\mathrm{d}p_B - \frac{\partial c}{\partial p_C}\mathrm{d}p_C = 0, \tag{B.1}$$

$$\left[(1-\rho)\left(x_F + p_F\frac{\partial x_F}{\partial p_F}\right) + w\frac{\partial x_L}{\partial p_F}\right]\mathrm{d}p_F + \left[(1-\rho)p_F\frac{\partial x_F}{\partial u} + w\frac{\partial x_L}{\partial u}\right]\mathrm{d}u - p_F x_F \mathrm{d}\rho = 0, \tag{B.2}$$

$$\begin{aligned}[p_B a_{BF} + p_C a_{CF}]\left(\frac{\partial x_F}{\partial p_F}\mathrm{d}p_F + \frac{\partial x_F}{\partial u}\mathrm{d}u\right) &= -\left[\left(a_{BF} + p_B\frac{\partial a_{BF}}{\partial p_B} + p_C\frac{\partial a_{CF}}{\partial p_B}\right)x_F - \frac{\mathrm{d}M^*}{\mathrm{d}p_B}\right]\mathrm{d}p_B \\ &\quad - \left(a_{CF} + p_B\frac{\partial a_{BF}}{\partial p_C} + p_C\frac{\partial a_{CF}}{\partial p_C}\right)x_F\mathrm{d}p_C,\end{aligned} \tag{B.3}$$

$$\mathrm{d}p_B/a^*_{LB} = \mathrm{d}p_C/a^*_{LC}. \tag{B.4}$$

To derive the optimal Lerner index, we use three relationships: $p_F(\partial x_F/\partial p_F) + w(\partial x_L/\partial p_F) = 0, (\partial c/\partial p_B) = a_{BF}$ and $(\partial c/\partial p_C) = a_{CF}$. Substitute the first relationship into (B.2) and the second and the third relationships with (B.4) into (B.1), and eliminate $\mathrm{d}p_F$, $\mathrm{d}\rho$ and $\mathrm{d}p_C$ from (B.1)–(B.4). By using Equations (9), (11) and (12), we have the following relationship:

$$\begin{aligned}-\theta\left(p_F\frac{\partial x_F}{\partial u} + w\frac{\partial x_L}{\partial u}\right)\frac{\mathrm{d}u}{\mathrm{d}p_B} &= \theta\left(a_{BF} + a_{CF}\frac{a^*_{LC}}{a^*_{LB}}\right)x_F \\ &\quad + \frac{\rho}{1-\rho}\left[\left(a_{BF} + a_{CF}\frac{a^*_{LC}}{a^*_{LB}}\right)x_F + \left(p_B\left(\frac{\partial a_{BF}}{\partial p_B} + \frac{\partial a_{BF}}{\partial p_C}\frac{a^*_{LC}}{a^*_{LB}}\right)\right.\right. \\ &\quad \left.\left. + p_C\left(\frac{\partial a_{CF}}{\partial p_B} + \frac{\partial a_{CF}}{\partial p_C}\frac{a^*_{LC}}{a^*_{LB}}\right)\right)x_F - \frac{\mathrm{d}M^*}{\mathrm{d}p_B}\right].\end{aligned} \tag{B.5}$$

Although the optimal Lerner index is determined when the home government maximizes the utility level u by controlling ρ, it has the same effect to maximize u by controlling p_B because $\mathrm{d}p_B/\mathrm{d}\rho \neq 0$ is supported by Yano and Dei (2003). Since the left-hand side of (B.5) is zero, the optimal Lerner index ρ^{opt} is written as (13).

Appendix C1. Optimal partial tariff policy under the special functional forms

Given the utility and cost functions (14)–(17), the partial derivatives are transformed into the following special forms:

$$\frac{\partial x_F}{\partial p_F}=\frac{x_F}{p_F}=\frac{x_F}{c},\quad \frac{\partial c}{\partial p_B}=a_{BF}=\frac{c\alpha\theta}{p_B},$$
$$\frac{\partial c}{\partial p_C}=a_{CF}=\frac{c(1-\alpha)\theta}{p_C},\quad \frac{\partial a_{BF}}{\partial p_B}=\frac{c\alpha\theta(\alpha\theta-1)}{p_B p_B},$$
$$\frac{\partial a_{BF}}{\partial p_C}=\frac{\partial a_{CF}}{\partial p_B}=\frac{c\alpha\theta(1-\alpha)\theta}{p_B p_C},\quad \frac{\partial a_{CF}}{\partial p_C}=\frac{c(1-\alpha)\theta((1-\alpha)\theta-1)}{p_C p_C}.$$

Substituting these specified partial derivatives and $\mathrm{d}u/\mathrm{d}p_B^*=0$ into (A.2′) and (A.3′), we have the following expressions:

$$\left[(p_B-p_B^*)\frac{2\alpha\theta-1}{p_B}\right]\frac{\alpha}{p_B}\frac{\mathrm{d}p_B}{\mathrm{d}p_B^*}=\frac{\alpha}{p_B}+\left[1-2(p_B-p_B^*)\frac{\alpha\theta}{p_B}\right]\frac{(1-\alpha)}{p_B^*},$$
$$\left[2(1-\alpha)\theta+\frac{(2\alpha\theta-1)}{(1+t)}\right]\frac{\alpha}{(1+t)}\frac{\mathrm{d}p_B}{\mathrm{d}p_B^*}$$
$$=\frac{\mathrm{d}M^*}{\mathrm{d}p_B^*}\frac{p_B^*}{c\theta x_F}-\left[\frac{\alpha}{(1+t)}+(1-\alpha)\right](1+\theta-\alpha\theta)-(1-\alpha)$$
$$\times\left[\frac{\alpha\theta}{(1+t)}+((1-\alpha)\theta-1)\right].$$

Eliminate $\mathrm{d}p_B/\mathrm{d}p_B^*$ from two equations above and substitute (4), (5), $p_B a_{BF}/c=\alpha\theta$, $p_C a_{CF}/c=(1-\alpha)\theta$ and $\eta^*=(\mathrm{d}M^*/\mathrm{d}p_B^*)(p_B^*/M^*)$ into these equations, and, then, the optimal tariff rate t^{opt} is formulated as (18).

Given (14)–(18), the elasticity of foreign import volume, η^*, and the trade balance equation in the optimal partial tariff policy given by (4) are transformed into (C2.3) and (C2.5), respectively, as shown in Appendix C2. Equations (5) (16)–(18), (C2.3) and (C2.5) are simultaneously solved with respect to $(p_B^*, p_B, c, c^*, \eta^*, t^{\text{opt}})$, and the optimal tariff rate is determined by the parameters.

Appendix C2. Trade balance equation and elasticity of foreign import demand in the optimal partial tariff policy under the special functional forms

The foreign consumer maximizes the Stone–Geary utility function (15) subject to the budget constraint $p_F^* x_F^* + w^* x_L^* = w^* L^*$. The foreign demand function for the final consumption good is written as

$$x_F^* = \frac{\mu^* w^* L^*}{p_F^*} - (1-\mu^*)\gamma^*. \tag{C2.1}$$

From $\psi^* = a_{AF}^*/c^*, p_F^* = c^*$ and $w^* = p_B^*/a_{LB}^*$, we have foreign import volume $M^* = a_{AF}^* x_F^*$ as

$$M^* = \psi^* \left[\frac{\mu^* L^*}{a_{LB}^*} p_B^* - (1-\mu^*)\gamma^* c^*\right]. \tag{C2.2}$$

Substituting the foreign cost function (17) with $w^* = p_B^*/a_{LB}^*$ into (C2.2) and differentiating M^* with respect to p_B^*, we have the elasticity of foreign import demand $\eta^* \equiv (\mathrm{d}M^*/\mathrm{d}p_B^*)(p_B^*/M^*)$ as the following expression:

$$\eta^* = \frac{\mu^* L^* p_B^* - (1-\psi^*)(1-\mu^*)a_{LB}^*\gamma^* c^*}{\mu^* L^* p_B^* - (1-\mu^*)a_{LB}^*\gamma^* c^*}. \tag{C2.3}$$

When the home government adopts the tariff policy, the home consumer maximizes (14) subject to (3). The home demand function for the final good is written as

$$x_F^t = \frac{p_B}{p_B - \mu\alpha\theta t p_B^*}\left[\frac{\mu w L}{p_F} - (1-\mu)\gamma\right]. \tag{C2.4}$$

From (C2.2) and (C2.4) with $p_B a_{BF}/c = \alpha\theta, p_C a_{CF}/c = (1-\alpha)\theta, p_F = c$, $w = 1/a_{LA}$ and $p_C = p_C^* = p_B^*$, we have the trade balance between $(p_B^* a_{BF} + p_C^* a_{CF})x_F^t = M^*$ as the following expression:

$$\theta\frac{(\alpha p_B^* + (1-\alpha)p_B)}{(p_B - \mu\alpha\theta t p_B^*)}\left[\frac{\mu L}{a_{LA}} - (1-\mu)\gamma c\right] = \psi^*\left[\frac{\mu^* L^*}{a_{LB}^*}p_B^* - (1-\mu^*)\gamma^* c^*\right]. \tag{C2.5}$$

Appendix D1. Optimal competition policy under the special functional forms

The functional specification of optimal competition policy is the same as that of optimal partial tariff policy. Substituting into e and ζ the specified partial derivatives shown in Appendix C1 and (12) with the assumption of $a_{LB}^* = a_{LC}^*$, we have the following expression:

$$e = 1 - \theta \text{ and } \zeta = \theta. \tag{D1.1}$$

Substituting (D1.1) into (13), we obtain (20).

Given (14)–(17), the elasticity of foreign demand η^* and the trade balance equation in the optimal competition policy (11) are transformed into (D2.1) and (D2.3) respectively, as shown in Appendix D2. Equations (16), (17), (20), (D2.1) and (D2.3) are simultaneously solved with respect to

$(p_B, c, c^*, \eta^*, \rho^{\text{opt}})$, and then, the optimal Lerner index is solved by the parameters.

Appendix D2. Trade balance equation and elasticity of foreign import demand in the optimal competition policy under the special functional forms

Since the foreign demand function for the final good x_F^* and the foreign import volume $M^* = a_{AF}^* x_F^*$ do not change by the home country's policies with $p_B^* = p_B$, the elasticity of foreign import demand, $\eta^* \equiv (\mathrm{d}M^*/\mathrm{d}p_B)(p_B/M^*)$ is written as

$$\eta^* = \frac{\mu^* L^* p_B - (1-\psi^*)(1-\mu^*)a_{LB}^* \gamma^* c^*}{\mu^* L^* p_B - (1-\mu^*)a_{LB}^* \gamma^* c^*}. \tag{D2.1}$$

When the home government adopts the competition policy, the home consumes maxmizes (14) subject to (10). The home demand function for the final good is

$$x_F^\rho = \frac{1}{1-\mu\rho}\left[\frac{\mu w L}{p_F} - (1-\mu)\gamma\right]. \tag{D2.2}$$

By substituting (D2.2) and (C2.2) with $\theta = (p_B a_{BF} + p_C a_{CF})/c, (1-\rho) p_F = c, p_B^* = p_B$ and $w = 1/a_{LA}$ into the trade balance equation, $(p_B a_{BF} + p_C a_{CF})x_F^\rho = M^*$, it can be written as

$$\frac{\theta}{1-\mu\rho}\left[\frac{(1-\rho)\mu L}{a_{LA}} - (1-\mu)\gamma c\right] = \psi^*\left[\frac{\mu^* L^*}{a_{LB}^*} p_B - (1-\mu^*)\gamma^* c^*\right]. \tag{D2.3}$$

References

Honryo, T., Yano, M. (2006), Short-run trade surplus creation in a two-sector setting. *Japanese Economic Review* 57, 476–482.

Ma, Y. (2005), Basic theorems of trade theory in a two factor vertical production chain model (in Japanese). Unpublished doctoral dissertation, Kobe University, Kobe. (For an English version, see Ma, Y. (2005), Vertical production chain, trade and tariffs in a two-factor model. Discussion Paper 2005-22. Graduate School of Business Administration, Kobe University.)

Ministry of Finance, Political Research Institute. (2005), *Zaisei Kinyu Toukei Gep-pou (Ministry of Finance Statistics Monthly) 640*. Ministry of Finance, Tokyo.

Ota, R. (2006), Adjustability in production and dynamic effects of domestic competition policy. *Journal of International Trade and Economic Development* 15, 431–439.

Sanyal, K., Jones, R.W. (1982), The theory of trade in middle products. *American Economic Review* 72, 16–31.

Takahashi, R. (2005), Domestic competition policy and tariff policy compared. *Japanese Economic Review* 56, 210–222.

Yano, M. (1989), Voluntary export restraints and expectations: an analysis of export quotas in oligopolistic markets. *International Economic Review* 30, 707–723.

Yano, M. (2001), Trade imbalance and domestic market competition policy. *International Economic Review* 42, 729–750.

Yano, M. (2004), Short-run trade surplus creation. *Journal of Difference Equations and Applications* 10, 453–461.

Yano, M., Dei, F. (1998), A trade model with vertical production chain and competition policy in the downstream sector. Keio Economics Society Discussion Paper Series 9804.

Yano, M., Dei, F. (2000), A trade model with vertical production chain and competition policy in the downstream sector. Kobe University Graduate School of Business Administration Discussion Paper Series 2001-10.

Yano, M., Dei, F. (2001), International game of domestic competition policies. Unpublished paper.

Yano, M., Dei, F. (2003), Trade, vertical production chain, and competition policy. *Review of International Economics* 11, 237–252.

Yano, M., Takahashi, R., Kenzaki, J. (2006), Competition policy or tariff policy: which is more effective? *Asia-Pacific Journal of Accounting and Economics* 13, 163–170.

CHAPTER 22

Free Trade between Large and Small: What's in it for the Large Country? What's in it for the Small?

Carsten Kowalczyk

The Fletcher School, Tufts University, 160 Packard Ave, Medford, MA 02155, USA
E-mail address: carsten.kowalczyk@tufts.edu

Abstract
This chapter provides a formal analysis of the economic welfare effects for large and small partners to free trade agreements. Michaely (1998) has demonstrated that large country welfare is U-shaped in the small country's size. I derive the welfare for the large country for all possible small country sizes, and show that the maximum possible loss for the large country is twice its tariff revenue. I identify the data necessary to estimate the welfare effects and consider how initial trade volumes, tariffs, and international price differences affect the large country's welfare.

Keywords: Small countries, large countries, free trade areas

JEL classifications: F00, F02, F10, F11, F13, F14, F15

1. Introduction

While the process of multilateral liberalization proceeds at a pace that at times seems almost glacial, recent years have seen much liberalization in the form of free trade areas, customs unions, or other types of preferential market access agreements. Many of these preferential arrangements are or will be between small and large countries. The United States has, for example, established free trade agreements with Israel, Chile, and several small Central American countries. The European Union has free trade agreements with Iceland and several small countries in the Mediterranean. Even Japan, a latecomer to preferential liberalization, has established a free trade agreement with Singapore.

There is no sign that this phenomenon is on the decline. The United States, the European Union, and Japan are all currently considering other

Frontiers of Economics and Globalization
Volume 4 ISSN: 1574-8715
DOI: 10.1016/S1574-8715(08)04022-0

free trade agreements. There have even been calls for pursuing such arrangements with increased vigor as the WTO Doha Round multilateral negotiations have failed to meet self-imposed negotiating deadlines.

This chapter presents a formal analysis of the effects on the economic welfare of a large country and on a small one from signing a free trade agreement with each other.

Wonnacott and Wonnacott (1981) demonstrated that a small country, in a world where trading blocs can be formed, can do better by signing a free trade agreement with a large country than from unilateral free trade. I (Kowalczyk, 2000) presented a formal analysis of the problem, and showed that the small country, under certain conditions, would even wish to sign free trade agreements with multiple large countries. These papers demonstrate also that the large country would lose real income from such an arrangement.[1]

In a first analysis that recognizes that not all small countries are of the same size, Michaely (1998) shows that the welfare of the large country is U-shaped in the size of the small trading partner: there is virtually no loss from integrating with a microstate or with a country that is almost the same size as the large country, but there is a loss from integrating with an intermediate size small country.

It could be important for countries to know the size of such a loss. A large country might, for example, request concessions, political or economic (on migration or security, for example) in return for entering into a free trade agreement with a small country. Or the small country might offer financial compensation.[2,3]

Michaely's (1998) analysis is diagrammatic and qualitative, and it applies a methodology, that of Jacob Viner's (1950) trade diversion and trade creation, that cannot be implemented empirically.[4] The purpose of the present chapter is to present a formal analysis of the issue of varying small country size and to identify the variables that would allow a quantitative assessment of the large country's change in welfare from a free trade agreement with a small country. Using the terms-of-trade

[1] In the absence of sidepayments, that is. I show, in Kowalczyk (2000), that there exist sidepayments from the small to the large country such that both countries would benefit from a bilateral free trade agreement.

[2] International sidepayments have been used at times of expansions of the European Economic Community. The creation of the European Economic Area in the early 1990s also involved sidepayments.

Kowalczyk and Sjöström (1994) and Konishi, Kowalczyk, and Sjöström (2003a, 2003b) show how international sidepayments could even support immediate global free trade in a world where countries instead could have chosen to form customs unions.

[3] Another possibility, not considered in this chapter, is that the large country government engages in such an agreement because of lobbying by some domestic industry.

[4] Kowalczyk (2000) offers a comprehensive critique of the trade diversion and trade creation approach, and demonstrates that the welfare calculus of tariffs, i.e., the terms-of-trade and volume-of-trade approach, is a useful alternative.

and volume-of-trade approach, I show that the U-shaped welfare locus can be expressed in terms of variables that can be observed or estimated, and I derive a precise value for the large country's maximum possible welfare loss from integrating with a small country.[5]

Section 2 presents the model and the welfare expression. Section 3 applies the welfare expression to assess the large country's welfare as well as the small country's welfare from bilateral free trade, and how the effect on the large country depends on the size of the small partner country. Section 4 discusses which information is required to determine the size of the large country's welfare loss, and Section 5 derives statements on the likelihood of welfare improving free trade as a function of such parameters as trade volumes, tariffs, and price differences. Section 6 concludes the chapter.

2. *The calculus of national economic welfare*

Consider a world where each of three countries a, b, and c, indexed by i ($i = a, b, c$), are inhabited by price-taking consumers and producers, who demand and produce goods 0 and 1 indexed by g ($g = 0, 1$). The variable m_g^{ij} denotes country i's net imports from country j of good g, and x_g^{ij} is country i's net exports to country j of good g; m^{ij} and x^{ij} are the corresponding vectors.

Let p_g^i denote the domestic price for good g in country i, and let $(p_g^e)^{ij}$ be the tariff-exclusive price paid by residents in country i for imports of good g from country j. If tariffs are specific rather than *ad valorem*, and if t_g^{ij} denotes country i's tariff on imports of good g from country j, then $p_g^i = (p_g^e)^{ij} + t_g^{ij}$ or, in vector notation, $p^i = (p^e)^{ij} + t^{ij}$.

Let Δ denote a change. Then, if pre-change values are given by subscript A and post-change values by subscript B, $\Delta(p^e)^i = (p_B^e)^i - (p_A^e)^i$ is the change in country i's tariff-exclusive prices, and $\Delta m^i = m_B^i - m_A^i$ is the change in its trade volume.

The minimum spending required by the representative consumer in country i to reach the level of utility u^i when the domestic price is p^i is given by the expenditure function $e^i(p^i, u^i)$.[6] If c_A^i is the initial expenditure-minimizing consumption bundle in country i, then $S_\gamma^i = p_B^i c_A^i - e^i(p_B^i, u_A^i)$ is the consumption effect in country i as the consumer, due to the price change, adjusts his or her bundle to reach the initial level of utility. If preferences are convex, S_γ^i is non-negative. Similarly, if y^i is the vector of profit-maximizing

[5] Kowalczyk (2006) compares the welfare effects for a small and a large country from three liberalization strategies: unilateral free trade by a small country, a free trade agreement between a small country and its large partner, and preferential access by the large partner to the small country's exporters. I show, among other results, that if the large country has granted preferential access to the small country then, paradoxically, a unilateral tariff reduction by the small country would reduce the large country's welfare yet further.

[6] See, for example, Dixit and Norman (1980).

output in country i, then $S^i_\pi = p^i_B(y^i_B - y^i_A)$ is the production effect as producers adjust their plans due to the change in domestic price. If production possibilities are convex, S^i_π is non-negative. I denote the non-negative sum of the consumption and production effects by $S^i = S^i_\gamma + S^i_\pi$.

Define $\Delta\eta^i$ to be the change in country i's welfare as measured in units of numeraire good 0. As discussed by James Meade (1955), and as formalized by Ronald Jones (1969) for small changes, and by Michihiro Ohyama (1972) and Earl Grinols and Kar-yiu Wong (1991) for large changes, the change in country i's welfare can then be written as

$$\Delta\eta^i = -\Delta(p^e)^i m^i_A + (p^i_B - (p^e_B)^i)\Delta m^i + S^i. \tag{1}$$

The change in welfare is hence the sum of a terms-of-trade effect, $-\Delta(p^e)^i m^i_A$, caused by any change in the cost of obtaining the pre-change trade vector; a volume-of-trade effect, $(p^i_B - (p^e_B)^i)\Delta m^i$, equal to a change in tariff revenue at post-change tariff rates; and the non-negative sum of the consumption and production effects, S^i. As I discuss in Kowalczyk (2000), and in contrast to the trade diversion and trade creation approach, data exist, or meaningful estimates can be generated, for all variables in expression (1), whether they be trade volumes, international trade prices, domestic prices, tariffs, or substitution in production and consumption due to changes in prices.

3. *Welfare from varying small country size*

I assume that each of the three countries applies non-discriminatory import tariffs in the initial situation A. I assume also that country a is large relative to country b but small relative to country c (the "rest of the world"), and that in the initial situation country a imports good 1 from both countries b and c in return for good 0, and that countries b and c do not trade with each other. I will now analyze a free trade agreement between large country a and small country b.

Consider Figure 1, which reproduces Michaely's Figure 2. The standard definition of a small country is that no unilateral action by such a country can affect the international prices at which it trades. If the large country engages in bilateral free trade with a small country of this type, then the domestic price in the large country would not be affected. Rather, the large country would experience a welfare reducing loss of tariff revenue with the size of this loss being a function of the size of small country b where size will be measured in terms of the amount of imports into large country a from small country b after the integration.[7]

[7] An example of this would be if country b were a microstate, in which case country a continues to obtain virtually all its imports from country c.

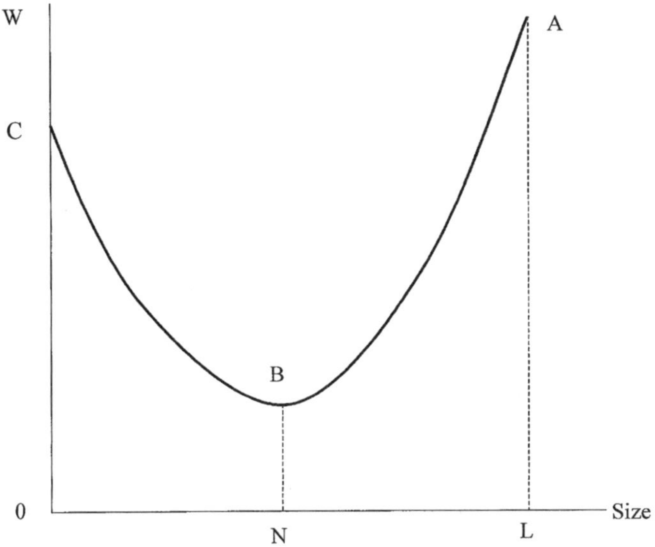

Fig. 1. Welfare levels and size of partner.

The largest size of small country *b* consistent with no effect on country *a*'s domestic price is where large country *a* obtains all its imports from small country *b*, but where the marginal unit of imports could be from the rest of the world *c*. Let point *N* in Figure 1 denote that size. For small country *b* sizes smaller than *N* the domestic price of imports in large country *a* equals the constant tariff-inclusive price on imports from the rest of the world *c*. Michaely (1998) refers to this range of country *b* sizes as "ultra small."

In a departure from conventional work on small countries, Michaely considers also when the size of a small country is large enough to affect the domestic prices in large country *a*. For a small country *b* larger than size *N*, large country *a* obtains all its imports from country *b* after establishing the free trade area. Michaely assumes that for country *b* sizes larger than *N* the domestic and tariff-exclusive prices of imports in large country *a* are lower the larger is small country *b* due to lower cost in country *b* of meeting the increase in import demand from country *a* due to the free trade agreement. I will refer to a country *b* falling in this unconventional size range as "price-affecting small." Michaely demonstrates that large country *a*'s welfare locus has positive slope in the size of the price-affecting small country, as illustrated in Figure 1 of this chapter.

I will now turn to the formal analysis of country *a*'s welfare. I do this by considering first that *a* integrates with a price-affecting small country, and I then explore how reducing the size of partner *b* would affect the large country's welfare.

In Figure 1, let L be the size of a price-affecting small country b which is so large that entering into bilateral free trade with country a will have no effect on country a's terms of trade. In this case, large country a experiences a loss of tariff revenue of $t_A^a m_A^a$ since there would be no importation from the rest of the world c. Large country a is also affected by a non-negative substitution effect, S^a, since the domestic price of imports in country a falls relative to the pre-free trade situation due to the elimination of the tariff on imports from small country b. The implied change in large country a welfare at point L is

$$\Delta\eta^a = -t_A^a m_A^a + S^a. \tag{2}$$

The effect on large country a's welfare is ambiguous. It loses tariff revenue but gains due to consumption and production effects. For a sufficiently small value of initial tariff revenue, the large country may even gain.

At small country size N country b switches from being price-affecting small to being ultra small. If integrating with a country b of size between L and N, the change in large country a's welfare can be written as

$$\Delta\eta^a = -((p_B^e)^{ab} - (p_A^e)^{ab})m_A^{ab} - ((p_B^e)^{ab} - (p_A^e)^{ac})m_A^{ac} - t_A^a m_A^a + S^a. \tag{3}$$

By assumption, integrating with a country b of this size implies a higher price for imports from small country b, i.e., a higher $(p_B^e)^{ab}$ than if country b is of size L. As long as $(p_B^e)^{ab} \leq (p_A^e)^{ac} + t_A^a$, large country a will continue to import from small partner b rather than shifting back to importing from the rest of the world c. Compared to the initial situation A of no free trade agreement, large country a experiences the volume-of-trade loss $t_A^a m_A^a$ and in addition a terms-of-trade loss equal to $[-((p_B^e)^{ab} - (p_A^e)^{ab})m_A^{ab} - ((p_B^e)^{ab} - (p_A^e)^{ac})m_A^{ac}]$. The reduction in country a's domestic price will be smaller than if price-affecting country b were larger, since $(p_B^e)^{ab}$ is higher than it would be at L, and any contribution from a non-negative S^a is therefore smaller than at L. Thus, any welfare loss to country a is larger if price-affecting partner country b is smaller, i.e., country a's welfare is increasing in the size of the price-affecting small country b if country b is larger than N.

At point N, small country b is so small, and the price large country a pays for its imports from small country b is so high, that large country a's tariff-exclusive price on imports from small country b is just equal to large country a's pre-integration domestic price on imports from rest-of-world c, i.e., $(p_B^e)^{ab} = p_A^{ac}$. Since $p_A^{ab} = p_A^{ac} = (p_A^e)^{ac} + t_A^a$, it follows that, $(p_B^e)^{ab} - (p_A^e)^{ab} = (p_B^e)^{ab} - (p_A^e)^{ac} = t_A^a$. Finally, with no change in the domestic price in country a, S^a vanishes. Thus, the loss in welfare consists of worse terms of trade, $-t_A^a m_A^a$, and lost tariff revenue, $t_A^a m_A^a$, and the change in large country a's welfare is

$$\Delta\eta^a = -2t_A^a m_A^a. \tag{4}$$

If large country a integrates with an even smaller country b, i.e., if country b is ultra small, only some of large country a's post-change imports will be from the small partner country b, since large country a will continue to obtain some of its imports from the rest of the world c even after entering the free trade agreement. The terms-of-trade loss for large country a will be smaller when b is ultra small, and the implied volume-of-trade loss will be smaller since country a's imports from country c will be reduced by only $(m_A^{ac} - m_B^{ac})$ rather than by the full initial volume of m_A^{ac}. Since the domestic price in large country a continues to be given by its initial value $p_A^a = p_A^{ab} = p_A^{ac}$, there is no welfare improving substitution effect, S^a. When integrating with a country smaller than N, the change in country a welfare, when compared to the pre-integration situation A, is therefore,

$$\Delta\eta^a = -t_A^a m_B^{ab} - t_A^a(m_A^{ac} - m_B^{ac}). \tag{5}$$

This expression implies that the smaller is partner country b, i.e., the smaller is m_B^{ab} and hence the smaller is the reduction in country a's trade with rest-of-world c and thus the larger is m_B^{ac}, the smaller is country a's loss in economic welfare. In the limit, country b reaches the size of a microstate where m_B^{ab} is approximately zero, and m_B^{ac} is approximately equal to m_A^{ac}, and there is approximately no effect on country a's welfare. Thus, country a's welfare is decreasing in the size of an "ultra small" partner. Combining this with the finding for the price-affecting small country, and the U-shaped welfare locus in Figure 1 follows with minimum welfare given by expression (4) when small country b is of size N.

Turning to the small country's welfare from the free trade agreement, expression (1) yields

$$\Delta\eta^b = -((p_B^e)^{ba} - (p_A^e)^{ba})m_A^{ba} + S^b, \tag{6}$$

where the sources of welfare change are a terms-of-trade effect and a non-negative production and consumption effect.

As discussed earlier, if country b is price-affecting small, the terms of trade improvement $(p_B^e)^{ba} - (p_A^e)^{ba}$ may be smaller than large partner a's initial tariff. However, if country b is ultra small, expression (6) becomes

$$\Delta\eta^b = t_A^a X_A^{ba} + S^b, \tag{7}$$

as the small country's export price increase is now the large country's initial tariff rate.

4. *Informational requirements for welfare assessments*

How difficult would it be to gauge the effects on large country a's welfare from integrating with a small country b? Expression (5) shows that if b is an ultra small country, the required information is country a's initial tariff rate t_A^a, country b's potential to export to country a, as given by m_B^{ab}, and country a's loss of imports from the rest of the world, $(m_A^{ac} - m_B^{ac})$.

If, instead, the small country is price-affecting, estimates of country b's export price, $(p_B^e)^{ab}$, and of the production and consumption effects, S^a, would be necessary as well.

The welfare expressions in the previous section can help provide answers to three queries by Michaely.

> The welfare level represented by OC may be higher or lower than that of LA. (Michaely, 1998, p. 79)

As discussed earlier, the country a welfare level at OC, where large country a integrates with the smallest possible microstate b, is approximately equal to the pre-integration welfare level. On the other hand, the direction of change in large country a's welfare from integrating with a price-affecting small country b of size L is given by expression (2), and hence requires knowledge of the size of the loss $t_A^a m_A^a$ versus the size of the gains, S^a.

> With no specific knowledge, we likewise cannot rank the welfare levels of a point on AB and a point on BC. (Michaely, 1998, p. 79)

Expression (3) gives the welfare from integrating with a country on AB in Figure 1, and expression (5) yields the welfare from integrating with a country on BC. Welfare on BC is higher than welfare on AB if:

$$\begin{aligned} -t_A^a m_B^{ab} - t_A^a(m_A^{ac} - m_B^{ac}) > &-((p_B^e)^{ab} - (p_A^e)^{ab})m_A^{ab} \\ &-((p_B^e)^{ab} - (p_A^e)^{ac})m_A^{ac} - t_A^a m_A^a + S^a \end{aligned} \tag{8}$$

The condition states that the required information is tariff rate, imports from each trading partner before the free trade agreement, and imports from price-affecting partner country b once an agreement is established, import price differential, and degree of substitution. The condition is more likely to be satisfied for small terms-of-trade and volume-of-trade losses from integrating with the ultra small partner as implied by the left-hand side of the inequality and for small values of substitution, S^a, and large terms-of-trade losses to large country a from integrating with a price-affecting small country b, as given by the right-hand side.

> Somewhere along [as price-affecting country [*b*] gets smaller; *my addition*], a welfare loss due to the preferential agreement turns from a possibility to a certainty; but where this is (i.e., at what level of "smallness" of the partner) we cannot generally say. (Michaely, 1998, p. 79)

Again, the answer lies with expression (3). Assuming that large country a trades with both b and c initially, $(p_B^e)^{ab} - (p_A^e)^{ab} = (p_B^e)^{ab} - (p_A^e)^{ac}$. Let $(p_B^e)^{ab} = \Phi(m_B^{ab})$ where $\Phi' < 0$, and $S^a = S^a(m_B^{ab})$ where $S^{a\prime} > 0$. Substituting these into expression (3), setting $\Delta\eta^a = 0$, and rearranging terms, using that $(p_A^e)^{ac} + t_A^a = p_A^a$, implies the following expression from which the critical value for m_B^{ab}, at which the large country switches from gaining to losing from integrating, can be derived:

$$(\Phi(m_B^{ab}))(m_A^{ab} + m_A^{ac}) - S^a(m_B^{ab}) = ((p_A^e)^{ac})(m_A^{ab} + m_A^{ac}) - t_A^a m_A^a. \tag{9}$$

5. *On the likelihood of welfare improving integration*

There have been attempts in trade theory at establishing simple predictors for when a preferential trade arrangement raises welfare versus when it does not. Initial levels of protection and initial trade flows have been given particular attention since both are observable.[8]

For free trade with a price-affecting small country, expression (3) implies that the initial tariff affects large country *a*'s economic welfare through affecting both the size of the terms of trade loss and the size of the positive contributions from the consumption and production effects. Thus, eliminating a higher tariff implies a larger preference to exporters from small country *b* and therefore a larger terms of trade loss for country *a*. However, the elimination of a higher tariff also reduces the domestic price of imports in large country *a* by more, and it raises, therefore, the potential magnitude of the welfare improving consumption and production effects S^a. Hence, the effect of the height of country *a*'s initial tariff on country *a*'s economic welfare from a free trade agreement with small country *b* is ambiguous. It follows also from expression (3) that large country *a*'s welfare falls by less the smaller is the difference between the initial trade price $(p_A^e)^{ac}$ and the post-change trade price $(p_B^e)^{ab}$; and the smaller are country *a*'s initial imports from the rest of the world, m_A^{ac}.

Proposition 1. *Conditional on the small country in a free trade agreement being price-affecting small, the large country's loss is smaller (or its gain is larger), (i) the smaller is the cost difference between partner country and the rest of the world, (ii) the smaller are initial imports from the rest of the world, and (iii) the more price responsive are large country production and consumption. The effect of the level of the initial non-discriminatory tariff on large country welfare is ambiguous.*

If country *b* is ultra small instead, expression (5) implies the following result:

Proposition 2. *Conditional on the small country in a free trade agreement being ultra small, the large country's loss is smaller, (i) the smaller are initial imports from the rest of the world, (ii) the smaller is the free trade partner's potential to export, and (iii) the smaller is the large country's initial non-discriminatory tariff.*

---

[8] See, for example, Richard Lipsey (1960) and Raymond Riezman (1979).

It is noteworthy that, in both propositions, initial trade flows relative to the rest of the world play a role for the size of any welfare loss but that initial trade flows relative to the partner country do not. It is also noteworthy that the effect of the size of the initial tariff is ambiguous: if country *a* integrates with an ultra small country *b*, a high tariff raises the welfare loss, but if country *b* is a price-affecting small country, the effect from a high tariff is ambiguous.

6. Conclusion

Using the terms-of-trade and volume-of-trade approach, I have shown why the large country's welfare locus is U-shaped as a function of the size of the small trading partner by reference to variables that are either observable or can be estimated. I have derived what is the large country's maximum possible welfare loss from integrating with a small country, and I have identified conditions that make increased large country welfare from a free trade agreement likely.

The effect on the large country from free trade with a small country, while likely to be negative, is an empirical issue. It is, for example, a maintained assumption in this study that all goods are homogeneous and produced under competitive conditions. If, instead, trade is primarily in varieties produced by monopoly firms, then the assumptions required for price-taking small countries would no longer apply, and integration with even very small countries could affect large country prices.

Returning to the analysis of the present chapter, if a large country does decide to integrate with small partners, it would be better for the large country to integrate either with few very small countries, or with a large number of small countries so that their aggregate size would make them appear as if they were a relatively large price-affecting small country. Integrating with small countries leading to medium aggregate size, which would reduce large country welfare the most, would have to be for other purposes than immediate large country welfare, such as, for example, to signal to negotiating partners an intention to pursue further liberalization in a multilateral negotiation.

Acknowledgements

This chapter was prepared for the City University of Hong Kong Conference in Honor of Professor Ronald Jones. I thank a referee and conference participants for comments, and I thank the City University of Hong Kong for financial support. This paper is part of the Globalization Project at the University of Aarhus.

References

Dixit, A., Norman, V. (1980), *Theory of International Trade*. Cambridge University Press, Cambridge.

Grinols, E.L., Wong, K. (1991), An exact measure of welfare change. *Canadian Journal of Economics* 24, 61–64.

Jones, R.W. (1969), Tariffs and trade in general equilibrium: comment. *American Economic Review* 59, 418–424.

Konishi, H., Kowalczyk, C., Sjöström, T. (2003a), Free trade, customs unions, and transfers. The Fletcher School, Social Science Research Network. Available at http://ssrn.com/abstract=428346.

Konishi, H., Kowalczyk, C., Sjöström, T. (2003b), Global Free Trade is in the Core of a Customs Union Formation Game. The Fletcher School. *Review of International Economics* (forthcoming).

Kowalczyk, C. (2000), Welfare and integration. *International Economic Review* 41, 483–494.

Kowalczyk, C. (2006), Liberalizing trade between large and small: the welfare from three different strategies. *Asia-Pacific Journal of Accounting and Economics* 13, 171–179.

Kowalczyk, C., Sjöström, T. (1994), Bringing GATT into the core. *Economica* 61, 301–317.

Lipsey, R.G. (1960), *The Theory of Customs Unions: A General Equilibrium Analysis*. Weidenfeld and Nicholson, London.

Meade, J. (1955), *Trade and Welfare*. Oxford University Press, London.

Michaely, M. (1998), Partners to a preferential trade agreement: implications of varying size. *Journal of International Economics* 46, 73–85.

Ohyama, M. (1972), Trade and welfare in general equilibrium. *Keio Economic Studies* 9, 37–73.

Riezman, R. (1979), A 3×3 model of customs unions. *Journal of International Economics* 37, 47–61.

Viner, J. (1950), *The Customs Union Issue*. Carnegie Endowment for International Peace, New York.

Wonnacott, P., Wonnacott, R. (1981), Is unilateral tariff reduction preferable to a customs union? The curious case of the missing foreign tariffs. *American Economic Review* 71, 704–714.

CHAPTER 23

Fragmented Trade and the Hub–spokes Game – Strategic Trade Under the WTO

An-Chi Tung[a] and Henry Wan Jr[b]

[a]*Institute of Economics, Academia Sinica, 130, Section 2 Academia Road, Taipei 11529, Taiwan*
E-mail address: actung@econ.sinica.edu.tw
[b]*Department of Economics, Cornell University, 470 Uris Hall, Ithaca NY 14853-7601, USA*
E-mail address: hyw1@cornell.edu

Abstract
In the Jones–Kierzkowski world of fragmented production, we address a strategic trade issue for development: how to industrialize under the WTO regime. One solution is to generate cross-border externalities, such as becoming the *hub* of a network of countries, so as to attract foreign investment with collective comparative advantage. Thus the small, remote and pre-industrial Singapore managed to organize a *hub–spokes* game: achieving a win-win solution for all and gaining the most as the hub. In servicing the spokes for fee, Singapore has earned First World income levels, by the twin patterns of the *flying geese* and the *triangular accord.*

Keywords: Fragmentation, flying geese pattern, foreign direct investment, industrial policy, network

JEL classifications: F13, F15, F21, F23, C72

1. Motivation

In the first sentence of his first article on international trade, Samuelson (1938, p. 261) traced the common origin of economic theory and trade theory and observed, 'International trade theory was developed by practical men, interested in normative, welfare problems'. Ronald Jones, a leader in international economic theory at the turn of this century, is such a practical man. Having devoted most of his effort to trade theory during the 20th Century, he has recently extended his attention to issues of trade policy facing the world of the 21st Century. Among various topics, his interest ranges over the fragmented production (Jones and Kierzkowski, 1989), technology transfers (Ruffin and Jones, 2007),

Frontiers of Economics and Globalization
Volume 4 ISSN: 1574-8715
DOI: 10.1016/S1574-8715(08)04023-2

economic take-off (Bond et al., 2005), and the provision of national service-links (Golub et al., 2007). To his honor, this chapter addresses a novel topic in strategic trade policy, which overlaps with all the above listed issues that he studied. And this topic is especially important in today's world under the WTO.

2. *Statement of the problem*

2.1. The topic

Today, a key issue for strategic trade theory is *whether* and *how* a country can influence cross-sector resource allocations with industrial policy. Traditionally countries hoping to industrialize would nurture infant industries with quotas and tariffs. But nowadays, by the spirit of the WTO/GATT, only under special circumstances, temporary trade restrictions are allowed as *safeguard*. Otherwise, other countries can complain, and then retaliate, once the complaint is upheld in hearings.

But actually there is more room for policy, on both conceptual and historical grounds. Conceptually, industrial policy is to overcome coordination failure, not to restrict trade. Historically, although its home market is too Lilliputian to protect, Singapore still manages to promote industry with policy, and becomes a showcase in that. In both contexts, trade restriction – the principal concern of WTO/GATT – is conspicuous by its absence.

In fact, any industrial policy is viable, if it neither restricts trade, nor triggers actionable complaints (Wan and Tung, 2006). In these two dimensions, Table 1 compares the alternative strategies of infant industry protection and cross-border alliance building (the latter option is studied below).

The implication of such an alliance is shown in the Venn diagram in Chart 1, motivated by a case of Itoh (1999). Set A represents the country which activates the alliance; Set C includes all coalition members; Set B denotes all those beneficiaries of the alliance; Set U includes all parties in the model.

The secret here is to design a win-win solution, and gain the most among all players. An appropriate illustration is the well-documented record of Singapore.

Table 1. A typology of industrial policy measures.

Industrial policy measures		Triggers actionable complaint	
		No	Yes
Restricts trade	No	Forming cross-country alliances	–
	Yes	–	Infant industry protection

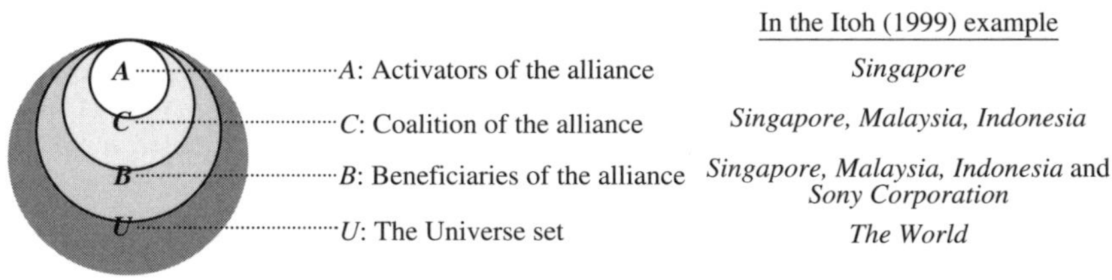

Chart 1. The implications of a cross-boundary alliance.

2.2. The exemplar

Singapore succeeded by harnessing the trend of international trade, namely, fragmented production, the topic of the seminal contribution by Jones and Kierzkowski (1989). The South industrializes by trading *with* the North, not *de-linking from* the latter.

Singapore defied export pessimism, the popular view after World War II and became 'fully developed' by means of a two-pronged strategy formulated around 1962–1964,

(a) 'To leapfrog the region', and
(b) 'To create a First World oasis in a Third World region',

in the succinct words of Lee (2000, pp. 75–76).

Regarding (a), for the small, remote and pre-industrial Singapore, industrialization needs a source of technology and a market for output: both lie in the developed world, half a globe away. Thus, there is the inherent disadvantage of distance – the transaction cost to interact with the industrial economies afar. This must be compensated somehow, if Singapore is ever to become 'fully developed'.

Regarding (b), the second principle answers the question raised by the first. With itself as the core, an 'oasis' organizes the desert nearby into an effective *hub–spokes* network, to seek outside opportunities on the basis of division of labor. Hopefully, sufficient compensation may come to the hub. To be a 'First World oasis' means becoming part of the First World.

The litmus test of being 'fully developed' that Singapore has passed is *to match the First World in real output per capita* by offering First World service.

Some elaboration follows naturally. First, throughout the developing world, producers suffer two disadvantages: an initially low productivity relative to the North and the costly transportation to the industrial center they depend on. Through learning by doing and the improvement of transportation, these drawbacks can be ameliorated partly, but never entirely.[1]

---

[1] See Proposition 1 (a).

Second, further progress can come only by building alliance. Thus, the *hub* may assist the *spokes*, trouble-shooting by its own experience, and receiving fee-for-service. Thus, away from the industrial First World, only this fee may allow the hub (but not the spokes) to reach the First World level of per capita income.[2]

A new era dawns only when the Southern development gains the critical mass.

This strategy of alliance-building entails two testable implications – in twin complementary patterns, *over time* and *across space*.

First, *over time*, the development proceeds in a *trilogy* along the *output ladder*: *the pre-industrial* stage (like being an entrepôt for natural resources gathered nearby), to the *industrial stage* (like focusing on the division of labor with the developed North), to ultimately the *post-industrial* stage (like providing service to industrialize neighboring economies). This parallels to the well-known *flying geese* pattern of Akamatsu and Kojima. See Tung (2003, 2006) for more detail.

Second, *across space*, there emerges a *tripartite* interaction among the country ladder: there is the First World, as the original locus for technology and market, and the Third World, as the source of inexperienced but low-cost labor, and finally, the experienced intermediary in between. This pattern of division of labor may take two alternative forms:

1. Intra-firm – inside multinational corporations. As an example, among Sony's branches in Singapore, Malaysia and Indonesia, workers with less skill but even lower wages can produce with the support of experienced workers from Singapore. In the bargain, Sony gains the cost advantage, and Singapore the concentration of high-skill and high-wage jobs (Itoh, 1999).
2. Cross-firm – among various enterprises. For example, the experienced Singaporean businessmen intermediate between the First World customers and Third World producers, to develop export platforms at Batam Island, Indonesia (Lee, *op. cit.*, 271ff), as part of the three-country Growth Triangle. This Singaporean episode is far from an isolated case. For its parallel, in the interaction between Chinese suppliers, Taiwanese intermediaries and their First World clients in a tripartite accord, see Liu and Tung (2007).

Having clarified some of the relevant conceptual issues, we are ready for the formal analysis in the subsequent sections. Before that, a brief might be helpful as a roadmap.

[2] See Propositions 2 and 3.

2.3. The organization of the analysis

The real world is characterized by three elements: (a) the world prices which clear the market, (b) the externalities which prevail over the network and (c) the policy interactions among various economies.

Effective policy analysis requires insight into the externality ridden general equilibrium. The general nature of such a model resembles the case of national and international returns to scale (Ethier, 1982). It is well understood but not readily tractable. We find it useful to develop insight in the next two sections through the pattern of hub–spokes network and a simple, a-temporal game over it. Next, we return to the framework of general equilibrium: to characterize both the dynamics in the development and the distribution of trading gains. Finally, it is then shown that the theoretic predictions are not contradicted by the available information. Some concluding remarks are offered in the last section.

3. The hub–spokes network

As shown in Figure 1, it is the fragmented production that allows for outsourcing, the North–South intra-industry trade, and hence the shipping of goods across long distance. An asterisk denotes the input or output located in the South.

Trade provides the North the access to the low-wage labor from the South, and the South the only practical chance to participate in industrial production.

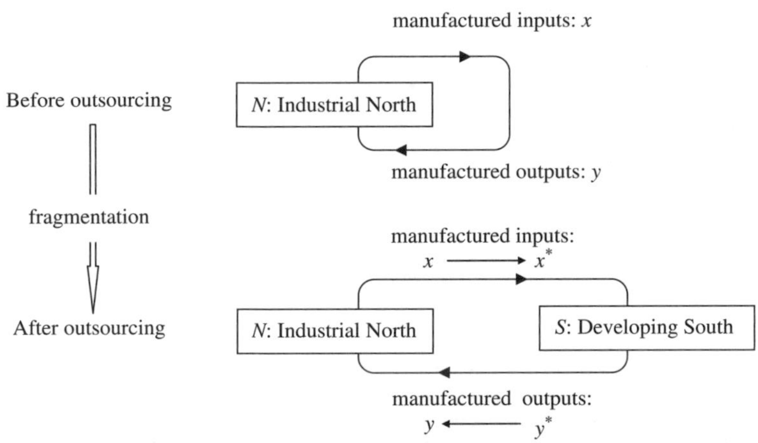

Fig. 1. The supply chain.

Table 2. Unit prices under the no-arbitrage conditions.

	Manufactured input		Manufactured output	
	In the North: x	In the South: x^*	In the North: y	In the South: y^*
Unit price	p	$p^* = T \cdot p$	1	$1/T$

To fix ideas, the following example is given under the assumption of a Leontief production function.[3]

3.1. An extended example

We begin by considering outsourcing between any two economies, one in the North and one in the South.

The (Leontief) production function for the output-numeraire:

$$y = \min(x/a_x, L/a_L), \tag{1}$$

where L is the Northern labor (supply of labor $= N$),

$$y^* = A \cdot \min(x^*/a_x, L^*/a_L), \tag{2}$$

where L^* is the Southern labor (supply of labor at each position $= 1$) and $A \in (0, 1)$ the output-augmenting efficiency index for the South.

As a first approximation, assume for simplicity that for both the manufactured input and output, on the average, every $T > 1$ units produced for shipping, $T - 1$ units must be spent as transportation cost, with only 1 unit available for use at the destination. T is here the parameter for transportation cost, about which, more will be said later. At any market equilibrium under outsourcing, a pair of no-arbitrage conditions must hold among the unit prices of the four manufactured goods which are shown in Table 2.

Thus, there are the competitive profit conditions for the manufactured outputs:

$$\begin{aligned} &1 \leq p \cdot a_x + w \cdot a_L, \\ &y \geq 0, \\ &y(1 - p \cdot a_x - w \cdot a_L) = 0, \end{aligned} \tag{3}$$

[3] More generally, at the micro-foundations, the principle of alliance-building may be also approached by means of the theory of 'coalition production' where the distributive problem is solvable, in the 'additive case' (Hildenbrand, 1974, p. 210). That is, unlike the proverbial case of 'the battle of the sexes' (Luce and Raiffa, 1957), there remain identifiable, externality ridden individual production sets, where income may be determined by competitive force.

where p is the price for x and w the Northern wage.

$$\begin{aligned} &1/T \leq (p^* \cdot a_x)/A + (w^* \cdot a_L)/A, \\ &y^* \geq 0, \\ &y^* \cdot [1/T - (p^* \cdot a_x)/A - (w^* \cdot a_L)/A] = 0, \end{aligned} \tag{4}$$

where p^* is the price for x^* and w^* the Southern wage.

Thus, (3) and (4) imply that, at equilibrium,

$$\begin{aligned} 0 \leq w^* &= (A/T - T \cdot p \cdot a_x)/a_L \\ &< (1 - p \cdot a_x)/a_L = w. \end{aligned} \tag{5}$$

By (5) one can derive the following proposition.

Proposition 1. *(The consequence of distance)*

(a) (The limit on catching-up in production.) As long as the same output is produced in both North and South, there is always a wage gap favoring the former;

(b) (The limit on outsourcing.) Outsourcing can go on only if

$$T \leq [A/(p \cdot a_x)]^{1/2}. \tag{6}$$

In fact, Southern workers would work for outsourcing only if their wage level, in terms of the output, exceeds some minimum level, $\underline{w}^*$. Thus, one has the more stringent constraint as follows.

Corollary. Outsourcing is possible, if and only if

$$(A/T - T \cdot p \cdot a_x)/a_L \geq \underline{w}^*, \text{ or } T \leq T^o, \tag{7}$$

where $(A/T^o - T^o \cdot p \cdot a_x)/a_L = \underline{w}^*$.

This is shown in Figure 2.

So, outsourcing takes place if the Southern productivity can justify the round-trip transportation cost.

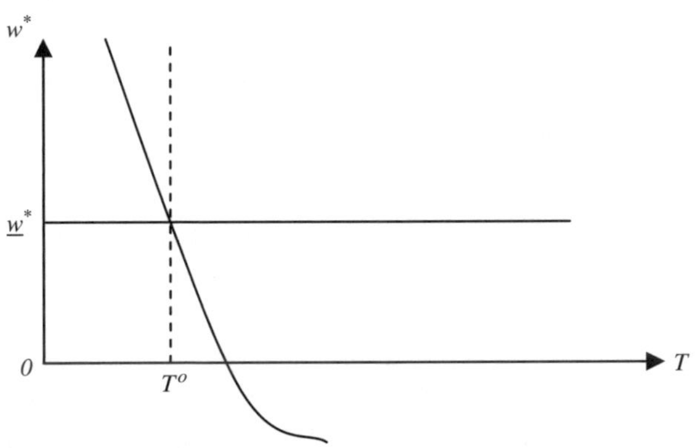

Fig. 2. The limit for T.

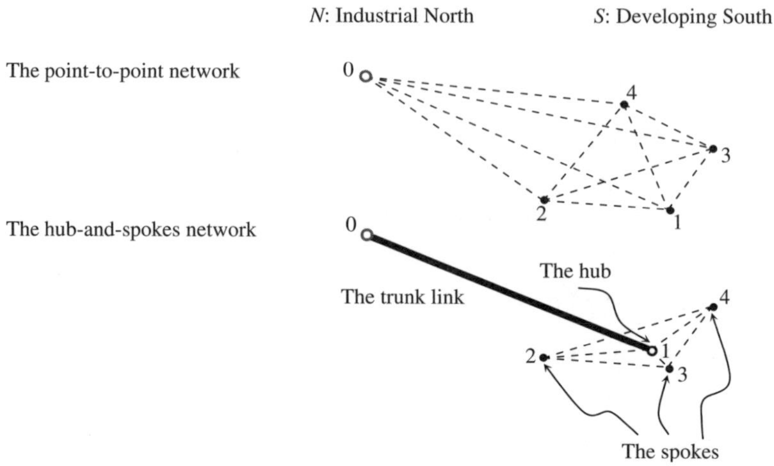

Fig. 3. The road networks.

Next, consider outsourcing with multiple Southern producers.

Here, the road network then decides the transportation cost. Two samples of networks are shown in Figure 3. For a description of the *hub–spokes* network, see for example, Markusen (1996). The hub is connected with the outside with a 'trunk link'. The shared use of that route results in efficiency gain, due to increasing returns in volume. Such a network reduces transportation cost for everyone, but the hub gains most by its direct 'trunk link' to the North.

To fix ideas, the following assumptions are made.

ASSUMPTIONS.

1. The distance between the North (at node 0) and any Southern node 1, 2, 3 or 4 is $m>0$ units; any two Southern nodes are of unit distance in between along the ordinary road.
2. The transportation cost increases at the rate $r > 0$ per unit of travel time. Hence a bill of goods of unit volume shipped for v units of time ends up with a net amount of $e^{-rv} = 1/T<1$ on arrival, or, $T = e^{rv}$.
3. Traveling each unit of distance takes one unit of time along the ordinary road, but only $1/q$ along the trunk link, with its better facilities, for some $q>1$.

Denoting the hub as node 1 without losing generality, one can derive the following results by routine computation.

LEMMA 1. The traveling time from the North to the South is:

$v = m$	to any Southern node in a point-to-point network
$v = m/q$	to the hub in a hub-and-spokes network
$v = m/q + 1$	to any spoke in a hub-and-spokes network

Consider the case that a trunk link joining node 1 to the North (at node 0) satisfies

$$m > q/(q-1) \qquad \text{(long distance, deep cost reduction).} \tag{8}$$

One can thus derive the following proposition.

PROPOSITION 2. *(Design a win-win game; gain the most among the players): To travel from any Southern node to the North (at node 0), the replacement of the point-to-point network with the hub-and-spokes network means*

(a) less traveling time, hence
(b) lower transportation cost, and
(c) higher wage, but
(d) the hub gains more than any spoke.

PROOF. About traveling time v, use Lemma 1.

Part (a),
for the hub, $m/q < m$, since $q > 1$;
for any spoke, since q is positive,
$m/q + 1 < m$ if and only if $m + q < mq$,
which is implied by condition (8).
Part (b) holds, since $\partial T/\partial v = rT > 0$.
Part (c) holds, since (5) implies $\partial w^*/\partial T < 0$, for all $T \leq T^{\circ}$.
Part (d) holds, since $m/q < m/q + 1$.

We next consider the effect of learning and trouble-shooting. So far the productivity A at various nodes is treated as exogenously given, where the productivity gap, $1-A$, may be understood as the *technological backlog* of Gerschenkron, which is the difference between the best practice 1 and the current practice A.

Adopt the following assumptions.

ASSUMPTIONS.

(a) the rate of relative reduction of the productivity gap is proportional to the current output, y, and
(b) under diminishing returns, one can commit a dosage of labor θ with production experience $Y_1 > 0$ at one location to trouble-shooting for inexperienced workers at another location and transfer a fraction of the experience,

$$Y_b = g(\theta)Y_1, \qquad g' > 0 > g''. \tag{9}$$

From Assumption (a),

$$\begin{aligned} dA/dt &= (1-A)fy, \text{ or, } A(Y) \\ &= 1 - [1 - A(0)]\exp(-fY), f > 0, \; Y = \int_{-\infty}^{t} y\, d\tau, \end{aligned} \tag{10}$$

so that one can have the following lemma.

LEMMA 2.

$$dA/dY > 0 > d^2A/dY^2.$$

The situation is seen in panels (a) and (b), Figure 4. In panel (a), the level of labor productivity at the North by workers accomplished in skill is marked by line α, as $1/a_L$. This is assumed to be constant for the present context. In contrast, the labor productivity at the North by workers who started at time 0 rises along line β, with their experience measured in accumulated output. This stands currently at the level of Y_1. To take account of the transportation cost in shipping to the North, the labor productivity at the hub is divided by the factor T, to arrive at the 'equivalent output per worker'. The relationship between this equivalent output per worker and cumulated output is shown as a thick dotted line γ.

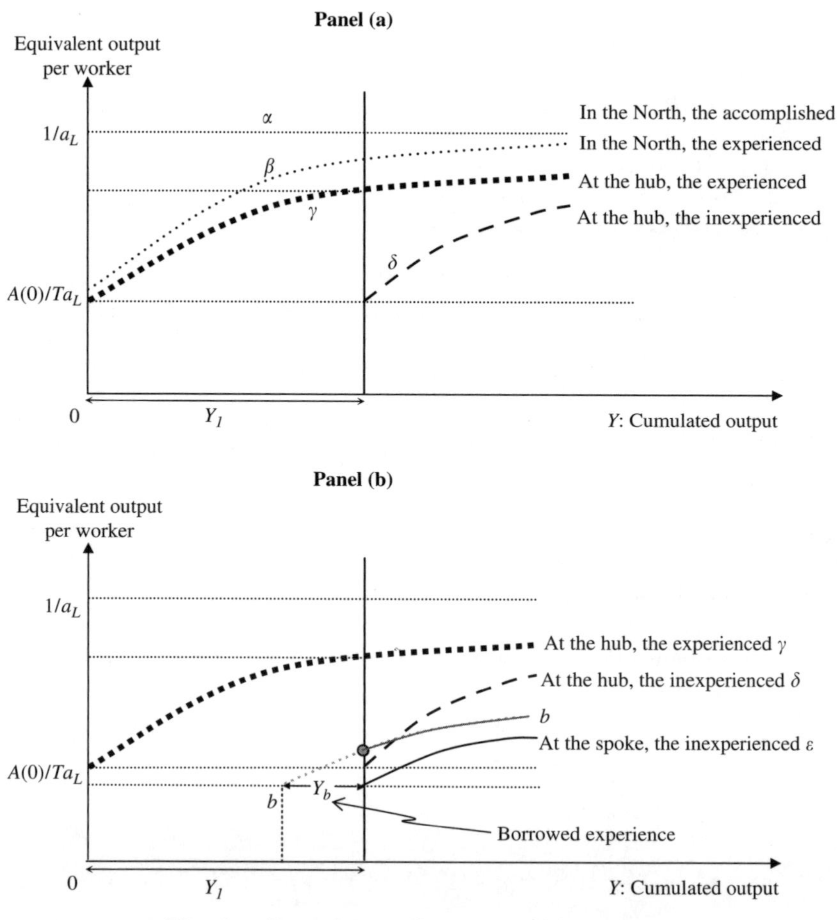

Fig. 4. Experience, distance and borrowing.

For comparison, if output is produced now at the hub without any experience, the situation is plotted as a broken line δ.

However, to start production now, at the spoke, the equivalent output per worker has to be reduced further, to account for the higher transportation cost at the spoke. This is shown in panel (b) as the solid line ε. Next, through trouble-shooting, one can raise productivity through 'borrowing' experience from the hub, by deploying some workers from the hub as trouble-shooters. Suppose the fraction borrowed is at the level of θ, and the experience level is Y_1 at the hub, one can obtain a particular level of equivalent labor productivity, $A[g(\theta)Y_1]/T_1 a_L$ shown at the intersection of the *bb* curve and the vertical line, $Y = Y_1$. It is the market force that determines the equilibrium level of trouble-shooting, that is the level of θ. This influences both labor allocation at the hub, and consequently the wage determination there, and the productivity level $Y_b = g(\theta)Y$ at the spoke, and hence the output at that location.

At the equilibrium, denote $L_{\text{h}}^* \geq 0$ as the labor at the hub used for direct production, and $\theta^o \geq 0$ as the labor at the hub sent to assist each spoke in trouble-shooting. Then with $G-1$ spokes, the full employment condition for the hub is:

$$L_{\text{h}}^* + (G-1)\cdot\theta^o = 1. \tag{11}$$

Denote the wages for labor at the hub and the spoke as w_{hh}^* and $w_{\text{hs}}^* \geq w_{\text{hh}}^*$ (in view of the 'hardship pay' of the hub labor at the spoke), respectively, and the wage of the spoke labor as w_{s}^*, then,

$$w_{\text{s}}^* = \max_{\theta\geq 0}\{A[g(\theta)]/T - T\cdot p\cdot a_x - \theta^o w_{\text{hs}}^*\}/a_L. \tag{12}$$

The above mechanism explains how the hub may assist the spoke, on the fee-for-service basis, and raise its own income. It is how the hub can match the income per worker of the First World.

4. The hub–spokes model

Ex ante, Singapore was no different from many ports nearby. Ex post, its development leads to a win-win outcome for all, with Singapore gaining the most, matching the First World in per capita real income. This path-dependent process locks in all parties in a market-enforced solution through the profit-seeking actions of the Multinational Corporations. As a parable, this section first presented the outcome below as a self-enforced, one-shot, coordination game: a hub–spokes game that generalizes the well-known battle of the sexes model. Next, details are given about how Singapore earns its current positing by decades of hard work.

4.1. A game theory parable

To focus attention to the strategic considerations underlying Proposition 1, consider a static coordination game for the Southerners, under the simplifying assumptions:

A. All parties are *symmetrical* to each other, *a priori*.
B. All parties interact in *simultaneous moves*, say, in sealed bids.
C. All parties engage with each other in a *non-cooperative game*.

There are G 'players', at distinct locations, or *nodes* $i \in S = \{1, 2, 3, \ldots, G\}$ in a network: all nodes are symmetric before the play. Each player marks one's choice among a list $(1, 2, \ldots, G)$ in a sealed bid and all bids are opened together.

The game may end with two outcomes: either (i) there will be no hub and the payoff for everyone is 0, or (ii) some node h becomes the hub by consensus with payoff a, leaving all others as spokes with payoff.

$$a > b > 0. \tag{13}$$

Proposition 3. *There are G symmetric Nash equilibria in pure strategies, each associated with a hub at some, h, and a payoff profile, $(b, b, \ldots, b, a, b, \ldots, b)$, with the entry a in the hth position.*

Proof. Straightforward.

Corollary. (*Implementation*). Without pre-communication, there is no assurance at all that any pure-strategy Nash equilibrium will be reached. This is more likely as G increases: out of all G^G possibilities, only G cases end up with a hub.

Corollary. (*Specialization*). For $G = 2$, the hub–spokes game becomes the game of *the battle of the sexes*.

Remark. This chapter studies alliance-building as industrial policy under the WTO regime, with Singapore as the referent. The hub–spokes game conveys the oasis quality of Singapore.

We now relax assumptions A and B in our hub–spokes game. For the present context, no attempt is made to explore such game-theoretic issues of mixed strategies and equilibrium refinement. These would be important for Singapore's investment decisions, against contemporary contestants of near-equal status.

4.2. The historical perspective

In his flight from Srivijaya to found the Melaka (Malacca) State, Prince Paramesvara, at the end of the 14th Century, spent five years at

Temasek-Singapoura. Melaka, Singapore and Srivijaya were then near equals as his base for operation. But by the time of its separation from Malaysia in 1965, Singapore was not only the center of transportation on the Malacca Strait, but also the main link of Peninsular Malaya astride the road between the East and the West shores.

Economic development being path-dependent, with all the facilities left by the British intact, it is natural for Singapore to play the first mover in the game[4] and hope it will become the regional base of multinational corporations for the Southeast Asia.

To portray the strategic situation, consider a three-player hub–spokes game in the familiar matrix form, for Indonesia (the row player), Malaysia (the column player) and Singapore (the matrix player). Taking advantage of its position of the first mover, Singapore would select the last matrix. Unless Indonesia and Malaysia both designate Singapore as the hub, all players would get the lowest payoff of zero. The asterisk sign shows the resultant solution.

In contrast, in taking the initiative to separate Singapore out of the Federation of Malaysia, it was not the wish of the latter at all to deepen the existing economic ties between the two. On the contrary, in *The Malay Dilemma*, Mahathir (1970) – later a long-serving leader of the Malaysian government – clearly prefers a fuller separation, in economics as well as in politics.

For its own economic survival, Singapore industrialized and expanded its infrastructure to support such development. As a natural extension of its industrialization, when wage rose with labor shortage, Singapore moved into high value-added activities to become a regional center in manufacturing, service and finance, also a headquarters town for multinational corporations.

It has then presented its Southeast Asian neighbors, Malaysia included, a virtual economic 'offer one cannot refuse': to industrialize together, with Singapore as the pivot. Closer economic association has since prospered, in an economic win-win game; as a virtual 'dominant player', Singapore has enjoyed faster growth than all its immediate neighbors, Malaysia included, in the process. Its own pace of development is only slower than China and India, in the most recent period, and outranks other economies at a similar level of per capita income.

We now return to the matrix game in Table 3, and ask whether or not the payoff values listed there are realistic. The answer seems to be no. Consider the payoff profile, (0,0,0), at the third row, second column of the third matrix. It implies all players will receive their status quo payoffs under the following scenario: Malaysia competes against the hub status of

---

[4] Often this is done just by signaling the willingness to host the multinational corporations, when other Third World countries were in riots and mass movements for confrontation.

Table 3. The three-player matrix game.

Indonesia		Malaysia's choice		
		Indonesia	Malaysia	Singapore
Indonesia's choice	Indonesia	(a, b, b)	(0, 0, 0)	(0, 0, 0)
	Malaysia	(0, 0, 0)	(0, 0, 0)	(0, 0, 0)
	Singapore	(0, 0, 0)	(0, 0, 0)	(0, 0, 0)

Malaysia		Malaysia's choice		
		Indonesia	Malaysia	Singapore
Indonesia's choice	Indonesia	(0, 0, 0)	(0, 0, 0)	(0, 0, 0)
	Malaysia	(0, 0, 0)	(b, a, b)	(0, 0, 0)
	Singapore	(0, 0, 0)	(0, 0, 0)	(0, 0, 0)

Singapore*		Malaysia's choice		
		Indonesia	Malaysia	Singapore*
Indonesia's choice	Indonesia	(0, 0, 0)	(0, 0, 0)	(0, 0, 0)
	Malaysia	(0, 0, 0)	(0, 0, 0)	(0, 0, 0)
	Singapore*	(0, 0, 0)	(0, 0, 0)	$(b, b, a)^*$

Singapore (say, by investing in the Multi-media Super Corridor), but Indonesia keeps on using Singapore as the hub. In all likelihood, both Indonesia and Singapore may end up to have some positive payoffs b' and a', respectively (above the *status quo*), even though the sum $a' + b'$ may fall below $a + b$, their aggregate payoffs if Malaysia had supported them. But Malaysia must compete alone against its peer, an Indonesia backed by Singapore, with the latter having made the first move on the strength of its existing infrastructure. The Malaysian payoff may well be negative. In short, compared against Table 3, non-cooperation of the *non-conformist* may not derail completely the plan by the others, yet the punishment for non-cooperation may be much more severe.

In short, compared against Table 3, deviation from the equilibrium by a player in real life does not completely derail the equilibrium outcome for other players, but causes a high self-inflicted penalty.

In contrast to the parable of the hub–spokes game, real life is unveiled with more discretion. As planned all along, Singapore offered services at the First World level, aiming to become 'a base camp for ... professionals who had business to do with the region' (Lee, *op. cit.*, p. 76). It was the multinational corporations of the First World who confirmed Singapore as the hub for fragmented production. With the exception of Myanmar, neighboring countries acquiesced by their move to join the worldwide supply chain of the multinationals. Everyone gained, but Singapore benefited the most.

The static game theory has its advantage in focusing on certain strategic aspects, namely, by effort of one's own, it is possible to become the hub of a win-win game and gain the most among all players. However, this model formulation can be misleading. National prestige being what it is, no leader of any neighboring country can ever accept in a self-enforced solution, in which Singapore has arrogated to itself the position of a 'dominant player', without the choice of the multinationals. To portray the dynamics of the problem in a tractable manner, we now return to the version of market equilibrium.

5. *The evolving world*

5.1. The labor market

Over time, from Equations (5) and (10), wage would rise, and labor allocation would vary. Figure 5 depicts these with the 'full employment condition' on the left panel via an indifference map and the 'labor allocation condition' on the right panel via a labor supply schedule. Each person has 3 units (24 h) of endowed labor time, with 1 unit (8 h) as the legal working day. Hence 2 units of time are enjoyed as leisure under full employment. Situations at instants t_1, t_2 and t_3 ($t_1 < t_2 < t_3$) are shown in dotted, broken and solid lines, respectively.

Case 1. (An interior solution) The wage rate w_1^* is low so households would work only part of the legal working day, and $\mu < 1$ units are spent as extra leisure, shown in the right panel by a vertical reservation demand line for labor, μ units left of the point 1. The limit case is $\mu = 1$ at $w = \underline{w}^*$ of Figure 2. No worker can be hired at lower wages.

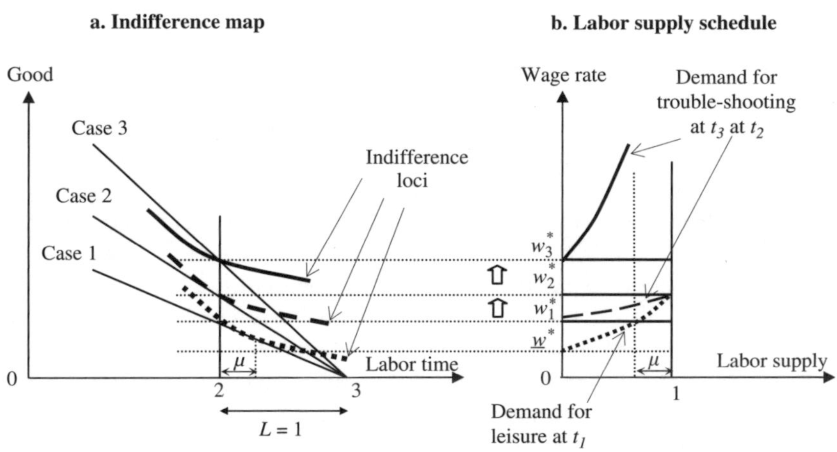

Fig. 5. The labor market.

CASE 2. (The knife-edge case: no trouble-shooting) At wage rate $w_2^* > w_1^*$, the worker chooses to work exactly the full legal working time. All time is spent on production, none left for providing the service of trouble-shooting.

CASE 3. (A corner solution: no direct production) The demand for trouble-shooting is so high at $w_3^* > w_2^*$ so the workers spend all their legal working time for trouble-shooting services to assist others, and none to produce goods.

In the right panel, the demand for productive labor is shown as a horizontal line, those for leisure and trouble-shooting, as sloping lines, measured from the right.[5]

5.2. Service income

For the present purpose, no attempt will be made in this study about the precise determination of service income at the equilibrium. Suffice to say, it is a fact in real life that some experienced individual at the hub offers trouble-shooting as a full time job, on a fee-for-service basis. Such well-paid services raise productivity in the spokes, and induce the hub toward the post-industrial stage. This fits well the extended example. The latter itself is no more than a useful parable. In real life, Singapore derives much income from a rich blend of services, making its neighboring countries more productive than otherwise.

5.3. The installation and expansion of the trunk link

This study focuses on industrial policy under the WTO, with Singapore as example, in organizing a hub-and-spokes network as the means to become 'fully developed'.

To become a hub and maintain such a position depends on the presence of trunk links and their expansion over time. This draws upon both Singapore's pre-industrial role as an entrepôt to ship natural resources, and the continued investment in its infrastructure. The economics of the entrepôt involves the making of complementary investment by the hub to host the most suitable mode of transportation, each mode being a technology with its quasi-fixed cost (Kakinaka, 2006). This is an issue not dealt with here.

Singapore earned its position as a hub by the quality of its service. Take civil air transportation for perspective. Facing the same clientele as BOAC, Qantas and the Malaysian Airline in transportation, and airports like Kuala Lumpur in airfields, Singapore has never been the sole player who

---

[5] The reservation demand is time-invariant; but the demand of labor for trouble-shooting is experience- (hence, time-) dependent.

could earn monopolist rent, astride some trunk link. For example, the Malaysia-Singapore Airline got London landing rights in 1970 from the UK only when Singaporean maintenance crew slowed down the servicing of BOAC (Lee, *op. cit.*, p. 229). The Singapore Airline emerged in 1972 after the split-up of the Malaysia-Singapore Airline. In the contest against the International Civil Aviation Policy (ICAP) of Australia in 1978, Singapore gave concessions to Malaysia to unite the entire ASEAN countries versus Australia so that the Changi Airport would not be bypassed on the 'kangaroo route' between Australia and the UK (*ibid.*, p. 373).

5.4. The Allyn Young externality – the Singapore version

Part and parcel of Singapore's success is due to the Allyn Young externality, a doctrine well cherished but not explained at its micro-foundations in the literature. The core notion is about *complementary industries* at the *same location*. In the context of Singapore, *same location* has to cover some area across the borders and fit well the hub–spokes theme, with transportation cost playing an explicit role. Likewise, *complementary* is particularly relevant along some country ladder – skill ladder axis, by experience, and induced training. Space limitation only allows this topic to be sketched, for the occasion.

At the basic level, production involves a large number of steps, and increasingly so, with fragmented production. Learning effect diminishes at varying paces. When experience brings insignificant productivity gain at a particular step, cost consideration justifies the replacement of the high-wage experienced workers with the low-wage and less experienced. If schooling improves productivity more effectively than experience, training is prescribed with the suitable curricula. On appropriate occasions, foreign labor is brought in with temporary working permits, or permanent residence status. Industries are set up to be mutually complementary, at locations dictated by transportation cost. In Singapore, what becomes the Allyn Young externality, *ex post*, often may be viewed as the planned outcome by the government and multinational corporations, *ex ante*.

Neighboring countries may plan for alternative hubs. But such projects can succeed only when they are compatible with the interests of the multinational corporations.

6. Some statistical facts

This is an analytic study of models with proposed structures. It is justified by practical relevance, and buttressed by events of a particular economy. Patterns of development are held up as testable implications. So there is a need to enquire whether or not such patterns are contradicted by broad observations in reality.

First off, one must decide *how* and *when* to test *whether* Singapore has become an oasis of the First World. For economists, per capita real income relative to the US appears a reasonable yardstick, showing how well the average person can afford to live. Countries like Italy, France, Germany and Japan are usually acknowledged members of the First World. Matching them by that yardstick is arguably acceptable for Singapore's membership. One would like to choose some early date at which the Singaporeans themselves perceived to have made the cut, and not by a fluke. The conference, 'Singapore: toward a developed status' was planned during 1996 in Singapore, after three decades of separate existence (Low, 1999). Chart 2 used the 1995 figures to confirm Singapore as part of the First World, by the standard of relative per capita real income. Singapore has maintained this status for the last dozen years.

Second, the over-time and across-space patterns are less easily documented, beside such case studies like Itoh (1999), but are at least not contradicted by the statistics in Chart 3. Both Malaysia and Indonesia have prospered, but Singapore has gained even more, which is what to expect about the virtual dominant player in a win-win game. Over time Singapore has developed into a regional center not only in transportation but also in finance and communications. It also has become the favorite regional headquarters of multinational corporations. On the one hand, rising prosperity in the services brings about rising cost in Singapore and leads to the departure of such industries from textiles to part of the hard disk drive manufacturing (the *flying geese* pattern). On the other hand, these services have been serving the worldwide economic development, in bridging the gap between Third World countries with the First World (the *triangular* pattern).

As in most economic matters, patterns may be prominent for certain duration, but not forever. Trade with Singapore gains importance in

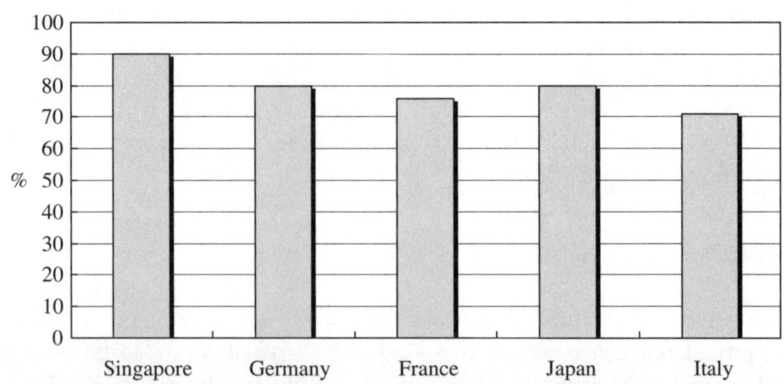

*: Real GDP per capita (in international dollar) relative to the US, by PWT 6.2

Chart 2. Real GDP per capita relative to the US, 1995.

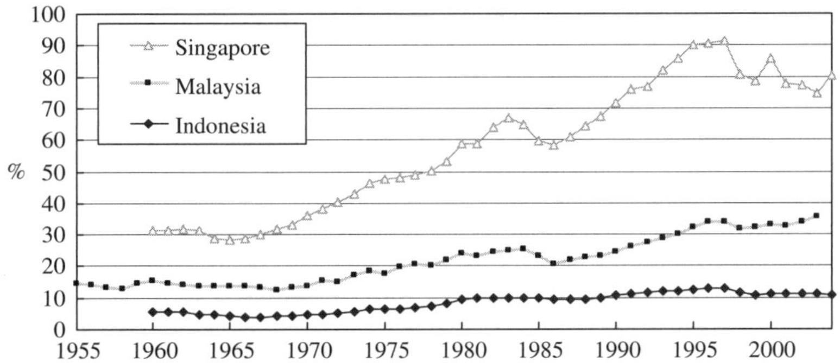

*: Real GDP per capita (in international dollar) relative to the US, by PWT 6.2

Chart 3. The hub-and-spokes pattern in macro-economic terms.

Malaysia and Indonesia in absolute level. This is also in relative shares, but only for some time, as these countries have gradually developed their own capabilities. As a win-win game, the hub–spokes network launches the spokes into industrialization, but does not saddle them with any permanent yoke.

7. *Concluding remarks*

This study explores the implications of fragmented trade on industrial policy. The hub–spokes game and the Singapore case by no means mark the limit of such investigation. The main thrust is that industrial policy rectifies coordination failure and remains potent under the WTO regime. Cross-country alliance is a natural instrument for furthering its goals.

Within this broader scope, policies encouraging foreign direct investment await study as a coordination game. Again the record of Singapore provides much grist for theorists' mill. The circumstance of Singapore is of special interest because its limited domestic market makes it difficult to pursue policy programs relying on trade restrictions. But surprisingly, a continent-wide domestic market is not the best for trade-restrictive policies either. The appropriate form of industrial policy depends upon the local circumstance, which differs from location to location, for countries such as China. So like Singapore, the Chinese policy also relies on foreign direct investment to further its policy goal. Such matters deserve investigation in future studies.

References

Bond, E., Jones, R., Wang, P. (2005), Economic take-offs in a dynamic process of globalization. *Review of International Economics* 13 (1), 1–19.

Ethier, W. (1982), National and international returns to scale in the modern theory of international trade. *American Economic Review* 72 (3), 389–405.

Golub, S.S., Jones, R., Kierzkowski, H. (2007), Globalization and country-specific links. *Journal of Economic Policy Reform* 10 (2), 63–88.

Hildenbrand, W. (1974), *Core and Equilibria of a Large Economy*. Princeton University Press, Princeton, NJ.

Itoh, M. (1999), Foreign direct investment, international trade and transfer of technology: a case study in South-East Asia. In: Piggott, J., Woodland, A. (Eds.), *International Trade Policy and The Pacific Rim*. St. Martin's Press, New York, pp. 370–391.

Jones, R., Kierzkowski, H. (1989), The role of services in production and international trade: a theoretical framework. In: Jones, R., Krueger, A. (Eds.), *The Political Economy of International Trade: Festschrift in Honor of Robert Baldwin*. Basil Blackwell, Oxford, pp. 31–48.

Kakinaka, M. (2006). Essays on optimal coordination management for investment competition, policy reform, and product design. Unpublished Thesis, Cornell University, Ithaca, NY.

Lee, K.Y. (2000), *From Third World to First: the Singapore Story, 1965–2000*. Harper Collins Publishers, New York.

Liu, B.J., Tung, A.-C. (2007). Experience-Based Outsourcing: East Asian Middlemen-Manufacturers in a Triadic Concord, SSRN WPS 977721.

Low, L. (1999), *Singapore: Toward a Developed Status*. Oxford University Press, Singapore.

Luce, R.D., Raiffa, H. (1957), *Games and Decisions: Introduction and Critical Survey*. Wiley, New York.

Mahathir, B.M. (1970), *The Malay Dilemma*. Times Books International, Singapore.

Markusen, A. (1996), Sticky places in slippery space: a typology of industrial districts. *Economic Geography* 72 (3), 293–313.

Ruffin, R., Jones, R. (2007), International technology transfer: who gains and who loses? *Review of International Economics* 15 (2), 209–222.

Samuelson, P.A. (1938), Welfare economics and international trade. *American Economic Review* 28 (2), 261–266.

Tung, A.-C. (2003), Beyond flying geese: the expansion of East Asia's electronics trade. *German Economic Review* 4 (1), 35–51.

Tung, A.-C. (2006). The Evolving Flying Geese Formation: Commodification and Export Outsourcing. Paper presented at the NEUDC, 2006.9.29-30, Cornell University, Ithaca, NY.

Wan, H., Jr., Tung, A.-C. (2006), Industrial policy in a globalized age – lessons from east Asian experience. *Singapore Economic Review* 51 (3), 267–281.

SUBJECT INDEX